NONCOERCIVE THREATS TO ACADEMIC, POLITICAL, AND ECONOMIC FREEDOM

NONCOERCIVE THREATS TO ACADEMIC, POLITICAL, AND ECONOMIC FREEDOM

EDITED BY
AKEEL BILGRAMI AND
JONATHAN R. COLE

Columbia University Press
New York

Columbia University Press
Publishers Since 1893
New York   Chichester, West Sussex

Library of Congress Cataloging-in-Publication Data
Names: Bilgrami, Akeel, 1950– editor. | Cole, Jonathan R., editor.
Title: Noncoercive threats to academic, political, and economic freedom /
    edited by Akeel Bilgrami and Jonathan R. Cole.
Description: New York : Columbia University Press, [2025] | Includes
    bibliographical references and index.
Identifiers: LCCN 2025009664 (print) | LCCN 2025009665 (ebook) |
    ISBN 9780231218559 (hardback) | ISBN 9780231218566 (trade paperback) |
    ISBN 9780231562348 (ebook)
Subjects: LCSH: Freedom of expression—United States. | Freedom of
    information—United States. | Academic freedom—United States. | Economic
    rights—United States. | Political rights—United States. | Duress (Law)—
    United States. | Disinformation—United States.
Classification: LCC KF4770 .N66 2025 (print) | LCC KF4770 (ebook) | DDC
    323.440973—dc23/eng/20250604

Cover design: Chang Jae Lee

GPSR Authorized Representative: Easy Access System Europe, Mustamäe tee 50,
10621 Tallinn, Estonia, gpsr.requests@easproject.com

For Edward

CONTENTS

PART VI. MEDIA

EDITORS' INTRODUCTION

AKEEL BILGRAMI AND JONATHAN R. COLE

1.

A few years ago, we published a collection of essays entitled *Who's Afraid of Academic Freedom?*[1] As can be gathered from the title, our subject was *freedom* in the academy, but our approach to it was via an analytic scrutiny of those who fear and oppose it, threatening or undermining the free pursuit of learning and research as well as the free presentation of research and learning in classrooms. This sequel volume retains that negative approach to freedom via a consideration of unfreedom but greatly enlarges the canvas to domains beyond the academy. Because "freedom" is such an omnibus term and because the concept it expresses is so variously theorized and so contested, we have thought it more tractable and more modest to approach it obliquely in this way, looking to what threatens and undermines it and seeking—from a study of those conditions and causes of its loss—to draw conclusions about its nature and about why we value it as we do. One of the striking and recurring features of the discussion in the earlier volume was that often academic freedom was undermined by methods or by conditions that are not in any obvious sense threatening to freedom *at first sight*. Examples of unfreedom were discussed at length that did not seem to have as their source any manifest or evident form of coercion, as that term is routinely understood. Yet, in these very examples, *freedom was undeniably being undermined*. This seemed to us also worth exploring in detail.

So, to put it in a word, the present volume (a) continues the approach to understanding the nature of freedom by looking to what makes for unfreedom, (b) does so on a very much wider canvas than the earlier focus on the academy, and (c) takes a much harder look at the ways freedom gets undermined in this wider domain that do not seem to be coercive or, at any rate, not obviously and manifestly, or not directly or overtly, coercive.

In proposing (a) as a topic to our contributors, we asked them to consider as an initial and only prima facie characterization of unfreedom that it consists in a reduction of our options. Some of the essays explicitly do so. We say "characterization" because it is obvious that it is in no way a "definition," and we say "prima facie" because it was our explicit intent to ask them to problematize the characterization. The problems are obvious. For instance, an abundance of options—a supermarket shelf laden with forty-three different brands of toothpaste, say—need not signal any presence of great freedom. Nor does a reduction of options *suffice* to count as unfreedom. Jeremy Waldron's essay in this volume looks in close philosophical detail at a case where a particular sort of reduction of options might indeed even be a way of exploring the nature of our autonomy and freedom. A similar sort of example is mentioned further below in this Introduction in the discussion of the essay by Jon Elster. Still, it is a schematic beginning in the characterization of freedom to see it as involving a reduction of options, a characterization that can then be made more complicated and problematized, as is done by several essays in this volume. Joseph Stiglitz's essay is a valuably detailed look at the complications and problems for this characterization in the economic sphere. The most general thing that might be said about how the complications and problems arise is this. Freedom is a normative notion. We don't really understand freedom unless we also understand that it is something we care for, something we want. It is a value. But then, like all values, it may conflict with other values and bringing it in alignment with those other values may, in fact, amount to articulating a richer conception of freedom than the initial characterization of a reduction of options suggests. Furthermore, freedom, viewed as a reduction of options may conflict internally in the sense that one person's freedom may engender another person's unfreedom, a reduction of my options, may lead to the increase in another's or others' options. Again, conceptually drawing solutions to such conflict may require complicating and substantially transforming what is claimed by the initial characterization.

Turning to (b), we can be brief. No special conceptual issues are involved, since (b) just seeks to extend this volume's study of unfreedom to areas well beyond the earlier volume's focus on the academy, reaching out to some of the most fundamental domains of social life. Though we still have a section on the academy, we have cast the net very wide to now include the economy, the law, the media, racial relations, as well as the sphere of the psyche and the spheres of public speech and moral behavior. With such a wide reach, the volume may quite properly be said to be a study of *political* unfreedom in the *broadest* sense of the term. But, political though the canvas of themes certainly is, we have not invited any essays on the most obvious sources of deprivation of political freedom—those that lie in one or other kind of manifestly authoritarian rule, whether of the past or the present. The volume rather is intended as a study of the many detailed sources of unfreedom within the institutions and public culture of a *liberal democratic framework*.

Taking on (b) has meant recruiting essays from a wide range of disciplinary angles: philosophy, psychology, sociology (including the sociology of science), law, and political economy so as to seek out and analyze these sources.

It is because our interest in unfreedom is within avowedly liberal and democratic institutions and culture, with explicit commitments to a range of familiar freedoms and a range of rights and other formal provisions seeking to ensure the implementation of those commitments, that (c), then, naturally comes to have a particular relevance for us. Where there is no authoritarian framework, where there is commitment to freedom and democracy, unfreedoms will very likely lie in unobvious places and will not take the brazenly coercive form they do under authoritarianism. And so, (c) is worth spelling out in greater detail before we conclude with very brief summaries of each essay. The issues around how freedom gets undermined in this wider domain, though familiar to philosophers, economists, and social and political theorists, are delicate and difficult and are, therefore, liable to be misunderstood, and they will need greater elaboration than (a) and (b).

There are relatively intuitive and clear examples of the kind of undermining of freedom that (c) is concerned with. Sticking for the moment with the academic domain, though sometimes academic institutions can coerce authors and teachers and prevent the publication or classroom presentation of their research, many essays in that earlier volume revealed that much of the time, academic freedom is threatened without any detectable coercion. As one author pointed out, given certain contextual conditions, freedom in the academy can often even be undermined by something as seemingly benign as *pity*, as when someone with socialist views in an economics department in a university in the United States is inhibited from airing or publishing his views, even perhaps to the point that he gradually abandons his views and moves on to other more "current" topics and approaches, when he hears remarks from his colleagues such as "Poor fellow, he is fifty years out of date!" On the face of it, anyone who knows something about the discipline of economics as it is pursued in most American universities (shaped as these universities have been under the long shadow of McCarthyism, and dominated as this discipline is by "neoclassical," indeed "neoliberal" tendency) might be forgiven for thinking that this is a case of having one's freedom undermined, even though there is no evident coercion—there is, after all, no directive nor rule backed by academic administrative sanction, nor even any kind of more informal but explicit warning that one should not pursue a particular point of view in one's research. This is just one example of what (c) is concerned within one domain, the academy; many essays in the present volume discuss examples in other domains of social, economic, and political life. That there are many such examples is undeniable.

One would only deny it on the one hand, (1) if one were quite simply insensitive to the subtler forms of undermining of freedom, failing to recognize the loss of freedom they reveal because some more directive and conventionally authoritarian intervention is missing; or deny it on the other hand, (2) because, although one agrees that freedom *is* being undermined in these cases, one insists that such undermining is not properly described as noncoercive; insists, in other words, that if freedom is undermined, coercion must be present.

We would strongly disagree with those who deny it on the basis of (1). Freedom is frequently and pervasively undermined even when no authoritarian element is present, and, as we just said, some of the book's most interesting contributions present a range of cases where this happens. A little further below we try to explain what might prompt the thinking in (1) and why it is unconvincing.

The disagreement with those who deny it on the basis of (2) is more rarified because both parties to the disagreement agree that freedom is being threatened and undermined in these cases.

Let us consider first the grounds of denial in (2).

The disagreement is over whether there are cases of the undermining of freedom which are not cases of coercive impositions by which those freedoms are undermined. That is, it is a disagreement over whether there is a *distinction* between coercive and noncoercive ways of undermining freedom. No doubt, it may well be that in some cases of this sort the distinction is not best expressed in just that way—as the last sentence does—but in those very cases, it will often turn out there will be other words by which the distinction can be quite appropriately and accurately described, words such as "not apparently coercive," "not directly coercive," not "overtly coercive." . . . If the denial of these examples persists, refusing *all* such words to make the distinction that the examples seem to exemplify, it begins to sound like a dogmatic stipulation that is counter to the facts that the examples describe and to the ordinary meanings of these words used in the description. There is no gainsaying, of course, that intuitions may vary regarding which exact words are apt and relevant to describing one or other such case. This is inevitable because in the study of human subjects and society, concepts—at least the nontrivial ones—almost never get elaborated in strict definitions. (As Socrates admitted at the end of his life, the only word he had ever succeeded in defining was the Greek word for "mud," which—if anyone is interested—he defined as "the mixture of soil and water.") Thus, some may feel that the word "coercive" should not be withheld in a given case but would allow "not overtly coercive." Other cases may more suitably get the description "not directly coercive." Yet others, "not apparently coercive." . . . A particularly interesting description might be *"not felt to be* coercive" by those who are rendered unfree. And, here too, it may turn out that once those who are rendered unfree, when they *come to understand* the subtler, more covert or indirect, sources of their unfreedom, may *begin to feel coerced,* so the description does not any longer apply. But even they must admit that the unfreedom of *others* faced with the same sources of unfreedom, but who have *not yet come to grasp* their nature, will still accurately be described in those words and other such appropriate words, depending on the case. So the point of significance is that there is a relatively clear and interesting *distinction* to be noted between freedom being undermined by remarks of that sort by a socialist economist's academic colleague and freedom being undermined by an administrative directive backed by sanction; and if it sticks in someone's throat to say that the former, unlike the latter, is a case of *noncoercive* undermining of freedom, then other words may be brought in to make the distinction that more aptly capture the distinction. To repeat, depending on the details of any given example of this sort of distinction, different words will seem more and less appropriate. The thing that is not deniable in such examples is that there is a distinction, however we settle the matter of which words to most suitably apply in making the distinction. To put it differently, there is agreement on both sides that there is an undermining of freedom in all such examples and that this is a bad thing, but we insist that not all such bad things are the *same* bad thing, and there are often grounds to not *equate* undermining of freedom with coercion or direct coercion, and so forth.

This prima facie distinction we are insisting on has been powerfully theorized in different philosophical traditions. It is at the heart, for instance, of Antonio Gramsci's notion of "hegemony."[2] The term "hegemony" in Gramsci's understanding is not the same as in our everyday, loose use of the word. It is, as philosophers like to call it, a "technical" term. Gramsci means by "hegemony" roughly that in liberal-democratic capitalist societies, the ruling class rules by convincing all other classes that *its* interests are the interests of all other classes. This suggests that in these societies, unlike authoritarian societies that wield coercion, the ruling class, by a wide range of methods, succeeds in fetching the *consent* for its rule from the classes it rules over. Gramsci shares with the entire Marxist tradition to which he belongs the conviction that this form of rule is oppressive, that the ruling class deprives working people of the sort of freedom that they would possess in a classless society, but his notion of hegemony is there to suggest, as we said, that this is done without coercion, without authoritarian rule, but rather is based on the consent of the ruled. So also, Foucault's acute insight that in the modern period (unlike many premodern societies), for all its sloganized commitments to the ideals of the Enlightenment, power is oppressively exercised in much subtler and more hidden and indirect forms by the cognitive and practical effects of a discursive field through the processes of what he calls "normalization," is a similar acknowledgment of the distinction which we have made one of our interests in this book.[3] Not all power need take the form of authoritarian rule such as in traditional monarchies, it need not even turn on explicit directives, but rather by new, silently circulatory forms of taboo and prohibition, which even if said to be coercive are much more *covertly* and *indirectly* so, working in the cognitive realm and generating a social *mentality*. Foucault's somewhat later inverted slogan, "politics is war by *other means*," again well captures the prima facie distinction that we are making one of our themes in this volume, as does his claim that an analyst might exercise power simply by sitting silently and listening to the patient. De Tocqueville too seems to be gesturing at the distinction when he said of America that for all its cherished commitments to the rights of freedom of thought and speech (if Chomsky is right, more cherished in America than in other democratic countries, many of which, for instance, have libel laws that undermine it), it is a country whose population shows very little "independence of mind."[4] And Marx's account of "false consciousness" is an early statement of what underlies later Gramscian ideas of hegemony that we mentioned earlier, and one fine philosophical work of recent times on "false consciousness" actually uses the slogan "Voluntary Servitude" as its title,[5] a slogan that flamboyantly conveys perhaps the most extreme version of the distinction in (c) that we asked some of our contributors in this volume to keep in mind. That is, if servitude is appropriately describable as *voluntary*, then it would seem it is appropriately describable as "noncoercively" wrought (or, if not "noncoercively," by one of the other descriptions we have mentioned above).

Many of the essays in this volume look at these subtler cases of power in generating unfreedom, the noncoercive, or the not overtly and not directly coercive forms of undermining freedom in one or other domain of social and political life. Some look at examples that might problematize the distinction because the lines are hard to draw. In fact, when we invited the essays, we explicitly sought analyses that displayed the detailed issues involved in the difficulty of precisely drawing the line that marks the distinction.

What, then, of (1), the other grounds for denying the distinction—not by denying that freedom is being undermined noncoercively (or not by overt or direct coercion) in these cases but rather by denying that these cases are to be counted as cases of threats or underminings of freedom?

Here the instinct for denial is to take the idea that we have ourselves appealed to—that not all bad things are the same bad thing—even further and claim that freedom is not being undermined in these examples at all, but rather some other value altogether is being unfulfilled. Isaiah Berlin was celebrated for expressing this instinct in no uncertain terms, especially against those who would argue—as Stiglitz does in his essay here and more elaborately in a recent book—that conditions of substantial *inequality* in a society undermine our freedom.[6] Why not just say, Berlin declares, that you are against inequality and be done with it? Why insist that freedom is being undermined?

Stiglitz himself gives impressively convincing reasons for resisting Berlin's instinct in his essay here, showing how much inequality reduces our options to pursue the most fundamental goals we have in life, even in liberal democracies where there is a self-congratulatory commitment to the ideals of the political Enlightenment, including especially freedom. And, of course, Gramsci and Foucault, whom we mentioned briefly, have provided subtle and powerful accounts of how power is indeed being exercised by the ruling elites in the modern period in liberal democratic polities and the economic formation they have embraced, depriving vast segments of a population of the freedoms that those very polities and economic formations, proudly claim as their achievements.

A more nuanced way than Berlin's of pressing (1), even perhaps providing the underlying considerations that lie behind Berlin's instinct, might go like this. Consider again the remark made about a socialist economist colleague in the academy. It may be said that this kind of example is not really a case of freedom being undermined but rather merely an example of socialization, the standard methods by which a member of a group acquires its norms by acculturation. For millennia, parents have done it with children, village elders with local communities, so why not, it might be said, professors with their colleagues? (A parent saying to a child, "Bilgramis don't do that sort of thing!" is in fact more clearly directive than "Poor chap, he is fifty years out of date!") The benign process of the acquisition of social norms is hardly a threat to freedom, it might be said. It is how human groups have sustained themselves—as groups, as traditions—through history.

Now, someone taking this view does not, in order to take the view, deny what is obvious: of course, some traditions of a group and its social norms can indeed undermine the freedom of individuals within the group and even do so coercively. Nor, in taking this view, need one deny something else that is also obvious: that in many groups the methods of acculturation can be overtly coercive forms of drill. So it is often true that there is nothing benign about this process of acculturation nor its outcomes. But this view can still surely insist that it would be a grossly crude inference to conclude from the fact that many traditions and social norms undermine freedom and bring about acculturation into those social norms by coercive methods, that there is no distinction to be made *in general* between coercion and acculturation, that is between coercion and the standard forms of conditioning that *every one of us* undergoes, just by the very fact that one is not Robinson Crusoe, just by the fact that one finds one-self in a social context, whatever that may be. Being social creatures, every sin-gle one of us inherits a tradition and norms by acculturation, by growing up in a culture and being conditioned by its mores. That sometimes the norms are coercive, and that sometimes the acculturation is coercively drilled, does not collapse the *general* distinction between conditioning and coercion. Even the most perfectly realized utopia, the most ideally free and socially and economi-cally egalitarian society, will sustain itself by a process of acculturation that its members undergo, by which its values and its traditions are imparted to them, and it is the truth of this perfectly *general* point that we are stressing when we play devil's advocate to present this view and this ground for the denial in (1). The ground for the denial in 1) under discussion, then, is: the socialist econo-mist who hears that remark by his colleague is just undergoing what happens—unless one is Robinson Crusoe—in the benign form of acculturation that might occur when someone finds oneself (whether by birth in a family, a neighborhood, a community, or by recruitment into an academy) in a social context. If *everyone* undergoes this social conditioning, just by the very fact of finding oneself in or growing up in a social context (whatever that might be), then this particular example of the academy, it will be said, seems to be like the benign cases of this ubiquitous, universal phenomenon.

Why then are we insisting that a colleague making a remark of that kind can, in some social and historical contexts—for instance the social context of a country which has had a longstanding social and intellectual ethos of hostil-ity to socialism, an ethos long shaped by the legacy of what was described as "the McCarthy period"—be a threat to freedom, and that the quality of the threat is only hidden from us because of its evident contrast with the coercive-ness by which that hostility was manifest in that earlier "McCarthy" period?

To begin to answer this question, let us first present what goes into *human* acculturation into social values and tradition, that is, what exactly is involved when such social conditioning involves the kind of subjects human beings are.

We have said that there is no gainsaying the fact of our social conditioning. Human beings are social creatures, not isolated subjects, and acculturation (sometimes benign, sometimes not) into society happens *to all*. But there is no gainsaying either that *human* subjects are *distinctive* as social creatures in one respect.[7] We are different from pack animals. At some point in their develop-ment to maturity, children are *able* to ask what cubs are not: "Should I be doing (or thinking) what the Bilgramis do (or think)?" What this means is that when asked why I do something, though I might answer "I did it because I was brought up to do it," that answer can amount to something much more than it *simply* sounds. This is because, unlike cubs, we have the *capacity* to ask *ourselves*, "Do I have *reason* to do what I am brought up to do?" So even if someone gives that answer to the initial question ("I did it because I was brought up to do it"), if she has exercised this capacity (even if only implicitly) and answered that further, embedded question in the affirmative "Yes, I have reason to do what I've been brought up to do," the answer to the initial question is much *more* than what it simply sounds. It amounts to much more than our saying of the grown wolf, "It does what it does because it was conditioned to do so." By the sheer possession of this capacity, we are, *in principle*, set apart from wolves and other creatures, in the kind of conditioning we undergo. And it is perfectly appropriate to say that to possess this capacity is to possess the distinctiveness of "reason"—after all, it is a capacity to ask and answer the question, "Do I have *reason* to embrace the social norms into which I have been acculturated?"

But this word "reason" needs to be carefully understood.

For one thing: wolves need not be denied reason in other senses of the term. A wolf can plausibly be said to have recoiled from a dangerous predator for *a reason*. But that use of the term is not "reason" in the sense that occurs when a subject is able to raise the question that a wolf is unable to: "Do I have reason to . . . ?" *This latter* capacity is distinctive, it is a capacity for "reason" that, so far as we know, only human subjects possess, a capacity that no doubt comes with our genetic endowment, but whose exercise emerges in the process of maturation.[8]

For another: special though this notion of reason is in this sense, it is still "reason" with a low profile, not with a capital R, not the "Reason" that has become the target of much recent critique of the Enlightenment's larger claims (Foucault himself being one of the best-known of such critics). Any effort to elevate this notion of reason into something grander—reflecting, for instance, some telos that is tracked in a "progressive" history, to mention just one such kind of grand elevation of it—distorts the common or garden status it has as a differentiating feature of human subjects among all the living creatures we know. Nothing self-congratulatory about the "human" is being claimed in claiming that human beings are distinctive in possessing *this* capacity for reason. Bees may have far greater capacities in *other* sorts of social practices. All we are doing, in mentioning this capacity, is saying that when it comes to their social habitus, human subjects possess what Gadamer called a "free, distanced, orientation," the capacity each one of us has to distance ourselves from our acculturation and ask about our social traditions and norms and habits, "Do we have reason to fall in line with them?"

Though Berlin does not present his instinct in just this way, what his view can be said to be exploiting is precisely this capacity we possess for *authorization* of what we are acculturated into. The capacity reflects that we are subjects who possess "autonomy" and so the instinct now can be elaborated fully. Since we have this capacity to raise questions about whether we have reason to embrace the social norms we are acculturated into and thereby authorizing them (or rejecting them) for ourselves, then—for subjects like us, with such a capacity—acculturation into social norms is not to be conflated with coercion of any sort.

That is the full articulation of the challenge (1) poses for us. How might we answer the challenge?

In resisting this challenge, there is no need to deny—as the cruder stipulations of (2) seek to do—the *general* distinction between acculturation and coercion. The general distinction is secure because when (from this "distanced" perspective—to use Gadamer's term—that human subjects are capable of) we ask the autonomy-reflecting question and answer it in the affirmative, we *at least some of the time* can properly be said to have authorized the norms that are questioned. And if that is so, then coercion is not present *at those times*, and so there *is* a *general* distinction between coercion and acculturation. The security of the distinction needs nothing more than such authorization (properly so called) on *some* occasions.

Our resistance to (1) must therefore say more about why we have left it open (in a way that Berlin's fully elaborated position is reluctant to do) that "authorization" or "self-authorization" is not automatically or exceptionlessly appropriate as a description of *all* human acculturation into social norms. On what conceptual ground can we locate the sources that sometimes *disallow* the aptness of the description "authorized" or "self-authorized" for the social norms we live by?

The most general way to approach that ground is to ask a further question: When I ask the question "Do I have reason to follow the social norms that I have been brought up to follow?," *what resources can I appeal to in answering it*? That is, what considerations, what standards, what values and beliefs, do I look to and apply in seeking to answer the question? And the answer to this *further* question can only be that there are no other resources (values, beliefs . . .) for me to appeal to than those that are given to me *in my social and historical situatedness*. There is no Archimedean or transcendent position from which to answer it—a point that Hegel crucially brought to bear on otherwise profound ideas about autonomy's relation to reason that we find in Kant. So, this autonomy-reflecting form of authorizing (or rejecting) social norms is necessarily done by an individual on the basis of values and beliefs acquired from *within* the norms into which she has been acculturated—standing in one place in our social context and looking to finding answers (reasons) to our question from another space, *also* within our social context. Both the question and the answer are asked and answered within the overall space of the social context in which we find ourselves.

And once we recognize that that non-Archimedean, immanent ground from which the autonomy-reflecting question is answered is the only ground there is, we have also to recognize that it may well turn out that the values and beliefs within our social and historical context that we appeal to in giving the answer, are *themselves* the product of a kind of social conditioning that is at odds with our impression that we are authorizing the initial social norms in question. In other words, in such cases, an affirmative (i.e., authorizing) answer to the autonomy-reflecting question may give us an impression of autonomy but that impression is misleading, and in fact it is an *illusion* of authorization. This is what (1) and Berlin are not leaving space for because they have not fully taken in the full weight and implications of the Hegelian point that must supplement Kant's notion of autonomy. The weight of that supplement is precisely to allow a space where unfreedom can enter to render a seeming authorization of our own social norms illusory. So, to sum up, the fact that we are in the first place under the impression that we have *authorized* the social norms is what makes it apt to say that (2) is wrong and there is no coercion or overt and direct coercion in play; and the fact that the impression of authorization is sometimes false and, when it is, we are under an *illusion* of authorization, is what makes it apt to say that (1) is wrong and these are genuine cases of our freedom being undermined by the social norms in question.

A number of the essays that follow discuss such cases of unfreedom that are opened up in the space that is created by Hegel's supplement to Kant's notion of autonomy, starting with the very first essay by David Bromwich's discussion of conformism, picked up in a different domain (the domain of the psyche) by Carol Rovane, and (the domain of the economy) by Prabhat Patnaik, and (the domain of the academy) by Kipnis and Ignatieff and Bilgrami; and the essays in the last section of the book touch on the question whether and to what extent the values and beliefs by which we seem to be authorizing our social norms are shaped by the media, thus rendering us unfree even in liberal democracies, where the media is supposed to be "free."

All of the foregoing we say by way of saying that it cannot be denied, as is done in (1), that freedom is being undermined in many cases where it does not seem to be done by coercion or direct or overt coercion. But one final point is worth emphasizing, if it is not already apparent. What is crucial to understanding this point is that, unlike as with wolves, it is precisely a certain capacity for distance from our social mores that makes us *vulnerable* to such *undermining* of freedom, a vulnerability and unfreedom that *cannot even be spoken of* about wolves and their acculturation into social propensities by their social mores. Wolves can, of course, be made unfree by being caged. But one can only speak of being vulnerable to unfreedom in these other ways because one is uniquely possessed of a certain capacity for autonomy and "reason" in this sense. All sorts of implications nest here, which call for explicit qualification. We won't elaborate on them here, except to say with a few more words what we say in note 7. This distinctiveness is not a basis for moral exceptionalism or an argument for privileges that are special to human subjects. Indeed, if there is any exceptionalism it is that such distinctiveness brings with it the freight and weight of responsibilities and duties toward subjects *not* possessed of this capacity but like human subjects possessed of the capacity to suffer and possessed of intrinsic value.

We have spent some time elaborating the detailed nature of what is intended by our focus on (c) because we have found in various exchanges on the subject that it is possible to be misunderstood or completely fail to be understood in rather elementary ways about the nature of (c) without such elaboration. Both (1) and (2) are manifestations of that failure.

One last, brief word on (c). It may seem to some that this is not the right time to be so concerned about (c), that it is a somewhat remote undertaking to explore these subtler, noncoercive (or not overtly or directly coercive) kinds of threat to freedom in *liberal democracies*, when various contemporary populisms and nationalisms have revealed the *authoritarian* side of politics. But the fact is that in the complex world that has emerged ever since constitutional democracy—at least in its formal aspects—came to be fairly widely embraced as a definitive framework for governance, some of this authoritarianism of our time works *not* by coercive state or military rule but by noncoercively manipulating that liberal framework in illiberal directions and by arranging, again quite noncoercively, for the media to acquiesce in, even sometimes cheerlead for, the illiberal outcomes.

We have divided the twenty-one essays of the volume somewhat artificially, for the sake of convenience, into six sections. There is an opening section that is broadly philosophical. Since, as we have said, noncoercive threats to freedom can simply consist in underlying conditions of a society, we have devoted one section to the economic conditions, and another to the abidingly vexed social conditions of racial inequality and oppression, and yet another to social issues of gender and public health and law. The media gets its own section, as does the academy.

2.

The opening philosophical section begins with an essay by David Bromwich on chapter 2 of John Stuart Mill's *On Liberty*. His central interpretative angle is that Mill is most deeply concerned in that chapter with the *pacification*—rather than the coercion—of the mind, in particular the pacification wrought by our own tendency to conform to intellectual trends in the air. This was a great concern of Mill's, but Bromwich's essay is by no means a mere stock-taking of that celebrated discussion of freedom of speech. It succeeds in saying fresh and illuminating things about Mill's argument, showing both why nothing in it leads to a relativism about truth or about value, and why nothing in it really encourages the image of a "marketplace of ideas," an image owing to Oliver

Wendell Holmes (even though Holmes never used exactly that phrase to express the image). The image that he eloquently brings to center stage instead is Blake's—of "mental fight." Mill's argument for liberty of speech takes for granted a Blakean ideal of human minds as restless and questing and seeking the stimulus of conflicting opinion. Bromwich then argues that the passive mind, seeking conformity to the currency of trends in the political and cultural zeitgeist, precisely seeks to avoid all such conflict and, as a result, inclines us to find anomalous views rude and offensive. But he insists that Mill would not have allowed the offence that is so often taken when confronted by anomalous views as falling within the "*harmful*" exceptions to the protections that speech is given when we declare it to be "free." This is because Mill sets the bar of what counts as "harm" very high. For related reasons, he would not have approved of any effort to make a right to free speech stand in conflict with any glibly claimed *right* to not be offended. To not wish to be offended is one thing, a natural thing. But to erect that natural and understandable wish into a right that matches *in the law*, the right to free speech, is quite another.

Jeremy Waldron's essay follows, raising the question of what philosophers call "practical necessity" and asks whether all cases of such necessity amount to a noncoercive threat to freedom. Like all necessity, it will remove options, but are all cases of that, cases of unfreedom? In an extended subtle and analytical comparative discussion of a pair of examples, he explores various ways in which an action that is compelled by considerations of a *felt* morality may, in fact, remove all other options from one's moral psychology, and yet be considered as quite distinct from other more routine cases of the elimination of options (which are viewed as examples of unfreedom) because it may actually be thought of as exemplifying one's *autonomy* in the Kantian understanding of that term. In carefully making its way to this claim, the essay crucially and insightfully stresses that it may be just as important (in the matter of whether reduction of options leads to unfreedom) to look at the nature of the existing options that get reduced as looking at what sort of thing reduces them.

Carol Rovane's is a philosophical exploration of the threats to human freedom that may be found in our responses to what is labeled "psychopathology," in particular the phenomenon of "multiplicity." She does so via a consideration of the work of Ian Hacking, who, influenced by Foucault's earlier ideas, has pioneered the philosophical study of this phenomenon. Rovane situates the issues at stake in a very much more general framework of philosophical questions about the nature of the self and self-knowledge, about the cultural effects of the human sciences, and about moral relativism. According to Hacking's Foucauldian metaphysical vision of human reality, our historical contexts supply us with categories through which we might make sense of ourselves, and in the process of employing those categories we actually *become* the sorts of things that instantiate them. While this might seem to constitute a form of *freedom*,

Hacking emphasizes that it is really more a case of *constraint*, insofar as we have no choice but to become instances of the categories that we happen to have available, through which to make sense of ourselves. This means that when the human sciences offer us new categories, this may impose a noncoercive threat to our freedom, in the form of a constraint, not only what we *can* become but what we *inevitably will* become. Against this metaphysical backdrop she provides a critical discussion of Hacking's historical account of how the category of *multiple personality disorder* emerged. She argues that there are interesting similarities between moral relativism and Hacking's metaphysical vision of human reality. Pushing these similarities, her reflection on the issue of moral relativism brings to light that there are social conditions in which a single human being might fail to be the site of a single unified self but instead host to multiple selves—only unlike the case of multiplicity that interests Hacking, this case is *not* pathological. She observes that in the nonpathological case, the inner condition of the multiple reflects a corresponding *external social* condition, and the same holds for the pathological case. This, therefore, gives us a new angle from which to contemplate what makes the pathological case *pathological*—why multiple personality disorder is indeed a *disorder*. Rather than merely focus on the inner condition of the multiple, we should (equally) focus on what is disordered about the social condition that their inner condition reflects. Thus, insofar as multiple personality disorder is a *dissociative* condition, it reflects, and also corresponds to, *dissociation at the social level*. Rovane makes *two* related claims in this connection: first, dissociation at the social level serves to keep the causes of dissociative psychiatric disorders hidden from view; but second, these hidden causes can generate an inner condition of multiple personalities or selves *only insofar as they remain hidden*. Thus multiple personality disorder not only reflects, but also *depends on*, dissociation at the social level. Note that if there is any threat to freedom here, that might derive from dissociation at the social level, it cannot be of the coercive variety—at least to the extent that we tend to think that threats are not coercive unless they are so perceived. The fact that multiple personality disorder both reflects, and also depends on, dissociation at the social level has generally been overlooked, even by Hacking himself. She closes by arguing that if we keep it in view, we can see better how, and why, phenomena having to do with multiplicity challenge certain moral values and ideals that center on the importance of the *human individual*—values and ideals to which Hacking remains attached, an attachment that, she suggests, is not always compulsory.

The section on political economy consists of three papers that are serially linked in a snug dialectic, the first concluding that only a *progressive* capitalism can steer us out of the seemingly noncoercive threats to human agency that have characterized the neoliberalism of our times, the second concluding that the only way in which a progressive path in political economy can withstand the constant innate tendencies of capital to *undermine* progressive constraints on it is by an adoption of economic *rights*, and the third seeking to present *what about* economic rights might be able to provide for such resilient constraints.

Joseph Stiglitz, despite his long and distinguished career in the mainstream of the discipline of economics, subjects the "neoclassical" economic theories that have dominated that discipline to a systematic and comprehensive critique. From a number of different angles, appealing to Keynesian ideas but very interestingly mixing and integrating them with more recent results of inquiry in behavioral economics, he turns the tables on the claim—in von Hayek and Milton Friedman—that keeping faith with the ideology of unfettered markets alone can promote the values of freedom and democracy that we have come to cherish since the political Enlightenment. It is precisely the faith in that form of freedom, he argues, that has consistently, even if often noncoercively, impoverished the options ("reduced the opportunity set") of citizens. A genuinely democratic culture that promotes a substantive conception of freedom requires capitalism to be constrained along lines that are "progressive."

Prabhat Patnaik takes the criticism of capitalism one step further in his essay by analyzing how Keynesian ideas of constraining capital are, from the point of view of the immanent ("spontaneous") tendencies of capital, intolerable. It is built into capital's trajectory that its spontaneous tendencies will constantly seek to undermine efforts to constrain it, rendering such constraints fragile, unstable, and, thus, not offering an *eventual* solution. He begins by expounding how under capitalism for the first time an economic formation emerged that (unlike the "monseigneur's whip" of earlier economic formations) resorted to noncoercive methods of "disciplining" to reduce options of working people, methods, for instance, such as arranging for a permanent force of labor reserves that will have the effect of substantially reducing the bargaining power of labor. He considers at length the extended Keynesian period after the Second World War that sought, through demand management, to generate employment and use up the labor reserves, and analyzes why it did not succeed due to the spontaneous immanent tendencies of capital. He concludes briefly with the proposal that a strategy of economic *rights* might be introduced to address these tendencies, at least initially.

Akeel Bilgrami's essay is an attempt to present a foundational philosophical grounding of economic rights, exploring why it might be that this grounding has not been attempted with the same long and profound tradition of justificatory foundational philosophy that the rights around liberty have had. He seeks to uncover the precise property of rights that might have the effect that Patnaik has claimed for them. The three essays, read together, provide a quite comprehensive discussion of economic threats to freedom coming from quite nonauthoritarian sources in liberal-democratic modernity and the prospects for addressing them.

The essays on society and the law cover three distinct social issues to which human freedom and unfreedom are central: abortion, public health, and the threats to freedom that some have thought come from cultural customs. Questions of law inflect all three topics.

Geoffrey Stone's essay, as its opening makes clear, is about how the Supreme Court decision in *Roe v Wade* in 1973, reduces the options of citizens in a liberal democracy.Submitted to us prior to the *Dobbs* decision, his essay focuses on the history of abortion practices and law in the United States in anticipation of the fate of *Roe v. Wade*. As he says, the way in which we got to *Roe* and subsequently to *Dobbs* provides us with context for how we have arrived at this moment in the divisive debate over abortion. Stone takes us back to the time of the creation of our Constitution—and still further back to the Greek Empire—to undermine the idea that the practice and right to abortion is a recent phenomenon. For example, in the middle of the nineteenth century, roughly 20 percent of pregnancies ended with abortions. He identifies a shift in public attitudes toward abortion. He goes further to discuss the role of the rise of religious evangelical groups that actively proselytized against abortion. He suggests that there has always been a battle between those who think that limits on abortion is a form of state-sponsored coercion, while at the same time others because of their religious or moral beliefs feel quite the opposite. Heated debate continues, of course, over when abortions may or not be permissible. The debate is not simply a legal one. It confronts individuals with ethical and moral questions about their own freedom and those of a fetus. It has also involved informal social control within local communities. There were clearly noncoercive efforts by the Catholic Church and allied organizations to redraw the legal lines of what was permissible for women when they contemplated terminating a pregnancy through an abortion. And the Church tried, using both noncoercive and coercive means, to alter the behavior of women's abortion decisions. In many Catholic families the normative mantra was: "The Smiths don't have abortions." Where do you draw an acceptable line in law when strong conflicting positions about the moral and ethical positions on abortion involve coercive and noncoercive efforts to extend or limit freedom of choice? The essay raises the question about how far legislatures and courts should or can go to abridge what most believe is an inalienable right—control over their own bodies.

The medical community in the late nineteenth century also played a role in asserting medical grounds, which the essay discusses, as a basis for anti-abortion values and behavior. Most of this medical work was grossly flawed. Despite the condemnation of abortion by a significant part of both medical and religious communities, women continued to terminate their pregnancies. Stone points out that early in the twentieth century, roughly two million women in the United States had abortions annually. By the end, we come away with a salutary reminder that women and their choices for how to deal with their own bodies has had a long, contentious, and divisive history. That divisiveness is, of course, more than ever with us.

Robert Klitzman addresses the salient conflicts that pit public health issues against individuals' perception and assertion of their rights and freedom. The question had already been raised briefly in Stiglitz's essay: How should we draw the line between individual autonomy—and the possibility that the autonomy can cause harm to others—with the way we try to control disease and pandemics? This is not a new dilemma, and Klitzman alludes to historical precedents of limitations on individual options. But, as we all know very well, these conflicts have become particularly salient recently during the COVID pandemic. Should individuals have the freedom *not* to wear masks when they are mandated to do so in public places during a pandemic? Should they have the right to refuse vaccinations based on their religious beliefs? Laws have been passed in many countries that restrict individual freedoms that could create great risks to public health and safety. The conflicts reflect the relative weights given to autonomy and to the common good and questions arise, therefore, as to whether the very notion of autonomy is in need of modification or whether this is just simply a matter of trade-off between two completely distinct values—individual freedom and the common good. Stiglitz explored this familiar theoretical issue in his chapter, but however we resolve it, courts, Klitzman reminds us, have in the judgments they articulate often quite simply seen it as a trade-off and favored the latter. He examines the underlying ethical and bioethical principles behind the decisions one has to make and extends the discussion to ethical issues related to basic and clinical medical research, where the individuals participating in clinical trials may not be adequately familiar with the risks associated with their participation in experiments. And where they do understand risks, should researchers be allowed to use monetary incentives to persuade individuals to participate in the experiment? When do the benefits of the clinical research outweigh the risks that individuals may be exposed to?

Richard Shweder raises questions about the scope of religious liberty and cultural diversity in the land of the free, with special reference to the appropriate legal status for gender-equal Muslim versions of the Abrahamic circumcision tradition. American Shia Muslim women of the Dawoodi Bohra religious denomination have recently been prosecuted because they customarily adhere to a gender-equal version of the Abrahamic circumcision tradition. By most accounts the circumcision procedure for girls amounts to a nick, abrasion, piercing, or small cut restricted to the female foreskin or prepuce (often referred to as "the clitoral hood"). From a surgical point of view the custom is less invasive than a typical male circumcision as routinely and legally performed by the Jewish, Christian, and Muslim descendants of Abraham in the United States. If (Abrahamic) circumcision is legal for boys, why shouldn't it be legal for girls?

If it is illegal for girls, why shouldn't it be illegal for boys (including Jewish, Christian, and Muslim boys)? Shweder gives special attention to two competing interpretations of the free exercise of religion clause of the First Amendment of the US Constitution. Should the clause be interpreted narrowly (and conservatively) as a "no religious persecution" clause, or more broadly (and liberally) as a "respect for religious conscience" clause. His essay explores the implications of each interpretation for religious and cultural freedom and for the future of Jewish and Muslim Abrahamic circumcision traditions in the United States.

The essays on race approach the long-standing unfreedoms of African Americans from perspectives that are historical, philosophical, and sociological.

Eric Foner, who has written extensively on the Civil War and Reconstruction—often comparing the nineteenth century with more contemporary history—declares in his essay that "no idea is more fundamental to Americans' sense of themselves as individuals and as a nation than freedom." He takes us on a short historical journey that exposes us to the varying meanings of freedom for different Americans; how it meant one thing for whites, another for Blacks. This was inevitable since Blacks were trying to acquire freedom, whites were fearful of it being taken away. Foner suggests that quite different ideas about freedom emerge in different generations, and that to this day, even with civil rights legislated and all the elaborate apparatus of liberal democracy in place, unfreedoms remain whose implications are still not always fully understood, so freedom is a still evolving idea in our own time.

Robert Gooding-Williams's essay brings philosophical analysis to a range of historical phenomena regarding race via an interpretation of Dubois's considered angle on a familiar question that can be put much more generally than the particular version of it, which Dubois himself takes up in detail. That general question is: on what ground and by what claimed right did the ideals of freedom articulated in the European political Enlightenment get viewed (even by their propounders) as compatible with European colonialism? In Dubois, race is explicitly introduced into the formulation of this overarching question. What explains the social ameliorations wrought by emerging democratizations in the modern period being restricted to the white working populations? Dubois considered this question both in the context of the failures of the Reconstruction period in America after the Civil War and with regard to European colonialism. The essay expounds Dubois's efforts to provide an integrated account of the relations between the economic and the racialist aspects of colonialism and the Reconstruction, exploring initially the extent to which the (conquest and) exploitation of darker peoples in the African continent, as well as of the freed Black population after the Civil War, is prompted by a complicity of white working populations in the metropole uniting with white property-owning classes to seek a mutual gain from the extractions and the markets that colonialism provides. A similar alliance is explored as one factor in accounting for the failures of Reconstruction. But it is the driving burden of Gooding-Williams's argument that the overarching question we mentioned earlier would not be adequately addressed, for Dubois, if we rested with these merely economic motivations. It can only be satisfactorily addressed when one probes the *moral psychology* of white supremacism that is shared by all white economic classes (capitalist and labor), an ideology that invokes a version of Christianity, Dubois argues, that is deeply inflected by *attitudes* of prejudice, such as hatred and contempt, against the colored races. This ineliminable element of moral psychology in explaining white supremacism is of deep underlying relevance to the theme of the next essay.

Bruce Western and Jessica Simms discuss the unfreedom that Black American men face in an era of mass incarceration, which emerged in the United States in the first decade of the 2000s. Their essay comes to conclusions after a careful look at the statistics on imprisonment, including solitary confinement. They note that the level of incarceration has risen from roughly 200,000 in 1970 to about 1.4 million in 2019—almost five times the historic rate during the twentieth century. The era of mass incarceration was jointly produced by conditions of mounting levels of violence and conditions of steep racial and class inequality, propelled by political and cultural projects of expansive social control. The essay, like Stiglitz's, reveals the extent to which and the depth at which issues of freedom are inextricably linked with issues of equality. But, as we said, they link thematically with Gooding-Williams's essay as well.

The *outcome* of current judicial practices of the present—incarceration—is obviously coercive. Since it puts people behind bars, how can it fail to be? But if *unjust* incarceration of the present survives the widespread embrace of a panoply of *civil rights*, we need explanations of how this is possible. And Gooding-Williams's Duboisian framework, which stresses the ineliminability of the *moral psychology* that explains the abidingness of white supremacist ideology to this day, is of obvious relevance. Prejudice embedded in the psychology of hatred and contempt surfaces in the *interstices* of avowedly liberal and egalitarian frameworks that have been adopted and generates the unjust carceral regime, generates the unjust application of laws in a society claiming to be ruled by just laws. These *subtler* interstitial sources of unfreedom are obviously not to be found in the *fact of incarceration* (an outcome) but in the (moral psychological) *causal conditions* that generate that outcome. This is the explanatory continuity between the claims of these two successive essays.

The section on academic freedom is diverse in its reach and the perspectives it offers.

Chapter 13 consists of two related pieces by Noam Chomsky. In his essay, he takes us back to the purposes of the great houses of intellect and how efforts to create a community of scholars and scientists have been under continual attack for more than a hundred years. He describes the historical context in which our universities have grown and considers the views of prominent early critics of universities in America during the First World War, Randolph Bourne and Sinclair Lewis, who lamented that they were led by a "liberal, technical intelligentsia," which endorsed the prevailing government mantra that those at universities who did not support the war effort had committed punishable acts of sedition. For Sinclair Lewis, these men were "*captains* of erudition." He then turns to a discussion of the principle of academic freedom and free inquiry formulated by J. B. S. Haldane, who believed that decisions on how to use funds for research should be made by scholars rather than by politicians, benefactors, or corporate givers to our universities. Looking to our time, he asks: Has the governance and power structure of universities changed over the past hundred years? How much of the Haldane doctrine have we achieved? Acknowledging the extraordinary discoveries produced by universities over the past century, Chomsky discusses how the American economy is based on public subsidy and private profit and explores the relationship between government policy and university-based research. Is academic freedom under the Haldane principle possible at American research universities, or does the economic and political system influence, even if without any overt coercion, what faculty members and researchers can explore? How much have the "technocratic and policy-oriented intellectuals" gradually come to gain greater centrality than the "value-oriented intellectuals"? How does governmental influence and corporate philanthropy pacify those young people and their teachers who believe in fundamental social change? What were the larger cultural and economic changes in the United States, beginning in the 1980s, that led to the renewed subordination of nonconformist ideas and social movements? Courage among leaders of our universities has always been in short supply. Today, as in the past, Chomsky suggests that we are witnessing another wave of cowardly, careerist leadership with a trained incapacity for understanding the values that lie at the very foundation of our universities, values that were always intended to be the basis of criticism of the deformations of existing societal formations.

The editors of this volume pursued some of the questions raised and conclusions drawn in this brief, thought-provoking essay in a follow-up conversation with Chomsky, which is also published here.

Michael Ignatieff's personal reflection considers the liminal state between freedom and coercion—a state of unfreedom where he places himself for most of his adult life. Ignatieff explains what he means by the state of unfreedom in terms of the extent to which one thinks for oneself and thus creates freedom. He speaks of being "adrift in a surging tide of opinion and counter-opinion, unwillingly imprisoned in other people's certainties." While registering the various states of unfreedom of various groups in our society, Ignatieff suggests that the most unfree individuals are those who are unable to think for themselves. The project of independent thought is difficult in free societies for reasons quite different from those of totalitarian nations, because the structure of these civil societies foster (through their values and culture) conformity. As Justice Oliver Wendell Holmes put it in his famous dissent in the 1919 *Abrams* case: "If you have no doubt of your premises or your power, and want a certain result with all your heart, you naturally express your wishes in *law*, and sweep away all opposition." Ignatieff explores the concepts of "manipulation" and of "persuasion" and the tension between these two ideas. He also elaborates on why free thinking requires more than free institutions for it to flourish in our society. Finally, based on his own position as a leader of an important educational institution, the Central European University, and after many years teaching at Harvard, he turns to the phenomenon of extreme opinions on the Left and the Right on college campuses, and the relevance of his remarks on persuasion are particularly interesting to bring to bear on this phenomenon.

Jon Elster's polemic provokes many questions. His overarching claim is that postmodern trends in academic inquiry and in art insulate themselves respectively from opposing arguments and from the demands of standards in the realm of "beauty" because arguments and standards are precisely what postmodernism eschews and undermines. This, says Elster, justifies criticizing them by ridicule, rather than argument—even ridicule that deploys deception and "sting" and "entrapment." In short, Habermas's dictum (which he cites) that, in intellectual inquiry, "the only legitimate means of persuading an interlocutor is the coercionless (*zwangsfreie*) force of the better argument" simply lapses when intellectual inquiry has been contaminated by postmodernism. Like all polemics, Elster's claims will no doubt fetch a lot of heated controversy, but—in a more sober register—there are two points worth observing, one on the theme of this volume (the nature of coercion and its relation to freedom) and one on Elster's claim about art.

Habermas's dictum is itself mildly paradoxical, combining the notion of *force* with the notion of *coercionlessness*. Can that combination possibly be right? If good arguments *compel* us to their conclusion, then, at least prima facie, they should surely be characterized as *coercive*. The question, then, is, does *this* kind of coerciveness have any implication for unfreedom? In other words, might it be not only that not all threats to freedom are coercive, but also that not all coercions generate unfreedom? And, of course, we might also then go on to ask: Does ridicule compel and coerce in the way that good arguments do? The other point worth remarking is that those who will immediately dismiss Elster's criticism of Duchamp, Warhol, and Cage might pause to consider that a celebrated philosophical art critic, Arthur Danto, himself declared that Duchamp's urinal signaled the "*end of art.*" But before Elster gleefully hijacks Danto as an ally, we should also note that Danto went on to add a crucial second point to his conclusion—that such works of art *transfigured art into philosophy*. This views Duchamp as a starter of a new conversation, whereas if Danto had not added this second point, he would have viewed Duchamp merely, as Elster does, as a conversation-stopper.

These essays are followed by two others that take up very current and rather urgent concerns that have arisen on American university campuses and are increasingly surfacing on campuses in other parts of the world.

After providing a historical and sociological background to "woke," as they are called, demands by students, Akeel Bilgrami suggests that these demands may well be steering one to a new model of inquiry in the humanities and in the social sciences, a transformation that is quite different from the earlier ("*verstehen*") transformation that had introduced hermeneutical and interpretive models to these subjects; he suggests, rather, that inquiry in these areas are being modeled more on inquiry in criminal law. But even such an emerging model, he argues, can be prevented from thwarting the commitment to free inquiry, if we shape that model along less forensic lines, thereby stressing *engagement* in the way that it was stressed in the application of criminal law in some celebrated cases of transitional justice.

Laura Kipnis asks whether American campuses bastions of supposed academic freedom and free inquiry have, today, become a "hotbed for craven snitches." Based upon actual cases, Kipnis raises the more fundamental issues about enforced surveillance and mandated reporting of alleged transgressions of sexual misconduct and "inappropriate" workplace behavior by faculty, students, and staff. She notes that in the past snitching was perceived as normatively inappropriate behavior. Today it may have become the norm with all members of an academic community who are now mandated to take online courses and quizzes about appropriate behavior of their colleagues and when, under threat of personal liability, faculty and others in the community are obliged to report on their colleagues. Kipnis questions where the line ought to be drawn between protecting observed behavior and the reporting of supposed inappropriate behavior. She questions whether the current system of control and power undermines fundamental values that lie at the very foundation of our academic communities—and she reflects on its consequences. She also raises the question: Who should act as the Grand Inquisitor when faculty are under attack for their views and their behavior that some believe go beyond the boundaries of acceptability? Implicitly, Kipnis questions whether universities and colleges have become surveillance communities.

The section closes with an essay by Jonathan Cole and Daria Franklin on women in academic science that examines why the fundamental norm of universalism, which enjoins members of the community to evaluate scientists solely on the quality of their scientific work—regardless of ascribed characteristics such as their race, gender, nationality, and other extraneous criteria—has been abridged by pervasively noncoercive measures and policies. On the basis of extensive personal interviews with female scientists conducted in the 1980s by Harriet Zuckerman and Cole, they review the changing status of women scientists during this period. Unsurprisingly, they find that women were largely excluded from this male dominated social system. Women were found, for the most part, in the outer circle of science—if they entered science at all. Discrimination against women was a part of this story, but Cole and Franklin go beyond that obvious explanation to explore how the culture and zeitgeist during this period, as well as the norms and values which universities embraced, generated fundamentally different opportunities and outcomes for women. Female scientists' options were far more limited than men who were their peers because of the *structural* bases for gender bias and because of what they describe as "particularism" in the academic community. They suggest that the social structure of science led to a definition of science as a community of *men*.

The media has long been recognized as quite possibly the most pervasively influential institution in shaping behavior without coercion and generating unfreedom by constructing what Gramsci calls "hegemony," though it must be pointed out that under certain unusual circumstances it sometime generates the opposite as well—conventional media, indeed just one television station, was to a considerable extent responsible for what we remember as the "Arab Spring," beaming into the homes of citizens of some Middle Eastern countries just how corrupt and brutal their rulers were.[9] When it comes to the hegemonic shaping of consent, the anxiety is whether the media which does this is *itself* really "free" or whether it does so because it is controlled, though again often without overt direction, by governments or corporations. Thus, the issue here is of embedded unfreedoms—the media's *and in turn* those whom it influences. Since the rise of unconventional, "social" media these questions have been intensified and rendered very much more complicated because of the entry of the *demos* in media activity, raising questions about whether this aspect of democracy itself generates unfreedom and whether to seek to regulate it is, in effect, undemocratic. Here again we are in the realm of the conflict of values, the conflict of freedoms, discussed as well in the essays by Stiglitz and Klitzman.

Two expert essays by Duncan Watts and his multiple collaborators cover a lot of the basic ground of current concerns. On offer in the first is an intriguing and somewhat counterintuitive look at the influence of social media on information flows and opinion formation. Since the 2016 US presidential election, the deliberate spread of misinformation online, and on social media in particular, has generated extraordinary concern, in large part because of its potential effects on public opinion, political polarization, and ultimately democratic decision making. Recently, however, a handful of papers have argued that both the prevalence and consumption of "fake news" per se is extremely low compared with other types of news and news-relevant content. Although neither prevalence nor consumption is a direct measure of influence, this work suggests that proper understanding of misinformation and its effects requires a much broader view of the problem, encompassing biased and misleading—but not necessarily factually incorrect—information that is routinely produced or amplified by mainstream news organizations. They propose an ambitious collective research agenda to measure the origins, nature, and prevalence of misinformation, broadly construed, as well as its impact on democracy.

In the second essay, which appeared initially in the journal *Science*, Watts and his collaborators further explore questions surrounding "fake news." "Fake news," broadly defined as deliberately false or misleading information masquerading as legitimate news, is widely believed to be pervasive on the web, especially on social media, with serious consequences for public opinion, political polarization, and ultimately for democracy. Using a unique multimode data set that comprises a nationally representative sample of mobile, desktop, and television consumption across all categories of media content, they seek to refute this conventional wisdom on three levels. First, news consumption of any sort is heavily outweighed by other forms of media consumption, comprising at most 14.2 percent of Americans' daily media diets. Second, to the extent that Americans do consume news, it is overwhelmingly from television, which accounts for roughly five times as much as news consumption as online, while a supermajority of Americans consume little or no news online at all. Third, fake news comprises, they argue, only about 1 percent of overall news consumption and 0.15 percent of Americans' daily media diet. To the extent that Americans are misinformed or uninformed about important political issues, their results suggest that a combination of ordinary news bias—especially on television—and avoidance of certain vital news are more serious concerns for democracy than any form of overtly fake news.

The volume concludes with Anya Schiffrin tellingly invoking an era some eight decades before the rise of social media to look at possibilities for resisting the distortions in information that we are now faced with at every turn. In that time, she says, despite a simpler vocabulary ("propaganda") to describe it, this phenomenon was a familiar tool exploited by states as well as by the newly emerging public relations industry. It was a cause of much concern among democratically minded public educators. She focuses on a particular institution that took up this concern in a systematic way, countering propaganda not by banning it (disavowing that as "not the American way"), but rather by educating the public into an understanding of how it works—what (more or less) exact forms the distortion takes and what its motives and goals are, and how one might guard against it. What drove Clyde Miller and his associates at the Institute of Propaganda Analysis is the idea that if one can explain to the public how it is generated and how works, then without violating the first amendment and without generating one's own counterpropaganda, one has implicitly taught citizens how to address the problem of disinformation. Throughout the essay, even as she acknowledges the immense complexity introduced by contemporary electronic media forms, Schiffrin seeks to draw lessons for our own time from these detailed efforts of that earlier period.

The editors would like to thank each one of our contributors, very busy people who nevertheless very kindly accepted our invitation to contribute to the study of one of the most interesting and vexing of questions—a question that, although it has been around for well over two thousand years, takes on new guises in our own most complex of times. We hope these essays will contribute measurably to advance our understanding of how this question must be addressed, and since the question of threats to freedom, especially in their non-coercive form, is not likely to ever completely go away, we hope these essays will at least provide analyses and answers that those who produce future work on the subject will profit from reading.

NONCOERCIVE THREATS TO ACADEMIC, POLITICAL, AND ECONOMIC FREEDOM

PART I

PHILOSOPHICAL ISSUES

CHAPTER 1

WHY FREEDOM TO SAY ENLARGES FREEDOM TO THINK

DAVID BROMWICH

Some hints in the second chapter of John Stuart Mill's essay *On Liberty* I think are worth spelling out, and the remarks that follow will mainly be a commentary on that text. Mill entitled the chapter "On the Liberty of Thought and Discussion," and he starts from two fundamental propositions he has laid down in his first chapter. To begin with: "the sole end for which mankind are warranted, either individually or collectively, in interfering with the liberty of action of any of their number, is self- protection." And second: "the only purpose for which power can be rightfully exercised over any member of a civilized community, against his will, is to prevent harm to others."[1] Mill holds a precise and narrow definition of harm: he nearly confines it to physical harm; in any case, as the tenor of his argument will make clear, the harm must be substantial and visibly threatening to life or livelihood.

Americans in the last generation have extended that definition of harm, perhaps inordinately. But the truth is that Mill left an ambiguity through which a troop of exceptions can pass. If "mankind" (to keep with Mill's own usage) "collectively" are allowed to impede the freedom of "any of their number" for the "self-protection" of men and women, a great deal depends on one's idea of legitimate self-protection. Under examination by reasonable persons, how small or local or conjectural may an alleged threat be in order to justify censorship or prior restraint? But we should not make too much of the grammatical loophole, for Mill seems to have taken on trust a standard of common sense. The record of any life will show unpleasant experiences, some of them caused by other people and theoretically classifiable as injuries; and there is no way for an ethic of liberty to screen out every sensation of insult or emotional setback to which people are susceptible. The conceptual inflation by which we may widen the field of words, signals, and verbal gestures that qualify as actionable "harms" is driven by a demand that grows stronger the more it is it is propitiated. Social anxieties are not less real for being the creation of new social conditioning; and when the anxieties flood the perception of a great many people or come to be credited by a sufficient number of institutions, a restriction or penalty that would once have seemed outlandish will be deemed acceptable and even desirable. The "Satanic Panic" of the late twentieth century, for example, became a matter of public concern from the supposed abuses at American child-care facilities. The accusations here required that credence be given to a previously inadmissible kind of evidence: the unconscious materials of "repressed memory," coaxed into articulate form by the ministrations of a psychotherapist. The rapid onset of that panic, and its gradual disappearance with jailed or slandered victims in its wake, reminds us of the speed at which an enlightened society can suddenly discard its customary manners along with its former practice of fairness and common sense. We saw a similar defection on a larger scale in the early twenty-first century, with the passage of the Patriot Act and the consequent narrowing of people's idea of their right of privacy.

Mill was an early reader and admirer of Tocqueville's *Democracy in America*. He published reviews of both volumes, and those articles show that he was especially struck by Tocqueville's observations on the despotism of manners that is peculiar to democratic life. Tocqueville spoke of "the omnipotence of the majority," and he warned: "A king's power is physical only, controlling actions but not influencing desires, whereas the majority is invested with both physical and moral authority, which acts as much upon the will as upon behavior and at the same moment prevents both the act and the desire to do it." Tocqueville goes on to make an unsettling observation: "I know no country in which, speaking generally, there is less independence of mind and true freedom of discussion than in America."[2] This can happen in a democracy, says Tocqueville, because of the extraordinary power of the majority in disciplining and stereotyping the opinions held by people in general. The warning may bring to mind, first of all, the power of a sheer *numerical* majority at election time, but a different kind of pressure is exerted between-times by articulate public persons—"influencers," as we now call them, who command lots of followers. These people have a power in democracy unrivaled by the office-holder in a traditional society. Tocqueville was directing his criticism not against popular sovereignty, as such, but rather the enormous authority accorded to the prominent persons or groups who shape the trend of opinion in democracy. For better or worse, these people control the public culture. We are governed, after all, by opinion more than by force, and our effort to act and talk in line with the right opinions seems part of our membership in society itself.

The danger is that people being governed by majority opinion can come to exert a *tyranny* of the majority. Mill, again following Tocqueville's lead, wanted to guard against the unfree habits of mind a tyranny of opinion fosters by the inhibition or elimination of alternative views. So strong is his belief on this point that he asks us to consider a hypothetical case that is unlikely ever to occur. Suppose a government is "entirely at one with the people" and wishes to conduct its policies always "in agreement with what it conceives to be their voice." On the face of it, that would seem sufficient warrant for a speech code delimiting what can and cannot be said; for, in Mill's hypothetical case, the government is following the wishes and tendency of all the people, or anyway a large and unfluctuating majority. But Mill recoils from the very possibility and surprises us by his vehemence:

> I deny the right of the people to exercise such coercion, either by themselves or by their government. The power itself is illegitimate. The best government has no more title to it than the worst. It is as noxious, or more noxious, when exerted in accordance with public opinion, than when in opposition to it. If all mankind minus one, were of one opinion, and only one person were of the contrary opinion, mankind would be no more justified in silencing that one person, than he, if he had the power, would be justified in silencing mankind. Were an opinion a personal possession of no value except to the owner; if to be obstructed in the enjoyment of it were simply a private injury, it would make some difference whether the injury was inflicted only on a few persons or on many. But the peculiar evil of silencing the expression of an opinion is, that it is robbing the human race; posterity as well as the existing generation; those who dissent from the opinion, still more than those who hold it. If the opinion is right, they are deprived of the opportunity of exchanging error for truth: if wrong, they lose, what is almost as great a benefit, the clearer perception and livelier impression of truth, produced by its collision with error.[3]

Mill supports this extraordinary assertion with a tactical argument. He says we can never be sure if a new idea is false; but even if it is false, we are wrong to stifle it.

All silencing of dissent, even of a negligible minority opinion, he says, amounts to an assumption of infallibility by those who prevent it from being uttered. We might reply, "No, it is only a way of saving time; we can't be arguing about details forever, when most of us agree and we want to get something *done*." Even so, Mill would disapprove any shortcut that prohibits an obnoxious view. The only profit in such a ban is a cheap economy of discussion that spares us the truth about our fallibility. This uncertainty, the fact of our fallibility and our reluctance to acknowledge it, I think is the reason Mill pushes the point so hard. For uncertainty will never be admitted after the fact. Our errors of judgment may raise a scandal once we translate them into action; but when the deed is done in conformity with triumphant opinion, it is as if the dissenting view had been refuted, whereas in fact it was merely outvoted.

So it seems that *a loss of truth* is a consequence of the exclusive acceptance of one sort of speech and the repression of counterspeech; but there is also loss of something less easily noticed: an active interest in *discovering* truth, which is a main element of our intellectual energy. Indeed, Mill extends his criticism beyond the censorship practiced by a high official or even an entire society. A whole era of the world may be as fallible as individuals are. To take an illustration close enough to our time: America in the 1950s, in its cultural imagery and prevalent mores, assigned to women certain everyday household functions and the raising of children; their social status was not thereby demoted or necessarily undervalued, but anything beyond that role—a working career, say, that lasted beyond the birth of children—was apt to be seen as peculiar and to invite an explanation. In this respect, the 1950s now appear to us less advanced than the generation of the 1930s and 1940s; you can notice the difference in the movies of the time. Or take a more recent example: after the fall of Soviet Communism and the collapse of the Soviet bloc in 1991, many Americans, especially in the sphere of foreign policy and economic planning, believed we had arrived at "the end of history." You can trace the extent of the delusion in the popular book of that title, published a year later. This misjudged confidence prompted Americans to think commercial democracy an arrangement impressed on the genetic code of humanity for the rest of time.

Mill, for his part, believed the Enlightenment had enlightened and that the prospects were good for the continued progress of science and the widening of human possibilities; but, writing in 1859, he was less certain about the future of liberal democracy. He attacks the presumption of those persons who accept, if only for convenience, the rightness of prohibiting certain opinions:

> We may, and must [they say], assume our opinion to be true for the guidance of our own conduct: and it is assuming no more when we forbid bad men to pervert society by the propagation of opinions which we regard as false and pernicious.
>
> I answer, that it is assuming very much more. There is the greatest difference between presuming an opinion to be true, because, with every opportunity for contesting it, it has not been refuted, and assuming its truth for the purpose of not permitting its refutation. Complete liberty of contradicting and disproving our opinion, is the very condition which justifies us in assuming its truth for purposes of action; and on no other terms can a being with human faculties have any rational assurance of being right.[4]

Moral progress, says Mill, can occur only if we recognize that we are never proof against error. We make mistakes. Fortunately, many of our mistakes are corrigible. But, for the necessary correction to occur, there must be discussion; and for the discussion to do all it can for the discovery of truth, it must be open and uninhibited.

Individually we may be timid from a natural wish to coexist in harmony with our neighbors; for we know we can satisfy them, and prevent friction, by being seen to hold similar opinions. But under an official or a tacitly understood regime of censorship, the constraints on discussion press much further. The presence of an external force disposes us to a speak timidly, and, by a sort of backward contagion that touches the roots of volition, our own habitual silence bends us to *think* timidly. What began as self-denial ends as self-stultification. Thoughts that lack an outlet in speech or that might, if permitted, have found expression in experimental speech, now recede to the background and are no longer detected by the thinker. The little inward concessions by which we allow this to happen are described memorably in the opening paragraph of Emerson's essay "Self-Reliance." Great works of art, Emerson says, give evidence of the genius that resides potentially in every thoughtful person: "They teach us to abide by our spontaneous impression with good-humored inflexibility then most when the whole cry of voices is on the other side. Else tomorrow a stranger will say with masterly good sense precisely what we have thought and felt all the time, and we shall be forced to take with shame our own opinion from another."[5] Emerson has in mind a listener who has already felt a glimmer of the true thought but never stepped forward to utter it. Mill finds a source of regret further along in the process of taking our opinion from another. Thoughtless acceptance even of a true opinion can become a habitual passiveness. The inward repression may gradually yield an outward acquiescence in censorship.

So great is the danger of such passive conformity that Mill devises a stratagem to stimulate active engagement with even the most established ideas. In continuing to accept such ideas, he says, a liberal society should follow the practice of the Catholic Church in approving the canonization of a saint. Society should appoint a person of appropriate knowledge and authority to act as *advocatus diaboli*. Resistance, opposition, or (to use Mill's favorite word) collision is good if the end in view is intellectual discovery and the elimination of error. "The usefulness of an opinion," he remarks, "is itself a matter of opinion"—meaning that different people may hold different ideas of what counts as useful. Note that this affirmation, even as Mill's idiom remains stubbornly utilitarian, opens his argument to broader criteria of value than the utilitarian calculus would allow. One person's settled hatred may be a vital touchstone to another, and so long as the loathed and admired thing is not evidently harmful, there is no possible warrant for banning it.

Socrates and Jesus are his leading examples of discoverers of truths who were condemned to death by their societies. Mill adds that even the wisest of Roman emperors, Marcus Aurelius, could not perceive that Christianity had brought the world a dimension of moral truth missing from the pagan philosophy. There are people who would convince us that persecution is a necessary ordeal, a sort of rite of passage for the recognition of a new and difficult truth. Mill sees the intuitive plausibility of that claim, but he rejects it on historical and psychological grounds. The advances of human and moral knowledge should not have to be achieved at an agonizing cost. Besides, persecution sometimes wins out; do we want to assent to its undeserved triumphs? "Men," he writes, "are not more zealous for truth than they often are for error." That skeptical verdict answers, by anticipation, Justice Oliver Wendell Holmes's optimistic judgment in *Abrams v. United States* that truth will *ultimately* win out and we should therefore let all views be aired, so long as they pose no clear and present danger to society.

An important phrase in Holmes's opinion is "free trade in ideas." This has come down to us, a bit slanted and garbled, as "the free market of ideas"; and with some further garbling, the phrase has been attributed to Mill. But if one looks closely at a famous passage from Holmes's opinion, one may notice the difference between Mill's idea of the collision of truth with error and the idea of market competition in ideas. The moral value of a discovered truth, for Mill, is quite distinct from the social value of betting on the ideas we find profitable. He may seem to set a market value on truth when he says "the truth of an idea is part of its utility"—a reassuring but also a confusing axiom, given his admission that usefulness is a matter of opinion and the fact that a new truth is liable to arouse anger or disgust. But Holmes anyway was saying something altogether different, namely that the present or potential utility of an idea *constitutes* its truth, just as the usefulness of a commodity is proved by its having fared well on the market:

> If you have no doubt of your premises or your power and want a certain result with all your heart you naturally express your wishes in law and sweep away all opposition. To allow opposition by speech seems to indicate that you think the speech impotent, as when a man says that he has squared the circle, or that you do not care wholeheartedly for the result, or that you doubt either your power or your premises. But when men have realized that time has upset many fighting faiths, they may come to believe even more than they believe the very foundations of their own conduct that the ultimate good desired is better reached by free trade in ideas—that the best test of truth is the power of the thought to get itself accepted in the competition of the market, and that truth is the only ground upon which their wishes safely can be carried out. That, at any rate, is the theory of our Constitution. It is an experiment, as all life is an

experiment. Every year if not every day we have to wager our salvation upon some prophecy based upon imperfect knowledge. While that experiment is part of our system I think that we should be eternally vigilant against attempts to check the expression of opinions that we loathe and believe to be fraught with death, unless they so imminently threaten immediate interference with the lawful and pressing purposes of the law that an immediate check is required to save the country.[6]

Holmes assumes, as Mill did not, that the best ideas will prevail, just as he also believes the best product will earn a profit in circumstances of open competition and free trade.

By now it should be clear that Mill's language about truth and liberty of discussion has some other guiding light than utility and some other criterion of truth than mere success against competing ideas. Truth is often defeated, sometimes martyred, occasionally suppressed for long ages of the world. The good of not silencing an idea you oppose is not simply that you want to take charge of the best ideas and promote your society's internal improvement and perhaps also its standing in comparison with other societies. Rather, Mill says, we ought not to silence an idea unless it threatens immediate harm to others, because we ought always to act so as to keep alive a spark of originality that exists preeminently in a few individuals, and so as to nurture a fugitive spark that may eventually show in others. As he puts it in his plain and unglamorous language, we should strive "to enable average human beings to attain the mental stature which they are capable of." The word *stature* matters more than can easily be seen from the neutral adjective with which Mill pairs it. Stature sounds like a merely physical term, but, of course, stature is something we would all wish to be known for; it denotes a kind of dignity, a moral worth resulting from rightly earned respect and self-respect.[7] Mill wants to promote a high average of human stature, despite the tendency of a democratic society to keep the average just where it is. As usual, Mill here is siding with energy against inertia, and with rational nonconformity against imitation. Epochs hospitable to original thought and feeling have been rare. He mentions the Reformation, the Enlightenment, and the Romantic age in German thought, and that is all.

As for mid-Victorian society, Mill takes it to be sunk in a torpor of moral and intellectual self-satisfaction:

Our merely social intolerance kills no one, roots out no opinions, but induces men to disguise them, or to abstain from any active effort for their diffusion. With us, heretical opinions do not perceptibly gain, or even lose, ground in each decade or generation; they never blaze out far and wide, but continue to smoulder in the narrow circles of thinking and studious persons among whom they originate, without ever lighting up the general affairs of mankind with either a true or a deceptive light. And thus is kept up a state of things very satisfactory to some minds, because, without the unpleasant process of fining or imprisoning anybody, it maintains all prevailing opinions outwardly undisturbed, while it does not absolutely interdict the exercise of reason by dissentients afflicted with the malady of thought. A convenient plan for having peace in the intellectual world, and keeping all things going on therein very much as they do already. But the price paid for this sort of intellectual pacification, is the sacrifice of the entire moral courage of the human mind.[8]

The real danger for Mill, then, does not come from the potential influence of less useful ideas when better ones are available. No: the enemy is what he calls intellectual pacification.

What we risk is the loss of the entire moral courage of the human mind—a collective endowment of the species, squandered for the sake of temporary comfort and harmony. A salient property of any original idea, whether true or false, is its power to irritate whose who find it strange or disconcerting. The idea breaks up habitual ways of thinking or doing; it unsettles and is to that extent repellent. Indeed, *that it disturbs* is always among the complaints heard from opponents of an original truth, which is not to say that anything that disturbs is bound to be new and true. The "us," however, is as significant an element of the interaction as the idea of a right not to be disturbed.

So fearful is Mill of the too-easy acceptance of habitual ideas that he proposes a kind of regimen to be followed by thinking persons. In order to value a given opinion as a living truth rather than dead dogma, it is not enough to have mastered the grounds of your own belief. You must throw yourself into the mental position of those who hold a view opposite to your own. To have earned the beliefs he professes, the thinker "must be able to hear [the opposing beliefs] from persons who actually believe them; who defend them in earnest, and do their very utmost for them. He must know them in their most plausible and persuasive form; he must feel the whole force of the difficulty which the true view of the subject has to encounter and dispose of."[9] This proposed therapy in defense of truth—the necessity of a mock encounter with a formidable antagonist—leads to Mill's generous sketch of what he calls the "many-sidedness" of moral truths. The danger always lies with one-sidedness and the way such simplicity appeals to our merely social intolerance.

What we should cultivate, according to Mill, is not tolerance for the sake of social blending, not the formation of personalities willing to countenance any idea because we are afraid of offending others, but instead a "lively apprehension" of the truths we have come to understand and approve. The alternative to this generous receptivity Mill captures in the image of the inherited creed as a sentinel over a vacant mind: "Both teachers and learners" he says, "go to sleep at their post, as soon as there is no enemy in the field." And yet, to keep in mind the many-sidedness of truths that are valuable for living, we must recognize that no moral idea that gains our respect will seem absolutely new. The Christian morality rejected Jewish tribalism but incorporated the Jewish morality of friendship. On the other hand, Christianity, admirable for its idea of equality in the eyes of God, erred in disdaining the idea of *honor*, which was central to the classical culture of Greece and Rome.

We would be wrong to take Mill's case for liberty of discussion as an endorsement of respectful etiquette and the reduction of social friction. He published his thoughts out of fear as much as hope—fear of the leveling and assimilative instincts that are especially keen in democracy; fear, that is, of his own society. Our merely social intolerance breeds "a low, abject, servile type of character," and even once we agree to abide by an ethic of open debate, the "formidable evil" is not "the violent conflict between parts of the truth, but the quiet suppression of half of it." Mill takes for granted a high degree of civility, and he knows that abrasive and offensive speech runs counter to the purpose of persuasion. Yet he is suspicious of those who, reducing the rules of discussion to a criticism of manners, would set up boundaries of politeness that rule out undesirable opinions: "Much might be said on the impossibility of fixing where these supposed bounds are to be placed; for if the test be offence to those whose opinion is attacked, I think experience testifies that this offence is given whenever the attack is telling and powerful, and that every opponent who pushes them hard, and whom they find it difficult to answer, appears to them, if he shows any strong feeling on the subject, an intemperate opponent."[10] Honest argument requires that you encounter the opposing argument in the fairest and strongest possible terms. To refuse your opponent a serious platform does an injustice to your own cause and weakens whatever truth may emerge from the collision of ideas in question.

Having canvassed a partly misleading interpretation of Mill's view by his fellow libertarian Justice Holmes, it may sharpen our view to hear the opposing voice of a rational conservative and antilibertarian. The most famous contemporary reply to *On Liberty* was James Fitzjames Stephen's *Liberty, Equality, Fraternity*. Stephen argued that Mill, with his all-out defense of liberty on behalf of individuality and variety, had confused the proposition "goodness is various" with the proposition "variety is good."[11] The latter proposition, when extended from personal life to society at large, Stephen believed to be a dangerous fallacy. He denies that free citizens should feel perpetually obligated to confront all ideas, since the clutter and tangle of superfluous nonsense can only distract us from the pursuit of rational progress. We want only the best ideas to survive. And Stephen does think there is a necessary ordeal of persecution or coercive resistance by which a new idea *should* have to fight against prejudice to gain a hearing. Surely it is only timid people who require the sort of protection Mill offers; trial by adversity builds a truth that is fit to last, and we can hardly want a society of the pampered and timid.

But recall now Mill's answer to this objection. Many truths have failed to pass the test initially. Do not suppose that you improve the chances for a better society by acting in your own time as the party did that condemned Socrates in Athens, or Jesus in Judea. Stephen, however, while recognizing the evident harshness of his analysis, remains unyielding. People need an orthodoxy in order to find their bearings in matters of right and wrong, and the process by which orthodoxy may be shifted ought to be difficult. He frankly sides with the Roman governors in the time of Christ, against the early Christians. Politically and judicially, the governors were right to act as they did in defense of their own morality; and in the same way, we are right to act on behalf of our morality. A striking fact emerges here. It is often said, against Mill's libertarian radicalism, that its doctrinal tolerance indicates an underlying relativism. It can seem to argue that anything anyone says is as permissible as, and therefore potentially as good as, anything else. We have seen that Mill was far from holding such a view: he sets an ultimate and nonnegotiable value on the "moral courage of the human mind" in its fight against "intellectual pacification." Nowhere does he defend liberty of thought and discussion on the ground that we do not mind what our fellow citizens say. We abide by a principle of liberty because we hate moral cowardice, we want to maintain our guard against spiritual deadness, and we find that in the field of ideas, the vices of prohibition and censorship obstruct our knowledge and self-knowledge, even as they intolerably lower our image of human nature.

In this comparison it is not Mill but Stephen—the advocate of force deployed on behalf of conventional morality—who appears as the relativist. When the Romans laid the early Christians under proscription, Stephen is willing to say, what they did was right for them. And when in our turn we require certain oaths of allegiance or censor what we deem to be dangerous speech, we are doing what is right for us. Stephen presents himself as a defender of the normal mind of his time, and he was indeed serving that function, as Mill was not. Accordingly, Stephen opposes not a decent respect for other opinions but rather *too much* tolerance, *systematic* tolerance; he says that Mill's immoderate stance betrays "a kind of Quakerism." Where Mill warned against intellectual pacification, Stephen accuses him of being a pacifist in the ordinary sense: someone who refuses to go to war for his society. Considered as a polemical tactic, "a kind of Quakerism" may be a cheap shot, but as far as it goes, the charge is true. Mill assumes that his society does a very good job defending itself. Meanwhile, people like him are needed to prevent its death from the tactics it deploys on its own behalf.

To return to the possible harm of speech, it bears repeating that Mill assumed a precise, limited, and commonsense definition of harm—an immediate threat of injury, or the impairment of life by damage to one's property or other necessities. Soften the definition of "harm" sufficiently—let it encompass a depression of mood or self-esteem in the listener—and the regime of energetic contest that Mill envisaged will be overruled by a code of coercive politeness. This has been the rule in most societies at most times, those committed to equality quite as much as those governed by theocratic edict. But Mill does not underrate the difficulty of practicing the form of liberty he defends. He tells us that there are two distinct but complementary tendencies in the development of any society, the pressure for order and the pressure for reform. A peaceable civil order, incorporating protection against demonstrable harm to life or liveli-hood, must be in place for reform to do its work. The rights of women, within and outside marriage; the ability of laborers to associate and organize to improve their working conditions; the reduction of the socially sanctioned prejudice against Jews and other religious minorities, including atheists—these were some of the reforms Mill advocated in an orderly society that was free enough to debate them openly.

From his own practice as well as the argument of chapter 2, it is clear his defense of liberty was meant to foster a generous practice of toleration even in the most heated controversies. How might such a defense work today in approaching contentious issues about which liberty of opinion is legally toler-ated but not socially practiced? For there are in America today social and polit-ical topics so divisive that members of one body of opinion can hardly bear to listen to a word said by the other side. Consider abortion and immigration. If we were to heed Mill's advice on the hearing owed to the opposing view, a pas-sionate advocate of the right to life of the unborn would have to listen patiently to, and to carry in her mind the strongest argument made by, the believer in a woman's right to have control of her body without interference by the superior power of the state. The advocate of a woman's choice in matters involving her body, in turn, would have to encounter and reason with the passionate belief of her opponent that the fetus is a being so close to human that it creates an obligation indistinguishable from our duties toward the living. I have tried to state these opposing views in terms their supporters would find credible and free of caricature, but Mill would ask that we also expose ourselves to appeals that may be far more emotional, more penetrating, more apt to disconcert. His thought is that something good may come of the result, whereas only stultifi-cation can come from excluding the forbidden view.

Or again, consider immigration. The radical defender of open immigration, whose slogan is "No borders, no walls," would be asked to hear out and inhabit the mental field of someone who believes that citizenship in a constitutional democracy is a sacred thing, and by establishing a permanent twilight category of noncitizen participants in the society, or else by making border crossing itself sufficient for the eventual attainment of citizenship, we degrade the civic ideal and usher in a social order whose rules are unknown to many of its members. On the other hand, the anti-immigration partisan would have to confront the fact that worldwide migration is increasing and will continue to increase in a time of planetary climate disruption; that there are places in the United States where new immigrants might be led to settle in an orderly and documented procedure; and that the variety brought to American culture by immigrants from Europe in the late nineteenth and early twentieth centuries, and from South Asia and East Asia in the late twentieth and early twenty-first centuries, and from Latin America at all periods, have contributed to an agreeable variety most Americans now think of simply as American. One thing we can say about these acts of imagining an opposite view is that they make it harder, in a scene of moral conflict, to retain the belief that one side or the other holds an exclusive claim to moral rectitude and political justice.

Mill argued for liberty because he thought our experience of divergent ideas could enlarge the humanity of individuals in a free society. The image of social and political understandings as the product of a clash of opposing ideas, so central to his way of thinking, may be the part of his argument most alien to us now. And perhaps it is misleading to suppose that without such collision our own cherished beliefs are apt to wither and die. They may only grow dormant and atrophy. In corporate life, in the media, and in universities, a commonly heard expression is: "They don't bother you if you keep your head down." By repeating what we are expected to say, or offering minimal assent to things we half believe, we allow our own ideas to slacken and grow less vital. Kierke-gaard, in *The Sickness Unto Death*, saw such a withdrawal from speech as the counterpart of despair. A possible occasion to *say* is ignored as the person relapses into silence, just as a possible occasion to *do* is sidestepped and action is displaced by indolence. But why call it a condition of despair rather than well-instructed prudence? "The despair," writes Kierkegaard,

> which not only occasions no embarrassment but makes one's life easy and com-
> fortable is naturally not regarded as despair. That this is the view of the world
> can also be seen in almost all the proverbs, which are merely rules for shrewd
> behavior. It is said, for example, that a man ten times regrets having spoken,
> for the once he regrets silence. And why? Because the fact of having spoken is
> an external fact, which may involve one in annoyances, since it is an actuality.
> But the fact of having kept silent! Yet this is the most dangerous thing of all.[12]

The self-subversion that Kierkegaard describes is another name for hopelessness—the elemental meaning of despair. By contrast, Mill's deepest motive in writing *On Liberty* was to offer a new basis of hope for the self as well as society.

CHAPTER 2

KANT AND "CAN'T"

Practical Necessity and the Diminution of Options

JEREMY WALDRON

1.

One's options have a way of simply evaporating. There you are, walking down a country road, fancy free, approaching the brow of a hill beyond which you know there's an intersection, any of whose paths you could take—you could go east to meet with your grandchild or west to go to the library. "What shall I do?" Then suddenly you see a person lying by the side of the road (*your* side of the road) gravely wounded, evidently a victim of violence. You are not the first to encounter him. It's a well-known story, a parable in fact.

> *Samaritan*
> A certain man went down from Jerusalem to Jericho, and fell among thieves, which stripped him of his raiment, and wounded him, and departed, leaving him half dead. And by chance there came down a certain priest that way: and when he saw him, he passed by on the other side. And likewise a Levite, when he was at the place, came and looked on him, and passed by on the other side. But a certain Samaritan, as he journeyed, came where he was: and when he saw him, he had compassion on him, And went to him, and bound up his wounds, pouring in oil and wine, and set him on his own beast, and brought him to an inn, and took care of him.[1]

Peter Winch, a twentieth-century English philosopher, glossed the story as follows in a paper called "Who Is My Neighbour?," published in his collection, *Trying to Make Sense*: "The Samaritan responds to what he sees as a necessity generated by the presence of the injured man." Winch continued: "What I mean by
introducing this word [necessity] can be brought out by considering what someone in the Samaritan's position, and responding as he did, might say if urged by
a companion to hurry on so as not to miss his important appointment. "But I
can't just leave him here to die." "The word 'can't,' as used in such a context,"
said Winch, "expresses [a] kind of necessity—in this case an impossibility." It
seems that the "Samaritan's conviction [was] that *nothing else was possible* in the
circumstances." One *must* stop and help the man. Evidently the "can't" is not
physical impossibility: the priest and the Levite in the parable experienced no
difficulty in passing by on the other side after they looked on the injured man
and saw his plight. Winch says if the Samaritan had a companion who responded
to his saying "I can't just leave him here to die" by saying, "Of course you can,
you can walk can't you?" that "he would not be meeting the Samaritan's point,
so much as making a black, tasteless joke."[2]

2.

What is the connection here between words like "must" and "can't" in "Samaritan" and the idea of unfreedom? Is Winch's Samaritan telling us that because
he feels morally constrained in the situation described in the parable, he is really
not free to pass by the injured man without helping? If we take him at his word
on that, what is the impact on our understanding of freedom? Is the Samaritan
saying that he is suddenly less of a free man in this encounter?

Our topic in this volume is unfreedom, and we are supposed to be examining
the independently quite plausible suggestion that unfreedom should be understood, not just in terms of a person's being subject to coercion but also in terms of
the impoverishment of a person's options.[3] Understanding lack of freedom in
that way casts a wider net, capturing and denouncing threats to freedom that
don't necessarily involve force or jail or chains. So consider the following case,
which might be regarded as a classic instance of this extended conception of
freedom.

Proletarian

Karl's boss, Adam, pays Karl a barely living wage for dirty and dangerous work.
But, says Adam, Karl is a free man nonetheless because he had and has a variety of jobs to choose from. He could work for Friedrich and be paid an even
lower wage for work that is dirtier and more dangerous. Or he could work for

Milton and be paid the same money that Friedrich offers for work that is as dirty and as dangerous as work in Friedrich's establishment. Karl claims to be unfree; working for any of the others, he says, is not a real option; he has no choice but to work for Adam; so he is not really a free man. Friedrich and Milton (and Adam) deny this.

Adam might note that no one is holding a gun to Karl's head to force him to work in Adam's factory; there is no direct coercion. And that is right. Karl has alternatives, and no one will harm him if he takes one of them. But Karl might also be right in insisting that he is not truly free, because he has nothing but impoverished options to choose from. Accounts of this kind are very common in Marxist theory, denigrating the vaunted freedom of capitalist society. They rely on an expanded understanding of unfreedom that takes account of the quality of the array of options that a person chooses among.[4]

Such an expanded understanding of unfreedom is important and, in my view, desirable. But if we cast the net this widely, what are we to say when it also captures the sort of phenomenon Winch described in the Samaritan parable? What if the impoverishment of options available to Karl in "Proletarian" is similar to the impoverishment of options in "Samaritan"? Karl says he can't work for Milton or for Friedrich; he has to work for Adam. And the Samaritan says he can't just walk on to the library or to his grandchild's house; he has to help the man who fell among thieves. In both cases, it may seem the central character has a choice, but the choice that he has is not real. Is this an equivalence we should be comfortable with?

I think that if we adopt the expansive conception of unfreedom, we have to be careful to distinguish the impoverishment of options in "Proletarian," which we might see as constituting a certain (deplorable) type of unfreedom, from the diminution of options characteristic of certain (laudable) feelings of moral necessity, in "Samaritan" for example. But drawing a distinction between the two cases is not easy. It is a subtle and difficult task, and it is my purpose in this paper to try to figure it out.

We might phrase the Samaritan's "can't" in terms of necessity.[5] One *must* stop and help the man. The other options—walking on to one of one's chosen destinations—are options that are *not possible* in the circumstances. I am pursuing the questions I have raised not just because of a possible equivalence in the use of "can't" as between the two cases, but also because the element of necessity in the two stories seems to have a different relation to freedom. In "Proletarian," the connection between Karl's experience of necessity and the Marxist imputation of unfreedom seems plausible. Other chapters in this book have explored the conditions of its plausibility.[6] In "Samaritan," by contrast, it not only seems implausible, but to some minds it seems to support the exact opposite conclusion. Think of the position, espoused most famously by Imman-uel Kant, that the practical constraint experienced by someone like Winch's Samaritan is best understood as the *epitome* of freedom, *true* freedom, not unfreedom at all.[7] It is true freedom in the sense of autonomy—maybe even noumenal autonomy—as one responds with reason and principle to a given sit-uation and allows alternatives based on mere inclination and feeling and our animal nature to fall away as ineligible. Though we "have no choice," we reveal ourselves as free in this response to the singular demand of a moral impera-tive. On the Kantian position, the Samaritan vindicates his moral autonomy in being necessitated in this way. So then: if there is anything to the Kantian position, we may want to be careful in the way we toss around the idea of unfree-dom in relation to the impoverishment of options. We think the position held by Adam, Friedrich, and Milton is inauthentic: what they call free choice for Karl is not really choice at all. But we should not throw out the Kantian baby with the capitalist bathwater.

But are the cases really on a par? As we proceed, two broad strategies sug-gest themselves: (1) we might discredit (or, more charitably, reinterpret) the sense of necessity that seems to be involved in "Samaritan," so that it no longer dis-tracts us in our consideration of cases like "Proletarian" in which a person's options are truly impoverished; or (2) if we still take the impoverishment of options in "Samaritan" seriously, we might distinguish between the way impov-erishment arises in that case and the way it works in a case like "Proletarian" and attribute some significance to that difference. I shall explore both options.

3.

Let's begin by reconsidering the attitude of Winch's Samaritan toward the avail-ability of the options that someone might say he has. No one is coercing him. But suddenly, with his sighting of the man who fell among thieves, the Samar-itan's alternate courses of action—walking on by to one of his possible destinations—have evaporated or at least for him they have become impover-ished. To pass by on the other side now seems like a hideous betrayal, a flat compromising of agency, a failure of the most important part of practical rea-son. Something that might have seemed like an attractive alternative—just walking on by to one of his possible destinations—no longer seems available to him.

Now perhaps this is just a subjective impression.[8] It's a matter of how the Samaritan perceives, how he would describe, his options: how it all feels to him. It is subjective too in the sense that not everyone will see them this way. We all know some people who would walk on cheerfully, unaffected in themselves in the way we are told the Samaritan is affected. The reaction seems intensely personal. So is this purely a subjective fact about the Samaritan's options? And does that distinguish it from the impoverishment of options that we see for example in "Proletarian"? Well, there is an element of perception in Karl's view also: the employment options seem ineligible *to him*. But what Karl sees are visible facts about the options: the real level of pay and the actual nature of the work. The Samaritan's view of the impoverishment of his options seems somewhat less tangible than that.

One way of interpreting the felt necessity—the "can't"—in "Samaritan" is as an aspect of the identity a person cherishes for himself. Those who can't shake off the grip of the "can't" are expressing and indulging their own identity, telling us something important about themselves. Think of Martin Luther's declaration at the Diet of Worms in 1521 when asked whether he was willing to revoke his writings criticizing the practice of selling indulgences, *"Hier steh' ich, ich kann nicht anders"* (Here I stand; I can do no other). Maybe all the emphasis ought to be on the *"ich"*—*"<u>ich</u>, Martin Luther, kann nicht anders."*[9]

The intense subjectivity of the practical "can't" and even its patent variation from person to person should not lead us to dismiss it as flighty or trivial. Its being personal in this sense does not preclude the "can't" from going very deeply into the self. The mode of assessment of options might go to the heart of who one is—it might be a matter of character—and its role in practical reasoning may express a robust sense of personal integrity.[10]

But a strong sense of necessity associated with one's identity as a person might still seem indulgent, at least until we add in a moral element. For some people morality is just another personal indulgence. But for many philosophers, bringing morality into the picture is not just an aspect of the way the Samaritan happens to sees himself in the situation; morality is a set of impersonal considerations—objective considerations—to which his involvement as an agent is properly responsive.[11] Winch's Samaritan will say: "It is not just a matter of how things seem to me or how I want myself to be in this situation. The impossibility that I experience here—I *must* help the man who fell among thieves; I *can't* just continue on to one of my other destinations—is the right response to have in the circumstances. It is not a personal option; it is a matter of duty. Not only that, but the Samaritan seems to have something like moral objectivity in mind. The sense of moral duty is not invoked here capriciously or arbitrarily. Though some may be blind to it, its force for the Samaritan has the characteristic not just of the right but the true.

This line of thought counsels against any easy dismissal of the Samaritan's position. At the same time, however, it may argue for a more straightforward rendering. For, if the objectivity of moral judgment really is what's at stake, then surely it would be better to talk transparently in a way that foregrounds this element of what we are saying, rather than cloaking it in the rhetoric of necessity (which is subject to all sorts of other interpretations). Why not admit that the "can't" in "Samaritan" is just rhetoric, embellishing what should really be understood as a very strong moral "ought" (or rather "ought not")? We use all sorts of terms to convey "ought"—a person faced with a strong "ought" may also say "I must," "I have to," "I have no choice." Faced with an "ought not" he may say "I mustn't" or we may say that for him "You mustn't." The moral "can't" may be nothing more than the result of mapping deontic logic onto the syntax of modal logic, which we all know can be done, but which has few if any substantive implications. So we shouldn't worry too much about these locutions. They are just words in the service of moral judgment, used to make an imperative appear inevitable or nonnegotiable. Use any words you like, we may say. But a perspicuous language of practical reason will deploy the well-understood vocabulary of "right' and "wrong," "ought" and "ought not," and the language of obligation and permission—not least because it invites us to offer reasons to back up the moral predicates.

Before we go on, a slight digression. Some moral philosophers may be reluctant to associate "Samaritan" with Kantian morality because the "can't" in "Samaritan" seems born of compassion rather than a strictly moral imperative. The Samaritan is moved by benevolent inclination rather than by austere Kantian duty. After all, his action is cited as an instance of love: "Love thy neighbor." It doesn't seem like an exercise of practical reason. As I have argued elsewhere, the Samaritan doesn't pause to reason anything out; he just acts.[12] Fair enough. But if the specific content of the parable is a distraction, we can easily set up a case in which austere moral duty is unquestionably at stake, with compassionate options being among those cast into shadow by the moral imperative.[13]

To resume: if we give "Samaritan" (or some case like it) this moral interpretation, will that sufficiently distinguish the parable from "Proletarian"? In some ways, yes: "Proletarian" is not really about Karl's *moral* choice. But "Proletarian" can be presented nevertheless as Karl's response to an overwhelming imperative, albeit a hypothetical imperative or perhaps what Kant would call an assertoric imperative.[14] The options that Karl allegedly has are utterly incompatible with his happiness or welfare; working for Adam is the only option that comes close. Still, we can put to Karl a version of what we put to the Samaritan: a perspicuous way of describing his options would just identify the relevant imperative, rather than imply that the options literally cannot be chosen. In that way the cases or our respective resolutions of them remain analogous.[15]

That conclusion is reinforced when we consider another way of pushing the two cases closer together, another way of lessening the apparent contrast between moral and nonmoral necessity.

Some philosophers have suggested that practical necessity of the sort we see in "Samaritan" is not so much a moral idea as a *proto*-moral one, a phenomenological response that morality builds on. Winch says this about the relation between the Samaritan and the idea of divine law. He argues that the parable is told to convey something that the relevant divine law was supposed to capture, not to repeat or represent its content: "The responses to moral modalities that we share with the Samaritan (however much they are modified or stifled by circumstance) are among the seeds from which, in some people, grows the conception of divinity and its laws."[16] Or, if we don't adopt a theistic conception at all, we might say that the feeling of necessity in "Samaritan" is a precursor to the power of the secular moral "ought"—something that morality builds on rather than something that reflects the already understood power of morality itself. As Robert Gay puts it, "it seems to be simply because we have this experience [of necessity] that we must act in this way. . . . We find ourselves responding to this in a way which involves the idea that we must so respond."[17] We organize our moral "oughts" and our "musts" to comprehend this phenomenology.

This order of argument is reflected in the fact that the "can't" of Winch's Samaritan does not line up perfectly with "ought." It works better with some "oughts" than with others. Some powerful "oughts" do not generate this sense of necessity. And the sense of necessity is sometimes associated with supererogatory actions, which we are reluctant to talk of as things that "ought to be done."[18] The true moral "ought" seems a little too well organized to be regarded as the source of the rather unwieldy Samaritan's "can't."

What this consideration of the "moral" character of the Samaritan's "can't" reveals is that it is less stable in its connection to practical necessity than we might think. And that impression is reinforced when we consider some other ways in which a practical "can't" can be generated.

The claim that "I can't do this," put forward in circumstances fraught with political controversy, has been subject to powerful analysis by the late legal theorist Robert Cover. In his 1975 book *Justice Accused* Cover considered the phenomenon of antislavery judges in the northern states faced with the task of administering fugitive slave statutes in the decades that preceded the Civil War. African Americans fled from their slave masters in the South and came north to Pennsylvania or Ohio seeking liberty.[19] The masters sent slavecatchers into the northern states, and when they apprehended fugitive slaves they sought to return them to their chains. Sometimes they were challenged in court, or sometimes they needed the assistance of northern or federal courts. A number of the judges who sat in these cases were known for their antislavery inclinations. And when they were reproached by their friends and family—their fellow abolitionists—they had to say why they didn't just exercise their judicial power to let the former slaves go free. Sometimes they did, because there was a range of cases, following the English decision *Somerset v Stewart*, that the Fugitive

Slave Acts couldn't touch.[20] But mostly they did not let the slaves go free. They said they couldn't. So, for example, in the 1853 case of *Miller v McQuerry*, a fugitive slave case from Ohio, Justice John McLean wrote this in his judgment:

> With the abstract principles of slavery, courts called to administer this law have nothing to do. It is for the people, who are sovereign, and their representatives, in making constitutions, and in the enactment of laws, to consider the laws of nature, and the immutable principles of right. *This is a field which judges can not explore.* Their action is limited to conventional rights. They look to the law, and to the law only. . . . If the law be injudicious or oppressive, let it be repealed or modified. But *this is a power which the judiciary can not reach.* . . . Upon the whole, no doubt can exist on the evidence, that the fugitive owes service to the claimant; and, under the law, *I am bound to remand him to the custody of his master,* with authority to take him to the state of Kentucky, the place from whence he fled.[21]

Here's what Cover said in response (with the benefit of 120 years of hindsight): "to say that one cannot perform an action is a definitive answer to the moral prescription that one ought to do it. . . . The impossibility . . . of an action keeps the question of whether to perform it (asked as a practical question) from arising. . . . But "cannot" may be used in many other senses than physical incapacity." Sometimes we use it in regard to the rules or convention of a game: you cannot move your bishop along a row or file in chess. You would be cheating, or it would no longer be chess. Legends occasionally arise of an activity changing its rules in midgame.[22] But it is pretty unusual. Another example Cover mentions are the conventions of a language. Linguistic rules are more flexible, and they can change in ways other than formal prospective legislation. The firm Staples may advertise itself as "a new way to office." If we say, "You can't use 'office' as a verb, they will say, "Just watch us." New usages enter the language by transgression. In these contexts, then, "can'ts" seem fragile and negotiable. At best, insistence on the "can't" could be understood only as a way of curating the integrity of a given conventional structure as it happens to be for the time being.

In the particular context that Cover is considering, the judicial "can't" seems to be predicated on something a bit more substantial—an understanding of official role and perhaps also the political morality that underpins it. Justice McLean says, in effect, that in his role as judge, it is not for him to call the institution of slavery into question. He cannot do that as a judge. To do it would involve hijacking his court as an institution and turning it into something like a Senate, an all-purpose censor of the laws. As Justice McLean went on, "A disregard of this, by the judicial powers, would undermine and overturn the social compact." McLean's "can't," then, may be translated into the following moral statement: A judge ought not explore the natural right of slavery unless he is prepared to destroy the social compact. He is not referring here to the social contract in the abstract, but to the basis on which the nation is trying to hold itself together in light of the looming danger of civil war. But then, as Cover suggests, what we surely want is more detail on the dilemma and a clear indication of what would be at stake if one of the "can't" options were actually chosen. A physical "can't" eliminates moral dilemmas and absolves the actor from choice: "Competing, inconsistent, moral demands, by contrast, do not resolve but define moral choices. The ethical man still must choose and choose well."[23]

4.

It is not my aim to denigrate the sense of options' having evaporated in "Samaritan." The accounts we have considered—subjective perception, personal identity, role, conventions, and the reflex of morality—don't explain it away, though they reveal the depth and possible complexity of the phenomenon. Equally, it should be pretty clear that we might subject Karl's "can't" in "Proletarian" to similar kinds of analysis, with similar kinds of result.

Instead, I want now to pursue a different approach, focusing on the dynamics of the respective cases rather than the specific content that underpins them. How do options become ineligible in the two cases? In the moral cases, how is that related to the striking compulsion of the one choice that morality requires? Alternatively, how does the compulsion of the one choice follow from the character of the other options or the work that has been done on them by some agency?

Both in "Samaritan" and in "Proletarian" we compare one apparently salient option with two others that seem ineligible. The structure is X versus Y or Z. In "Samaritan" the salient option (X) is helping the man who fell among thieves, and the two ineligible options (Y and Z) are walking on to the library and walking on to meet a grandchild. In "Proletarian" the salient option (X) is working for Adam, and the two ineligible options (Y and Z) are working for Milton and working for Friedrich. There is an apparent difference, though, between the way the Y and Z options become ineligible in the respective cases.[24] In "Proletarian" Y and Z are ineligible in large part because of their own characteristics: a lower-than-living wage and particularly dirty and dangerous work. Though the availability of a slightly less unattractive option (X) highlights these characteristics of the ineligible options, they would be unattractive in themselves whether X was available or not.

In "Samaritan," by contrast, the Y and Z options become ineligible only by virtue of the presence and compelling character of X. Visiting a grandchild or visiting the library are, in themselves, fine things to do, and the choice between them would be regarded as quintessentially a matter of ordinary autonomy. It is only in light of the sudden necessity for help for the man who fell among thieves—the apparently compelling duty to choose X—that the other options become ineligible, become choices that the Samaritan *cannot* make. The Samaritan *must* choose X; that is why he cannot choose Y or Z. In "Proletarian," by contrast, the worker really cannot choose Y and Z (working for Milton or Friedrich); that is why he must choose X (working for Adam). The background impoverishment of options—due to capitalist conditions as background—is what renders the options ineligible and the choice wretched.

Notice, however, that in "Samaritan" the shadow cast by option X also colors the characteristics that, in and of themselves, might make each of the other options attractive. Once they have been made ineligible by the compelling presence of X, they can no longer be seen in an attractive light. If the Samaritan were to take up the desirability of a visit to the library, he would find it tainted by consideration of what he ought to have been doing instead; and the same would happen to the joys of visiting his grandchild. These actions, these choices become awful to him in this character even though there is nothing awful about what they intrinsically involve. Nothing like that happens in "Proletarian." But it is characteristic of the way that moral imperatives work. For example, an absolute prohibition like the ban on torture not only makes it necessary to forego coercive interrogation; it also poisons anything people might want to enjoy by using this forbidden means. Suddenly what we seek and even actually achieve by torturing somebody is tainted by the way we pursued it. The security that we sought is less easy to enjoy when we know it was obtained on the back of a waterboard or at the end of a live electrode. Again there is a contrast with "Proletarian," where the Y and Z options are mainly unattractive in themselves, apart from the shadow cast by X. I cannot pursue this in detail in the present chapter, but I believe this phenomenon is too often overlooked in consequentialist defenses of torture.[25]

I think this distinction between the different dynamics involved in our two leading cases helps us with the relevance of political freedom—which, remember, is supposed to be our main concern. Freedom is a value. We want people to be free, and we want this as much for the Samaritan as for Karl. Lack of freedom for Karl, situated as he is in "Proletarian," is a shame and something to be deplored. He ought to have had more and better options. But is the impoverishment of options for Winch's Samaritan to be *deplored* in same way that it is in "Proletarian"? Is the unfreedom (such as it is) in "Samaritan" a matter of concern in the same way as it is in "Proletarian"? Is the Samaritan's case to be regretted as a loss of freedom?

We can distinguish them by noting that Karl's predicament in "Proletarian" seems to be someone's fault—the fault of some individuals or a class—in a way that the predicament in "Samaritan" is not. It is often said not only that freedom is an evaluative term but also that a charge of unfreedom has to be accusatory, voiced when we think there is someone to blame for an agent's predicament. And that seems appropriate in "Proletarian." Adam, Milton, and Friedrich could agree to raise the wages on offer to give people like Karl a real choice, or they could withdraw their opposition to a state-mandated minimum wage. So long as they refuse to do that, they are responsible for the impoverished options that Karl currently faces. They are culpable, and the claim that Karl is unfree reflects their responsibility.

By contrast, no one is really responsible for the Samaritan's predicament—I mean for the fact that he now has no choice but to help the man on the side of the road. It is no one's fault that he cannot just go on cheerfully to visit his grandchild or the library. Now that's not quite true. Can we not blame the priest or the Levite? If one of them had done his duty, the Samaritan's predicament would not have been so acute. They are certainly to blame for their failure to help the man by the side of the road. But it seems odd to blame them for the Samaritan's unfreedom.

I suppose we could blame the thieves who attacked the man by the side of the road, who beat him and left him half dead. They surely have some responsibility, though again perhaps not for the predicament of the Samaritan—I mean not for the evaporation of his options. Except that they must have known that actions like theirs would confront subsequent passersby with stark choices. (It seems after all to have been a well-traveled road.) If you like, we could take the thieves out of the equation and just posit the classic case of a baby found drowning in a shallow pool—no one's fault, but there it is—and again a Samaritan comes along and sees what is happening by the side of the road, and when he is urged to hurry on by his companion, he says, "I can't just leave the baby to drown." Same "can't," but nobody's fault. We could take the priest and the Levite out of the equation too. It's just the Samarian and he can't just walk by. Perhaps the absence of fault is the basis of a clear distinction between "Proletarian" and (let's call it) "Child-in-the-Pool." Is that a good explanation of why talk of unfreedom is appropriate in the former case, but not the latter?

Some, we know, will talk of structural inequality in Karl's case, eschewing all sense of responsibility and blame. Does that bring "Proletarian" and "Samaritan" back together? Does it reestablish some equivalence between them? Not quite. It remains the case, as we noted a little while ago, that it is the quality of the other options in "Proletarian" that drives the necessity to which Karl is subject. And that combines with the point we have just developed a moment ago, that our understanding of political freedom in "Proletarian" moves from the options to the necessity (of his choosing to work for Adam) whereas in "Samaritan" the movement is in the opposite direction. Even if there is no agent to blame, the quality of Karl's other options remains deplorable and should be thought of as something to fix if fixing is possible (even if necessary by large-scale social change). The link between talk of unfreedom and negative evaluation remains important even when it doesn't surface in a reproach to any particular individual.

5.

What I conclude from all this is that the expansion of the idea of unfreedom, which is the topic of this book, ought to focus on what happens (or has happened) to the options a person might have faced to bring him to a situation in which he has no real choice. Our analysis should not turn on the sheer number of eligible options facing the agent or the proportion of his options that are ineligible. Freedom is not a matter of option-counting. What matters is how the ineligibility of options, such as it is, came about. Has someone been working on the options themselves rendering some or all of them ineligible? If so, there is a case to be made for deploying the expansive sense of unfreedom. Or is the ineligibility of some of the options just a reflection of the importance of some other choice facing the agent. If so, then one's ability to apprehend the necessity of the choice that is left should be regarded as a mark of freedom rather than as something that detracts from it.

We should be careful, in other words, not to draw the wrong moral from "Proletarian." Of course Karl is made unfree by the quality of options that he has. And of course there is something in Joseph Raz's insistence that normally "autonomy requires the availability of an adequate range of options."[26] A person's autonomy is characteristically defined by the way in which this choice rather than that choice is opted for, when either might have been chosen. But in the circumstances of human life, the starker choice of the kind faced by the Samaritan cannot be ruled out. And though we may deplore the circumstances that led to it, we should not deplore its having to be faced. It may be no one's fault, but sometimes there is only one acceptable thing to do, and other putative options have to be set aside in the light of that fact. Neither the fact nor its recognition is incompatible with freedom. Such situations—many unacceptable options and just one of them recognized as acceptable—can't be ruled out. They can't even realistically be expected to be exceptional. We might even say that in the collapsing world we have to address, particularly in the face of climate change, cases like these will become typical, and good people will increasingly face choices arrayed like this in which it is appropriate for us to engage the idea of moral necessity.

CHAPTER 3

FREEDOM AND UNFREEDOM IN HUMAN CATEGORIES

The Case of Multiplicity

CAROL ROVANE

I n his insightful and searching work, Ian Hacking offers us a rich—
and I think largely true—vision of what it means, in our time, to
undertake the task of coming to know ourselves.[1]
He tells us that it is inevitable that we will turn to the human sciences, and
most especially to psychology. He is concerned, however, that we not misconstrue what the human sciences can deliver, or should aspire to deliver. He echoes
Rousseau's caution against thinking that we can ever discern what belongs to
human nature per se, conceived apart from, or in abstraction from, the effects
of human history. This is not because he doubts, any more than Rousseau
doubts, that there *is* an underlying nature common to all human beings; it is
rather because he rightly sees that we can only investigate human beings as they
are, which is to say, as they have actually been formed by history. So, the sen-
sible thing to do is to accept that what we human beings have become is perfectly real, and fully worthy of investigation.

Hacking offers several reflections about what it means to pursue this sen-
sible course.

First, psychologists must accept that the concepts and categories that they
employ in their research may be *confined* to the historical contexts in which
those categories emerge and are applied. In other words, there are real limitations on whether it is ever appropriate to apply our current psychological
concepts and categories to human phenomena that arose in other historical
contexts. Hacking even goes so far as to argue that these limitations point to a
kind of *indeterminacy of the past.*

Second, the confinement of human concepts and categories to historical contexts derives from a complex human phenomenon that is arguably at work in *all* historical contexts, which consists in a form of feedback that attends the process of trying to make sense of ourselves. Whenever we try to make sense of ourselves, we are bound to employ the concepts and categories that are ready to hand in the particular historical context we occupy. Hacking contends that we are also altered in the process, so that we *become* the sorts of things to which our ready-to-hand concepts and categories apply. If he is right, this affords a somewhat deeper, or at any rate a more detailed, explanation of why human beings are not stable objects for scientific investigation, which goes beyond the general point that they are changed and shaped by history. In his view, even when we turn to psychological science in order to make sense of ourselves, we are affected by our own efforts and are transformed into things that fit the scientific concepts and categories that we apply to ourselves.

This human responsiveness to what psychology delivers poses a challenge to its self-image as a science, because scientific investigation is normally conducted from a realist standpoint that takes for granted that its objects are *mind-independent*, and that the scientific goal must therefore be to represent reality *as it is in itself*, conceived apart from our efforts to know it. Whereas, if Hacking is right, this realist standpoint is not appropriate in the human sciences. We cannot coherently aim to know human reality as it is in itself, apart from our efforts to know it, because *what it is* is altered by our efforts to know it. Of course, no one can coherently deny that there are some aspects of human reality toward which it would be appropriate to adopt the realist standpoint, because they really are what they are in themselves, independently of our efforts to know them. The underlying chemistry, biology, physiology, neurology, and so forth of the human organism are obvious candidates.[2] And some of the "subpersonal" processing that goes on in the human mind—what Kant referred to as "blind functions of the soul"—are also good candidates. But Hacking puts into doubt whether very many other aspects of the human mind are good candidates, owing to how they will be affected by our efforts to know them.

This metaphysical vision of human reality lands contemporary psychologists with new questions that are not strictly speaking *scientific* questions, at least not as science is ordinarily conceived. These new questions have their source in longstanding ethical questions concerning how we should live, and how we can live *well*. For at least two millennia the assumption in the West has been that it is central to this ethical project that we should come to *know* ourselves—our human nature. It is hardly surprising that many now turn to the human sciences when they seek such knowledge. Yet when they do so, they do not regard science as a source of knowledge about what our ethical goals should be. They take for granted that our ethical goals must be set independently, and then what science can contribute is instrumental knowledge about how to achieve those goals. So, for example, if they believe that happiness is the key ingredient in the good life, then they might hope that psychological research will shed light on what does and does not conduce to human happiness. But they would not expect that psychology will afford any ethical insight into why happiness should be our primary ethical goal—why it should matter more than other ethically significant goods we might pursue. Intuitively, this may seem to be just the right division of labor between scientific psychology and ethical inquiry. But Hacking's metaphysical vision does not accommodate it. The knowledge psychologists produce will bring forth human phenomena that were not there before, and as a result, they will bear significant responsibility for the new human reality that emerges. So they cannot—or perhaps I should say, ought not to—proceed without considering whether what they are bringing forth is a way of living well. I would say that this is not an *ethical* concern, insofar as ethics tends to be a personal matter of figuring out for oneself how to live; this is rather a moral concern about how to proceed while bearing in mind our effects on others.

Hacking keeps this moral concern very much in view when he undertakes to investigate a relatively new phenomenon in human history, namely, multiple personality disorder, along with its more recent descendent, dissociative identity disorder. He ends his book on the subject with genuine wonder about whether it is indeed a good thing that it has become possible to live as a multiple—a possibility that he sees as being afforded by what he refers to as "multiple therapy."

His investigation into multiple personality disorder owes much to Foucault, who lays great emphasis on how certain institutions emerged in the nineteenth and twentieth centuries, such as hospitals, asylums, and prisons.[3] These institutions are maintained by the activities of experts who draw their expertise from the human sciences, and the effect has been to introduce a new form of power into human life that does not fit older models of power. On the older models, power is maintained deliberately: the strong aim to dominate and control and oppress the weak. In contrast, the experts through whom the new forms of institutional power are maintained do not personally aim to oppress anyone, but on the contrary, they typically aim to improve various aspects of our current human condition. So, like a great many other outcomes of historical processes, these newly emerged forms of power were not explicitly intended by anyone. Furthermore, it is extremely unlikely that gaining historical understanding of how they emerged will put us in a position to exert intentional control over them in the future. They will operate much as historical conditions generally do, more as background conditions in which we exercise our agency than as things we can realistically hope to control through our agency.

Hacking's debt to, and agreement with, Foucault makes his position two-faced—not in a false way, but in a true way.

One face is the face of freedom. Hacking emphasizes how newly emerged institutions, along with the expertise that maintains them, have supplied us with conceptual resources through which to *become* something new. This strongly suggests that we human beings possess a kind of freedom that makes us very different from the rest of nature—because our efforts to know ourselves give us an opportunity to change, and to some extent, it seems that we can always aim to change for the better. Of course, this freedom is limited by the conceptual resources we have available, through which we can frame our intentions and actions. For example, we cannot intentionally become Buddhists unless we have the concept of such a thing in the first place. And so it is with all of our intentional activities, both within own personal spheres of individual agency and in the larger spheres of institutional and political agency. But our conceptual resources are not fixed. They can be expanded, and this would appear to be an expansion of our practical possibilities, an expansion of our freedom. It would seem to follow that when Hacking enjoins psychologists—and all of us really—to consider what we are bringing forth when we bring conceptual resources to bear in human life, he is enjoining us to exercise our freedom well.

But the second face of Hacking's position is the face of *limitation*. He agrees with Foucault that our conceptual resources do not lie within our intentional control because they emerge in, and remain embedded in, institutions and practices that were brought forth by various contingencies and accidents of history. So when he claims that human reality changes with changing concepts, he is drawing attention to changing conditions that do not lie within our intentional control, but figure as conditions within which we must operate; and then he tends to emphasize a negative point, about what differently situated human beings cannot be, owing to the unavailability of certain conceptual resources. He is emphatic, for example, that there was no such thing as multiple personality disorder before the nineteenth century. On his account, the phenomenon arose with, and through, new ways of conceiving and studying the human mind that arose in that century, which he labels the *sciences of memory*.

It is worth remembering that Foucault does not give up on the aspiration to freedom, or on the idea that the human individual is an important site of moral effort. Hacking is quite reticent on moral matters and generally prefers to gain historical perspective on the moral terrain than to make explicit moral recommendations. Nevertheless, at the end of his book on multiple personality disorder he does finally raise some moral concerns, and there his moral gaze is also on the individual, and more specifically, on the lived meaning of multiple personality disorder for the individual human beings who are diagnosed with it and treated for it.

My own suggestion in this chapter, however, is that the case of multiplicity calls into question both the viability, and the appropriateness, of keeping our moral gaze primarily on the human individual. It gives us a new lens through which to contemplate the human being, so that we may reconsider: How does a human being come to be—or as I would prefer to say, become the site of—an *individual in the morally significant sense*? What social conditions are required for this achievement? What kind of a good is this achievement? What kind of loss is incurred when human beings do not achieve it? When Hacking struggles with the last two questions, he expresses serious reservations about whether offering distressed people a new way to be, as actively multiple, has led to better lives, or even *can* lead to better lives. But we ought not to try to address his reservations without first undertaking a careful reexamination of the social conditions that have afforded this new human possibility. My own reexamination of these social conditions here strongly suggests the following: they are not merely enabling conditions for the sort of dissociation that we find in individuals who suffer from multiple personality disorder; they are themselves *sites of dissociation* at the social level. In other words, the inner condition of human beings who develop multiple personality disorder corresponds to, and reflects, their external social conditions. So if Hacking is at all on the right track in suggesting that it may be better not to live as an active multiple, nothing much follows unless there are measures we can take to address the social conditions to which human beings are responding, and which they are internalizing when they develop multiple personality disorder.

My argument takes up two philosophical issues that are not usually discussed together. One is the issue of moral relativism, and the other is the issue of personal identity. It should be clear that the latter issue is pretty well unavoidable in any serious philosophical investigation into multiple personality disorder. It may be less clear what relevance the former issue has. We shall see that the case of multiplicity actually puts these two philosophical issues into interesting relation, and it is their relation that will help us to see how, and why, the inner condition of multiplicity is indeed a reflection of external social conditions—with the result that, insofar as the inner condition of multiplicity is ever disordered, so too is the external condition that it reflects.

Hacking's metaphysical vision of human reality has a great deal in common with the moral relativist's metaphysical vision. On my understanding of moral relativism,[4] the moral relativist can allow that there are perfectly real and objective matters to investigate in the domain of morals, but then insists that the truths that emerge from our moral investigations hold only locally, within a given context—in other words, moral truths are not *universal* truths that hold for all persons in all times and places. This is very much how Hacking understands the domains investigated by psychological and social science: there are real and objective matters to investigate, but the truths we discover hold only within a given historical context, and not universally across all historical contexts.

I will clarify what stance the relativist should take toward other moral contexts and how it differs from the stance we take when we suppose that truth is universal. Although Hacking does not describe himself as a relativist, he does implicitly adopt a relativist stance when he discusses psychological concepts and categories belonging to other historical contexts. Furthermore, when he makes paradoxical-sounding claims about the indeterminacy of the past, he is really highlighting how difficult it can be to describe the local truths that hold in other historical contexts from the vantage point of our own—and this is a difficulty that moral relativists also face.

As I have said, Hacking is particularly sensitive to the difference between the cases of multiplicity that interest him, and other cases of multiplicity that have arisen in other times and places, such as mediumship and possession. He is interested in a disorder of personality, or as we now say, identity, which in his view could only have arisen after the sciences of memory took shape in the nineteenth century. And he takes the same view of psychological disorders in general: according to him, there simply were no such things until after the birth of scientific psychology, via the sciences of memory. But I want to interrogate more carefully *why* multiple personality counts as a disorder. It might seem that it should suffice to note that multiplicity is an abnormal condition of the human being, whose *normal* condition is be a site of one individual self or person. The diagnostic criteria for *dissociative identity disorder* specified in the DSM-V are complex and varied. But I will suggest that the entire entry is premised on an implicit assumption that it is indeed normal for each individual human being to exhibit the sort of unity that is characteristic of the individual self or person through the whole of its life.

I will also introduce an account of the self or person that contravenes this assumption.[5] On this account, the unity of the self/person/personality does not arise as part of the natural development of the human being but is rather an achievement. I think many clinical psychologists would say that it is both—that while yes, it is an achievement, it is one that it is natural and normal for any human being to achieve, much as it is natural and normal for human beings to learn how to walk and to talk. But my suggestion is that the achievement of overall unity within the whole of a human life *optional* and may be forgone in favor of multiplicity. Furthermore, reflection on the issue of moral relativism brings to light a certain kind of social condition, in which this is not only feasible, but positively invited. This would be a social condition in which a single human being must navigate and live within multiple social contexts, and while there may be no reason to achieve the sort of unity that is characteristic of the individual self or person overall, within the *whole* human life, it is both feasible and pointful to achieve such unity within the distinct portions of that live that are lived in distinct social contexts—thereby giving rise to an inner condition of multiplicity. I see nothing pathological in this development. On the contrary, it is a perfectly appropriate response to the human being's lived social reality, which is also in a very real sense, multiple.

Lessons from moral relativism

There is a lot of philosophical confusion about what the moral relativist's position is supposed to be, and what reasons there are to take it seriously. So let me be as clear as I can be. I take the moral relativist to be denying that moral truths are universal, in the sense that they hold for all people in all times and places. The reasons to take moral relativism seriously stem from the action guiding character of moral truths. What a person morally ought to do depends upon what morally significant options they face, and knowing a moral truth cannot help them navigate these options unless it speaks to those options. This will generally require the use of what Bernard Williams calls *thick* moral concepts as opposed to *thin* ones.[6] Thick moral concepts make detailed reference to aspects of a given moral context—the specific institutions, projects, relationships, etc. around which the person's life is organized. Thin moral concepts are abstract concepts devised by moral theorists who want to say something completely general about what makes every right action right and every wrong action wrong. But according to the moral relativist, when moral truths are couched in thin terms they are too remote from the specific options we face to give us any real guidance.

To illustrate, let me sketch two distinct moral contexts in which people require guidance from different thick moral truths. One is the moral context of liberal individualism as it is lived in the contemporary United States. In this moral context, the primary values are organized around oneself: each individual is in charge of their own life; each individual must take responsibility for their own life; each individual is a locus of rights and liberties; what individuals primarily owe to others is due recognition of their rights and liberties. Compare this to the moral context of traditional Indian values as they are lived in rural villages in India. In this moral context, the primary values are organized around one's position within an extended family that resides in a small, close-knit community; and each member has many special duties, which go by the name *katarvya*, which are owed to many specific others depending on their specific relationships with them. Among these special duties is this one: one should defer to one's parents' wishes. The sort of deference to parents that is owed in the moral context of traditional village life in rural India is not owed to parents in the moral context of New York City, which affords such rich opportunities for, and also encouragement of, liberal individualist aspiration. This is true even while children are still of school age. Of course, the city's children are forced to go to school, and of course, some parents are obtrusive and overbearing. But nevertheless, the educational culture is one that aims to offer students opportunities to identify and develop their own interests, talents, and projects. Thus, deference to parents is not actually owed to parents in New York City, though it is owed in rural India.

To those who oppose relativism, the situation I just described might appear to be an ordinary moral disagreement, in which one moral position or the other must be right and the other must be wrong: deference to parents either is, or is not, owed! This appearance of disagreement goes together with a conception of moral truth as universal, according to which what is true anywhere is true everywhere, for all people in all times and places. It follows from this universalist conception that all of the moral truths can be embraced together within a single point of view. So, for example, if a New Yorker found that they could not embrace and live by the view of traditional village-dwelling Indians, on which deference to parents is owed, then they are committed to rejecting that view as false and mistaken, whereas the moral relativist interprets the situation quite differently. It is not a situation of disagreement but of difference. In order for the situation to be one of disagreement, the parties must be affirming and denying the very same proposition—in this case, that deference to parents is owed. But the moral relativist invites us to look more closely at the situation. When we do, we will see that the two parties do not mean the same thing by what is owed, or to put it another way, they do not share a common conception of what moral duty consists in. Traditional Indians owe specific relationship-based duties of *katarvya*, which is a thick moral value that can be action guiding only in places where those relationships, and the form of life in which they arise, are present. Although liberals do not like to think so, the moral relativist will construe the rights-based liberal duties that are owed in places like New York City along similar lines, as thick moral values that can be action guiding only in places where life is organized around individualist pursuits and social arrangements. So there is no disagreement between the traditional Indian and the New Yorker, about whether children owe deference to parents, because they are not affirming and denying the same proposition. If they were, then they would indeed be in disagreement, and only one of them could be right. But they do not disagree. They embrace different moral truths that are couched in terms of different thick moral values—the special duties of *katarvya* vs. the liberal duties that follow upon a recognition of individual rights; and these very different thick moral values are embedded in, and action guiding within, different moral contexts—or as I would recommend we say, different moral *worlds*.

The moral relativist makes a further point about this sort of moral difference: if the two parties are not in moral disagreement, they are not in moral agreement either. It might appear that they are, insofar as both parties can certainly *say* that traditional Indians owe a kind of duty to their parents called *katarvya*, whereas New Yorkers do not owe a duty of deference to their parents, or really to anyone at all. But this falls short of a moral agreement according to the relativist, because the moral truths that are being articulated are not universal but are confined to a given moral world. It goes together with this claim that traditional Indians and New Yorkers should adopt a relativist stance toward one another. When they adopt this stance, they thereby recognize that the thick moral values by which each party respectively lives in their own moral world do not hold in the other's moral world, and that the inhabitants of the other moral world need different thick moral values to live by. This shows that they are not really in moral agreement about how to live, for they respectively embrace and live by different moral truths. And yet, even though neither party can embrace the moral truths by which the other party lives, they are not in a position to deny that those truths are indeed truths that the other party can embrace and live by. So their situation is a peculiar one: they are not in a position to either teach or learn from each other about morals, practically understood as a guide to life; for although each can learn about the other's moral world and the thick moral truths that hold there, this is not moral learning per se. To recognize this situation is to adopt the relativists' stance toward one another; and to adopt this stance is to recognize the independence and separateness of their moral worlds—a relation I have elsewhere called *normative insularity*. The opposite of the relativists' stance is a stance of universal engagement, where we take for granted that if anyone anywhere has a true moral belief, then we can embrace it for ourselves as a basis from which to live; and if we come across someone whose moral beliefs we cannot consistently embrace together with our own, then either we must reject theirs as false, or else we must revise our moral beliefs so as to accommodate theirs.

The idea of universal engagement within the moral domain is undeniably attractive. But that doesn't mean that it is always feasible. The reasons why it isn't feasible are the reasons I have already given in favor of moral relativism: moral values must be action-guiding; this requires thick moral values that speak to the options we actually face in life; differently situated moral agents might face quite different options and require the guidance of quite different thick moral values. Admittedly, it does *seem* as though we can always engage with others about moral matters, even if they occupy a moral context that is different from our own; and insofar as we find that our attempts to engage such differently situated others should fail, we typically feel free to sit in moral judgment on them anyway. My example of life in a rural Indian village vs. life in New York City, seems to afford ample opportunity for precisely this sort of external judgment, and indeed, I think many actual New Yorkers do sit in moral judgment on other moral contexts in which Western liberal individualist values are not embraced. But the moral relativist insists that if these cross-context judgments are to qualify as moral judgments, then they must register an ought that can be action guiding. And the moral relativist denies that such judgments are normative in this way, because they agree with Foucault, and Hacking, and many others, that the course of history itself, which includes the processes though which forms of life and culture arise, is not subject to our intentional control. So while a New Yorker may appropriately register that they do not find an alternative form of life appealing for themself, this is a very different thing from pronouncing moral judgment on it. It bears mention that the moral relativist can easily explain this lack of appeal: we are all morally formed in the moral worlds that we actually occupy, and this places limits on our capacity to move into other moral worlds and take up life there, because it would require a very substantial personal transformation to do so! This does not mean, however, that our reactions to alternative forms of life will generally be negative. We may also romanticize them, and if they are in the past, we may regard them with nostalgia. But to have these experiences is not to engage in *serious moral inquiry into how to live in the moral world one actually occupies.*

Thus, according to the moral relativist, when we take an interest in learning about alternative forms of life that are not available to us, and over which we cannot exert real intentional control, we should not confuse this interested response with the form of universal engagement that opponents of moral relativism wish to promote. In their view, every encounter is an occasion for agreeing or disagreeing and can never be an occasion to simply register difference. Of course, it might be argued that we ought to engage with others whenever it is feasible. But this argument would leave the relativist's point still standing, which is that there are, or at least can be, cases of difference where engagement is not feasible. The relativists' recommendation is that when we encounter others who do not share our views, we should not automatically presume that moral engagement with them is feasible, but instead, we should pause to consider whether it is feasible while bearing in mind that for anyone to seek a moral truth of the matter is to seek a truth that will be action guiding for them in the moral world where they actually live.

History has shown that distinct moral worlds do not always remain distinct. When there are large movements of groups of human beings into new territories—conquerors, refugees, and so on—a new form of life may emerge that is shared by everyone who has come to together, so to speak. In this new form of life, there will be common problems to solve. The process of solving these common problems will likely involve rather complicated moral engagements about the various thick moral values that had formerly been effective guides in what had formerly been quite distinct moral worlds. There will likely have to be some sheddings, and revisions, and admixtures of these thick moral values, in order to cope with the new circumstances. But we should not infer from the fact moral engagement may become feasible when circumstances change, that it is *always* feasible for *all* people in *all* times and places—that is, we should not infer that the relativist's stance is never appropriate.

In fact, the relativist's stance is sometimes appropriate even after distinct moral worlds have come into close spatial proximity with one another. I think this often happens in cities like New York that attract and accommodate large numbers of immigrants. Recently arrived immigrants often maintain family and community networks that remain quite insulated from the moral world they have come to live right next to, in which it is possible and appropriate to continue living by their traditional moral values.

Moral relativism and multiplicity

Imagine a young immigrant from rural India, whose parents still live by their traditional values but who also gains entry into one of the elite public high schools of New York City. When this young immigrant is at home, they find that it is good and right to live by the traditional values that prevail there, and more specifically, to fulfill their special relationship-based duties (*katarvya*). When they are at school, they find it is good and right to live by the liberal individualist values that prevail there, by working out how best to conduct themself according to their own interests, talents, ambitions, etc. Thus, our young immigrant is living by very different thick moral values, depending upon where they find themself—that is, which moral world they are navigating at the moment. The upshot is that they never have occasion to develop a single, unified, point of view from which to reason and act as one. Instead, they develop *two* such points of view, each of which is constituted by a different set of attitudes from which deliberation and action proceed in a rationally unified way. Of course, there will be much in common between these two points of view, just as there is among all of us who know a lot of the same things about the world at large (the sky is blue, and grass is green, and so on). But in the case we are imagining, there is a great deal that is *not* in common as well, for it is no exaggeration to say that our young immigrant reasons and acts from two separate sets of thick moral values. Insofar as that is what they are doing, they are reasoning and acting from two quite different moral points of view, in spite of the fact that there is a lot of common knowledge between them.

There has been a longstanding presumption in the West that the achievement of a significant kind of unity within the whole of a human life is central to the ethical project of living well. I daresay it is generally regarded as being just as important as, and maybe even more important than, coming to know oneself. But the prospects for achieving this particular human good appear to be bleak for our young immigrant, because they are faced with having to navigate two distinct moral worlds on a daily basis. The question arises, how might they try to achieve such unity? One way would be to choose to live in only one of the moral worlds that they face, and to forsake the other. But it may well be that both of these moral worlds beckon to our young immigrant. That is, it may well be that, on the one hand, home, family, community, and tradition all matter, while on the other hand, so does the space of practical possibilities opened up by attending the elite public high school.

A decision theorist might suggest that it should still be possible for our young immigrant to achieve unity within the whole of their human life, by arriving at a single, transitive, ordering of all the goods among which they might ever have to choose (all of the options they might ever face), in terms of the *better than* relation. One can see the point of the suggestion for, arguably, such a transitive ordering would afford a unified basis from which to make consistent choices across many different choice situations. It should be conceded, however, that this sort of unity would fall short of the kind of unity that moral philosophers typically have in mind when they portray the best human life as unified. They typically portray a unified life as one that is organized around a life project that can give overarching purpose or meaning to it. By contrast, the kind of unity that is achieved by conforming to the rational requirements of decision theory is merely formal—a purely rational unity. This brings me to a second, and crucial, claim that I want to make about the situation we are now imagining: Not even this formal, or rational, unity is available to our young immigrant as I have described them. They are confronted with having to navigate two distinct moral worlds, and in each of those worlds, what counts as right and wrong and good and bad is determined by a set of thick moral values that do not apply in the other world. More specifically: There simply is no opportunity to live by *katarvya* at school, and so it is quite false to the situation to describe it as one in which our young immigrant judges that it is better to live by the values of liberal individualism instead. Likewise, there is no opportunity to live by the values of liberal individualism at home either, because *katarvya* rules there! Thus, the practical issue of which thick moral values to live by is not determined by a comparing them all and then ranking them together on a single scale in the way that decision theorists envisage. The issue is entirely determined by *current moral location*.

What I am claiming, then, is that our young immigrant will end up developing an internal duality of moral point of view, that reflects the dual nature of their social conditions—that is, the fact that they are faced with having to navigate two separate moral worlds. The effect of their social conditions upon them is that they are not of one mind with respect to moral questions concerning what is right and wrong and good and bad, but rather two. The moral philosophers who value overall unity within the whole of a human life may be inclined to argue that this is not the best way to live. My response to this argument is that we must make the best of life as it comes, and what life has brought to our young immigrant is two moral worlds—so it is a perfectly fitting response to proceed by developing two moral points of view, a separate moral point of view from which to navigate each separate moral world.

This is what I mean when I say that there can be *nonpathological cases of multiplicity.*

To say that these are cases of multiplicity is to say that they are cases in which a single human being is the site of more than one self. I am claiming that such multiplicity will arise whenever human beings enter into spheres of activity that are distinct in the following sense: a human being will have to navigate one or another of them at any given time, but never all of them together at once. Although a human being who enters into such distinct spheres of activity cannot be a site of overall rational unity of the kind that decision theorists describe and study, within the whole of their life, it is possible to achieve such unity within each portion of their life that is lived in a distinct social space. I am claiming each unified portion of such a life qualifies as a separate self because it has a separate point of view, and each such point of view consists in the set of attitudes from which that self deliberates and acts. Social psychologists would not typically characterize these different portions of a human life as distinct selves; they would characterize them in terms of different social roles that the human being plays in different social contexts. But that characterization gives the impression that there really is a single unified self there, who then puts on different hats for different occasions. I am claiming that this impression is false. There is indeed a single human being there. But when a human being is faced with having to navigate many distinct social conditions, there is no opportunity to develop a single unified self; what is called for, and called forth, is a kind of inner multiplicity that corresponds to the external multiplicity of the human being's social conditions. Some philosophers come close to capturing the kind of inner multiplicity that I have in mind, when they claim that a human being can have multiple identities owing to many different social involvements—in their families, in their work, in their institutional settings, and in their group affiliations.[7] It is unclear whether their use of the language of identity is intended to be taken literally. My arguments here invite a literal interpretation: a human being may possess multiple identities in the sense that they are literally a site of multiple selves, each with its own point of view, and its own identity.

To repeat in closing: the condition of multiplicity that I have just elucidated is not pathological, because the condition is a perfectly fitting response to a human being's social reality—though really I should speak in the plural, of social realities.

With this point in hand, let me turn to Hacking.

Hacking's account of multiple personality disorder

As I have said, Hacking and Foucault, and many others before them, believe that we are products of history, and that we cannot hope to know ourselves without knowing our history. Before recounting Hacking's history of multiple personality disorder, I want to step back and to ask a general question, about whether the project of tracing the history of particular concepts and categories helps to advance *normative* understanding—where by this I mean not only moral understanding, but any other normative understanding we may need in order to cope with the practical matters we face. I think that most everyone is inclined to answer yes, and this is so regardless of whether they are putting forward histories with a positive and progressive message, as we find in Hegel and Marx, or whether they are putting forward histories with an undermining message, as we find in Nietzsche and Foucault. In the case of Nietzsche, it is to undermine *moralität*, as a self-deceived and self-serving project of the weak. In the case of Foucault, it is to undermine the self-conception of certain institutions as benevolent, for while these institutions may officially have aimed to exploit the human sciences for a project of human betterment, what they have managed to accomplish is to bring a new form of power into human life whose consequences have not been good—and it is a particularly intractable form of power. I would not challenge any of these thinkers on the matter of whether their histories, if they were true, would hold the normative significance claimed for them.

I do want to emphasize a contrast, however, between the sorts of normative significance that have been claimed for these varied histories and genealogies, and the normative significance of moral relativism. The moral relativist agrees that we are products of history. But rather than try to reassess our current normative situation in the light of its historical origins, it aims to focus our moral attention on the possibility that differently situated human beings may face such different moral problems that they require guidance from different thick moral concepts. This may happen even among human beings who live at the same time. But I want to emphasize that when such difference arises consecutively over the course of history, moral relativism is predisposed *against* the progressive understanding of this phenomenon, as we find in the historical visions of Hegel and Marx, which anticipate that a single truth will emerge at the end of history. Moral relativism does not look very favorably upon the revisionist normative project of a Nietzschean genealogy either, which would call for a "revaluation" of values. And finally, it does not promote any normative re-understanding of the sort that might follow upon Foucault's archaeology. Instead, it takes real moral practices in their real moral contexts more or less at face value and locates all of the normative action *within* them. This is why there is room for what I am calling the relativist stance and its recognition that there is such a thing as normative insularity. To recognize normative insularity, is to recognize alternatives that do not stand in any normative relation at all to one's own point of view—they cannot be embraced together with what else one thinks as true, and they cannot be ruled out by what else one thinks as false. It is a situation that trucks neither agreement nor disagreement, but only otherness.

Hacking shares this normative orientation of the moral relativist, even though he doesn't use the language of relativism. When he moves from his historical excavation of the human category of multiple personality disorder to normative reflection, he confines his moral attention to the lived consequences of the category; and he is very clear that these lived consequences are confined to the historical context in which the category became most fully developed, which would be North America in the late twentieth century. As I have said, he is prepared to grant that in other historical contexts, other forms of multiplicity have been recognized, such as mediumship and possession. But these are no more pathological than the sort of case to which I drew attention in the preceding section. It required various scientific, medical and institutional developments in the West, in the nineteenth century, before this new human category could emerge and afford room for a new way to live, as someone who suffers from a dissociative condition that counts as a disorder—meaning that the condition is a psychological abnormality that should be cured if at all possible, and if cure is not possible then it should at least be ameliorated.

Significantly, when the category of multiple personality disorder finally made it into the *Diagnostic and Statistical Manual* that came out in 1980, DSM III, the policy at the time was to specify conditions and symptoms that should serve as the *criteria* for diagnostic categories that did not make mention of their causes. As the American Psychiatric Association says on their website: "*DSM-III* introduced a number of important innovations, including explicit diagnostic criteria, a multiaxial diagnostic assessment system, and an approach that attempted to be neutral with respect to the causes of mental disorders."[8] Yet, as Hacking notes, the cases of dissociation that were observed and studied in the nineteenth century generally carried strong intimations—and many would say, indications—of a personal history of what we would now call child sexual abuse. He traces how these two human categories, of multiple personality disorder and child sexual abuse, became ever more closely associated over the next century and a half and more, until finally there was a great profusion of both in late twentieth-century North America, which generated a great deal of controversy— and judging by Hacking's account, a certain amount of *social hysteria* as well.

Let me briefly summarize the main points in the historical progression that Hacking traces in his book, *Rewriting the Soul*. We tend to overlook how varied the phenomena have been, that we now try to track with the word soul. The primary connotation here and now is of an immortal soul that is distinct from the body—a point in common between East and West, insofar as it seems equally central to theories of reincarnation as to theories of an afterlife with God. Hacking reminds us that the Aristotelian conception was much more biological by comparison: the soul is what *animates* the human being. But that conception was obscured by the metaphysical dualism that had come to prevail when Descartes became perplexed by whether the new physics that he was helping to usher in could ever explain how the mind, qua immaterial soul, interacts with the material human body. Previously, it had seemed more important to explain how the soul could survive the death of the human body, than to explain how it could interact with it. But there were perplexities concerning life after death too, that Locke brought out with great force of logic. He wanted to know how one could stand before God on the Great Day as oneself, so as to be held to account for one's earthly deeds. And he argued that neither the resurrection of one's body, nor the persistence of one's soul, would suffice without personal consciousness of what one had done. This logic led nineteenth-century psychologists to doubt that there is anything more to the soul—the ego, the self—than a series of thoughts that are sufficiently interconnected by memory relations. On Hacking's account, this is how the sciences of memory were born. They counted as science because they fastened on observable, and measurable, and quantifiable, psychological facts to do with the workings of memory.

Once the sciences of memory got going, there were bound to be investigations into the many ways in which memory can be disrupted, one of which was hypnosis, and then hypnosis became a primary focus of research in its own right. Some of the most interesting human subjects for this research were women who had been diagnosed with various nervous conditions, most prominently, hysteria; and it was among these distressed women that the first cases of multiple personality were observed, generally with the help of hypnosis. After an initial period of fascination with multiple personalities, attention shifted to other mental disorders, and other ways of thinking about mental disorders, including psychoanalysis.

It was not until 1970 or so that attention got redirected back to dissociation and multiplicity, with the help of two other new human categories: child abuse, where this carries a definite connotation of child sexual abuse, and trauma. Hacking charts the emergence of these other categories in order to expose the contribution they made to the conception, and eventually to the lived reality, of multiple personality disorder. He notes that incest and other forms of child sexual abuse were in evidence in many of the early cases of multiplicity, and the linkage between the two continued right through the rise and proliferation of cases that culminated in what he refers to as the multiple movement. But it made a great difference when the concept of child abuse got sharpened and given an official place in the law as a crime that could be attested to by doctors who had been properly trained to detect it. This development effectively displaced an earlier concept, cruelty to children, which had belonged to morals rather than to the institutional settings of law and medicine. Alongside these institutional developments and conceptual innovations, a body of research grew up around the topic of trauma. After World War I soldiers were being diagnosed with posttraumatic stress disorder, which was sometimes treated with the same tool that had been used on those fascinating female hysterics of the nineteenth century, hypnosis. After World War II, concentration camp survivors were diagnosed with other varieties of trauma. So too were the survivors of child sexual abuse. This last development brings us full circle back to Hacking's ideas about the sciences of memory. It is now generally accepted that there are many kinds of dissociation, and that there is a particular kind that is produced by child sexual abuse, namely, *traumatic amnesia*. It is also generally accepted that when such abuse begins early, and is repeated often over many years, the conditions are ripe for multiple personality disorder, or as it is now called dissociative identity disorder.

The DSM-V specifies the following criteria for the diagnosis of this disorder:

300.14 (F44.81)

A. Disruption of identity characterized by two or more distinct personality states, which may be described in some cultures as an experience of possession. The disruption in identity involves marked discontinuity in sense of self and sense of agency, accompanied by related alterations in affect, behavior, consciousness, memory, perception, cognition, and/or sensory-motor functioning. These signs and symptoms may be observed by others or reported by the individual.

B. Recurrent gaps in the recall of everyday events, important personal information, and/or traumatic events that are inconsistent with ordinary forgetting.

C. The symptoms cause clinically significant distress or impairment in social, occupational, or other important areas of functioning.

D. The disturbance is not a normal part of a broadly accepted cultural or religious practice. (Note: In children, the symptoms are not better explained by imaginary playmates or other fantasy play.)

E. The symptoms are not attributable to the physiological effects of a substance (e.g., blackouts or chaotic behavior during alcohol intoxication) or another medical condition (e.g., complex partial seizures).[9]

I want to pause to underscore that these criteria for the disorder are premised on an implicit assumption, that it is normal for a human being to exhibit the kind of unity that is characteristic of an individual self, or person, throughout the entire course of its life.

We should not be surprised that the DSM-V fails to be explicit about this assumption. The manual's purpose is to offer diagnostic categories for various mental disorders, and so *that* is what it needs to be explicit about. It would be a less pressing task, and I daresay a more controversial and daunting task, to say positively what it is for a human being to be in good mental order. But also, in the case of the particular assumption I am attributing, I think most everyone finds it so natural and plausible that it would hardly need stating. I nevertheless want to belabor the point that the DSM-V does indeed make the assumption, so that it can serve as backdrop against which to set the following further points for which I am arguing: first, when we make the assumption, phenomena to do with multiplicity are bound to be appear pathological; second, there are compelling reasons to reject the assumption, and thereby to make room for the possibility of nonpathological forms of multiplicity such as the one I described; third, when we keep the nonpathological forms in view, we can gain a more complete understanding of what makes the pathological forms pathological; and finally, we can put Hacking's own deep ambivalence about multiplicity into interesting perspective.

In general, we can learn a lot about what the DSM-V implicitly assumes about the normal human condition by working back from the abnormal conditions that it cites as criteria for various categories of mental disorder. So let us reconsider the criteria it offers for dissociative identity disorder with this aim.

Criterion A refers to a "disruption of identity." When it proceeds to tell us that the disruption is characterized by "two or more distinct personality states," we may safely infer that a human being who does not suffer from dissociative identity disorder has one personality state instead of two or more. And when it says that a disruption of identity "involves marked discontinuities in sense of self and sense of agency," we may safely infer that a single personality with an undisrupted identity has a continuous sense of self and agency. And when it says that the discontinuities that disrupt identity are accompanied by "alterations in affect, behavior, consciousness, memory, perception, cognition, and/or sensory-motor functioning," we may safely infer that a single personality with an undisrupted identity does not exhibit such alterations—its psychological traits and dispositions are more stable and enduring. This all adds up to a fairly familiar conception of the psychological condition that many philosophers have argued constitutes an individual self or person—that is, it is adds up to the sort of psychological *unity* that constitutes a single unified self.[10] There cannot be any doubt that this is the condition of identity that is referred to at the start. There cannot be any doubt either, that the DSM-V assumes that this condition is normally satisfied in human life, unless it is disrupted by dissociative identity disorder (or perhaps some other disorder).

Criterion B introduces what is generally referred to as traumatic amnesia. There cannot be any doubt that DSM-V takes a high degree of memory connectedness to be normal by contrast—and of course, memory connectedness is generally taken to be necessary for the broader condition of possessing a single unified self.

Criterion C is not particularly illuminating about what DSM-V implicitly takes to be normal, for it merely notes a typical consequence of the abnormality of the symptoms catalogued in A and B, which is that they cause "distress" and "impaired. . . . functioning."

Criteria D and E are more directly concerned with what is normal. They clarify that not all cases of apparent dissociation indicate the presence of dissociative identity disorder. There are three such exclusions: when the "disturbance" is "a normal part of a broadly accepted cultural or religious practice; when it is better explained in terms of "imaginary playmates or other fantasy play"; when it is "attributable to the physiological effects of a substance . . . or another medical condition." It is obvious that the second and third exclusions do not countervail the implicit assumption I am attributing—no one supposes that children who engage in imaginary play thereby cease to possess a single unified self, and ditto for adults who suffer from temporary blackouts or seizures. The first exclusion does not countervail the assumption either, but it merits separate discussion.

The reference is clearly to shamanic practices in which dissociative phenomena are taken to involve mediumship or possession. Although these dissociative phenomena are indeed accepted as a "normal part" of shamanic practices, they are not regarded as part of the normal human condition. On the contrary, the capacity for mediumship and possession is regarded as a rare gift that is possessed by a select few. But more directly to my overall point: when a shaman is "visited" or "possessed," it is not supposed that their own personal identity has somehow been "disrupted" or "disturbed"; it is supposed, rather, that other selves—selves who are not the shaman—speak and act through the shaman's body. Hacking is quite right to emphasize that this is a profoundly different conception from the conceptions of *multiplicity* that have been elaborated in the history of Western medical science, first in connection with multiple personality disorder, and then later with dissociative identity disorder. With criterion D, the DSM-V is registering agreement with him on this point. But the point I want to underscore is that cultures that recognize and value the sorts of dissociative phenomena that arise in the context of shamanic practices actually share the assumption I am attributing to DSM-V, that it is *normal* for a human being to be the site of a single unified self.

In any case, we ought not to lose sight of the fact that both the authors of DSM-V and its users do not participate in a culture that recognizes mediumship and possession. The cultural context in which psychiatry and psychotherapy developed, and still thrive, is that of Western liberal individualism, which places an especially high value on the unity of self or person, construed as the unity of a whole human life. In this cultural context, there is very little room for a human being to satisfy criteria A and B for dissociative identity disorder without also suffering in the ways that are described in C, and this would likely go hand in hand with feeling themself to be suffering from a disorder. For such human beings, the concession that DSM-V makes about cultural contexts in which dissociative phenomena are taken to be a normal part of certain practices, is quite irrelevant.

Unlike DSM-III, DSM-V does not cleave to absolute neutrality about the causes of disorders, for it is willing to discuss at least some of them under the rubric of "risk factors." In this connection, it notes that dissociative identity disorder is "associated" with a history of trauma, most especially a history of early and repeated child sexual abuse.

Hacking delights in recounting the fairly wild controversies that arose after Americans became familiar with the bundle of ideas surrounding multiple personality, child sexual abuse and traumatic amnesia. Could there really be such things as alter personalities? Had the human beings who seemed to "host" them really been subjected to the childhood horrors they were reporting? How could a human being forget such horrors? And even supposing that they could forget them, how could they ever recall them later in adulthood? Where were the memories stored? Why weren't they accessible before they were recovered? And how could one ever verify that it was indeed real remembering, as opposed to fantasy or delusion? Equivalently, how could one ever rule out the presence of what became known as *false memory syndrome?*

In North America, multiple personality disorder entered the popular imagination after the publication of the biography *Sybil* in 1973, along with other portrayals in books and movies. This led to an explosion of interest, both in the public at large, and among the clinicians who had led a successful campaign to get the disorder recognized in the DSM-III. But there was also a great deal of suspicion, prompted in part by the questions I just recounted. Even much later, in the 1990s, it was quite common for psychiatrists to feign open-mindedness about the category while also insisting that they themselves had never seen a case, and adding that they suspected that many of the diagnosed cases had been misdiagnoses, with the result that what might have appeared to be multiple personality disorder was really a case of bipolar disorder, or borderline personality disorder, or the like.[11]

One of the charges against the clinicians who regularly made the diagnosis of multiple personality disorder was that their preferred methods of treatment actually manufactured the forms of multiplicity that they claimed to be finding. These methods included the use of hypnosis, both in order to uncover a hidden past of abuse and in order to expose the continued existence of alter personalities who had suffered the abuse. The methods also included forms of talk therapy in which these alter personalities would be given names, and engaged as conversational partners in their own rights, as distinct from the personality who had initially come in for treatment. Typically, the latter personality remained in the dark about the existence of the alters during the early phases of treatment.

It is perhaps a fair worry that hypnosis can be intrusive and suggestive, and that it may not be the best method for uncovering a hidden past of child sexual abuse. But it would be rash to rule out the syndrome that goes by the name traumatic amnesia on that account. A remarkable French study reviewed the medical files of adults who reported recovered memories of child abuse much later in life, after a long period of apparent traumatic amnesia.[12] The study found that there typically was a record of childhood injuries to indicate that remembered abuses probably had occurred. Moreover, the study found that recovered memories are about as accurate as ordinary memories. In contrast, Hacking is rather reserved on the matter of how reliable recovered memories of child abuse might be, while taking the time to recount, at some length, the pushback that occurred at the height of the multiple movement, in which reports of recovered memories of traumatic child sexual abuse were dismissed as belonging to a false memory syndrome. This is not to say that Hacking would deny that child abuse has gone on and continues to go on—any more than he would deny the DSM-V's claim that repeated traumatic sexual abuse in early childhood puts a human being at risk for developing dissociative identity disorder. But as I noted at the outset, he does have reservations about the forms of treatment for this disorder that he calls multiple therapy, which I will address briefly at the very end of the chapter. We shall see that his reservations reflect a moral perspective that dovetails with DSM-V's implicit commitment to the idea that multiplicity undermines the *normal* human condition of overall *unity*.

There are other reservations that Hacking does not raise but perhaps deserve to be aired at this point. Traumatic amnesia is often described in ways that assimilate it to the Freudian phenomenon of repression. According to these descriptions, a traumatized subject forgets in order to protect themself from what is too painful to remember, by repressing the memories of it. But there is an air of paradox in the Freudian conception of repression: How can something that started out as conscious become unconscious? How can we ever cease to know what we once knew? Wouldn't the knowledge still have to be present somehow even though it is not conscious? Note that these are the very same questions that led many to posit a false memory syndrome rather than believe reports of recovered memories of child abuse. I think it is fair to say that, in the case of psychoanalytic theory, we have simply gotten used to the air of paradox that surrounds the phenomena of unconscious, or repressed, thoughts. We might reasonably expect, then, that if similar paradoxes were to arise in connection with traumatic amnesia, we might get used to them there as well. However, we shall see that the theorist of multiple personality disorder does not have to get used to them, owing to *two* reasons. One has to do with the specific nature of trauma, and with some consequent differences between trauma-induced dissociation and Freudian repression. This reason is now well in view for at least some theorists and clinicians. But the other reason is not generally visible—it owes to the role that social conditions play in generating pathological forms of multiplicity, and the nature of those social conditions.

Making sense of multiplicity as a disorder

To speak of amnesia and recovered memories is to speak of a single subject who once knew, and then forgot, and then later remembered. But that is not the way trauma and dissociation work, according to more recent accounts.[13] What is traumatic presents as a mortal threat, which then induces an emergency response on the part of the whole human being, in which all resources are marshaled in order to deal with the mortal threat via one of three standard animal responses, of fight, flight, or freeze.[14] By *all* resources, I mean even the resources that would normally be devoted to the sort of cognitive processing that yields a perception of events in real time, which will be available for recollection at future times via memory. Typically, all that gets retained in situations of trauma is an unprocessed jumble that includes some powerful emotions along with some fleeting images in various sensory modalities. Both the emotions and the images can recur in the mind of a traumatized human being without giving them much sense of what happened, and for this reason, the emotions and images do not present as memories, but rather as intrusive thoughts. The traumatized human being does not, therefore, need to forget. What the traumatized human being needs to do—if it is even possible to do, and it may not always be possible—is to arrive at a belated sense of what happened, by carrying out a great deal of uncompleted cognitive work, which they had not been able to carry out in real time as the traumatizing events unfolded.[15]

The primary effects of traumatic child sexual abuse that I just described do not themselves amount to the sort of multiplicity that psychologists had in mind when they posited multiple personality disorder and dissociative identity disorder. Therefore, it may seem that nothing stands in the way of positing a single self in such cases—so long as we are prepared to concede that this single self is in a state of genuine ignorance about its traumatic past, as opposed to having forgotten it. But before we go that route, we ought to consider more carefully how, and why, traumatic child sexual abuse might actually put a human being at risk of being truly multiple. For this purpose, it will be helpful to return to the argument for the possibility of a nonpathological form of multiplicity. I will begin by further elaborating the conception of the self on which the argument relies and then turn to the role of social conditions in the generation of multiple selves.

On just about any conception, a single unified self possesses a special relation to their thoughts and actions, which is a first personal relation of ownership. Elsewhere, I have argued for a thoroughgoingly normative conception, of both the self and the ownership relation that a self bears to its own thoughts and actions.[16] Thus, one's own thoughts are the thoughts that one embraces as a proper basis for deliberation and action—they are what one ought, by one's own lights, to take into account when one deliberates about what it would be best to do; correlatively, one's own actions are the actions that one ought (or ought not) to have done by one's own lights—which is to say, by the standard of what would be best in the light of all that one thinks. We often portray deliberation and action as proceeding from a point of view. On the normative conception, one's point of view is nothing else than the thoughts that one embraces as the normative basis of one's own deliberations. I have argued that the possession of a point of view in this normative sense is not something that merely happens but is rather an achievement. In other words, it takes effort and will to forge a point of view, where this involves appropriating the various thoughts from which one deliberates and acts as all belonging to one's self. Furthermore, the intentional activities by which a point of view is forged, are also activities through which a self comes to be. One might ask, but doesn't there have to be an original self who is already there, who performs all of these intentional acts of appropriation? My answer is no. The self is an emergent thing, which comes to exist through the thinkings and doings that seek and create the self's unity and, therewith, the self itself.[17]

A self in this normative sense does not emerge in a vacuum, but in response to surrounding social conditions. When I argued for the possibility of a non-pathological form of multiplicity, I argued that some social conditions invite the formation of multiple selves within a human life, as opposed to a single unified self that spans the whole of a human life. In these social conditions, a human being must navigate separate social spaces, which call for deliberation and action on the basis of quite different attitudes and values, with the result that many distinct points of view may get forged, one for each such space—as in the case of the young immigrant who must navigate two very different moral worlds each day.

Now compare the social situation of a child who is at risk for developing the form of multiplicity that qualifies as pathological, and hence as a disorder. Such a child has been subjected to ongoing and traumatic sexual abuse from a very early age. If the child is not thoroughly overwhelmed during the entire time they are trapped with their abuser, the abuser will very likely talk to them in ways that are intended to ensure that the abuse will remain hidden. The child must be given reasons to keep the secret—perhaps they are shamed into silence, or perhaps they are threatened with terrible consequences if they tell. The situation of such a child is in some ways comparable to the situation of the young immigrant who must navigate two different moral worlds each day. For the victim of child sexual abuse is faced with two very different social worlds—the hidden world of abuse and the world of normal life. In the world of normal life, the abuse is never acknowledged as real. Therefore, no one is helping the child to learn to process it, or to remember it, or to become the site of a single self that functions as the *same* self in both of the social worlds with which they are confronted, in which knowledge of what happens in both worlds is embraced together from a single point of view. So we should expect that insofar as there is any scope for *self-formation* in the hidden world of abuse, it will be a self who is distinct from the self that is formed in the world of normal life. I do think there is *some* scope for this, in cases where the child is not actively abused through the entire time they spend in the hidden world where the abuse goes on. Insofar as some amount of cognitive processing and self-formation can get under way in the actual context of abuse, there may even be scope for some additional, albeit belated, cognitive processing when the child is alone and undisturbed. In this way, a separate point of view might be forged, that is dedicated solely to navigating the hidden world of abuse.

However, a great deal of belated processing of child sexual abuse is likely to happen very belatedly, often in the context of talk therapy during adulthood—what Hacking refers to as *multiple therapy*. I would venture that much of our knowledge of pathological forms of multiplicity is derived from this particular therapeutic context. As I have noted, some have objected that these forms of multiplicity are themselves generated by the therapeutic process, and they have gone on to raise skeptical doubts about whether we should regard the multiple selves or personalities that emerge in this way should be counted as real. In response, I want to insist that such skepticism is entirely misplaced. After all, none of the selves that these skeptics do count as real—selves of roughly human size—could have emerged without social interactions of a similar kind. In other words, if no one had ever named a human being, or engaged them and treated them as one, then the human being could never have become the site of a single unified self. It would be inane to infer that such a single unified self, that spans a whole human life, was not real owing to the role of social interactions in its development. So if we are to be consistent, then, we must not infer that the multiple selves who emerge in talk therapy are not real, merely on the ground that they develop through social interactions too. Of course, it makes some kind of difference when multiple selves emerge in a specifically therapeutic context. But the point remains, it is not a difference that has to do with the reality vs. unreality of the condition of multiplicity itself.

Hacking would agree with this last point, that the consequences of multiple therapy are perfectly real, even though there is also a real difference between the condition of being multiple vs. the presumptively normal condition of being a single unified self of human size. So far as I know, he is not aware of the other possibility for which I have argued, of a nonpathological form of multiplicity. Yet if we take his own work on multiple personality disorder as our guide, we can easily see that one crucial difference between the pathological vs. nonpathological cases of multiplicity is that the former are situated in the specific history that eventually led to the diagnostic categories of multiple personality disorder and dissociative identity disorder. I would suggest that the reason why Hacking does not recognize the possibility of a nonpathological form of multiplicity is that this very history does not leave any conceptual room for it. It has left us with a presumption, that the normal human condition is a condition of overall unity within a whole human life, and so any departure from this normal condition is, by definition, abnormal.

Since I have raised the possibility that this history has led us to overlook, of a nonpathological form of multiplicity, I am left with the question, what distinguishes it from the pathological forms?

I have indicated that I think we should look to social conditions in order to answer this question. Yet there is no denying that any form of multiplicity is an inner condition, and this may naturally incline us to focus solely on the inner differences mark the pathological cases—differences that are very real indeed, such as the presence of traumatic amnesia, dissociation, flashbacks, and so forth. Moreover, it may seem that we can retain this inward focus even as we acknowledge the social role that a therapist might play when an adult survivor of traumatic child sexual abuse begins to exhibit multiple selves in the therapeutic context. I observed earlier that such adult survivors may experience flashbacks, and I speculated that the reason why flashbacks do not present as memories even though they concern past events, is that the experiences could not be fully processed in real time, because the processing was interrupted by traumatic overwhelm. This led me to suggest that flashbacks might best be viewed as experiences that are picking up where they left off when they were interrupted. It would be natural, then, for a therapist to try to facilitate some belated processing in order to achieve greater clarify about what happened, and to make way for some belated emotional responses as well. Insofar as what was interrupted was being experienced by a child, with a child's level of psychological development, it is unclear that the adult who is experiencing the flashback has the right mindset to complete the psychological processing that the child never had a chance to do. This, I think, is a good reason why a therapist might try to address the child who underwent the traumatic abuse, and to engage that child as a personality who is distinct from the adult who is seeking therapy—it would be in order to help facilitate the belated processing that the child had not had a chance to do. This therapeutic strategy may seem especially appropriate in cases of so-called traumatic amnesia, where the adult spent much of their life not knowing about the abuse. All of these aspects of multiple therapy help to bring out there is indeed something internally disordered about the form of multiplicity that emerges through such therapy. Nevertheless, I will argue that the dissociation that characterizes the inner condition of multiple personality disorder (or as it is now called, dissociative identity disorder), is due to an *original dissociation that exists at the social level.*

Before I can proceed with this argument, I need to clarify the notion of dissociation. As I have already noted, sometimes the notion is not properly distinguished from Freud's more paradoxical notion of repression, which seems to require that a single subject first knows something and then manages to hide the knowledge from their own self by repressing it. It is not clear how this feat could be accomplished deliberately without still knowing what one is supposed not to know. In Freud's view, the knowledge somehow becomes unconscious. But the word "dissociation" was used in nineteenth-century scientific psychology (Hacking's "sciences of memory") long before Freud introduced his notions of the repressed and the unconscious. In that earlier usage, it connoted a failure of association among thoughts, all of which were assumed to be conscious. Thus, dissociated thoughts were conceived as perfectly conscious thoughts, though they are not co-conscious. Thus, in contrast to Freudian phenomena, there is no undoing or losing of knowledge. It is rather the case that there are separate centers, or streams, of consciousness within a single human organism. For those early psychologists, the clearest cases of dissociation were induced by hypnosis, though they also recognized other cases that are now recognized as the earliest cases of multiple personality.[18]

It appears that what trauma induces is much more like what the nineteenth-century psychologists meant by the word "dissociation" than what Freud meant by his term "repression." However, there is one important qualification to be made about the difference between the case of trauma and the case of hypnosis. As I have said, more recent work on trauma indicates that when a young child is subjected to ongoing sexual abuse, there is no opportunity to process the traumatic events in real time. So in these cases, there aren't any fully processed representations of those events—no perception-based beliefs—that remain unassociated with the rest of the child's conscious thoughts. Whereas that is exactly what is happening when a subject is hypnotized—there is plenty of mental processing going on, only it remains unassociated with the rest of the subject's waking life. So let me be as clear as I can be here, about what I mean when I use the term "dissociation" to describe the inner condition of human beings who suffer from a pathological form of multiplicity: I am using it to refer to the condition I just described in connection with hypnosis—which, to repeat, is not repression, rather a failure of association. I have just explained that this failure of association among thoughts can occur only if the thoughts are sufficiently processed to count as thoughts to begin with, and this must happen from within a point of view, or as Williams James would say, from within a stream of thought. There are plenty of associations among thoughts that occur within the same point of view or stream of thought; the *failures* of association occur only among thoughts that occur in distinct points of view or streams of thoughts. I am asking, what is responsible for this form of dissociation, which consists in a failure of association among thoughts that occur within different points of view or streams of thought? And I am arguing that we should look to social conditions for our answer to this question.

I have already emphasized that, in order that child sexual abuse can go on uninterrupted and unimpeded, it must be shrouded in *secrecy*. Sometimes it may be a family secret that is kept from the surrounding community, and sometimes it may be a secret *within* the family. In either case, there will be people who are very close to the events, but who nevertheless do not acknowledge them. We may wonder: is this generally due to simple, innocent, *ignorance* of the occurrence of child sexual abuse, or is there a certain amount of denial on the part of those who are close enough to at least suspect that it is going on, but who prefer to look away from it rather than look into it? We know that institutions, especially church and school, have chosen to look away from it. We also know that when it has been forced on their attention, their first impulse has been to cover it up—this would obviously be in their interest, since if it ever became known that they had allowed abuse to go on the negative repercussions would be terrible. It is fairly obvious that mendacious public denial would have been much more dangerous than cover-up, because denial would have invited closer scrutiny. But I would like to suggest that if cover-up would afford greater protection than public denial, here is what would afford the greatest protection of all: promote the attitude that child sexual abuse does not go on because it could not possibly go on! It makes sense that abusers themselves would promote this attitude. It also makes sense that it would be the declared attitude of other adults who do not themselves abuse, but who are willing to provide cover for the abusers. We can safely assume that this will be so in any setting where child sexual abuse goes on, whether it be home, church, school, or some other institution: the best course for all the adults involved will be to proceed as if the abuse does not go on because it could not go on. Wherever this attitude is the official position, it will circumscribe, and perhaps even define, one social space that the victim of child sexual abuse must navigate. It is the space of the so-called normal, in which such children engage in the ordinary activities of daily life; but what I want to emphasize is that it is also a space in which the abuse they are undergoing is officially unreal, because it is impossible. Alas, such a child will be returned again and again to another social space, in which the abuse is not only real, but also, pretty much all that there is. As I said above, the prospects for developing a single unified self in such social conditions are not very good. But as I also argued, there may be some scope for developing multiple selves instead, insofar as there is enough opportunity to do enough psychological processing in the social space in which the abuse is carried out. Why *multiple* selves? Because the more effectively this other social space is separated from the space of the normal, and indeed kept hidden from it, the less chance a child will have to forge a single point of view that spans what goes on in both spaces.

Consider how different matters would be if the abuse were exposed and acknowledged in the space of the normal. Then it would at least be possible to acknowledge all that had been happening in the distinct social spaces that the child must navigate, as having happened to a single self. But note that this would mean that there was no longer any effective separation of the two social spaces that the child had been navigating. A common social space would have emerged, in which nonabusive adults were reacting to what the abuser(s) had been doing and vice versa. In this common space, the many injuries done to the child could then be identified and treated, whether they be physical injuries, psychological injuries, or moral injuries. This might afford a process of healing, and into the bargain, it might help to increase the chances that the child could come to achieve a unified self, with a unified perspective on all that they had been though. However: a common social space in which all of this could happen would be a social space in which the abuse itself would not likely continue— for it is too morally outrageous to be tolerated within any well-functioning community, once it is officially acknowledged.

Before proceeding further, I want to pause to address a worry about whether there is a consistent moral outlook informing my various arguments here. Twice I have invoked moral relativism—first in my efforts to clarify and sharpen aspects of Hacking's metaphysical picture of human reality (his dynamical nominalism, and his thesis about the indeterminacy of the past), and then later in my description of social conditions that conduce to a nonpathological form of multiplicity. In contrast, the last claim of the paragraph immediately above may seem to be registering a moral truth that is *universal*. I suspect that, to many readers, it may seem important that it does—important, that is, to register that child sexual abuse is always wrong, in all times and places, with no exceptions. I have found that this strong sense that we have—that certain actions and practices would be morally wrong, no matter what the context—is often put forward as a decisive refutation of the moral relativist's position. But we should take care not to caricature the moral relativist's position, or to misconstrue its implications. The moral relativist is not claiming that anything goes, but merely denying that moral truths are universal. And the point of denying that moral truths are universal is not to allow that what is morally wrong in one context might be right or permissible in another context; the point is rather to underscore that the concepts or terms in which certain moral truths are framed are neither universally available, nor universally applicable. But let me try to put the moral relativist's point more positively. The moral relativist insists that moral principles must be action guiding; and in order to be action guiding, they must speak to the morally significant options that we actually face, given our actual situation, embroiled as we are in particular relationships, pursuits, institutions, political and legal frameworks, and so on; and this requires that moral principles be framed in terms of thick values that take due account of all this specificity of our context. With these points in hand, let me return to the issue of child sexual abuse. The moral relativist agrees with Hacking that the very concept of child sexual abuse, like the concept of multiple personality disorder, has arisen in a very particular historical and cultural context, in which both legal and medical institutions have helped to define them. And while there may be other morally unacceptable offenses against children in other contexts (Hacking mentions "cruelty to children"), the particular offense of child abuse is confined to this particular context. My last claim in the foregoing paragraph should be understood accordingly. The claim is that the contexts in which child sexual abuse *can* occur are ones in which it must remain hidden, for it will not be morally tolerated once it is known.[19]

To return to my account of the social conditions that would engender a pathological form of multiplicity: child sexual abuse necessarily goes on in social spaces that are effectively separated from, and indeed hidden from, the other social space(s) that its victims must navigate; in these social conditions, a child has no hope of forging a unified point of view that encompasses the world of abuse and the world of the normal. For when the child travels from the former world to the latter, it will come up against the official attitude that prevails there, according to which the abuse that it is undergoing does not go on because it *cannot* go on, at least not in the vicinity of that particular child. Between the power of that attitude, and the overwhelming character of trauma, and the motives of abusers to enforce secrecy, there really is no hope of forging a single point of view from which the child could learn to deliberate and act as one.

Let me now contrast the sort of social separation that leads to nonpathological cases of multiplicity. When small communities form within large metropoles like New York City in order to maintain their own traditions, they do indeed keep themselves separate from the social spaces that surround them. But such separation does not require that they adopt the attitude I just described, which tries to pretend that what goes on in other spaces does not go on because it could not possibly go on. The members of an insulated immigrant community know perfectly well what goes on elsewhere and can readily acknowledge it—they knowingly coexist with it. If they remain separate nonetheless, it is because they are committed to their own way of life, and not because they have retreated to an untenable position from which other ways of life are relegated to the status of being unreal. Correlatively, those who are committed to other ways of life have no reason to keep their ways of life secret, or to deny the reality of alternative ways of life. Implicitly, the inhabitants of such separated social spaces are adopting the position and stance of the moral relativist. They may not have at their disposal the philosophical language with which to make this explicit, but it is nevertheless what they are implicitly doing. What I want to emphasize is that *there is nothing disordered or pathological about the social conditions in which the moral relativist's stance is appropriate.*

In contrast, *there is something disordered and pathological about the social conditions in which traumatic child sexual abuse can go on.* What makes it so is not just that there is some kind of separation between distinct social spaces or worlds—that is so in *both* pathological case and nonpathological cases of multiplicity. The difference is that the activities of ongoing child sexual abuse do not constitute an alternative form of life that can go on side by side with—and in clear view of—other forms of life; they are activities that must remain hidden, because they are too morally outrageous to be tolerated. To some extent, the separation of the social space in which the abuse goes on is achieved through secrecy on the part of abusers. But the separation could not be effectively maintained without some degree of cooperation, if not collusion, on the part of other, nonabusive, adults in the victims' lives. Minimally, there must be a disposition to look away from it. But there is also the impulse to cover it up as soon as it starts to appear. Most crucially and depressingly of all, there is the official attitude that *it does not go on because it could not possibly go on.* This looks rather like Freudian repression at the social level. Only it is less paradoxical and puzzling. Rather than being asked to suppose that a single individual both knows and doesn't know something, we are only being asked to suppose that *some* individuals know something, and these individuals pretend to others that they don't know, and they back up their pretense with the official attitude that *there is nothing to know because it is not possible.* Through this pretense, backed up by this official attitude, a social space is created in which the other social space, in which child sexual abuse occurs, disappears from view as entirely unreal. I am arguing that this condition deserves to be called *dissociation at the social level.* I am also arguing that this dissociation at the social level is a disordered and pathological condition, because it enables morally outrageous activities that the society should not tolerate and would not tolerate were it not for its dissociative condition.

I have contrasted two kinds of social conditions that may lead to the formation of multiple selves within a single human life. In both cases, the human being's inner condition of multiplicity corresponds to, and reflects, a multiplicity of social worlds that the human being must navigate. When those social conditions are themselves pathological and disordered, then the inner condition of multiplicity that they engender is pathological and disordered too. When we diagnose human beings with the condition that is now called *dissociative identity disorder*, we ought to take due account of the fact that they have internalized, and are reflecting back to us, a parallel dissociation in their outer social condition. However, I am not suggesting that child sexual abuse always leads to this pathological form of inner multiplicity—for as I have already explained, such abuse may be so traumatic and overwhelming that there is no opportunity for much conscious cognitive processing to go on in the world of abuse. When a human being is a site of such traumatic overwhelm, that too is a disordered inner condition. But it falls short of what I have characterized as a pathological form of *multiplicity*. And the point still stands, that when a human being develops this form of multiplicity, they are internalizing and reflecting back to us a pathological form of dissociation at the social level.

The official attitude that I am claiming affords this sort of dissociation at the social level—according to which child sexual abuse does not go on because it cannot go on—has extended to the very topic of child sexual abuse, which for the longest time was not a topic for research.

I would go so far as to speculate that the official attitude helps to explain what happened to Jeffrey Masson, after he argued that Freud's early seduction theory, which takes seriously the charges of incest made by Freud's patients, is more plausible than Freud's later theory about repressed infantile desire for the father. Since I am not a Freud scholar, I have no standing to register a view about whether Masson was right. But the point I am making now does not turn on whether he was right. My point has to do the nature of the reaction to his work rather than the work itself. Masson was promptly fired from his position as Projects Director at the Freud Archives, and in the following years he drew extraordinarily aggressive and sustained criticism from the psychoanalytic community. It seemed important that he not merely be shown to be wrong or mistaken—his reputation had to be destroyed and his character impugned, leading eventually to an unsuccessful libel suit on his part.[20] It defies credibility that this strong reaction was motivated entirely to protect Freud's reputation and ideas; I think it bespeaks an underlying determination to blot out any suggestion that the reports by his patients of incestuous abuse during childhood—reports that Freud himself had initially taken seriously but later rejected—could possibly have been true.

The official attitude has not been confined to the psychoanalytic community but has extended to the wider psychiatric and psychotherapeutic establishment. An Australian psychiatrist named Warwick Middleton has spent his life treating survivors of long-term incestuous abuse, all of whom developed some form of multiplicity. He writes movingly about how in his early days treating these patients it was hard to find any useful information in the psychiatric literature about the disorders that he was trying to diagnose and treat, and in the end he had to turn journalism—to news reports of particularly shocking cases of incest, as well as child sex trafficking—in order to find out more about the nature of the abuses to which his patients had been secretly subjected.[21] He claims to see a continuum between the systematic forms of oppression and domination that we find in patriarchal culture generally, and in the homes of survivors of long term incestuous abuse. Thus, although we have learned that schools, churches, prisons, hospitals, and the like are all places where child sexual abuse has occurred and been kept hidden, we have not yet looked hard enough at the family as the site of it. In Middleton's assessment, so long as child sexual abuse can be kept hidden it will go on. In my assessment, this hiddenness has been facilitated by dissociation at the social level, and to such an extent that it has touched clinical practice as well as research. Even after the diagnostic categories of multiple personality disorder and dissociative identity disorder were introduced, clinicians were slow to embrace it and work with it. I cannot help but speculate that one of the stumbling blocks was that it required going against the official attitude, by accepting the reality of child sexual abuse in the lives of their clientele.

Of course, there has been progress in exposing the phenomenon, and in addressing it. There is the work of toilers in the psychiatric field like Middleton, who went so far as to found a journal called *Trauma and Dissociation*. And there is the work of Hacking himself, who has written so much about the social conditions in which the very category of child sexual abuse first arose and started to gain traction. However, he seems to have been more interested in exposing an escalation of reports and charges that eventually led to a kind of social hysteria surrounding the topic in North America, than in exploring the extent to which the phenomenon has historically been under reported, with dire consequences for victims whose psychiatric conditions were misdiagnosed. Indeed, it was not so very long ago that, when female psychiatric patients reported that they had been subjected to child sexual abuse, these reports were taken as evidence of delusion on their part, rather than as evidence of abuse. Thus, the official attitude then was the same attitude that continues to maintain dissociation at the social level: child sexual abuse is not very widespread because it is simply impossible that it *could* be very widespread. And even when we are forced to allow that it is real after all, we still presume that it could not be going on very near, among people whom we know.

What I find sad and upsetting about dissociative identity disorder is that when we try to respond humanely to it, we continue to regard it solely in its internal aspect. The internal aspect is certainly there: dissociation is part of psychological reality as we now know it, and so is the traumatic nature of the experiences that help to generate the pronounced forms of it that we find in cases of dissociative identity disorder. But I believe we will not be able to come to grips with this inner condition until we acknowledge the ways in which it is a response to, and indeed a reflection of, an outer social condition.

Hacking, for all his interest in social history and social reality, concludes his book with the usual regrettable focus on the inner aspect of multiplicity. He offers these approving words about those who quietly doubt the wisdom of employing the diagnostic category of multiple personality disorder and engaging in multiple therapy: "[They] suspect that the outcome of multiple therapy is a type of false consciousness. This is a deeply moral judgment. It is based on the sense that false consciousness is contrary to the growth and maturing of a person who knows herself. It is contrary to what the philosophers call freedom. It is contrary to our best vision of what it is to be a human being." In response, I can only say that, with these words, Hacking is retreating to an ancient model of what it is to live well, which endures in liberal individualist ideals and in the institutions of psychiatry and psychotherapy that are informed by those individualist ideals. Alas, anyone who retreats to this ancient model thereby fails to engage with some further facts about multiplicity, beyond the hidden history Hacking has so helpfully brought to light: facts about how, and why, certain complex social conditions may invite nonpathological forms of multiplicity; and facts about how, and why, the pathological forms of multiplicity that now go by the name "dissociative identity disorder" reflect a disordered social condition that is well described as *dissociation at the social level*.

PART II

POLITICAL ECONOMY

CHAPTER 4

FREEDOM AND COERCION, OPPORTUNITY AND THE ECONOMY

Neoliberalism, the Individual, and Society

JOSEPH E. STIGLITZ

There is a simplistic reasoning that sees freedom and coercion as simple antitheses of each other.[1] An individual has the freedom to wear a mask or not, to get a vaccine or not, to contribute financially to the defense of the country or not, or to voluntarily give money to a poor person. The state has the power to take away these freedoms. It may compel or coerce me to wear a mask, get a vaccine, pay taxes to help support a defense force or support the poor. Taking away these freedoms of action is often referred to as coercion.

The same dichotomy exists at the level of the nation-state in its relation to other nation-states. States may feel that they are forced into doing what they don't want to do by the threat of military action or through actions that have an impact on their economy so severe they feel they have no choice.

In at least some of these cases of coercion, though, economists might reframe the issue. All individuals (all states) face constraints. One might say, "I am coerced into living within my budget," but one could just as well say, "I am not entitled to live beyond my budget," or "no one else can be coerced to give me resources beyond those that my budget allows me to enjoy." Few would use the vocabulary of coercion to describe the constraint of living within one's means.

But defining freedom as spending one's income the way one wants and coercion as having constraints put on how one spends one's income subtly gives primacy to markets and market-determined prices. Markets are a particular system of allocating resources that generates wages and prices and interest rates, and those prices determine individuals' budget constraints. If prices were different, I would have the "freedom" to consume more of some good—but that might constrain me at the same time to consume less of other goods. By contrast, if wages were low enough, I might have to work more to survive; I might rightly feel that I am being coerced into working. And there has, indeed, been a long history of exactly this kind of coercion. For instance, in South Africa, Black South Africans were not allowed to farm in an economic regime *designed* to force the workers to toil in the mines at low wages.

Perhaps in this context the word coercion may not be helpful. We can simply think of a "tighter" budget constraint as one of many *noncoercive* ways in which a person's freedom to act is reduced.

What matters is a person's *freedom* to act. Changes in an individual's opportunity set—the set of options a person has available—affect the freedom to act. Any reduction in the scope of actions that can be undertaken is, in this sense, a loss of freedom.

From the perspective of an economist, the language surrounding this loss makes no difference.[2] All that matters is the set of available options from which the individual can choose. Taking this point of view, it makes no difference whether one induces someone to behave in a particular way by *incentivizing* the person through rewards or *punishing* the person through fines, even though we champion the former as "noncoercive" (praising economic systems that design clever incentive systems to efficiently induce the desired behavior) and castigate the latter as coercive. Of course, modern behavioral economics has explained that most individuals *perceive* the two as markedly different; "framing" matters, and that means the words we use matter. A bonus for doing the right thing is perceived as different from a penalty for doing the wrong thing even though in classical economics, so long as the opportunity sets are the same the two are equivalent. In the first part of this essay, I take the economists' traditional view. In the second, I explore some of the ways that behavioral economics changes our thinking on these matters.

This essay approaches the question of freedom and liberty from the perspective and language of economists and quite naturally focuses on *economic freedom* (as opposed to what is usually referred to as political freedom, though I will discuss some of the relationships between the two). I address, too, the critical question of what kind of economic system is most likely to enhance the economic freedom of most citizens.

As I will note again, both the meaning of liberty and freedom and its relationship to the economic system are questions that economists have long addressed. I believe that the economists' lens has much to add to the discussion. But the answers provided by many earlier economists I believe are markedly misguided, in some cases because they wrote before modern advances in economics provided new insights into the functioning of the economic system, in other cases because ideological convictions overwhelmed their ability or willingness to do the required analysis. (I want to emphasize, too, that while looking at these issues through an economist's lens may be enlightening, it is also limiting; there is much more to the subject that is not well captured within an economics framework.)

Major themes

The language of coercion and freedom has become an emotive part of our political vocabulary, with the Right claiming that governments have restricted our freedom, *and unnecessarily so*. The thesis of this essay is that well-designed government actions are, in a fundamental sense, *liberating*; at least they can be for a large proportion of the population. That government action can be liberating is obvious: The end of slavery removed the shackles clamped on the many by a few. In more subtle ways, a few within our economic system have exploited many, either by depriving them of their lives or by reducing their freedom to choose. But once we look at the world through the lens of how one person's actions might impinge on others, we enter the world economists define by *externalities*. These are pervasive, not just at the individual level where what I do may harm you, but also at the societal level, where what one set of firms does may harm other large groups (for example, oil producers in relation to the greater population harmed by the burning of fossil fuels).

Whether or not the vocabulary of coercion helps in our analysis, our discussion undermines the libertarian view that argues any such intervention is "morally wrong" since it represents a loss of liberty. Market-based coercion, such as fines for not wearing a mask, is simply a change in the budget constraints faced by an individual. To argue that there should be no government intervention in budget constraints is to argue that there is something sacred about market prices. But I have seen no persuasive argument for why that should be so— and the preceding discussion and the following strongly suggests that it should not be so.

This, then, is the second theme: *One person's freedom is another's unfreedom.* The most obvious example is murder. My liberty to kill you deprives you of your freedom to live. This seems so obvious as to be banal, but it is an observation unrecognized by the Right. To one extent or another, the hard choices facing society are but variants of this theme. Your right to carry a gun increases *probabilistically* the infringement of my right to live. As does your right not to wear a mask or not to be vaccinated. In some cases, the balancing of rights is obvious. In all societies, killing another is prohibited, except in narrowly defined circumstances. There are many other instances where, I think, the balancing of rights *should* be obvious, if we would only clear away the cobwebs created by the false rhetoric of freedom and coercion. For instance, with the exception of someone for whom being vaccinated poses a health threat, the dangers of an unvaccinated person spreading a dangerous and perhaps deadly disease far outweigh the "inconvenience" or the "loss of freedom" of an individual being compelled to get a vaccination.

Even in simple societies there was a need for regulations—most of the Ten Commandments can be viewed as the minimal set of regulations required for a society just to function. As our economy has grown more complex and as we have become increasingly urbanized, we have become increasingly interdependent—far more than was the case in the simple agrarian economies of several centuries ago. The benefits are clear: standards of living and life expectancies have soared.[3] Greater interdependence, though, means one individual's actions are more likely to have effects on others—effects that they imperfectly take into account. There are huge externalities, and in one way or another individuals must be coerced or constrained into taking them into account. Traffic lights are a simple regulation, easily enforced, that allow drivers to take turns going through an intersection. In their absence, there would be gridlock. Everyone would be worse off. (Of course, there is a price—but not a market price—for defying traffic lights: the probability of a collision, and a fine, to account for the possible harm caused to another.)

These changes in our society and economy also mean there is greater opportunity and need for collective action. For instance, basic research underlies most of the important advances in recent decades, and the private sector will undertake too little research, because knowledge is what economists refer to as a public good, the benefits of which cannot by fully appropriated by the party making the expenditure. And when there are advances that are privately financed, there will be too little dissemination of that knowledge, as firms seek to make rents from their monopoly on knowledge. But financing these public goods requires taxation—"coercion"—even if *all* individuals' opportunity sets were improved, that is, even if in a more fundamental sense everyone had more freedom, *net,* considering the decrease due to taxes, and the increase due to the gained knowledge.[4]

Earlier economists' perspectives

Economists have long weighed in on the discussion of liberty and freedom, from John Stuart Mill in his *On Liberty* to Milton Friedman in his *Capitalism and Freedom* and Friedrich Hayek in his *Road to Serfdom.*[5] But the latter two looked at the set of issues from an ideological perspective, an attempt to defend unfettered markets, and took little note of the externalities and market imperfections that are at the center of the analysis here. Indeed, all three wrote before our understanding of the limits of markets became widely accepted and before the pervasive nature of externalities and the harms an individual or group can impose on others became well understood.[6] They wrote about a mythical world with perfect information and no market power, where no one could exploit someone else. Even then they recognized there might be no moral or ethical justification for the inequalities generated by the market economy—but they argued that, if it were desirable to ameliorate these inequities it could and should be done within a market framework through the imposition of what economists referred to as lump-sum taxes, which are taxes that imposed no distortions at all. Of course, the assumption that such taxes could be used to redistribute income is another convenient assumption for those who try to defend the market economy, and it is an assumption that is markedly different from reality.[7]

Once one recognizes that these economists' understanding of the nature of economics and the relationship between economics and society was badly flawed, one has to reappraise their conclusions and the arguments by which they reached those conclusions. They wanted to provide an economic argument for the market economy—that it was efficient. Hayek's analysis was more subtle than Friedman's: he and others of his school argued that the dynamics of markets, the evolutionary process, would lead to better outcomes, which meant a wealthier society. Neither Friedman nor Hayek, though, succeeded in proving their claims, and modern research has shown that those claims were, in general, wrong. Markets are never efficient, even in the limited sense that economists use that term (no one can be made better off without making someone else worse off), and there is no teleology in evolutionary processes, that is, there is *no* presumption that they result in the overall long-run dynamic efficiency of the economy.[8] Quite the contrary. There are well-known shortcomings.[9]

That unfettered markets, or even inadequately regulated markets, lead to socially undesirable outcomes should be obvious to anyone living through the late twentieth century or the early twenty-first century. Think of the opioid crisis, created in no small measure by drug companies and pharmacies exploiting people who sought relief from their pain; think of the cigarette companies making addictive and sometimes lethal products; think of the financial companies bringing on the financial crisis that caused so much economic devastation in the early years of the century; think of the multiple scams preying on the elderly and others; and think of the oil and coal companies making billions as they endanger the future of our planet. My intent is not to engage in a tirade against modern capitalism; it is, at this point, more modest: to argue that any theory of liberty and freedom, like Hayek's or Friedman's, that rests on the contention that markets on their own are efficient and not exploitative obviously rests on a weak reed. We need to rethink the relationship between "capitalism and freedom."

But Hayek and Friedman wanted to go beyond the *efficiency* argument for capitalism. It was a moral argument, that it enhanced individual freedom. There was something morally desirable about individuals getting rewarded based on their contributions to society—a theory called "just deserts." Indeed, these moral arguments have probably had as much or more force than the technical arguments put forward by economists.

The argument of this essay, while seeking to repudiate Hayek's and Friedman's analysis of economic freedom within a more modern context and with the use of more recent economic tools, is, however, somewhat more ambitious.

First, I want to explore some of the implications of modern behavioral economics. Economists emphasize the role of incentives in shaping actions. By using incentives, we don't *compel* people to act in the desired way, but we *induce* them to do so. Both the private and the public sectors employ such mechanisms; most would eschew at describing these as "coercive." I think there is a blurry line between "inducement" and "coercion" (a point to which I will return later). Obviously, having the *power* to structure such inducements matters—thus power matters. Standard competitive analyses in economics *that assume no one has any power* do not discuss such questions; they assume them away. And it is almost obvious in today's world that there are some individuals and corporations with power.

There is a particular aspect of this power that I want to emphasize: The power to shape preferences and beliefs. If one can do that, one can induce people to behave in certain ways *without* coercion, or even without the inducement of (costly) incentives. "Modern" economics has *assumed away* the power to shape preferences by assuming that preferences are fixed and given. Indeed, it is claimed that (under certain conditions) markets are not just the best allocators but are seen also as *the best "revealers" of these fixed and given preferences* of citizens. As these market proponents argue for the informational efficiency of markets, they ignore completely the preference-shaping role of markets through, for instance, advertising media.[10]

Powerful actors within the market can also shape beliefs, say about the consequences of certain actions. When individuals change beliefs, in the standard theory, they do so because (and only because) of better (more) information. But in reality, shaping preferences and beliefs is *more* than just a matter of providing more and better information, something to which every parent and every person working in marketing or advertising can attest.[11]

Such seemingly noncoercive behavior may, of course, sometimes be good for society: The belief that it is *wrong* to litter may be more effective in reducing littering than fines for littering. Recently, development economists have shown that changing beliefs may be far more effective than traditional economic incentives, such as subsidies, in inducing behaviors that promote development or societal well-being, such as reducing fertility rates or gender discrimination.

But beliefs and preferences can also be affected in ways that are antisocial, such as the campaigns waged against the COVID-19 vaccine. More broadly, the beliefs about liberty discussed earlier—giving primacy to one's selfish interests over the harm these interests might have on others—provide a prime example.

Because behavior and choices (including in the political arena) are so affected by beliefs, the power to shape beliefs is critical; and unfortunately, in twenty-first-century capitalism, that power is concentrated and held by the relatively few who control the media.[12] In some cases, as in social media, they act as "gate-keepers," determining what information users are allowed to disseminate on their platforms. The content published and promoted on the various media platforms clearly shapes individuals' thinking and affects their behavior, including actions that individuals take that affect others. But the platform algorithms are in some sense more invidious, because they even shape the information that different users are given. Consequently, individuals are induced to behave in a certain way. It might seem this is not coercive, but how is this indirect use of power different from the more direct use of power via coercion? Individuals lose agency. At least to some extent, they become puppets of others.

Particularly problematic is inducement to *political behavior*, prodding voters to cast their ballots in favor of legislation that then induces or coerces citizens to behave in particular ways, expanding the freedom of some, but often at the expense of others. Shaping the beliefs of enough voters that abortion is "wrong" and should be prohibited leads to laws and regulations that are directly coercive, preventing those who would have an abortion from having one. So, too, allowing corporations to exploit others, through market power or deceptive trade practices, expands the freedom of corporations at the expense of others. Thus, a seemingly noncoercive loss of freedom leads to a directly coercive loss of freedom. In thinking about freedom and power, we must take a systemic view.

Second, the failures of the neoliberal economic system within countries described earlier have been replicated in the failures of the international order. There is a parallel between the sovereignty of countries and "freedom" or "liberty of individuals," and the neoliberal system of international rules and institutions that has expanded the economic opportunities of rich countries at the expense, especially, of poor countries.

Third, and perhaps most important, I want to show that there is an alternative way to organize society (the economy) that is better at expanding the opportunities of individuals—of enhancing their freedom. I call it *progressive capitalism* or a rejuvenated social democracy. It provides better prospects of creating what might be thought of as the "Good Society" than neoliberal capitalism, which is the kind of capitalism envisioned by Friedman or Hayek.

This essay is divided into five parts, beyond the introduction and a brief concluding section. The first presents the basic analysis of economic freedom, and the second discusses the special problems presented by the endogeneity of beliefs and preferences. The third explains why neoliberalism, despite its name and its pretense to enhance freedom, did just the opposite, while the fourth explains a parallel failure as those same flawed ideas were applied to the relations among countries. The fifth presents an alternative economic and political framework that I believe is more likely to enhance freedom: progressive capitalism, a rejuvenated social democracy.

I. Basic principles underlying individual economic freedom

The argument presented in the introduction that, in the presence of externalities, one person's freedom is another's unfreedom, seems sufficiently obvious that it should not be controversial. But my argument against Friedman, Hayek, and libertarians more broadly who believe that taxation is an infringement on individual liberty, is more general, and I develop it in the next eight sections. In section 1, I begin by repudiating their argument in what might seem to be the most favorable set of circumstances for their case, where there are competitive markets and no externalities. I then develop the argument further in the case where there are externalities (section 2), concerns about inequality (section 3), and market exploitation (section 4). A central economic argument of economists like Hayek is that freedom unleashes the innovative spirit, and infringements on liberty curtail growth and possibly the well-being of all citizens, including those for whom redistributive taxation and regulation are supposed to help. Section 5 addresses such concerns, while section 6 shows in a sense the opposite, that underlying all innovation is basic research, which necessarily is publicly financed. Coercion—forcing all citizens to contribute to support innovation and other public goods—can enhance the opportunities of all, even those taxed. In this sense, coercion can enhance economic freedom.

Section 7 considers the question of freedom through the lens of contracts, including social contracts, pointing out that all contracts constrain but that individuals willingly agree to such constraints because they are welfare-enhancing—much like the other constraints that I have discussed in this section are "freedom enhancing."

To many, discussions of freedom center around political freedom, and the final section of part I addresses some aspects of the relationship between political and economic freedom.

1. Competitive markets and freedom

The market always constrains what we can do. Or, more accurately, scarcity constrains what we as individuals and as a society can do. We do not naturally call these constraints a loss of freedom, but when the government, or market power, steps into the allocative process we often describe the *additional* constraints thereby imposed as a loss of freedom.

We can clearly see how such public interventions in the natural workings of the market or such deviations from competitive markets may seem "coercive," restricting our choices from what they otherwise would have been. But, as we observed in the introduction, this view gives primacy to the prices that might be derived in a perfect competitive market, and why should we do that? Competitive markets are only one way by which resources might be allocated.

The primacy of "competitive prices" is to be questioned even were it the case that markets were perfectly efficient and there are no "market failures" or imperfections. Consider the not unrealistic case in which a few individuals inherit a large fraction of a country's wealth from parents who acquired that wealth by taking it from others (the case of landowners in many countries where European colonizers displaced the previous inhabitants). The "moral claim" to wealth in this context is obviously weak; few would say that a policy of redistributing that wealth to citizens with lower incomes—especially if the land were stolen from those citizens or their forebears—is a fundamental infringement on freedom. Many might claim that a policy of restitution would be morally justified. But that would raise questions about the moral claims to the land of those from whom the land was taken. Perhaps they also took the land from others.

We can similarly question the moral claim to high income by people whose income is high because of the way the market values their assets. In a competitive market, relative prices reflect the preferences of people with income and wealth; the returns on certain assets may be high simply because of the demands of those whose moral claim to wealth is questionable.

Historically, as we have seen, economists attacking redistribution have claimed that incomes are the "just deserts" of individuals' efforts. The justification put forward by Nassau Senior, one of the great economists of the early nineteenth century, of the wealth of capitalists was that it was the just reward for the "abstinence" of their saving, not consuming, which generated the capital accumulation that was at the center of capitalism. The analysis just provided should, however, make clear that while it is true there may be strong moral and economic arguments that those who work or save more should be rewarded for their work or savings, even in perfectly competitive markets, the *magnitude* of those rewards may have no fundamental moral justification.[13]

This is even more the case as we have come to understand the multiple "distortions" in the economy—no market economy even approximates a competitive ideal, with perfect competition, perfect information, and perfect risk and capital markets. These are not trivial assumptions. Each "failure," even a very small one, can have large effects on prices and therefore on the opportunity sets of different individuals.

There are two important sets of market failures to which I want to call attention, and which are particularly germane to the question examined here: market power and externalities.

2. Externalities and freedom

The examples with which I began this essay illustrate the externalities that are pervasive in our economy and society. Earlier economic analyses gave short shrift to externalities, with examples like the orchard and the beekeeper, smokers and nonsmokers, suggesting that they were not at the *core* of economic analysis.[14] The number of bees affects pollination in the orchard, hence the profits of the owner of the orchard; the number of trees in the orchard affects the opportunities for pollination, hence the profits of the beekeeper. Smokers affect the health and happiness of nonsmokers; but nonsmokers' attempts to restrict smoking affect the (short-run) happiness of the smokers.

But as the world today faces the challenge of living within its planetary boundaries—with climate change representing an existential threat—environmental externalities have taken on a first-order importance. Likewise, as we moved into a knowledge economy, informational externalities have taken on a first-order importance.

The pandemic brought home the importance of public health externalities—how one person's actions affect the well-being of another in ways they won't take into account unless they are other-regarding and won't take *sufficiently* into account unless they are *very* other-regarding. The hypothesis underlying almost all economic analysis is that individuals are not so other-regarding (indeed, most economic analysis is predicated on the hypothesis that they are completely selfish). The presence of such externalities means (in the vocabulary that I used in the beginning of this chapter) that one person's actions (a group's actions) affect the opportunity set of others in ways that are markedly different from the manner in which they would be mediated in an ideal, perfectly working, competitive marketplace without externalities.

Externalities are everywhere. We are experiencing them globally in public health and the environment. Conflicts, especially armed conflicts, have enormous impacts, as Russia's invasion of Ukraine reminds us. Standard economics argues that government intervention is justified by the presence of externalities; interventions that reduce the magnitude of these externalities are desirable.

While the externalities that I have noted (surrounding pollution, military conflict, and health) are obvious, they are far more pervasive. In work with

Bruce Greenwald, I showed that whenever there is incomplete and asymmetric information and imperfect risk markets—that is, always—there are pecuniary externalities that matter, that is, that affect the efficiency of markets. As I have often put it, the reason Adam Smith's hand is invisible (arguing that the pursuit of self-interest would lead, as if by an invisible hand, to the well-being of society) is that it's not there.

Coase's conjecture and another absurd stance

Earlier in this chapter I explained why the libertarian position that individuals should just be left to do as they please, even when their actions hurt others, was absurd. Economists who argue for unrestrained markets have put forward another argument—that markets on their own will address the problems of externalities that we have identified *if only government (society) assigns appropriate property rights*. Ronald Coase, who won a Nobel Prize for his work in 1991, followed by a host of others, argued that this was *the* solution to problems of externalities.[15] He was wrong on two accounts. As I have already noted, and as I will elaborate more fully, regulation can be just as effective and efficient, and in practice more equitable. And Coase's solution can't work when we have a pure public good—something from which *everyone* benefits—like combatting climate change.[16] Nor does it work well more generally when there are transactions costs, incomplete information, and some have disproportionate bargaining power.[17]

3. Freedom and distribution

A particular set of trade-offs and externalities is of special importance in this context: those associated with inequality.

In a society with a fixed number of resources, expanding one individual's budget constraint—enhancing the freedom to spend—necessarily entails constraining others' budgets. Redistributive taxation, of course, does this. Libertarians focus on the restraints that taxation imposes on the rich (they have less to spend) rather than on the loosening of the constraints of those whose opportunity set has been expanded (who have more to spend). In such a setting the vocabulary of freedom is not helpful in guiding critical choices. Why is the initial "endowment" (distribution of assets) "natural," and the incomes generated from that endowment not to be deviated from? The discussion of the previous two sections discredits such views.

Indeed, we can look at the issue much as we did through the lens of externalities, where one person's freedom was another's unfreedom: Taxation can expand the opportunity set of one person—increasing the person's "freedom to act"—as it contracts the opportunity of another. It is not possible to say whether liberty, in the particular sense we have been using the term, is greater or lesser in the society with or without the redistribution.

Whether such a "redistribution of freedoms" is desirable is a matter of judgment. The examples given in section 1 show that there are at least some situations in which there is no moral justification for existing inequalities, and indeed, there is a moral justification for redistribution.

Standard welfare analyses, in which we identify circumstances in which social welfare is increased, may be helpful in reaching a judgment. There may be a broad consensus that *a nondistortionary* redistribution from a rich to a poor person is desirable. This is the perspective of nineteenth-century utilitarians, "Benthamites," who argued that society should maximize the sum of the welfare (utilities) of the individuals in society.[18] In *A Theory of Justice* (1971) John Rawls argued that, behind the veil of ignorance, "justice" required that the well-being of the worst-off person be maximized, providing thereby an even stronger argument for these specific redistributions.

He argued that inequalities, *in general*, may be tolerated if they result in an increase in the well-being of the worst off. The claim that is the case has been used by many on the Right to defend inequalities under the rubric of "trickle-down economics." Make the rich richer and the poor benefit. The reality is otherwise. As the top's income has soared, the average income of the bottom 90 percent has stagnated, and (adjusted for inflation) the income of the bottom has done even worse. This should not come as a surprise. There never was a strong theoretical basis for trickle-down economics—and the argument was especially weak for the form and extent of inequality in America, where much of the inequality is associated with rent-seeking, which actually undermines total income as it decreases the well-being of the poor.[19] With political power linked to economic power and economic power to the economic rules that determine income inequalities, as I will describe shortly, what has happened is what was to be expected.

Some on the Right make a more limited claim: taxes are distortionary—they disincentivize work or savings—and are costly. Even if it were the case with costless redistribution, social welfare would be increased, with costly redistribution that is not the case. The losses to the rich, and society more broadly, from the distortionary taxation exceeds the social benefits of the redistribution.

Such costs may impose a limit on the amount of redistributive taxation that is socially desirable—they should be part of the analysis of the trade-offs, of how we assess the expansion of freedoms of the poor against the losses of the freedoms of the rich. Research on the responsiveness of labor supply, for instance, to taxation suggests that with "reasonable" social welfare functions, marginal tax rates at the top should be 70 percent or more.[20]

Moral claims and redistribution

The desirability of redistribution is especially compelling when there is no moral basis for the initial inequality, for example, if it arises simply out of luck or inheritance, and even more so if it arises out of exploitation.

Arguments such as Amartya Sen's in *Development as Freedom* would strongly press for public interventions that expand individuals' capabilities and thus their opportunity sets, their freedom to act. This would occur not by transferring income or changing returns on assets but by increasing human capital and what they can do. Expanding opportunities by providing health care and education to the poor can expand their opportunity sets far more than it contracts the opportunity sets of the citizens who are taxed.[21]

There is also a broad consensus on even the greater desirability of at least some redistribution when inequality itself gives rise to an externality—where inequality adversely affects economic performance or has social and political consequences. My book *The Price of Inequality* (2012) emphasized the multiple ways in which inequality has such adverse economic, social, and political effects. Since then, there has been a wealth of evidence supporting the existence of systemic macroeconomic externalities arising from inequality.[22] I shall touch on many of these.

4. Exploitation and freedom

Imperfect information and competition provides opportunities for some—large corporations, for example—to exploit others by taking advantage of information asymmetries and individual's vulnerabilities. No real modern economy even approximates the idealized pure, competitive market economy. And it is hard to see how an economy that is so distorted as ours—that deviates so much from the competitive "ideal"—provides a normative basis for analyzing infringements on freedom that arise from market interventions.

To the extent that wages are below what they would be in such a world or food prices are higher than they would be, there is a sense in which individuals are coerced into working more. Is there much difference between what is occurring in these situations and the situation in South Africa, where workers were coerced into working in the mines because they were prohibited from working the land? Or the coercion to work in those places where individuals have to pay poll (lump-sum) taxes?

In many cases, one form of exploitation gets piled on another. In South Africa, wages of miners may have been lowered still further—coercion still greater—as a result of the monopsony power of the mines, their market power over workers; or even worse, the mining companies may have colluded. The legal framework may have made matters still worse: workers were inhibited from unionizing, thus weakening their bargaining power.

Many libertarians might agree with government interventions designed to limit deviations from the competitive equilibrium. For instance, a monopolist's "right" to exercise that power by raising his price to whatever level he wants obviously affects my budget constraints; it reduces my "liberty" to spend. If I want to buy so much of his good, I am forced to give up more of the consumption of other goods. Perhaps more telling: If the monopolist has a monopoly over a drug I need to live, he has real coercive power. He could force me to give him all my goods just to survive. To what extent is this different from being held up at gunpoint?

But others argue that markets are self-correcting, that monopolies cannot persist, that eventually, competition will prevail. Modern economics has shown that that is not true; even with arbitrarily small sunk costs, for instance, monopolies can persist.[23] And even if it were true that *eventually* there would be competition, the harm from exploitation in the interim can be enormous.

The exploitation that I have focused on in this section arises from market power; but there is a myriad of other forms of exploitation—taking advantage of asymmetries of information or individuals' vulnerabilities—that can generate incomes for the exploiter at the expense of the exploited. The arguments for "coercion," restricting the exploiter's ability to exploit, are even more compelling in some of these cases than where there is just market power.

5. Curtailing monopoly power and rewarding innovation

Does it make a difference whether an innovator was given the magic elixir, purchased it from another, found it by chance, or discovered it by dint of hard work and genius? Is the innovator's claim to being rewarded well for a societal contribution the same in each of these instances? Some of these distinctions raise difficult philosophical issues.

In the last case, I think, there would be a societal consensus that the innovator should be justly rewarded for the work, but even then, it is morally wrong—coercive—to abuse that power. Consider the case in which the innovator has discovered a drug that can save my life. Most would say that it is abusive if the innovator uses market power (say, granted by a patent) to demand all my goods. We would say that a Good Society would find better ways of discovering these medicines and/or constrain the market power of private parties that make such discoveries—even if in doing so there might be some reduction in innovative activity.

This example also highlights the fact that it is not "nature" or "natural law" that determines the distribution of income and wealth but the laws of people, and as such, the laws can be changed. Intellectual property rights can take on a multitude of forms, with different consequences for different individuals. Individuals have no intrinsic rights to the income generated by a particular patent law. When society adopts an intellectual property regime, it may well think of the distributive consequences, limiting the ability to charge abusive prices or redistributing the gains from excessively high prices.

Rawls's difference principle tolerates inequalities in society if they end up making the *worst off* better off. Thus, to the extent (and only to the extent) that additional rewards to the innovator increase the well-being of the worst-off individual should they be tolerated; and to the extent that they do not, constraining the ability of the monopolist to raise prices (thus benefiting the poor) is welfare-enhancing.

But Akeel Bilgrami has argued for another view. One should reward talented innovators more because they *deserve* more, because they have contributed more, not because giving them more leads to more innovation, because to reward them only *because* such reward incentivizes them to work harder is "to treat them as a mere means. In the end, treating people as a means is to undermine them as persons with autonomy and goes against the ideal of their freedom, which is closely tied to autonomy and personhood . . . Freedom and equality have a built-in tension because desert and reward are intrinsically connected with recognizing a person's autonomy and agency and freedom, seeing her or him as an end in themselves, but at the same time such desert and reward for talent and enterprise and effort can lead to inequalities."[24]

Of course, if the discovery is just a matter of luck, there is little argument that they deserve more. But what if talent itself is itself just a matter of luck—the roll of the genetic dice? Is someone with the good fortune to be born more talented deserving of greater reward by that account alone? I suggest that this is just another form of luck, and no more deserving of reward.

And if the innovator is more deserving because of the hard work that translates the talent into achievement, how much should that additional effort be rewarded? Rawls's theory (and other similar utilitarian approaches) provides a clear answer: to the extent that additional rewards induce additional effort from which others benefit. Our earlier analysis clearly shows that the rewards generated by the market on their own have no moral claim.

Parsing the extent to which the innovation is the result of talent, hard work, or luck is virtually impossible—even more so because each innovation rests on a myriad of innovations that preceded it, and talent would amount to nothing without effort.[25] How much profit should Pfizer and Moderna be allowed to reap from their mRNA COVID-19 vaccines, which rested on public investments in the development of mRNA vaccines more generally and especially when the companies received large injections of public money from the United States and Germany? And does the answer to that question depend on whether their freedom to charge monopoly prices and restrict production not only constrains the opportunity set of others but actually leads to the death of some? Again, when put this way, I suspect most would subscribe to the notion that restrictions on the freedom of the drug companies to charge as they will is more than justified—it is small compared to the effects on the "liberty" of others that results from the unconstrained behavior of the monopolies.[26]

6. Public goods, the free rider problem, and individual economic freedom

So far I have focused mostly on instances where seemingly coercive government action is directed at limiting the harms that one individual imposes on another, or at enhancing the capabilities, and hence freedoms, of others. In this subsection I consider another important case where there are benefits from *collective action* through the provision of a public good from which all benefit—including the individual who is taxed. Coercion is required, even though the result of such coercion is to expand the budget constraint of the taxpayer, and in that sense the person's economic freedom (the set of things that he or she can do) is unambiguously enriched.

There are many instances of this. Most important, in our twenty-first-century economy we have all benefited from public investments in basic research. Research on DNA was followed by research on messenger RNA, and that was followed by the development of the mRNA platform that proved so important in rapidly developing the highly effective vaccine against COVID-19. Just imagine where we would have been had the disease struck a century ago. Similarly, the success (and wealth) of Silicon Valley tech entrepreneurs rests on publicly funded foundations—the development of the internet, including the first browser.

In spite of these enormous benefits, there is a "free rider problem." Since everyone benefits from such public goods, no one has any incentive to contribute toward its provision.[27] They benefit as much whether they do or do not support it, and in a large economy people might reason that whether they provide support will have a negligible effect on the supply. Thus, they have a strong incentive to become free riders on others. But obviously, if everyone attempts to be a free rider there will no provision; and even if only some are so selfish as to be free riders, there will be an underprovision of the public good to the detriment of all.

So in this key arena of public goods (a more expansive list of which includes not just research, but public investments in infrastructure, education, and health), we obtain the seemingly ironic result that coercion can expand individual economic freedom for all. But there are other areas in which government interventions that appears coercive in restricting the actions of some (or possibly all) individuals actually increase the *equilibrium* set of things that all (or most) individuals can do. Again, some seeming coercion enhances freedom of action.

This is the characteristic of a wide class of situations that economists have identified as "coordination problems." Of course, all interactive activity can be viewed as entailing some degree of coordination. The competitive equilibrium model argues that prices do all the coordination that is needed, and the Nash equilibrium, when individuals maximize their well-being given the prices (themselves reflective of the actions of all others), is an efficient outcome. But the thrust of research since the precise formulation of that model by Kenneth Arrow and Gerard Debreu in the 1950s is that the conditions under which that is so are highly restrictive.[28] When those unrealistic conditions are not satisfied, however, in general the outcome is inefficient, and there are interventions—sometimes seemingly coercive—that can make everyone better off.

A well-known example is sometimes labeled the tragedy of the commons, where citizens in a society share a common grazing ground or a common lake or another resource. The problem is that each doesn't take into account the externalities: If one person takes more fish out of the lake, there may be fewer fish for others, and they will have to exert more effort to obtain the same number of fish that they previously caught. Even worse, each may take out so many fish that the total fish population declines. *All* are then worse off. Conservative economists advocated privatization of the commons; a privatized commons would, they argued, be efficiently managed so that there was the optimal amount of fishing. In principle, everyone could be made better off. In practice, grazing land commons were privatized by Scottish lords, who shared none of the gains with those who had previously had access to the commons, many of whom were unambiguously worse off. But as Nobel Prize–winning political scientist/economist Elinor Ostrom pointed out, there is another way of dealing with the commons, fairer, and potentially just as efficient: regulation, restricting the number of cattle or sheep or goats that each could graze (or limiting the number of fish that each could catch).[29]

In a sense, both privatization and regulation are coercive. Privatization completely constrains ordinary Scotsmen from doing what they previously could have done, letting their animals graze freely. They are either forbidden or charged a price. In the absence of compensation, they are unambiguously worse off. Regulation restricts what ordinary Scotsmen could do, but far less. Neoliberalism taught us to see the issue through the eyes of the Scottish lords, who obviously were less constrained. But if we look at it through the eyes of the ordinary Scotsman, regulation would have been far less coercive: Each *ordinary* Scotsman would have had more freedom, a larger opportunity set.

There are some instances in which government solves a coordination problem in such a way that everyone is better off and yet no one feels coerced—even though it imposes (what turn out to be nonbinding) regulations. Consider what would happen in the absence of a rule or convention concerning which side of the road one drives on. There would be chaos—even worse than the gridlock that arises in a world without stoplights.

In some cases, what is required is only a one-time intervention: a government regulation saying that everyone *must* drive on the right-hand side solves the coordination problem. But after its initial imposition, it is noncoercive: if everyone is driving on the right-hand side, I want to do so too.

The coordination of many Europeans around taking vacation in August may be another example. Given that my spouse has been given August as a vacation, I want to have August as a vacation. This coordinated equilibrium is Pareto superior to the uncoordinated American equilibrium, where the value of vacation days is diminished because of the difficulty of both spouses getting vacation simultaneously, and as a result both take fewer vacation days. Not only are both individuals worse off, but productivity (and therefore profits) may be lower.[30]

There are a host of other coordination problems that economists have studied in recent decades, where coordination enhances well-being, but individuals would rationally (pursuing their own selfish self-interest) deviate from the welfare-maximizing coordinated equilibrium so that government intervention *seems* coercive. But we again get the conundrum that "coercion frees": the limited amount of coercion allows all to have an expanded opportunity set. The most famous of these is the "prisoners dilemma." Everyone wants to take off from work on Sunday and enjoy a day of rest, consistent with the biblical injunction. (It is not clear whether the objective of the fourth commandment was to solve this coordination problem or, more likely, to prevent excessive exploitation of workers.) But if all other stores are closed, it pays me to open my store—I get all the customers who want to buy on Sunday, some of whom may stick with me. But knowing that the other store(s) will be open, I too keep my store open lest I lose sales and profits. The equilibrium that emerges is one where all stores are open on Sunday and all storeowners are miserable. In total, they get no more sales than if they were all closed on Sunday. Government interventions, *forcing all businesses to close on Sunday*, make storeowners better off. Of course, those customers who really wanted to shop on Sunday are worse off. In some circumstances, there might be a better equilibrium where stores that are open on Sunday charge a higher price on Sunday, compensating storeowners for their having to work on that day. But this may not be possible because changing the price labels may be costly, or customers may feel this is "unfair," a form of price gouging against those who have to shop on Sunday. More generally, the decentralized market equilibrium will not be efficient, and some government intervention can be welfare-enhancing.[31] The regulation solves the prisoner's dilemma, making all the "players" better off. Each feels coerced—he would like to cheat, to deviate. But the coercion enhances the opportunity set of all—it is "freeing."

Bilgrami asks: Doesn't the problem recur one step up too?[32] Regulation requires policing. There has to be punishment of noncooperation (cheating and deviation). But policing and punishment *themselves require cooperation*. If individuals can avoid policing and punishment by offering bribes to or making threats against those who police and punish or those who cooperate with policing and punishing (witnesses, for example), that may be the rational thing for individuals to do. But there are ways to structure society that avoid this seeming dilemma, for instance through punishing those who do not punish (and punishing those who do not punish those who do not punish, ad infinitum), so that it is individually rational to comply with the regulations.[33]

There is a myriad of examples of this form and especially so if we consider interventions that increase the welfare of almost all individuals, but not necessarily of *all* (and which are therefore not Pareto improvements). Knowing whether it is going to rain tomorrow may enable a speculator to buy up umbrellas, selling them at a high price the next day. But access to this information is just *redistributive*, that is, the speculator gains at everybody else's expense. Even though there is nothing anybody can do about the weather, they all will be induced to spend money to find out whether it will rain so they won't be ripped off by the speculator. Society is worse off because of the wasteful expenditure on information that doesn't have any social value—it just enables some speculator to earn rents. And a simple seemingly coercive rule—no price gouging when it rains—solves the problem. Only the speculator is worse off.

Elsewhere, I have shown that flash trading—where speculators try to garner information a microsecond before others, spending millions of dollars to get this informational advantage—is of precisely this form.[34]

7. Contracts and freedom

When individuals sign a contract they agree to do something (thus constraining their "freedom" to act in the future) in return for something from the other party or parties to the contract. Individuals willingly agree to such constraints, because the entire "deal" is welfare-enhancing—just as the "coercion" that the state may impose to regulate certain actions (like polluting or driving recklessly or getting a vaccine) is welfare-enhancing. In a fundamental sense, such constraints expand opportunities. Without credit contracts, individuals could not get access to the funds they need to make high-return investments; but in return they accept constraints, including on how they can use this money and possibly even constraints on *other* aspects of what they can do (e.g., not borrowing still more from others).

(The fact that a contract is "voluntarily" entered into does not mean it is not exploitive. An individual might sign an exploitive labor contract if it is the only way the worker can survive. In such a situation, one might even say the person is coerced; and even more so if the employer has done something to deprive the individual of alternatives, as in the case of South Africa, noted earlier, where Black Africans were deprived of the right to farm. There is in this sense a big difference between contracts among those of roughly equal power and contracts between those where there are large differences in power.)

Social philosophers have long viewed the relationship between individuals and society as governed by a similar *social contract*, which constrains individuals but in ways that enhance their overall freedom and well-being.

Obviously, what I have been discussing in this chapter has been the set of provisions of this social contract that, in some sense or under some criteria, maximize societal welfare, which may, for instance, enhance all or at least most individuals' opportunity sets and in that sense enhance their freedom. I have argued that individuals would want to accept regulations or taxes that seemingly restrict their freedom because, ultimately, they expand their opportunity sets.

The Right often has a peculiar and very limited view of the nature of this social contract. There are a limited number of restrictions on actions that are accepted as part of the social contract (killing, stealing); under the principle of *freedom to contract*, the social contract entails an agreement to have government enforce *private contracts* no matter how exploitive they may be; cooperative actions undertaken in certain forms (through legal entities—corporations) where relations are defined by contracts are allowed; but other cooperative actions (workers getting together to advance their interests through unions) are either enjoined (as collusive) or discouraged (as interfering with the "right to work"). This selection of what might be viewed as central provisions of the social contract cannot, I believe, be justified on the basis of any reasonable theory. There are, however, clear consequences of this particular set of choices for the distribution of power and wealth.

Moreover, in keeping with these analytics, part of what I would view as a desirable social contract is not allowing, let alone enforcing, certain contracts and contract provisions, such as those related to child labor.

8. Economic and political freedoms

During the Cold War there was much debate about the relative importance of economic versus political rights, with the West claiming the primacy of the latter and the Communist world, the former. The West did less well in providing equality of political rights than it claimed, the Communist world less well in providing economic equality than it claimed. There is, moreover, more than a little grain of truth in the claim that political rights have little meaning to a person starving to death or dying unnecessarily from a disease. These individuals would gladly trade their political rights for an increase in the most basic of economic rights, the "right to live."

In fact, economic and political rights/equality are more intertwined than either side admitted, one of the central propositions in my book *The Price of Inequality*. The argument is simple and obvious: There is really no such thing as a "free market" or pure capitalism. Markets don't exist in a vacuum. There have to be rules and regulations. Rules and regulations can favor large corporations, or they can favor ordinary citizens and workers. But the rules are set by the political process. And in almost any political process, those with more income, wealth, and education have a greater voice in the political process and therefore greater opportunity to shape the economic game in ways that favor them. But making matters even worse is that they can help shape the political process in ways that enhance the political power of the wealthy. The United States is Exhibit A for this process.

Thus, while at least in that era, the West championed *voting* and a free press as the hallmarks of a democracy, democracy is about more than going to the polls every few years. And in recent years we have seen a rash of democratically elected authoritarian figures, Recep Tayyip Erdogan in Turkey, Narendra Modi in India, Jair Bolsonaro in Brazil, Viktor Orban in Hungary, and Vladimir Putin in Russia. Most might have received a majority vote even without voter suppression and with a free media. But none of them believe deeply in democracy and showed themselves willing to do anything that would help ensure their ability to stay in power, including imprisonment and other forms of suppression of the opposition. (In some cases, such as Brazil, they fortunately failed. In other cases, such as India, the end is still not clear, but there is little doubt the country is on the road to fascism.)

The links between "voting," democracy, and freedom have accordingly been broken. What has been happening in the United States itself has also undermined our understanding of the meaning of democracy and its links with political freedoms. Widespread voter suppression—with Georgia even passing a law making it illegal to give water to people waiting in long lines, part of a multipronged effort to make voting more difficult—is just a slightly softer version of what prevailed in that state before the passage of the Voting Rights Act in 1965.

II. Beyond an individualistic analysis

In this part of the chapter, I go beyond the individualistic analysis to discuss the implications for our understanding of freedom and coercion when our beliefs and preferences are endogenous, that is change, affected by our experiences, and most importantly, when they are largely shaped by others within our society. This is one of the obvious but still important insights of modern behavioral economics (section 9)—a perspective that was excluded from economics for some two hundred years. These endogenously formed preferences sometimes provide an efficient way to internalize externalities, but sometimes they are coercive. Section 9 then explores the implications of social coercion and social cohesion for the meaning and nature of coercion. This and the other sections of this part explore how the endogeneity of preferences and our concern about the views of others (peer pressure and social coercion) might shape views of freedom. Section 10 then extends that analysis to some of the unsavory aspects of endogenous preference formation, associated with advertising, China's social credit system, and other aspects of social control. Both traditional and social media play important roles in shaping preferences and beliefs. Section 11, noting the dangers posed by unregulated media and by a media controlled by the wealthy, considers public interventions, especially in the case where there is market power, thus pursuing our general theme of how curbing the freedom of some may effectively expand that of others. Section 12 considers the special role that education plays in shaping beliefs, preferences, and understandings—including how enhanced understandings of how we are "shaped" can itself be liberalizing. Section 13 turns to the key Enlightenment value of tolerance. Finally, section 14 discusses a key consequence of moving beyond an individualistic framework: the necessity of revisiting normative analyses.

9. Insights from modern behavioral economics: Social coercion and social cohesion

The standard welfare analysis is conducted within an individualistic framework, in which individuals' preferences and cognitive lenses are fixed; but a new strand of behavioral economics has emphasized that both are endogenous, and most importantly, to a large extent, are socially determined. To use the economists' jargon, there are large social externalities.

An aspect of the social shaping of preferences and beliefs central to the topic is whether peer pressure, cultural norms, and so on constrain individual freedom. Of course they do. What we view as "acceptable" is shaped in no small measure by our society. In some societies it is acceptable to litter, to go unmasked during a pandemic, or to beat one's wife; in other societies, such behaviors are viewed as unacceptable. One might say in each instance that the norms constrain what the individual could do without the imposition of social sanctions—no less constraining and in some cases far more constraining than a government fine—and in that sense could be viewed as coercive.

In some cases, the benefits of this kind of peer pressure from a social perspective are clear and large. Sometimes such norms can help address an externality. Peer pressure and social norms can lead to less littering, less drinking, safer driving. To the extent that a social norm succeeds in internalizing an externality, seemingly more intrusive—coercive—public interventions to regulate externalities are less necessary.

Peer pressure and social norms can be important, too, in creating and maintaining a Good Society, for example, by discouraging wife-beating or encouraging tolerance.

There are two nuances of these more positive perspectives on peer pressure to which I wish to call attention.

First, while there is an obvious negative overtone to social coercion, social cohesion (with its positive overtones) and social coercion may be close to observationally equivalent. Again, certain behaviors, which we may call for simplicity pro-social, are part of the social formation of beliefs and preferences—of our identity. It is part of who we are. We think of ourselves as good citizens, members of a community, doing our part. It is not that we are coerced to behave well. It is part of our being that we show respect for others by not loitering, for example. Again, to the extent that there is this social cohesion, it is not coercive to be required not to exert negative externalities—as I have noted, viewed in this way, a regulation requiring wearing a mask is not coercive. But it is not even coercive to be required to contribute to the support of those who are less well off, to pay taxes to support redistribution. We might do it on our own, but society as a whole is better off if we do it collectively so that no one can be a free rider in creating the kind of shared prosperity that is central to a Good Society.

Indeed, if individuals fully adopt the norms as their own values there is no constraint. They would not want to violate the norm; and a constraint that is not binding is not effectively a constraint. In well-functioning societies, as I have noted, most of the efforts at "socialization" (the social formation of preferences) entail inducing individuals to internalize externalities. But the transmission of norms across individuals is imperfect. Some individuals will not have fully adopted the norm and then the constraint is binding—a seeming reduction in those individual's freedom to act. Ironically, from this perspective, the loss of freedom is associated only with the imperfect transmission of preferences, the imperfect adoption of norms, and, when those norms are appropriately directed at internalizing an externality, at the imperfect internalization of such externalities.

The view that sees peer pressure as coercive can be criticized from another angle: We are sentient human beings, able, at least to some extent, to make judgments about whether and to what extent we will be influenced by others. There have always been individuals who have stood against the herd, who have used "reason" to understand that, for instance, certain preferences and beliefs are, in one way or another, undesirable. The capacity for reason is a critical part of an individual's autonomy, agency. We have the ability to make judgments about whether we *ought* to follow the herd—either for our own long-term interest (especially important in the case of peer pressure on a teenager) or for societal well-being (entailing moral reasoning). As Bilgrami has put it, "an embrace of prevailing social norms is something that one, with one's reason, allows oneself to be trained or acculturated into. That is why there is no intrinsic or essential link between individual autonomy and the self-regardingness that is so central to the standard economic outlook."

But in arguing in this way, Bilgrami may be going too far: We do not freely choose the lenses through which we see the world. They are largely, though not completely, determined by our environment, and especially in our most formative years that environment is largely determined by others (our parents). Much of the shaping of our perspectives and beliefs occurs subconsciously, without our even being aware of it.[35] The question is, when that is the case do individuals really have the *capacity* to choose a different lens? The fact that *some* individuals, possibly as a result of a liberal education (as we will see), have been able to recognize the special lens through which they see the world and even understand how they came to see the world through those lenses doesn't mean that all individuals have the capacity to reach that understanding, particularly in the absence of the exposure to the knowledge of "lens formation."[36]

Second, much of peer pressure is not directed at curbing externality-generating activities or encouraging pro-social actions. Some of it may even generate social harms—for instance, when it is directed at enforcing exclusionary behavior, as was the case with Jim Crow.

10. Social control, social credit, advertising, and individual freedom

In the same vein, while we may applaud socialization of individuals, making them, for instance, better adapted to the workplace, there may be a more problematic side to this social engineering, exemplified by Orwellian attempts to shape individuals toward social conformity. There has long been a concern that, for instance, corporations can use insights of modern behavioral economics and social psychology to make individuals behave in ways that are in *their interests* or consistent with *their views of how others should behave.*

Today this is not just a matter of speculation; it is a reality, not of perfect control but of moving at least parts of society in certain directions. China's system of social credit supported by mass surveillance intends to incentivize people to act in the way that that country's leaders want; its real intent is more than to incentivize, it is to create internalized social norms.

Westerners feel revulsion about this twenty-first-century version of *Nineteen Eighty-Four*, but they have done something of (almost?) equal concern. They have allowed some in the private sector to have similar impacts but with greater subtlety, through advertising designed to induce us to take actions that, in our more rational moments, we would not undertake. Has the compulsive gambler who is enticed to gamble away his wealth lost, in some sense, his "freedom to act" by this seemingly noncoercive method? In one sense, he was "free" to resist the enticement. But in another sense, the enticers knew that he was not likely to resist. There are enormous social harms that arise from this kind of inducement. Think of food companies inducing children and adults to eat harmful foods that have contributed to the epidemic of childhood and adult diabetes, or the Sackler-owned drug companies that contributed to the opioid crisis, or the cigarette companies that made their products more addictive without consumers even knowing it. Each of these can be thought of as a noncoercive threat to the individual's freedom.

I believe that public interventions in the "free" market to limit these antisocial activities is called for, and while they restrict the freedom of, say, the Sackler family, they expand the freedom of others in ways that enhance the well-being of society.

Social media and the internet have amplified all the problems to which I have called attention and added several more. It has led to the incitement of violence, the spread of hate speech, and massive amounts of mis- and disinformation that have had viral spread, inducing antisocial behavior such as the refusal to wear masks and a reluctance to get vaccinated. In our world of social media, with its multiple social harms and multiple aspects of what many might label noncoercive reductions in freedom (like cyberbullying), we again confront the dilemma noted earlier, that one person's freedom is another's unfreedom.

The companies have a business model that profits from "engagement," and engagement is increased when individuals are emotionally enraged. AI algorithms have targeted different individuals with different information designed to enhance their engagement. This fragments the information structure beyond anything that had previously been possible and in ways that have enhanced polarization, which is itself a social harm. The ability to create separate communities and reinforce disparate beliefs has made matters still worse. Virality meant information could spread quickly, more quickly than "antidotes" to the misinformation could be designed. The lack of transparency in who gets what messages has meant that the antidotes could not be effectively delivered in the relevant time span, if at all. Social media companies' claim that they are just neutral is obviously false. Their algorithms make decisions about which messages to promote to which people, and they do so in ways that enhance profits and polarization; there might be alternative algorithms that lead to less polarization, indeed some that might enhance social harmony.[37] What is privately profitable does not coincide with what is socially desirable.

There is an increasing consensus over the need to regulate social media. The EU, for instance, has adopted the Digital Services Act. A central question in the design of these regulations (a full discussion of which is beyond the scope of this essay) is how to prevent harms within democratic frameworks that emphasize, for instance, freedom of speech (First Amendment rights). Societies (even the United States), however, have not taken absolutist positions. There are prohibitions against fraud ("lying" in commercial contexts where the lie results in harm), false advertising, child pornography, and crying "fire" in a crowded theater. Some countries ban hate speech. In each of these situations there is a recognition that one person's freedom is another's unfreedom; that the social cost of the absence of a constraint is high. Clearly, the greater harms emanating from mis- and disinformation on social media, for example, change the "balancing" entailed in the design of all regulations toward greater intervention, especially when such intervention is directed at the extent of virality.

11. Market power, the media, and the shaping of society and individuals

Making matters worse is the strong interaction between information and market power. Information economics in all its dimensions (including the creation of information asymmetries) can lead to market power, and market power enhances the ability to exploit limitations in information. Elsewhere, I have pointed out how information economics helps explain the limited competition in media, including social media. As they garner more information through traffic on their platform, social media companies gain a competitive advantage over others, enhancing their market power.

In many countries, control of both traditional and social media is highly concentrated and lies disproportionately in the hands of the very wealthy. This gives them the power to shape beliefs, perceptions, and even preferences. They have enormous power over societal metanarratives, the lens through which large portions of the population see what is going on. They shape views about whether the government is "the solution" or "the problem," about whether material incentives matter, about whether mask requirements are an infringement on one's liberty. And, of course, these metanarratives have enormous political implications. In the United States, there has been considerable success in convincing individuals that the bequest and estate tax is a tax on death rather than a means of preventing the perpetuation of wealth inequality. As behavioral economists and psychologists have long recognized, how issues are framed affects how they are seen. By unwittingly becoming prey to how the media and social media are shaping us, we lose important elements of our freedom.

There is another way, perhaps a more subtle way, that mis- and disinformation in the traditional and social media reduces our freedom: If they *pollute* our information environment they impose costs on society, necessitating expenditure of time, effort, and possibly money to undo the effects of their activities. They thereby adversely affect our budget constraints, which I have characterized as a loss of freedom.

12. Education, the social formation of beliefs, and the liberalization of individuals

I have discussed several ways by which individuals and their beliefs and preferences are shaped. In a modern society, the formal education system plays a central role in shaping individuals, including in the intergenerational transmission of values and beliefs. Schools do more than just impart skills ("human capital").[38] The widespread support of public education in the nineteenth century was in no small measure directed at creating a workforce suitable for the industrial economy then emerging, requiring individuals sufficiently socialized that they behaved appropriately (and efficiently) in the workplace. All over the world, schools try to inculcate values, including national, and in some cases religious, identities, with school days beginning with singing the national anthem or, as in the United States, pledging allegiance. History is taught in a way that glorifies the past, sliding over the atrocities that the country may have committed. All of this is an attempt to shape individuals, to affect their behavior especially in particular situations and at particular times, for instance in wartime, when individuals are called on to fight for their country.

Whether we call all of this building social solidarity/cohesion or imposing social coercion may seem just a matter of semantics. It is obviously both. Both the benefits and the dangers are apparent. Education can be used to impart scientific knowledge about climate change, but it can also be used to convey climate skepticism. The challenge, briefly considered toward the end of the chapter, is how education can be designed to create a Good Society rather than an Orwellian dystopia.

Education plays another role, in creating what Bilgrami calls "social commons."[39] We are social beings and want and need to communicate with each other. (Such communication is an obvious prerequisite for the implementation and enforcement of regulations and the undertaking of other forms of collective action.) Educational systems help create these common understandings; good educational systems provide broader common understandings, with greater nuance that enables differentiated meanings.

Educational systems—and our knowledge system more broadly (including research universities and think tanks)—play a quite different role, which helps to "free" individuals from social coercion and enhance their autonomy. I noted that the lens through which we see the world is influenced by those around us and the events that confront us in ways of which we are usually unaware. A good "liberal" arts education helps us to understand these forces and sometimes gives us a new and different lens through which to see the world. It is fundamentally liberating. And it is why those in favor of current norms persisting (such as restricted gender roles), regardless of the merits, fight so strongly against a liberal education.

13. Tolerance and freedom

In all the examples I have given so far, the norms are related to individual actions that have externalities on others; they are ways by which society internalizes the externality, increasing social welfare. But in many societies norms go well beyond that, to actions and even beliefs that have no direct impact on the well-being of others aside from knowing that there are other people with beliefs and actions different from those we think appropriate. Enlightenment values, themselves social norms shared by many and to which I subscribe, say that one should not allow such beliefs and actions to affect one's well-being and that, whether they do or not, others should be free to choose for themselves. No one should impose social sanctions on someone else simply for holding different beliefs; even if one does not want to interact with such people, public policy should certainly not discriminate against them and there should be no public sanctions.

Bilgrami has suggested that one of Christianity's greatest tyrannies was to go beyond saying "Thou shall not commit adultery" to saying (in the Book of Matthew) "You have heard that it was said, 'Do not commit adultery.' But I tell you that anyone who looks at a woman to lust after her has already committed adultery with her in his heart." Even earlier, the Ten Commandments enjoined "coveting thy neighbor's house. You shall not covet your neighbor's wife, or his male or female servant, his ox or donkey, or anything that belongs to your neighbor" (Exodus 20:17). Coveting is about one's inner thoughts.

Perhaps one could justify this intolerance of thought within the logic that thinking such thoughts increases the likelihood of actions that induce social harms. (The Bible is explicit, warning about being "ensnared.") But such a view gives short shrift to human agency. We don't act on every idea that passes through our minds.

There are many dimensions to what I refer to here as "Enlightenment tolerance." It entails the toleration of ideas and values (both social and political) that may be antithetical to one's own. (Here we face the inevitable conundrum of the extent of tolerance for those whose value systems are antithetical to tolerance, or more broadly, to Enlightenment values.)

Whether the evolutionary view that better ideas will dominate is correct or not, that is, whether Enlightenment values *eventually* predominate, is of no matter. As Keynes put it, in the long run we are all dead. The reality is that these values are not shared by a significant fraction of the population. Maintaining them is a constant struggle, even though the principles of tolerance that I have just described would be widely agreed on, and I suspect any Constitution written today would attempt to enshrine such values for public action. (As one of my colleagues in the Clinton administration put it, he felt like he had to relitigate the Enlightenment every day.) Deep and universal adoption of the Enlightenment value of tolerance is difficult, for it entails the commitment to a certain mindset, and there seems a natural proclivity to shun those who do not share our values. Still, one of the marked changes of the past fifty years (until the arrival of the Trumpian movement) has been what I see as the advancement of this kind of tolerance.

14. Rethinking a Good Society

The objective of any political and economic system is to create a Good Society. The way any political or economic system should be evaluated rests on the extent to which it helps us achieve that. But that raises the fundamental question: What is a Good Society?

For the past century or so economists have tried to avoid that issue by focusing on Pareto optimality. A good economic system is one in which no one's well-being could be made better off without making someone else's worse off, a situation labeled as Pareto efficient after the great Italian economist of the early twentieth century, Vilfredo Pareto.[40] The positivist economics agenda, beginning at least from my teacher Paul Samuelson, tried to eschew all of these judgments, both on the nature of preferences and on interpersonal comparisons. Economists shied away from discussions of social justice. So long as the economy was Pareto efficient, the question was left to moral philosophers to decide whether an economy in which most of the income went to a few was better than one in which incomes were more equally shared.

Some economists, like Nobel Prize–winning Chicago economist Robert Lucas, went further, claiming that "of the tendencies that are harmful to sound economics, the most seductive, and in my opinion the most poisonous, is to focus on questions of distribution."[41] I obviously think Lucas was wrong, and that the market, especially the neoliberal capitalist market with its "freedom to exploit," generates neither efficient nor socially acceptable outcomes.[42] A society with a given amount of goods, with those goods more equally distributed, is a more just and better society than one in which those goods reside in the hands of a few. It is a more just society, in terms of how a moral philosopher like John Rawls might look at the matter (behind a veil of ignorance), but it is also a society where more individuals have more freedom—freedom to do more and greater opportunities to realize their human potential.

The positivist economics agenda could only go so far, and in many ways it was misleading, and indeed misled policy for more than a third of a century. Paretian criteria are simply insufficient for guiding moral judgments and public policy. Almost all public policy decisions involve some trade-offs. Someone—even if it's just the exploiters and speculators—is worse off with a regulation prohibiting such antisocial behavior. Earlier I argued in favor of government actions limiting cigarette advertising and the sale of opioids or circumscribing the foods that give rise to childhood diabetes. Whether such interventions were a Pareto improvement is no matter. The broad consensus on the desirability of such interventions only reinforces the conclusion that economists' obsession with Pareto interventions is misguided.

But the arguments of this part of this chapter have also exposed another limitation within the standard economic approach that assumes fixed preferences. These expansions of the lens through which we look at society have profound normative implications, for it means that the standard economists' framework, focusing on (constrained) Pareto efficiency, does not suffice. When preferences can change, when they are endogenous, standard welfare economics becomes rudderless. Should we be concerned with the initial preferences (say where we value only consumption today) or the later preferences (where we have come to value the future, and so become concerned about what climate change might do to our planet)?

Economic analysis can describe policies that might best achieve each possible desirable outcome, but without knowing what we desire—since that itself is subject to change, possibly by the policies themselves—it cannot ascertain which of the alternative policies is ultimately preferable.

Consider two possible scenarios. The first a capitalism that breeds selfish people who exploit each other and who get enormous "disutility" out of regulation—so Pareto optimality entails allowing them to exploit each other. The other, a cooperative society that breeds other-regarding people who cooperate with each other while at the same time exercising their individualism, but who accept the need for and desirability of regulations to prevent harmful activities and to encourage still greater thoughtfulness and cooperation. Twentieth-century economics said that we can say nothing about the relative merits of these two societies. In each society preferences are different, and we can only ascertain how good an economic system is in delivering well-being *given those preferences.*

(Hume famously distinguished between preferences and cognition. The latter he argued is subject to reason—although, to use modern terminology, when the world is ever changing, we may have no way to be sure that our judgments of relative frequencies are "correct."[43] Preferences, however, he argued are not. As George Stigler and Gary Becker argued, following Hume, *De Gustibus Non Est Disputandum*: Preferences are just given, not subject to reason.[44] Hume's famous slogan was "Reason is the slave of the passions," a view not inconsistent with modern behavioralist theories of confirmatory bias, and with its implication of "equilibrium fictions.")[45]

But I think there is more one can say about preferences, as well as cognition, related to an individual's ultimate well-being. One can ascertain, for instance, whether particular actions are consistent with our stated objectives—whether, for instance, certain actions, appearing to reflect our preferences *today*, are consistent with our seeming long-term well-being; one can similarly uncover other instances of seeming dissonance.[46] Time inconsistency, in fact, has been a major theme in behavioral economics.[47] But even here there is an ambiguity. While tomorrow we may regret that we did not save as much money as yesterday, acting on our tastes (preferences) *as they were then* was not in any sense wrong. There is a sense in which we should not even feel regret. We may even know that we will have different preferences in the future. Still, we act today in terms of what gives us pleasure, and that may well "rationally" take into account some notion of regret tomorrow that our behavior today had not been different. Only if we are not fully cognizant of what is going on can we be said not to be rational.[48]

In a world with endogenous and changing preferences, there is no way around asking the deeper question that economists have been trying to evade for a century: What do we mean by a Good Society? Of course, this is a question not to be answered just by economists. We, as a society, must address it. It should be at the forefront of our democratic discourse and dialogue. This is not the place for an articulation of the full meaning of the Good Society. I want, however, to comment on two aspects of the Good Society: social justice and tolerance.

It is intuitively clear to me that a society marked by greater equality (other things being equal) is better than one marked by huge disparities; that one marked by cooperation and tolerance is fundamentally better than one marked by greed, selfishness, and intolerance; extreme versions of the latter that have appeared on the American scene in recent decades are truly loathsome.

Of course, economists can be useful in helping us understand why that might be so, for instance by showing how trust enhances social cooperation, economic performance, and general societal well-being. Economics has also shown that societies with greater equality perform better. There are negative macroeconomic externalities that arise especially from excessive inequality. But the arguments for a society based on trust, tolerance, and social justice go beyond the instrumental. Such societies are, I believe, preferable and not just because they can deliver more goods. Fully arguing this would again take us beyond the confines of this chapter.

Freedom, coercion, and the Good Society

I want to return to the theme of coercion and freedom. Historians of economic thought looking at the totality of Adam Smith's writing, including his *Theory of Moral Sentiments* (published in 1759, twenty-seven years before his better-known *Wealth of Nations*), suggest that Smith was focused on individuals' well-being, *broadly construed*, including individuals' sensibilities for the welfare of others. If individuals care about each other, then a mask requirement is *not* coercive. As I put it earlier, they have internalized the externality. They may have done so perhaps because they realized that they themselves might be worse off. The spread of COVID-19 may, in the end, increase their own probability of death, so that it is in their own narrow self-interest to pay attention to the social consequences of their actions. But, alternatively, they may have done so because of their empathy with others. I think it could be well argued that a Good Society is one in which individuals feel this kind of empathy, at least to some extent.

The two perspectives are, of course, normally intermingled and cannot be easily separated. Consider, for instance, the question of progressive taxation. A society with high levels of inequality may be marked by high levels of crime, forcing the superrich to live in gated communities. The quality of life of the wealthy may be enriched were they to live in a society with less inequality. Moreover, there is evidence that economic growth is greater in economies with less inequality, and while there is little evidence of trickle-down economics—faster growth does not necessarily improve the welfare of the poor—there is evidence of trickle-up economics, those at the top do better if there is faster growth.[49] At least on average, they may be better off with at least some degree of progressive taxation.

Summary

Let me summarize my argument thus far. Earlier notions had it that a Good Society was one that allowed the maximum freedom of each person so long as that freedom did not infringe on another's. At the center of such a dictum is *tolerance*. It explicitly says that one person's views about what is desirable or good should have no bearing on what is allowed, encouraged, or discouraged. Only actions adversely affect others. (This doctrine itself does not resolve one of the major issues dividing the United States, abortion, because it does not define what another "being" is, a question at the center of the debate.) It is clear that the Right, at least in the United States, has repudiated such notions of Enlightenment tolerance.

Putting that aside, what I have argued is that most of the central issues of policy today entail, to use the economists' jargon, trade-offs in freedoms, with the expansion of one person's freedom coming often at the expense of another's. As I have put it, one person's freedom is another's unfreedom. Libertarianism itself gives us no guide on how to weigh such trade-offs, but common sense and a sense of societal well-being may.

And libertarianism doesn't address the important set of situations where "constraints are liberating," that is, where collective action can expand the *opportunities of all.* We don't even face trade-offs, but successful undertaking of the desired collective action requires constraints on each individual taking advantage of others.

We have also seen that the distinction sometimes made between coercive and noncoercive constraints on freedom may be less important than typically imagined. Both entail a reduction in the individual's opportunity set.

In this part of the chapter, I have emphasized that our beliefs and preferences are shaped. That this is so seems to be at the heart of many current political controversies, including much of the "culture" war going on in the United States and elsewhere. The Left has internalized the externalities associated with wearing masks and getting vaccinated. They see it simply as showing respect for others in one's community; they would wear masks and get vaccinated even if there were not mask and vaccine mandates. Because they recognize that not everyone has internalized these externalities, they believe (rightly in my view) that there should be—there needs to be—regulation. But the Right see these mandates as an infringement on their freedom, and in a sense it is, because they have not internalized the externalities; they have not even recognized that their freedom is others' unfreedom.

I have considered here briefly the various mechanisms by which we are shaped and examined the constraints on freedom imposed by social sanctions or peer pressure. While social solidarity and cohesion can promote pro-social behavior, which enhances societal well-being, including individual freedoms, without imposing seemingly restrictive regulations, it does not always work that way.

Education plays an important role in shaping our preferences and actions, and a better understanding of how our preferences are shaped and how they are affected by peer pressure can be "freeing."

But a good and just society would not, I believe, give so much power to the wealthy to shape society's beliefs and preferences—especially because they have done so in ways that have been costly for everyone. So, too, market power in the media is far more invidious than in other areas of the economy.[50] The growth of social media has exacerbated long-standing abuses associated with advertising.

I should be clear: I am appealing to considerations of the Good Society and social justice to adjudicate between freedoms when they conflict, as they often do. It is *not* a matter of balancing the ideal of freedom with the ideal of the Good Society and a just society; for an intrinsic part of a good and just society must be freedom and liberty—but that cannot be uncircumscribed precisely because, as I have emphasized, one person's freedom is another's unfreedom.

III. Neoliberal capitalism and freedom

The principles I have enunciated suggest a more nuanced view toward evaluating alternative economic systems than has traditionally been used. The standard economic perspective of Pareto efficiency simply doesn't suffice. Here, I want to look at the issue through the lens of "freedom" or "individual liberty."

As its name suggests, neoliberalism sought to reduce government regulations, freeing up markets and thereby increasing economic prosperity and societal well-being. It was predicated on "market fundamentalism," the notion that *free* markets would, through Adam Smith's invisible hand, "deliver" on societal well-being. Critical advances in economics in the second half of the twentieth century showed that that was not generally the case. One needs strong regulations to ensure that markets are competitive, and even then, with imperfect and asymmetric information and incomplete risk markets, free markets are essentially never constrained Pareto efficient. As I have put it, the reason the invisible hand is invisible is that it's not there.

COVID-19 and climate change have focused our attention on the importance of externalities, to which neoliberalism gave short shrift. Regulations proscribing actions that generate negative externalities may reduce an individual's freedom to act, but enhance others' freedoms, expanding their opportunities. Externalities are pervasive in a modern economy: enhanced "freedom" given to banks under financial market liberalization led to a financial crisis that imposed enormous costs on others, requiring a huge government bailout.

COVID-19 has also focused our attention on the importance of collective action, to which neoliberalism also gave short shrift. For example, public investments in basic research allowed the development of vaccines, including the highly effective mRNA vaccine, tests, and therapeutics. Much of this was based on basic research funded by the government. "Free markets" on their own will not invest sufficiently in basic research. But such public investments require resources in the form of taxes, which reduce the opportunity set of some individuals and their freedom to consume certain things, even as it expands our society's opportunity set in many other ways.

Neoliberalism recognized that there might be externalities, but they went the other way. Trickle-down economics said that if (through liberalization) the economy grew more, *everyone would benefit*. There never was a theory that supported this hypothesis, and in fact evidence over the past forty years shows the opposite. Liberalization overall led to slower growth, and the fruits of what limited growth occurred overwhelmingly went to those at the top.[51] People in the middle saw their incomes stagnate, and many toward the bottom saw real incomes fall, especially in the United States. In a sense, while the freedom of banks to act was expanded, the freedom of others contracted.

The history of the last four decades has discredited other tenets of neoliberalism.[52] In 1979, Milton Friedman wrote, with his wife Rose, the highly influential book *Free to Choose*. As its title suggests, it championed the virtues of a free market economy, with limited regulations and limited redistribution. But, of course, those with limited income are *not* free to choose; they do what they can to survive. Their effective choices are greatly circumscribed. And the unbridled capitalism that these ideas gave rise to is perhaps better described by *Free to Exploit*. The examples given earlier in this chapter have shown how corporations have taken full advantage of this freedom to exploit.

Friedman put forward another idea that became a central tenet of capitalism, American-style, enshrined in the laws of many states: shareholder capitalism, or the notion that the managers of firms should maximize shareholder value and only shareholder value. They had no responsibility to pay attention to workers, customers, the community, or even the environment, except to the extent that their actions, with respect to those "stakeholders," affected share prices. Even as Friedman enunciated that doctrine in a famous article in the *New York Times* in 1970, I, together with others like Sandy Grossman, was analyzing the conditions under which shareholder maximization would lead to societal well-being.[53] We showed that those conditions were extraordinarily restrictive—not satisfied by any real economy. But our articles, published in venues like *Quarterly Journal of Economics* or *Journal of Finance*, were far less influential than Friedman's.[54] He was an apostle of the free market, someone of enormous persuasive abilities, putting forward arguments that people like Ronald Reagan and Margaret Thatcher *wanted* to hear. He was little concerned about whether there were analytics behind these arguments.

Every modern economy has to be decentralized, with a multiplicity of establishments producing the goods and services that society needs and wants. Neoliberal capitalism was predicated on a particular view of how such a decentralized society should be organized: unregulated profit-maximizing firms. Advocates like Friedman argued that such a system was not only efficient but fair and even more important enhanced freedom, giving the system a moral legitimacy. He was concerned that the economic system of the time (late mid-twentieth century) was not sufficiently reflective of neoliberal principles. He wanted more freedom for the economy, which would result in more freedom of individuals. He was wrong on every count, both theoretically (as I discussed earlier) and empirically. But he was wrong at an even deeper level conceptually. As I emphasized earlier (section 8), there is really no such thing as a "free market" or pure capitalism. Markets don't exist in a vacuum, there have to be rules and regulations, and those rules can favor one group at the expense of others.[55] The so-called deregulation of the banks, getting government out of the way, didn't do that. It got government *temporarily* out of the way, as bankers reaped huge rewards for themselves; but then with the 2008 financial crisis government took center stage, with the largest taxpayer-funded bailout in the history of the universe. Thus, bankers gained at the expense of the rest of society.

Most important from the perspective of this essay, the worsening of the economic prospects of a very large proportion of Americans meant their freedom to act was constrained, not expanded, and with enormous political consequences: it has set the country off not on the road to greater liberty and freedom, but *on the road to fascism*, with the liberties not just of the poor but of the entire society constrained.

IV. Freedom, sovereignty, and coercion among states

As I suggested in the beginning of this essay, many of the issues concerning freedom and coercion play out, often in related ways, at the level of nation-states, though the language is sometimes slightly different. Countries worry about their loss of sovereignty in international agreements, such as the one establishing the World Trade Organization. Countries accepting funds from the International Monetary Fund feel coerced into accepting the conditionalities that come along with the money.

It may be useful to distinguish two kinds of situations. The first is true coercion—the threat of violence with which the colonial powers exerted their control. They were clearly intruding on the liberty and freedoms of those they colonized, even if the colonized signed an agreement giving up their rights. That was a mere facade.

The second is an agreement among two equals, made for *mutual* benefit, either to stop each from exerting negative externalities on the other (as might arguably be the case with climate) or to facilitate their exerting positive externalities on each other (as might be the case from a mutually beneficial expansion of trade). In both cases each party agrees to do or not to do something if and only if the other does similarly. While freedom to act in some dimension is constrained, the expansion of the opportunity set of each as a result of the agreement (assuming the other side complies) increases freedoms to act in many other ways. There is no coercion in such truly voluntary agreements, even if they circumscribe "sovereignty." These agreements can be viewed on the international scale like the contracts among individuals discussed in section 6.

In the late twentieth and early twenty-first centuries, the agreements between advanced countries and emerging markets and developing countries have the appearance of being voluntary—there typically is no physical coercion—supported by a rhetoric of mutual benefit; but that is not always how they are perceived by developing countries, which invoke the language of "economic coercion."

Just like the deprivation of outside opportunities by the oppressive South African regimes induced Black South Africans to "voluntarily" work in the mines at low wages, colonialism left a legacy of deprivation in many countries, in which the best alternative was to accept economic relations on terms that were advantageous to the advanced country, terms that would not have emerged in a fully competitive global economy (whatever that might mean). Much of my writing over the past two decades has been to show the exploitive nature of international agreements and the exploitive workings of the international economic institutions, the disparity between the rhetoric of "free market mutually advantageous fair agreements" and the reality of unfair agreements written to promote the interests of advanced countries' multinationals, including their large financial corporations.[56]

In many cases the international agreements (exemplified by investment agreements) brought little if any benefits and yet constrained what those signing the agreements could do. These are the clearest cases of economic coercion, a loss of economic sovereignty and freedom.[57] Some countries, such as South Africa, finally realizing this, are walking away from such agreements. In some cases, the international institutions have talked about cross-border externalities, but externalities from small developing countries or even emerging markets are *de minimus*, while those originating from the major advanced countries are large; yet agreements have sought to circumscribe the behavior of the developing countries and emerging markets, for example, in their imposition of capital controls, while doing next to nothing about the large externalities emanating from the advanced countries, such as through quantitative easing by their central banks. What is going on here is little short of coercion—an attempt by the advanced countries to use "power" (broadly defined, the power they have, which is not unconstrained but is still real and large) to advance their own interests at the expense of the less developed countries and emerging markets.

V. Progressive capitalism and social democracy

I hope this is the moment in which neoliberalism's failures are so apparent that it will be abandoned. Gabriel Boric, elected president of Chile in 2022, captured the spirit of the moment on the eve of his primary victory when he said, "If Chile was the birthplace of neoliberalism, it will also be its grave!"

Earlier discussions have drawn attention both to analytic flaws of the economic theory underlying neoliberalism and to its immense failures. We should learn from these experiences, as well as successes in countries that have explored other economic models.

Here I want to discuss an alternative framework, one that I develop more fully in my book *People, Power, and Profits: Progressive Capitalism for an Age of Discontent*. (Had I been writing the book for a European audience I would have emphasized more a rejuvenated social democracy.) I focus in particular on two themes: power, which I see as undermining individual freedom; and collective action, which, when appropriately channeled, as *empowering* individuals.

Power and the competitive paradigm

Modern economics begins with a model of perfect competition, in which the economy is in a harmonious equilibrium and no one has any power, no one exerts any negative or positive externalities on others. The underlying assumptions are such that there is no need for government or regulations except to enforce contracts. Indeed, in the extreme view of neoliberalism, not even competition policy is required because the economy will be *naturally* competitive.[58] Here they depart markedly from Adam Smith, which shows that they champion him only to the extent that he agrees with their views (or what is in their interests).[59]

In reality, power relations are central to understanding economics, politics, and society. America's economy was built on slave labor—hardly a manifestation of a free market, although there was a market for the buying and selling of enslaved persons, and the country's legal structure was designed to enforce slavery. When enslaved people were freed, the concern in most places was the loss of the property rights of slaveholders, not the compensation of the denial of the rights of those who were formerly enslaved.

Power relations have historical inertia. In the United States, constitutional debates center on the interpretation of a document agreed on by a group of largely rich, white males, many of whom were slaveowners. Those excluded—the vast majority of American citizenry—ask why what those men thought of as important should dictate public policy today, including the delicate balancing of freedoms that has been at the center of today's discussion.

The economy is not naturally competitive, in the narrow sense in which economists use that term, that no firm has the power to raise prices or impose contractual terms on others. The power and profits of the digital giants are apparent and persistent. At the same time, the evisceration of the power of workers is also apparent, and it is worsening.

Evidence and theory argue that these power relations are central to understanding what has been happening, both in terms of growing inequality and slowing economic growth, and that rebalancing these power relations is necessary. From the perspective of this discussion, it is essential to understand that this imbalance of power may have expanded the "freedom" of big corporations even as it has constrained the freedom—the opportunity sets—of ordinary citizens. They feel it intensely in the frustration in dealing with their internet provider or telephone company or bank. There is no real choice, each company as exploitive as the next, with noxious contract provisions like mandatory arbitration of disputes and usurious fees for late payments. And on top of that, there are often two-hour waits to talk to a "service" representative.

The harmoniousness of the equilibrium trumpeted by neoliberalism is also obviously false. It has, in fact, created the divides that make cooperation so difficult, and even helped create the selfish mindsets that make cooperation all but impossible. Moreover, there is *no* equilibrium: the economy is always evolving, and not necessarily in ways that lead society to be better off. There is no teleology in evolution, contrary to the Social Darwinism of an earlier era.[60] The development of social media may be a "mutation" that, unless better controlled, could have disastrous effects.

The challenge, then, is to design a social and economic system that expands freedoms and, more broadly, well-being, in a socially just way that helps create a Good Society. We know that neoliberalism failed on virtually all accounts—it was neither efficient nor stable, it was not socially just, and it led to a divided society that cultivated greed, selfishness, short-sightedness, materialism, intolerance, dishonesty, and other characteristics that seem the antithesis of the Good Society. So doing better than that is a low bar.

Key elements of progressive capitalism

In my book *People, Power, and Profits*, I set out some of the features of one example of a society and economy that might create wider societal and economic well-being. First, it would entail a broader ecology of institutions, going well beyond the usual division into private and government. This includes NGOs, cooperatives, civil society institutions, and unions. Indeed, just thinking again about the United States, arguably the most successful institutions that explain a lot of the overall achievements of the United States are its great research universities, which are either foundations, like Harvard and Columbia, or public. Exemplary of for-profit universities is Trump University, which excelled only in the exploitation of those who want to get ahead. Likewise, the cooperative part of the U.S. financial system was the only part that, for the most part, behaved in a socially responsible way both before the 2008 financial crisis and after. Before, these institutions did not take part in the kind of predatory lending that marked most of the country's major banks; after, they continued to lend to small- and medium-sized enterprises while the big banks withdrew funds just when they were needed most.

Second, it entails a greater role for collective action in all its forms (class action suits, unions, and government), and a better balance between the private sector and collective action, including government at all levels. If communism went too far in one direction, Reagan-Thatcherism went too far in the other, and the Third Way reflected by the triangulation of Clinton, Blair, and Schroeder was an insufficient correction. It embraced neoliberalism, materialism, and markets and ignored concerns of social justice to a degree that might not have been acceptable in a world in which communism and market economies were competing for hearts and minds.

As I have emphasized, this better balance entails regulation to curb the agglomeration of power and pervasive negative externalities—including those associated with the devastation of our environment—that are inevitably associated with unfettered markets.

Another key component of collective action is more public investments, including in research, in children, and, more broadly, in social and physical infrastructure. These investments will not just promote growth, they will enhance the opportunities (the freedoms, the capabilities) of ordinary citizens.

Still another vital component of collective action is social protection against the vicissitudes of life, including those arising from markets even when they are tempered and tamed. Social protection is itself liberating, for it frees individuals to undertake risks that they otherwise would fear to engage in lest they fail and be left destitute. That is why societies with better systems of social protection can actually be more innovative.

An agenda of social justice—one that attempts to reduce the levels of inequalities from the extremes to which they have risen in recent decades, and which is especially attentive to inequalities that arise from various forms of exploitation—has to be part of an alternative system.

There is a further set of arguments for the social justice agenda that centers on who we are as individuals and as a society. Inequalities breed a divided society that leads to individuals at the top with a sense of entitlement and individuals at the bottom who live in despair, without hope or aspirations.

I believe a social consensus can be reached on this, even if, in the abstract, we can't agree about the "optimal" amount of inequality, or even precisely the circumstances under which inequalities are inconsistent with or antithetical to a Good Society. In the *Price of Inequality* I argued that indeed, much of extant inequality arises from rent-seeking and exploitation and could be reduced without impairing overall economic performance.

Progressive capitalism and social democracy

Progressive capitalism calls for an expanded, or at least a different, role for the state. As I have repeatedly noted, research over the past half-century has shown the pervasiveness of "market failures"—that markets are not in general efficient—and that there is no "moral legitimacy" to the distribution of income and wealth that emerges. But critics of our perspective suggest that it pays insufficient attention to "government failures." As flawed as economic processes may be, political processes are even more flawed.

Any American living through the Trump administration knows about government and political failures. I am not pollyannish. I know that creating a strong, effective state that advances economic progress and social justice—and not just special interests—is not easy. But I also know that there has been little or no social and economic progress in the absence of a strong and effective state. Collective action is essential. So we have no choice but to try to make our democracy work in ways that advance the interests of society as a whole. At times and at places, societies have had considerable success in doing just this.

VI. Concluding comments: Democracy, freedom, and equality

This essay has largely been about economic freedom, about individuals' "freedom to choose," including how one person's freedom impinges on others. As noted earlier, much of the discourse in the West has been about political freedom. In these final paragraphs, I come back to the links between the Progressive or Social Democratic agenda and its focus on equality and democracy.

The *democracy* part of the agenda is crucial, but rejuvenating it necessitates rejuvenating the social justice part, too, in all its dimensions. The reason is obvious and has already been noted: If there are excessive economic inequalities, the wealthy will use their money to advance their own interests at the expense of the rest of society. They will do it in every venue possible, including in the political arena. There is a persuasive argument that the free market, unfettered capitalism, is a system that devours itself. It creates *by itself* sufficient economic inequalities that get translated into political inequalities, which lead to rules that are not really "free market" rules but simply serve the interests of large, corporate special interests. At the same time, their political power enables them to write political rules that perpetuate their economic and political power. The persistence of the power of money in American politics is but one example. At least in the United States, we have created a vicious circle between economic and political inequality, one that cements more "freedom" for the rich, including freedom to exploit others, and less freedom for the poor.

There are many ways that economic power gets translated into political power. In some countries it's as crude as buying votes. In "advanced" countries the wealthy use their influence in the media and elsewhere to create narratives—and they are in the best position to make their narratives become the "conventional wisdom"—for instance, that certain rules and regulations and government interventions that are in the interest of the rich and powerful are in fact in the national interest.

Is it a free society when a few dictate the terms of engagement to the rest? When a few control the major media, including social media, and use that control to determine what news individuals see? Few would deny that there is an important loss of freedom in an Orwellian world; people in the West have long criticized the propaganda spewed out by the Nazis and the Communists. But we are embedded in a world of Murdochian propaganda and worse; we have as a result moved into a polarized world in which different groups live in different universes, disagreeing not only on values but on facts and how they can be ascertained and verified. As I suggested earlier, one challenge facing progressive capitalism and social democracy in coming years is how to move away from this emerging dystopia in a way that is consistent with democratic values.

Thus, constraints put on the financial sector in the aftermath of the Great Depression, restraints that led to five decades of no financial crisis, were torn up as the financial sector propagated the idea that self-regulation and financial innovation would, by themselves, stabilize the economy. It was called "deregulation," part of the broader agenda of "liberalization," *freeing the economy*, which would enable faster growth from which all would benefit. The vocabulary was chosen to appeal to the universal love of "freedom." But it wasn't really about getting the government out of the financial sector—in the end, as I have noted, there was massive government intervention, a massive bailout. There were, to be sure, key elements of freedom: the freedom of banks to exploit and to discriminate, the freedom of banks to engage in reckless risk-taking, with ordinary taxpayers picking up the tab for their misdeeds.

I could cite multiple other examples.

This raises critical questions: besides circumscribing excessive inequalities, which we know are corrosive to the sustenance of democracy, is there anything else we can do to prevent capitalists' interests from distorting our social, economic, and political system? Is there anything that can be done to make democratic capitalism more sustainable, or more likely to be sustained? There is no easy or obvious answer, certainly no easily implementable magic formula. We can attempt to inculcate more deeply democratic values, which are suspicious of the agglomeration of power in any form. We can inculcate more strongly a commitment to freedom of the press—and to the notion that there needs to be a diversified press and media where the wealthy do not have disproportionate say—to ensure that actions that undermine democratic values and processes are exposed. We can more broadly strengthen systems of checks and balances in our society. It is not just one branch of government checking other branches, but it is the private, public, and civil society checking each other, and the fourth estate checking all of them.

And, of course, we have to ensure that we have a democracy. While earlier concerns were about a majority suppressing minority rights, today the concern is about a minority suppressing majority rights. Voter suppression, extreme gerrymandering, and a host of other antidemocratic actions by Republican extremists have put America's democracy in danger. There are multiple reforms in our political processes that would ensure greater democracy.

More generally, a rights-based agenda—which takes as a basic underlying assumption that we are endowed with certain inalienable rights, including economic rights and political rights—may have the potential to hold at bay the extremist agenda of today's Right. But I am not sure. The Right in the United States has used its distorted interpretation of basic economic and political rights as an instrument to foist its agenda on the rest of the country and used what influence it can to extend the reach of that agenda around the world.

For more than two hundred years, lip service has been paid to freedom and liberty, but what that means in our complex, integrated society is not so easy to answer. I have looked at the subject through the lens of an economist—seeing in particular how externalities imply that one person's freedom is another's unfreedom, and how, by collective action, we can expand the opportunity sets for all. But I have argued that the models employed by economists in recent decades excessively narrowed our vision, resulting in a set of doctrines, loosely referred to as neoliberalism, that has circumscribed the freedom of many, perhaps the vast majority, while bestowing freedom on a few to exploit others. This has led to a dysfunctional, materialistic, and divided society that has failed even in terms of the limited claims of efficiency made for it.

There is an alternative, which I have referred to in shorthand as progressive capitalism, that expands the freedoms of the vast majority. We should aspire to this kind of society.

CHAPTER 5

CAPITALISM AND THE QUESTION OF FREEDOM

PRABHAT PATNAIK

I

All precapitalist societies with the exception of primitive communistic ones are characterized by the use of physical coercion against direct producers. This is obvious in the case of slavery where the person of the slave itself was the property of the master, on which the master could inflict whatever torture he wished, and of feudalism, where the monseigneur's whip was freely used against recalcitrant serfs. In medieval India, where the system of production differed from European feudalism, coercion was used not only against the peasants to extract a surplus for the imperial nobility but also against agricultural laborers who typically belonged to the *dalit* castes to ensure that they continued to work for the peasants in the village and did not run away to cultivate fallow land that was available outside; Mughal troops were sent to bring back fugitive laborers.[1]

The use of such coercion played two distinct roles. One was to extract a surplus for the propertied class. In European feudalism this surplus could take the form of labor rent, or produce rent, or, later, money rent; but this rent was extracted from producers in the name of "custom," behind which was force. The second role was necessary for production itself. All production requires the coordinated application of collective labor at least for some constituent activities, for which work discipline and work motivation have to be ensured among those laboring. This is obvious in the case of the cultivation of the landlord's land; but it is even needed in the case of small-scale farming by individual peasants whose viability is in the interest of the landlord, even after rent gets received in the form of produce or money. The use of physical coercion ensures work discipline and work motivation, not just under slavery, where its need is obvious, but even under feudalism.

Capitalism by contrast does not depend on physical coercion. The labor contract is worked out between consenting individuals, the capitalist and the worker, who meet in the marketplace as equal participants. How then does the capitalist extract a surplus from the workers, and how are work motivation and work discipline ensured in the process of production, which under capitalism is necessarily a wholly collective endeavor? Schumpeter's critique of Ricardo and Marx was that competition between employers under this system would not only ensure full employment of labor but drive profits down to zero and raise wages to absorb the entire output.[2]

Marx's answer to this question, in contrast to Ricardo, who had invoked the Malthusian theory of population that Marx saw as a "libel on the human race," relied on the concept of the "reserve army of labor," considered by many to be his greatest contribution to economic theory. The entire available workforce at any time does not find a place in the active army of labor, and the competition between the employed and the unemployed (and underemployed) keeps wages down, ensuring a positive rate of surplus value for the capitalists. Any tendency for the reserve army to get exhausted raises wages and lowers the rate of surplus value, whose fall below a threshold chokes off accumulation, thereby spontaneously replenishing the reserve army. The reserve army can thus never disappear, and its perennial existence explains why surplus value continues to be extracted from the employed workers.[3]

While all this is well known, the role of the reserve army in instilling work motivation and work discipline is less discussed. The threat of the "sack," of throwing out workers who are suspected of being laggards, hangs like a Damocles sword over the workers' heads, forcing them to keep the "boss" satisfied with their work; and this threat will lose its sting in the absence of a reserve army of labor. The reserve army in short plays the same role under capitalism, where there is no exercise of explicit coercion, as the monseigneur's whip, or the torture of the slave, had played in earlier systems.

This is a point hardly recognized in economics to this day. Much of "mainstream" economics believes that the capitalist system, through the operation of the market, reaches an equilibrium with full employment of all "factors of production." It does not reckon with the fact that in such a case work discipline and work motivation will disappear. It does not in short reckon with a system of *production*, instead extrapolating what may happen in the market equilibrium in a purely *exchange* economy to one with production, without looking at the sui generis nature of production. Even Keynes who recognized that the capitalist economy scarcely ever reached full employment through its spontaneous working, believed that state intervention could push it toward such a state, without pausing to ask if production under capitalism was at all compatible with the complete disappearance of what he had called "involuntary unemployment."[4]

The reserve army of labor is not a spontaneously devised means of disciplining *only* the active army of labor, that is, *only* the employed workers. *It has a generally disciplining effect on the system as a whole.* This is for the following reason.

Capitalism is characterized by pervasive competition within the workforce and also among capitalists; even when competition is sought to be suppressed through the formation of combinations, it never can be fully suppressed. The formation of trade unions, while it may suppress competition among employed workers, cannot suppress competition between the employed and the unemployed, that is, between the active and the reserve army of labor. Likewise, the suppression of price competition through the formation of cartels, or price agreements, among monopolists, only shifts competition to a different terrain: monopolists compete against one another through introducing new processes and products, through advertising, and such other means.

This competition however is much more than what is normally recognized in economics, which relates to the price of a product being equalized everywhere or the wage rate and the rate of profit being equalized across sectors. Such equalization however is typical only of free competition capitalism, as distinct from monopoly capitalism, and does not constitute an abiding characteristic of the system. The competition that is ever present in capitalism is competition in the Darwinian sense, where the losers completely lose their place within the system.

"Losing one's place within the system" means being consigned to some place outside of it. Competition in the Darwinian sense thus presupposes the existence of an "outside" of the system. The reserve army of labor constitutes this "outside," which is why its existence acts as a disciplining device for all agents within the capitalist system. All agents in capitalism are engaged, in different ways, in a Darwinian competitive struggle for survival, for which they have to act in specific ways, play specific roles, independent of their volition.

II

Capitalists accumulate not necessarily because they like accumulating capital, but because not doing so would cost them their place within the system. They would get pushed out of the system by others who have accumulated capital. This is because introducing technological progress at any time requires capital of a certain minimum size; and this size keeps increasing over time. Hence larger capitals succeed in introducing new techniques and new products and thereby outcompete smaller capitals. As large capitals destroy small capitals, every capital seeks to become large through accumulation, which thus becomes the key to survival.

Even the capitalists in other words have to act in a manner that is independent of their own volition. It is not just the workers who are alienated under capitalism, but also the capitalists, though the alienation of the workers and that of the capitalists are not of an identical nature. Capitalism is a system of universal alienation, where every economic agent is forced through a Darwinian struggle for survival to act in a way that is not of his or her own volition. It is not just a system formed through the interactions of atomized individuals (that would at best produce anarchy, as Keynes recognized); it is a system where the actions of the atomized individuals are not of their own volition but are dictated by a Darwinian struggle for survival.

If the actions are not of their own volition, then the overall outcome of these actions too is not what the individual agents either foresaw or intended. These overall outcomes can be analyzed in terms of a set of *tendencies* that are produced through the actions of individual economic agents who did not consciously visualize these tendencies. The system can thus be seen as a "spontaneous" or a self-driven system whose tendencies emerge through the actions of individuals each of whom acts in a way that is independent of his or her own volition. This set also includes the capitalist, whom Marx had called "capital personified," that is, the person through whose actions the immanent tendencies of capital realize themselves.

An important tendency already alluded to is the tendency toward centralization of capital, that is, the formation over time of fewer but bigger blocs of capital. Even though there is a pressure for capital accumulation arising from the need for survival (such accumulation does not have to be in a physical form but can take a monetary form, whence the possibility of overproduction crises or what Keynes had called "involuntary unemployment"), not all capital succeeds in surviving. Even though each capital is driven by the Darwinian struggle for survival, each does not necessarily succeed in this struggle for survival. Some still fall victim to displacement by larger capitals, their space taken over by the latter. This causes centralization of capital. And against this background there is also a fusion of capitals, small capitals coming together to form larger blocs, which is another source of centralization.

One can think of other tendencies: the tendency toward the subversion and hegemonization of precapitalist modes of production; the tendency toward a rise in the technical (not necessarily value) organic composition of capital, that is, the tendency for each worker to work with an ever increasing mass of capital; and the tendency for capital to control the entire globe, that is, not to leave out any "empty" space free from the control of capital. These tendencies spontaneously work themselves out through the mediation of human agents who are forced to act in ways not of their own volition.

III

How is the spontaneity of capitalism related to the question of freedom? There are three obvious ways in which this spontaneity implies a denial of freedom. One, in the realm of the economy at least, the individuals who constitute economic agents have no freedom to act according to their volition; there is no exercise of free will in this realm that constitutes the essence of freedom. Two, the economic *destinies* of people, that is, the overall outcome of the functioning of the system, are beyond people's control. Whether they face unemployment, or inflation or expropriation (if they are petty producers), is a matter that is determined by the spontaneous, self-driven system; it simply "happens" to them without their having any say in the matter. And three, the tendency of capital to go all over the globe necessarily implies an imperialist drive for domination over distant people in which the domestic economic agents become unwittingly complicit; and, as Marx had put it, "a nation that dominates others cannot be free."

But even if individuals in their capacity as *economic* agents are driven by the spontaneity of the system, can they not intervene as *citizens* in a democratic society to influence the state to intervene in the functioning of the economy, to mitigate the effects of its spontaneous functioning? Can they not use their *political* clout in a democracy to influence their *economic* destiny? That they can and should was the core of Keynes's prescription and remains central to much liberal thought. But a necessary implication of the spontaneity of capitalism is that "economics" under this system drives "politics," instead of being driven by "politics."

To start with, of course, political intervention in the functioning of the economy that goes *against* its spontaneous functioning is not easy to bring about. Against the background of the spontaneously functioning economic system, there is a political struggle around intervention; it is not easy for those advocating *pro–working people intervention* to win this struggle. Keynes's own ideas had to wait for over a decade after the *General Theory* to find acceptance in his own country, and that too happened because of the greater assertiveness of the working class in postwar Britain that led to Churchill's defeat and brought social democracy to power. His advocacy of public works financed by a fiscal deficit to overcome unemployment as early as in 1929, had fallen on deaf ears.[5] Keynes himself had attributed this reluctance of the establishment to accept suggestions for overcoming unemployment, which would also bring higher profits to capitalists (since overcoming "involuntary unemployment" is a non–zero sum game), to a lack of theoretical understanding; but it has to do with class positions and the balance of class power.

If perchance such intervention is effected, however, it makes the system dysfunctional, which poses before the intervening government a choice: either carry intervention further forward or backtrack on the intervention effected until then. A government that remains steadfast in its support for intervention, will then have to keep enlarging its intervention, until such recursively strengthened interventions lead to a transcendence of capitalism itself; if such transcendence is found scary then the government will backtrack on the intervention it has already effected. There is no equilibrium halfway house, no "reformed " or "welfare" capitalism that can be *permanently* instituted. True, the dysfunctionality engendered by state intervention may often take long to manifest itself, creating the impression that the reformed system, reformed by such intervention, has become a permanent phenomenon, a new "normal"; but this impression proves illusory.

The fate of Keynesian demand management establishes this point. While obviously the entire unemployment of the Great Depression years could not be considered essential for the system and hence ineluctable, the permanent institution of a regime of state intervention that would eliminate "involuntary unemployment" ultimately proved impossible. The elimination of the reserve army of labor eventually caused an acceleration of inflation that left the government with having to choose between two options; either raise the level of intervention to include a prices and incomes policy (backed by selective nationalization in cases of willful violation), or to re-create the reserve army with a vengeance. The first course was tried for a while (without any punishment for violation, that is, it was tried as a "corporatist" strategy), but its inevitable failure brought Thatcherism to the fore that recreated mass unemployment as the means of overcoming inflation.

The tendency to backtrack from pro–working people state intervention (intervention in keeping with the spontaneous tendencies, as a means of hastening them, does not create such dysfunctionality) is strengthened by another factor. Even during the period when such intervention is in place, the immanent tendencies of capitalism continue to operate, in particular the tendency toward centralization of capital. The coming into being of larger blocs of capital tilts the balance of class forces against such intervention, so that the original balance that had made such intervention possible is disrupted. In the case of postwar capitalism, the period of Keynesian demand management, sometimes called the "golden age of capitalism," had witnessed centralization of capital through the formation of a massive agglomeration of finance in banks and other institutions that wanted to go all over the globe in search of investment opportunities.

This had two effects. One was to put pressure that was unprecedented for "opening up" all countries to free financial (and trade) flows, thereby negating the Bretton Woods system that had allowed them to impose capital (and trade) controls; and two, since finance dislikes inflation, the pressure to control the 1970s inflation through the generation of mass unemployment became intense. In short, a state of affairs that Keynesianism had taken for granted as being permanent was overturned by the logic of the system, by its need for a reserve army and by its immanent tendency toward centralization that arises from its spontaneous operation.

IV

The coming into being of a neoliberal regime, in the place of the earlier, dirigiste regime that in the advanced countries had witnessed state intervention under the aegis of social democracy, and in the third world a burgeoning public sector and various forms of "planning," not only shows the eventual untenability of using politics to affect economics within a capitalist framework but also implies an unprecedented restriction on freedom. In fact, under neoliberalism the very possibility of using politics to affect economics is foreclosed.

In a neoliberal regime with relatively unrestricted flow of commodities and capital, including finance, we have a peculiar dichotomy, namely globalized finance capital facing individual nation-states. In this situation the nation-state is compelled to act in conformity with the demands of globalized finance, for otherwise finance will leave the country en masse, and that too with great speed, precipitating a financial crisis. The policies of the nation-state therefore are tailored to keep globalized finance happy, to retain what is euphemistically called the "confidence of the investors."

This has two obvious implications. One, no matter which political formation comes to power, as long as the country remains trapped within the vortex of global financial flows, it pursues the same policies as its predecessor, namely policies approved by globalized finance. Even formations that promise a different set of policies before coming to power change course after coming to power, if they do come to power, when confronted with the threat or reality of capital flight. The electorate therefore is denied any effective choice between alternative political formations as far as the economy is concerned; this is a denial of democracy.

The second implication is that the state itself, instead of appearing as an entity that presides over all classes looking after the interests of all, as was the case during the dirigiste period, becomes exclusively concerned with defending and advancing the interests of the corporate-financial oligarchy that is integrated with globalized capital. This means a withdrawal of state support and protection from the peasants, the petty producers, the fishermen, the craftsmen, and the workers, both urban and rural, that they had enjoyed earlier. The question of any authentic pro–working people state intervention simply does not arise under neoliberalism; state intervention is merely to further the interests of big capital, that is, in the same direction as the immanent tendencies of capitalism.

Neoliberalism entails in a sense a recreation of the "old capitalism," that is, the pre-dirigiste capitalism that Keynes had critiqued, though there is now much greater mobility of capital from metropolitan to third world economies. By restricting the people's capacity to intervene even as citizens to change their economic destiny, the neoliberal regime denies democracy. Such a denial of democracy obviously means an attenuation of freedom.

Neoliberalism, even as it denies any scope for pro-people political intervention against the spontaneous economic tendencies of capitalism, creates in the realm of the economy the very conditions that Keynes was "beginning to despise,"[6] conditions involving greater distress for the working people and heralding an overproduction crisis. The reason for this trend is the following.

The mobility of capital from advanced countries to third world economies under the current globalization links wages in the former to those in the latter. Not that the wages are equalized in the two regions, but any widening of the difference encourages greater relocation to the third world, thereby preventing further divergence. Globalization therefore makes advanced country wages subject to the baneful effects of the massive third world labor reserves. Joseph Stiglitz has found that, taking 1968 and 2011 as the two endpoints, the real wages of an average male American worker scarcely increased between them.[7]

At the same time, however, such relocation and the high rate of growth in third world economies experienced under globalization do not lead to an exhaustion of third world labor reserves. This is because the opening up of economies to free flows of goods and services, intensifies competitive struggle among countries and hence leads to more rapid introduction of technological progress resulting in a much higher rate of growth of labor productivity. The rate of growth of employment, therefore, which is the excess of the output growth rate over the labor productivity growth rate, remains constricted, even declines, compared to the dirigiste period, even where output growth rate accelerates greatly. In most third world economies, and in the aggregate for the third world as a whole, the growth rate of employment falls below even the natural rate of growth of the workforce, enlarging the relative magnitude of the labor reserves, instead of using up the labor reserves, which keeps real wages more or less stagnant at their near-subsistence level.

Because of this, both in individual countries and in the world as a whole, the vector of real wages falls behind the vector of labor productivity, to say the least, resulting in a rise in the share of surplus in output. It is this which underlies the increase in income inequality in most countries that economists like

Piketty have been underscoring (though the reason they adduce does not stand scrutiny).[8] And such increase in income inequality in the third world has the effect of bringing about structural changes in the economy with sectors catering to elite consumption growing relatively faster, and, since they are characterized by relatively lower employment intensity, of further raising labor productivity growth and lowering employment growth.

A second factor aids this increase in the relative size of labor reserves. The withdrawal of government support from the peasant and petty production sector under neoliberalism has already been noted. This makes these sectors, at least significant segments of them, unviable, driving many who are employed in these sectors to towns in search of employment; the scarcity of employment there, however, means that they just add to the labor reserves, though this may take the form of a given amount of work being shared among more people.

The impoverishment of petty producers, including peasants, without their getting absorbed into the active army of labor, increases the relative magnitude of absolute poverty in the population of the third world as a whole, which expresses itself emphatically in particular countries. In India for instance, between 1993–1994 and 2011–2012 (both years of large sample surveys), the percentage of the rural population not having access to 2,200 calories per person per day (the original benchmark for defining rural poverty) increased from 58 to 68; the percentage of the urban population unable to access 2,100 calories per person per day (the original benchmark for defining urban poverty) increased over this period from 57 to 65. And this happened even when India was being hailed for achieving a significant acceleration in its GDP growth rate compared to the dirigiste period.

Even in countries—and this would include advanced capitalist countries—where absolute poverty did not increase under neoliberalism, income and wealth inequality did; and this, we have seen, was a universal phenomenon. Since the working people consume a much higher proportion of their income at the margin compared to the rich, the rise in the share of surplus in world output (which underlay this increased inequality) meant *ceteris paribus* a fall in the share of consumption in total output, and hence an *ex ante* tendency toward overproduction; investment cannot compensate for this fall, since it responds primarily to the growth of the market, and hence itself slows down in the wake of such a fall. The tendency toward an overproduction crisis therefore is immanent in the rising inequality that is a feature of neoliberalism.

This tendency, however, was kept in check for a while in the world economy by the formation of asset price bubbles in the United States, first the dot-com bubble (a rise in the prices of stocks of dot-com companies) and then the housing bubble. Such bubbles, by artificially boosting private wealth when they lasted, stimulated consumption as well; but with the collapse of the housing bubble, the underlying tendency toward overproduction ensured that the entire capitalist world was engulfed in a crisis even before the pandemic had struck. The effects of the pandemic were superimposed upon this underlying crisis.

What is noteworthy is the fact that within the parameters of neoliberal capitalism, even state intervention cannot overcome this crisis, that is, cannot prevent the *ex ante* crisis from becoming an *ex post* reality. This is because for state expenditure to increase aggregate demand, it has to be financed either by a fiscal deficit or by taxes on the rich; financing an increase in state expenditure by taxing the working people who consume the bulk of their incomes anyway adds little to aggregate demand: it only substitutes one kind of demand (state expenditure) for another (working people's consumption). But both these ways of financing additional state expenditure are anathema for globalized finance capital whose dictate is decisive under neoliberalism. Taxing capitalists and other surplus earners is anathema for obvious reasons. And increasing state spending through a larger fiscal deficit is anathema because it tends to delegitimize the role of capitalists, including especially financiers; it becomes obvious to all that they do not have to be wooed to undertake investment to get the economy out of stagnation or recession. This indeed is why virtually all countries, other than the United States, have legislation limiting the ratio of fiscal deficit to GDP. The crisis of stagnation caused by the immanent inequalizing tendencies of neoliberalism is therefore insurmountable within the parameters of neoliberalism.

V

It is in this context that there is a pervasive tendency toward the emergence of neofascism and the formation of an alliance between neoliberalism and neofascism. Fascist or neofascist elements exist in all modern societies but as fringe phenomena; they move center stage in periods of existential crisis of the system when they get the financial and the media backing of big capital. As long as the world economy was growing rapidly, and with it the economies of most individual countries, the working people, despite being relatively or even absolutely worse off than before, could entertain the hope that they would eventually get some benefits from this growth through a process of "trickle down." But when this growth itself comes to an end, this hope vanishes; the system then turns to an alliance with neofascism in order to buttress its position.[9]

Neofascism helps in shifting the discourse from issues of material living to the so-called injustice perpetrated by the "other," typically some hapless minority religious or ethnic or linguistic group. This has the effect of dividing the working people and thereby incapacitating collective praxis, and of shifting their attention away from the issues over which collective praxis could be organized to those whose sole purpose is to generate hatred on the one hand and fear on the other. In a swathe of countries across the world, neofascist elements are in power with the support of the corporate-financial oligarchy (that is, integrated with globalized capital); elsewhere, despite their rise to prominence, they still have not succeeded in acquiring power, though this is by no means impossible.

Even neofascist governments, however, unlike the fascist governments of the 1930s, are incapable of overcoming the economic crisis that underlies their ascendancy. This is because within the parameters of neoliberalism, they too are as hamstrung as the preceding liberal bourgeois governments in stimulating the economy, being caught in the contradiction between the nation-state and international capital; they too cannot increase state expenditures by taxing the rich (which they would not like anyway) or by borrowing (as 1930s fascism had done), owing to the opposition of international (globalized) capital. This *may* push the neofascist elements occasionally out of power, especially since a democratic shell may continue to be preserved by neofascism; but they would also come back to power later and have a lingering presence in society and the polity, leading to their becoming increasingly fascistic over time.

Thus the constriction of freedom under capitalism reaches its limit under neoliberal capitalism, where its alliance with neofascism implies much more than the lack of agency, or the lack of control over one's economic destiny, arising from the spontaneity of capitalism: together with the denial of freedom for these reasons, there is even a loss of basic civil liberties. Overcoming neofascism must be the obvious first step toward acquiring freedom. But overcoming neofascism requires overcoming the conjuncture that gives rise to it, namely, the conjuncture of crisis of neoliberal capitalism, which we have seen cannot be done within the parameters of neoliberal capitalism itself. It requires a transcendence of neoliberal capitalism itself. Such transcendence, if it is not merely to turn the clock back to dirigiste capitalism from whose ashes neoliberal capitalism has arisen, would entail going beyond capitalism itself to an alternative more humane society that is free of "spontaneity" altogether.

VI

The neoliberal arrangement, however, is not easy to shake off. The problem of capital flight has already been mentioned, which begins the moment a political formation that favors "delinking" from the neoliberal universe is predicted to come to power. Even if that formation stands firm despite such capital flight and introduces capital controls upon coming to power to stem such flight, the inflows of finance into the country dry up, which makes meeting the current account deficit nearly impossible. This leads to a depreciation of the currency and hence an acceleration of inflation, which necessitates the imposition of trade controls as well.

All this affects not only the affluent but even the ordinary working people in whose interests "delinking" was undertaken in the first place. Their support for the government begins to wane, even as the big bourgeoisie and the urban middle class, votaries of neoliberalism, step up their struggle against "delinking." The government in short finds itself cornered and isolated, and under immense pressure to surrender.

If it still does not surrender, then the advanced capitalist countries get into the act and impose sanctions against the recalcitrant country. These sanctions particularly hurt the poor, as they cut off supplies of essential commodities, including even basic medicines, which further reduces support for the government among the very classes whose interests it sought to represent while embarking on "delinking." The pressure to surrender becomes even more intense.

The neoliberal regime, even as it brings distress to the working people in the high growth phase itself and compounds this distress in the period of stagnation, even as it undermines democracy in the high growth phase itself and unleashes neofascist repression when it gets into stagnation, seeks thus to create a "no-exit" situation for countries caught in its grip.

Escape from this grip is essential for freedom, not just of the working people but even of the capitalists and the affluent who too are alienated under capitalism and hence under neoliberal capitalism. Such escape is especially difficult for small economies that are not sufficiently diversified and therefore have to depend on imports for much of their essential requirements; the impact of sanctions would be particularly severe on such economies. They have to unite with other economies to form blocs so that they can collectively attempt to exit from the grip of neoliberal capitalism.

This point relates only to the size of the unit that can realistically attempt "delinking." But it is clear from the foregoing that several essential conditions have to be fulfilled if "delinking" is to have a chance of succeeding. The first condition for exiting this apparently no-exit situation is the creation of full awareness on the part of the working people of the difficulties of transition, so that they can face up to these difficulties. Freedom, in other words, cannot be visualized as a largesse to the people from some benign political formation; freedom must be earned by the people, who may use a particular political formation as their instrument for doing so.

The second condition is a prioritization of the needs of the working people over all other demands on resources, so that there is no reneging on promises made to them while acquiring power. For this a set of constitutionally guaranteed, universal, justiciable economic rights must be instituted. These must include, at the very minimum, the right to food, the right to employment, the right to free health care, the right to free education, and the right to non-contributory old-age pensions and disability benefits. By their very nature these rights cannot be guaranteed under capitalism, which is why their institution, or even striving for an agenda incorporating their institution, constitutes a way of making people aware that a society beyond capitalism, a society free of spontaneous economic tendencies over which they have no control, is possible. The struggle for the institution of these rights is a means of transcending capitalism.

CHAPTER 6

WHITHER ECONOMIC RIGHTS?

AKEEL BILGRAMI

In his essay in this volume, after a scathing critique of the influence of orthodox, ideological positions in macroeconomics which have generated serious (even if noncoercive) threats to human freedom, Joseph Stiglitz offers a version of capitalism that he describes as "progressive capitalism," constrained by progressive measures that would go some distance in overcoming those threats.

Prabhat Patnaik's essay follows with a somewhat more pessimistic analysis of capitalism, in which he argues that capital has built-in spontaneous tendencies that—again with no coercion involved but rather with a set of disciplinary social conditions—undermine all attempts to place progressive constraints on it. Such optimism as Patnaik is prepared to offer, he says toward the very end of his essay, will depend on whether a regime of *economic rights* can be adopted and implemented. In another paper he presents in detail a proposal for such rights in one particular economy, the Indian economy.[1] He proposes that such *fundamental* economic rights ("rights," properly so called, rather than merely gestural "directive principles," as currently exist) should be inserted into India's constitution, thereby redeeming a commitment made during the freedom movement in the Karachi Resolution of 1931 and subsequently ignored by the constitutional developments in independent India.[2]

In this chapter I will not be discussing the Indian economy but rather will speak to the general appeal to economic rights (made by Patnaik for India, in particular) as an initial step in setting us on the path to progressive developments in political economy. I will first situate the notion of economic rights in a rudimentary exploration of the well-mined philosophical foundations of *the very idea* of rights, quite generally, and then try to diagnose the relative neglect in providing such foundations for economic rights, in particular. With this in place I will turn to the larger canvas of the analysis of capitalism that Patnaik presents in his chapter in this volume, with a view to exploring *what about* the nature of economic *rights* in a capitalist society, analyzed along these lines, makes them conducive to the prospects for a path to progressive developments in political economy suggested by Stiglitz.

As I said, Patnaik's proposal is a quite *specific* one, both in being about economic rights in particular and because it is intended for a particular nation (India) in a particular time (the present, even though it traces the proposal's genealogy to a resolution adopted in 1931). But when it comes to a subject like rights, however specific the proposal under discussion is, the force and rationale of the proposal, even in its specificity, cannot be fully explored without first getting clear in a quite *general* way about certain foundational questions regarding what rights *are* and *why* we speak of them at all. The specificity of the proposal may cancel *some* detailed points that surface in such a discussion of the foundational questions about rights in general (and, in what follows, I will mention where such a cancellation seems apt), but it cannot cancel all of them without changing the topic from rights to something else. Patnaik, after all, is not talking about economic and social welfare *policies* that are the outcome of a government's *cabinet* deliberations or the routine deliverances of a *legislature*. He is rather proposing (economic) *rights* that a *constitution* should adopt. So, there is no avoiding a more foundational discussion of two questions: What is *meant* by this quite distinctive suggestion that they be rights and not mere policies; and *on what grounds* do we posit such a distinctive thing as rights in the first place?

Let me take up both these questions in turn.

1. What are rights? Two features

Since whole books have been written on the question of what is meant by "rights," it would be foolish to undertake any extended answer to it in a short essay, but let me at least try to state some of the more elementary and defining features of rights so as to set the general context within which the idea of more specifically economic rights can be raised.

Even a glance at a good dictionary will tell one that rights are *entitlements* that all or some members of the public have and, as such, these entitlements entail *duties* (sometimes in the form of prohibitions) for others. If someone is entitled by right to something, it is standardly implied that others (individuals, institutions, including the state . . .) are required to or made to do or not do something. My right to privacy entails that others have a duty to not do some things—set up apparatus for surveillance in my drawing room, for instance.

But bare definitions of this kind tell us very little about what rights are. We need to conceptually explore what features such—barely defined—rights have before we come to a full understanding of what rights mean.

This conceptual exploration can proceed from various angles.

One angle is to see what rights should be distinguished from. They are distinct from "the good." A way to put this distinction is to say that a right is the sort of thing that cannot be violated in order to maximize the good under any understanding of what is "good." In the intellectual history of the subject, maximization of the good, understood in utilitarian terms, is the usual source of contrast with rights. But the contrast is not restricted to that; it holds for all conceptions of the good. This is because rights are, to use a phrase from John Rawls, *"prior to the good."*[3] What this means is that the value we put on nonviolation of rights cannot be weighed on the same scale as the good. Why not? Rights stand outside of considerations of the good and serve—from the outside—as a form of *constraint* on the pursuit of the good. That is to say, one cannot pursue the good when doing so violates a right. So, for instance, if one is seeking to maximize social aggregate utility, rights cannot ever be the object of a negotiation appealing to considerations of utility—or, indeed, any other good being maximized. This point about rights being a constraint is even more radical than I have put it so far because it is not restricted to constraints on the pursuit of the good or goods. It is a constraint on *any* maximization project. Hence, it is not just that rights cannot be weighed on the same scale as the good; they cannot be weighed *at all*. Even if the violation of a *particular* right were to serve the maximization of the nonviolation of *rights in general*, the violation will not be justifiable. To think that it could be justified would be to confusedly treat the notion of a constraint as being on a par with what it is a constraint on. A category confusion.

A second feature of rights is that in a society that adopts them, there is some sort of *obligation* that they be implemented. Since "implement" is a success verb, perhaps the more cautious way to put the point is that in that society, there must be some institutions (formal or, at the very least, informal) that strenuously *seek* to implement them, even if there is no guarantee that the attempt will be successful. So it is not as if their implementation is guaranteed, but what is guaranteed is some determined institutional attempt at correction or redress or protection, if it looks as if rights are being violated or threatened. Sometimes the term "justiciable" is used to capture this feature of rights. Institutions in a polity, such as independent judicial courts, for instance, are *obliged* to take up the matter if rights are violated or threatened.

This feature of rights implies that they presuppose some authority, formal or informal, which undertakes these obligations that rights generate. There are two possible objections to this claim. First, it may seem that the long-standing talk of *natural* rights comes with no such presupposition, it is only conventional rights that do, because in a state of nature there is no authority of the state or courts, which emerge only after and as a result of a social contract. As John Locke puts it in his *Second Treatise on Government* (1689), in a state of nature, "every man is a judge in his own case," simply making a claim to a right on the basis of an appeal to its justification *in (our) nature*. But given the fact that conflicts may arise between natural rights and given also that there will be unequal relations of power in the state of nature (some individuals are just stronger than others), some sort of (at least informal) authority that assesses and adjudicates these conflicting rights claims and navigates these differentials of power is presupposed, if natural rights are to be effectively implemented. A second objection might be that individuals may justifiably be said to have some rights *against* the actions and judgments of a state and its institutions such as the judiciary, so talk of rights presupposing an authority such as the state to implement them cannot be conceptually quite right. But I don't believe this sort of case should be viewed as a *counterexample* to the claim that a right presupposes some statelike authority or state-related institutions like the courts, which undertake the obligation we call "justiciability." Rather, this sort of case provides a *limiting or degenerate* case of such a presupposition. The presupposition *is* in place, even if in a degenerate form, in these cases. Constitutions, which have escape clauses for conscientious objection, implicitly acknowledge this.

I will proceed, then, assuming that these two features of rights (their priority over the good and their justiciability) are necessary and defining features. A third feature, which I will divulge at the end of the chapter, is much less discussed in the literature on rights but it is of vital importance in the context of Patnaik's more general analysis of capitalism.

2. The foundations of rights: The rights of liberty and economic rights

Turning from what "rights" means to the other foundational issue, we must ask *why* do we introduce the notion of a right (understood as having these features that I have mentioned) into the discourse of politics in the first place? This is a much more difficult and complex question than the question of meaning and will need far more detailed attention and elaboration. It is also a question of the utmost significance because without a satisfactory answer to it, rights are not likely to be taken seriously, a point I will take up again. Without a satisfactory answer there will be a tendency either to uncritically proliferate rights or to dismiss the need for rights altogether. Both tendencies are noticeable in recent times, and both should be resisted. On the one hand, because they rest on foundations that plumb beyond the more superficial aspects to the deepest and most fundamental features of humanity, rights will (and should) be very restricted in number. On the other hand, the hostility shown by an increasing number of political and legal theorists, who would happily allow the concept of the good to exhaust the realm of political morality, without any constraints coming from rights, leaves far too much to political negotiation, a form of latitude to which I do not subscribe. It leaves too much to the consensual judgments that emerge in politics, and, in a sense, I think that is to be too idealistic about human beings and the effects of the institutions they construct. One does not have to be a cynic to think that it is *not up for negotiation* that on certain matters of fundamental moral and political and economic importance, human beings and the institutions they adopt need to be constrained—that is, need to be made to or required to do certain things or prevented from doing other things, by some fundamental constitutional commitments that stand apart from all the other commitments. Rights are where those principles are enshrined, and, given the emphasis on their nonnegotiability, one has to give them at the very outset firm foundations in considerations that speak to what is fundamental about human beings. It is these foundations that a satisfactory answer to our second question must provide.

So something special is being done when we introduce talk of a right into the discourse of morals and politics. In doing so we are elevating *a value* to a *special* status among all the other values we have and pursue. We pursue all sorts of values that we have each day of our lives. But some of these values (such as *freedom* of speech, say, or *privacy*, or the value implicit in Patnaik's proposal— the *security* we gain from food and shelter and health), we are told, are to be elevated into something special and to be called "rights." And what that second question is asking is: *On what grounds* is this elevation of some values being made? What makes these particular values special and deserving of this status and this name?

When it comes to a value such as free speech, we find that the question we have just posed about the grounds on which it is elevated to a right, has been getting answers (of varying degrees of soundness and sophistication) going as far back as Periclean Athens, with its notion of "parrhesia," and again and again through the centuries since then—with Milton's *Areopagitica*, Locke's *A Letter Concerning Toleration*, Kant's profoundly deep discussion of autonomy, Mill's widely influential *On Liberty*, and so on providing only some of the most prominent answers. This entire rich tradition of thought grounds not just the right to free speech but a wide range of other rights tied to the notion of liberty in general, that is, such personal freedoms as the freedom of association, the freedom of religion, and even the right to privacy. (The right to private property is frequently bundled with these, but that is restricted to liberal doctrines, since socialist political ideals have long put it into question.)[4]

My own view is that the deepest source of such a grounding for these rights of personal freedom lies in the notion of *autonomy or self-governance* and this idea of autonomy is itself ultimately *grounded in the fact that human beings, by their very nature, are unique in possessing "reason."* That shows just how basic the ground is on which these rights stand. By tracing it all the way to the idea of human reason, what I mean is this. Individual human subjects are born into social contexts of one or other kind and are, from very early in their development, acculturated and habituated into its mores and customs and ways of thinking. But unlike other social creatures, say wolves, they are possessed of the capacity to ask of any social acculturation or social conditioning that they have been brought up on—*should I be doing (thinking) what the pack is doing (thinking)?* This just comes with the capacity for "reason." It defines human subjects *uniquely* (as far as we know). To possess reason is to be able to ask questions of this kind. And it is from this capacity to raise such a question that *self*-governance or autonomy (initially, autonomy from the established conventions of one's upbringing, one's social background and influences, and the like) emerges as a fundamental human trait that defines human subjects, and is exercised in our choices of what we speak and express, of what we worship, of whom we form associations with, etc. By protecting these in rights we thus preserve what is unique in human nature or what defines human subjects. Although the point has not been put in just this way, all the many details that have been traversed in the liberal tradition of thought on this subject (as I said, from ancient Greece through Milton, to Kant and Mill and after) stem, I believe, from these very fundamental considerations tied to human reason as it yields notions of autonomy or self-governance.

I should add that nothing in what I have said here about these rights being grounded in this notion of autonomy is intended to be individualistic in any dogmatic or invidious sense. Let me in particular distance what I have said from two such senses of individualism with which it might be confused.

First, autonomy, so conceived as intrinsically linked with the human capacity for reason, does not in the slightest amount to a conception of the individual as seeking his or her self-interest rather than the interest of the group to which he or she, as an individual, belongs. Just because reason from its earliest onset disposes us to ask, "Should I be thinking or doing as the social group is doing?," it does not follow at all that it is asking whether it is in my *self-interest* to think or do what the group is thinking or doing. It *could* take that form, but it does not *have* to do so. In its most general form, exercising autonomy consists in asking "Do I think what the group is thinking or doing, is *right*?" (This use of the word "right" is synonymous with "correct" or "morally correct" and obviously should not be confused or conflated with talk of "*a* right"). That the notion of "right" here is to be thought of as being elaborated as "in my self-interest" is a very specific and substantive reading of what is right or correct. Some might well think of right that way, but many might not. So, there is no *logical tie* between the autonomy-reflecting question and a self-interested form of individualism. As it happens, it is quite possible that our reason itself might tell us that pursuing one's self-interest is *not* right. In short, nothing about autonomy, so conceived, generates free riders. One can put this point by saying that the notion of reason or rationality in question, the one that underlies autonomy or self-governance, is a "thin" notion of reason.[5] It can be developed into "thicker" ideas of rationality in various directions (in the direction of individual self-interest, in the direction of the group's interest, or indeed in several other directions yet that are orthogonal to these), but such thick ideals should not be confused with what is the source of autonomy or self-governance and, therefore, what underlies the rights of personal liberty. What underlies these is "reason" in the thin and most minimal sense that I expounded earlier.

Second, despite the example I gave of the autonomy-reflecting question ("Should I do or think what the group does or thinks?"), there is nothing in what I have said about reason and its conceptual tie with autonomy that suggests that the notion of autonomy can be exercised only by individual human beings. That question can also be asked (and, therefore, autonomy can also be exercised by) a social *group*. A group can ask the same sort of autonomy-reflecting question. Of course, it is not (ex hypothesi) the *same* question that is asked by an individual human being; but it has the same general form as that question. Thus, a collective might ask, "Should the group be following the customs or traditions that it has formed over the long past?" Now, of course, if the group does ask such a question and exercises its autonomy in this way, it is thinking (cognitively functioning and deliberating) as an individual, a *group-individual*, as it were, rather than an individual human organism. There is no reason why only the latter should count as individuals, capable of individual deliberation. There certainly can be rational deliberation carried out by more abstract kinds of individuals, such as a group-individual. Rousseau was precisely suggesting this possibility when he spoke of the "general will." That will was intended by him to be both "general" (all the citizens in the polity) *and* "individual" (i.e., singular). And since Rousseau, the idea has been metaphysically developed and considerably refined.[6] Thus, though, in political contexts, the reference of the terms "individual" and "human organism" mostly coincide, they can come apart in the case of group-individuals. I say all this to make clear that what I have said about autonomy is not any kind of dogmatic stand against collective forms of deliberation and autonomy. It is not insisting on a *liberal* individualism that restricts itself to individual *human beings*. So, perhaps the best way to put the general lesson here is this: autonomy (and ultimately "reason") is the fundamental grounding notion for the rights of liberty and both individual human beings and group-individuals can exercise autonomy (and reason) in the sense I have briefly outlined.

To see autonomy in this way, as being reflected in the notion of reason that itself is exercised in its most elementary and fundamental form in the raising (whether by an individual human being or a social collective) of questions of this kind, is a particularly attractive formulation, because it combines Kant's notion of autonomy with Hegel's (and Marx's) ideas about how autonomy and reason are to be seen in two respects that find no central place in Kant's thinking. By tying autonomy to questions of this kind, questions that are always asked by one about what is *given to one in one's socially and historically situated condition*, makes for the Hegelian and Marxian correction of Kant—always situating our subjectivity *in a historical context*. And by allowing the question that reflects autonomy to also be asked by a *collective* or group-individual, it corrects for Kant's liberal individualism in just the way that Hegel and Marx sought. Thus, there is a fine balance to be maintained between the Kantian and Hegelian insights. To repeat: that individuals are constituted by the social relations into which they are acculturated from an early age is the insight we owe to thinkers such as Rousseau and Hegel and Marx. That we nevertheless possess autonomy from the social because, unlike pack animals, our capacity for reason allows us to ask questions that reflect this autonomy is an insight that Kant made central. Kantian ideas of autonomy do not cancel the Hegelian insight because any *answer* that these autonomy-reflecting questions (Should I be doing or thinking what the group is doing or thinking? Should the group be following the traditions it has been for so long been shaped and defined by?) get will unavoidably be given from *within* the situated perspective of the society (or tradition) within which the individual (or group) finds itself when asking that question. There is no transcendent perspective or source from which these answers can be provided. In that sense, reason, even when it questions society or tradition, does so without losing its place in society or tradition. Autonomy, therefore, can be genuinely *autonomy* even as it is exercised only within history and within a social context. One cannot step outside of these contexts. Precisely what Hegel and Marx sought as a correction of Kant is thus preserved. In Hegel and Marx this preserved element is famously presented in a notion of social and economic transformation that follows an *internal dialectic* of contradictions emerging in a society or economy and passing over into transformative resolutions of those contradictions. This is just their (more diachronically indexed) version of my more synchronically formulated point that answers to the questions that reflect one's autonomy from one's social context or one's tradition are nevertheless given from within the perspective of one's social context and one's tradition.

Since I am not a liberal, I am particularly concerned to stress both these caveats I have made because they both reveal that one can be committed, as I am, to these particular rights around the value of liberty and freedom, without a commitment to liberalism, as it is standardly understood.[7] Liberalism does not have exclusive claims to the notion of liberty nor to its enshrinement in various of these rights. To drive home this point, I should add that although the discussion of this notion of autonomy or self-governance, which grounds the notion of certain rights of liberty and freedom, has indeed been dominated in the modern period by a liberal tradition of thought, there have been very interesting dissenting offshoots: one claiming that the deepest notion of freedom at stake is best exemplified in a long *republican* tradition going back to ancient Rome, recently inventively revived with meticulous scholarly detail by Quentin Skinner, and another, owing to Rousseau and culminating in Marx, putting somewhat different points of pressure on the liberal tradition as being too exclusively focused on the negative notion of liberty (liberty as "noninterference") and offering, by contrast, various more "positive" elaborations of the notion of liberty.[8] All of these diverse ideas and doctrines, not just liberalism, can be mobilized into answering foundational questions about the rights surrounding liberty.

Nothing like this long-standing (and outstanding) intellectual history is to be found in the efforts to lay foundations for the rights that Patnaik's proposal is concerned to promote. Explicit foundational discussions of it are really only detectable as recently as the late 1940s and mostly owing to the fact that the United States Declaration of Human Rights in 1948 contained some clauses (see in particular articles 22–26) about the right to food, work, shelter, and so forth.

Why is this kind of inquiry such a latecomer in political philosophy and social theory? Why should the value of liberty and autonomy get a foundational discussion for some twenty hundred years while the value of security in the basic necessities of life is more or less entirely neglected until measurably less than a century ago? Given this striking differential, it is hardly surprising that such rights have to get the kind of special advocacy that Patnaik is urging for them now, while rights around the concept of freedom and liberty such as, for instance, free speech, need no such advocacy since they are already widely and deeply entrenched in the constitutions of liberal democratic polities.

Part of the reason for this curious neglect of economic rights may be due to the fact that they are the kind of rights that the Left, rather than standard forms of liberalism, are likely to take up, and yet much of the Left, especially the Marxisant Left, has shown an abiding hostility to the notion of rights in general. In fact, I cannot resist saying that when Patnaik's essay, which made the proposal for economic rights for India, was published in *Economic and Political Weekly*, a friend of mine wrote to me to ask, "Why is a Marxist like Patnaik going soft and liberal?" This question, though it was put to me in a somewhat offhand manner, is not without point since Marx, as everyone knows, had famously written with dismissiveness about the very idea of rights precisely because it was embedded in a liberal ideology that, according to his analysis, had evaded aspirations to a more profound emancipation.[9] However, Marx, it must be remembered, was writing in what Hobsbawm had dubbed "the Age of Revolution" (1848 was palpably in the horizon of his thinking, 1789 was not a very distant inspirational antecedent, and it is these very dates that serve as the bookends of Hobsbawm's "Age").[10] So, quite understandably, he had hopes for Europe leapfrogging over an extended period of incubation in rights that were, in any case, predominantly theorized only in liberal doctrine, to a more radical transformation of society. But, as the question that was put to me reveals, Marx's skeptical attitude toward rights has influenced generations of Left thinking on the subject, even when the Age of Revolution has receded into a distant past and there does not seem much scope for what I called the leapfrogging that Marx held out hopes for. Yet his skepticism about rights seems to persist in much of the radical Left. It is partly this skeptical challenge that has prompted me to write the reflections of this chapter.[11]

Though, as I said, this is in part no doubt responsible, the main reason why considerations of autonomy (and the various values of liberty and freedom that it underwrites) have occupied philosophers and thinkers for longer and more deeply is because they are considered *more fundamental* than the value of security that comes from the provision of food and shelter and health and so forth. This is so for various reasons, and it is not at all obvious that the reasons are good ones. But before I get to those reasons, I will need to make some preliminary analytical points regarding the foundations of rights, including, particularly, economic rights.

As a terminological point, let me just quickly say that I think we need another term than "security" to describe the value or values that are attained through these provisions that economic rights demand. The entire rhetoric around "security" has been ruined by its recent association with the "war on terror," which was said to be carried out in the name of attaining "security" for one's people. It is not obvious what alternative vocabulary should replace it. In an earlier rhetoric these provisions were described as the fulfilling of our "basic needs" and the term "well-being" was often used to describe the value that was served by fulfilling basic needs. This term is not entirely satisfactory either, since it may seem as if much more than the fulfilling of basic needs goes into bringing about our "well-being." But whatever word we use, the question remains: How can it be that what such a word represents can be *less* fundamental than autonomy? What it represents, that is, what is brought into effect by the fulfilling of basic needs, is just about the most fundamental value that human beings could seek since, without such basic needs being fulfilled, we could not function as the human beings we are. This point is surely very well understood and hardly needs to be said. (As a matter of fact, it has been said in such foundational discussion of economic rights as exists in the philosophical literature.)[12] Nevertheless, it has to be admitted, that there seems to remain a very strong strain in philosophy that views the basic needs and their fulfillment as less fundamental in underpinning rights foundationally than considerations of autonomy. That is one reason why economic rights remain without philosophical foundations unlike say, the right to free speech and other rights of liberty. And that, in turn, it would seem is why economic rights seem to be excluded from constitutions and need the special kind of advocacy that economists like Patnaik are seeking.

A more important preliminary point of analysis requires me to lay down in a very elementary *schematic* form the nature of the answers that might be given to our second question, the question that asks about how rights are to be grounded. In any schematic answer, we have to say which value is being elevated by the rights in question, as well as what in human nature grounds the rights and the value being elevated.

With one set of rights regarding speech, association, worship, privacy, and so on, which have received long and careful answers over the centuries, we have already presented the following schema: The value that these rights *elevate* is liberty or freedom (for the purposes of this essay, I use these two terms synonymously); and these rights and this value are *grounded* in the notion of autonomy, which itself is grounded ultimately in the very idea of human "reason."

What matching schema can we present for the other set of rights, economic rights, which have received far less long and careful attention? We have resisted saying that they elevate the value of "security." We have also resisted saying that they elevate the value of "well-being." Perhaps, then, it is best to simply say this as a matching schema: these rights *elevate* the value of "basic needs fulfillment" (since the rhetoric of basic needs was widely used in the discussions of economic rights a few decades ago, we can simply describe the fulfillment of basic needs as itself the value that such rights speak to); and they are *grounded* in the notion of human vitality, that is, the living of a human life at its most fundamental existential level. (Sometimes this is described in terms of human "survival" but, for reasons that I will not elaborate here, I prefer to put it in terms of life and vitality.)

The idea of economic rights speaking to the value of the fulfillment of basic needs, and finding its constitutive ground in the very existence and sustenance of human life and vitality, is perhaps rather obvious. In the literature, needs and rights have often been said to have a close conceptual tie, and the schema offered here merely makes the tie explicit. But, obvious though it may be, this schema and this tie are not intended, at least not by me, as taking a misleadingly direct form. I am not suggesting that the very concept of a "need" is such that one cannot hear that something is a need (or someone has a need) without feeling the tug of obligation to fulfil it. There is a temptation to say this because the concept of a need stands in contrast with the concept of a "want" or "preference." And so it may seem that it directly entails an obligation (on the part of the state, say, as propounded in the feature of rights that is called "justiciability") to ensure that they are fulfilled. Wants, we all know, just by the fact of being wants, are not the sort of thing that impose any obligations on any one to gratify them, not even on the possessor of the wants, leave alone on others or on the state. On the contrary, we say of many wants that they *ought not* to be gratified. As I said, even those who have the wants might sometimes say that. So it might be thought that one contrast with wants that needs stand in is that needs *do* impose such obligations to fulfill them. But that is not how the schematic argument for the foundation of economic rights presented earlier proceeds. This is because that is not the correct way to make the contrast between needs and wants. The contrast between needs and wants, no doubt, does turn on the fact that the former are more objective than the latter: If one *wants* something because it has a certain property, one necessarily believes that it has a certain property—but it could turn out that the belief is false. But if one *needs* something because it has a certain property, it *does* have that property and if one also believes that it has the property (which, unlike in the case of wants, one might not), the belief *is* true. But needs being more objective than wants in this way does not directly give us any obligatory claim to having the needs fulfilled by way of right or rights. Why not? Because needs, despite being objective in the way just expounded, nevertheless are needs *for a purpose*. That is, when we say someone needs something, we can always be asked the question: Need it for what? And not all answers to this last question yields an obligation (in the form of a right) to have the need fulfilled. For instance, I might say, "I need a cricket bat." And, I will be asked: "Need it for what?," to which I answer: "To go out on to the pitch and face the bowling." None of this, obviously, raises any issues about rights. It is only some answers to the question "Need it for what?" that yield obligations of that sort. The schema we gave for economic rights suggested that the answer to this "What for?" question, when applied to the needs that underlie economic rights, is: human life and vitality. It is only when the answer goes as deep as that into the nature of human beings do we get into the terrain of rights with the obligatory feature we call "justiciability." All this suggests that the foundational relation between needs and rights is much more indirect than it might initially seem. They ground rights only via a justificatory grounding argument of the sort that the matching schema here tries to provide. There is no more direct certification that needs can provide for rights.

The point of these schemas is to bring out that the foundations of *both* sets of rights (one in notions of autonomy/reason, the other in notions of life/vitality) go as deep as *fundamental* aspects of *human nature* itself and so it is not surprising that they have, for so long and recurringly, been described as "natural" rights. If the foundational discussion takes us to a level as deep and fundamental as that, then whether or not we actually call them natural rights (a matter that turns on rather arcane issues), we can at least understand why many have thought it apt to call them that.

A final point of preliminary analysis requires me to explain why, since I am making the familiar appeal to basic needs and their fulfillment in the foundational discussion of economic rights, I have tended to focus on only three of the five economic rights that Patnaik mentions (and most others mention) when they speak of economic rights. I have restricted myself to talk of food, shelter, and health and omitted the right to work or employment and the right to education. These are not omissions due to neglect. Let me take up the deliberate reason for each omission in turn. The reason I have not mentioned the right to employment at the outset is that unlike food and shelter and health, it does not speak *immediately* to the value of basic needs fulfilment, it only *secondarily* speaks to it via the undeniable fact that food, shelter, and health are only available in a productive economy, and such an economy requires that citizens be variously employed in production, distribution, and so on; moreover, even in a society that has adopted economic rights there will be some minimum costs that citizens may incur in the purchase of food, the maintenance of shelter and health, and so forth, costs that to be paid by citizens will require that they have income that presumably has its source in employment. So a full understanding of what makes possible the implementation of the rights to food, housing, and health requires one to see the secondary place of the right to employment within the schema that grounds these rights. Over and above this secondary place in the schema for economic rights, some may wish to argue (plausibly enough, though because this is a matter that could be debated, I have not stressed it) for a more immediate grounding of the right to work in considerations of human vitality, claiming that idleness goes against the vitality of a human existence and work is essential to vitality. As for the right to education, it has a slightly more complex and rather more interesting foundational base. It is important to make clear that the right to education should not get a very specific elaboration since what gets counted as a necessary education is highly contested—thinkers ranging from Gandhi to Paulo Freire to Bertrand Russell have argued that orthodox education of one or other kind prevalent in modern societies, far from being a right, is detrimental to human development. But even if one describes the education to which one must have a right in general enough terms to avoid these controversies, I would argue that unlike the other economic rights, the grounding for such a right is not primarily and immediately tied to considerations of human vitality that underlie basic need fulfillment. Rather, the right to education is the one right which has a foot in each of the two schematic foundational grounds I outlined. Like the rights to liberty, it has essential ties to the idea of human reason since education is essential for the nourishing and flowering of the capacity for human reason. But, equally, education is needed for some aspects of the functioning of productive economies that make possible the provision of food and housing and health—so, just as I said about employment, it too is secondarily related to the values of basic need fulfillment that are grounded in considerations of vitality necessary for a functioning human life.

3. A philosophical bias and its sources

With these preliminary analytical points in place, let us return to the two schemas we had elaborated for the two sets of rights (the rights of liberty and economic rights) and ask again: Why, if these two sets of rights reach down to foundational values and notions that reflect something as fundamental as human nature itself, has one set of these grounding values and notions (liberty and autonomy/reason) been thought to be *more fundamental* than the other (the fulfillment of basic needs and human life and vitality)? I will present four factors (there may well be others) that are responsible for this bias.

One factor that may account for it being considered less fundamental is that, though these needs tied to the life and vitality of functioning human beings are defining of human beings, they are *not unique* to human beings and hold of the entire animal kingdom, indeed of the entire living environment. By contrast, "reason" of the sort that goes into self-governance and underlies the rights of freedom *is* uniquely possessed by human beings. But this cannot be the basis for thinking that basic need fulfillment is less fundamental than freedom. If anything, it is a reason for making these rights based on the fulfillment of basic needs *wider* in scope so as to include the rights of animals and of nature. (It is not as if this point has not been registered quite widely by those who have been arguing for animal rights and the rights of the natural environment.) Something does not become more fundamental just because it is grounded in something that human beings distinctively possess. To say that it does would reflect a kind of parochialism about the human species that has no justification, no more than any other parochialism (of race or gender or caste or religion or nation) has a justification. To repeat the introduction to this volume: "This distinctiveness is not a basis for moral exceptionalism or an argument for privileges that are special to human subjects. Indeed, if there is any exceptionalism it is that such distinctiveness brings with it the freight and weight of special responsibilities and duties toward subjects *not* possessed of this capacity but like human subjects possessed of the capacity to suffer and possessed of intrinsic value." For all our distinctiveness, they are nevertheless our *fellow* creatures and we have obligations and duties to them as well.

I will return to discuss another possible philosophical use of human distinctiveness, equally fallacious, a little later.

A *second* factor behind the tendency may be the fact that the threshold for what are *basic* needs shifts around, depending on how economically advanced the society is. This may make it seem as if rights tied to basic human needs are tied to something too indeterminate to be the grounds for something as fundamental as rights. To this sort of objection, either of the following two responses seem to me to suffice. We could on the one hand simply relativize the notion of what is "basic" to different societies and tie rights to basic needs, so relativized. On the other hand, one could say that if the idea of a basic need is grounded in the very idea of *human* life and vitality which, in turn, is uniform wherever human beings are found, then rights are tied to basic needs in some absolute and nonrelativized sense, and some societies may wish to make commitments (not in the form of rights but of policies) to higher thresholds once the rights to the basic needs, defined in these absolute terms, have been justiciably established. I am allowing either of these responses to this challenge with this kind of airy indifference only because *neither* answer, nor the challenge itself, is relevant to Patnaik's proposal. The entire controversy about the indeterminacy of the notion of "well-being" or of basic needs is beside the point in the context of his proposal, because he is, as I said at the outset, making a claim for a *very specific society and polity*, the national site of India in the present. Even though he may need to take up (as we have in this essay) foundational questions turning on universal considerations about human beings that ground the economic rights he is proposing, he is not making the proposal for all the human beings in the entire globe living in enormously diverse societies with very different levels of social and economic development. Therefore, if the foundational questions are answered by an appeal to the idea of basic needs, he can with confidence *assume* a relative *determinacy* of basic needs for the site he specifically has in mind.[13] The crucial point to keep in mind is that although the notion of rights (including economic rights) needs a foundational discussion of the kind we are exploring, and although any foundational discussion is going to be raising issues of *universal* human concern and relevance because (being foundational) they trace back fundamentally to features of human nature (such as autonomy, basic needs, and so on), *the "universal" here should not be conflated with the "global."* This point is utterly obvious and the mistake of such a conflation, if made, would be elementary, but it may still be easy to slip into it because, as we know, rights (and economic rights particularly) came to have a new prominence a few decades ago at a global site as a result of being included in an *international* charter adopted by the United Nations. Moreover, on that global site and in that international charter, they were (and are) spoken of as "*human*" rights to be contrasted with rights of citizens of particular nations. But the very use of the word "human" there might give the impression of doing a quite different duty than just making this contrast. It may give the impression that the term "human" there was intended to suggest a universality of the kind that has been in evidence in the foundational discussion of the foregoing pages in which we have spoken of autonomy, basic needs, and so on, as fundamental facets of human nature that ground these rights. That is the confusion to be avoided. I repeat: the United Nations charter—with its international status, standing over and above particular nations—spoke of these rights as "human" rights primarily with a view to contrasting them with the particular rights enshrined in the constitutions of particular nation-states. Thus, the ambiguous role of the term "human" here makes it quite easy to fall into the confusion between "global" and "universal" when interpreting the charter's talk of "human" rights. Patnaik's proposal, unlike the charter's articles on economic rights, is intended for a specific nation in the present time. Despite its specificity, we have been trying to explore the *universal* foundations for such rights. But if we refuse the confusion of the universal with the global, that universality does not mean that the proposal, therefore, loses its specific earmark for a nation, and becomes a proposal in the global arena. And if earmarked specifically for a particular nation, it is not vulnerable to the objection that societies and countries with different levels of development will have different thresholds for what is *basic* in the understanding of "basic needs."

This last series of remarks (about the internationalist context within which the notion of economic rights has been discussed in recent years, ever since they were listed in three or four articles in the United Nations charter) leads into a *third* factor that has led to the neglect of serious discussion of the foundations of these rights. At the international level, rights talk is *necessarily merely aspirational*. This is for the simple and widely recognized reason that there is no state/judicial authority at the global level of the kind necessary to carry through the implementability or justiciability feature of rights that we had mentioned earlier. A rhetoric of rights that is merely aspirational is not "rights," properly so called. It may be worthy rhetoric and it may be used (with a marginal degree of success sometimes, as by the Indigenous people of Chiapas, Mexico, and the Basques in Spain) to mobilize particular nation-states to implement rights, but this does not amount to "justiciability." That kind of success entirely depends on the extent to which national governments are willing to listen to and be shamed by chastising reports on human rights by international bodies such as the United Nations, and the plain fact is that most national governments committing human rights violations—such as in India today or Israel ever since 1967, to name just two—are shameless. What all this obviously reflects is the complete lack of authoritative sites of governance at the global level. In fact, when it comes to economic rights, it is a curious thing that ever since its financialization in the neoliberal period, the only global phenomenon of real significance in the last few decades is capital. Far from being a site of governmental authority, it is a phenomenon that desperately needs to be *constrained* by governmental authority, if any economic (or for that matter, environmental) rights are ever going to be implemented. But, as we know, there is no such authority at the global level to constrain capital. At the global level, there is only a highly patchwork form of governance consisting of a toothless United Nations (and its Security Council), the international credit agencies and trade organizations, various multilateral and bilateral treaties and arrangements, and various elite associations (G20, G7), whose tendency has been to brazenly promote the hegemony of finance capital rather than to constrain it.

When rights talk is necessarily only aspirational in this way, lacking the feature of justiciability, the foundational considerations we appeal to will be unlikely to ground anything that is potentially effective. It will only ground rights as, at best, recommendations. This point applies to all rights, of course, not just economic rights. But since articles 22–26 of the United Nations charter brought attention to economic rights in a serious way for the first time, this merely aspirational element of rights at the global level made them ineffectual, a sort of window dressing of loftiness while a capitalist political economy generated deprivations on the ground, especially from the 1980s onwards. As Sam Moyn's *Not Enough* (2018) has ably demonstrated, it is not exactly accidental that *global* level economic rights talk under the rubric "human" rights has coincided almost perfectly with the phenomenon of global finance capital that we call neoliberalism. But what Moyn does not recognize (because he provides no analysis capitalism in the way that Patnaik does) is that what this should lead us to explore is the possibility that we begin to think of political economy for particular nations in ways that decathect from global finance capital and explore further how economic rights on distinct *national* sites, as clauses in the constitutions of national governments rather than in an international charter, may play a central role in such a transformation of their political economies. That is indeed Patnaik's proposal, restricted as it is to India, but as a proposal it really makes sense only if one situates it in Patnaik's own analysis of the political economy of capitalism, to which I will turn shortly.

Before I do, I want to mention a *fourth* and final factor that prompts the tendency to view freedom and autonomy (which underlie the rights related to speech and association and privacy, etc.) as more fundamental than basic needs fulfillment and considerations of the vitality of human life (which underlie economic rights). This fourth factor is a much more sophisticated one than the previous three and derives from work that quite deliberately and explicitly seeks to deny a place of centrality to the idea of basic needs fulfillment, making it secondary by *folding it into notions of freedom and agency*. The most prominent and influential figure to take these issues in this direction is Amartya Sen, whose notion of "capabilities" was first formulated via a critique of "needs."[14] I want to be clear that Sen's replacing "needs" on center stage with "capabilities" is not a denial on his part that the fulfillment of basic needs is an important goal. He has spent much of a lifetime of thought and writing addressing the concerns of poverty and deprivation. The sense in which he makes needs secondary is not by denying the importance of fulfilling needs—rather, as I said, he makes them secondary, in a more sophisticated sense, by *subsuming* the notion of needs under another notion, the notion of capability. He does this because he thinks that capabilities have a property that makes them more fundamental than needs. That property is precisely the property of human autonomy and freedom. And since I am looking to diagnose why the considerations that ground one set of rights—considerations of freedom and autonomy—are generally considered more fundamental than the considerations that ground another set of rights—considerations of basic need fulfillment and human life and vitality—this sophisticated turn in the discussion of these issues is of immediate and direct relevance. Sen's refinement (words like "refinement" and "sophistication" are well chosen here since Sen is explicit in saying that the notion of needs is too crude for the purposes at hand) of the notion of needs via their subsumption under notions of freedom and autonomy is at once a reflection of the long-standing tendency to view freedom as more fundamental than basic needs fulfillment I am trying to diagnose and (because of Sen's great influence) a perpetuation of that tendency in our own time.

The basic idea in Sen is to knit together two notions that he labels "functionings" and "capabilities." The former consists of human behavioral states as well as states of being. Someone voting is an example of a behavioral state. Someone being a cricketer is an example of a state of being. Both are examples of what he calls "functionings." Now, a society can arrange it so that I have the *option* to vote and the option to be a cricketer and in doing so it gives me some capabilities. By stressing options, capabilities stress freedom and autonomy. The subsumptive effect this has on the notion of needs is that something like the need for food or shelter, necessary for one's vitality in living a human life, is now filtered through options: fulfilling these needs is an option that one has, and one can choose to exercise this option and fulfill them. Freedom is thus primary; basic need fulfillment is folded within it.[15]

An obvious criticism of Sen might take the form of saying that attributing a need to someone summons a certain sense of urgency and it makes one sit up to the moral importance of addressing it, whereas capabilities lack that urgency and normative force.

But we have to proceed slowly here. As we saw earlier, the urgency and normative force of someone needing x only really arises when the question "Needs x for what?" gets some answers rather than other answers, gets answers that speak to such fundamental considerations as human vitality requisite for the living of a human life. That is why economic rights speak to *basic* need fulfillment. But Sen can, then, respond by seeking to finesse this objection by speaking of "*basic capabilities*" (which, in fact, he has, though by this category he also has in mind to track innate human capacities such as the capacity for language), and he can declare that these are marked as having a certain urgency and normative force that other capabilities do not have. So where does that leave us on the matter of the difference between capabilities and needs?

This objection to Sen will thus have to be reformulated with greater care. There is a substantive *political/legal* difference between saying

(a) If a citizen opts to have their basic needs fulfilled, then a good society and polity will seek to arrange it so that they are fulfilled

and

(b) A good society and polity will seek to arrange it so that the basic needs of its citizens are fulfilled, though, of course, it is up to particular citizens whether they opt to fulfill their basic needs.

It should be clear that (a) expresses the basic capability view and (b) the basic needs view. And now, the objection must go on to claim that the difference between (a) and (b) is that (b) seems to have greater moral force and thus not only puts greater pressure on a state and society to make the requisite arrangements, but it motivates more than (a) does its own insertion into constitutions. Moreover, as a formulation, it is better suited to such an insertion than (a), which is formulated with a clause that gives a covering primacy to optionality and choice rather than to the basic needs. The differences between (a) and (b) are essentially differences in where the *default* or priority is taken to lie and where the default lies makes all the difference to the political compulsions it necessitates via the constitutional status that it is given. And proponents of the superiority of the formulation in (b) can clinch their case by pointing out that, *in any case*, there are *other* aspects of constitutions (the other set of rights, the rights of liberty) that can recuperate the optionality that fails to find a place in (b). It is just this recuperation that is reflected in the secondary clause in (b), once the default clause is already in place, that is, the secondary clause which reads "though, of course . . ."

It is, I suppose, still possible for Sen to say that although he can hear these subtle differences between (a) and (b), these differences do not show his initial response to be false. He can point out that what he was saying in his initial response was that basic needs and basic capabilities are *coextensive*. These differences do not overturn that response because they only show that basic needs and capabilities are not *cointensive*. To put it less cryptically, (a) and (b) are such that although they do not *convey the same idea* (i.e., are not cointensive) because the idea of basic capabilities sophisticates the idea of basic needs in the direction of freedom and autonomy by filtering it through optionality, they nevertheless *pick out the same things* (i.e., are coextensive) with their different respective concepts "basic capabilities" and "basic needs." Be that as it may, the objection can still claim that not being cointensive is significant because it has implications for politics if a greater moral pressure is exerted by the basic needs approach of (b) to make the requisite arrangements that fulfill those needs.

I think, so formulated, this objection does show that one should not be treating the foundational ground in autonomy for one set of rights as more fundamental than the foundational ground in basic need fulfillment for the other set of rights.

As I said, while discussing the first of the four factors underlying the bias being discussed in this section, one may be tempted to think with Sen that this filter via optionality is dictated by our acknowledgment of the fact that our experience of basic needs and their fulfillment is a richer experience in human beings than it is in nonhuman animals because such experience is embedded in a rich capacity to reason that reflects our possession of a kind of freedom that animals do not possess. But the thrust of my foregoing remarks has precisely been that no such dictation is justified by the acknowledgment of this fact. We no doubt experience our basic needs and their fulfillment in a sense that is qualitatively different from the experience of these things in animals because we distinctively possess freedom and reason, but it is a non sequitur to think that a constitutional (social and political) commitment to fulfilling basic human needs of citizens should, as a result, be viewed merely as a commitment to providing for their freedom to exercise their *options* to fulfil them. To see the default as it is presented in (b) rather than as in (a) is to suggest that they need to be fulfilled *anyway*.

The only question that remains, then, is whether Sen's urge to impose this filter of optionality on needs is not a kind of obsession with freedom and autonomy. And it particularly seems to be a kind of fetishization of freedom when it comes to viewing even *basic* needs through the filter of optionality; a sort of *bias* toward freedom over basic needs fulfillment. The only grounds I can think of, on Sen's behalf, for insisting on this filter of optionality is the somewhat strained possibility that someone might actually choose to exercise the option of *not* having his basic needs fulfilled, for example, an artist who feels that he cannot really do justice to his art unless he is existentially deprived—starving, say, or homeless, or suffering ill health. I say "strained" for more than one reason. First of all, such examples seem to be highly exceptional. Moreover, it might also plausibly be said that the artist needs the vitality of a basically functioning human life in order to make his art and this may require that the artist is *not* starving or homeless or suffering ill-health. And finally, as I said, constitutions (in any case) have the rights of liberty, so the optionality is (in any case) recovered there for this kind of exceptional artist. In response, Sen would have to say that this sort of "in any case" recuperation somewhere else is not good enough. The optionality should be present *in* the formulation about basic needs and (b) does not do that. Without that, (b) is philosophically deficient. But I would think this demand is working with a very rarified and quite unreasonable conception of what is philosophically adequate and what is philosophically deficient. For all these reasons, I do find the example of the artist and the work it is being put to here, quite strained.

Even so, Sen can claim that his filter, which places freedom and autonomy in a more fundamental role than basic need fulfillment, has the advantage of allowing in examples of this kind, however strained they might seem. But even if this is the response of last resort in favor of Sen's view, it is not decisive in establishing freedom and autonomy as being more fundamental than the vitality considerations underlying basic need fulfillment. This is because one can summon other examples (no doubt, also strained) that point in the opposite direction. Someone living in the hellish deprivation of chronic and severe malnutrition in India may think that life in Havana, even if he would be deprived there of the freedom and autonomy to speak freely, is a kind of paradise compared to the deprivations he is suffering. Anyone who has read Hegel will be alerted by this sort of example to one strand of thought behind the philosophical myth of the master-slave dialectic, in which the existential struggle between Self and Other results in one person placing the value of life above the value of freedom and becoming the slave while the other, with these values inversed, becomes the master. Geist's dialectical development emerges from the pervading instability of this relationship because the master cannot get the recognition and acknowledgment from the slave. And one way to read Marx's upending (or upturning) of Hegel's idealism is precisely as seeing through to the point that nothing short of placing what I have called the value of "life and vitality" *on a par* with the value of freedom and autonomy will yield the mutual recognition that sets history on the path to dissolving classes in an ideal state—not, in that case, the Prussian state, but the socialist ideal of an unalienated life formed by the appropriate distributive movement from abilities to needs.[16]

But putting aside this suggestive philosophical messianism, one could just simply say, in a more sober register, that since (strained) examples can be given, in this way, in two opposing directions, what this implies is that the most plausible view would be an ecumenical one in which considerations of reason, freedom, autonomy *and* considerations of basic need fulfillment and vitality, *both* speak *equally* to fundamental aspects of human nature; and the urge to place the one as having more fundamental status and the other as having a merely subsumed status within it, comes from a misguided attempt at moral and political sophistication of the more elemental needs to which economic rights speak, revealing a philosophical bias in favor of autonomy and freedom.

There may be a temptation here to refuse my attribution of a bias of this sort by invoking a point discussed a little earlier about the *distinctiveness* of human subjects, possessed as they are of a distinctive conception of reason that sets them apart from all other animals. Though in that discussion I said that one would be parochial to draw conclusions about moral exceptionalism from the fact of this distinctiveness, I will not deny that the *experience* of basic needs (and the experience of vitality that their fulfilment makes possible) is a richer and more meaningful notion of "experience" than that undergone by nonhuman animals precisely because it is embedded in the human possession of reason in its full, sophisticated sense not possessed by other creatures. Embedding in a rich conception of reason makes the experience of (indeed the very idea of) needs and their fulfillment a qualitatively different phenomenon and so, as philosophers like to say, it is wrong to think that there is a "highest common factor" notion of "experience" and "needs" that captures both what is undergone by human and by nonhuman animals.[17] So the temptation is to say that Sen's filtering the notion of basic needs through optionality and freedom is a reflection of this distinctiveness of the experience of basic needs and their fulfillment. But the temptation is based on a non sequitur. When giving the philosophical foundations of rights we are theoretically engaging with what is justified and what is possible in the political arena. The case for economic *rights* is a case that has to be made in the political and constitutional arena. The disagreement is over whether in the matter of the fulfillment of basic needs, *which Sen himself is committed to achieve*, we should or should not be filtering the idea of basic needs through notions of optionality and autonomy. I have argued that *in the political and constitutional arena*, Sen's stress on capabilities and my refusal of that stress respectively yield two different conditionals with two different formulations of what the default or priority should be, and that—in the political and constitutional arena—it makes all the difference in arranging for the fulfillment of basic needs, which default or priority is in place. This latter conclusion is not overturned by the fact that the experience of basic needs in human beings is distinctive because of their distinctive possession of autonomy and "reason." And what primarily matters in the political and constitutional arena in which we are seeking a philosophical foundation for economic rights is *this latter conclusion*. The thicker or richer texture of *human* experience of basic needs is not a sufficient ground to integrate or assimilate the *political* case for rights grounded in basic human needs with the rights grounded in human possession of "reason" and "freedom."[18]

Though all of the foregoing may sound like a sustained criticism of Sen, in a sense it is not. By this I mean that there is an understandable reason why Sen does not see his way to the kind of ecumenism I have been arguing for. This ecumenism of letting the fulfillment of basic human needs stand side by side with human autonomy (rather than get folded into it) comes into view only when one is focused, as I am in this essay, on the subject of *rights*. Sen's discussion of these issues is most often within a quite different focus, which is his long-standing and recurring interest in questions of *equality* (and inequality).[19] Given that focus, Sen is aspiring for something more ambitious than the fulfillment of basic needs. In one place he even hints at something stronger than what I have just expressed in my last sentence, pointing out that often the advocacy of the fulfillment of basic needs might be a ploy to deflect away from the more ambitious goal of equality. (This is quite of a piece with Samuel Moyn's conclusion that I mentioned a little earlier—that the entire movement of human rights grounded in the idea of basic needs of some decades ago nested quite comfortably with neoliberalism's widespread inegalitarian effects.) Sen's turn to capabilities, within the focus on that more ambitious goal of equality, can then be seen as a way of trying to ensure that equality is not at odds with freedom and autonomy and also that it is not conceived in the routinely rigid terms of equality of, say, income, but rather of ensuring that people are provided with what they, with the exercise of their autonomy, chose to value. The relation of capabilities to equality is perhaps that equality, when approached via capabilities, amounts to a dispersed version of "equality of opportunity," where by "dispersed version" I mean that unlike the usual appeal to equality of opportunity, which targets particular domains (as when we say: everybody should have the opportunity of the same *education* or everybody should have the same opportunity for getting *bank loans* . . .), Sen's version leaves the targets to the values that individual citizens opt for.

The overall point, however, is this. Whatever we think of the efficacies that capabilities yield in the aspiration to equality (there may be many who think that equality of opportunity is not the primary form of equality one should be seeking), the focus in this chapter, the question of economic rights, is on *a quite different set of concerns*. Though it can hardly be doubted that the implementation of economic rights will go some ways in reducing inequalities, it is just as clear that their implementation will yield and will aspire to yield something that falls distinctly short of equality. Why then have I been concerned that this distinctly less ambitious goal of economic rights is being deflected by placing the values of freedom and autonomy above the values of basic needs fulfillment that these less ambitious goals aspire to? Why, in general, am I concerned with and focused on the much less ambitious goal (than equality) that Patnaik's proposal for economic rights speak to? This is a good and sharp question. And we can only answer it, if we turn finally, as promised, to Patnaik's analysis of capitalism.

4. The tendencies of capital

To begin with, it is worth trying to get to grips with how Patnaik's analysis of capitalism is relevant to understanding why his proposal that there should be economic rights is intended for a very specific national site, India in the present.

In two successive books, *A Theory of Imperialism* (2016) and *Capitalism and Imperialism* (2021), coauthored with Utsa Patnaik, he argues that economic imperialism—the economic domination of one region of the world by another—is not a late-coming development in the history of capitalism, but an essential feature, built into the tendencies of capital from its earliest beginnings as an economic formation in Europe. On this analysis, capitalism in the metropole (Europe initially and then, by diffusion, other parts of the temperate belt such as North America, the Antipodes . . .) is a dynamic system characterized by an incessant competitive drive, as a result of which an *external* stimulus is indispensable for the reproduction of capital. As a matter of empirical fact, due to the availability of essential primary commodities in the tropical and subtropical regions of the world (commodities which are not grown or not grown year-round in the North due to its climactic conditions), as well as because of the extensive external markets the populations of these southern nations provide,[20] the chief external source of this stimulus needed to sustain capital accumulation (and capitalism as the economic formation it is) is provided by these distant lands. Imperialism, in the familiar traditional form of colonialism, was motivated by this need to secure this external source for capitalism and—until decolonization in roughly the middle of the last century—for its entire long duration it did so with methods and economic policies that imposed a range of economic hardships on the population of the colonized lands. In the period immediately after decolonization, there was a hiatus in this entire systemic relation between the metropole and its erstwhile colonies. This was due to independent sovereign states that had emerged in the latter seeking to gain greater control over their national economies than colonialism had allowed to these regions of the South, so as to pursue policies that would improve the conditions of their working people. This hiatus lasted no more than three and a half decades after which, as a result of measures adopted that made for the increasing financialization of capital and the globalization of finance, the ability of these newly emerging nation-states to exercise sovereignty over their own economies was drastically weakened in what has come to be called the "neoliberal" period of capitalism; and thus the external element that is required to sustain capital in the form it requires was restored. This restoration amounts once again to imperialism because, though it employs methods and economic policies that are somewhat different from traditional colonialism due to the transformed nature of capital in the neoliberal period of financial globalization, nevertheless at a more abstract level of description (some of Patnaik's own descriptions at this abstract level are "income deflation" and "demand compression") they have the same essential features that imposed hardships on the populations during the colonial period.

For reasons of space, in an essay that is primarily about rights, I have put the analysis very abstractly and without any detail. Despite that, it is still easy to infer from this skeletal description that if one were to seek to oppose imperialism in this new formation of capitalism that we call neoliberalism, a first step will have to be that these nation-states of the southern regions of the globe will have to find ways to reacquire greater control over their own economies. Since this cannot be attempted along the lines pursued immediately after decolonization because of the financialization and globalization of capital in recent decades, Patnaik argues that they can now only really do so by "delinking" very substantially from the global economy of finance capitalism. It is in the context of this argument (an essentially antiglobalization argument, as the very notion of "delinking" makes clear) that Patnaik's proposal about economic rights is made for *particular* nations, nations of the South suffering from this renewed imperialism; and his focus has been primarily on India. The idea presumably is that if India were to adopt a constitutional regime of economic rights, which had the two features mentioned earlier (justiciability and nonnegotiable priority over the good), then in order to implement those rights the state would willy-nilly have to adopt policies that in the end would amount to an assertion of control over their own economies by imposing constraints on global finance capital. Human rights articulated in a global arena, such as the United Nations charter, are simply not justiciable for lack of any serious structures of international governance. The only structure of governance that exists, with articulated constitutions and the requisite judicial and executive authority to implement rights, is on the site of the nation. It is hardly surprising, then, that, as Moyn has shown, the *global* human rights movement was entirely compatible with the form of imperialism that neoliberalism exemplifies. In the neoliberal period the global mobility of capital that its financialization has wrought weakens the states of countries like India and prevents them from pursuing policies that uplift the conditions of life of their working populations. Under neoliberalism these policies, which would necessarily have to put constraints on capital, are hostage to the constant anxiety that capital will find these constraints intolerable, and, given its newfound global mobility, it will move to other parts of the world which have not imposed the same constraints. For considerations such as these (and also familiar counterpart considerations having to do with trade in the neoliberal period), countries like India are helpless while linked to the global economy. Delinking from the global economy is the only form of resistance to the hegemony of finance capital, and setting up a constitutional regime of economic rights with the two features I mentioned earlier is the first substantial step in such resistance. In a word, in the current period of neoliberalism, economic rights on the site of the nation and delinking from the global economy to gain greater national sovereignty are *of a piece*.

The *full* extent to which they are of a piece, however, comes into view only if we understand another ineliminable aspect of capitalism that Patnaik has emphasized in his analysis and, once we do, we will be in a position to conclude this essay by specifying a third feature of rights which we left unspecified in the earlier discussion. This third feature, though it is a feature of all rights, not just economic rights, has a particularly vivid point and significance for economic rights, once we grasp this ineliminable aspect of capitalism.

Borrowing an expression of Oskar Lange, Patnaik characterizes capital as possessed of certain "spontaneous tendencies," a prominent one of which is that *capital, by its very nature, is disposed to undermine all constraints that are put on it, rendering all such constraints unstable and impermanent.* Thus, under capitalism, human subjects do not have a certain kind of freedom, the freedom to impose permanent and stable constraints on capital. The undermining of the constraints that were imposed during what I called the period of "hiatus" after the Second World War is just one prominent example of this tendency. But the tendency is in general everywhere detectable on the surface of politics, as we well know, when governments that pursue social democratic policies (that require imposing constraints on capital) are never able to do so with much stability, even in the Scandinavian countries, and are constantly susceptible to being undermined and overthrown because such constraints are simply not tolerable, from the point of view of capital, given its built-in spontaneous tendencies. From this, Patnaik draws an interesting theoretical conclusion.

Given such tendencies, any effort to oppose capitalism is left with a disjunction. *Either* you transcend capitalism *or* capitalism will undermine the constraints you try to impose on it. To put it in terms of freedom and determinism, we, as human subjects in the modern period with its unique economic formation, are determined in the sense that we cannot (we are not free to) constrain that formation, but we are also *free* to *transcend* the formation. It is just *within* capitalism that we are determined and are not free to constrain it.

This leaves one with the question about how this transcendence is to be achieved. As the discussion earlier of Marx and Hobsbawm makes clear, we are not in an "Age of Revolution," so, realistically speaking, a revolutionary transformation to another economic formation—such as socialism, say—is not in the cards. What options remain, then?

Patnaik himself does not answer this question in very detailed or elaborate terms. What he does say, though, is certainly in the right direction. He submits that one should *continue* to put constraints on capital and then, rather than leave things there (since, given his analysis of capital, we know that they will be sooner or later undermined), we should *"build on them recursively"* (those are his own words) until eventually capital is transcended. He does not specify what the further recursive steps would be because, as he says, they will depend on and be dictated by the contingent forms the crises and dysfunctionalities the constraints on capital will bring about, the exact nature of which cannot be predicted.

Though this is, as I said, a good schematic statement of the general direction of the answer to our overall question (the question, what options remain if the prospects of a revolution are nil?), an unanswered, indeed unasked, more specific question is: Even if the further recursive steps cannot be predicted, what should the *initial constraint* or constraints on capital be, on which the recursive steps must build? One should be able to specify these with some minimal theoretical description since we already have his analysis of capitalism in hand. What, then, is that significant minimal description? Clearly, the initial constraint will have to be carefully chosen so that it *addresses the central claim of his analysis of capitalism.* That means that one must seek to put a constraint on capital, which, *by its very nature,* confronts *explicitly and directly* the spontaneous tendency of capital to undermine constraints placed upon it. Previous constraints on capital were not constructed with a full awareness of the disjunction mentioned earlier, they were not constructed with a full awareness of the spontaneous tendency of capital to not tolerate constraints placed upon it. But if a constraint *is* constructed with such a full awareness (and I will say more about this constraint in a moment), it *would* address that tendency directly and explicitly and may therefore possess a *relative* stability, not hitherto present in other constraints that have been placed on capital in the past. This in turn will allow scope (even as we know that the constraints are not going to be allowed to be permanent) to do what Patnaik thinks should next be done—recursively build on this initial constraint in the future until capitalism is transcended. And even if, as he says, these *further* recursive constraining steps that build on this initial constraint cannot be specified at the outset because the dysfunctionality and crisis that will be generated within capitalism by the imposing of this initial constraint cannot be predicted, one can nevertheless, if one chooses the *first* constraint along the theoretical lines I have just mentioned, be sure that *it will* generate a crisis and dysfunctionality. This is because, on the one hand, as Patnaik has pointed out, capital will not cease in its tendency to try to undermine the constraint and, on the other hand, the constraint in question (by its very nature, as I said) explicitly and directly addresses this tendency since it is self-consciously constructed with full awareness of the susceptibility of constraints on capital to being undermined. This, then, would be an unprecedented confrontation in the history of capital, creating conditions for a chronic crisis and dysfunctionality, which, although we cannot predict their exact nature, will be fertile ground for recursively strengthening this initial constraint with whatever future constraining steps those conditions of crisis and dysfunctionality will demand, until such point as transcendence from capital emerges as a serious possibility.

We have arrived at a crux point in the dialectic of this chapter and must ask: What kind of initial constraint is dictated when it is theoretically conceived as self-consciously addressing an innate spontaneous tendency of capital to undermine constraints upon it?

It will come as no surprise that its underlying nature is to be found in the insertion of economic rights in the constitution since I have already said that it is this insertion that will force nation-states to recover sovereignty over their own economies by imposing necessary constraints on capital. (I say "force" because these economic rights will not be implementable—justiciable—if capital is not constrained.) But what exactly is it about economic rights that speak to the very specific nature that this initial constraint is supposed to have that distinguishes it from all previous constraints put on capital, namely, that it is a constraint constructed out of a self-conscious awareness of the spontaneous tendencies of capital to undermine constraints put upon it and that, as a constraint, it contains properties that explicitly and directly address that tendency and oppose it. What about economic rights speak to *this theoretical desideratum?*

It is to answer this crucial question that we need to introduce a third—relatively neglected—defining feature of rights, which I have so far suppressed.

5. What are rights? A third feature

Apart from the two features of rights that we had outlined earlier (priority over the good, and justiciability), rights, properly so called, possess a third defining feature that I will call the "Ulysses and the Sirens" feature.[21]

Ulysses, at a crucial moment in his travels, had tied himself to the mast because he was deeply and fundamentally committed to the value of marital fidelity (in his case, fidelity to Penelope), and he was concerned, knowing himself, that he might weaken and be seduced when the sirens sang their song. The idea is that even when he is weakened and seduced and no longer values fidelity, he is living by the value of fidelity. Commitments of this sort are, thus, relativized to times. At time t_1, a commitment to a value has the "Ulysses and the Sirens" feature if, those who have the commitment, knowing that they might weaken at some future time t_n and might cease to be committed to the value, arrange at t_1 to entrench the commitment to that value in such a way that they are living by it at t_n, even when they have weakened and ceased to be committed to it at t_n.

When we elevate some values to rights, properly so called, we entrench the value and our commitment to it in constitutions in just this way. Take the fundamental right to free speech in many constitutions. Apart from putting a constraint on various pursuits of the good in the way described earlier, and apart from its justiciability, making the value of free speech a fundamental right also amounts to saying that if at some point in the future, we find ourselves very upset by some offensive form of speech and allow those hurt feelings to weaken our commitment to free speech and demand that the speaker or writer to be censored, our demand should not and would not be indulged. By making the value of free speech a right, we have tied ourselves to the mast with it, and this future weakening and demand for censorship by us is thus going to be denied.

Similarly, if economic rights are rights, properly so called, we will tie ourselves to the mast with them and will resist all tendencies to undermine them, because of a fundamental constitutional commitment to them in this "Ulysses and the Sirens" form. *This feature of rights, then, explicitly and directly speaks to and resists what Patnaik calls "the spontaneous tendencies" of capital.* If the effect of implementing economic rights in a particular nation-state like India will inevitably require the state to impose certain constraints on capital (for instance, to name just two, raising taxes on corporations and wealth and inheritance and imposing capital controls to prevent capital flight that would otherwise ensue), and if, moreover, the economic rights are understood as having the "Ulysses and the Sirens"–like structure, then this *latter* feature of rights will necessarily amount to a more stable and sustained resistance against the spontaneous tendencies of capital to undermine the constraints placed upon it. Thus, economic rights (so understood as possessing this third feature) bestow on these constraints on capital that are required for their implementation, just the property that ought to be the first step in a recursive process of strengthening the constraints on capital till such time as capital might be transcended. If the tendencies of capital are to constantly destabilize constraints upon it, and if tying oneself to the mast with something, whose implementation require, *as a result of being so tied*, those very constraints on capital *to be more stable than they have hitherto been*, we are set on a path which holds real possibilities for the recursive process that Patnaik's account envisages.

Various questions of detail remain.

Some will be general questions about the consequences of delinking from the global economy. One such is whether the envisaged delinking will not impose its own great hardships on the Indian economy. Patnaik's writings consider this issue in detail, warning against caving in to the punitive responses that global finance is bound to make and making detailed proposals about how to address the hardships. What should be added is that the populations of nations of the south, which have undertaken such a delinking, must be persuaded to stay the course, despite the initial hardships that will follow upon delinking. This would mean a constant campaign of public education that would apprise them of the temporary nature of such hardships and of the mid- and long-term efficacy of the proposals to address them.

Another question will be whether the economies of some nation-states of the South will not be too small to survive such a delinking, and Patnaik addresses this too, though only briefly, by suggesting that there be South–South links whereby a system of cooperation between larger and smaller economies of the South will emerge.

A third question, an anxiety really, about delinking is that it is a form of nationalism and nationalism is associated with a reversion to aggressive, narrow-minded ideologies, often driven by ethnic pride or religious bigotry, and often characterized by autarchic concentrations of power. Even Yannis Varoufakis, the radical economist and cabinet minister who walked out of the Greek government because it would not resist the domination of the banking elites set up in Brussels, refused delinking from Europe and a common currency as an option, saying he did not believe in autarchy. This anxiety is based on a fundamental confusion. There is no rational ground to conflate a delinking of the form that Patnaik is suggesting with nationalisms characterized along these lines, nor even any reason to think that they will generate such nationalisms. Indeed, there is good reason to think that delinking will, after an initial period of hardship, result in the upliftment of the conditions of the poorest sections of the working population of nations, a result that is likely to diminish their tendency to embrace the aggressive forms of nationalisms that prompt these anxieties. There is much more reason, in fact, to expect (as recent developments all over the world have manifestly shown) that if there is no delinking, and neoliberalism and hegemonic finance continues to hold sway, that working people suffering under its policies will have nothing else to turn to than nationalism of this anxiety-inducing form.

Other questions will be more immediately connected with the idea of economic rights. For instance, how can a country like India afford to adopt and implement these economic rights? This is an obvious question and without an answer to it, the feature of justiciability of these rights is going to ring hollow. Patnaik considers the question of affordability in careful detail, makes highly specific assessments of the public expenditures entailed and how they will be provided for—in particular, what percentage of the GDP will be tapped by the extra expenditure entailed by introducing economic rights, and which segments of the population and which institutions will be targeted for taxation and for how much. Such details apart, at a more philosophical level it seems at first sight that these questions arise only for economic rights and not for the other rights of personal liberty and freedom we discussed in our foundational discussion earlier in the chapter. The rights of liberty are to a large extent rights of *noninterference* and thus negatively formulated rights. By contrast, economic rights are more positively formulated as entailing *provisions* to the nation's citizens. For citizens to be left alone from interference, no questions seem to be raised about whether a state can afford their implementability. But when it comes to feeding and sheltering and sustaining the health of citizens, all sorts of issues arise because doing these things requires food to be grown, houses to be constructed, hospitals to be set up, doctors to be trained. . . . So it must be granted that the rights of liberty, unlike economic rights, seem to be rights that don't bring out immediately the extent to which individual citizens are embedded in contexts of social production and distribution. But this seeming difference is only a matter of degree. In fact, a very substantial regulatory force of policing and protection is involved in seeking to guarantee the rights of liberty. Just consider the enormous numbers of a police force that may have to protect publicly made speech that is controversial and generates conflict within a population; or consider the vast amount of public expenditure by the government of the United Kingdom, which, in order to implement its free speech rights, gave Salman Rushdie twenty-four-hour police protection for years following the threats he received in the aftermath of the publication of *The Satanic Verses*. The implementation of *all* rights (the rights of liberty and economic rights) reflect to some (if varying) degree the fact that citizens are embedded in infrastructures of regulation, production, distribution, and so on. Rights may owe their foundations to our fundamental nature as human beings, but rights are not implemented for human beings in a state of nature, they are implemented for human beings in these highly embedded social, political, and economic contexts.

A final question is about the third feature of rights, which I have named the "Ulysses and the Sirens" feature. What exactly does it mean to tie oneself to the mast with a right? It cannot, of course, be that masts—at least as understood in the constitutional context of rights—can simply *never* be untied. But even if that is so, the idea, in general, is that to the extent that one thinks these rights are fundamental rights and are to be deeply entrenched, then to that extent at least, one must make it as difficult as possible to undermine them. All sorts of detailed suggestions can be made regarding this entrenchment that I cannot possibly elaborate here in a chapter that is already too long. But I will say this. No routine form of what often passes for "judicial review" will suffice for such entrenchment. What may be required, if economic rights are going to be central to the initial set of constraints that will amount to a sustained resistance against the tendencies of capital, is a clear understanding that they will not be amended in their *basic structure* as commitments (even if they are periodically updated in the *detail* to adjust to changing contexts of needs) by anything more expedient than deliberations carried out after a re-formation of a constituent assembly of the sort that initially debated and then formulated the Indian constitution. That is how seriously we have to take fundamental rights.[22] That is what distinguishes them both from policies and from the variable forms of pursuit of the good.

6. Concluding remarks

This chapter, resisting current developments in political and legal theory (primarily critical race theory and critical legal theory), has proceeded on the assumption that rights are a necessary element of any rational understanding of a political framework for our time. Such an assumption equally stands in contrast with the overly idealistic political outlook that puts faith in the moral judgment of citizens to construct not just a theory of the common good but to put that theory into practice, without any framework of rights (possessing the three features I have outlined in the foregoing pages) that would, in some fundamental spheres of human life, *make* citizens and the institutions of governance they adopt do certain things and *prevent* them from doing other things. Policies and routine laws devised by the executive and legislative institutions of governance do not possess these three features and therefore cannot be counted on to be the deep commitments that will do the sort of "making" and "preventing" that rights are intended for. At the same time, as the expression "fundamental spheres" that I have just used makes clear, this chapter has been careful to restrict the scope of rights to only those things that can get a foundational grounding in considerations of the most basic aspects of human nature. Rights cannot be proliferated (except as merely aspirational rhetoric and gestural, heuristic, principles) at the will of citizens. Rights are firm commitments, but they are *few* because they are chosen with the utmost rigor and care in such foundational discussion, some of which I have briefly presented.

It has been a central concern of this chapter to include among these few and carefully chosen and defended rights, a range of economic rights. The extended discussion that sought to justify this inclusion had to situate economic rights in a foundational discussion, which inevitably led to detailed comparisons of the foundations of such rights with the foundations of the rights to liberty. But even if economic rights were foundationally grounded along the lines this discussion brought out, the relevance of such rights for the political economy of our times does not come into view until we situate these rights further in an analysis of capitalism, one systematic example of which is provided by Prabhat Patnaik himself. This chapter briefly expounded that analysis and found, as a result, first that economic rights only get to have any bite in our time if they are inserted into the constitutions of *particular nations*, and second that they can address the economic obstacles that capital constantly and effectively places in the path of the pursuit of the common good, if we stress a *third* defining feature of rights that has been relatively neglected in the discussion of the meaning of rights.

One recurring concern of this chapter has been to try to diagnose why the rights surrounding liberty have received so much more foundational attention and discussion than economic rights. I have discussed at considerable length the factors that might lie behind this neglect of such a significant set of rights that speak to such fundamental aspects of human life and existence. That discussion raised a very wide range of issues. But one issue—perhaps the most obvious one—was not discussed earlier because its significance is manifest only once we have an analysis of capitalism, which we did not have at that stage of the chapter. So let me conclude, then, with just one or two very brief remarks about it. I can do no better than to approach the issue by relating a conversation that I had with Ronald Dworkin. Quite some years ago, Dworkin had given the Dewey Lectures at Columbia University on the subject of equality, in which he had made an elaborate case for a view of equality that stressed what he called "equality of resources." I had chaired the last of the three lectures and was expected to raise the first question to break the ice and get a public conversation going. I asked him about why he had not mentioned the possibility that economic rights might be a first step in the direction of achieving greater equality. His answer came immediately, almost unreflectively, but it is obvious that he had long reflected on the subject. He said rights are rights only if they can be guaranteed to be implemented. Economic rights, he added, cannot be guaranteed to be implemented, so we should pursue them not as rights but as social welfare policies, to which he, as a liberal with social democratic commitments, was certainly committed.

Dworkin, however, did not pause to consider what was being presupposed by his avowed reason for excluding economic rights from rights proper. I believe that if we consider the relation between Dworkin's remark and the analysis given by Patnaik of the political economy of our time, it becomes quite clear that Dworkin's reason for saying that they should be the target of policies and not rights implicitly presupposes that liberal democratic polities are always to be situated in a capitalist political economy, and it is precisely in a capitalist economy that they are not implementable.

This then presents us with a choice: *either* restrict the goal of fulfilment of basic needs to social welfare policies that, in effect, require putting constraints on capital *or* attempt—via the recursive strategy that includes adopting economic rights, outlined in the last few pages—to transcend capitalism. Dworkin opts for the first, Patnaik for the second. Some wag, perhaps it was none other and none less, than G. E. Moore, once said, "One man's modus ponens is another man's modus tollens." The relation between Dworkin's view and Patnaik's view does not quite fit this snowclone—because it is not a premise, but a background presupposition or assumption of Dworkin's that Patnaik is rejecting—but it is a close enough cousin of it.

Patnaik does not discuss the foundations of economic rights in much detail, and to the extent that he does in the work I have cited, he grounds them in the idea of democracy. I find this does not help as much as he thinks it does because notions of democracy are very variable and very contested, while the foundations we need for rights need to be much less variable and contested if they are going to justify adopting commitments with the three features I have said are defining of rights. That is why in probing their foundations I have appealed to considerations that go to the most fundamental aspects of human nature, which are uniform among human beings and cannot be contested. But the strength of his discussion really lies in the fact that, unlike the philosophers who have discussed it foundationally, he motivates his proposal for economic rights, both in principle and in detail, within a deep and persuasive analysis of capitalism. A crucial element in that analysis is a disjunction, which I presented earlier. This disjunction has obvious bearing on the options, just mentioned, that are thrown up by a consideration of Dworkin's remarks. To repeat, the disjunction that Patnaik's analysis leads to is: *either* you transcend capitalism *or* capitalism will undermine the constraints you try to impose on it. To repeat, the options that Dworkin's remarks lead to are: *either* restrict the goal of fulfilment of basic needs to social welfare policies that in effect require putting constraints on capital *or* attempt—via the recursive strategy elaborated some pages ago—to transcend capitalism. The second of Patnaik's two disjuncts reveals exactly why one should not take the first of the two options that a consideration of Dworkin's account throws up.

All of this reveals a point of the utmost significance: unless one situates the discussion of economic rights in a sound analysis of contemporary capitalism, as Patnaik does (but much recent discussion, whether it is by Dworkin or Sen or Moyn, does not), one will not find the really persuasive reasons for adopting economic rights, and one will have no answer to those (the very same gentlemen mentioned in the last parenthesis) who have expressed one or other sort of skepticism about economic rights and the foundational basis for them. At the same time, ironically, though not altogether surprisingly, it is precisely such an analysis of capitalism that satisfactorily addresses the other familiar quarter where skepticism about economic rights is most prevalent, those on the radical Left who view Marx's historically contextual dismissive remarks about rights to be everlasting truths.

PART III

SOCIETY AND LAW

CHAPTER 7

ROE V. WADE

Freedom of the Woman Versus Freedom of the Fetus

GEOFFREY R. STONE

The Supreme Court's 1973 decision in *Roe v. Wade* presents a particularly vivid example of the sort of unfreedom that this volume is concerned with—the impoverishment of a citizen's options or choices. It raises the question whether a woman should have the freedom to choose whether to remain pregnant, or whether she should be compelled to carry an unwanted pregnancy to term. Those who have supported the landmark decision in *Roe* view their opponents as impoverishing the options of women. Those who have opposed the decision have implicitly viewed fetuses as potential citizens, possessing (potential) options that the decision in *Roe* has impoverished. This is a dispute that has sharply divided our nation. Indeed, for five decades, it has been one of the most bitterly divisive issues in American politics.

Opponents of *Roe* maintain that in that decision the Supreme Court invented a constitutional right out of whole cloth, without any legitimate justification. Supporters of *Roe* maintain that it was a perfectly sound decision that correctly recognized a fundamental constitutional right of the woman. Whether one agrees or disagrees with *Roe*, contemporary understandings of the decision and of its historical origins are often confused and incomplete. The story of how we got to *Roe* is important to remember, for it gives both content and context to the ever more divisive debates of the present and to the Court's 2022 decision in *Dobbs v. Jackson Women's Health Organization*, which overruled *Roe*.

I

So, let us begin at the beginning. At the time our Constitution was drafted, abortion was often relied upon by single and widowed women to avoid the consequences of illegitimate births. In that era, contrary to what many people today assume, abortion before quickening, that is, before the point at which the woman could feel movement—usually at around four and a half months—was perfectly legal. Indeed, this had been the unbroken state of the law at least as far back as the ancient Greeks. The ancient Hippocratic treatise *Diseases of Women*, for example, recommended a number of abortifacients, Plato commended abortion as an important means of ensuring population stability, and Aristotle advocated abortion, as long as it occurred prior to quickening.[1]

Although the Church in the Middle Ages condemned abortion as a sin, the law did not treat abortion as a crime. To the contrary, those who did not share the faith were free to do as they wished. Abortion was also common—and legal—in England in the years leading up to the American Revolution. As Lady Caroline Fox wrote her husband in the 1740s upon learning that she was pregnant for the third time in as many years, "I'm certainly breeding. I took a great deal of physic yesterday in hopes to send it away." Soon thereafter she wrote her husband that she had been successful, noting, "Is not that clever?" At this time, a wide variety of "female pills" were readily available in London shops for the purpose of inducing abortion.[2]

The American colonies embraced the same approach to abortion as the English common law, and abortion before quickening was both common and legal. Moreover, even abortion after quickening was almost never punished, and this was the state of the law at the time the Constitution was adopted. Over the course of the nineteenth century, abortion became ever more common. This was evident in the fact that the birth rate in the United States fell dramatically from 1800 to 1900. In the colonial era the average family had nine children. By 1900 that number was only three. The reason for this change was clear. In the agrarian world of the eighteenth century, children were an important economic asset; but by the end of the nineteenth century, with greater urbanization, children were increasingly seen as a financial burden that could cause a family's economic ruin. Thus, for most families, birth control had become essential, and because contraception was generally unreliable, abortion was seen a critical way of managing family size.[3]

Indeed, by the middle of the nineteenth century, approximately 20 percent of all pregnancies ended in abortion. At this time, abortifacients were readily available from mail-order firms and pharmacists; daily newspapers regularly ran ads for abortifacients; and those who provided abortion services did so quite openly. The flamboyant Ann Lohman Restell of New York, for example, who was popularly known as "Madame Restell," maintained a highly profitable abortion business serving a genteel middle- and upper-class clientele. She touted her "celebrated powers for married ladies," and, like many of her competitors, she broadly advertised her services in the penny press of the day. Here is an example of one her widely distributed advertisements:

> To married women: Is it but too well known that the families of the married often increase beyond what the happiness of those who give them birth would dictate? In how many instances does the hard-working father, and more especially the mother, of a poor family remain slaves throughout their lives, urging at the oar of incessant labor, toiling to live, living but to toil. . . . Is it desirable, then . . . for parents to increase their families, regardless of consequences to themselves, or the well-being of their offspring, when a simple, easy, healthy, and certain remedy is within our control?[4]

The general acceptance of abortion as an appropriate method of managing family size began to change, however, in the latter part of the nineteenth century. Two factors in particular contributed to this shift. First, religious perspectives on abortion began to change during the evangelical explosion of the Second Great Awakening. The traditional Protestant conception of the fetus assumed that it was not a human life until the point of quickening. Abandoning that view, evangelicals during the Second Great Awakening began to preach that a separate, distinct, and precious life came into being at the very moment of conception.

Second, medical professionals in this era increasingly came to the view, based partly on religion and partly on half-baked science, that human life begins at conception. A professor at the University of Pennsylvania Medical School, for example, published a pamphlet in which he confidently asserted that newly conceived embryos could think and perceive right and wrong, and in the late 1850s the Boston doctor and religious moralist Horatio Storer initiated a concerted "Physicians Crusade Against Abortion." Storer decried the growing frequency of abortion and maintained that the primary cause of this phenomenon was the "general demoralization" of women and "wide-spread . . . ignorance of the true character" of abortion. Storer insisted that many women who have an abortion "become confirmed invalids" and develop "serious and often fatal organic disease." He added that some women who have an abortion die, either immediately or shortly thereafter, as a result of "moral shock from the very thought" of what they have done, while many others are driven to insanity. Storer charged that children born to a woman after she has had an abortion are often "deformed or diseased," and that they too therefore bear the burden of their mother's "heinous" act. Storer emphatically rejected the notion that a woman should decide this question for herself because, he explained, during pregnancy a "woman's mind is prone to . . . derangement."

As a result of Storer's campaign, in 1859 the newly founded American Medical Association adopted a resolution condemning abortion "at every stage of gestation," except when necessary to save the life of the woman. Over the next several decades, the AMA, working hand-in-hand with religious moralists during the late nineteenth century's "social purity" movement, launched an aggressive and successful campaign to rid the nation not only of abortion but of contraception as well. As the leading voices of this movement explained, the sole purpose of women is to "produce children," and women must therefore remain within their "God-given sphere."[5]

By the end of the nineteenth century, in a complete reversal of the world of the Framers, every state had enacted legislation prohibiting the distribution of any product designed for purposes of contraception, and every state had enacted legislation prohibiting abortion at *any* stage of pregnancy, unless a doctor certified that the abortion was necessary to save the life of the woman. Thus, for the first time in Western history, abortion was unlawful even before quickening, and women who sought abortions were now themselves subject to prosecution. Opponents of birth control insisted that the issue was simple: "If a woman didn't want to get pregnant, then she shouldn't do anything that might get her pregnant." It was as simple as that.

But despite the threat of criminal sanctions, the medical profession's often perverse warnings about the dangers of abortion, and the preaching of religious moralists, women in the late nineteenth century continued to seek abortions in record numbers. Indeed, by the turn of the twentieth century, approximately two million women had illegal abortions each year, and almost a third of all pregnancies ended in abortion. Now, though, for the first time in history, these abortions had to be performed illegally, in secret and unsafe circumstances, and by much less reliable practitioners than in the past.[6]

By the 1950s, with improvements in contraception, which was now increasingly but still not universally legal, the number of unwanted pregnancies gradually declined. But even then, approximately one million women each year resorted to illegal abortions. The vast majority of these women continued to turn either to self-induced abortion or to the dark and often forbidding world of "back-alley" abortions. Women who resorted to self-induced abortion typically relied on such methods as throwing themselves down a flight of stairs, or ingesting, douching with, or inserting into themselves a chilling variety of chemicals and toxins ranging from bleach to turpentine to gunpowder. Knitting needles, crochet hooks, scissors, and coat hangers were among the tools most commonly used by women who attempted to self-abort.

Approximately 30 percent of all illegal abortions at this time were self-induced. Women who sought abortions from "back-alley" abortionists encountered similar horrors. To find someone to perform an illegal abortion, women often had to rely on tips from elevator operators, taxi cab drivers, salesmen, and the like. Because of the clandestine nature of illegal abortions, the very process of finding an abortionist was dangerous and terrifying. Women who sought "back-alley" abortions were often blindfolded, driven to remote areas, and passed off to people they did not know and could not even see during the entire process. Such abortions were performed not only in secret offices and hotel rooms but also in dank bathrooms, in the backseats of cars, and, literally, in "back alleys." The vast majority of these abortions were performed either by persons with limited medical training or by rank amateurs, including elevator operators, prostitutes, barbers, and unskilled laborers.

In the 1960s an average of more than two hundred women died each year as a result of botched illegal abortions. In addition to those who died in the course of illegal abortions, many thousands more suffered serious illness or injury. The stories of women who suffered through this nightmare are legion. One woman recalled how a fellow college student who had had an illegal abortion was too frightened to tell anyone what she had done. She locked herself in the bathroom in her dorm and quietly bled to death. In another incident, twenty-eight-year-old Geraldine Santoro bled to death on the floor of a Connecticut hotel room after she and her former lover attempted an abortion on their own. The former lover, who had no medical experience, used a textbook and some borrowed tools. When things went terribly wrong, he fled the scene, and Santoro died alone.[7]

The occasional visibility of such incidents led some religious organizations that had previously been silent on abortion to address the issue more directly. Protestant churches varied in their opinions. The United Methodist Church, for example, acknowledged "the sanctity of unborn human life" but nonetheless proclaimed that because "we are equally bound to respect the sacredness of the life and well-being of the woman, for whom devastating damage may result from an unacceptable pregnancy," its leaders "support the removal of abortion from the criminal code." Similarly, in 1968, the American Baptist Convention came to the conclusion that abortion should be a matter of "responsible personal decision."[8]

The Catholic Church, on the other hand, insisted that abortion was always and unequivocally forbidden, even when necessary to save the life of the woman. This led the politics of abortion to play out in interesting ways. Because Catholics had traditionally identified with the Democratic Party, and because Catholics were more likely than others to oppose abortion, Republicans at this time were more "pro-abortion" than Democrats. Although we often forget this fact, it is interesting to recall that 59 percent of Democrats and 68 percent of Republicans in early 1972 thought that "the decision to have an abortion should be made solely by a woman and her physician." Indeed,

Republican politicians spearheaded some of the earliest efforts to liberalize abortion laws. Barry Goldwater, for example, one of the Republican party's conservative icons, supported abortion rights, and in 1967 California Governor Ronald Reagan signed a bill liberalizing that state's abortion laws. But because of other, more liberal elements in the Democratic Party, the Democratic Party itself was officially more pro-abortion than the Republicans.

Seeing an opportunity to draw disaffected Catholic voters away from the Democrats, Republican leaders began to move toward a more anti-abortion stance. They knew that, if they could succeed in this effort, they could bring about a profound shift in American politics. This strategy was clearly evident in President Richard Nixon's policies during the 1972 election. With a clear sense of the political ramifications of the abortion issue, Nixon embraced an anti-abortion stance in a strategic effort to draw Catholics into the Republican camp. Nixon knew what he was doing. In the 1972 election, large numbers of Catholics who were prepared to cast single-issue votes on the issue of abortion voted Republican for the first time in their lives, helping Nixon win an overwhelming victory in that year's presidential election.[9]

At roughly the same time, though, the rising voice of the women's movement began to shape public discourse on abortion. In February 1969, for example, Betty Friedan, the founding president of the National Organization for Women, delivered a rousing address in Chicago at what was billed as the First National Conference on Abortion Laws. Friedan declared that "there is no freedom, no equality . . . possible for women until we assert and demand the control over our own bodies, over our own reproductive process." At the end of the conference, the participants founded the National Association for Repeal of Abortion Laws (NARAL) on the premise that what was needed was a complete overhaul of America's abortion laws. "Recognizing the basic human right of a woman" to control her own reproduction, NARAL declared that it was "dedicated to the elimination of all laws . . . that would compel a woman to bear a child against her will." Later that year, Planned Parenthood and the American Public Health Association also called for repeal of America's abortion laws and declared abortion to be a fundamental personal right of the woman.[10]

As these organizations moved to the forefront of national debate, the law began to change. In 1970 four states—Hawaii, Alaska, Washington, and New York—legalized abortion in the first trimester, thus restoring the law to more or less what it had been at the time our Constitution was adopted. Opponents of these laws quickly mobilized their forces. Adding fuel to the fire, in early 1972 Congress approved the Equal Rights Amendment and submitted it to the states for ratification. This immediately led religious and conservative activists to tie the issue of abortion to even larger conflicts about the appropriate role of women in American society and to the meaning of "family values." Suddenly, the legislative progress on abortion that had begun only a few years earlier ground to a halt. Despite growing—and clear majority—support for legalizing abortion, no state legislature now acted on that view.

Several factors contributed to this legislative paralysis. The most important was that the initial round of pro-abortion legislative victories energized abortion opponents, and they organized with extraordinary effectiveness. Those opposed to abortion threatened to act as single-issue voters, and they communicated that intention to elected officials with perfect clarity. Legislators knew all too well that, although a substantial majority of citizens supported legalizing abortion, when election day rolled around committed single-issue voters could effectively vote them out of office.[11]

Faced with this sudden paralysis in the legislative arena, pro-choice advocates began for the first time to think about challenging the constitutionality of anti-abortion laws in the courts. Initially this seemed a long shot because, in the words of *New York Times* columnist Linda Greenhouse, the idea of a constitutional right of abortion seemed somewhat "illusory." But with legislative change effectively blocked, the courts now seemed the only realistic alternative.

In 1970, after the Connecticut legislature repeatedly refused to amend its nineteenth-century anti-abortion statute, a group of women activists formed a new organization, Women Versus Connecticut, to challenge the constitutionality of the law. "We want control over our own bodies," they declared. "We are tired of being pressured to have children or not to have children. *It's our decision.*" Six weeks after Women Versus Connecticut filed its complaint in federal court on behalf of 858 women plaintiffs, the federal court held the Connecticut law unconstitutional. Judge Edward Lumbard, a conservative Eisenhower appointee, held that in this law, "Connecticut trespasses unjustifiably on the personal privacy and liberty of its female citizens in violation of the Constitution," and that the state's purported interests in banning abortion "are insufficient to take from the woman the decision . . . that she, as the appropriate decision maker, must be free to choose."[12]

Cases challenging anti-abortion laws now started popping up everywhere. In Georgia, a group of twenty-four plaintiffs, including doctors, nurses, social workers, and members of the clergy, challenged the constitutionality of Georgia's anti-abortion statute. The federal court in Georgia also held the statute unconstitutional, explaining that the constitutional "concept of personal liberty embodies a right to privacy" that is "broad enough to include the decision" to terminate an unwanted pregnancy. At roughly the same time in Texas, Linda Coffee and Sarah Weddington, recent graduates of the University of Texas Law School, teamed up with a plaintiff identified only as "Jane Roe" to challenge the Texas anti-abortion statute. On June 17, 1970, the federal court held that the Texas law violated the "fundamental right" of women to decide for themselves "whether—or not—to have children." What, though, would the Supreme Court do?

II

A year later, the Supreme Court of the United States announced that it would hear the case of *Roe v. Wade*. The Court held the Texas abortion statute unconstitutional by a vote of seven-to-two. In his opinion for the Court, Justice Harry Blackmun began by acknowledging "the sensitive and emotional nature of the abortion controversy" and the "deep and seemingly absolute convictions that the subject inspires." The Court's task, he explained, "is to resolve the issue by constitutional measurement, free of emotion." Blackmun added that to put the issue in its proper context, it was necessary to understand the historical evolution of attitudes toward abortion over the centuries.[13]

Turning to that history, Blackmun observed that the criminalization of abortion was a relatively recent phenomenon. Laws prohibiting the procedure, he explained, were not of ancient origin but derived from legislation in the late nineteenth century. It was thus apparent, he concluded, that "at the time of the adoption of our Constitution, and throughout the major portion of the 19th century, . . . a woman enjoyed a substantially broader right to terminate a pregnancy than she does in most States today."[14]

After reviewing the history of medical views on abortion, Blackmun identified the three arguments that had most often been advanced in the late nineteenth century to justify strict criminal laws against abortion. First, some anti-abortion advocates had insisted that such laws could be justified in terms "of a Victorian social concern to discourage illicit sexual conduct." Blackmun dismissed this justification as plainly inadequate, noting that no legal authority today takes this argument "seriously" as a legitimate justification for banning abortion.[15]

Second, some defenders of restrictive abortion laws had argued that such laws were necessary to protect pregnant women against the temptation to submit to dangerous procedures that might place their lives "in serious jeopardy." Although noting that abortion had indeed been risky prior to the "development of antisepsis," Blackmun emphasized that modern medical techniques had clearly altered this situation and that by 1973 it was well established that abortion prior to the end of the first trimester was generally a very safe procedure. At the same time, though, Blackmun noted that states have a legitimate interest in ensuring that abortion, like any other medical procedure, is performed under appropriate circumstances. He therefore concluded that states retain an interest in protecting the woman's own health and safety when an abortion is proposed "at a late stage of pregnancy," when the medical risks to the woman are potentially greater.[16]

Third, Blackmun noted that some defenders of anti-abortion laws had argued that such laws were necessary to protect the lives of unborn children. Without attempting to resolve the question of when human life begins, Blackmun acknowledged that the government has a legitimate interest at stake when "at least *potential* life is involved."[17]

Having thus laid out the state interests in regulating abortion, Blackmun turned next to identifying the constitutional interests on the other side. Although noting that the Constitution does not explicitly enumerate a right to privacy, Blackmun pointed out that, in a line of decisions going back to the 1890s, the Court had repeatedly recognized that "a right of personal privacy" exists under the Constitution.[18] As examples, Blackmun cited a long list of decisions, including *Skinner v. Oklahoma*, in which the Court had recognized a fundamental right not to be sterilized; *Stanley v. Georgia*, in which the Court had recognized a fundamental right to possess obscenity in the privacy of the home; *Griswold v. Connecticut*, in which the Court had recognized a fundamental right of married couples to use contraceptives; *Loving v. Virginia*, in which the Court had recognized a fundamental right to marry; and *Eisenstadt v. Baird*, in which the Court had recognized a fundamental right of individuals to decide for themselves "whether to bear or beget a child."[19]

"This right of privacy," Blackmun maintained, whether grounded in the Ninth Amendment or in the due process clause, "is broad enough to encompass a woman's decision whether or not to terminate her pregnancy." Blackmun explained that the harm that a state inflicts upon a woman when it denies her this choice is obvious:

> Specific and direct harm medically diagnosable even in early pregnancy may be involved. Maternity, or additional offspring, may force upon the woman a distressful life and future. Psychological harm may be imminent. Mental and physical health may be taxed by child care. There is also the distress, for all concerned, associated with the unwanted child, and there is the problem of bringing a child into a family already unable, psychologically and otherwise, to care for it. In other cases, as in this one, the additional difficulties and continuing stigma of unwed motherhood may be involved.[20]

On the other hand, Blackmun made clear that recognizing the existence of a right does not mean that the right is "absolute." Rather, as with other constitutional rights, there are circumstances when the right of privacy might be regulated, consistent with the Constitution, in the face of compelling government interests. Turning specifically to the regulation of abortion, Blackmun declared that in at least some circumstances, the government's interests "in safeguarding health, in maintaining medical standards, and in protecting potential life" might be "sufficiently compelling" to justify restrictions on a woman's right to terminate an unwanted pregnancy. The next question, of course, was which, if any, of the state's asserted interests in regulating abortion met that standard.[21]

In defense of its absolute prohibition on abortion except when necessary to save the life of the woman, Texas maintained that human life begins at conception and that its interest in preserving the life of unborn children was sufficiently compelling to override any constitutional right of the woman. Blackmun rejected this argument. Noting that even "those trained in the respective disciplines of medicine, philosophy, and theology are unable to arrive at any consensus" on the profound religious, moral, and scientific question of when human life begins, Blackmun reasoned that neither the state of Texas nor the Supreme Court is "in a position to speculate as to the answer." In such circumstances, he concluded, the state, by merely asserting "one theory of life," cannot declare a purported interest to be "compelling" in order to set aside "the rights of the pregnant woman."[22]

Blackmun turned next to the government's interest in regulating abortion to protect the health of the woman. Although recognizing that this interest is clearly legitimate, Blackmun held that it becomes "compelling" only at the end of the first trimester. This was so, he explained, because until that point abortion was now a relatively safe and simple medical procedure—safer even than childbirth. Thus, during the first trimester the woman and her attending physician must be free to decide, without government interference, whether the pregnancy should be terminated.

Blackmun also held, however, that after the first trimester, as the possible health risks to the woman increase, the government can *reasonably* regulate the abortion procedure in order to protect the woman's health. He noted, for example, that after this point in a pregnancy the state can reasonably regulate such matters as the qualifications of those who are authorized to perform an abortion and the types of facilities in which an abortion may be performed.

Blackmun finally turned to the government's interest in protecting "potential life." This interest, he concluded, becomes compelling at the point of fetal viability. Blackmun explained that this made sense because, at this stage in a pregnancy, the fetus has the ability to live "outside the mother's womb," and the government can therefore protect fetal life at that point without intruding on the right of the woman not to be pregnant. Blackmun emphasized, however, that even after this point in pregnancy the government cannot constitutionally forbid a woman to have an abortion if the procedure "is necessary to preserve the life or health" of the woman.[23]

Justice Byron White, joined by Justice William Rehnquist, dissented. In a brief opinion, White, who was generally quite conservative on such issues as obscenity, contraception, and abortion, maintained that the Court was simply making up "a new constitutional right for pregnant mothers," insisting that, in an area as "sensitive" as abortion, the matter "should be left [to] the political processes the people have devised to govern their affairs."[24]

III

Many Americans today think of *Roe v. Wade* as a radical, left-wing decision, but that was not at all the view at the time. By 1973 a substantial majority of Americans supported the right of a woman to decide for herself whether to remain pregnant, and Gallup polls showed that "two out of three Americans think abortion should be a matter for decision solely between a woman and her physician." Moreover, as we have seen, the lower courts were already moving sharply in a direction that anticipated the decision in *Roe*. Moreover, three of the four justices appointed to the Court by Richard Nixon, who had dedicated himself to appointing "conservative" justices, joined the decision. Indeed, without their support, *Roe* would have come out the other way. That Warren Burger, Harry Blackmun, and Lewis Powell joined the decision in *Roe* speaks volumes about the mainstream nature of the decision. Indeed, five of the six Republican appointed justices on the Court when *Roe* was decided voted to recognize a woman's constitutional right to terminate an unwanted pregnancy.

The plain and simple fact is that, at the time *Roe* was decided, the justices did not view the abortion issue as posing a particularly divisive *ideological* question. Although the justices certainly understood the stakes, none of them imagined that *Roe* would later come to be a central flashpoint of American politics. This understanding of *Roe* is consistent with both the news coverage and the public reaction at the time. Because Lyndon Johnson died on the same day that the Court announced its decision in *Roe*, newspapers, magazines, and news shows treated *Roe* as only a secondary headline. *U.S. News & World Report*, for example, did not even mention *Roe* on the front page of that week's issue. As the editors observed forty years later, "the far-reaching effects of the decision simply weren't evident at the time." This view is also consistent with the editorials and commentary about *Roe*, which were overwhelmingly approving. Even newspapers in traditionally conservative states took this view. The *Atlanta Constitution*, for example, characterized the decision as "realistic and appropriate," the *Houston Chronicle* called it "sound," and the *San Antonio Light* gushed that although the ruling was "not perfect . . . it was as close to it as humanly possible."

Moreover, the American people clearly endorsed the decision. In polls taken at the time, only 41 percent of Americans disapproved of the Court's decision. To put that in perspective, it is useful to compare the public's reaction to *Roe* with its reaction to other more controversial decisions. In 1962, for example, after the Supreme Court held prayer in public schools unconstitutional, 79 percent of Americans disapproved of the decision. In 1967, after the Court held laws prohibiting interracial marriage unconstitutional, 72 percent disapproved. In 2010, after the Court held laws limiting corporate campaign expenditures unconstitutional, 80 percent of Americans disapproved. But only 41 percent of Americans disagreed with *Roe*. An additional measure of just how uncontroversial *Roe* was at the time is the fact that, when President Gerald Ford nominated John Paul Stevens to succeed Justice William O. Douglas in 1975, not a single senator asked Stevens a question about *Roe* or about his views on abortion. Even most evangelicals did not challenge the decision, for in 1973 most evangelicals still regarded abortion as a Catholic issue.

The one group that did strongly condemn *Roe* from the very moment of the decision were Catholics, who disapproved of the decision by a margin of 56 to 40 percent. Indeed, within days of the decision, thousands of telegrams and letters of protest from Catholics began pouring into the Court, many of them form letters from Catholic school students denouncing the justices as "murderers" and "butchers."[25]

Of course, as we know, *Roe* eventually emerged into a bitterly divisive issue, but this did not happen until the end of the decade, as the culture wars exploded over such issues as the Equal Rights Amendment, gay rights, obscenity, and women's liberation, thus inflaming the evangelical community. By this time, polls showed that more than a third of all Americans identified themselves as "born again." Evangelicals had become the nation's largest religious demographic. When the Rev. Jerry Falwell founded the Moral Majority in 1979, he brought together for the first time the many disparate elements of Christian fundamentalism into a single, unified, political movement. Falwell explained that *Roe* had awakened him from his slumber, and he preached that if evangelicals worked together they had the power "to take control of the national government."

The Moral Majority raised huge amounts of money to support political candidates, and in state after state its members wrested control of the state Republican apparatus from party regulars. By the summer of 1980, Republican Party leaders were treating Falwell, more than any other religious figure in American history, like the leader of a powerful political constituency. The Christian broadcaster Pat Robertson boasted that the evangelical community now had "enough votes to run the country," and in his pursuit of the presidency, Ronald Reagan now called for a constitutional amendment to overturn *Roe* and promised to appoint pro-life judges at all levels of the judiciary, thus ushering in a historic era of judicial nominations shaped in no small part by religious conceptions of constitutional law. With Reagan's election, James Dobson, the founder of Focus on the Family, proclaimed that evangelicals had finally "come home," and that "home was the White House."[26]

IV

In the years since 1980, a succession of Republican presidents, have sought religiously to appoint Supreme Court justices who would overturn *Roe v. Wade*.

Interestingly, though, three of those nine justices—Sandra Day O'Connor, Anthony Kennedy, and David Souter—disappointed those who appointed them. Demonstrating both a respect for precedent and an understanding of the fundamental right at issue in *Roe*, O'Connor, Kennedy, and Souter consistently reaffirmed *Roe*, despite repeated efforts to overturn the decision. The most important decision was handed down in *Planned Parenthood v. Casey* in 1992.

The drama leading up to that decision cannot be overstated. By 1992, several states, including Utah and Louisiana, had defiantly enacted laws that outlawed almost all abortions that were not necessary to save the life of the woman. Shortly before the argument in *Casey*, which involved the constitutionality of a series of Pennsylvania restrictions on abortion, more than half a million people marched on the nation's capital to demand that *Roe* be overturned. Once again, a Republican administration, this one led by President George H. W. Bush, urged the Court to overrule *Roe*.

In his brief for the United States in *Casey*, Solicitor General Kenneth Starr left no doubt of the Bush administration's position: "*Roe v. Wade* was wrongly decided and should be overruled. . . . The protection of innocent human life—in and out of the womb—is certainly the most compelling interest that a State can advance. In our view, a State's interest in protecting fetal life throughout pregnancy . . . outweighs a woman's liberty interest in an abortion."[27]

Moreover, the Court now consisted of eight justices appointed by Republican presidents and only one justice—Byron White, who had dissented in *Roe*—appointed by a Democratic president. The conventional wisdom assumed that the newly constituted Court was finally poised to overrule *Roe*. Indeed, as the *New York Times* journalist Linda Greenhouse observed, "with the new makeup of the Court, *Roe* had never looked so imperiled."

At the Court's conference after the oral argument in *Casey*, five justices seemed ready to change the course of history. With the support of Justices White, Antonin Scalia, Anthony Kennedy, and Clarence Thomas, Chief Justice Rehnquist assigned the opinion to himself. In the words of the legal journalist Jan Crawford, it was the opinion "he had waited eighteen years to write." But two days after Rehnquist circulated his draft majority opinion to the other justices, Justice Kennedy, who was raised in an Irish Catholic family and had been appointed to the Court by President Reagan, sent a rather cryptic note to Justice Blackmun. Kennedy's note to Blackmun read, "I need to see you as soon as you have a few free moments. I want to tell you about some developments in *Planned Parenthood v. Casey*, and at least part of what I say should come as welcome news." It was, for Blackmun, "welcome news," indeed. When the two justices met the following day, Kennedy informed Blackmun that he, O'Connor, and Souter "had been meeting privately and were jointly drafting an opinion that, far from overruling *Roe*, would save it." Ever after, pro-life conservatives would cast Kennedy in the "role of traitor."

In a 5–4 decision, with Justices Blackmun, Stevens, O'Connor, Kennedy, and Souter in the majority—all five appointed by Republican presidents—the Court concluded, in a stunning turn of events, that "the essential holding of *Roe* v. *Wade* should be retained and once again reaffirmed."[28] After ratifying the underlying constitutional rationale of *Roe*, the Court explained that, even if some members of the majority had reservations about *Roe*, there was no sufficient justification for overruling it. In short, none of the traditional reasons for overruling a precedent—that it had proved unworkable over time, that it could be jettisoned without upsetting settled expectations, or that subsequent decisions had eroded its rationale—was present in the case of *Roe*. Moreover, even if a justice were inclined to overrule *Roe*, there were important institutional reasons not to do so. This was so, the Court observed, because when viewed against the continuing political controversy over abortion, such a decision would inevitably be seen as "a surrender to political pressure" that "would subvert the Court's legitimacy."[29]

Although reaffirming "the essential holding" of *Roe*, Justices O'Connor, Kennedy, and Souter then parted company with Blackmun and Stevens and jettisoned the trimester framework of *Roe*. In an unusual opinion authored by the three of them jointly, O'Connor, Kennedy, and Souter maintained that the trimester framework was unduly "rigid" and was "unnecessary" to protect the core of the right guaranteed in *Roe*. In their view, the critical "line should be drawn at viability," because viability marks "the time at which there is a realistic possibility of maintaining and nourishing a life outside the womb." At that point, which shifts over time with medical advances, the state's interest in protecting human life "overrides" the woman's interests in privacy and personal liberty. This is only fair, they reasoned, because "it might be said that a woman who fails to act before viability has consented to the State's intervention on behalf of the developing child."[30]

O'Connor, Kennedy, and Souter concluded further that although a woman has a right to decide for herself whether to terminate a pregnancy before viability, the government can constitutionally impose regulations "to ensure that this choice is thoughtful and informed." Even in the earliest stages of pregnancy, for example, the government may enact regulations designed to inform the woman that there are "arguments of great weight that can be brought to bear in favor of continuing the pregnancy" and that there are alternatives available to abortion, including adoption and, in some cases, financial assistance if the woman chooses to raise the child. Thus, "only where state regulation imposes an *undue burden* on a woman's ability" to decide to terminate a pregnancy previability does it violate the Constitution. Government measures "designed to persuade" a pregnant woman "to *choose childbirth over abortion*" *are therefore constitutional, unless they "constitute an undue* burden" on her "freedom of choice."[31]

Applying this newly fashioned standard, O'Connor, Kennedy, and Souter, joined by the four dissenting justices—who called for *Roe* to be overruled—upheld the constitutionality of several relatively modest restrictions on the right of women to obtain pre-viability abortions. Although dissenting from the Court's decision to uphold these restrictions, Justice Blackmun nonetheless commended O'Connor, Kennedy, and Souter for "an act of personal courage and constitutional principle" and for reaffirming that "the Constitution protects a woman's right to terminate her pregnancy in its early stages."[32] Although relieved, Justice Blackmun, looking to the future, saw much "to fear." "I fear for the darkness," he wrote, "as four Justices anxiously await the single vote necessary to extinguish the light." "I am 83 years old. I cannot remain on this Court forever, and when I do step down, the confirmation process for my successor well may focus on the issue before us today. That, I regret, may be exactly where the choice between the two worlds will be made."[33]

V

Having learned an important lesson from the decision in *Casey*, Republican presidents grew ever more determined not to replicate that mistake, and with the appointment of justices like Antonin Scalia, Clarence Thomas, John Roberts, Samuel Alito, Neil Gorsuch, Brett Kavanaugh, and Amy Coney Barrett, the Supreme Court finally overruled *Roe* in the *Dobbs* decision. In an opinion by Justice Alito, the Court held that *Roe* should be overruled because its reasoning was flawed, there was no history of a constitutional right to abortion, the undue burden standard had proven difficult to apply, and the Court in *Roe* and *Casey* had failed to respect the interests of states in protecting the interests of the fetus.

So, where are we today? Although abortion rates in the United States declined over time, due largely to improvements in contraception, before *Dobbs* more than 20 percent of all women had at least one legal abortion during their lives, and approximately 620,000 legal abortions were performed in the United States annually. In the aftermath of *Dobbs*, some states have recognized a woman's right to terminate an unwanted pregnancy under state law, but others have not. As a result, hundreds of thousands of women, mostly poor and minority, will once again be thrown each year into the dark and dangerous world of back-alley abortions. With their decision in *Dobbs*, the conservative justices have cast hundreds of thousands of women each year into the dark and dangerous realm of unfreedom. As Justice Sonia Sotomayor asked during oral argument, if the conservative justices in *Dobbs* overrule *Roe*, "will this institution survive the stench that this creates in the public perception—that the Constitution and its reading are just political acts?"

CHAPTER 8

FREEDOM AND COERCION IN PUBLIC HEALTH

ROBERT KLITZMAN, MD

A s the COVID-19 pandemic has painfully revealed, desires for individual freedom can at times clash with the interests of public health. Challenges emerge ranging from battles over mandates to wear masks or undergo vaccination to dilemmas regarding financial incentives to recruit study subjects into medical experiments. Ethical, legal, and social consensus has prevailed that at times public health safety should outweigh individual freedoms—when individuals are at high risk of directly harming others (e.g., in the case of secondhand smoke). In clinical trials and other research experiments on humans, fears also arise of coercion and undue influence, and disagreements can ensue, given that these concerns involve inherent subjectivities—for example, determining the point at which participants may take risks that they would not otherwise take. In addressing these tensions, bioethical principles of autonomy, beneficence, nonmaleficence, and justice can provide useful and helpful guides. However, in each specific case, these principles must be carefully evaluated, weighed, interpreted, and applied, along with scientific evidence concerning the benefits and risks involved. Unfortunately, scientific knowledge of the short-term and long-term benefits and harms of any intervention are frequently limited, due to uncertainties and the fact that science is ever-evolving. As COVID has demonstrated, these decisions can spark controversies, and public discussion and education are critical.

Freedom and constraints on public health before COVID-19

Historically, public health in particular has long wrestled with these conflicts. Individual freedoms are obviously essential in civil societies and functioning democracies, but an individual's behavior can at times endanger the health and well-being of multiple other people. Hence, at times, government need to constrain individual choices in order to avoid widespread harm to others. For instance, after the dangers of secondhand tobacco smoke were demonstrated, municipalities in the United States began to prohibit smoking inside public places such as restaurants and airplanes. In seeking to uphold individuals' rights to smoke whenever they wanted, tobacco companies, restaurants, and other entities have sued municipalities.[1] Yet courts agreed that the dangers to which smokers were exposing other individuals outweighed this freedom.[2] Similarly, laws require car passengers to wear seat belts and motor cyclists to wear helmets, since otherwise they can be severely and permanently injured in accidents, requiring costly hospitalizations and long-term care at public expense.[3] Likewise, medical diagnoses are considered confidential—except if these may suggest possible harm to the collective.[4] Local health departments require, for instance, that physicians divulge identifying information about any patient diagnosed with a sexually transmitted disease (STD) in order to contact his or her sexual partners, to inform these partners that they have been exposed to the disease and should themselves get tested. The health department thus violates the patient's right to privacy since other individuals (the patient's sexual partners and in turn these partners' other sexual partners, if any) may now have a deadly disease that might not be immediately symptomatic but is treatable if detected early.

Similarly, cancer diagnoses are considered confidential information. Yet governments routinely require that doctors disclose these in order to track and monitor whether clusters of cases are occurring that may indicate the presence of particular environmental toxins (e.g., toxic wastes in a particular location).

Still, public health mandates that restrict certain individuals' freedoms have historically sparked opposition. Western industrialized countries have therefore varied, for instance, in whether and how they have instituted such decrees, such as bans on smoking in public places. Several European countries, for instance, continue to permit smoking in such environments. Impingements on individual freedom in the interest of public health can thus end up getting negotiated in various situations. Partly, in certain countries, smoking in cafés and bars may be culturally more deeply entrenched, and inextricable from such public establishments.

Vaccine requirements, especially, continue to engender opposition among some members of the public. Such immunizations can help avoid serious and potentially deadly diseases in oneself and others but require jabbing a healthy person with a needle, which hurts, even if momentarily, and literally punctures the thin protective coat of our skin covering our very bodies, in order to prevent a disorder that we don't now have and may never get.

But these immunizations can provide immense benefits both to the individual and to society as a whole, and lack of vaccination can cause widespread harm. Thus, the Supreme Court has upheld needs for mandatory inoculations in certain situations. In 1902, as an outbreak of smallpox was killing thousands of Americans, Cambridge, Massachusetts, required vaccination against this disease. Henning Jacobsen, a pastor, refused, claiming that he and his son had had "bad reactions" to earlier shots, which he thought might result from their genetics. He argued that the mandate was "unreasonable, arbitrary and oppressive." Cambridge fined him five dollars, but he appealed. His case reached the Supreme Court, which upheld the mandate, arguing that, "in every well-ordered society charged with the duty of conserving the safety of its members the rights of the individual in respect of his liberty may at times, under the pressure of great dangers, be subjected to such restraint, to be enforced by reasonable regulations as the safety of the general public may demand."[5]

Still, resistance to such vaccination has persisted.[6] For decades, in order to attend, elementary school, children must first receive certain shots, such as those for measles, mumps and rubella. But starting in the 1980s, groups of parents have increasingly fought these requirements, arguing, falsely, that these vaccines cause autism. The only alleged evidence to support this claim was, in fact, wholly fabricated.[7] Nonetheless, so-called antivaxxers persist. Since scientific data has unequivocally rejected claims that these inoculations cause autism, many parents have then sought religious exemptions. Unfortunately, due to lowering rates of vaccinations, outbreaks of measles subsequently occurred at Disneyland and elsewhere.[8] As of this writing, five states have eliminated such religious exemptions, while thirty states and Washington, DC, permit these exemptions, and thirteen states allow "philosophical" exemptions.[9]

Not surprisingly, the notion that public health benefits may at times warrant restrictions on individual freedoms disturbs many people on both sides of the political divide. Given several centuries of forced suppression of freedom by authoritarian leaders from Hitler and Stalin to Mao and now Putin, many Western thinkers understandably hesitate to see *any* encroachment on freedom as justified. The Left fears dictatorship and authoritarian rule. On the right, libertarians argue that individual freedoms should essentially trump all other priorities.

But as the COVID pandemic has clearly shown, many individuals feel they are thus free to spread infectious diseases or engage in other activities that harm people around them and the public as a whole. In such situations, safety measures prove vital for making society as healthy as possible.

Unfortunately, political leaders have also at times used the language of public health discourse to pursue their own agendas that in fact harm broad swaths of a society. Dictatorial leaders have censored critics, for instance, arguing that these opponents threaten the public safety.

Hence, any use of public health principles must clearly be carefully examined and justified, supported by both scientific evidence and bioethical principles, with minimization of any unintended harms or impingements on individual freedoms, or on the welfare of disadvantaged groups.

The roles of bioethical principles

The field of bioethics and the subdiscipline of public health ethics within it have thus developed and articulated ways of addressing these complexities, evaluating and balancing competing claims in any particular situation. Specifically, bioethics has developed principles to weigh these competing ethical considerations of freedom and public safety, drawing on several principles: particularly, respect for persons (upholding individuals' rights to autonomy), beneficence (maximizing the benefits to individuals), nonmaleficence (minimizing risks and harms), and justice (seeking to reduce inequities and avoid undue burdens on any vulnerable or disadvantaged groups).

These principles can help in vital ways in balancing claims for freedom in various public health, research, and clinical settings. Yet dilemmas can also emerge. These principles therefore need to be carefully assessed, interpreted, and applied in any particular situation, depending on the specific contexts and scientific facts involved. Autonomy is critical, for instance, but different stakeholders may claim rights that then need to be examined.

The case of COVID-19

The many controversies triggered by the COVID-19 pandemic regarding public health and individual freedom highlight both the importance of using these principles as guides and the challenges that can emerge. Unfortunately, public health officials often need to make decisions in the face of wide uncertainties in scientific knowledge, such as how severe future additional mutations in the COVID virus might be.[10]

With COVID, debates erupted regarding both positive and negative rights—that is, involving obligations either to engage in certain activities, or to refrain from others. Controversies surfaced entailing positive rights concerning, for instance, how to respond to individuals' claiming rights to certain scare resources (e.g., how to allocate limited supplies of ventilators and intensive care unit and other hospital beds) and whether governments or various types of employers should mandate quarantines for individuals who were either infected or exposed, and if so, when, for whom, and for how long and whether and how to enforce these. Conflicts regarding negative rights raged over whether to require masks, repeated COVID negative tests, and vaccinations or other such preventative measures, and if so, when and for whom—whether to include all employees and customers. These challenges varied by types of employer and situation, given differing potential risks of exposure, from hospitals to subways, buses and airplanes (where social distancing may be hard to maintain) to restaurants, and stores.

Especially at the beginning of the pandemic, hospital administrators feared that they had insufficient numbers of ventilators and ICU beds to provide one to all patients who might benefit from one. Given surges of COVID cases and resultant staff shortages, physicians sought to develop revised standards of care for crisis emergencies. ICU nurses, for example, who ordinarily treated four patients in a shift now had to care for ten. Such reduced standards in emergency situations created undesirable strains, and, not surprisingly, frustration and debate.

With COVID, patients (or families on their behalf) argued that they had rights to a ventilator, though the numbers of such machines were insufficient. Hence, such claims of rights could not always be honored, and public health officials had to decide *whose* rights should prevail. While a priori everyone may have an equal right to treatment, unfortunately supplies can at times be insufficient. From a utilitarian perspective, allocating such limited treatments through, for instance, a lottery or a "first come, first serve" approach, do not allow hospitals to provide "the greatest good to the greatest number." Providing ventilators to those who could most afford them would also raise concerns about social justice.

During the Napoleonic Wars, military physicians developed principles of triage to determine how to best allocate scarce resources on the battlefield—specifically, which wounded soldiers should receive treatment, when supplies were inadequate to care for all of those in need.[11] Emergency rooms routinely use such triage approaches, not treating all patients in the order in which they arrive but prioritizing the sickest patients over healthier ones who could potentially wait longer to receive care.

With COVID, doctors similarly had to decide how to allocate limited resources and drew on these established principles of triage. According to these principles, in distributing scarce medical supplies, doctors should prioritize patients who are most likely both to perish without treatment and to recover if they receive it. Patients who are most likely to survive *without* the intervention receive lower priority. Severely ill patients who are unlikely to recover, even if they receive the intervention also receive lower priority. Secondary considerations that might serve as "tie breakers" can also then be included as well. With COVID, for instance, healthcare workers received additional priority, since they could then help other patients.

Yet making these determinations is not always easy. Assessments of who will be more or less likely to benefit from an intervention is not always wholly predictable. Initially, in the United States and elsewhere, masks, ventilators, and COVID vaccines, for instance, were in short supply, posing dilemmas about who should get them first. For ventilators, physicians developed Systemic Organ Failure Assessment (SOFA) scores, which gauged the degrees to which various organs (such as the heart and brain) had impairments prior to COVID. COVID patients with higher scores would then receive lower priority for receiving ventilators. But these scores turned out to disproportionately favor Caucasians over African Americans and Latinos, underestimating impairment among Caucasians and overestimating it among African Americans. In part, Caucasians had had better prior access to healthcare and therefore fewer preexisting chronic health problems. Suggestions have thus been made to adjust these scores accordingly to benefit patients from disadvantaged backgrounds.[12]

Yet, once the supply of masks, for instance, was adequate in the United States and other industrialized countries, it soon became apparent that many people refused to wear them. No one likes to don masks;[13] they impede our breathing, fog our glasses, and make us hot. During the pandemic, we had to remember to always carry them with us when we went to stores, restaurants, and other public places. At times we forgot. In restaurants, airplanes, and medical facilities, fights erupted when customers refused to wear a facial covering.[14]

But uninfected employees and customers also had rights to safe environments that were free from harms, including dangerous and potentially fatal infections from unmasked personnel. Many antimaskers insisted, "It's my right *not* to wear a mask," ignoring the fact that they were thereby endangering others.

Governments had to grapple with these challenges, deciding whether to impose fines or other punishments on individuals who refused to comply with such requirements. Quebec, for instance, opted to fine store owners if any customers did not wear masks.[15]

With quarantines as well, governments struggled with balancing individuals' freedoms against group safety. Hong Kong, for one, sought to ensure that COVID-exposed individuals remained quarantined by requiring them to wear electronic bracelets that, if these individuals illegally left their apartments, alerted the police.[16] Other countries relied on the "honor system" to maintain quarantines, hoping that citizens would comply.

Thus, governments and employers faced quandaries about not only *which* health prevention measures to adopt but also whether to monitor these, and if so, how, and what to do if individuals fail to comply.

About one-third of the population declined vaccines, raising difficult questions about whether governments or companies should then mandate these interventions.[17] Certain individuals also argued, for instance, that they had a right not to wear a mask. Several hospitals, in particular, sought to vaccinate all employees who might otherwise infect patients, who commonly have other medical conditions that heighten susceptibilities to severe COVID. Yet innumerable hospital workers sought religious exemptions. As of 2022, 12.7 percent of healthcare personnel received the primary COVID vaccine series, and 32.9 percent had not received a booster dose. Such nonvaccination was higher in long-term care facilities/home health care (20% for the primary series and 39% for a booster). Employer requirements and recommendations significantly increased rates of immunization.[18] As of 2024, only 31.3 percent of healthcare workers had received the updated 2023–24 COVID vaccine, including 52.7 percent of physicians and 29.8 percent of nurses.[19]

Under Title VII of the Civil Rights Act of 1965, employers should accommodate workers who have "sincerely held" religious beliefs,[20] if such accommodation does not unduly pose hardship on the employer. Yet religious beliefs can be vague and hard to pin down. And unfortunately, many people may use religion as an excuse. Some antivaxxers argued wrongly that the vaccines were made using fetal issue. The Johnson & Johnson vaccine used fetal cell lines (derived from fetal cells taken in 1985 and replicated innumerable times in labs).[21] Yet the Pfizer and Moderna immunizations did not.[22] Some antivaxxers then argued that the Pfizer and Moderna vaccines were developed using technologies that had in the past used fetal cells. But in fact, almost all medications used today were developed employing knowledge derived from such cells.[23] These antivaxxers commonly took these other medications without comment or complaint. Other employees argued that they didn't want any "unnatural products" inside them. Or they said that they believed only in natural herbal treatments.

Yet such exemptions could harm coworkers, family members, and customers (or patients, in the case of hospitals). Indeed, the Occupational Safety and Health Act requires safe and healthy workplaces, and the Centers for Disease Control and Prevention and Equal Employment Opportunity Commission classified COVID-19 as a "direct threat" in workplaces.[24]

Moreover, despite many individuals' claims that their religion prevented them from getting vaccinated, Pope Francis and the national leaders of many faiths, including the National Association of Evangelicals and the Church of Latter-Day Saints strongly encouraged vaccination.[25] Even Christian Science, which generally encourages natural treatments, urged its adherents to "respect" public health agencies and follow "the laws of the land, including those requiring vaccination."[26] No national religious leaders opposed vaccination. Jesus, after all, encouraged helping rather than harming other people.

Individuals have rights to their religious beliefs, but not to endanger other people. As Supreme Court Justice Oliver Wendell Holmes Jr. stated, even free speech has limits when falsely yelling "fire" in a crowded theater.[27]

Given the complex tensions entailed, courts adjudicated on several proposed mandates. Private establishments (e.g., a theater or restaurant) could require that visitors wear masks or show proof of vaccination.[28] President Biden initially proposed, for instance, that all employers with more than one hundred workers should mandate vaccines.[29] However, on January 13, 2022, the Supreme Court struck this law down, arguing that "the challenges posed by a global pandemic do not allow a federal agency to exercise power that Congress has not conferred upon it."[30] Federal, state, and local governments also wrestled with mask mandates and varied significantly.

Some employers, such as hospitals, decided not to mandate vaccines because of fears that many nurses and other employees would quit. Hospitals hence struggled to balance competing concerns and priorities—maximal prevention against COVID through vaccination mandates for employees against fears of losing nurses and other staff, which could impede patient health in other ways.

Governments confronted ethical conundrums, too, about society-wide lockdowns due to COVID. At the outset of the pandemic, Sweden, for instance, decided not to lock down but to stay open, realizing that this decision would likely result in the deaths of thousands of citizens.[31] Similarly, in the United States, some states decided to prioritize freedom and avoidance of economic slowdown over the prospects of thousands of citizens dying. In conjunction with these decisions, certain political leaders minimized the threat of the pandemic, some even so far as to deny it.[32] President Trump and some of his supporters in fact initially called COVID a "hoax."[33] Yet counties that in the 2020 presidential election were pro-Trump rather than pro-Biden had much higher COVID death rates, given their less aggressive intervention efforts.[34]

Such undervaluation of patient deaths, however, posed additional problems since vulnerable groups, especially poorer people of color, were much more likely to be hospitalized or die due to COVID.[35] These inequities stemmed in large part from prior disparities in access to care, and therefore in preexisting medical conditions that also predisposed people to develop more severe COVID. Hence, political leaders who pushed for individual freedom from preventive measures and avoidance of economic difficulties over the lives of certain citizens were frequently in fact prioritizing the freedom and economic advantages of *wealthier* individuals, at the expense of the death and suffering of the poor, who were also disproportionately people of color.

The fact that the COVID virus remained relatively new and that knowledge about it thus remained incomplete and evolving fueled these battles.[36] Especially at the outset of the pandemic in 2020, no one knew how widely the virus would spread, with what short-term and long-term effects and costs, whether vaccines or treatments might be developed, and if so, when, how effectively, and for whom (e.g., whether infants, children, the elderly or patients with serious pre-existing conditions). Hence, uncertainties surfaced about the short- and long-term effects of interventions, including "lockdowns," quarantines, hand-washing, mask wearing, and social distancing, since the full effectiveness of these measures depended on how many people participated in them. A mask mandate, for instance, has little effect if few people comply with it. Researchers developed and studied multiple vaccines, not knowing which, if any, would work, and if so, to what degree—whether 30 percent, 50 percent, 70 percent, or 90 percent of the time—and how long it would take to know.

Governments were obviously wary of lockdowns that shut down the economy, since long-term economic effects could pose enormous burdens, especially on poorer, vulnerable people. Unfortunately, lockdowns can disproportionality burden groups that are already disadvantaged, such as poor people of color and blue-collar workers who cannot telecommute and have to rely on mass transit and may have more difficulty obtaining food and essential healthcare and other services. Lockdowns could also hamper children's education.

Consequently, governments needed to balance the possible future benefits of any such proposed intervention against the possible future risks, though such predictions were fraught with potential errors. Dilemmas arose about the degrees of risks and benefits, the understandings of which evolved during the pandemic, and how to balance these, and who should decide.

Implementation of such public health policies was also difficult because much of the public misunderstood and/or opposed them. Given understandable wariness of any potential impingements on liberty, many citizens became suspicious of public health officials' efforts to protect the health of the community as a whole. Public distrust of government has grown over recent decades, especially since the 1960s and the Watergate scandal and more recent polarizations, fueled by social media echo chambers.[37] Hence, public health proposals were often not only unpopular but also distrusted, presenting barriers that needed to be overcome.[38]

Lack of understanding of science and of the fact that it constituted a *process* rather than *a final stable set of answers* further fueled misunderstandings. Many people wanted and expected black-and-white definitive answers rather than seeing science as consisting of evolving, complex, and slowly accumulating knowledge involving trial and error—especially when the problem, such as COVID, was itself new and literally mutating and evolving.

Thus, public health efforts that may impinge on individual freedoms need not only to be well supported by both scientific evidence and ethical principles but also to be implemented in ways that engage the public as early as possible to understand and respond to community concerns and potential wariness in order to effectively communicate the rationale for these measures. Unfortunately, public health measures occur in emergencies, making communication difficult, although that is not always the case.

Coercion in research ethics

Concerns about tensions between freedom and coercion arise not only in broad public health policies, but in conducting medical and public health research. Investigators and research ethics committees (or institutional review boards) face quandaries about how to advance science by encouraging people to enroll in experiments without impinging on these human subjects' voluntariness. Yet participation in medical research frequently entails undergoing discomfort and even risks—for instance, of being enrolled in studies of new experimental drugs that have never been tried in humans or have been administered only in smaller doses or in relatively few healthy volunteers. Unfortunately, scandals have occurred. Most notoriously, the Nazis conducted horrific, often lethal experiments on concentration camp prisoners without any consent.[39] More recently, some individuals in studies have not known or understood that they were in fact "human guinea pigs."[40]

Institutional review boards thus seek to ensure that research subjects both receive adequate informed consent about participation in studies, and volunteer freely. Yet these committees face challenges in achieving these goals. Clinical trials commonly require that participants take risks and undergo inconvenience. As part of a study, participants may need to undergo various medical tests, including lumbar punctures (or spinal taps), and may not benefit at all, especially if they are given a placebo or if the experimental drug proves to be ineffective or even harmful. Patients with serious medical conditions, especially, may be at considerable risks of serious side effects.

Many subjects enter such studies because of altruism—wanting to help advance medical science in ways that may aid future patients. But such generosity usually proves insufficient to recruit sufficient numbers of participants to remain in a study over several years to determine if a drug works or not.

Therefore, researchers routinely provide compensation to such study subjects. But doing so presents dilemmas. If the amount of payment is too low, too few participants will enter the study, and the results will fail to be meaningful. However, if the amount of compensation is too high, other problems can ensue. Some potential participants may lie about their symptoms in order to gain entry into the study. For instance, a patient with few if any symptoms of headache or depression may claim that he or she has severe symptoms in order to enter the study and receive a relatively large sum of money. Other people may be persuaded by a large amount of compensation to take undue risks. In the Philippines and several other countries, for instance, many poor people agree to sell their organs in exchange for cash.[41] These individuals sell a kidney, for instance, hoping to thereby significantly improve their socioeconomic situation and/or permanently escape poverty. However, studies reveal that many such organ sellers subsequently suffer significant side effects from the surgery and permanent lack of a kidney and feel too tired to work or function fully.[42] Hence, they end up in worse poverty. In such cases, the lure of a seemingly large amount of money has led these individuals to agree to undergo an intervention that does not help them at all medically, is not in their long-term financial interest, and in fact harms them over time.

Institutional review boards are therefore concerned about patients entering experimental drug trials when unduly swayed by similar financial motives. Moreover, in recruiting subjects into studies, researchers often have inherent conflicts of interest, wanting to enroll adequate numbers of participants to be able to obtain valid results. Unfortunately, investigators have thus at times encouraged patients to enter trials that were not in these patients' best interest. As a result, these committees strive to uphold participants' voluntariness and to avoid any coercion or undue influence.

But deciding at what point an amount of money may "unduly influence" a potential study participant is inherently subjective and hard to determine. In part, individuals vary greatly in their socioeconomic status and desires. A poor person might see a particular amount of money as extremely large and thus attractive and worth accepting in return for undergoing certain risky procedures, while a middle- or upper-middle-class person might not. Institutional review boards consequently struggle with how much to give subjects, whether subjects should receive different amounts based on their income, whether the amount should be in cash or coupons to particular stores or for particular items (such as clothing or food), whether the provision of free medical care as part of the trial will unduly influence potential participants, and whether compensation will skew the type of people who enter the study (e.g., attracting only poorer people, who have limited access to healthcare and thus have different types and degrees of diseases, making the data less generalizable to other groups). These review boards, facing tensions, may fear subjects' participating "just for the money" and wrestle with whether that motivation should be prevented and, if so, how.[43] Disagreements can occur within and between committees. In part, scientists commonly feel that science should be "pure" and avoid the "taint of money," but this principle should pertain to scientists themselves and may not be appropriate to apply to study subjects who bear the risks of experimental interventions. More explicit awareness of and increased attention to these tensions could help.

There is also a lack of social science research and understanding of when people become unduly influenced by money and act "against their better judgment" and what that phrase means. Committees may therefore rely on "gut feelings" that may or may not be correct.[44]

Conclusions

Medical research and care and public health thus frequently confront questions regarding potential constraints on individual freedom, and bioethics provides a framework for addressing such tensions. Challenges arise ranging from battles over mandates to wear masks or undergo vaccination to dilemmas regarding financial incentives to recruit study subjects into medical experiments. In the ensuing debates, bioethical principles of autonomy, beneficence, nonmaleficence, and justice can provide useful and helpful guides.

Ethical, legal, and social consensus has prevailed that at times public health safety should outweigh individual freedoms when individuals are at high risk of directly harming others. At times, constraints on freedom are warranted and even crucial (as in the case of secondhand smoke). However, in each specific case, these principles must be carefully evaluated, weighed, interpreted, and applied, along with scientific evidence concerning benefits and risks. Difficulties emerge since scientific knowledge of the short-term and long-term outcomes, benefits, and harms of any intervention are frequently limited due to uncertainties, and the fact that science is ever-evolving. Gray areas clearly emerge—for instance, when the scientific evidence about the extent of future harm remains limited. Balancing competing principles of advancing public health and medical research on the one hand and avoiding unnecessary restrictions on individuals' freedom on the other thus requires careful assessment, analysis, monitoring, and examination to ensure that ethical principles and scientific evidence support restrictions on individuals' freedoms. Public education about these tensions and challenges is consequently also essential, especially as these issues become distorted and polarized in social media.

In research as well, fears of coercion and undue influence arise and disagreements can ensue, given that these concerns can involve inherent subjectivities—for example, determining the point at which individuals might take risks that they would not otherwise take.

In a functioning democracy, public health and medical care and research require careful weighing of the rights of certain individuals against the rights of others, short- and long-term risks to others, medical and broader social benefits, and avoidance of disproportionate burdens to vulnerable and disadvantaged groups. As COVID has demonstrated, these decisions can spark controversy but be vital to societies and the health and survival of millions of people at local, national, and global levels.

CHAPTER 9

THE PROSECUTION OF GENDER EQUAL ABRAHAMIC CIRCUMCISION

Implications for Jews and Muslims

RICHARD A. SHWEDER

Congress shall make no law [1] respecting an establishment of religion, or [2] prohibiting the free exercise thereof . . .

—The two famous religion clauses of the First Amendment to the US Constitution

Introduction: "The free exercise thereof" in liberal pluralistic societies

This essay is about the free exercise of religion and culture in a liberal plural-istic society such as the United States. Liberal pluralistic ideals and narratives have led some Americans (and I am one of them) to imagine the history of their country as a haven for religious freedom and cultural diversity; as a land where the state does not take official or public positions (and hence is "neu-tral") concerning the particular religious beliefs and related practices and cultural traditions of its citizens; and as a place where citizenship as an American has relatively weak and limited implications for the way you lead your private life, for the type of associations you form, and for the way you raise your children.

More specifically, the essay is focused on the recent criminal prosecution of Jumana Nagarwala, an American physician who performed customary female circumcision ceremonies for families in her Muslim religious and cultural community, which is known as the Dawoodi Bohra. The essay discusses two alternative interpretations of the free exercise of religion clause of the First Amendment of the US Constitution and considers the implications of *United States v. Nagarwala* (350 F. Supp. 3d 613) for the toleration of religious and cultural diversity in the United States and for the future of the Jewish and Muslim custom of Abrahamic circumcision.

Not all liberal societies have a pluralistic history or have evolved their social, political, and legal norms to accommodate a multireligious, multicultural, multiethnic, or multiracial domestic population. Denmark and Sweden are examples of societies that are liberal but not historically plural. In the face of contemporary immigration and asylum seeking (approximately 5 percent of the current Danish population and 8 percent of the current Swedish population is Muslim) it remains to be seen whether the historically evolved social, political, and legal norms of those countries are able to accommodate religious, cultural, ethnic, and racial diversity.

Conversely, not all pluralistic societies are liberal. China comes to mind as an example of a plural society that is not liberal.

Nevertheless, within those societies that are both plural and have liberal ethical and legal traditions (such as the United States) one is likely to discern certain values and organizational principles designed to protect diverse minority groups from the so-called tyranny of the majority and also to help sustain the plural character of that society.

I have in mind country-specific ethical and legal principles such as the free exercise of religion, the separation of church and state, a robust notion of family privacy and strong parental rights (the idea that the upbringing of the child is primarily the right and responsibility of parents not of the state), expressive and associational liberties, and some kind of balance between individual autonomy and the autonomy of the society's diverse religious and cultural communities to carry forward their way of life without too much interference from the state. I have long had an interest in how those ethical and legal principles get interpreted and applied (or not applied) within particular countries; and I have wondered: To what degree do those ethical and legal principles expand domestic toleration for religious and cultural differences?

I realize those comments are quite general. Rest assured; I am going to spend much of this essay describing and discussing a specific case. Although the case concerns the legality of gender-equal Abrahamic circumcision as practiced by a particular Muslim denomination, I believe it carries potentially ominous implications for the future liberty of all Jewish and Muslim denominations in the United States to honor the biblical Abrahamic covenant for boys and to do so exclusively on religious, aesthetic, or cultural (rather than medical) grounds.

This is a case that has absorbed much of my attention over the past few years, and one I can precisely date to April 12, 2017.[1]

April 12, 2017: Why it matters

On April 12, 2017, Jumana Nagarwala, a forty-four-year-old Shia Muslim woman born in the United States, the valedictorian of her high school class, the class speaker at her college graduation, a medical doctor trained at the Johns Hopkins Medical School, the mother of four children, and an admired member of her local religious community, was arrested by the FBI in Detroit, Michigan, and charged under a 1996 (never before used) federal statute (18 U.S. Code § 116) with the crime of "female genital mutilation." It took nearly four and a half years for her case to run its course, and it came to an end only on September 28, 2021.

I became interested in the case for several reasons. Let me start by mentioning at least one source of my interest. Fortunately for American Jews, their traditional rite of entrance into the covenant of Abraham has not yet been the focus of government surveillance, administrative regulation, or legal prohibition and subsequent criminal enforcement in the United States. The traditional rite I have in mind, of course, is neonatal male circumcision as prescribed (indeed commanded by the voice of "God") in Genesis 17 of the Hebrew Bible.

For several thousand years childhood male circumcision has been experienced as a transgenerational obligation and as a symbol of ancestral community identity by most Jews. That sense of obligation and identity persists in the contemporary world, even among highly educated secular Jews who have never read the Hebrew Bible or heard of Genesis 17. When thinking and writing about Jumana Nagarwala's arrest and prosecution, the following question has been on my mind: Looking toward the future from a legal perspective, how secure is the liberty of Jews and Muslims to carry forward (from generation to generation) their ancient Abrahamic circumcision tradition in the United States?

In this essay I am going to suggest that the arrest and prosecution of Jumana Nagarwala is not only a provocation to think deeply about the scope and limits of religious and cultural freedom in liberal pluralistic societies. It is also a wake-up call about the future of Abrahamic circumcision for Jews and Muslims in the United States. Indeed, it is noteworthy that one of the earliest voices reacting to her arrest and incarceration came from the American Orthodox Jewish rabbi Philip Lefkowitz and was published in the *Times of Israel*. The rabbi sensed that April 12, 2017, was a moment of truth for Jews. He wondered what her prospective federal criminal trial portended for religious liberty in the United States. His was the kind of admonition familiar to many Jews: First they came for the 'other' and I did not speak out; then they came for me![2]

First they came for the other: A bit of background to the legal case

So-called Abrahamic circumcision, so named because of its origin in Genesis 17 of the Hebrew Bible (the famous biblical encounter between Abraham and God when Abraham, the first Jew, was given his Jewish name and commanded to circumcise all the male members of his tribe) is not *just* a Jewish practice. It is also embraced by Muslims around the world. Indeed, with regard to global prevalence, most Abrahamic circumcisions occur in Muslim communities. There are 14 million Jews in the world. There are 1.8 billion Muslims.

For Jews the custom is passed on through an ancestral descent line flowing from the biblical Abraham to his secondborn son Isaac, son of Abraham and Sarah, and onward through Jewish generations. For Muslims the custom flows from the same biblical Abraham through his firstborn son Ismael, son of Abraham and his mistress Hagar, to the Prophet Mohammed (viewed as a descendent of Abraham and Ismael) and then onward through Muslim generations.

Historically the Abrahamic circumcision tradition has been gender-exclusive for Jews (all males and only males). Not so for all Muslims. Ever since the Prophet Mohammed's incorporation of the Hebrew Bible and the New Testament into the Qur'an and his revelatory updated report of God's will in the seventh century CE, an alternative gender-inclusive interpretation of the ancient Abrahamic tradition has evolved in several (although certainly not all) denominations of Islam. Among the Muslim religious communities adopting a gender-inclusive version of the tradition is the Shia Muslim Dawoodi Bohra denomination, which is a small, cosmopolitan, and highly educated denomination of about one million people with an international presence and a pre-eminent religious leader who resides in India and exercises supreme authority over the religious community.[3] Observant Dawoodi Bohra parents customarily circumcise both girls and boys, with mothers controlling and managing the circumcision of their daughters and arranging for the religious procedure to be done by a qualified female circumciser. In the case of *United States v Nagarwala* that qualified circumciser was Jumana Nagarwala.

By most accounts the Dawoodi Bohra ritual procedure for girls amounts to a nick, abrasion, piercing, or small cut restricted to the female foreskin or prepuce (often referred to as the clitoral hood). From a surgical point of view the custom is less invasive than a typical male circumcision as routinely and legally performed in the United States.

This is my understanding of the procedure for girls as performed in the United States, which takes place around seven years of age. A local anesthetic is applied to the genitals by a female specialist (a traditional circumciser or trained physician), who then raises the foreskin with tweezers and pinches off a few millimeters of skin using scissors or a similar instrument. The amount of skin that is removed is tiny (the size of a sesame seed) but is preserved (for example, in gauze) for further use in a religious ceremony. The surgery heals without the need for stitches, diathermy, or cauterization. The purpose of the tradition is the donation of a piece of foreskin tissue, not the nicking, piercing, or cutting per se. I won't describe an equally vivid typical male circumcision in the United States, which is generally considered a minor surgical procedure but involves a much more complete removal of the foreskin tissue.

It is worth noting that Dawoodi Bohra women who embrace this gender-equal circumcision tradition avow that the surgical procedure for their daughters is medically safe and surgically less invasive than a standard circumcision procedure for their sons. A recent survey of the opinions of 786 randomly selected Dawoodi Bohra women from several countries, conducted by the London barrister Zimran Samuel, discovered overwhelming female support for this religiously based gender inclusive approach to circumcision. Most of the women in the survey viewed the custom as a meaningful religious procedure that is not physically harmful and does not affect a woman's sex life.

In light of this description of the female procedure, and assuming its fidelity, questions arise about the scope and limits of tolerance for religious and cultural diversity in the land of the free and home of the brave. Related questions arise about the appropriate legal status for religiously based gender-equal versions of the Abrahamic circumcision tradition. If Abrahamic circumcision is legal for boys, why shouldn't it be legal for girls? If Abrahamic circumcision is illegal for girls, why shouldn't it be illegal for boys (including Jewish, Christian, and Muslim boys)? If gender-equal Muslim versions of the Abrahamic circumcision tradition are prohibited in the United States, how long will it be until gender-unequal versions of the ancient tradition are prohibited as well? Already in Europe, Jewish and Muslim parents who circumcise their sons are being described as "mutilators" (or "assailants" or "batterers") of their children, thereby reviving reproachful and vilifying epithets from the historical past.

The legal proceedings in Michigan: A short summary

Jumana Nagarwala was arrested by the FBI in Michigan on April 12, 2017. As noted, she was charged with violating the 1996 federal statute (18 U.S. Code § 116) prohibiting "female genital mutilation." The initial federal criminal complaint included reference to a physical examination of two seven-year-old Dawoodi Bohra girls by a medical doctor, a pediatrician whom the FBI had relied on in the past in cases of child abuse but who had no prior experience conducting a genital examination of this type. She stated that for one of the girls "her clitoral hood has a small incision, and there is a small tear to her labia minora." For the other girl she claimed that her clitoral hood is abnormal in appearance and "her labia minora has been altered or removed." During the State of Michigan Child Protective Agency hearing (which was designed to evaluate the agency's petition to remove Dawoodi Bohra children from their parents), that account by the prosecution's medical doctor was disputed by the defense. The defense relied on expert testimony from their own witness, an international expert on genital development in girls who had decades of medical experience conducting examinations of this sort and who reviewed recordings of the physical examinations of the Dawoodi Bohra girls. The defense claimed that Nagarwala's procedure conformed to Dawoodi Bohra religious injunctions calling for a small nick or superficial abrading of the foreskin and the removal of a tiny amount of skin. Those original descriptions by the prosecution's medical doctor did not appear in the subsequent "superseding" version of the criminal indictment prepared by the prosecutor. Instead, the "superseding" indictment referred (without any specifics) to the occurrence of "fgm procedures."

Nagarwala was denied bail by a magistrate judge and held in pretrial captivity pending a federal criminal trial. Among other charges she was also accused of conspiring with Dawoodi Bohra mothers to transport their daughters across state lines to commit a sexual offense. She was denounced as a monster in the popular press. She was fired from her job by her medical employer. If convicted of all the charges leveled against her she faced the prospect of spending the rest of her life in prison. Throughout this process of vilification, Nagarwala maintained her innocence. She claimed that no crime had been committed and that she was merely performing a medically safe religious ritual using a procedure of the type described earlier, which she claimed was not female genital mutilation.

Five months later, on September 19, 2017, her prospective federal criminal trial was postponed until June 2018. At that point Bernard Friedman, the federal district (trial) judge who had been assigned to the case, ordered an end to her incarceration. Despite strenuous objections from the federal prosecutor, who argued that Nagarwala was a flight risk and a threat to the community, he ordered that she be released on bail. Her release (pending a federal trial) commenced on November 21, 2017, seven months after her original arrest.

Nagarwala's delayed pretrial release from jail was conditioned on various reconnaissance and shadowing requirements. These included a tracking device on her ankle, a twenty-four-hour chaperon, residence in a hotel rather than at home, restrictions on contact with her children, no internet access, and a prohibition against all communication with members of her religious community. Her bail was ultimately secured with a $4.5 million bond, the largest ever required in the Eastern District of Michigan and perhaps the most unusual. Sixteen of her friends and supporters pledged their own homes and personal finances as collateral. Over the next nearly four years of pretrial legal motions and countermotions, she was not allowed to speak with any member of the Dawoodi Bohra community.

Then, on January 14, 2018, Judge Friedman dismissed the prosecution's sexual conspiracy allegation. In response to requests to further delay the trial the judge rescheduled it for January 2019. (Later the trial was rescheduled again for April 2019.)

On August 7, 2018, the judge relaxed one of Nagarwala's bail conditions and allowed this notably devout defendant a bit of space for the free exercise of her religion. In response to a request from her lawyer Shannon Smith, he gave Jumana Nagarwala permission to watch twenty-two specific hours of live-streamed religious sermons on her computer during a period of remembrance celebrated by Shia Muslims around the world. This is a high holy holiday when members of her religious community collectively mourn the death of the Prophet Mohammed's grandson Husain. That modest request on behalf of the defendant for a circumscribed grant of liberty to live stream a series of religious sermons was opposed by the federal prosecutor.

By then another significant legal event had transpired. A separate State of Michigan proceeding had taken place months earlier (on April 13, 2018) in front of a Wayne County circuit judge. At that proceeding the State of Michigan's Child Protective Service petition to permanently separate Jumana Nagarwala from her children was denied by the judge. Instead, the judge assumed legal authority over her family and granted her permission to leave the hotel where she had been residing and go home and live with her husband and children while awaiting her eventual fateful day in a federal criminal court.

The federal trial never took place. On July 27, 2018, criminal defense lawyers Shannon Smith, Mary Chartier, and Matthew Newberg, representing three Dawoodi Bohra defendants in the case, submitted a motion to dismiss the central charges in the original federal indictment. They argued that within the framework of the enumerated powers granted to Congress in the Constitution, Congress lacked the authority and should not be allowed to generalize its police power to criminalize the noneconomic behavior of private actors. Legislating criminal laws of that sort, they argued, is a constitutional function reserved to the states, which have the sole right to exercise police power to regulate and promote the health, safety, and welfare of citizens within their borders. In other words, the defense lawyers contended that enacting the 1996 "female genital mutilation" statute exceeded the enumerated powers granted to Congress.

The defense lawyers further developed that argument. They argued that the statute was not designed to regulate the economic activity associated with interstate commerce. The power to regulate interstate commerce is explicitly granted to Congress in Article I, section 8, clause 3. Valid federal law supersedes state law, so it was necessary for the defense to argue that Nagarwala was not engaged in interstate commerce when she performed the procedure for which she was being tried. Similarly, international treaty obligations are federal law. Defense argued that no such treaty obligations applied in the Nagarwala case. Finally, the defense argued that the statute could not be rescued by claiming that it was an application of the due process clause of the Fourteenth Amendment, which has been interpreted to permit federal regulation of state officials and agencies but not private individuals. Thus, argued the defense, the case fell outside the legitimate purview of the federal government. In other words, the federal prosecutors had been engaging in a criminal investigation that was not the business of the federal government to pursue.

Four months later, on November 20, 2018, Judge Friedman ruled on the dismissal motion. In a judgment that went to the very heart of the original indictment, he declared that the central legal basis for the arrest, the 1996 federal statute criminalizing female genital mutilation, was indeed unconstitutional. The legislation of the statute was not based on an enumerated congressional power; Congress did not have the authority to enact it.

That ruling, however, was not the end of the story. A chain of federal attorneys filed a succession of superseding indictments and allegations unrelated to the now disqualified 1996 statute—for example, lying to a federal officer, witness tampering, obstruction of justice. They kept the case going for an extended period of time, apparently hoping to convict and imprison Jumana Nagarwala and the other defendants one way or another to achieve some kind of victory after their high-profile (and embarrassing) loss of the main statutory foundation for the original arrest. They gave the impression that they would not take no for an answer. Finally, on September 28, 2021, Judge Friedman said, in effect, that enough is enough. In the face of a fourth superseding indictment and a motion from the defense lawyers claiming that their defendants were being punished for having prevailed on the central charge in the case, the judge dismissed all remaining charges and chastised the federal prosecutors for persisting in what he agreed was a "vindictive prosecution" and due-process violation of the rule of law. Shortly thereafter Shannon Smith, Nagarwala's lawyer, posted a powerful message about the conduct of the prosecutors, the character of her client and what it meant for her to be a criminal defense lawyer in a case such as this one, which turned out to be the biggest win of her career yet one that other defense lawyers and trusted friends did not want her to take.

A Pyrrhic victory

Jumana Nagarwala and the other defendants ultimately went free, but it was a Pyrrhic victory for the Dawoodi Bohra community, and a religious freedom defense was never tested.

In 1996 the original federal "female genital mutilation" statute was unanimously endorsed in Congress by voice vote in the context of legislating the "Illegal Immigrant Reform and Immigrant Responsibility Act of 1996." The statute was then attached to an Omnibus Appropriations Bill without any discussion or public hearings. The enactment process for the statute was hardly a model of deliberative democracy. In accordance with the demands of anti-FGM activist organizations the statute itself was designed and tailored to criminalize only one particular form of childhood body alteration, namely, procedures involving female genitalia. With specific attention to girls who are under eighteen years of age the statute prohibited all nonmedical procedures on particular itemized parts of female genital anatomy: specifically, the clitoris, the labia majora, and the labia minora. No explicit mention was made of the sheath of skin (the prepuce, foreskin, or hood) surrounding the clitoris, which is a distinct and separate part of genital anatomy. No comparable statute was proposed concerning nonmedical procedures on the genitals of boys. Quite crucially the statute made no exceptions and offered no exemption for medically harmless female genital procedures that might have religious, spiritual, aesthetic, or social benefits. With the enactment of the 1996 law all such procedures (for example, cosmetic labiaplasties) became vulnerable to prosecution as federal crimes.

Anti-FGM activist organizations and their supporters had been caught off guard and were shocked, disappointed, and outraged by Judge Friedman's ruling that the 1996 statute was unconstitutional. They pressed for replacement legislation. In 2020 Congress enacted a revised statute, asserting that the procedures in question require the use of materials that are transported in interstate commerce. (The 2020 revised statute includes an expansive notion of what counts as engagement in interstate economic activity such that if the tweezers used in a circumcision rite was manufactured in another state the religious ritual becomes subject to congressional regulation). This revised statute was named the Stop FGM Act of 2020. Again the vote was treated as a politically cost-free "no brainer." It was passed unanimously without any public hearings or debate. In the revised statute Congress added even greater draconian penalties for violation of the law and expanded the definition of "mutilation." The revised law now criminalizes any and all nonmedical female genital procedures (including procedures involving the foreskin, prepuce, or clitoral hood). As in the earlier 1996 version, such procedures are deemed criminal no matter how minor or harmless, and regardless of their aesthetic, religious, cultural, or social purpose. The revised Stop FGM statute now explicitly rules out the free exercise of religion or culture as a defense against prosecution and describes itself as a constitutional regulation of interstate commerce. That claim remains to be tested in court.

It should be noted that in the wake of the arrest of Jumana Nagarwala the federal prosecutors and the FBI were cheered on by some leading feminist organizations. Equality Now and the AHA Foundation (named after Ayaan Hirsi Ali) submitted amicus briefs supporting the roundup and incarceration of Dawoodi Bohra mothers. In our liberal pluralistic democracy, anti-FGM activists champion a policy of intolerance without limits, which they celebrate every year on February 6 with a well-publicized observance called Zero Tolerance Day. In 1996, they successfully used their political networks and influence in lobbying Congress to pass an anti-FGM statute. On April 12, 2017, those in the thrall of the moral force and emotional power inherent in the expression "female genital mutilation" were thrilled that the statute bearing that name was finally going to be applied in a federal court case—the first of its kind. Although they were shocked and devastated when the statute was declared unconstitutional, anti-FGM organizations viewed Judge Freidman's decision as a legal technicality and temporary setback. They were certainly not going to be deterred from their cause. In addition to pressing Congress to revise and reenact the law, activist organizations got busy lobbying state legislatures to pass similar laws.

The very expression "female genital mutilation" is of course a horror-inducing accusation. Strident critics of Islam and influential media personalities seem to love the word "mutilation" and have been shouting it at Muslim communities. The World Health Organization (WHO) uses the term "mutilation" by definitional fiat as a label for any and every nonmedical genital procedure for females (although not for males), from a minor nick of the prepuce (the logic of their approach implies that the use of genital jewelry by young women is a "mutilation" of their body) to an infibulation (which, across Africa and Southeast Asia is a relatively infrequent and geographically limited custom yet has become the core element in the horror inducing and falsely stereotyping picture of genital procedures in Africa). Conclusion-demanding headlines were pervasive in media coverage of Jumana Nagarwala's arrest and prosecution. "Lock her up," "she's a monster," "increase the maximum prison sentence," "throw away the key" were not uncommon reflexive responses to the "M" word stimulus inscribed in the very name of the 1996 federal statute. Nevertheless, it is a hazardous word when used to incite a rush to judgment.

In the 1990s a medical committee at the Harbor View Medical Center in Seattle proposed to do something that (little did they know) Dawoodi Bohra women have been doing for many centuries. Male circumcision was already routinely available for children at the Medical Center. As a way of respecting the spirit of gender equality requested by their clients from a local immigrant refugee population the physicians on the Harbor View committee wanted to make a minor physical procedure available for girls as well. They recommended a symbolic circumcision involving a nick or tiny incision of the prepuce or clitoral hood, which looking back appears to be similar to the Dawoodi Bohra "circumcision" procedure for girls. The doctors at the Harbor View Medical

Center in Seattle believed the procedure was safe and harmless, although due to hostile media coverage their proposal was not implemented.[4]

To date no one, including the World Health Organization (WHO), has proved them wrong. In June 2017, soon after Jumana Nagarwala was arrested and denied bail, a Dawoodi Bohra journalist, Jamila Najmuddin, at a South Asian news service pressed the World Health Organization to supply her with credible scientific evidence that the type of religious rite practiced by the Dawoodi Bohra was actually harmful or damaging to girls. The WHO staff came up with nothing.

One can discern a very basic ethical principle in the recommendation of the Seattle Harbor View Medical Center committee: One should protect those who are vulnerable and in one's charge from harm and damage. One can also detect a liberal pluralistic willingness to make space for the religious obligations and cultural traditions of diverse groups. That same disposition was seen more recently in an essay by two gynecologists, Kavita Arora and Allan Jacobs.[5] They proposed a classification of female genital procedures based on scientific evidence of harm and damage rather than on the power of the "mutilation" label to trigger an intense emotional response among members of dominant groups in a multicultural society.

In categorizing types of genital procedures (and deciding whether they should be permitted in a liberal society) Arora and Jacobs wanted to know whether a particular procedure actually produced any lasting disfiguring morphological changes in genital anatomy. They wanted to know whether the procedure was actually associated with significant sexual or reproductive dysfunction. Given their harm-based criteria it seems likely that the Dawoodi Bohra Abrahamic circumcision procedure for girls, precisely because it is less invasive than a typical male circumcision in the United States, resides well within the pale of a safe zone.

Cautioning against the hazards of the "mutilation" label, the same harm-based approach to the classification of genital procedures was also advocated by the former director of the Program on Medicine and Religion at the University of Chicago Medical School, Aasim Padela, and his associate, Rosie Duivenbode. In a commentary published in the Hastings Center Bioethics Forum they suggest that the Dawoodi Bohra religious rite is not a "mutilation." They write: "The ritual involves the nicking of the prepuce, or clitoral hood, and is, for this community [the Dawoodi Bohra], grounded within Islamic scriptures and aimed at gender equity; young males are circumcised and females are nicked."[6]

The rush to judgment after the arrest of Jumana Nagarwala and the other female defendants from her religious community also produced some strange bedfellows. Cheering on the federal prosecutors and the FBI and rooting for a conviction were not only global feminists but also "intactivists" (individuals and groups opposed to male circumcision) and right-wing American nativists, who were anti-immigration and anti-Muslim and depicted Dawoodi Bohra women as aliens who should be locked up and did not belong in US society in the first place.

Ultimately, as noted earlier, the legal case against the Dawoodi Bohra defendants unraveled, but slowly. The case was undone but in such a way that there was no opportunity to address the ominous portent in Rabbi Lefkowitz's opinion piece in the *Times of Israel* about the fate of religious liberty in the United States. Never addressed over that 4.5-year period during which the case collapsed were the broader moral and legal implications of the Dawoodi Bohra gender-equal Abrahamic circumcision tradition for religious liberty and cultural diversity, or for the future of male only versions of Abrahamic circumcision in the United States. Some of those implications have recently been discussed in a special open access issue of the journal *Global Discourse*, which poses the question: "Gender Equality in Abrahamic Circumcision: Why or Why Not?"[7]

Divergent interpretations of religious liberty in the United States

Looking toward the future of Abrahamic circumcision from a legal perspective, how secure is the liberty of Jews and Muslims to carry on from generation to generation with their ancient tradition in the United States?

That issue has recently been raised in a US Supreme Court concurring opinion written by Justice Samuel Alito and joined by Justices Neil Gorsuch and Clarence Thomas, *Fulton et al. v. City of Philadelphia, Pennsylvania, et al.* (2020). The case concerned a City of Philadelphia policy forbidding participation in foster care referrals by a Catholic agency that refused on religious grounds to refer children for placement with same-sex couples. The justices unanimously overturned the city's policy. A majority did so on narrow procedural grounds. Justice Alito wrote a concurring opinion raising deeper constitutional "free exercise of religion" issues. (Note: Because we currently live in a highly partisan political world, I pause here to caution the reader not to rush to judgment or be misled by one's prior views of particular members of the court.) Over the past several decades there have been liberal justices as well as conservative justices on both sides of the deep question addressed in Justice Alito's concurring opinion. That question concerns the correct interpretation of that concise, highly consequential, yet elusively vague clause in the First Amendment of the US Constitution which states that "Congress shall make no law . . . prohibiting the free exercise . . . [of religion]."

How broadly should we interpret the free exercise of religion clause? Does it have a narrow meaning or a broad meaning? Was it specifically (and exclusively) aimed at prohibiting Congress from engaging in state-sponsored religious per-secutions? If that is its intent and the free-exercise-of-religion clause should be read as a no-religious-persecution clause, then perhaps it should be interpreted narrowly and conservatively as merely forbidding legislation that explicitly expresses an animus toward religion or is deliberately scripted to discriminate against particular (or even all) forms of religious exercise.

Or alternatively, was the religious liberty clause designed to accomplish something broader. Was it perhaps designed as a more proactive principle sup-portive of ideological (religious and cultural) pluralism in the United States? At the time the free exercise clause was written the various regions of the coun-try were culturally and religiously distinct and thus heterogenous, and (one assumes) each region had an interest in being free to retain their local beliefs and customs.[8] If that was the intention and the clause should be read as a respect-for-religious-conscience clause, then perhaps it should be interpreted more liberally as requiring some degree of deference in our secular law and order society to the claims and authority of sacred personal obligations, sincerely held moral convictions, and religious conscience.

The no-religious-persecution interpretation of the free exercise of religion clause reads it narrowly, conservatively, and thinly. The respect for religious conscience interpretation reads the clause broadly, liberally, and thickly. Accord-ing to the narrow, conservative, thin reading no citizen is ever beyond the reach of a valid law, and the only types of laws that are invalid and forbidden by the First Amendment's religious liberty clause are those that on their face (as written) directly display hostility toward religious beliefs and conduct.

A rather consequential corollary flows from that interpretive perspective, namely, that there is no constitutional religious liberty grounds for a conscien-tious objection to a facially neutral law of general applicability that serves some secular purpose (for example, a statute requiring formal schooling for all chil-dren until sixteen years of age; a statute requiring all eighteen-year-old males to perform military service; a statute requiring everyone, without exception, to be vaccinated against every contagious disease for which vaccines are available; or a statute requiring that all nonessential businesses remain closed on some des-ignated "day of rest"). By the lights of that no-religious-persecution interpreta-tion of the religious liberty clause, if a law is generally applicable (applies to everyone regardless of their religious convictions), is neutral toward religion on its face, serves some legitimate government interest (it need not even be a com-pelling government interest, just a legitimate one), and was enacted by a demo-cratic legislative process, then religious liberty objections to the law on (sup-posed) constitutional grounds are misguided and not even entitled to judicial review. This is the view expressed in *Employment Division v. Smith*, 494 U.S. 872 (1990), in a majority decision written by Justice Antonin Scalia that forms the basis for Supreme Court free exercise jurisprudence at the present time.

Much has been written about the Smith decision and its doctrine. And there have been ongoing debates about whether Justice Scalia's interpretation of the Constitution's free exercise clause is persuasive.[9]

The Supreme Court's religious liberty doctrine as expressed in the Smith decision has been incendiary. It provoked a legislative revolt in Congress, where, in opposition to the courts' decision, our elected federal legislators overwhelmingly passed the 1993 Religious Freedom Restoration Act (RFRA), which was quickly signed into law by President Clinton. In rebellion against the Supreme Court's Smith doctrine, Congress and the president thereby gave statutory authority to the broader respect for religious conscience interpretation of what religious liberty means in the United States. Subsequently, the Court's opinion in *City of Boerne v. Flores* (621 U.S. 507) restricted applicability of the Federal RFRA statute to federal law, though states remain free to enact similar provisions under their own legal codes. Twenty-one states have done this. In Justice Alito's concurring opinion in the recent case of *Fulton et al. v. City of Philadelphia, Pennsylvania, et al.* (2020), he expressed the constitutional view that Smith should be overturned. He, along with Justices Gorsuch and Thomas, identified the problem with Smith's interpretation of the free exercise clause this way: "Even if a rule serves no important purpose and has a devastating effect on religious freedom, the Constitution, according to Smith, provides no protection." It was that type of concern and opposition to Justice Scalia's reasoning in the Smith case that led Congress in 1993 to pass the RFRA, with strong bipartisan support.

Smith was a watershed case: an established interpretation of the free exercise clause (namely, the respect for religious conscience interpretation) was abandoned and replaced by the no-religious-persecution interpretation. From 1963, with the case of *Sherbert v. Verner* (374 U.S. 398), the respect for religious conscience interpretation had become the court's recognized free-exercise-of-religion doctrine. The Court allowed claims for religious exceptions and applied the standard of strict scrutiny: Limitations of religious liberty required a compelling government interest, and that limitation had to be as narrowly tailored as possible. Evaluating a religious liberty case thus required several judgments: First, was the claim a religious claim? Second, was it sincere? Third, was there a compelling government interest that required limiting the religious practice? Finally, was the scheme for limiting religious practice as narrowly tailored as possible?

In other words, between 1963 and 1990 the Court did not rule out the granting of exemptions from neutral laws of general applicability. As a matter of principle, such exemptions might be granted if certain conditions were met, namely, the incidental and unintended burden on religious exercise created by the law was real; the government interest served by the neutral law of general applicability that was creating the burden was not a compelling government interest (distinctions were drawn between valid or legitimate government interests, important government interests, and compelling government interests); and the burden created by the law (even by a law serving a compelling government interest) was more burdensome than necessary to serve that government interest. Taken together, those conditions for granting exemptions from neutral laws of general applicability were known as "the Sherbert test." Taken together, they were a manifestation of the court's respect for the religious conscience interpretation of the free exercise clause.

During that era (between 1963 and 1990) the Court was willing to consider (on a case-by-case basis) whether a devout and conscientious plaintiff should be granted an exemption from a majoritarian law of general applicability on the grounds that the law incidentally placed an unacceptable burden on that person's constitutional right to religious liberty by compelling conduct forbidden by the person's religious conscience or sacred obligations. The Court subscribed to the view that the formal features of a statute (in particular, its generality and facial neutrality, and hence apparent nondiscrimination against religion) were insufficient for dismissing a religious liberty claim. For example, in the 1972 case of *Wisconsin v Yoder* (406 US 205), a decision that exempted Amish Mennonite families in Wisconsin from the state's requirement that children attend school until age sixteen, the Court majority wrote: "A regulation neutral on its face may, in its application, nonetheless offend the constitutional requirement for government neutrality, if it unduly burdens the free exercise of religion." The Court reinforced *Sherbert*'s call for doctrinal flexibility and a pragmatic case by case-based application of the First Amendment's religion clauses. The opinion went on to say, "The Court must not ignore the danger that an exception from a general obligation of citizenship on religious ground may run afoul of the Establishment Clause [favoring Amish Mennonites over other religions, who have not been exempted from the law, for example], but that danger cannot be allowed to prevent any exception no matter how vital it may be to the protection of values promoted by the right of free exercise."

Then, in 1990, the Sherbert test was shelved by the reasoning of the majority in the Smith decision and superseded by Justice Scalia's no-religious-persecution interpretation, which narrowly defined the free exercise of religion clause as a constitutional shield against intentional religious discrimination and persecution by the state. With Smith the respect for religious conscience interpretation became defunct as a constitutional principle.

RFRA: The congressional phoenix of religious conscience

Nevertheless, as noted, after the Smith decision was announced the respect for religious conscience interpretation of the free exercise clause managed to rise up from the ashes through legislation. It lives on as a potential religious liberty exemption claim wherever there is a Religious Freedom Restoration Act (RFRA), either federally legislated or enacted by a state. Notably, conspicuously, astonishingly, in the wake of the Smith decision, the respect for the religious conscience interpretation was resurrected and reactivated by an act of Congress with its 1993 RFRA legislation. Thus, today in the United States "religious liberty" means one thing from the point of view of Supreme Court constitutional doctrine yet has a very different meaning from a congressional (or state) statutory perspective.

In effect and with intent, the Religious Freedom Restoration Act (RFRA) reinstituted the Sherbert-test religious exemption regime, whose purpose is "to make sure that broad statutes, sound as they may be in general, aren't applied in situations where they both (A) interfere with religious practice and (B) aren't really necessary, given the specific facts of the case." In other words, RFRA "provides that the government (A) may not substantially burden people's religious beliefs unless such a burden is (B) the least restrictive way of serving a compelling government interest."[10]

To reiterate, in 1990, with the Smith decision, the Supreme Court abandoned the respect for religious conscience interpretation of religious liberty and disposed of the Sherbert test. Three years later, by endorsing RFRA, Congress legislatively recommitted the country to the respect for religious conscience interpretation of religious liberty (and the Sherbert test). Currently, that broader reading of the free-exercise-of-religion clause lacks constitutional authority in the eyes of the Supreme Court. That broader reading is currently nonoperational as a potential *constitutional* defense against neutral laws of general applicability that incidentally burden one's sacred obligations and religious conscience; and that broader reading will remain nonoperational at least until five justices vote to revisit and overturn the doctrine behind the Smith decision. At the same time, RFRA explicitly grants *statutory* authority to the broader interpretation of religious liberty and provides a legal path to conscientious objections to neutral laws of general applicability, which, if and when Sherbert-test criteria apply, permits the courts to grant exemptions from majoritarian laws of general applicability.

Who wants to restore respect for religious conscience: Liberals or conservatives?

It is noteworthy, as I mentioned earlier, that the Supreme Court's shift from the respect for religious conscience interpretation to the antireligious persecution interpretation did not neatly divide conservative justices from liberal justices. The conservative Justice Scalia was joined in his doctrinal reasoning by the liberal Justice Stevens. He was opposed by the liberal Justices Brennan, Marshall, and Blackmun. He was joined in his reasoning by the conservative Justices Rehnquist, Whyte, and Kennedy, but not by conservative Justice Sandra Day O'Connor, who was so vehemently opposed to his reading of the meaning of the free exercise clause that she argued it was "incompatible with our nation's fundamental commitment to religious liberty." Liberal Justice Blackmun (joined by Justices Brennan and Marshall) began his dissent this way: "This Court over the years painstakingly has developed a consistent and exacting standard [the Sherbert test] to test the constitutionality of a state statute that burdens the free exercise of religion. Such a statute may stand only if the law in general, and the State's refusal to allow a religious exemption in particular, are justified by a compelling interest that cannot be served by less restrictive means. Until today, I thought this was a settled and inviolate principle of this Court's First Amendment jurisprudence. The majority, however, perfunctorily dismisses it as a 'constitutional anomaly.'"

And ever since the Smith case there have been liberal justices (e.g., Justice Souter in his concurring opinion in *Church of the Lukumi Babalu Aye, Inc. and Ernesto Pichardo, Petitioners v. City of Hialeah*, 508 U.S. 520, 1993) and conservative justices (e.g., Justice Alito) who have made it clear they are uncomfortable with the Court's current interpretation of the religious liberty clause and would like to see the reasoning of the Smith majority and its no-religious-persecution doctrine overturned. As Justice Souter opined in his concurrence, "the [Smith decision] rule that a neutral, generally applicable law does not run afoul of the free exercise clause even when such a law prohibits religious exercise . . . ought to be re-examined by the Supreme Court in a case presenting the issue." These critics, whether they are liberal justices or conservative justices, have favored of a broader, thicker (dare I say more "liberal") reading of the free exercise clause; one that is more open to claims of religious conscience and sincerely held sacred obligations. They would permit the court to implement case-by-case exemptions from laws designed to be generally applicable. Justice Alito expresses displeasure with the Smith decision, and notably (given a main topic of this essay) does so with reference to a hypothetical (and by his lights, odious) ban on neonatal male circumcision as practiced by Jews and Muslims. To wit:

> There is no question that Smith's interpretation can have startling consequences. Here are a few examples. Suppose that the Volstead Act, which implemented the Prohibition Amendment, had not contained an exception for sacramental wine. The Act would have been consistent with Smith even though it would have prevented the celebration of a Catholic Mass anywhere in the United States. Or suppose that a State, following the example of several European countries, made it unlawful to slaughter an animal that had not first been rendered unconscious. That law would be fine under Smith even though it would outlaw kosher and halal slaughter. *Or suppose that a jurisdiction in this*

country, following the recommendations of medical associations in Europe, banned the circumcision of infants. A San Francisco ballot initiative in 2010 proposed just that. A categorical ban would be allowed by Smith even though it would prohibit an ancient and important Jewish and Muslim practice. (My emphasis)

Categorical bans on gender-equal Abrahamic circumcision: Is there a legal defense?

The original 1996 federal "female genital mutilation" statute initially appeared vulnerable to legal challenges on several grounds. In the Michigan case Judge Bernard Friedman declared the statute unconstitutional on the grounds that it exceeded the enumerated legislative powers granted to Congress in the US Constitution. In 2021 Congress reenacted the law and explicitly claimed authority to do so under its constitutional power to regulate interstate commerce. Michael Rosman has suggested that unless the courts revisit the expanding scope of application of congressional interstate commerce regulatory powers the new "Stop FGM Statute of 2020" might well survive constitutional challenge.[11]

Nevertheless, if there had been a federal criminal trial and subsequent court appeals of Jumana Nagarwala and her Dawoodi Bohra gender-equal Abrahamic circumcision tradition, that 1996 federal statute might have been challenged in other ways. The statute most certainly did burden a religious custom of conscientious members of a Muslim religious denomination and expanded the capacity of federal governmental agencies to intrude into the family privacy of parents from disfavored minority groups.

The statute also failed to provide equal protection for both boys and girls before the law: Observant Muslim and Jewish males were permitted to have their religious obligations honored while observant religiously motivated Muslim women were not. And this was so even in the absence of any showing of physical injury or serious harm and without any concern for the non-medical religious benefits of the custom for women. As Michael Rosman has suggested, "The Due Process Clause of the Fifth Amendment to the US Constitution has been held to have an 'equal protection' component that restricts the federal government in a way similar to the restrictions that the Equal Protection Clause of the Fourteenth Amendment imposes on state government (*Adarand Constructors v. Pena*, 515 U.S. 200, 213–18 [1995]). Thus, to the extent that Section 116 [the federal anti-FGM statutes of 1996 and 2021] treats female circumcision differently from male circumcision, it is subject to a challenge under that provision."

That equal protection argument of course cuts in both directions. Imagine a federal statute, written as a law of general applicability categorically criminalizing female circumcision. If it were upheld, then the equal protection argument might carry disastrous implications for the future liberty of Jews and Muslims to honor the biblical Abrahamic covenant for boys exclusively on religious, aesthetic, or cultural (rather than medical) grounds. Imagine in this instance that a Fifth Amendment due process clause equal protection argument then resulted in the enactment of a general and categorical law serving some postulated government interest that criminalizes all nonmedical genital procedures on children regardless of gender or religion. As Justice Alito feared, such a result might very well be consistent with the Supreme Court's current Smith doctrine, "even though it would prohibit an ancient and important Jewish and Muslim practice."

Justice Alito's comment highlights the point that the court's current Smith doctrine leaves little room for an American citizen to contest (on First Amendment religious liberty grounds) a general federal (or state) statutory ban on childhood circumcisions. This is one reason the Dawoodi Bohra Michigan case inevitably draws our attention to divergent interpretations of religious liberty in the United States, and to current debates about the legal scope for the free exercise of religion in our liberal pluralistic society.

What if Congress or any of the fifty state legislatures enacted a categorical generally applicable ban on all childhood circumcisions (female or male)? On what legal grounds might religiously motivated Jews or Muslims (including the Dawoodi Bohra) object? At least two prominent legal advocates, Eugene Volokh and Michael Rosman, think the RFRA might provide the answer, but that remains to be seen.

Then they came for me

I suppose it must be obvious by now that I have written this essay as a cautionary tale. I have written it as an anthropologist who believes we have a responsibility in our plural (multireligious/multicultural/multiethnic) society to try to understand the unfamiliar customs of others before we decide to "other them," treat them as aliens, or charge them with a serious crime. I have written the essay as a cultural psychologist of morality who believes we should be slow to judge a little known and poorly understood minority group such as the Dawoodi Bohra, whose women (we discover upon investigation) find spiritual significance in a customary Abrahamic rite that is gender inclusive and for girls is less invasive than a male circumcision.

Admittedly, I have also written this essay motivated by an ancestral consciousness and legendary collective memory of times when Jewish mothers were persecuted because of their attachment to Torah-based practices such as male circumcision. Permit yourself to imagine what it must be like for loving parents who are members of a religious minority group to be charged with the "M" word, accused of being "mutilators" of their own children, and demonized because of a custom at the heart of their personal and communal identity. Envision an FBI surveillance of Jewish institutions, the interrogation of Jewish children, forced inspection of their genitals and separation from their families, led by a federal prosecutor who views their parents as threats to society. Picture the arrest of observant Jewish parents who live in Minnesota and arrange for a mohel who usually practices in Michigan to conduct a circumcision ritual, whose religiously motivated action then gets represented in court filings as a criminal conspiracy to transport children across state lines to commit a sexual offense. In our land of the free and home of the brave that has been the recent experience of American Muslim women of the Dawoodi Bohra faith.

Perhaps one way to make the Dawoodi Bohra custom seem less alien is to recognize the similarity between the procedures associated with the female side of their tradition and the Jewish conversion ceremony called *hatafat dam brit*, a rite of entrance into the covenant of Abraham arranged by conservative and orthodox Jewish parents (and by some Reform Jews as well) when they adopt a non-Jewish child who has been previously circumcised. Viewed as a physical and symbolic process *hatafat dam brit* (for boys) resembles the Dawoodi Bohra custom (for girls). In both instances the central physical procedure is a mitigated cut, nick, or piercing. In the Jewish case it is aimed at drawing a drop of blood from the head of the penis (where the foreskin had already been excised). In the Dawoodi Bohra case it is aimed at excising a few foreskin cells. In both instances the physical procedure is a symbolic act in the sense that it simulates a circumcision with the hope of binding generations to the ancient revelation and to each other and to continuing the relationship to the divine it is designed to evoke. In both religious traditions, Jewish and Muslim, an insignificant physical procedure conveys transgenerational obligations and communal identity meanings that run deep.

To date, the Jewish rite of entrance into the covenant of Abraham has not been an object of moral panic, topic of widespread concern, or focus of government attention in the United States. Europe, however, is quite another story. Childhood male circumcision has been under attack by the Council of Europe and by regional courts, legal activists, political parties or medical associations in Germany, Holland, Denmark, Norway, Finland, and Sweden.[12] In 2018 a legislative ban on male circumcision, one comparable in its aim to the 1996 FGM statute in the United States, was under consideration in Iceland. The proposed bill criminalized any childhood male circumcision that was not medically required. Not surprisingly, the bill provoked strong religious freedom objections from Jews and Muslims living there.

Clouds are on the horizon even in the United States. The "M" word is now the idiom of anti-"male genital mutilation" ("MGM") activists, the so-called intactivists. With a tactical interest in the Jumana Nagarwala case, they too supported her 2017 arrest and prosecution and welcomed her prospective trial as an opportunity to further their cause, which amounts to being saviors who liberate baby boys from their "mutilating" parents.

Jewish and Muslim male circumcision procedures have not (yet) been the target of federal legislation in the United States (to date there has been no anti-male genital mutilation bill). Nevertheless, in 2010–2011 there was a ballot initiative to prohibit male circumcision in the city of San Francisco. One of the leaders of that initiative, the intactivist Matthew Hess, achieved notoriety by creating and publishing a comic book series featuring a blond, Aryan-looking, superhero named Foreskin Man, "who saves babies from being circumcised and fights their would-be circumcisers" (with special attention to Jews, Muslims, and Africans).

The San Francisco ballot initiative was quashed by a California judge on the grounds that male circumcision was a State of California medical procedure that could be opposed only by a statewide ballot initiative. All bets are off, however, if one day an American Dawoodi Bohra mother legally circumcises her son and is then arrested and convicted of a serious crime for performing a medically safe less intrusive excision procedure on the foreskin of her daughter. The intactivist movement already has adherents and ideological visibility on social media. One of their calls to action reads "Equal Rights for All Sexes: Say 'No' to Forced Genital Cutting." Had Jumana Nagarwala been convicted of the crime of "female genital mutilation," it is not unimaginable that the verdict would have added energy and force to political mobilization efforts and legal arguments for equal protection before the law for boys as well. The result might well have been an increase in demands to criminalize or interdict childhood male circumcision as well as female circumcision.[13] Down the road (and not necessarily in the distant future) the fate of Jewish and Muslim male circumcision is likely to be in the hands of our courts, and thus rest on a judicial interpretation of the true meaning of the promise of religious liberty in the United States.

Conclusion: Imagining the future of the rites of Abraham

Seth Rozin is an award-winning playwright, the artistic director of the Philadelphia based experimental InterAct Theatre Company, and the courageous author of an eye-opening one-act play titled *Human Rites* (2019), which challenges us to come to terms with cultural diversity in conceptions of gender, sex, and "normal" genitals. At the very end of his essay "A Dramatic Interpretation of the Fragilities of the FGM Narrative," he describes his idea for another play that could serve as a kind of thematic sequel to Human Rites. It would follow a pair of US Department of Justice lawyers—one a Jewish man, the other a Christian woman, neither particularly religious—who are prosecuting a Dawoodi Bohra mother and her family physician for practicing FGM. The two attorneys are politically liberal and fervently anti-FGM, and as they dig deeper into the ritual—its origins, its basis in religion and its spiritual and social meaning in the Dawoodi Bohra community—they begin to craft the most compelling arguments for prosecution. But in doing so, it becomes clear to the Jewish lawyer that if successful, the exact same line of thinking could, and probably will, be employed against the Jewish (and broader Western) practice of circumcising infant boys at some point down the road. Conflict between the lawyers intensifies, as the Jewish man begins to reconsider his desire to prosecute the case and even whether the case might do more harm in the world than good. In the end, Christians, Muslims, and Jews, along with the secular and non-religious alike, must grapple with the consequences of judging and prosecuting such practices on separate and unequal terms.[14]

The playwright's essay concludes: "As the practice of circumcision and its corollary risks and benefits for both males and females inevitably gain greater attention and scrutiny, I anticipate that there will be more and more plays, as well as books and movies, bringing to life stories that chronicle the evolving moral attitudes around this most visceral of human rites."

In addition to plays, books, and movies, I anticipate more and more prosecutions and legal debates about the meaning of religious liberty in the United States, with potentially serious consequences for the future of Abrahamic circumcision customs.

PART IV

RACE

CHAPTER 10

FREEDOM IN THE AMERICAN CENTURY AND AFTER

ERIC FONER

O ne of the most revealing episodes in the history of American freedom took place in the immediate aftermath of World War II. On September 16, 1947, the 160th anniversary of the signing of the US Constitution, the Freedom Train opened to the public in Philadelphia. A traveling exhibition of 133 historical documents, the train, bedecked in red, white, and blue, soon embarked on a sixteen-month tour that took it to more than three hundred American cities. Never before or since had so many cherished pieces of Americana—among them the Mayflower Compact, Declaration of Independence, and Gettysburg Address—been assembled in one place. After leaving the train, visitors were exhorted to dedicate themselves to American values by taking the Freedom Pledge and adding their names to a Freedom Scroll.

The idea for the Freedom Train, perhaps the most elaborate peacetime patriotic campaign in American history, originated with the Department of Justice. President Harry Truman endorsed it as a way of contrasting American freedom with "the destruction of liberty by the Hitler tyranny." Since direct government funding smacked of propaganda, however, the project was turned over to the nonprofit American Heritage Foundation, whose board of trustees, dominated by leading bankers and industrialists, was headed by Winthrop W. Aldrich, chairman of Chase Manhattan Bank.

The Freedom Train was an enormous success. It attracted more than 3.5 million visitors and millions more took part in the activities that accompanied its journey, including labor-management forums, educational programs, and patriotic parades. Behind the scenes, however, the Freedom Train demonstrated that the precise meaning of freedom was not uncontroversial. The liberal staff members at the National Archives who proposed the initial list of documents included the Wagner Act of 1935, which guaranteed labor's right to collective bargaining, and President Roosevelt's Four Freedoms speech of 1941, which listed as the Allies' aims in World War II freedom of speech and religion, freedom from fear, and the vaguely socialistic freedom from want—that is, the guarantee to all of a basic standard of living. These documents, however, were eliminated by the more conservative American Heritage Foundation. Also omitted were the Fourteenth and Fifteenth Amendments to the Constitution, which had granted civil and political rights to Black Americans after the Civil War but had been essentially nullified by the white supremacist South, and Roosevelt's order of 1941 establishing the Fair Employment Practices Commission. In the end, nothing on the train referred to organized labor or to any twentieth-century social legislation, and of the 133 documents, only three related to Blacks: the Emancipation Proclamation, the Thirteenth Amendment, and a 1776 letter criticizing slavery.

Black Americans, indeed, had virtually no voice in planning the exhibit and many were initially skeptical about it. On the eve of the train's unveiling, the poet Langston Hughes expressed the hope that there would be "no Jim Crow on the Freedom Train." "When it stops in Mississippi," Hughes wondered, "will it be made plain / Everybody's got a right to board the Freedom Train?" In fact, with the Truman administration about to make civil rights a major priority, the train's organizers announced that they would not permit segregated viewing. In an unprecedented move, the American Heritage Foundation canceled visits to Memphis and Birmingham when local authorities insisted on separating visitors by race. But the Freedom Train visited forty-seven other southern cities without incident and was hailed in the Black press for breaching, if only temporarily, the walls of segregation.

If the Freedom Train reflected a growing sense of unease with overt expressions of racial inequality, its journey also revealed the Cold War's impact on the definition of freedom. Conceived as a way of underscoring the contrast between American freedom and Nazism, the Freedom Train quickly became caught up in the emerging ideological struggle with communism. In the spring of 1947, a few months before the train's dedication, Truman had committed the United States to the worldwide containment of Soviet power. Soon, attorney general Tom C. Clark was praising the Freedom Train for helping to prevent "foreign ideologies" from infiltrating the United States and for "aiding the country in its internal war against subversive elements." The Federal Bureau of Investigation began compiling reports on those who criticized the train or seemed unenthusiastic about it. The Freedom Train inaugurated a period when the language of freedom suffused American politics and culture. At the same time, it revealed how the Cold War subtly reshaped freedom's meaning, identifying it with anticommunism, "free enterprise," and the defense of the social and economic status quo. The story of the Freedom Train reveals in microcosm a crucial fact about freedom: far from being fixed, the definition of freedom has changed many times and has been the subject of persistent conflict in American history. It also points to the three major issues that debates about freedom have revolved around: the meaning or definition of freedom; the social conditions that make freedom possible; and the boundaries of freedom, that is, who is entitled to enjoy it.[1]

No idea is more fundamental to Americans' sense of themselves as individuals and as a nation than freedom. The central term in our political vocabulary, freedom—or liberty, with which it is almost always used interchangeably by ordinary Americans—is deeply embedded in the documentary record of the nation's history and the language of everyday life. The Declaration of Independence lists liberty among mankind's unalienable rights; the Constitution announces as its purpose to secure liberty's blessings. The United States fought the Civil War to bring about a new birth of freedom, World War II for the Four Freedoms, the Cold War to defend the Free World. In the early twenty-first century, the administration of George W. Bush gave the title Operation Enduring Freedom to the global war on terrorism and Operation Iraqi Freedom to the invasion of that country. Americans' love of freedom has been represented by liberty poles and liberty caps and acted out by burning stamps and burning draft cards, running away from slavery, and taking to the streets to demand the right to vote. Obviously other peoples also cherish freedom, but the idea does seem to occupy an unusually prominent place in public and private discourse in the United States. "Every man in the street, white, black, red or yellow," wrote the educator and statesman Ralph Bunche in 1940, "knows that this is 'the land of the free' . . . [and] 'the cradle of liberty.'"[2] And as groups from nineteenth-century abolitionists to modern-day conservatives have realized, to "capture" the word freedom is to acquire a formidable position of strength in political debates.

Perhaps because of its very ubiquity, the history of what the historian Carl Becker called this "magic but elusive word" is a tale of debates, disagreements, and struggles rather than a set of timeless categories or an evolutionary narrative toward a preordained goal. Definitions of freedom relegated to the margins in one era have become dominant in the next, and long-abandoned understandings have been resurrected when circumstances changed. Instead of a fixed concept, freedom is what philosophers call an "essentially contested concept," one that by its very nature is the subject of disagreement.[3] And the many meanings of freedom have been constructed not only in congressional debates, court decisions, and political treatises, but on plantations and picket lines, in parlors and even in people's bedrooms.

If freedom has been a battleground throughout our history, so too has been the definition of those entitled to enjoy its blessings. It is hardly original to point out that the United States, founded by declaring to the world that liberty is an entitlement of all mankind, blatantly deprived many of its own people of freedom. When the Constitution was ratified, fully one-fifth of the American population consisted of African American slaves. Efforts to delimit freedom along one or another axis of social existence have been a persistent feature of our history. More to the point, perhaps, freedom has often been defined *by* its limits and exclusions. The master's freedom rested on the reality of slavery, the much-celebrated autonomy of men on the subordinate position of women. By the same token, it has been through battles at the boundaries—the efforts of racial minorities, women, workers, and other disadvantaged groups to secure freedom as they understood it—that the meaning of freedom has been deepened and transformed and the concept extended to realms for which it was not originally intended. Time and again in our history the definition of freedom has been transformed by the demands of excluded groups for inclusion.

These themes are powerfully illustrated by the changing meaning of freedom during the "American Century," a phrase coined by the prominent American publisher Henry Luce during World War II. Of course, Americans in the twentieth century were inheritors of ideas of freedom forged many decades earlier. The struggle for American independence gave birth to a definition of nationhood and national mission closely linked to freedom. The new nation defined itself as a unique embodiment of liberty in a world overrun with oppression. The fate of freedom thus rested with what Thomas Jefferson called "this empire of liberty." The sense of American uniqueness, of the United States as an example to the rest of the world of the superiority of free institutions, remains alive and well even today as a central part of our political culture.

But the Revolution also revealed the persistent inner contradiction of American freedom, by giving birth to a republic rhetorically founded on liberty but resting economically in large measure on slavery. As Tyler Stovall writes in his recent book *White Freedom*, the Age of Revolution witnessed both the crystallization of many modern ideas of freedom and the rapid spread of Atlantic slavery and European empire. This combination led to the idea of freedom being increasingly "racialized," defined, that is, as an entitlement of whites alone.[4] Some of the most famous philosophers of freedom either profited from slavery (including John Locke, an investor in the slave-trading Royal African Company), owned slaves (Jefferson held well over one hundred when he drafted the Declaration of Independence), or spoke of slavery primarily as a metaphor—being subjected to intolerable laws such as taxation without popular consent—rather than as a living reality that made a mockery of the idea of a universal entitlement to freedom.

"Those who are taxed without their own consent," said the founder John Dickinson, "are slaves."[5] Indeed, to the revolutionary generation, the right of self-government and the protection of property against interference by the state were essential to freedom; taken together, these principles suggested that it would be an infringement on liberty to deprive a man of his property (including slave property) without his consent. To divest owners of their slaves would reduce *them* to slavery.

During the decades between the Revolution and Civil War, slavery expanded rapidly in the United States. Southern slaveowners dominated the federal government, and the profits derived from slave labor fueled the entire country's economic growth. Slavery's powerful presence helped to define American understandings of freedom. Even as whites celebrated their own freedom, the "imagined community" of the American republic—the definition of those entitled to enjoy the "blessings of liberty" protected by the Constitution—came to be defined by race. Only one state (Maine) that entered the Union between 1800 and the Civil War allowed Black men to vote, a crucial disability in a nation that prided itself on political democracy. No Black person, declared the Supreme Court on the eve of the Civil War in the *Dred Scott* decision, could ever be an American citizen or had any rights "which the white man is bound to respect." Yet at the same time, the struggle by outcasts and outsiders—white abolitionists, slaves, and freed people, often employing the larger society's language of freedom, reinvigorated the notion of freedom as a truly universal ideal. The principles of birthright citizenship and equal protection of the law without regard to race, which became central elements of American freedom, were products not of the nation's founding, but of the antislavery struggle and the Civil War.

During the postwar era of Reconstruction, freedom for the first time became a concrete matter of public policy rather than simply an abstract principle. Once slavery was abolished, the status of the former slaves became the central issue in American politics. What did it mean to be a free person in the United States? The Civil Rights Act of 1866 began to answer that question by mandating racial equality in the rights essential to compete in the economic marketplace—owning property, going to court, and so on. There followed constitutional amendments and legislation expanding the definition of freedom to include citizenship for all those born in the country, the equal protection of the laws, the right of all men to vote regardless of race, and the absence of racial discrimination in access to transportation and public accommodations. For a moment, a powerful federal government, feared by many of the founders as a danger to liberty, became what the abolitionist senator Charles Sumner called the "custodian of freedom."[6] Yet a violent racist backlash soon followed that wiped away many of the gains of Reconstruction and, in the South, restored the racial boundary that limited the enjoyment of freedom to whites.

After decades of the slavery controversy, which had somewhat tarnished the sense of a special American mission to preserve and promote liberty, the Civil War and emancipation reinforced the identification of the United States with the progress of freedom. In the 1880s the British visitor James Bryce was struck not only by the power of Americans' commitment to freedom but also by their conviction that they were the "only people" truly to enjoy it.[7] Even as the United States emerged from the Spanish-American War of 1898 with an overseas empire akin to the empires of Europe, traditional American exceptionalism thrived, yoked ever more tightly to the idea of freedom by the outcome of the Civil War.

At the turn of the twentieth century, its social conditions dominated discussions of freedom. American disciples of Herbert Spencer such as William Graham Sumner argued that law by definition restricts freedom and that the free market is the true domain of liberty. The Supreme Court, embracing this view in its "liberty of contract" jurisprudence, overturned numerous state laws regulating conditions of labor and the behavior of corporations as interference with the freedom of employers to manage their property as they desired and of laborers to decide for themselves when and where to work. Labor, said the union leader John L. Mitchell, was being guaranteed freedoms it did not want and "denied the liberty that is of real value."[8] Mitchell and other critics raised the question whether meaningful freedom could exist in a situation of extreme economic inequality. In the nineteenth century, economic freedom had generally been defined as autonomy, usually achieved via ownership of property—a farm, artisan's shop, or small business. The man who worked for someone else his entire life was not truly free. The transformation of the United States into the world's foremost industrial economy rendered this understanding of freedom increasingly obsolete. When early twentieth-century reformers forcefully raised the issue of "industrial freedom," they insisted that economic freedom had come to mean not so much the independence that came with property ownership but economic security—a living wage, the right to a say in management, or, in a phrase that became ubiquitous in these years, an American standard of living.[9] To secure economic freedom thus defined required active intervention by the government.

This belief achieved a remarkable popular reach, especially during World War I and again in the 1930s. During the war, as the Wilson administration spoke of making the world safe for democracy, employers worried that workers were "taking the idea of emancipation" too literally. "It has been impossible to fight Kaiserism abroad without some introspection at home," one wrote. The rhetoric of democracy and liberty used to promote World War I echoed among workers seeking "industrial emancipation" at home.[10] During the 1920s this expansive notion of economic freedom was eclipsed by a resurgence of laissez-faire ideology. But in the following decade, Franklin D. Roosevelt sought to make the word freedom a rallying cry for the New Deal. As early as 1934, in his second fireside chat, Roosevelt juxtaposed his own definition of liberty as "greater security for the average man" to the older notion of liberty of contract, which served the interests of "the privileged few." Roosevelt consistently linked freedom with economic security and identified entrenched economic inequality as its greatest enemy. "The liberty of a democracy," he declared in 1938, was not safe if citizens were unable to "sustain an acceptable standard of living."[11]

If Roosevelt invoked the word to sustain the New Deal, "liberty," in the sense of limited government and liberty of contract, became the fighting slogan of his opponents. The principal conservative critique of Roosevelt's policies was that they restricted American freedom. When conservative businessmen and politicians in 1934 formed an organization to mobilize opposition to the New Deal, they called it the American Liberty League. The fight for possession of the "ideal of freedom," the *New York Times* observed, was the central issue of the presidential campaign of 1936.[12] Opposition to the New Deal planted the seeds for the later flowering of an antigovernment conservatism bent on upholding the free market and dismantling the welfare state. But as Roosevelt's landslide reelection in 1936 indicated, most Americans had for the time being come to accept the view that freedom must encompass economic security, guaranteed by the government.

If for most of the nineteenth century America's encounter with the outside world had been more ideological than material, the twentieth saw the country emerge as a persistent and powerful actor on the world stage. And at key moments of worldwide involvement the encounter with a foreign antagonist subtly affected the meaning of freedom in the United States. One such episode was struggle against Nazi Germany, which not only highlighted aspects of American freedom that had previously been neglected but also fundamentally transformed perceptions of who was entitled to enjoy the blessings of liberty in the United States. It also gave birth to a powerful rhetoric, the division of the planet into free and unfree worlds that would long outlive the defeat of Hitler.

Today, when asked to define their rights as citizens, Americans instinctively turn to the privileges enumerated in the Constitution's Bill of Rights—freedom of speech, the press, and religion, and so forth. But for many decades, the social and legal defenses of free expression were extremely fragile in the United States. A broad rhetorical commitment to this ideal coexisted with stringent restrictions on speech deemed radical or obscene. Dissenters who experienced legal and extralegal repression, including abolitionists, labor organizers, World War I–era socialists, and birth control advocates, had long insisted on the centrality of free speech to American liberty. But not until the late 1930s did civil liberties assume a central place in mainstream definitions of freedom. It was only in 1939 that the Department of Justice established a Civil Liberties Unit. In 1941 the Roosevelt administration celebrated with considerable fanfare the one hundred and fiftieth anniversary of the Bill of Rights, whose fiftieth anniversary and centennial had passed virtually unremarked.

There were many causes for this development, including a new awareness in the 1930s of restraints on free speech by public and private opponents of labor organizing. But the "discovery" of the Bill of Rights on the eve of American entry into World War II owed much to an ideological revulsion against Nazism and the invocation of freedom as a shorthand way of describing the numerous differences between American and German society and politics. During World War II, the Nazi counterexample was frequently cited by defenders of civil liberties in the United States, among them the Supreme Court when it reversed an earlier decision and overturned the conviction of Jehovah's Witnesses who refused to salute the American flag in public schools. Freedom of speech took its place as one of the "four essential human freedoms"—President Roosevelt's description of Allied war aims endlessly reiterated throughout the conflict. Not only did the Four Freedoms embody the "crucial difference" between the Allies and their enemies, but in the future, Roosevelt promised, they would be enjoyed "everywhere in the world," an updating of the centuries-old vision of the United States instructing the rest of mankind in the enjoyment of liberty.[13]

If World War II embodied a transformation, in the name of freedom, of the country's traditional relationship with the rest of the world, it also reshaped Americans' understanding of the internal boundaries of freedom. The abolition of slavery had not produced anything resembling racial justice, except for the brief period of Reconstruction. By the turn of the century, Jim Crow, a system of inequality resting on segregation, disenfranchisement, a labor market rigidly segmented along racial lines, and the threat of lynching for those who challenged the new status quo, was being consolidated in the South, with the acquiescence of the rest of the nation. At the turn of the century not only the shifting condition of Black Americans but also the changing sources of immigration spurred a growing preoccupation with the nation's racial composition. Beginning in the 1890s, more than half of the immigrants who entered the United States hailed not from northern and western Europe, the traditional sources of newcomers, but from Italy and the Russian and Austro-Hungarian empires.

Among middle-class native-born Americans, these developments inspired an abandonment of the egalitarian vision of freedom spawned by the Civil War. By 1900 the language of "race"—race conflict, race feeling, race problems—occupied a central place in American public discourse. The idea that mankind is divided into "races," each of which possesses inborn capacities and incapacities, had become foundational to the study of history and political science, just emerging as academic disciplines. The boundaries of nationhood, expanded in the aftermath of the Civil War, contracted dramatically. The law of 1924 that banned all immigration from Asia and severely restricted that from southern and eastern Europe reflected the renewed identification of nationalism and freedom with notions of Anglo-Saxon superiority.

The First World War challenged the idea of white freedom. Many thousands of people of different races fought for a nonracial ideal of liberty. But the hopes engendered by the conflict for an end to the Jim Crow system in the United States were dashed by the violent race riots that followed the war and the resistance of the white South to any changes in the Jim Crow system. At the Versailles peace conference the principle of national self-determination, a key wartime commitment of Woodrow Wilson, was extended only to subject peoples of the now defunct Hapsburg and Ottoman empires, not to Britain and France's colonial subjects.

The struggle against Nazi tyranny and its theory of a master race discredited ideas of inborn ethnic and racial inequality and gave a new impetus to the long-denied struggle for racial justice at home. A pluralist definition of American society, in which all Americans enjoyed equally the benefits of freedom, had been pioneered in the 1930s by leftists and liberals associated with the Popular Front. During the Second World War, this became the official stance of the Roosevelt administration. The government self-consciously used the mass media, including radio and motion pictures, to popularize an expanded narrative of American history that acknowledged the contributions of immigrants and Blacks and to promote a new paradigm of racial and ethnic inclusiveness. What set the United States apart from its wartime foes was not simply dedication to the Four Freedoms but the resolve that they could and should be enjoyed by Americans of all races, religions, and national origins. Racism was the enemy's philosophy; Americanism rested on toleration and equality. By the war's end, awareness of the uses to which theories of racial superiority had been put in Europe helped seal the doom of racism—in terms of intellectual respectability, if not social reality.

Rhetorically, the Cold War was in many ways a continuation of the battles of World War II. The discourse of a world sharply divided into opposing camps, one representing freedom and the other its opposite, was reinvigorated in the worldwide struggle against communism. Once again the United States was the leader of a global crusade for freedom against a demonic, ideologically driven antagonist, and American exceptionalism now suggested a national responsibility to lead the forces of the Free World in the containment of Soviet power. From the Truman Doctrine to the 1960s every American president would speak of a national mission to protect freedom throughout the world, even when American actions, as in Iran and Guatemala in the 1950s and Vietnam in the 1960s, seemed to jeopardize freedom rather than enhance it.

As the USSR replaced Germany as freedom's antithesis, freedom from want, central to the Four Freedoms of World War II, slipped into the background. Whatever Moscow stood for was by definition the opposite of freedom, and not merely one-party rule, suppression of free expression and the like, but anything to which the word "socialist" could be attached, such as public housing, universal health care, full employment, and other policies that required strong and persistent government intervention in the economy. Economic freedom came to be defined as the enjoyment of consumer choice in an unregulated market. Economic libertarians advanced this view as an alternative to the welfare state as well as to communism. Indeed, they insisted, the former would lead inevitably to the latter and so must be stigmatized as a danger to freedom. If freedom had an economic meaning, it was "free enterprise" (often called the Fifth Freedom by conservative businessmen) and the ability to choose from the cornucopia of goods produced by the modern American economy. Internationally, the goal of the United States became to remodel Europe and eventually the entire world in the image of modern American capitalism.[14]

The high or low point of the equation of freedom with consumerism came in 1959 at the famous Kitchen Debate, an iconic moment of Cold War America. "What Freedom Means to Us," Vice President Richard Nixon's speech opening a US exposition in Moscow, focused not on political and civil liberties but on the country's fifty-six million cars and scores of labor-saving devices. Throughout the exchange Nixon used the words "women" and "housewives" interchangeably. Pointing to a little robot that swept the floor in the model of a suburban kitchen that was the exposition's centerpiece, Nixon remarked, "In the United States you don't even need a wife"—inadvertently making plain the role women were expected to play in the consumer culture. It was left to Soviet Premier Nikita Khrushchev to suggest that freedom involved a national purpose larger than consumption. Yet in announcing that the Soviet Union would soon surpass the United States in economic production, Khrushchev in effect conceded the debate. If the battleground of freedom was the consumer marketplace, American triumph was inevitable.[15]

As Louis Menand observes in *The Free World*, his recent study of art and thought during the Cold War, freedom was "the slogan of the times," invoked "to justify everything." This included, incongruously, the ability to discriminate against other Americans. The 1964 referendum in California that resulted in the repeal of a law outlawing racial bias in the sale and rental of housing was organized by realtors acting, they claimed, to secure homeowners' "freedom of association" or simply "freedom of choice."[16] Yet the glorification of freedom as the essential characteristic of American life in a struggle for global dominance opened the door for others to seize on the language of freedom for far different purposes. Most striking was the civil rights movement, with its freedom rides, freedom schools, freedom marches, and its insistent cry, Freedom Now. The movement voiced an expansive definition of freedom. When Martin Luther King Jr. ended his great oration on the steps of the Lincoln Memorial with the words of a Black spiritual, "free at last, free at last, thank God almighty, I'm free at last," he was not referring to getting the government off his back or paying low taxes. Freedom for Blacks meant empowerment, equality, and recognition as a group and as individuals. Central to Black thought has long been the idea that freedom involves the totality of a people's lives and that it is always incomplete. To oversimplify, most white Americans believe that freedom is something they possess and that some outside force is trying to take away. Most African Americans view freedom not as a possession to be defended but as a goal to be achieved. From what the political theorist Nikolas Rose calls a "formula of power," the Black movement made freedom once again "a formula of resistance," a rallying cry of the dispossessed.[17]

The 1960s also witnessed the emergence of social movements in which private self-determination assumed a new prominence in definitions of freedom. The expansion of freedom from a set of public entitlements to a feature of personal life had many antecedents in American thought (Jefferson, after all, had substituted "the pursuit of happiness" for "property" in the Lockean triad that opens the Declaration of Independence). But the New Left was the first movement to elevate the idea of private freedom to a political credo. The rallying cry "the personal is political," driven home most powerfully by the second wave of feminism, announced the extension of claims of freedom into the arenas of family life, social and sexual relations, and gender roles. While the political impulse behind Sixties freedom has long since faded, the decade fundamentally changed the language of freedom of the entire society, identifying it firmly with the right to choose not only in the consumer marketplace but in a whole range of private matters from sexual preference to attire, music, and what was simply called "lifestyle." More recently, the most striking expansion of the idea of freedom into new private realms came in 2015 with the Supreme Court's decision requiring states to allow gay couples to marry. Writing for the majority, Justice Anthony Kennedy reaffirmed the idea that the American Constitution is a living document whose protections expand as society changes. "New dimensions of freedom become apparent to new generations," he wrote, "often through perspectives that begin in pleas of protest. . . . [The] generations that wrote and ratified the Bill of Rights and the Fourteenth Amendment did not presume to know the extent of freedom in all of its dimensions."

Although Cold War rhetoric eased considerably in the 1970s, it was reinvigorated during the presidency of Ronald Reagan, who effectively united into a coherent whole limited government, free enterprise, and anticommunism, all in the service of a renewed insistence on American exceptionalism based on the idea of freedom. Consciously employing rhetoric deeply embedded in the American experience, Reagan proclaimed that "by some divine plan . . . a special kind of people—people who had a special love for freedom" had been chosen to settle the North American continent. (This narrative, of course, wrote the Black population, whose ancestors arrived in chains, out of the American story.) Its exceptional history imposed on the nation an exceptional mission: "We are the beacon of liberty and freedom to all the world."[18]

Since Reagan's presidency the dominant constellation of definitions of freedom in the United States has consisted of a series of negations—of government, of social responsibility, of restraints on individual self-definition and consumer choice, of any activities with broad social aims that might interfere with the creation of a free market in capital, natural resources, and labor. After the collapse of the Soviet Union and the end of communism in Eastern Europe, a series of administrations, aided and abetted by most of the mass media, embraced the idea that the operations of the global free market embodied the essence of freedom and that the economic life of all countries should be refashioned in the image of the United States—the latest version of the nation's self-definition as model of freedom for the entire world. But the financial crisis of 2008 and the recession that followed, the worst economic crisis since the Great Depression, drove a stake into the heart of this doctrine, sometimes called "neoliberalism," which had been embraced by governments around the world in the 1990s and 2000s. Like a zombie, neoliberalism still walks the earth. But its failure opened the door for new understandings of freedom to gain wider acceptance, most strikingly exemplified in the widespread popularity, especially among young Americans, of Senator Bernie Sanders of Vermont, a self-proclaimed democratic socialist who helped propel to center stage of political debates the idea that economic inequality is a threat to American freedom.

Meanwhile, in the aftermath of the tragic events of September 11, 2001, freedom quickly emerged as an all-purpose explanation for the attack itself, and as the battle cry of a new generation of war hawks. Freedom itself is under attack, President George W. Bush announced in his speech to Congress ten days after September 11. In later speeches he repeated this theme. Why did terrorists attack the United States, he repeatedly asked. His answer: "Because we love freedom, that's why. And they hate freedom. . . . They hate us because we are free." (Actually, while Osama bin Laden, who planned the September 11 attacks, condemned the United States on many grounds, including the stationing of American troops in Saudi Arabia, the spiritual homeland of Islam, he never actually identified American freedom as the motivation for his self-proclaimed war against the United States.) To his credit, Bush insisted that the "war on terrorism" was not a conflict with Islam itself—a religion that claims more than one billion adherents, in countries across the globe. But many Americans rejected this part of his message and embraced the idea that the Cold War had been followed by a new global conflict—the "clash of civilizations," the latest iteration of the racialist ideology that sees the enjoyment of freedom as something which only certain persons (whites) and societies (Western)—are capable of enjoying.

As in past wars, the invocation of freedom proved, for a time, a powerful means of rallying public support for military operations. But Bush's uses of the idea of freedom went well beyond military combat. In 2002 the administration issued the National Security Strategy, a document that dealt with global military and political affairs. It opened not with a discussion of weaponry or geopolitics but with a brief essay on freedom, which it defined as a combination of political democracy, freedom of expression, religious toleration, and free enterprise. These, it proclaimed, "are right and true for every person, in every society." There was no sense that other people may have given thought to the question of freedom and arrived at their own conclusions about it. During the seven years of his presidency following September 11 Bush referred to the idea of freedom with amazing regularity. In his first inaugural address, in January 2011, he had used the words "freedom," "free," or "liberty" seven times. In his second, in 2005, they appeared forty-nine times in a ten-minute speech.

Like other wars, the "war on terrorism" raised anew the problem of balancing security and liberty. In the immediate aftermath of the attack, Congress rushed to passage the USA Patriot Act, a mammoth bill (it ran to more than three hundred pages) that conferred unprecedented powers on law-enforcement agencies, including the authority to wiretap and in other ways spy on citizens, open letters, read e-mail, and obtain personal records from third parties like universities and libraries. Large numbers of Americans approved of the government's limitations on freedom in the aftermath of September 11, a reminder that in an atmosphere of fear the cry of necessity can undermine the commitment to freedom. It also underscores that strong protection for civil liberties is a recent and still fragile historical achievement.

By the time Bush's second term ended, the war in Iraq had become extremely unpopular in the United States, and the economy was in a shambles. In this environment, Bush's incessant reliance on "freedom" to justify the unjustifiable had achieved the almost impossible result of seeming to discredit the very idea of freedom itself. One illustration of this was Jonathan Franzen's novel simply entitled *Freedom*, published in 2010. In Franzen's book every character wants freedom, speaks of freedom, and abuses freedom—all with disastrous results. The search for personal freedom leads to family disintegration. The quest for political freedom leads to the invasion of other countries and what would later be called "forever wars." The search for economic freedom leads to greed, inequality, and the decay of any sense of a larger social good.[19]

During his presidency, Bush's successor, Barack Obama, did not speak very often of freedom. (The exceptions mostly came when he was trying to rally support for sending more troops to the ongoing war in Afghanistan.) Obama preferred to invoke the ideals of community, equality, and responsibility. In his inaugural address in January 2009 Obama used the words "freedom" and "liberty" only four times. But he issued a direct challenge to the culture of "greed and irresponsibility" that, in the name of freedom, had prevailed in the United States for the previous three decades. Nor did freedom appear to be a major concern of Donald Trump, who followed Obama in the White House. Trump preferred to speak the language of raw military and economic power. He spoke of putting "America first"; national self-interest, not the promotion of freedom or the remaking of other societies in the American image, would be the hallmarks of his policies at home and abroad. But his political appeal also rested on an effort to redraw freedom's boundaries along nativist and racial lines. He launched his campaign for president with a diatribe against immigrants from Mexico, whom he characterized as murderers and rapists. Trump had first come to attention in politics by charging that Obama was not really an American citizen, since he was born in Africa (in fact, Obama's birthplace was Hawai'i). This charge recalled the idea, common in the days of slavery, that Blacks are aliens who can never be true Americans. Soon Trump was advocating repeal of the provision in the Fourteenth Amendment that establishes the citizenship of virtually anyone born in the United States. The eclipse of the language of freedom during the presidencies of Obama and Trump was a remarkable development in a country where devotion to freedom had long been a standard claim of movements from all parts of the political spectrum.

Nonetheless, freedom, however defined, is too central to American political culture to be permanently abandoned. Competing narratives of freedom, each rooted in the nation's past, have helped to shape recent public debates. One, with echoes of the biblical story of Exodus, sees freedom as a struggle to overcome inequality. This outlook was powerfully reinvigorated in 2020 by the demonstrations demanding racial justice that followed the murder by a white police officer of George Floyd, an African American resident of Minneapolis. A competing narrative of freedom focuses on untrammeled individual choice. This understanding of freedom predominates among conservatives of one kind or another, from advocates of unimpeded free enterprise to armed militias insisting that the right to bear arms is the centerpiece of American liberty. Most recently it has been widely invoked to support the claim that freedom includes the right to refuse to wear a face mask and to be vaccinated against the COVID-19 virus. In the name of freedom, that is, the right to expose fellow citizens to a deadly disease.

Today the meaning, boundaries, and future of American freedom remain as contested as ever. As in the past, the struggle to define the meaning of freedom is a contest for intellectual, political, social, and economic power and ultimately the ability to define what kind of country the United States should be. Which is why freedom, in the United States and across the globe, is always the subject of debate, forever a work in progress.

CHAPTER 11

FREEDOM THROUGH UNFREEDOM

W. E. B. Du Bois's Theory of Democratic Despotism

ROBERT GOODING-WILLIAMS

"**D**emocratic movements," W. E. B. Du Bois argues, "are . . . efforts to increase the beneficiaries of the ruling [of men]," and they are always taking place "inside groups and nations." In eighteenth-century Europe, he adds, a new, modern democratic movement emerged, aiming to give "universal expression" to these efforts. Indeed, the "philosophy of the movement said that if All ruled they would rule for All and thus Universal Good was sought through Universal Suffrage." On Du Bois's account the modern democratic movement aspires to universalize the benefit of ruling, to extend that good to all, and it promotes universal suffrage as a critical means to that end. Its efforts have been stymied, however, by ignorance and selfishness. During the eighteenth century "ignorance about the action of men in groups and the technique of industry in general" constrained successful democratic struggles to "restricting menial service, securing the right of property in handiwork and regulating public taxes; distributing land ownership; and freeing trade and barter." Meanwhile, as selfish interests opposed these efforts, "a whole new organization of work suddenly appeared"—the "'Industrial Revolution' of the nineteenth century"—largely though not exclusively due to the "determination of powerful and intelligent individuals to secure the benefits of privileged persons, as in the case of foreign slave trade." Confronted with this "vast and unexampled development of industry," the "new democracy stood aghast and impotent," unable to rule what "it did not understand." Thus "an invincible kingdom of trade, business, and commerce ruled the world, and before its threshold stood the Freedom of 18th century philosophy warding the way. Some of the very ones who were freed from the tyranny of the Middle Ages became the tyrants of the industrial age."[1]

The historian Eric Hobsbawm has written that "if the economy of the nineteenth century world were formed mainly under the influence of the British Industrial Revolution, its politics and ideology were formed mainly by the French."[2] Du Bois embraced a similar view, I propose, but also held that there is a fundamental contradiction between the tyranny of the industrial age and the "Philosophy of Democracy handed down from the 18th century."[3] To be sure, he recognized that the latter can be adduced to rationalize and protect the former, but the contradiction between democracy and tyranny, between freedom and unfreedom, whether political or industrial, was critical to his thinking. When Du Bois published "Of the Ruling of Men" (1920), he held that the history of the modern world had largely been propelled by a conflict between the essentially democratic impulses animating the French Revolution and the antidemocratic, capitalist, and essentially self-interested forces driving the slave trade and the Industrial Revolution.[4] With the triumph of the latter, captains of industry and philanthropists ruled the world, but soon the "lowest laborers," including the "American Negroes" who revolted against slavery, took up the democratic fight for freedom. Still, he insists, the Civil War was *not* "a war for Negro freedom, but a duel between two industrial systems, one bound to fail because it was an anachronism, the other bound to succeed due to the Industrial Revolution." After the war, the philosophy of democracy reasserted itself against the newly consolidated capitalist order, for with Reconstruction there "was a chance . . . to try democratic rule in a new way, against the new industrial oppression with a mass of workers who were not yet in its control . . . a unique chance to realize a new modern democracy in industry in the southern United States which would point the way to the world." But the effort to make good on that prospect—to enfranchise Black and white labor, to redistribute land and capital, and to establish a public school system—ultimately failed, due to the resistance of "former slaveowners" and the "owners of the industrial North." The result, Du Bois writes, "was the disenfranchisement of the blacks of the South and a world-wide attempt to restrict democratic development to white races and to distract them with race hatred against darker races." "This program," he continues, while "it helped raise the scale of white labor, in much greater proportion put wealth and power in the hands of the great European Captains of Industry and made modern industrial imperialism possible."[5]

It is precisely with reference to "this [antidemocratic] program" and to white European workers' later, "renewed efforts" democratically to "control" modern industrial imperialism that Du Bois, during the decade of the Great War, conceptualized the mode of rule structuring the modern world.[6] In Du Bois's narrative of the history of democratic struggles stretching from the eighteenth century, the year 1877 marks a pivotal juncture marked by the end of Reconstruction and Stanley's arrival at the mouth of the Congo River. According to the story Du Bois tells, the demise of Reconstruction and the beginning of the scramble for Africa gave rise to a mode of global governance essentially characterized by two, interrelated dynamics: the ongoing democratic development of the white working class—its success, that is, in reforming the prevailing imperialist political order by promoting polices that reduced the capitalist domination and exploitation of white workers in Europe and America; and the persistent suppression of the democratic development of the world's "darker races"—thus, their ongoing subjection to domination and exploitation by white workers united with white capitalists.[7] Du Bois's term for this mode of governance, the advance of democracy and freedom at the expense of unfreedom and tyranny, is "democratic despotism."

Du Bois's moral psychology of white supremacy is part of his attempt to explain the conjunction of these dynamics—that is, to say why the moral norms advanced by the modern democratic movement, while effective in constraining capitalist interests when they targeted white workers, were not effective in fettering those interests when they targeted the world's darker peoples. Du Bois means his moral psychology to serve two purposes. The first, relying on a third-person perspective, is social scientifically to explain democratic despotism. The second, relying on a first-person perspective, is to articulate the Christian white supremacist's ideal, guiding conception of her life as a Christian, to which conception she holds herself accountable.[8] Du Bois's third-person depiction of the white supremacist's moral character is nuanced and complicated, and Du Bois invokes it, again, to explain the dynamics of modern, global governance. The white supremacist's tendency to act from anti-Black malevolence, whether his ill will finds expression in nasty displays of hostility or explicit acts of murder, is essential to Du Bois's portrait. Certain cognitive and affective tendencies are equally essential, however, for when the white supremacist acts malevolently he is assuming the truth of a wide range of firmly held beliefs—that Blacks are subhuman, that whiteness is "ownership of the earth," for example, which he regards as authorizing his actions; and expressing a wide range of intensely felt affects—contempt and hatred, for example, which lend emotional texture to his actions. In Du Bois's view, a combination of interrelated motivational, cognitive, and affective dispositions—including but not limited to ill will directed against Blacks—comprises the white supremacist's morally vicious character, a formation of habits and dispositions that is typically implicated whenever the white supremacist mistreats Black people, and which is likewise implicated in the increase of white freedom at the expense of Black unfreedom.[9]

Du Bois contra Hobson

Quoting Pliny the Elder's pronouncement that out of Africa there is always something new, *Semper novi quid ex Africa*, Du Bois opens "The African Roots of War" by remarking that "the Roman proconsul . . . voiced the verdict of forty centuries." Published in the May 1915 issue of *Atlantic Monthly*, Du Bois's essay makes the case that the cause of the then ongoing world war was to be sought in Africa—and, indeed, in the advent of something *new* in Africa. While Pliny's proclamation has been historically verified through any number of events, including, the essay argues, the first welding of iron and the emergence of Christianity as a world religion, Du Bois's interest is the comparatively recent event of Europe's colonial expansion into Africa, a "prime cause" of the World War and a world-historical catastrophe of "lying treaties, rivers of rum, murder, assassination, mutilation, rape, and torture [that] have marked the progress of Englishman, German, Frenchman, and Belgian on the dark continent." Like J. A. Hobson, with whom he attended the "First Universal Races Congress" held at the University of London in 1911, Du Bois described this catastrophe as "the new imperialism."[10]

Nine years earlier, in his book on the new imperialism, Hobson had argued that "the novelty of recent Imperialism regarded as a policy consists chiefly in its adoption by several nations." Hobson's epitome of the "root idea of empire," of the "conception of a *single empire* wielding political authority over the civilized world," was the hegemony that Rome exercised over the entire "recognized world . . . under the so-called pax Romana." With the fall of Rome, he tells us, this conception "did not disappear," but survived in the ambitions of Charlemagne, Rudolph of Hapsburg, and Charles V, as well as in "the policy of Peter the Great, Catherine, and Napoleon." In contrast to the initially Roman idea of empire, Hobson's "essentially modern" notion is exemplified by the competitive "scramble" of several European nations (Belgium, Britain, France, Germany) politically to absorb "tropical or sub-tropical lands in which white men will not settle with their families." The "new imperialism," Hobson writes, is "driven more and more into the annexation and administration of tropical countries."[11]

With his opening reference to Pliny, who, during the early years of the Roman Empire, seems to have spent part of his career as a procurator in Africa, Du Bois tacitly echoes Hobson in contrasting an older, Roman imperialism to "the new Imperialism"; that is, to the efforts of England, France, Germany, and Portugal, in the aftermath of the Franco-Prussian War, to seek "power and dominion away from Europe." The upshot of these efforts, of the "scramble for Africa," he argues, is that "a continent where Europe claimed but a tenth of the land in 1875, was in twenty-five more years practically absorbed." Du Bois reminds us that the scramble for Africa began with Stanley's explorations of

Central Africa and King Leopold's establishment of the Congo Free State, whose murder, mutilation, and robbery of Black Africans "differed only in degree and concentration from the tale of all Africa in this rape of a continent already furiously mangled by the slave trade." But while Stanley's explorations were "the occasion" of European nations seeking dominion away from Europe, "the cause lay deeper." "Why was this?," Du Bois asks, "What was the new call for dominion?"[12]

The new imperialism caused the war, Du Bois will argue, but what caused the new imperialism? Du Bois's answers to these questions, his accounting for the new imperialism, involve two components. The first is his explanation of the impetus to European imperial expansion, of the new call for dominion per se. The second is his explanation of Europe's realization of this impulse through its amoral, antidemocratic expansion into territories occupied by Black and other "darker" peoples notwithstanding the modern democratic movement's success in promoting moral norms that had otherwise been effective in taming capitalist self-interest. Conceptually, we can think of the distinction between these components of Du Bois's accounting for the new imperialism in terms that Max Weber famously invokes, arguing that "material and ideal interests, not ideas, directly dominate the actions of human beings. But the 'world views' created by 'ideas' have often served as switches, setting the tracks along which the dynamics of interest moved the actions forward."[13] For Weber, the valid attribution of causal significance to a particular worldview relied on counterfactual reasoning to show how that worldview, through its embodiment in our practices, had made a difference to the determination of the actual course of events through which material or ideal interests had been realized; or, to put the point otherwise, *to establish that the direction of historical development would have diverged from the actual course of events had that world view not acquired efficacy.*[14] Now, Du Bois explains the impulse to European expansion per se in terms of material economic interests. But the targeting of Black Africa and other areas inhabited by darker peoples for imperial expansion he explains in terms of the beliefs and affects constituting the moral character of the Christian white supremacist—her "worldview." Absent the historical efficacy of Christian white supremacy, Du Bois argues, Europe would not have expanded into Africa, or, if it did, its expansion would not have been at the expense of the democratic development of the world's darker peoples. In terms of Weber's "train switches" metaphor, he proposes that Christian white supremacy was the "switch" that accounts for Europe's antidemocratic, imperialist involvement in Africa, for, absent the cultural practice of Christian white supremacy, that involvement, had it still occurred, would not have been a moral disaster.[15] More precisely, and as we shall see, he argues that the "switch" of Christian white supremacy functioned as a "switch off" as well as a "switch on"—that it not only served to trigger violence against Black

Africans but effectively to rule out and halt the application of the moral norms that the modern democratic movement had advanced to curb the domination and exploitation of white workers to white Europeans' treatment of Black Africans.

* * *

"It is admitted by all business men," Hobson writes, "that the growth of the powers of production in their country exceeds the grown in consumption, that more goods can be produced than can be sold at a profit, and that more capital exists than can find remunerative investment." It is "this economic condition of affairs," he adds, "that forms the taproot of Imperialism."

Owing to deficient demand—to underconsumption—among Europe's domestic working classes, capitalists and financiers have a material, economic interest in opening up new markets for goods that can be sold at a profit. In each of several nations, these potential beneficiaries of investment abroad press the nation, the state, to annex foreign territory for the purpose of satisfying that interest. When this pressure succeeds, when, more exactly, the capitalists and financiers "secure the active co-operation of statesmen and political cliques," persuading them to confound class-specific economic interests with the nation's interests, the upshot is the nation's acquiescence to imperialist foreign policies and a consequent "fight" among European nations "for foreign markets or for-eign areas of investment." This dynamic could be halted, Hobson proposes, were each nation to follow the lead of the trade unionists and the socialists by redistributing income to the working class, or to public expenditure, thus rais-ing "the general standard of home consumption" and abating "the pressure for foreign markets."[16]

Like Hobson, Du Bois conceptualizes the nation as an agent of material, eco-nomic interests. On three critical points, however, Du Bois breaks with Hob-son. The first is Du Bois's rejection of Hobson's explanation of the genesis of the new imperialism. The second is his rejection of Hobson's analysis of the rela-tionship between nations' interests and the material interests that drive the new imperialism. For example, Du Bois denies that European imperialism is driven by a false identification of the interests of the nation with the interests of capitalists and financiers. The third is Du Bois's rejection of Hobson's view of the sort of remedy the dynamic of the new imperialism requires. In Du Bois's argument these three points belong together, for each of them stems from his effort in "The African Roots of War" clearly to formulate "the theory" of the "new democratic despotism."[17]

Du Bois presents his formulation of that theory as the solution to a philo-sophical paradox. "Most philosophers," he writes, "see the ship of state launched on the broad, irresistible tide of democracy, with only delaying eddies here and there." "Others," however, "looking closer, are more disturbed. Are we, they ask, reverting to aristocracy and despotism—the rule of might?" The paradox is not simply conceptual, but readily observable in the world, for it has "reconciled the Imperialists and captains of industry to any amount of 'Democracy,'" while allowing "in America the most rapid advance of democracy to go hand in hand . . . with increased aristocracy and hatred toward darker races." Du Bois's solution is straightforward: "The paradox is easily explained," he writes, "the white workingman has been asked to share the spoil of exploiting 'chinks and niggers.'"[18]

As we have seen, Du Bois conceptualizes democratic political movements as "efforts to increase the number of beneficiaries of the ruling [of men]."[19] In "The African Roots of War," he argues in a related vein that from the eighteenth through the twentieth centuries the advance of European democratic movements has led to an *increase* in the numbers of those who benefit from government, with the "dipping of more and grimier hands into the wealth bag of the nation, until to-day only the ultra stubborn fail to see that democracy in determining income is the next inevitable step to Democracy in political power." Economic democracy is an ideal that Du Bois explicitly endorses, but the intra-European tendency toward the realization of that ideal has in practice nationalized and radically altered the structure of exploitation: it is no longer the "merchant prince" or the "aristocratic monopoly" or simply "the employing class" that dominates and exploits the world in order to reap "dividends," but "the nation; a *new democratic nation* composed of united capital and labor." For Du Bois, the paradox of modern democracy is explained by the circumstance that democratic progress within Europe and America for white laborers has entailed the despotic exploitation in America and elsewhere of "chinks' and 'niggers.'" "The present world war," he maintains, is "the result of jealousies engendered by the recent rise of armed national associations of labor and capital whose aim is the exploitation of the wealth of the world mainly outside the European circle of nations."[20]

According to the theory of democratic despotism, material interests in the accumulation of profits through foreign investment gave rise to the new imperialism and explain the impetus to European expansion. Against Hobson, however, Du Bois's theory claims that European nations have become the agents of imperialist economic interests not because underconsumption has led capitalists and financiers to secure the assistance of statesmen and other political allies to advance them, but because the democratic gains of white workers have eliminated the possibility of extracting inordinate profit through the exploitation of those workers. Against Hobson, Du Bois also argues that the material interests sustaining the new imperialism are the true interests of the new democratic nations, each constituted through a unification of capital and labor, not the interests of capitalists and financiers that have been mistaken for these nations' true interests. And against Hobson, finally, Du Bois implies that a downward redistribution of income from white capitalists to white workers cannot possibly remedy the new imperialism, for precisely that sort of democratic redistribution has led to the emergence of democratic despotism and the new imperialism in the first place.[21]

The new imperialism and the moral psychology of white supremacy

I turn now to a more detailed analysis of Du Bois's explanation of Europe's expansion into Africa and elsewhere in terms of white supremacist beliefs, feelings, and motivational dispositions. Consider first a paragraph from "The African Roots of War," which focuses on beliefs:

> Whence comes this new wealth and on what does its accumulation depend? It comes primarily from the darker nations of the world—Asia and Africa, South and Central America, the West Indies and the islands of the South Seas. There are still, we may well believe, many parts of white countries like Russia and North America, not to mention Europe itself, where the older exploitation still holds. But the knell has sounded faint and far, even there. In the lands of darker folk, however, no knell has sounded. Chinese, East Indians, Negroes, and South American Indians are by common consent for governance by white folk and economic subjection to them. To the furtherance of this highly profitable economic dictum has been brought every available resource of science and religion. Thus arises the astonishing doctrine of the natural inferiority of most men to the few, and the interpretation of 'Christian brotherhood' as meaning anything that one of the 'brothers' may at any time want it to mean.[22]

The new imperialism generated stupendous wealth from the darker nations (the answer to the "Whence . . ." question), but, Du Bois suggests, the targeting of those nations for the extraction of wealth depended on beliefs about the world's darker peoples (the answer to the "on what . . ." question). As the older exploitation (of the merchant prince, aristocratic monopoly, and so on) waned in Europe, the knell tolling its demise likewise sounded in other, predominately white areas of the globe—like Russia and North America. But in the land of the "darker folk"—of the Chinese, East Indians, Negroes, and South American Indian—no such knell was even softly heard; indeed, it is precisely the exploitation of the nonwhite peoples inhabiting these lands that generated stupendous wealth for the European metropoles. Why, then, did the knell that otherwise tolled faint and far sound *not at all* in these lands? Du Bois's rejoinder is that the new democratic nations have given their common consent to the profit yielding dictum that nonwhite peoples are *for* governance by white folk and *for* economic subjection to them. New democratic nations targeted nonwhite peoples for exploitation, while slowly ceasing to exploit their white inhabitants, because the citizens of these nations held that their core, white supremacist beliefs—that nonwhites may be directed and used as whites are pleased to direct and use them; that they are naturally inferior to whites; and that they need not be regarded as the virtue of Christian brotherhood would dictate[23]—entailed that the moral considerations that had gradually persuaded them to repudiate the "rule of might," to curtail their exploitation of each other, and more and more to embrace the egalitarian demands of the modern democratic movement simply *did not apply to the treatment of nonwhites*. Again, Du Bois's reasoning is counterfactual: causal significance can be attributed to the new democratic citizens' core, white supremacist beliefs, he suggests, for absent those beliefs, and thus absent the limitation of valid moral judgments to the treatment of whites, the knell would likewise have sounded in the lands of darker folk, thus precluding Europe's realization of its material economic interests though an amoral, antidemocratic expansion into these lands.[24]

The larger story Du Bois tells is complex. As we have seen, he believed that the demise of Reconstruction and the advent of the scramble for Africa engendered a mode of global governance featuring the democratic development of the white working class and the suppression of the democratic development of the world's darker races. In *The Negro* (1915), published the same year as the "The African Roots of War," Du Bois elaborates this thesis in terms that resonate with his analysis of democratic despotism. "The middle of the nineteenth century saw the beginning of the rise of the modern [white] working class," he observes, for by means of "political power the laborers slowly but surely began to demand a larger share in the profiting industry." It was "natural to assume" that the "uplift" of emancipated "dark workers" would follow the same path, he adds, but the "new colonial theory" shaping the "new" colonialism "transferred the reign of commercial privilege and extraordinary profit from the exploitation of the European working class to the exploitation of backward races under the political domination of Europe."[25] In "Of the Culture of White Folk," published just two years later, Du Bois not only elaborates his understanding of modern global governance, but explicitly recurs to his earlier suggestion that white supremacist beliefs help causally to explain it:

> It is plain to modern white civilization that the subjection of the white working classes cannot much longer be maintained. Education, political power, and increased knowledge of the technique and meaning of the industrial process are destined to make a more and more equitable distribution of wealth in the near future. The day of the very rich is drawing to a close, so far as individual white nations are concerned. But there is a loophole. There is a chance for

exploitation on an immense scale for inordinate profit, not simply to the very rich, but to the middle class and to the laborers. This chance lies in the exploitation of darker peoples. It is here that the golden hand beckons. Here are no labor unions or votes or questioning onlookers or inconvenient consciences. These men may be used down to the very bone, and shot and maimed in "punitive" expeditions when they revolt. In these dark lands "industrial development" may repeat in exaggerated form every horror of the industrial history of Europe, from slavery and rape to disease and maiming, with only one test of success,—dividends!

This theory of human culture and its aims has worked itself through warp and woof of our daily thought with a thoroughness that few realize. Everything great, good, efficient, fair, and honorable is "white"; everything mean, bad, blundering, cheating, and dishonorable is "yellow"; a bad taste is "brown"; and the devil is "black." The changes of this theme are continually rung in picture and story, in newspaper heading and moving-picture, in sermon and school book, until, of course, the King can do no wrong—a White Man is always right and a Black Man has no rights which a white man is bound to respect.[26]

As the white working class inevitably advances, through political power, but also through education and so on, and as it wins an increasingly equitable distribution of wealth—as it dips its ever "grimier" hands into the wealth bags of the nations, in the words of "The African Roots of War"—European capitalists' interest in accumulating "extraordinary," now "inordinate" profit through the exploitation of European white working class ceases to be viable. But there is "loophole," the essence of which was expressed in Judge Taney's remark, in the Dred Scott decision, that "a Black man has no rights which a white man is bound to respect." On Du Bois's account, white culture, in all its varied, quotidian manifestations (school books, newspapers, moving pictures, etc.), denies that the moral considerations that animated and won wide acceptance through the modern democratic movement—that supported white workers' rights to organize and to vote and, more generally, that supported the protection of white workers from the murderous exploitation required to extract inordinate profit—bear on whites' actions regarding Blacks. Put differently, he maintains that white culture places all such actions beyond the pale of moral scrutiny—for, again, Blacks have no rights that whites must respect. Echoing "The African Roots of War," Du Bois further suggests that by so limiting the scope of legitimate moral judgment, white culture's loophole allows for levels of exploitation that would not have obtained had Blacks enjoyed moral standing in the eyes of whites. But because Blacks enjoyed no moral standing, because whites regarded Blacks as rightless subjects to be directed and used as white whim dictated, European capitalists looked to Black Africans and other darker peoples to realize their material interests in inordinate profits with a vengeance. White workers benefited from European imperialism, for in addition to winning larger and larger shares of the profits that European capitalists extracted from their labor, they were "practically invited to share in this new exploitation," and "flattered by popular appeals to their inherent superiority to 'Dagoes,' 'Chinks,' 'Japs,' and 'Niggers.'"[27] Accepting the "invitation," white labor entered into alliance with white capital, thus forging and strengthening the armed, national associations of labor and capital that sustained the new imperialism.[28]

In our analysis of Du Bois's explanation of Europe's expansion into Africa and elsewhere, let us consider two paragraphs, versions of which appear both in "Of the Culture of White Folk" and the *Darkwater* version of "The Souls of White Folk." Like "The African Roots of War," the first focuses on the Christian white supremacist's cognitive commitments. The second focuses on his feelings and motivational dispositions:

> With the dog-in-the-manger theory of trade, with the determination to reap inordinate profits and to exploit the weakest to the utmost there came a new imperialism—the rage for one's own nation to own the earth or, at least, a large enough portion of it to insure as big profits as the next nation. Where sections could not be owned by one dominant nation there came a policy of "open door," but the "door" was open to "white people only." As to the darkest and weakest of peoples there was but one unanimity in Europe—that which Herr Dernburg of the German Colonial Office called the agreement with England to maintain white "prestige" in Africa—the doctrine of the divine right of white people to steal.
>
> Thus the world market most wildly and desperately sought today is the market where labor is cheapest and most helpless and profit is most abundant. This labor is kept cheap and helpless because the white world despises "darkies." If one has the temerity to suggest that these workingmen may walk the way of white workingmen and climb by votes and self-assertion and education to the rank of men, he is howled out of court. They cannot do it and if they could, they shall not, for they are the enemies of the white race and the whites shall rule forever and forever and everywhere. Thus the hatred and despising of human beings from whom Europe wishes to extort her luxuries has led to such jealousy and bickering between European nations that they have fallen afoul of each other and have fought like crazed beasts. Such is the fruit of human hatred.[29]

The new imperialism was a competition among multiple new democratic nations to own and profit from the ownership of as much of the earth as possible; but where no nation could establish exclusive control over some section of the earth, the competing nations agreed to a nonprotectionist (non-dog-in-the-manger) "open door" trade policy that allowed them *jointly* to exploit it. Du Bois characterizes the open-door policy as for "white people only," for it extended only to white nations—the new democratic nations— not to "the darker nations." The dynamic of interests driving the new imperialism dictated that, where no nation was dominant enough to own some part of the earth, an open-door trade policy was needed. Why, however, did white European nations limit the scope of the trade policy on the basis of race? Why did they decide to realize their interests by opting to exclude rather than include the darker nations under the aegis of the open-door policy?

With respect to the scramble for Africa, Du Bois replies to these questions by referencing a December 1915 speech delivered by a former German colonial minister, Bernhard Dernburg. During the course of the war, Dernburg argued, England had undermined the "prestige" of the white race (in essence, peoples of color's sense that "the will of the white man is good, unshakeable, unconquerable"), as well as its solidarity against Black Africans, by bringing Black colonial subjects to fight in Europe.[30] In Du Bois's eyes, Dernburg's plea on behalf of white prestige and anti-Black solidarity was predicated on the belief that white people have a "divine right . . . to steal" from "the darkest and weakest of peoples," a sarcastic formulation alluding to the white supremacist's supposition that "whiteness is ownership of the earth," or, as I have put it, that whites have an exclusive right to possess, enjoy, and dispose of the earth. That belief, Du Bois now suggests, explains why the new democratic nations endorsed a racially discriminatory trade policy during the scramble for Africa. Material interests gave an impetus to a nonprotectionist trade policy where ownership by a single nation was impossible, but a belief that Black Africa belongs to and is to be exploited by whites alone explains why that policy followed the path of excluding rather than including nonwhites. Had the denizens of the darker nations been white, Du Bois implies, those nations would have been welcome to participate in the open-door trade policy.

Christian white supremacist beliefs about darker peoples and about Blacks, specifically, may have functioned as switches, conditioning the realization of capitalist economic interests, but the satisfaction of those interests had prerequisites. Thus, the satisfaction of an interest in "inordinate," "big," or "abundant," profits required a market where labor is cheap and helpless. Under the rule of democratic despotism, the new democratic nation was a profit seeking enterprise that pursued profit in Africa because African labor was cheap and helpless. But African labor was not *naturally* cheap and helpless, Du Bois reminds us, rather it was *kept* cheap and helpless "because the white world despises 'darkies'" or, more expansively, due to its "hatred and despising of human beings from whom Europe wishes to extort her luxuries." In "Of the Culture of White Folk," Du Bois claims that African labor had been kept cheap and helpless through policies that denied it the opportunities—educational, political (the vote), and self-assertive (unionization?)—that the European and American white working classes had used to advance democracy. With this observation, he extends an argument, already evident in "The African Roots of War," that African labor had been kept cheap and helpless through the ongoing violence of primitive accumulation, what Karl Marx famously characterized as "the historical process of divorcing the producer from the means of production."[31] Thus, Du Bois observes that "all over Africa" there has been a "shameless monopolizing of land and resources to force poverty on the masses and reduce them to the dumbdriven-cattle stage of labor activity," adding that "the Union of South Africa has refused natives even the right to *buy* land . . . a deliberate attempt to force the Negroes to work on farms and in mines and kitchens for low wages."[32] In stressing the coercive role of primitive accumulation through white Europeans' expropriation of the lands, resources, and labor that Black Africans used to sustain themselves, Du Bois echoes Rudolph Hilferding's and Rosa Luxemburg's prewar Marxist theories of imperialism more than Hobson. For Hilferding, capital "has recourse to the power of the state and uses it for forcible expropriation in order to create the required free wage proletariat. . . . These violent methods are of the essence of colonial policy." For Luxemburg, "each new colonial expansion is accompanied . . . by a relentless battle of capital against the social and economic ties of the natives, who are forcibly robbed of their means of production and labour power."[33]

Importantly, Du Bois differs from Hilferding and Luxemburg in maintaining that the attempt to keep Black labor helpless and cheap—whether through primitive accumulation or policies that denied Black labor opportunities enjoyed by white labor—is impelled by the ill will animating the affects of contempt and hatred; that is, by the desire to injure and do violence to Black life. The white world despises "darkies," and the destruction of Black life required to make darkies profitable, no less than the jealousy and bickering that led to the Great War, is part of the "fruit of human hatred." Here again, then, we find Du Bois arguing that the moral character of the Christian white supremacist, of which white culture is the expression, plays a key role in explaining the new imperialism. Again, it seems, Du Bois's causal reasoning entails the counterfactual claim that had the moral character animating white culture been defined by different tendencies—in this case, had it not been defined by anti-Black contempt, hatred, and ill will—then African labor would not have been kept sufficiently cheap and helpless to incentivize armed associations of white capital and labor to boost their profits through exploiting it. It is difficult, of course, to know exactly on what alternative paths European capital would have embarked to realize its material interests had the "switch off" of white supremacist belief not functioned, historically, to rule out the application of the moral considerations embraced by modern democratic movements to white Europeans' treatment of Black Africans; or had the "switch on" of white supremacist hatred and ill will toward Blacks not trig-gered the violence of primitive accumulation. Perhaps the result would have been a dissolution of the union of white labor and white capital, as white capital struggled to extract higher profits notwithstanding the moral norms animat-ing modern democracy. Or, perhaps, as I suggested, European capital would have found its way into Africa, but with less morally disastrous consequences. Or, perhaps, and finally, and as Du Bois seems to envision in "The African Roots of War," democratic movements would have progressed by leaps and bounds as the "principle of home rule" was extended to "groups, nations, and races" throughout the world and the advance of freedom at the expense of unfreedom met its demise.[34]

CHAPTER 12

THE DENIAL OF FREEDOM AND PUNITIVE EXCESS

BRUCE WESTERN AND JESSICA T. SIMES

T he punitive turn in criminal justice policy represents America's greatest contemporary experiment in freedom and captivity. Dating from the early 1970s and extending through to the current period, punitive criminal justice policy is indicated by the ready use of police powers and incarceration in Black and brown communities. From 1970 to 2019, the US prison population increased from 196,000 to 1.4 million. The US incarceration rate rose to being the highest in the world, and for a decade it has been about four to five times higher than its historic average throughout most of the twentieth century.

Throughout this period, Black men have been four to eight times more likely to be incarcerated than white men. The sociologist David Garland coined the term "mass imprisonment" to describe this period in which incarceration rates reached historic levels and were so socially concentrated as to confine not individuals, but whole social groups.[1] Although the prison attracted the greatest attention from researchers, growth in state prison populations was just the most striking indicator of a fundamental shift in the use of state power by criminal justice agencies. Jail populations for defendants awaiting court action also escalated, and conditions of confinement in prison and jail became harsher.

We use the term "punitive excess" to capture this broader trend in punishment that is comparatively and historically unusual and that also encompasses policing, jails, and projects of criminalization that lie beyond the prison. The unequal distribution of penal control is the essential social fact of punitive excess. Racial and economic inequalities in punishment have dominated the attention of researchers, but these are closely correlated with vulnerabilities of housing insecurity, poor health, and untreated addiction. Poor people of color are punished, yes, but they are also vulnerable in a variety of other ways that, in the absence of other social supports, exposes them to contact with police, the courts, and the penal system. This is punishment as social policy.

In this chapter we draw together some recent research that describes the great limitations on liberty in Black communities that have been imposed by punitive criminal justice policy. This empirical investigation describes the exposure of Black communities, and Black men in particular, to control through three distinct kinds of institutions: jails, prisons, and solitary confinement within prisons. We focus on a single statistic—called the period prevalence or cumulative risk—that describes the proportion of a population that have ever been exposed to an event, like incarceration. The period prevalence is often used in epidemiological studies of disease. In the study of incarceration, cumulative risks describe size of the group that have been subject to penal confinement. Although only a small number are locked up at any point in time, vast segments of Black and brown populations in the United States have lost their freedom to the penal system, for a time, by midlife.

The empirical evidence offers four lessons about punitive excess. First, the denial of freedom through incarceration is fundamentally social in nature. As Erving Goffman observed for the total institution, incarceration involves a displacement of the intimate bonds of family and community.[2] Second, the US experiments in mass criminalization and incarceration were overlaid on long-standing patterns of socioeconomic inequality. Racial gaps in schooling and employment, particularly among men, provided the social divisions along which penal inequalities emerged. Third, great projects in punishment are political in the sense of expressing extreme differences in social power between in-groups and outgroups. Reflecting the power dynamics, punitive excess answered the social problems of outgroups—interpersonal violence, untreated mental illness, and substance use, for example—with punishment. Finally, punitive excess is also a cultural project. Large-scale confinement often under harsh conditions of deprivation depends to an important degree on a cultural project of dehumanization that asserts the irredeemability of those who are locked up.

Demographic dimensions of the era of punitive excess

We describe the punitive era by drawing together several lines of research that measure the exposure of the population to the criminal justice system. This discussion focuses on a specific kind of statistic, called a period prevalence or a cumulative risk. Often the scale of a penal system is measured by an incarceration rate, which records the proportion of a population or demo-graphic group who are locked in prison on a given day. The US incarceration rate in 2021 was 537 per 100,000. Figures like this indicate the annual growth in the incarcerated population from the early 1970s until peak incarceration in 2008, and the slow decline since that time.

In contrast to the point-in-time incarceration rate, cumulative risks quan-tify the prevalence of criminal punishment over the life course, indicate racial and ethnic inequality, and illuminate the aggregate effects of criminal justice contact. Instead of describing the probability of incarceration at a point in time, cumulative risks describe the probability of incarceration usually during an age span. The statistic has been borrowed from social epidemiological studies in which a small number of people may have a disease at any point in time but many more may have been exposed to the disease over a period of time. Know-ing how many people have been exposed is important because it quantifies how many experience the consequences that flow from exposure. With disease, the consequences may be secondary health risks or immunity to further infec-tion. With incarceration, a large research literature details a wide variety of negative effects that descends on individuals who are incarcerated, and also on their families and communities.

Criminal justice contact creates an "eternal criminal record" with endur-ing negative effects.[3] Cumulative risks measure the footprint of the criminal justice system suggesting the aggregate effect of adverse outcomes observed at the individual level. The negative effects of incarceration include large num-bers of legal exclusions that attach to a felony record. These so-called collateral consequences limit rights to social welfare benefits, occupational licenses, and political participation such as voting. For example, a felony record can prevent access to Section Eight housing benefits or food stamps. In many states people with felony records can be denied licenses needed for skilled occupations involv-ing health care or finance, for example. At this writing, eleven states limited voting rights among those who have served criminal sentences. Another six-teen states denied voting rights to those in the community on probation or parole.

Beyond the legal limitations of collateral consequences, research on the socioeconomic effects of incarceration have examined economic opportunities, health, and family life. Researchers have found extremely low levels of employ-ment after release from prison, and incarceration is associated with large reductions in earnings. Formerly incarcerated people are also at high risk of mortality and drug overdose immediately after release. Research on families finds that children with incarcerated parents experience greater material hardship (poverty and homelessness) and diminished school achievement.[4] As a tool for investigating the links between incarceration and social inequal-ity, the cumulative risk specifies the size and social contours of groups at risk of the effects of incarceration.

Estimates of cumulative risks thus occupy a special place in research on criminal punishment and socioeconomic inequality. Researchers have estimated the cumulative risk of imprisonment for different racial and education groups across birth cohorts.[5] Other high-prevalence criminal justice contacts that fall short of imprisonment—like misdemeanor and felony conviction, and probation—have also been the focus of cumulative risk estimates.[6] Related research has estimated the prevalence of parental imprisonment among children.[7]

We describe the cumulative risk of incarceration for jails, prisons, and solitary confinement within prisons. At its core, the criminal justice system is a social control institution that applies the coercive power of the state to surveil and confine its citizens. But confinement varies greatly in degree. Each year in the United States about ten million people are arrested by police, and about a third of these arrests are for driving under the influence, drug violations, or simple assaults (less serious physical altercations). People who are arrested are taken to court, where some are released, but others are incarcerated while their cases are pending in the courts. Municipal and county facilities that detain people with pending criminal cases are called jails. In 2019 there were 2,850 jail jurisdictions in the United States, and jails on any given day held 740,000 people.

Defendants who are convicted of serious offenses, felonies, are committed to state or federal prisons. Prisons are the deep end of the punishment system, typically incarcerating people for at least a year. In 2019 the US prison population numbered 1.4 million, and about 50,000 of those had life-without-parole sentences for which there is no possibility of release. (Compare incarceration in Europe, where life without parole has been outlawed by the European Human Rights Court.) Prison facilities vary in their physical design from minimum security prisons that impose few restrictions on physical movement to supermax prisons that lock people alone in a cell for twenty-three hours each day.

Supermax incarceration is an example of solitary confinement where incarcerated people face round-the-clock incarceration. Nearly all prisons have solitary confinement units, and about 5 percent the whole prison population is locked in solitary confinement on a typical day. Solitary confinement is sometimes described as the prison within the prison, partly used for punishment for misconduct such as fighting or drug use and partly used as a way of controlling the prison population.

The jail

Members of the public are held in locked custody in a wide variety of institutional settings.[8] Police precincts and courthouses have lockups in which people are forcibly confined before appearing in court. State psychiatric hospitals have secure wards that hold people, sometimes with civil commitments, with mental illness who may pose a risk to others. Family courts send children under the age of eighteen to juvenile detention facilities. Immigrants who are staying in the country without lawful immigration status may be held in immigration detention facilities while their cases are resolved or while awaiting deportation. The largest custodial footprint, however, is created by the local jail. Unlike the prison, which incarcerates people convicted of felony crimes, jails detain many defendants who are awaiting court action. Many are held for low-level misdemeanor offenses. In 2017 US prisons admitted about 600,000 people, but 10.6 million were sent to jail.[9]

Perhaps even more than imprisonment, jail detention is closely linked to socioeconomic disadvantage. Those living in poor and minority neighborhoods face high risks of misdemeanor arrest. A system of cash bail and a perfunctory court process for low-level offenses make jail incarceration likely for poor defendants who have few resources for legal defense.[10]

Although duration is usually brief, jail incarceration has been found to adversely affect court outcomes, crime, and socioeconomic life. Natural experiments that exploit the random assignment of judges suggests pretrial detention in jail increases the probability of conviction, lengthens custodial sentences, increases court fees, and increases the likelihood of rearrest.[11] Studies also report reduced earnings and household income, increased risk of separation among parents, and reduced voter turnout following jail incarceration.[12] Because of the large number of jail admissions, researchers have argued that the aggregate effects of jail incarceration on life chances may also be proportionately large. As Kristin Turney and Emma Conner write, "Understanding jail incarceration has important implications for understanding how the criminal justice system creates, maintains, and exacerbates social inequality."[13]

Current understanding of the jail has been shaped by research from the 1970s and 1980s. Pretrial incarceration mostly for low-level offenses was concentrated among very poor urban residents who were often contending with homelessness and drug addiction. John Irwin's classic account, The Jail, described the jail as an adjunct to skid row. The jail managed "the rabble," incarcerating "petty hustlers," "derelicts," "junkies," and others that were distinguished not by their threat to public safety but their offensiveness to conventional norms and institutions.[14] The main empirical expectation of the rabble management perspective is a highly concentrated pattern of incarceration for a small group that returns repeatedly to jail.

Since Irwin's research on the jail, a new line of analysis has described a process of mass criminalization that emerged through the 1990s and 2000s. Mass criminalization involved increased contact between police and minority residents of poor urban neighborhoods. We use the term mass criminalization to describe a style of urban governance in which the police, the courts, and penal institutions exert a pervasive influence in disadvantaged communities in response to social problems linked to poverty and racial inequality. Whereas research on mass incarceration has focused on the "back end" of the criminal justice system, on the prison and prison reentry, mass criminalization describes the front end—the expansive role of police, misdemeanor courts, and jails in their attempts to regulate disadvantaged communities. In the era of mass criminalization, jail incarceration is a by-product of widespread arrests for drug and public-order offenses concentrated in low-income communities of color. Mass criminalization encompasses broken windows policing and the "managerial justice" of the misdemeanor courts that reserves wide discretion for police, prosecutors, and judges.[15] A key empirical expectation of the mass criminalization perspective is that jail incarceration is extensive, particularly in disadvantaged communities, and repeated jail admissions are experienced widely.

We can see the scale of jail incarceration with New York City data for the period 2008 to 2017. Jail incarceration in New York City is supplied by five county jurisdictions, but defendants are detained in a single municipal system, a sprawling array of detention facilities and razor wire located on Rikers Island just to the north of the borough of Queens. Rikers Island has a long history of serious violence, and reports of disorder and brutality at the jail were widespread during the period of our analysis, from 2008 to 2017.[16] Popular pressure to close the jail escalated following reports of a suicide of a young man named Kalief Browder who had been held for three years, seventeen months in solitary confinement, while awaiting trial.[17] The chief medical officer of the jail described a culture of violence in which detainees were regularly beaten by correctional officers, yielding large numbers of head injuries, facial fractures, and lacerations requiring sutures.[18] Solitary confinement was widely used at Rikers Island. About 7.5 percent of the population was held in punitive segregation on an average day in 2013, with an additional number diagnosed with mental illness in a facility dedicated to "restricted housing units."[19]

By the time of our study period, conditions at Rikers were still brutal, but the jail population had fallen by about two-thirds since its peak of 21,000 in the early 1990s. In fact, New York's jail incarceration rate by 2017 was among the lowest of large cities. The jail incarceration rate in New York City was under 200 per 100,000 in 2017, compared to roughly 600 per 100,000 in Philadelphia.[20]

Table 12.1 reports the cumulative risk of jail incarceration by age thirty-eight in New York City. Among white men, about 3.4 percent are estimated to have been incarcerated on Rikers Island at least one time by age thirty-eight. Among Black men by contrast, over a quarter had been incarcerated on Rikers by their late thirties. Cumulative risks are also very high for Hispanic men, about one in six of whom had been jailed by age thirty-eight. Cumulative risks are much lower for women, but even so, nearly 5 percent of all Black women in New York have been incarcerated by their late thirties.

TABLE 12.1 Percentage cumulative risk of multiple jail incarceration by age 38, New York City, 2008–2017

	Number of incarcerations		
	One or more	Five or more	Ten or more
Men			
White	3.4	0.6	0.2
Black	26.7	10.0	4.4
Hispanic	16.2	3.6	1.5
Other	5.7	0.6	0.1
Women			
White	0.7	0.1	0.0
Black	4.9	0.6	0.2
Hispanic	2.3	0.2	0.1
Other	0.6	0.0	0.0

Periods of incarceration in jail are relatively short, often for a week or two. With short periods of incarceration, the risk of repeated incarceration increases. The estimates indicate that 10 percent of all Black men in New York City have been incarcerated at Rikers five times or more. The cumulative risk of being incarcerated ten times for Black men exceeds the risk of being incarcerated even one time for white men. In short, in the era of punitive excess, New York City's jail functions as an instrument of mass criminalization and jail incarceration is a pervasive presence in the lives of Black men.

The prison

The jail represents the shallow end of the penal system, typically detaining people for several weeks while they await court action on their criminal cases, often misdemeanor offenses that offend propriety more than safety. At the deep end of penal confinement lies the state prison where people are incarcerated following conviction for felonies. Whereas jail detention often lasts for several days or weeks, the median period of imprisonment is twenty-eight months.

The growth in imprisonment rates is often taken as the leading indicator of the punitive turn in US criminal justice institutions. The significant growth in prison populations dates from the early 1970s and has been attributed to a complex combination of social forces. Researchers often single out four main causes. First, a decade of vigorous civil rights activism often accompanied by mass mobilizations and disturbances, infused with frustration at the slow pace of change, triggered a political backlash. Law-and-order politics that supported more police and tougher sentences surfaced in national political campaigns and was a cornerstone of the Republican Party's Southern Strategy in the 1968 presidential election. GOP presidential candidate Richard Nixon and segregationist third-party candidate George Wallace regularly conflated crime and civil rights protest on the stump and demanded a strong police response. The electoral success of tough-on-crime policy was reflected in the emergence of bipartisan consensus by the 1990s around increasing the federal funding of local police departments and long prison sentences.

Second, these political trends played out in a social landscape in which enduring employment problems emerged for young Black men with little schooling in central city neighborhoods. US poverty in urban areas was harsh by international standards, diminished relatively little by the kinds of safety net programs for healthcare and housing that contributed significantly to poverty reduction in Western Europe. Urban poverty was also highly spatially concentrated, following the pattern of racial segregation in housing. Spatial concentration of socioeconomic disadvantage became a magnet for spatially concentrated policing, which in turn produced highly spatially concentrated patterns of incarceration. Reflecting the close connection between urban poverty and mass incarceration, imprisonment rates rose significantly from the early 1970s to the 2000s, but nearly the entire growth in prison populations was concentrated among those with no more than a high school education, precisely that group that faced the most serious unemployment problems. Because of the large racial disparities in both poverty and incarceration, historically high prison populations produced astonishing levels of imprisonment among poor Black men who were drawn overwhelmingly from low-income neighborhoods in central cities.

Third, violent crime increased substantially from the early 1960s to the early 1980s. The national homicide rate more than doubled from 4.5 (per 100,000) in the early 1960s to its peak year of 10.2 in 1980. The increase was even larger in cities, rising in Chicago for example from 10.3 in 1960 to 25.0 in 1975. The murder rate for African Americans was 6 to 10 times higher than for whites;

Tedd Robert Gurr found the increase in violence in the 1960s and 1970s to be associated with a disproportionate rise in Black murder rates.[21] Murder rates for young Black men in particular, reached extremely high levels—around 150 per 100,000 in 1980—making homicide the leading cause of death among Black men and women aged fifteen to thirty-four by the early 1990s. Serious violence and concentrated poverty in Black neighborhoods are closely linked. Urban sociologists find that such neighborhoods can struggle to provide the informal social controls of family and community particularly when faced with decades of public policy neglect and segregation.

Some scholars have argued that crime rates bear no relationship to the scale of punishment, that punishment is a pure of expression of state social control for which the mission of crime control is just a fig leaf.[22] It is true that the scale of punishment doesn't track the crime rate in lockstep, but it is equally true that the distribution of violence across the population is closely correlated with the distribution of imprisonment. The level of violence also provides the context for political debate. Tough-on-crime political rhetoric, which often dominated the national stage from the late 1960s to the early 1990s, coincided with a period in which violent crime increased significantly.

Finally, a racialized tough-on-crime politics combined with fears of crime in an electorate facing high rates of violence contributed to changes in sentencing policy in the 1980s and 1990s. Through these two decades prison time became the presumptive sentence for a felony conviction. In part this involved the widespread adoption of prison sentences for drug crimes. Intensified policing efforts against drug crimes and prison sentences for people convicted for the possession and sale of drugs—collectively called the War on Drugs—is estimated to have contributed about to about half the increase in imprisonment from 1980 to 2000. Sentences for violent offenses also became longer as measures like three-strikes enhancements and truth-in-sentencing policies were widely adopted across the states. The increased rate of prison admissions for drug crimes, and the longer sentences for violent crime also drove up the racial disparity in imprisonment.

The results of these four social trends can be seen in the emergence of pervasive imprisonment in recent cohorts of Black men who never finished high school. We examine one cohort that was born between 1945 and 1949 and reached their mid-thirties before the emergence of mass incarceration. We compare them to a younger cohort, born between 1975 and 1979, who grew up during the US prison boom and reached midlife in 2009, near the peak of US imprisonment.

The risk of imprisonment is about seven times higher for Black men compared to white. Estimates indicate that about 9 percent of Black men in the older cohort are imprisoned by midlife, compared to around 1 percent of white men. In the bottom half of the educational distribution among those with no postsecondary education, nearly one in eight Black men born in the late 1940s had been to prison by their mid-thirties. In the cohort born a generation later, one-fifth of all Black men had been to prison by their mid-thirties. Among those without college education, the cumulative risk of prison was a third. The prevalence of imprisonment reached astonishing levels for Black men who had not completed high school. Among those without a high school diploma, fully 70 percent had been to prison by their mid-thirties in 2009. From the early 1990s, US crime rates fell dramatically as prison populations continued to rise. Thus pervasive incarceration emerged among low-education Black men born in the late 1970s at a time when crime was falling to historically low levels.

The prison within the prison

Incarceration in the United States is distinguished not just by the scale of the penal system but also by the severity of prison conditions.[23] The use of solitary confinement in US prisons is a key indicator of harsh conditions. In a given year, around one in five US prisoners is held in solitary confinement, with about half of those in solitary confinement for thirty days or more.[24] Legal scholars view solitary confinement as an unusually restrictive aspect of US incarceration, possibly violating international standards for human rights.[25]

Solitary confinement is the highest level of penal custody where prisoners are typically locked in their cells for twenty-three hours each day, with an hour of relief for recreation, showers, or appointments with medical staff. The twenty-three-hour lockdown characteristic of solitary confinement is generally imposed as punishment for misconduct, such as fighting, possessing contraband, or defiance of authorities. Besides its punitive function, solitary confinement is also used to manage conflicts and to ensure the immediate physical safety of the vulnerable, such as very young or mentally ill prisoners.

Solitary confinement is used more widely and for longer periods in US prisons than in other liberal democracies. Whereas European law limits solitary confinement to no longer than several weeks, US prisoners are incarcerated in solitary units for months and even years at a time.[26] Solitary confinement provides a case of penal severity in the United States, where the main harms of incarceration—material deprivation, social isolation, and psychological distress—converge in their most extreme form.

First, solitary confinement intensifies material deprivation. Solitary confinement deprives prisoners of the ability to obtain supplies, food, and other materials.[27] Released for only an hour or so a day, prisoners in solitary confinement generally cannot visit the prison commissary for supplies, nor can they eat in the dining hall. Prison staff typically pass meals and basic supplies through a slot in the cell door or through prison bars. With the extreme bureaucratic management of human needs, material hardships like hunger or temperature extremes become more likely.[28] Although staff provide regular meals and supplies, interactions with staff in a context of extreme dependence create painful feelings of deprivation and hardship.

Second, solitary confinement increases social isolation. Daily confinement in a cell for up to twenty-three hours severs communication with the rest of the prison population. Human contact is limited to brief, tightly controlled interactions. Prior to medical visits, recreation time, or showers, prisoners may be searched and shackled before being released from their prison cells.[29] The exact protocols of isolation vary from prison to prison, but in general solitary confinement expands the control of staff, increasing risks of arbitrary treatment and abuse.[30] Contact with friends and family outside prison is also restricted. One study found restrictions on visits and phone calls in solitary confinement for all forty-seven prison agencies that were surveyed.[31] Solitary confinement thus weakens the social relationships of those who are incarcerated and the connections of their families too.

Third, some researchers have found that solitary confinement is a significant source of psychological distress. Through a series of clinical assessments, Stuart Grassian observed a variety of symptoms associated with extreme social isolation. Being in a mental fog, obsessive thoughts, perceptual distortions, hallucinations, and other distress are indicators of what Grassian called "SHU syndrome," named for the special housing units in Massachusetts where he conducted his research.[32] Evidence for the negative effects of solitary confinement appears to be strongest for those with prior mental illness.[33]

In fieldwork we conducted in a solitary confinement unit in a maximum-security prison in Pennsylvania, respondents spoke both about the idleness and subjective feelings of isolation in extreme isolation. Michael was a white respondent in his early thirties who had returned to prison from a halfway house after violating the conditions of his release by relapsing to his heroin addiction. Entering prison on a misconduct charge for drug use, he had been placed in solitary confinement for thirty days. To break the ice with respondents, we began interviews by asking about the best thing and the most challenging thing in their day. Michael told us that the most challenging thing was "waking up too early." Waking up each morning at 2:00 a.m. meant "having to wait four or five hours for breakfast." Like many respondents we interviewed, Michael was regularly hungry, and hours were spent each day waiting for meals.

Michael spoke about how there was little to do in solitary confinement so he tried to spend his time sleeping: "I mean, your day is wake up, for me at least, I try to figure it out how I can sleep the most. I mean you just lay there, and you just think a lot. Sometimes you might get a little energy and try and do something, but there's only so much you can do. It might last fifteen minutes, it might last an hour." Sleep was an important strategy for passing time, mentioned in forty-five out of ninety-nine of the baseline interviews. The quality of sleep, however, was widely reported to be poor. Respondents traced their poor sleep to inactivity through the day and noise in the solitary unit at night. Half of the respondents reported that they had trouble sleeping either "all of the time" or "most of the time."

Michael left his cell several times a week for recreation in the small enclosed cages adjoining the solitary confinement unit. We asked him how often he did so: "I've been trying to sleep through one or two days on the schedule, so I forget. But I think it's five days a week, two hours a day, and then if I get the chance, I go. It's supposed to be an hour . . . some guys like to be out there for an hour and then being out there for two hours in a cage just drags on."

Many respondents asserted their status as "human beings" in a setting they felt denied their humanity. A total of forty-nine out of ninety-nine respondents either asserted their humanity ("I'm human like everybody else") or likened their treatment to animals ("I feel like I'm a dog in a motherfucking cell"). Material deprivation and social isolation were sources of distress in part because they were experienced as humiliating and degrading.

The isolation imposed through lengthy periods of lockdown and the denial of visits and phone calls also threatened the respondents' sense of self. Describing differences between solitary confinement and the general prison population, one respondent linked the dehumanization of solitary confinement to psychological distress: "I don't think that anybody should be isolated for such lengthy times as they were doing. Just because human interaction is kind of like a basic necessity. And it's already taken away from us to a degree in [the general prison] population. And then to completely be deprived of that down here, it affects the mind a little bit, regardless of what kind of mind you possess."

Another respondent similarly described the difficulties of being a loving person during incarceration as an affront to his moral worth. When asked what it was like to be incarcerated at the baseline prison, he said: "It's tough. It's tough—it's rough. There's no sympathy, no compassion. It's just, you know, for somebody who comes from any type of a loving background or something like that—you almost have to lose your sense of humanity. Because there is none. Not none that, you know, demonstrated, publicly or anything like that." Similar to Gresham Sykes's observation in his classic field study *Society of Captives*, "thwarted goals, discomfort, boredom, and loneliness" ultimately threaten "the very foundation of the prisoner's being."[34]

With administrative data from the Pennsylvania Department of Corrections, for the period 2006 to 2018, we can calculate the cumulative risk of solitary confinement. With the available data we are able to calculate the chances that a resident of Pennsylvania would ever be imprisoned and be incarcerated in solitary confinement by age thirty-two. For men in Pennsylvania, figures on imprisonment are similar to those we saw for the nation as a whole (table 12.2). About 20 percent of Black men in the state, and about

TABLE 12.2 Percentage cumulative risk of solitary confinement by race and gender, Pennsylvania, 2006–2018

	Men		Women	
	Imprisonment	Solitary confinement	Imprisonment	Solitary confinement
White	2.8	1.4	0.5	0.1
Black	19.1	11.1	0.8	0.4
Hispanic	6.6	3.4	0.4	0.2
Other	0.6	0.3	0.1	0.0
All	5.3	2.8	0.6	0.2

7 percent of Hispanic men had been to prison by age thirty-two compared to less than 3 percent of white men. In Pennsylvania, about 40 percent of men go to solitary confinement at some point during a prison sentence. The relatively high likelihood of solitary confinement contributes to significant cumulative risks. More than 10 percent of all Black men in Pennsylvania have been incarcerated in solitary confinement by age thirty-two. Further calculations show that about 1 percent of all Black men in the state have been locked in solitary confinement for a full year. Similar racial disparities are observed for women, but the level of incarceration and solitary confinement is much lower.

Conclusion

The punitive turn in US criminal justice policy, emerging in the 1970s in the wake of the gains to Black citizenship won by the civil rights movement, produced widespread incarceration in communities of color. In New York City where jail incarceration rates are now among the lowest in the nation, a quarter of all Black men are estimated to have been locked up in Rikers Island jail by their late thirties. National estimates for prison show that most Black men born since the late 1970s who never finished high school have been incarcerated in state or federal facilities. Conditions within prison are often actively harmful. More than 10 percent of Black men in Pennsylvania have experienced the extreme isolation of solitary confinement, and around 1 percent have been spent a year or longer in solitary confinement. Although the overall incarceration rate in the United States is less than 1 percent of the entire population, cumulative risks of jail, prison, and solitary confinement among men in Black communities are vastly higher.

Classical theories of punishment and legal practice also treat incarceration in individualistic terms. In the classical social theory of Bentham and Kant, punishment is the state's infliction of pain on the condemned man. The individualistic character of punishment is expressed in Bentham's utilitarianism for whom individual suffering might deter crime. Kant's retributivism views punishment as a leveling of the moral playing field between the victim and the offender, after the offender's wrongdoing. These individualized conceptions of punishment are also reflected in law, where incarceration is narrowly seen as a deprivation of liberty and prosecutors and defenders compete over the liberty interests of the individual defendant.

In sociology, on the other hand, the loss of freedom entailed by incarceration is deeply social. Incarceration diminishes status in a community. The stigma of a prison record has been well documented by researchers in a variety of domains.[35] Research on the transition to community life after incarceration makes a similar point, that regaining freedom involves reestablishing the social connections with family and friends that mark one's integration back in to society. Because of the spatial concentration, prison has a collective effect that shapes social dynamics across neighborhoods. Erving Goffman has argued that the penal institution itself displaces the household. Whereas the household satisfies the singularity of human needs for food and shelter through the intimate ties of family, food and shelter in the prison are provided through an impersonal bureaucracy that strips people of their individuality to make them more manageable for the institution. Replacing intimate bonds of kin with the uniform treatment of bureaucracy risks creating enormous harm. What people need for personal comfort and to be safe and fed are difficult to deliver at scale, particularly in the steep power relations that divide guards from incarcerated people. The prison researcher Allison Liebling studies whether prisons are meeting standards of humane and decent treatment and aims to measure their "moral performance." From this perspective, not only is the loss of freedom through incarceration a core social event, but the prison itself is also situated in a larger moral landscape. In Eighth Amendment jurisprudence that constitutionally prohibits "cruel and unusual punishment," courts acknowledge the unusual status of prisons as moral institutions by appealing to standards of decency and civilization in which incarcerated people are due a measure of respect.[36] Of course, the protection to incarcerated people provided by these standards has varied, but prisons in liberal democracies must stake a claim—in the courts, to oversight authorities—to maintaining the dignity of incarcerated people. All this reflects the fundamentally social character of freedom and its denial through incarceration.

The elimination of freedom and its accompanying social connections has taken place in a context of deep socioeconomic inequality, it has been a political project reflecting the power of contending social groups, and it has been cultural project in which criminalization is tantamount to dehumanization.

First, social inequality. It is a long-standing observation that punishment descends upon those who have the least. "The law," wrote Anatole France, "in its majestic equality, forbids rich and poor alike to sleep under bridges, to beg in the streets, and to steal their bread." We have seen that incarceration in its many forms has been consistently characterized by large racial disparities in which Black men in particular face the highest risks of incarceration. Race and economic disadvantage are tightly coupled together. The growth of imprisonment rates was concentrated among the non-college men whose economic opportunities deteriorated most in the period of punitive excess. Increasing class inequality in incarceration had a racially disparity producing extraordinarily high levels of imprisonment among Black men who never finished high school. Racial disparity is partly a product of residential segregation. Policing is largely spatially organized, and segregation concentrates arrest and incarceration in a relatively small number of communities of color.[37] The social disadvantage to which incarceration attaches is not described just by the lines of race and class. Penal institutions enforce social conformity. In part this can mean incarcerating those who harm others, but it also includes the adjacent nonconformities of poverty that include homelessness, untreated mental illness, and uncontrolled addiction. These social problems of poverty also became targets for the penal project.

Second, politics. The punitive project had deep historical roots in the use of criminal law to enforce control and confinement in Black communities but rapidly gained momentum in the 1970s and 1980s following the passage of voting and antidiscrimination protections through the Civil Rights Acts. The political struggle over Black citizenship played out in the realm of criminal justice policy. Critics might rightly observe that crime too, was a severe social problem in those communities, and getting tough on crime was a legitimate policy response. Punishment, however, is reserved only for the less powerful. We can see enormous harm perpetrated by powerful insiders, for which punishment has rarely been the solution. For example, in the run-up to the 2008 financial crisis, trading irregularities became normalized in the financial industry, and no major criminal prosecutions were mounted against those who pushed the global economy into a historic recession. College campuses provide another example of the impunity of the powerful. Studies of sexual violence on campus indicate around a third of female undergraduate students are sexually assaulted by graduation. Drug use is also common. Criminal prosecutions on college campuses for sexual assault or drug use or dealing are rare. The point is that there is no natural connection between crime and punishment. Crime by itself cannot explain who is punished. Instead, punishment reflects the balance of power between authorities and those who might be subject to their control.

Finally, culture. Similar to Orlando Patterson's sweeping account of slavery in world history, Slavery and Social Death, we argue that the large-scale loss of freedom entailed by mass incarceration has depended on a cultural project that involves the dehumanization of the poor and the powerless. Harsh punishment requires a profound suspension of human compassion. Black citizens have long-standing vulnerability to cultural projects of dehumanization. In his book by the same title, historian Khalil Muhammad traces a "condemnation of Black-ness" that dates at least from the nineteenth century in which Black men were seen as constitutionally prone to violence. Modern psychological research reports evidence of contemporary Black dehumanization where experimental subjects associate Black men with apelike images, and Black children are perceived as much older than they really are.[38] Tough-on-crime talk runs hot and angry, tapping into fears and other emotional insecurities. The language of super-predators, jungles, and savages, in political speech from Nixon and Wallace to Bill Clinton, draw from this same well of dehumanization. In a striking formulation from the heyday of the tough-on-crime era, William Bennett and his colleagues described children from poor inner-city neighborhoods as a new generation of criminal super-predators: "radically impulsive, brutally remorseless youngsters . . . who murder, assault, rape, rob, burglarize, deal deadly drugs, join gun-toting gangs, and create serious communal disorders. . . . To these mean-street youngsters, the words 'right' and 'wrong' have no fixed moral meaning."[39] For Bennett, the super-predators live in a world beyond the human community. Bennett's writing shows that the cultural project of dehumanization rests not just on the erasure of humanity but also taps into the motivating emotion of fear. Often the criminalization of Blackness, similar to Bennett's example, has conjured fears of violation, takeover, and chaos.

America's punitive excess has wound all these threads together—a history of racialized social inequality, political economy, and culture—in a way that sets it apart from every other society. The many degradations of punishment are visited on the poor and the powerless, while the powerful live with what sometimes seems to be mortal fear of threats to racial and class supremacy. A vast archipelago of prison and jails stands in the way of freedom, and human dignity is denied not just to the captives, but to the captors as well.

PART V

THE ACADEMY

CHAPTER 13

THE UNIVERSITY IN A TIME OF CRISIS

NOAM CHOMSKY

Ioften have to schedule talks well in advance and sometimes am
asked to propose titles. The request raises obvious difficulties in a
world that is always changing, often rapidly.

There are, fortunately, a few fallback options—titles that never fail. One, I've
discovered, is "The Current Crisis in the Middle East." That's sure to be appropriate. Another is "Academic Freedom is Under Threat"—and a closely related
one, "The University in a Time of Crisis," the title chosen for these remarks.
These too never fail.

The title for these remarks was just chosen a few days ago, but in fact it could
have been chosen half a century before. In fact, it was. It happens to be the title
of an article of mine in the late 1960s. And it also could have been chosen half
a century before that—and in fact was, by the great social critic Randolph
Bourne.

As the First World War was grinding to a miserable close, Bourne wrote an
essay about the impact of the war on the intellectual culture. He wrote that the
war had brought to leadership a liberal, technical intelligentsia "immensely
ready for the executive ordering of events, pitifully unprepared for the intellectual interpretation or the idealistic focusing of ends," pragmatic intellectuals who "have absorbed the secret of scientific method as applied to political
administration" and who readily "line up in the service of the war technique."

Turning to the university, Bourne described it as "a financial corporation,
strictly analogous, in its motives and responses, to the corporation which is
concerned in the production of industrial commodities. . . . The university

produces learning instead of steel or rubber, but the nature of the academic commodity has become less and less potent in insuring for the academic workman a status materially different from that of any other kind of employee." The trustees define their obligation as "to see that the quality of the commodity which the university produces is such as to seem reputable to the class which they represent." "Under trustee control the American university has been degraded from its old, noble ideal of a community of scholarship to a private commercial corporation."

That was a century ago.

If the lament sounds up-to-date, it's because it is. A century after Bourne, the British cultural critic Stefan Collini condemned the educational programs of the Tory government that were seeking to impose market discipline on the academic institutions. So if Oxford wants a classics department, show that it can survive in the market. In Collini's words, The Tory government was seeking to convert first-class educational institutions into third-class commercial operations, repeating Bourne's lament in close paraphrase.

The Tory government was threatening the cherished Haldane doctrine, which dates from the time Bourne wrote during World War One: the doctrine that use of research funds should be made by the researchers themselves, not by politicians, or for that matter by other donors.

We can certainly ask whether these ideals are actually realized in practice. Just as we can ask whether Bourne's "old, noble ideal of a community of scholarship" ever existed as more than an ideal. The answer is mixed. Looking over the centuries, the ideal was often upheld, but it has been a constant battle to try to sustain it in the face of external social, economic, and ideological pressures. The relation to academic freedom is too intimate and apparent to require further elaboration.

I happen to have had a good vantage point to observe the struggle during the post–World War II period. Most of my life was spent at MIT, the world's leading technological institution. During these years, MIT changed from an engineering school to a university based on science, with concomitant development of humanities and social sciences—a natural outgrowth of the transition from engineering to science, from making things to understanding them.

Interestingly, this transition took place almost entirely under Pentagon funding, which in fact kept quite strictly to the Haldane principle and its corollary regarding internal structure of educational programs. The reasons become clear when we look into prevailing socioeconomic and doctrinal realities.

There is a familiar doctrine that capitalist societies rely on private enterprise for innovation, risk-taking, discovery, and creating the economy of the future. The doctrine is mostly myth. Most of this work takes place in the public sector or with public funding. That includes what we are now using: computers, internet, satellites, microelectronics, and most of the rest of the high-tech economy—and also the vaccines that are rescuing us from the most recent plague. The results of this creative, innovative and risky work are then handed over to private enterprise for adaptation to the market. Although this brief summary draws the lines too sharply, it is not much of an exaggeration to describe the economy as based on public subsidy, private profit.

That was understood by US planners during World War II. They could see the achievements of state-funded research with their own eyes during the war years. Looking forward to the postwar era, national planners recognized that the United States must have a highly developed state-based industrial policy if it were to maintain its position of global power. Much of the work was directed by Vannevar Bush, who directed the highly productive research and development programs during the war years and soon after became, in effect, the country's first presidential science adviser, and a highly influential one.

As Bush and others understood, it was necessary to have a highly developed state-based industrial policy. But there was a doctrinal problem. The notion "industrial policy" is anathema according to official doctrine. It conflicts with reigning myths about free enterprise.

There was, fortuitously, an easy solution: implement industrial policy under Pentagon cover, selling it to Congress and the public as defense against savage enemies seeking to conquer the world and destroy us.

It worked very well, not only in science and technology. The interstate highway system, for example, is called the "Dwight D. Eisenhower National System of Interstate and Defense Highways"—and Eisenhower, no fool, was surely aware that the pretense of needing highways to transport missiles around the country was a marketing gimmick for Congress.

The planners also understood that the way to achieve results is hands-off: the Haldane principle. Pentagon funding had no strings attached. After many years, some concerns began to be raised in Congress about the observance of the Haldane principle. In 1969, the year of my article on the crisis of the university, Congress passed the Mansfield Amendment, which barred the Pentagon from using its funds "to carry out any research project or study unless such project or study has a direct and apparent relationship to a specific military function."

The narrow effect was that grant proposals were rewritten to fake a military function, but far broader developments were underway that had a much greater impact on the universities. These were the early years of a major transition of the socioeconomic system: from the regimented capitalism of the New Deal period, which persisted through the postwar years of very high and relatively egalitarian growth, to the neoliberal system that took off under Reagan and Thatcher and has prevailed since. There were major effects throughout the social order, not only in the United States and United Kingdom but throughout the world under the impact of overwhelming US power and shared elite interests, initiating a major chapter of world history in which we are living right now. The universities were not spared.

In research universities like MIT the transition led to a shift from government funding and the Haldane principle to corporate funding, which does not even have a formal commitment to the principle. Hence a shift toward more short-term applied projects under tighter funder control and for the first time, secrecy: corporate funding, after all, makes no pretense of being for the common good. Funding is, for me, the hallmark of the neoliberal ideology. That leads to the vulgarization that Collini describes, echoing Bourne's lament a century earlier.

This is very much a thumbnail sketch, omitting a great deal of nuance, but I think the general contours are accurate. There are implications for university independence and academic freedom. Whatever the source of funding, something like the Haldane principle should prevail. It is undermined in principle under the rule of private power. The reasons are not obscure. They were articulated clearly enough as far back as Adam Smith. He recognized that those he called "the masters of mankind," in his day the merchants and manufacturers of England, would pursue their "vile maxim: All for ourselves, nothing or anyone else." And they are often honest enough to make it explicit. The most respected academic neoliberal economist, James Buchanan, instructs us that economics must accord with human nature and its fundamental principle: that "Each person seeks mastery over a world of slaves."

Your highest goal, if you hadn't noticed.

Unlike private funding, government support is not bound in principle by the vile maxim, but one can ask how far it strays from it, in the light of another insight of Adam Smith's: the masters of mankind, he wrote, are the principal architects of government policy, and they make sure that their own interests are "most peculiarly attended to," no matter how "grievous" the effect on others.

Sometimes the masters feel that they can achieve a higher level of control. Reagan-Thatcher neoliberalism is guided by that goal. Its basic principle, shared by associates elsewhere, is that decision making should be shifted from governments, which are at least to some extent under public influence, to concentrated private power, which is totally unaccountable to the public. The doctrine is masked in terms of the alleged miracle of markets, but the reality is what I've just described, as we have seen vividly since the 1980s. I'll return briefly to that, but let's keep now to the crisis of the university system.

Socioeconomic power and organization are closely linked to major currents of intellectual culture. Returning to Randolph Bourne a century ago, recall that he linked the dismal fate of the university ideal to a shift in the general intellectual culture, the rise of a liberal, technical intelligentsia, pragmatic intellectuals committed to "the executive ordering of events" in political administration and "service of the war technique."

Bourne could have been describing the Kennedy intellectuals during the glory days of Camelot and the years that followed. They hailed themselves as "technocratic and policy-oriented intellectuals" as they micromanaged the escalation of the Vietnam War, among other achievements. They distinguished themselves from the "value-oriented intellectuals," old-fashioned types who haven't grasped the spirit of the age and wander in the mists of justice and rights and morality—"wild men in the wings," as they were described in 1968 by Kennedy-Johnson National Security Adviser McGeorge Bundy, former Harvard dean, referring to those fringe creatures who go beyond criticizing the tactics of war planners to raising questions of motives and legitimacy.

Bourne, too, was a wild man in the wings. There were a few such figures in all of the warring countries, but for the most part intellectuals rallied with remarkable unanimity and fervor to the call of the war machine. The more prominent ones who resisted the patriotic hysteria mostly ended up in jail: Bertrand Russell, Eugene Debs, Rosa Luxemburg, and Karl Liebknecht, among others. Bourne himself was lucky. He was not jailed, only thrown out of the liberal intellectual journals of the John Dewey circle. They were hailing the American intervention as the first war in history initiated and run by the intelligent men of the society, who deliberated rationally and determined the best path—much like their Camelot descendants.

Through the 1960s there were conflicting tendencies developing in the general intellectual culture: sophisticated intellectual discourse reflecting on the era adopted the framework I have just quoted. It distinguished the "technocratic and policy-oriented intellectuals"—sober, realistic, pragmatic—from the "value-oriented intellectuals," the wild men in the wings.

The value-oriented intellectuals may be a fringe, analysts recognized, but they are dangerous. To quote prestigious sources, the value-oriented intellectuals pose "a challenge to democratic government which is, potentially at least, as serious as those posed in the past by aristocratic cliques, fascist movements, and communist parties." Among other misdeeds, these dangerous creatures "devote themselves to the derogation of leadership, the challenging of authority," and they even go so far as to cast a critical eye on the institutions responsible for "the indoctrination of the young"—primarily the universities. Succumbing to challenges from then wild men, these institutions failed miserably in their task of indoctrination during the time of troubles, the standard phrase referring to the terrible 1960s. The failure of indoctrination was evident from the clamor in the streets demanding an end to the Vietnam War, the rising feminist agitation, and the other popular movements of the 1960s.

These popular movements posed a serious "crisis of democracy." The crisis was that the state could not respond to the demands of these "special interests," as they were called: the young, the old, women, workers, farmers, in brief the general population. It is therefore necessary to have more "moderation in democracy," a return to passivity, obedience, and conformity, so that the "responsible men" can return to the management of public affairs without disruption. As for the universities, they must take themselves in hand and devote themselves effectively to indoctrination of the young if the crisis of democracy is to be overcome.

I have been quoting from a crucial document of the mid-1970s, the first publication of the Trilateral Commission, constituted of liberal internationalists from the United States, Europe, and Japan—the left end of the respectable spectrum; the Carter administration was drawn almost entirely from their ranks. For lack of time, I'll ignore here the right end of the spectrum, the main business community, which was far more severe in its condemnation of the terrible crimes of the 1960s, which included a fall in the rate of profit and a rise in labor militancy, particularly among the young, often led by women and minorities.

To the guardians of established order, these were frightening times. The "crisis of democracy" was real: across a very broad spectrum, popular groups were organizing and pressing their demands in the public arena. They were not quietly accepting the principles of liberal democratic theory: that the public are spectators, not participants in political action. They have a "function." It is to appear every few years to select a member of the intelligent minority, who must be protected from the roar and trampling of the bewildered herd, the stupid and ignorant majority—benighted creatures who must be saved from their irrational whims. We must put aside democratic dogmatisms about people understanding their own interests. They do not. We do. They should return to their function of passive conformity.

I'm quoting the icons of liberal democratic theory, Wilson-Roosevelt-Kennedy liberals: Walter Lippmann, the leading twentieth-century public intellectual; Reinhold Niebuhr, known as the theologian of the liberal establishment; Harold Lasswell, a founder of modern political science. The Trilateral Commission study of the crisis of democracy was echoing these sentiments, which have deep roots in intellectual culture.

For the universities, the implications were evident and not concealed. Discipline must be restored, indoctrination made more rigid. With the neoliberal reconstruction of the social order, it was only natural that universities should be subjected to a business model, with a sharp growth in many layers of administration, a shift from faculty to administrative control, and imposition of business-style efficiency. One element of efficiency is to seek cheap and easily disciplined labor, replacement of tenured faculty who run their own affairs by temporary labor paid a pittance and with no security: adjuncts and graduate students. A concomitant has been radical defunding of public education, sharp

rise in tuition, greater reliance on private funding with the anticipated consequences. Not just colleges but mass public education as well.

This is particularly ironic in the United States. One of the great achievements of American democracy was initiation of mass public education and
publicly funded higher education. Now it must be smashed under the neoliberal hammer. All fully in the spirit of the neoliberal assault on the general
society.

The term "assault" is properly chosen. It is not our topic here, but it is the
essential background to the current crisis of educational institutions and
shouldn't be entirely ignored. Just keeping to the United States, the quasi-
governmental Rand Corporation once released a study of the wealth transferred from the working class and middle class—the lower 90 percent of the
population—to the superrich since Reagan. About $50 trillion, not small change.
Meanwhile, the top 0.1 percent has seen their wealth doubled to 20 percent of
the country's wealth.

The Rand conclusions are actually a vast underestimate of the wholesale robbery, a more accurate term than the polite "transfer." Its scale about doubles
when we take into account the other forms of robbery unleashed when Reagan
opened the spigots: tax havens, shell companies, rules allowing CEOs to select
the board that determines their remuneration, sharp cutback of government
monitors so that the rich can evade taxes at will, and much more.

The tax system has been radically modified to the benefit of extreme wealth
and corporate power. The pretext is that this would increase investment and
jobs. The effect is the opposite, as reviewed in detail in the current issue of the
main establishment journal, *Foreign Affairs*, by economist Joseph Stiglitz and
colleagues. They write that "nothing could be further than the truth" than this
pretext. "In fact, what is truly extreme is the experiment in taxation that began
during the Reagan era, when tax rates on the rich and corporations began their
dramatic descent. The results have been clear: slow growth, high deficits, and
unprecedented inequality."

Much the same has been true elsewhere under the neoliberal hammer blows,
leading to anger, resentment, contempt for political institutions, and the rise
of demagogues who channel justified anger toward scapegoats—immigrants,
minorities, the usual targets. There's plenty of work to be done to overcome the
impact of this assault.

Meanwhile, academic freedom is under attack in more conventional ways.
There is no more crucial issue in the United States than more than four hundred years of vicious racist repression, with a hideous legacy; and along with
it, the persistence of savage doctrines of white supremacy. Decades of hard work
of education and popular organizing have significantly raised understanding
of these crimes, in scholarship and the public domain, a significant even if partial achievement.

And there is a backlash. In Republican-run states, legislation is being passed to ban instruction in "critical race theory," the new demon, replacing Communism and Islamic terror as the plague of the modern age. "Critical race theory" is the scare phrase used for the study of the systematic structural and cultural factors in the hideous four-hundred-plus -year history of slavery and enduring racism. Proper indoctrination in schools and universities must ban this heresy. What actually happened for four hundred years and more and is very much alive today must be presented to students as a deviation from the real America.

This is not the only current "massive blow to academic freedom"—I'm borrowing the words of a remarkable letter published in the *British Medical Journal*, written by a scholar from the Irish Centre on Human Rights and two distinguished associates and titled "Political Censorship in Academic Journals Sets a Dangerous New Precedent."

The topic of the letter is what they describe, quite accurately, as in that title, as an unprecedented act of political censorship in academic journals. They are referring to a decision of the world's leading medical journal, the *Lancet*, to withdraw from its website a report it had published on "the potential [of the COVID-19 pandemic] to devastate one of the world's most vulnerable populations." The report provided details of the shocking health conditions in Gaza prior to the recent Israeli bombings, which had a devastating impact on the open-air prison where two million people, half children, have been subjected to a crushing siege by the occupying power since 2010, so severe that there is virtually no potable water, the health system is wrecked, international monitors warn that the territory is on the verge of becoming unlivable.

But the facts cannot be reported because of threats of boycott by doctors, mostly from the United States. The authors term the outcome "'epistemicide' of Palestinian history and present realities." It can stand alongside the epistemicide of American history and present realities under the rule of the Republican party, which mainstream political commentators describe as no longer a parliamentary party, but a "radical insurgency" that has abandoned democratic practices.

Epistemicide—a useful concept—is now rampant, including the most powerful state in human history. To mention only the most consequential illustration, Yale University carries out regular studies of popular opinion on global warming, the most important issue that has arisen in human history, with the fate of the human experiment at stake and not much time to determine whether the experiment is reaching an inglorious end. A study released in 2021, titled "Politics & Global Warming," reports that "over the past year, there has been a sharp decline in the percentages of both liberal/moderate Republicans and conservative Republicans who think developing sources of clean energy should be a priority for the president and Congress. The current numbers are all-time lows since we first asked the question in 2010."

That is the result of epistemicide with a vengeance, a campaign carried out with particular fervor since 2010. At that time, the Republican Party was beginning to toy with mild measures on climate change. In his 2008 presidential campaign, Republican candidate John McCain had a limited plank on the topic. That set in motion a juggernaut launched by the huge Koch energy conglomerate to end any such deviation from its commitment to end organized human life on Earth in the interests of short-term profit. The party capitulated, totally, and since has been completely denialist. Trump only carried the crime to caricature. The capitulation carried along with it the Party's echo chamber, Murdoch's Fox News, along with the talk radio network owned by far-right corporations and the rest of the disinformation system that has exploded during the neoliberal years.

Throughout the storm, the university system, with all its internal problems, remains an island of relative sanity. The noble ideal that Bourne invoked is battered but resilient. To ensure its survival and expand its reach is a task of prime significance in these deeply troubled times.

Editors' interview with Noam Chomsky

Akeel Bilgrami and Jonathan R. Cole: The Haldane principle, as you point out, is threatened by what Stefan Collini calls (in the words you quote from him) "the turning of educational institutions to third-rate commercial enterprises," as happened in Thatcherite Britain. Can the Haldane principle be threatened by noncommercial interests, too? Congresspeople meddling not with the interests of corporation and commerce motivating them, but with *state* interests. Or as with the lobbies that seek to silence criticism of Israel, and so on. How serious are these threats, would you say? And what are the best ways to protect universities against them?

Noam Chomsky: There are cases of state legislatures imposing demands on university instruction and research. In Illinois, a proposed bill compels universities to bar "delegitimizing the State of Israel by denying the Jewish people their right to self-determination and denying the State of Israel the right to exist." That would, for example, bar courses on the Middle East that discuss the proposals for a democratic secular state in the former Palestine that are advocated by prominent scholars or research on how to implement such a proposal. It would also, arguably, bar teaching of international law, which grants no state an abstract "right to exist." States are recognized, but to my knowledge Israel is alone in demanding a "right to exist."

An interesting project would be to determine when this exorbitant demand became prominent. I suspect it might have been in the mid-1970s, when Israel ferociously opposed a Security Council resolution supported by the main Arab states, vetoed by the United States, which called for Israel's "right to exist within secure and recognized borders," meaning basically the Green Line, alongside a Palestinian state with the same right.

There have been very serious abuses, even the targeting of faculty, leading to expulsion, by the disgraceful COINTELPRO activities of the national political police during the Kennedy-Johnson-Nixon administrations. But for the most part, at the federal level interference with the Haldane principle is implicit in research funding, sometimes on legitimate grounds but sometimes not—a distinction that is hard to establish.

The main effect of the lobbies and the authorities who cater to their wishes is indirect: intimidation, harassment, violent disruption or canceling of meetings, denial of appointments, many other devices. I could give a long list just from my own experience, which is misleading because I have enjoyed more protection than most of the "wild men in the wings," to borrow the phrase of McGeorge Bundy, referring to critics who went beyond raising questions about US tactical decisions in Indochina.

There is a long and disgraceful history of punishment of the "wild men," with plenty of recent examples. Not just from the right. In their call for the public to withdraw from the political arena, the liberal internationalists of the Trilateral Commission—in the United States, Carter liberals—denounced the universities for failing in their task of "indoctrination of the young," so that they stay disciplined and don't disrupt good order by demonstrating for free speech, ending the Indochina war, women's rights—almost as bad as corrupting the youth of Athens by asking too many questions.

Bilgrami and Cole: Also, could you say a little bit about whether, if academic institutions had the autonomy to control and use the funds as their faculty and researchers thought fit (as the Haldane principle sought), a quite different set of questions about threats to freedom of inquiry emerge? So, for instance, could you say a little bit about whether and when you think peer review (one way in which such autonomy is pursued) can indirectly lead to such a threat—as, for instance, when funds can be refused to those who think or who are engaged in projects outside "the paradigm" or the guild?

Chomsky: It certainly happens. Peer review can have the effect of imposing established doctrines and barring innovation and challenge. Again, I could give many examples just from my own personal experience. But I don't see any formal way to avoid such abuses. Professional review is unavoidable. One can work to overcome prejudice, the all too familiar pattern of protection of one's turf, an understandable but often improper defensiveness about challenges to received doctrine. But that's a matter of education, often following the advice attributed to Max Planck that what's important is not to try to change the minds of established scientists but rather of their students.

Bilgrami and Cole: You are certainly right about "epistemicide" and the two examples you mention (the attacks on critical race theory and *Lancet*'s capitulation over Gaza) are brazen and shocking assaults on scholarly freedom. On the issues of race and gender and diversity, generally, some academics (John McWhorter and David Bromwich, among others) have argued that academic freedom is being threatened from the other side as well, with many (students, especially) making demands that are unreasonable and amounting to what has come to be called "the cancel and call-out culture." These critics have argued that university administrations are not showing a strong enough resolve to preserve academic freedom in the face of these demands. In the continuing shadow of Trump's form of populism, there is no doubt that the greater threat (greater because it has the power of money and influential backers behind it) lies in the attacks on the politics of diversity represented, for instance, by the writings of some of the critical race theorists. But the threat to academic freedom from what I called "the other side," though considerably less backed by privilege and power and, though it is, as a result, *already being criticized* by the privileged and powerful, is nevertheless non-negligible. I find myself strongly disagreeing, for instance, with a very wide range of Steven Pinker's writings in the past many years (and many very knowledgeable scholars have questioned his conclusions—about the history of violence, for instance), but still I feel that some of the attacks on him are a real threat to academic freedom, even having recognized the asymmetry of the position of power and privilege of those attacking him. Bromwich and McWhorter are not academics who play into the hands of the powerful and privileged, and their concerns seem entirely genuine and honorable. So, this is a very hard and delicate issue. Can you say a little bit about how you think this new form of "culture wars" should be addressed, since cool heads have gone missing on both sides?

Chomsky: The new participants in the long-standing practice of "cancel culture" and "culture wars" are wrong in principle and suicidal in choice of tactics. They are mostly students who are going overboard in pursuing worthwhile concerns about social justice and suppression of history. NB: long-standing. This has been common practice, but directed against the "wild men," so passing with little notice. Again, I can give many examples.

To repeat, the practice of the new participants is wrong in principle, as it always has been. And it is suicidal. It's a welcome gift to the far right, which they relish and exploit. Fantastical exaggerations of practices that merit criticism are now a leading feature of the campaigns of the Trump-owned Republican party.

The abuses should be criticized. Reasoned discussion should be undertaken, as much as possible, to lead to recognition that the abuses are wrong in principle, and, secondarily, suicidal in practice. I don't know of any other way. It's nothing new. Those with memories going back to the 1960s will recall the efforts to keep very fine and deeply engaged young people from being trapped in Maoist and Weather Underground illusions, sometimes with dire consequences.

Bilgrami and Cole: You make a distinction between the years of social democracy soon after the Second World War and the neoliberal period that began roughly from the 1980s. Putting aside for a moment how this distinction made a difference to the universities and educational policy, can we pose a more general question of political economy to you about the distinction? What, in your opinion, is the underlying source of the *chronic instability* that is faced by governments pursuing social democratic policies? Even in the Scandinavian countries, social democratic policies are threatened with instability (though because they are a peripheral belt of capitalism, they seem to be a little more stable). This might, on the face of it, even be said to be a puzzling and seemingly contradictory aspect of capitalism because the thirty or so postwar years until that neoliberal period are in fact often known as the golden age of capitalism, with measurable economic growth—and economic growth is what capitalist economies seek. Is it not perverse, then, for capital to seek to destabilize and constantly seek to end social democracy wherever it exists? Why does capitalism so clearly favor growth in the form of bubbles that are destined to burst rather than the more stable form of growth that social democratic policies in fact did allow, as Keynes argued they would?

Chomsky: Capital seeks profit, and particular sectors of capital sometimes differ in policies they prefer to pursue this aim. Thomas Ferguson's research found that in the 1930s, capital-intensive internationally oriented business tended to be supportive of the New Deal, while labor-intensive domestically oriented business was bitterly hostile, for understandable reasons. We see similar differences today with regard to China policy.

From the short-term perspective of the business world, the neoliberal assault against the general population, targeting mild social democracy, has been spectacularly successful. One measure is given by a Rand Corporation study of "transfer of wealth" (more accurately, highway robbery) from the working class and middle class (the lower 90 percent of income) to the very top (in fact, mainly a fraction of 1 percent) during the forty-plus neoliberal years. Their estimate is close to $50 trillion. That qualifies as pretty successful class war. Reaganite deregulation of financial institutions predictably led to bursting bubbles, each worse than the last, but so what? The perpetrators can expect to be treated royally in our "bailout economy" (as it's called by economists Robert Pollin and Gerald Epstein) while their victims are left to fend for themselves—as when Obama decided to implement only one part of the TARP legislation, the part that compensated the banks and insurance companies, ignoring the part that offered some help to those who suffered from their criminal practices.

The short-term perspective is implicit in a market system, even one as distorted by state intervention as ours. A competitor who plans for the long run is not likely to be around to benefit from it.

Bilgrami and Cole: Moving from education, which is the main theme of your essay, to another basic public good, health, can you say a little bit about another seemingly puzzling and perverse feature of the American economy? As you have repeatedly pointed out, polls show that most ordinary people declare themselves in favor of a single payer healthcare system. That this does not happen, even so, as you have pointed out is how substantially undemocratic America's polity in fact is, despite the formal commitment to democracy. But we'd like to raise with you a slightly different question, which is in some ways continuous with the previous question. The fact is that most *corporations* are also groaning under healthcare costs. So, it would seem that even by the lights of the interests of *capital*, it would be beneficial to have a national health service in the United States. Yet it never happens. We were intellectually brought up to believe that in capitalist societies, what most corporations want, happens. And since it would seem most corporations (excluding the pharmaceutical industry and the insurance business, which even if one calculates the interests spawned by their multiplier effects, likely don't amount to more than a fifth of the corporate sector) *do* want public healthcare of the sort that exists in so many other countries, this is a contradiction in the heart of capitalism in the United States. Do you have an explanation for this puzzling phenomenon?

Chomsky: I haven't seen evidence that most corporations want public health care. Mostly they seem to oppose it, to my knowledge. The costs, it seems, are effectively paid by their employees through lower wages. In their comprehensive study of the actual tax system and how it is radically regressed under the neoliberal class war (my term, not theirs), *The Triumph of Injustice*, Emmanuel Saez and Gabriel Zucman estimate that on average workers pay more than $13,000 annually for health care through employers, a figure that has skyrocketed in recent years.

These considerations aside, it's in the class interests of capital to undermine any faith in government so that decisions will shift to their hands—outcomes concealed by fables about "economic rationality." The revered guru of neoliberalism, Ludwig von Mises, was ecstatic when the protofascist Austrian state violently destroyed Austrian social democracy and the vibrant labor movement in 1928. In his major work *Liberalism* a year earlier, he had extolled Mussolini for having saved Western civilization (meanwhile crushing labor and independent thought): "The merit that Fascism has thereby won for itself will live on eternally in history," Mises wrote.

Mises's acolytes plead that he expected the blackshirts to go home after they had completed their necessary work, presumably the same expectation that induced them to lend their enthusiastic support to the vile Pinochet dictatorship as it pursued similar objectives.

The same ideas motivate Reagan's famous exhortation that "the nine most terrifying words in the English language are: 'I'm from the government, and I'm here to help.'" For the more dedicated advocates of the rule of unaccountable private concentrations of power, the really terrifying words are that a democratic government could be an instrument for advancing the common good, not a slave of private capital.

Bilgrami and Cole: Returning to concerns about the academy: in many countries of the south—India is an especially conspicuous case—higher education is being increasingly privatized in these last few decades of neoliberal period. Most of the research, however, has always happened in public universities, and it is not at all obvious that these private institutions will be committed to the research that these countries need to pursue. However, even a number of academics have had their heads turned by the prospects of the private turn in the academy. In some sense this is the "Americanization" of higher education in these countries. Many have argued that this is a good thing. What do you think are the pitfalls of this direction that higher education has taken in these countries? Can it be reversed, or is it inevitable?

Chomsky: In the United States, the privatization of higher education has created a system of elite schools with substantial endowments (meaning rich alumni, hence preference for their children for admission) and sharp defunding of public institutions. Radical defunding in many cases. That is the neoliberal ideal. Milton Friedman publicly advocated eliminating public education. As he put it, we should "abolish the public school system and eliminate all the taxes that pay for it." Though surely not a racist himself, for this noble end he was quite willing to cooperate with the segregationist movements that arose to undermine Supreme Court decisions on integration by developing private alternatives, as Nancy MacLean has documented.

There's a good deal of irony in all of this. Free public mass education was one of the great American contributions to modern democracy, but from the neoliberal-"libertarian" perspective, a step backward.

With regard to research, I think we can make some reasonable predictions. Private capital naturally seeks to socialize costs and privatize profits. Really innovative and creative research is risky and costly. From capital's perspective, the risks and costs should be assumed by the public, and if something useful is developed, it should be handed over to the private tyrannies for marketing and profit: a system of public subsidy, private profit. That's the ideal, and not too far from the reality.

The modern high-tech industry largely developed this way. During World War II, state funding led to many technological breakthroughs, and planners, especially Vannevar Bush, recognized that there would be great advantages to carrying the program forward in the postwar years (nothing new, apart from scale). There was a problem: US dogma opposes "industrial policy," in keeping with free market mythology. A deus ex machina saved the day: the Pentagon. Everything from development of computers and the internet to the interstate highway system was sold to Congress as being for "defense." By 1969, some rumbles were disturbing the neat arrangement. Congress passed the Mansfield Amendment, requiring that military grants have some discernible military purpose. I suspect that the main effect was on how grant proposals were written, with some fake military purpose in the first paragraph.

This was however the beginning of the period of transition from highly successful regimented capitalism to the neoliberal disaster. One effect was replacement of government funding by corporate funding. The effect was quite visible at places like MIT: a shift to more short-term applied work and, for the first time, secrecy. Corporate funding is for me, not for the society at large.

Another shift reflected changes in the cutting edge of technological development, from electronic- to biology-based. Accordingly, government funding shifted toward biology-based institutions, like NIH. And the corporate installations clustering around research universities, like MIT, shifted from electronics firms to pharmaceutical, genetic engineering, and the like, to draw what they can from government-funded research.

Turning to predictions, as long as neoliberal policies and values are in the ascendant, I presume there will be more short-term applied corporate funded research along with continuation of the public subsidy/private profit system of industrial policy rather than research and development directly for the public good. The kind of distortion of the economy that our late friend Seymour Melman so effectively analyzed and exposed.

CHAPTER 14

PERSUASION, MANIPULATION, AND UNFREEDOM

MICHAEL IGNATIEFF

One privilege of life in a free society is that we get to take freedom for granted. One form that this complacency takes is to assume that freedom is binary. You're either free or you're not. I've always assumed I was free, but lately I've become aware of a liminal in-between state—call it unfreedom—where, it turns out, I've spent some of my intellectual life. The core experience of unfreedom is a queasy sense of being adrift in a surging tide of opinion and counteropinion, unwillingly imprisoned in other people's certainties. Storm surges have swept through intellectual life since the 1960s: the Vietnam era student radicalism and its attendant ideological enthusiasms; then academic Marxism; then structuralism, poststructuralism, deconstruction, and so on through the 1970s and 1980s. The latest tides of critical race theory and intersectional gender analysis are only the latest storm surges to buffet the moorings of intellectual life.

To be buffeted is no bad thing. As a graduate student, I remember with nostalgia, the times when I as a North American liberal was buffeted—and made a more consequential historian—by the wonderfully ecumenical and open-minded British socialist historians, inspired by Eric Hobsbawm and Edward Thompson, whom I met in the 1970s.[1] With less open-minded colleagues, however, intellectual life for a liberal in that era felt like trying to keep your boat tied to a dock in the middle of a violent storm. Sometimes I felt that the boat was ripped from its moorings and ended up beached on an alien shore. Each passing wave of intellectual fashions has left its imprint on me, sometimes benign, sometimes malignant. Fifty years on, I wonder what remains of the sovereignty of my intellectual judgments. I did resist these tides, but does resisting them, staying away from fashionable trends, as I hope I have done, signify that I've thought for myself, or is it nothing more than the stubborn narcissism of an old liberal still stuck in the 1960s?

Thinking for oneself may be the test of whether one is free or unfree, but let's not equate a free thought with an original one. That would set the bar too high. I would settle for thoughts that gloss the work of others but still count as a contribution that I arrived at on my own steam. Nor do we always need to think for ourselves on every occasion. Most of the time, it makes sense to take our opinions secondhand, to defer to those who know more than we do, provided we have good reason to trust them. But there are occasions when we need to turn opinion into belief, and to do that we need sound evidence from trusted sources and some process of deliberation in which we decide what we do believe.[2] These occasions are sometimes intellectual, as when, on a project in which we've invested time and effort, we have to decide what the evidence, testimony, or experience is actually telling us; sometimes it's personal, as when we have to decide whether to trust someone to embark together on a major life project, like a marriage; sometimes these occasions of choice are political, as when we have to decide what side to take on an important public issue. These consequential cases, when we need to legitimize our choices to ourselves and to others, when we shift from mere opinion to settled belief, are when we test whether we do exercise any sovereignty in our judgment.

If I cannot securely claim to have thought for myself on these consequential occasions, it casts a doubt, not on the desirability of free societies and their institutions in general, but on the question of whether I, as a free citizen, have made use of those freedoms as I should have done.

If this question raises troubling uncertainties about my intellectual sovereignty as an individual, it also leads me to ask whether the institutions I've spent my life in—universities in particular—have helped or hindered me to think freely. The current debates ricocheting through our campuses about academic freedom and free speech raise the disquieting possibility that our supposedly free institutions and our presumptively liberating discourses are creating a new generation of the unfree.

There are plenty of "unfree" people in our society as it is, those citizens whose poverty, race, or precarious status denies them the chance to exercise the rights they nominally enjoy. Unfreedom may also confine those who face no such obstacles, but who never manage to think a free thought of their own. Thinking for yourself, of course, is the very hardest freedom to exercise at all. The famous motto of the British Royal Society, *Nullius in Verba*—take nobody's word for it—has always been an injunction easier to admire in theory than to observe in practice.

It's hard to think for yourself in free societies, first because free institutions may themselves foster a climate of conformity hostile to intellectual independence. Nominal commitment to academic freedom and institutional autonomy in universities, for example, can go hand in hand with an academic culture that smothers robust debate. Second, even when a climate of freedom is encouraged, thinking people may allow themselves to become so convinced of the rightness of their positions that they lock themselves into a state of intellectual closure and what Daniel Kahneman has called confirmation bias.[3] Unfreedom can be self-imposed. We fit the chains to our own minds.

A third source of unfreedom is manipulation. If all free thought arises from persuasive encounters between free minds, manipulation is the opposite: tacit attempts to change minds, to shape them, to make them believe certain propositions, without the persuasive consent of the person involved. Since the dawn of free societies, in ancient Greece, thinkers have worried about manipulation. In the twenty-first century, new technologies—artificial intelligence, social media, and the algorithmic reinforcement of preferences—revive these ancient concerns and make them more pertinent than ever. We may have allowed ourselves to be enslaved to the very technologies that promise us unparalleled freedom.

One of the strengths of the liberal tradition has been its attention to "unfreedom." In the 1830s, Tocqueville insisted that democratic freedom in America was producing not robust pluralism of opinion but mass conformity of mind. The authoritarian tyrants of old enforced conformity with punishments inflicted on the body, Tocqueville said. In a democracy, it was the soul that the majority took captive.[4] Mill's *On Liberty* is a resonant plea on the same theme: to fight the unfreedom nesting amid freedom.

Isaiah Berlin is in this tradition. In thinking about "unfreedom," it helps to remember a point he made in *Two Concepts of Liberty*, back in 1958.[5] His epochal encounter with the Russian poet Anna Akhmatova in Leningrad in 1945 left him aware, as never before, how morally attractive intellectual freedom was, but Akhmatova's example also made clear that there was no necessary relation between free institutions and free thinking. If free thought could survive even in Stalin's terror, it could survive anywhere.

The converse was also true. In the free Oxford to which he returned after his visit with Akhmatova, there were still a fair number of what Czeslaw Milosz was to call "captive minds," free men and women who had allowed themselves to be seduced by the lure of Communism.[6]

Eastern European intellectuals like Milosz and the Yugoslav dissident Milovan Djilas were recurrently astonished that captive minds could emerge in free societies and their critique of totalitarian thought did something to break the chains, at least after 1956, that held so many minds in self-inflicted confinement.[7] In the resurgence of Cold War liberalism, epitomized by Karl Popper, Isaiah Berlin, and others, the key problem for a liberal society was to ensure that free institutions did indeed foster free minds.[8] A free society, they believed, links free thought in turn with moral ideas of dignity and autonomy. Accordingly, to think for yourself is to be a dignified person: to stand on your own two feet, to be your own master. This moral valuation of dignity and autonomy was one reason, the liberals of the 1950s and 1960s believed, to feel attachment to a free society itself. It encouraged us to be the kind of people we would like to be.

There may be a considerable distance, however, between the way a society promotes these ideals in theory and whether it allows us to exercise them in practice. Here is where the idea of "unfreedom" becomes useful. "Unfree" captures this uneasy, liminal state of mind in which our thoughts are structured for us by forces of convention, cliché, ideology, and partisan conviction.

Free thinking needs more than free institutions to flourish. A cultural climate that encourages, rewards, or at least does not punish contrarian or independent thought is just as important. Just as liberal constitutional thought since James Madison argues that a balance of powers is essential to freedom, so a liberal theory of culture and communication would also call for balance, in which contending ideas and visions of reality can compete for allegiance and demonstrate their truth from a position of roughly equal strength.

The conditions for this, from a liberal standpoint, were laid out long ago in John Stuart Mill's *On Liberty* (1859) and Oliver Wendell Holmes's dissent in *Abrams v. United States* (1919).[9] They are the canonical statements of the need for a "marketplace in ideas," where free and equal competition of opinion forces individuals to test their beliefs against contending dissents and where, through this process, truth is winnowed from falsehood. Unfortunately, societies with free, democratic institutions too often tolerate or do nothing to regulate cultural or intellectual monopolies that impede the free circulation of ideas. This may be our situation today.

Those who criticize the ascendancy of liberal and progressive opinion on US campuses today are saying, in effect, that liberal political correctness has achieved an oppressive monopoly of opinion. This feeling of pervasive suffocation of free thought in "woke" or "politically correct" liberal campuses has inspired some academics to support the foundation of a new university, the University of Austin, where the monopoly of the progressives, so its founders promise, will be broken. Its founding president, Pano Kanelos, claims a new institution is necessary because "illiberalism has become a pervasive feature of campus life." He adds, "faculty are being treated like thought criminals." And further, "fear can become endemic in a free society."[10]

The question is not whether these allegations may be true in this or that instance, or whether instances of harassment or silencing of teachers and students are not a very serious matter. The issue is whether progressive opinion on US campuses amounts to a monopoly.

Speaking from my own experience, it seems excessive to argue that progressive opinion has established anything like a monopoly position in these institutions. Those promoting progressive ideologies, like the waves that have swept the university in the past can be accused, at most, of intellectual arrogance, overreach, and occasional misuse of power. But the idea that progressives have secured a coercive monopoly of thought exaggerates its negative potential while underestimating its positive potential to provoke us all to rebel against progressive conformity.

It makes more sense to see American campuses today as the site of a profound debate about how universities should teach race, empire, gender, and nation. The problem, if there is one, is not a coercive liberal monopoly but an intellectual revolution that is overturning fixed boundary markers and threatening entrenched intellectual interests. This revolution in thought has not thrown a blanket over free thinking but rather has issued a discomfiting challenge to think for yourself.

Instead of letting these new intellectual fashions sweep through campuses and entrench themselves, all of us ought to subject all the new claims to critical scrutiny. My discipline, history, should welcome new narratives about the history of empire, and the role of enslavement, for example, and ask the standard questions any discipline should ask of new analysis: Does the research support the claims? If so, new narratives can be absorbed into the discipline, but if they don't, they should be kept at arm's length. Failure to critically evaluate progressive reevaluations of history would allow new narratives to entrench themselves as ideology, with inevitable damage to the integrity of the discipline itself.

It may seem strange to argue that freedom of thought depends on the curatorial functions of academic disciplines, but it is a paradox at the heart of any university education. Before you can think freely, you need to learn how to think, and this is the critical curatorial role of academic disciplines. A teacher who respects intellectual freedom uses their teaching to lead students up to the frontier of established knowledge, point out where the frontier lies and where, beyond it, lie the unanswered or controversial questions. In this way, learning a discipline frames the student's very capacity to strike out on their own. Liberals should have no reluctance to embrace the conservative claim that there is no originality of thought without respect for a tradition, no progress or development in ideas without the curatorial functions of disciplinary training. The challenge, of course, is to ensure these curatorial functions are exercised not to suppress the new, but to encourage the new to find its place amid the old. Achieving this balance inside our institutions is extremely difficult when every academic discussion turns into an exchange not of truth claims but of identity claims, that is, claims that what is true is true because they are articulated by persons with a particular identity, racial, gender, class, or the like.

So if we are to defend freedom of thought, we will need to adhere to the norms of persuasion. Persuasion implies a conversation among equals in which minds are changed through evidence and rational argument. Persuasion is most likely to occur when a certain self-discipline governs our exchanges, a self-discipline that tries, as best we can, to separate truth claims and identity claims, that is, to keep our identities out of the conversation.

The self-disciplines of persuasion are, of course, easier to preach than to practice. In highly divided, partisan political environments it becomes ever more difficult to stand apart from your tribe, your club, your party, your friends, and stand up for inconvenient yet evident truths that your side does not want to see. This is the experience of "unfreedom" characteristic of societies divided by toxic partisanship, although those who are under the spell of partisan intoxication may not feel "unfree" at all. They may on the contrary feel validated by their own emotions, so convinced of their rectitude that they experience what is in fact a certain enslavement to dogma as pure freedom. To anyone witnessing these *enrages* from the outside, they look like people taken hostage by their own ideology.

What appears to happen when we get intoxicated by our own convictions is a fusion between our identities and our beliefs. Free thought has to be able to stand on its own two feet, to be able to vest itself in the authority of truth rather than the authenticity of a lived identity. Otherwise our thoughts, when we express them, imprison us in intoxicating self-deception. We feel our thoughts are expressing, at last, who we truly are, free of inhibiting conventions and cliches from the past. We feel released, we feel authentic, we feel, in effect, that we are thinking for ourselves for the first time in our lives. An impartial observer might look at us and think, these people have lost themselves, perhaps forever.

In polarized conditions, common identities—being a citizen of a country, for example—begin to fragment into the more primordial elements from which they are composed: race, ethnicity, and gender. As civic belonging fragments, thinking compartmentalizes, commonality wanes, and what appears to be free thinking begins to look and feel like thinking within the supposedly safe confines of racial, ethnic, or gender identities, with the counterpart thought that no one can understand you properly unless they also belong to these identities themselves. You are free, in other words, when you are expressing who you truly are, and who you truly are is defined by your skin tone, your gender identity, or your ethnic origins. This is a state of exaltation that can rise to the level of "unfreedom." You may feel that you are at last free, when in fact you have just surrendered to the drumbeat of tribe or ideology. You allow yourself, in other words, to be manipulated.

Manipulation is the opposite of persuasion.[11] Persuasion models the democratic debate as an exchange of rationally grounded reasons, and models the interlocutors as self-governing agents, who, as the saying goes, "will take some persuading," that is, need to have good reasons before they will align with a political cause or give their assent to a political program. Persuasion, obviously, is then closely aligned with the idea of informed consent, with the proposition that authority is legitimate to the extent that it secures the consent of the governed by rationally grounded arguments. This in turn connects to a basic idea of freedom. We are free in a democratic society to the extent that we persuade ourselves to give consent to programs and courses of action for which we have been given good, or good enough, reasons.

When we are manipulated, as opposed to persuaded, someone is trying to sell us something, to work on our emotions, to slip by our reason altogether and get us to do something or think something that, if the matter were left to our unimpeded judgment, we might not agree to at all. There is benign manipulation, as when a spouse works on us with words and phrases he or she knows will work on us, to get us to do something that might turn out to be good for us, but that we may be resisting.

Seduction may be another form of benign manipulation, benign because we know that it's happening and because, when it becomes persuasive, we feel like surrendering to it. The key to whether it is benign or not is whether we give consent and whether we know it's happening.

There is malign manipulation—Iago's manipulation of Othello—in which a person plants a suspicion of betrayal in an unsuspecting mind. The critical feature of malign manipulation is that the person being manipulated is not aware or fully aware that their emotions, instincts, reason-giving capacities are being worked on. There is a lack of transparency, a lack of plain speaking, that distinguishes manipulation from persuasion.

Bad manipulation hides its purpose because if its target knew what was going on, they would resist. What is going on, fundamentally, is an attempt to make a person do or think something that they would not want to do or think if they knew what was happening, and the ultimate purpose of this maneuver is to strengthen the hand of the manipulator and weaken the hand of the manipulated. Manipulation, in other words, is a deceitful attempt to wrest power from someone else for one's own benefit. When we are manipulated in this way, we are unfree.

From the earliest days, Western reflection on politics and political speech has been troubled by the question of where and when persuasion shades into manipulation. The issue that triggered this discussion was how to think about political rhetoric. Plutarch says admiringly of Pericles, for example, that the great Greek statesman had the ability to play with the minds of the Athenians the way a great musician plays a stringed instrument. Pericles knew "the pitches and strings of the mind" that required "plucking and strumming in just the right way."[12] Plutarch praises Pericles's rhetorical skill, but is this persuasion or manipulation? Plato thought it was manipulation. In the *Phaedrus*, Plato has

Socrates saying of teachers of rhetoric "those whom you have heard, who write treatises on the art of speech nowadays, are deceivers and conceal the nature of the soul, though they know it very well."[13]

Thomas Hobbes carried into modern political theory this ancient suspicion of rhetoric as a form of manipulation. He spoke sarcastically in *De Cive* of "eloquence, whose end, as all the masters of rhetoric teach us, is not truth (except by chance) but victory; and whose property is not to inform but to allure."[14] Hobbes, of course, was no democrat, but even in a monarchical system ruled by a single ruler it was a critical issue how to safeguard truth in political argument from the wiles of rhetoric.

The very definition of a demagogue—and the Greeks and Hobbes shared a fear of them—was their fiendish intuition for what the mob wanted to hear, as opposed to telling them, as a good statesman should, what they needed to hear. Yet it seems impossible to do without persuasion that makes use of some of the techniques of rhetoric. Democracy requires the simplifications of complex ideas so that they remain in the memory and create the grounds for rational consent. How else can you keep the attention of the crowd unless you have mastered some basic techniques of rhetoric? Even the plain-speaking style that purports to disdain rhetoric, carried to sublime expression by Abraham Lincoln, for example, is another form of rhetoric itself. But when do these techniques shade into manipulation, when do they obstruct the persuasion necessary for deciding for yourself? When does this kind of manipulation make us unfree? And how do we free ourselves once again?

To the last question, there have been two very different answers. The first answer has been collective. For Enlightenment figures like Condorcet, religious superstition was the paradigm of manipulation: priests telling credulous people what to believe and making them fear eternal damnation if they disagreed.[15] People wouldn't be able to realize justice on earth, the French revolutionaries argued, if they kept believing that justice was attainable only in heaven at the throne of the Almighty. But they couldn't liberate themselves from superstition on their own. The revolution must free the people from their mental chains. The monasteries would be emptied; the riches of the church would be distributed; the priests would be defrocked; only a collectively enforced catharsis, involving the destruction of religious institutions, could free men's minds from the manipulation of the priesthood. Marx inherited these ideas and in the 1840s argued that working people could only be liberated from the chains of "false consciousness" and organized manipulation by the property-owning classes if there was a collective rising from below that, having shattered the chains of exploitation, would free men and women once and for all from manipulation.[16]

The collective answer to manipulation has not fared well. The societies created by radical revolution—France under the rule of the Committee for Public

Safety, Russia under Lenin and Stalin—scarcely fostered intellectual freedom. Free thought survived not because of their attempts to stamp out superstition but despite them. The inevitable conclusion is that a return to persuasion, and hence to freedom, cannot be imposed or legislated. Regulation, yes, by consent, but not by imposition.

Since the French Revolution, antirevolutionary liberals—Benjamin Constant, Alexis de Tocqueville, John Stuart Mill—worried constantly about manipulation, particularly by popular demagogues of the kind let loose by the French Revolution, and they concluded that there was only one possible return to persuasion as the model of democratic communication, and that was individualized emancipation.

The liberal answer to manipulation has always bet on the intransigent sovereignty of individual judgment. We alone can reclaim sovereignty over our own minds. We are the only ones who can strike the fetters off. No matter how devious the manipulation, we can force ourselves awake and realize, before it's too late, that that Iago is trying to pull one over us. Either we come to suspect the motives of those seeking to influence us, or we discover that what they are telling us about the external world just isn't true. Reality is the test against which manipulation often, though not always, breaks down. At no point are we helpless victims of the manipulator. We remain agents, with the added energy and ire that comes from realizing that we have been duped.

On this account, manipulation works only so long as the picture the manipulator wishes us to believe appears to correspond to what the world looks like to us. When we heed our uneasy feeling that someone is pulling the wool over our eyes, we can begin the process of repossessing the sovereignty of our own judgment.

Recovering the freedom of our judgment is never a once and for all process. It is a recurring struggle to defend the sovereignty of our own minds, to maintain a space of discernment and reflection that we can call our own, but without it, we risk experiencing our own lives as a succession of temporary enslavements to the fashionable opinions of our contemporaries.

The second side of the liberal answer to manipulation was public education. "We must educate our masters," as British politician Robert Lowe, Viscount Sherbrooke, famously said in a debate on the passage of the Reform Bill in 1867.[17] The idea that education can create free minds, and in so doing anchor democracy against the pernicious manipulations of demagogues, is evidently paradoxical. In great texts like George Orwell's "Such, Such Were the Joys," his savage recollection of his school days in a British boarding school, the very idea that education can create free minds was treated with fiery scorn.[18]

Great institutions manage the paradoxical relation between the learning that they impose on students and the free thought they reward by promoting teachers who push the discipline to its limits. Great schools both teach the canon of a discipline and expose their students to its limitations, and in this way take their students to the frontier line beyond which only original thinking can penetrate. Mediocre institutions, on the contrary, teach disciplines as orthodoxy and dogma, as comforting if illusionary certainty. They reproduce the state of mind we are trying to describe, of unfreedom.

Most of us, myself included, will not achieve free thought in the sense of pathbreaking originality, but with enough effort, over a lifetime, we can still learn to think for ourselves. In this enterprise we will have to learn and relearn the complex idea of keeping our identities out of arguments and not let ourselves give way to the temptation of believing that authenticity is the equivalent of or a substitute for veracity. We can be authentically ourselves when expressing our ideas, and we can channel our identities when we do so and still be wrong. To live by this ideal means being as conscientious as you can to be sure your own opinions are backed by evidence and to assess the opinions of others, especially those with whom you usually agree or feel kinship with, with as much care as you subject your own. It also requires taking a certain responsibility, in so far as we can, for the institutional or public conditions in which thinking occurs. So we want to work and live and teach in universities that reward, encourage, or at least do not punish free thinking. We want our social media free of manipulation, that is, we want to know what and why our social media are feeding us information, what privacy protections we can count on. It's not up to us alone. We need institutions that do not manipulate our freedom and leave us "unfree."

We cannot forget, when thinking about the challenges to free thought, to take a hard and questioning look at the technologies that we use to communicate with each other. Ever since the creation of the mass press in the nineteenth century and the mass advertising that sustains it, democracy has had to struggle to maintain a public sphere where opinion and belief could be formed free of manipulation. The key service providers who own our twenty-first-century public sphere, especially Google and Facebook, follow in the manipulative path pioneered by Hearst and McCormick and Rothermere, but the new digital technologies allow them to weaponize manipulation. Their algorithms canalize our own preferences as we register them in our countless daily interactions on the internet, so that we end up receiving only the information we want to hear, and we communicate only to those who are inclined to share our opinions and preferences. If it is a condition of free thought that we allow our thoughts to be submitted to falsification and contradiction, prolonged enclosure inside the "filter bubbles" of social media may leave us "unfree."[19]

Social media leaders, the men who own Facebook and Google, argue that any manipulation that occurs on their sites is benign, since it is not creating our preferences for us, merely reacting to preferences already expressed and giving us more of what we already say we want. In this way, we have given our consent to be manipulated.

But no manipulation is benign if it is untransparent. We do not understand how algorithms shape our preferences, and how these algorithms might be shaping our thoughts, if as is clear, our construction of our daily world view depends utterly on the information we receive from social media.

Here then is an expanding area—our daily immersion in social media— where the sensation of being "unfree" seems to deepen the more time we spend there. Those seeking to preserve the sovereignty of their own opinions and beliefs may well want to disconnect from the internet or at least to police their own interactions with it by, for example, turning off intrusive settings that track your locations, lay bare your preferences to other users, or violate your privacy rights. Beyond these private actions there are political solutions, which is for citizens to insist on disclosure, transparency, through legislation if necessary, so that we are possessed of the facts we need to understand how these monopoly powers are using this information. If we are unfree, and sometimes we most certainly are, we need democracy badly. We need publicly discussed and implemented regulation so that we cease to be manipulated. And when we cease to be manipulated, we cease to be unfree.

Beyond the issue of how to regulate our digital public square, any liberal, worried about the waning appeal of liberal ideals and the rise of clamorous forms of intellectual authoritarianism to the Left and to the Right, needs to address, more honestly than we have done so far, the erosion of freedom itself. It is, after all, liberalism's guiding value, the one, for example, that makes us privilege individual autonomy and sovereignty over the claims of equality or even fraternity. If we cannot say we actually exercise freedom of thought in nominally free societies, if we have to confess to ourselves that we have spent some portion of our intellectual lives in a state of unfreedom, then the reason for liberalism's waning appeal begins to become apparent, and the task of renewing and reviving the institutions that are supposed to help us to think freely becomes essential to the revival of liberalism's entire project.

CHAPTER 15

RIDICULE AND ARGUMENT

JON ELSTER

S cholars have mostly internalized Jürgen Habermas's principle that in academic and other serious discussions the only legitimate means of persuading an interlocutor is "the coercionless (*zwangsfreie*) force of the better argument." In this chapter I shall discuss whether and when other means can be legitimate. Specifically, can it be legitimate to make fun of an opponent?

Scholarly statements aim at *truth*. In principle, for any empirical proposition there is *a fact of the matter* by virtue of which if true it is true, or if false it is false. (Those who disagree can stop reading here.) Artistic (literary, musical, visual) productions aim at *beauty* or, perhaps more neutrally, aesthetic value. Broadly speaking, *postmodernism* embraces both statements that do not aim at truth and artistic productions that do not aim at beauty. The "truth" part of this claim is easy to sustain. The "beauty" part is difficult, perhaps impossible, to justify with any rigor, since most proposed criteria for aesthetic value are vague, controversial, or both. I shall nevertheless try to support the claim by drawing attention to some important features of artistic practice.

Freedom of expression, including academic freedom, is affected when profession-specific social norms make it costly to criticize those who do not seek truth or beauty. The costs range from the personal discomfort of criticizing colleagues with whom one interacts on a regular basis through various form of ostracism to failures in the relevant market. To avoid these costs, many participants in scientific or artistic arenas refrain from criticism and sometimes, through slow and insidious socialization, from the pursuit of truth or beauty.

Sometimes even those who do pursue these values find it difficult to be published or exhibited if the postmodernists control the relevant platforms.

Truth

Many who have tried to *argue* with a postmodernist by asking for explicit definitions or falsifiable implications of key theoretical statements will know the peculiar feeling of hopelessness generated by the answers. Instead of clarification, they offer deeper mystification, *obscurum per obscurius*. In a contribution to an earlier volume on academic freedom, I referred to these practices as *soft obscurantism*.[1] I also discussed and criticized *hard obscurantism*, the futile mathematization of human behavior. Although I believe that this strand generates many of the same social pathologies as its soft cousin (and, in fact, enemy), I shall not consider it here. I believe postmodernism both in the sciences and in the arts is characterized by an inscrutable arbitrariness, whereas hard obscurantism has at least the virtue of being governed by explicit criteria.

The natural starting point is the "Sokal Hoax," which I also discussed in my earlier contribution. In brief recapitulation, in 1994, Alan Sokal, at the time a physics professor at New York University, submitted the article "Transgressing the Boundaries: Towards a Transformative Hermeneutics of Quantum Gravity" to *Social Text*, a well-known journal in the humanities. It was accepted with revisions (one wonders what they were) and published in 1996. Sokal then revealed the hoax in *Lingua Franca*. The hoax is not only "the most famous spoof in the history of physics,"[2] but apparently is also the first spoof produced with the intention to expose intellectually substandard editors and reviewers. Except for the social-science emulations I shall discuss shortly, almost all other spurious articles submitted for publication are intended to expose predatory journals that will accept articles unread if the author is willing to pay a submission fee.

From the meaningless title to the 109 endnotes, many of them deliciously absurd, Sokal's article is a masterpiece of ridicule. In their reply, the editors wrote that they were "distressed at the deceptive means by which Sokal chose to make his point. This breach of ethics is a serious matter in any scholarly community, and has damaging consequences when it occurs in science publishing." The question then arises whether this form of "entrapment" or "sting," while completely legal, is condemnable on moral grounds.[3] The editors argued that it is, because "less well-known authors who submit unsolicited articles to journals like ours may now come under needless suspicion, and the openness of intellectual inquiry that *Social Text* has played its role in fostering will be curtailed." The first alleged consequence implies a confession of editorial incompetence to judge submissions on their merit. The second is incomprehensible. One would not of, course, expect the editors to applaud Sokal for having performed a public service by exposing their manifest disregard for truth and possibly dissuading some scholars from entering this particular dead end.

Some twenty years later, Peter Boghossian, James Lindsay, and Helen Pluckrose submitted twenty ludicrous articles to respected peer-reviewed academic journals.[4] For instance, the sample article I will discuss at some length in a moment was accepted by *Gender, Place and Culture*, which in 2020 had an impact factor of 2.032 and was ranked fifteenth out of one hundred journals of gender studies. According to the three submitters, it is even ranked as the top journal in feminist geography. Seven of the articles were accepted, six were rejected, and seven were under review when the *Wall Street Journal* revealed the hoax and the project was stopped.

The article I just referred to was titled "Human Reactions to Rape Culture and Queer Performativity in Urban Dog Parks in Portland, Oregon." Its thesis was that "dog parks are rape-condoning spaces and a place of rampant canine rape culture and systemic oppression against 'the oppressed dog' through which human attitudes to both problems can be measured. This provides insight into *training men out of the sexual violence and bigotry* to which they are prone" (my italics).[5] One of three favorable reviews stated,

> This is a wonderful paper—incredibly innovative, rich in analysis, and extremely well-written and organized given the incredibly diverse literature sets and theoretical questions brought into conversation. The author's development of the focus and contributions of the paper is particularly impressive. The fieldwork executed contributes immensely to the paper's contribution as an innovative and valuable piece of scholarship that will engage readers from a broad cross-section of disciplines and theoretical formations. I believe this intellectually and empirically exciting paper must be published and congratulate the author on the research done and the writing.

The article was chosen as one of twelve papers to celebrate the journal's twenty-fifth anniversary.

The article suggests two questions. First, why should there be a research field of "feminist geography?" The ingrown nature of this alleged field is illustrated by the titles of two recent articles in *Gender, Place and Culture*, "A Shelf of One's Own and a Room with Good Views: The Importance of Place in Negotiations of the Status of Feminist Scholarship" and "The Home-Based Postdoctoral Mother in the Neoliberal University." To be sure, I cite these "autoethnographies" only to make fun of them. To argue against them is impossible, since they do not contain statements with clear truth conditions. Second, how can this substandard journal receive a decent impact factor? Since I do not know how the number 2.032 is constructed, I can only speculate that the journal is highly cited by other substandard journals.

One of the authors of the spoofs, Peter Boghossian, was taken to task by the institutional review board of Portland State University, with which he was affiliated at the time of the spoofs.[6] One charge was that he had violated the university's informed-consent rules for research on human subjects.[7] The IRB determined that the spoofs qualified as "research" in the sense of "a systematic investigation designed to develop or contribute to generalizable knowledge." It also determined that editors and reviewers of the journals qualified as "human subjects." These determinations did not immediately imply that Boghossian had violated the rules, since exemptions are given for studies that are "of no more than minimal risk" to the subjects and that do not include a "vulnerable population." The section in the rules on "potential risks" explicitly includes "discomfort or embarrassment."

For an outsider like myself, the rules and their interpretation are largely a black box. The rebuke of Boghossian may have been due to the fact that exposure of the spoof would cause a more-than-minimal risk of embarrassment to editors and reviewers. It could also have a more objective justification, namely that the authors caused editors and reviewers to invest pointless time and effort in reading and commenting on the articles. In some cases, inducing wasteful behavior can perhaps be seen as misbehavior, as when an author submits an article to multiple journals simultaneously. It is wasteful, however, mainly because of the opportunity cost for the reviewers, who might have invested their time and effort more productively. In the case of the substandard journals, however, the opportunity costs are zero, at least for the reviewers who accept and praise nonsense. For reviewers who recommend *rejection* of the articles, the opportunity costs may well be positive, although the fact that they have been chosen by a substandard journal suggests that by and large they could not have spent their time more usefully. As I noted already, this scholarly literature is a closed universe.

In my opinion, the censure of Boghossian is a clear violation of the academic freedom of expression. When argument has no purchase on scholarly writings, ridicule can be the best substitute. In a famous critical review of Robert Nozick's *Anarchy, State, and Utopia*, Brian Barry wrote that there are "occasions when an emotional response is the only *intellectually* honest one" (his italics).[8] On other occasions, such as the ones discussed here, ridicule may work better.

So far, I have discussed how editors and administrators deal with the exposure of soft obscurantists. The Sokal hoax offered rich materials for understanding how these obscurantists try to shield themselves from sunlight.[9] Here I shall only mention some confrontations of Jacques Derrida with his opponents.

Sokal cites the following gem from Derrida's writings: "The Einsteinian constant is not a constant, is not a center. It is the very concept of variability—it is, finally, the concept of the game. In other words, it is not the concept of some*thing*—of a center starting from which an observer could master the field—but the very concept of the game." To my knowledge, Derrida never tried to explain what he meant by this statement. In what seems to be his only public comment on the hoax, he referred condescendingly to "le pauvre Sokal" and alluded opaquely to various irrelevant issues, including his writings on Gödel's theorem, a topic where fools rush in.[10]

Derrida simply did not know what an argument is. Instead, he used ridicule against his opponents. He made fun of John Searle by consistently referring to him as SARL, an abbreviation for Société à Responsabilité Limitée or Limited Liability Company.[11] Puns and wordplays were his stock-in-trade. Anthony Kenny describes his frustration after repeated attempts to interact with Derrida on intellectual matters:

> Like the skillful rhetorician that he is, Derrida keeps his readers awake by bringing in sex and death. Talking to oneself, we are told, stands in the same relation to talking aloud as masturbation stands to copulation. No doubt it does. A no less apt comparison would have been with solitaire vs. whist: but that would not have tickled the reader in quite the same way. Again, at the of the book of Revelation, we read: "And the Spirit and the bride say, Come! And let him that heareth say, Come" (22.17). Derrida has written at length on this text, making great play with the double entendre that attaches, in French as in English, to the word "come." If one were churlish enough to point out that the Greek word for "come" cannot possibly have the sense of "achieve orgasm," one would no doubt be told that one had missed the whole thrust of the exercise.
>
> It may appear unseemly to criticize Derrida in the manner just illustrated. The reason for doing so is that such a parody of fair comment is precisely the method he adopted in his own later work: his philosophical weapons are *the pun, the bawdy, the sneer, and the snigger.* Derrida himself rejected the idea that his work can be encapsulated in theses, and sometimes even disclaimed the ambition to be a philosopher. It is unsurprising that his fame has been less in philosophy departments than in literature departments. (My italics)[12]

We have come full circle. To expose those whom argument cannot reach, one must use ridicule. Those who do not know how to use argument against their opponents resort to ridicule.

Beauty

I feel reasonably confident in my criticism of soft obscurantism in scholarly work. The criticism I shall now make of certain artistic productions is much more tentative, because the criteria for aesthetic value are, as I said, much vaguer and more controversial than the criteria for truth value. Some will dismiss my comments as both uninformed and philistine. I plead somewhat guilty to the first charge but shall try to defend myself against the second.

Sergei Diaghilev told his dancers "*Étonne-moi!*" (astonish me). I believe that a more appropriate instruction would have been "*Enchante-moi!*" (enchant me). More conceptually, creativity should be valued above originality. This is not to deny that originality may be valuable in conjunction with creativity, only to assert that unlike creativity it has no value in itself. Classical examples of originality dissociated from creativity include Marcel Duchamp's urinal, Magritte's painting *Ceci n'est pas une pipe,* John Cage's four minutes and thirty-three seconds of silence, Andy Warhol's soup cans, the "automatic writing" of the surrealists, the use of randomization in the choice of words or musical notes, monochromatic paintings, all-white, all-black, or all-red, and the e-only and e-less novels of Georges Perec. The last, though, might conceivably be seen as a creativity-enhancing device.[13]

For some readers, this enumeration of allegedly worthless artistic productions will be enough to classify me as a philistine. They will be reinforced in their opinion if I go on to denigrate, as I shall, whole classes of such productions in the visual arts. These include conceptual art, installations, and performance art. They do not *represent* anything but are supposed to *communicate* something. Viewers may need help to decipher the message by the title of the production, by a statement by the artist, or by curatorial instructions. Because the human mind is endlessly prone to self-suggestion and because everything is a little bit like everything else, viewers will easily find the message they are told is there. Marcel Proust refers to the "aptitude which enables you to discover the intentions of a symphonic piece when you have read the program."[14] If the composer named it *Spring Symphony*, the audience is primed to hear a rustling stream; if he called it *Fall Symphony*, they will hear the wind in the trees. If a rough bloc of granite is exhibited as an installation and the curator explains that it conveys the idea of hungry Ethiopians, viewers will see it as a symbol of utter destitution. If told it is an image of raw strength, they will see it as an immovable and reliable source of support.

I cannot propose a theory of aesthetic value that would support these negative judgments. Instead, I shall appeal to the implicit value criteria of the artists themselves. Key terms are *skill, fine-tuning,* and *drafts.* Painters, sculptors, composers, musicians, and (historically) poets acquire a *craft* before they can be artists. (To a smaller degree this is also true of playwrights and writers of fiction.) They do so because they know that only by deploying a skill can they *get it right.* With some exceptions, they don't get it right immediately but experiment with small variations and successive drafts until they are satisfied. Proust wrote sixteen drafts of the opening chapter of *À la recherche du temps perdu*. Picasso filled sixteen sketchbooks with drawings in preparation for *Les demoiselles d'Avignon*. In discarding one draft or sketch and preferring another, they must have applied criteria that may not have reached the level of consciousness. I am agnostic as to the "objective" value of these criteria. My claim is only that artists have criteria that guide their work.

It will be obvious that the artists I referred to in the last paragraph do not include the makers of conceptual art, installations, or performance arts. The latter form a closed universe, similar to the soft obscurantists I discussed earlier. It is hard to imagine that installation and performance arts, in particular, are the result of fine-tuning, except perhaps for the purpose of maximizing shock value. After a urinal, actual urination or defecation may be needed and have in fact been "produced."

I hesitate to invoke a standard argument for the existence of objective value, namely the fact that certain works of art seem to have perennial value, be they the plays of Sophocles or the music of Beethoven. After all, it took a long time for Bach to be recognized for the genius he was and for Walter Scott to be demoted from being a novelist for adults to a writer for adolescents. There may be geniuses waiting in the wings. I am also hesitant to use a related argument, namely that it is "obvious" that, say, the music of Bach is superior to, say, the Muzak we hear in elevators. The often-cited criteria of higher internal differentiation and complexity of structure would presumably also give high marks to the fake Mozartian compositions generated by computer programs. My personal criterion, the capacity of a work to art to generate strong emotions, will almost certainly not generate intersubjective agreement.

Let me conclude by returning to the two terms in the title: argument and ridicule. As I see it, aesthetic theory has not reached and may never reach a stage or level where it can generate reliable assessments of the value of a work of art. Nor can we assume, as one can for truth, that there is a "fact of the matter" by virtue of which a work if beautiful is beautiful and if not isn't. There will be endless and irresolvable disagreement. The disagreement itself will help some to see values in a work that they had not perceived and others to understand that their appreciation was shallow. Yet the debates will always take place on a shared assumption that the artists did their best to get something right.

To expose postmodern artists and their promoters or interpreters it would be easy to use entrapment, a method that has in fact been used many times. However, in the absence of hard criteria and a "fact of the matter," I doubt that spoofs will have much of an impact. In addition, the fact that substandard— the term is too weak—works of art are sold for high prices as investment objects confer a spurious value on them to which nothing corresponds in the domain of truth.

Conclusion

Soft obscurantists and postmodernist artists form, as I said, closed universes or *sects*. In this respect they are similar to hard obscurantists, conspiracy theorists, and the Maoist political movements that flourished briefly in Western Europe in the 1970s. Different as they are in some respects, they have in common a disregard in practice for the standards they profess to uphold. Soft obscurantists rarely deny that the concept of truth is meaningful, since in doing so they would cut the ground under their own feet. Postmodern artists rarely deny that their productions are intended to have aesthetic value, since in doing so they might lose gallery access and prospective buyers.

How do sects affect the freedom of expression? Nobody has a *right* to have their opinions published or their artistic productions shown. Yet their freedom can be affected when rejections are done not on the merit of submissions but on their conformity with criteria that undermine the raison d'être of their activity—the pursuit of truth or beauty. They may be able to find an outlet elsewhere, but not if the field is dominated by obscurantists or postmodernists. Tenure in many American economics departments depends on publishing in hard obscurantist journals. (This is slowly changing.) Tenure in the anthropology departments of many American universities depends on publishing in soft obscurantist journals. English literature as taught in many American universities seems to be a subfield of obscurantist anthropology. In France, soft obscurantism has caused something of a brain drain in the social sciences. In Norway (and probably elsewhere), painters in the figurative tradition find it difficult to have their work accepted in official showings. Good work may prevail, but often with a delay. These statements rely on personal experience and secondhand reports. I have no reason to think that these data points are representative, but they are sufficiently numerous to make me confident that obscurantism and postmodernism constitute a substantial threat to the freedom of expression.

CHAPTER 16

IS WOKEISM CHANGING THE NATURE OF INQUIRY?

AKEEL BILGRAMI

T
he politics of diversity in currency has generated a quite remarkable transformation in American universities in recent years, with
some evidence of spread in universities in many countries abroad
as well. This has been the subject of intense debate on campuses, with cool heads
increasingly gone missing on both sides. In this essay, I would like to briefly
explore what changes this politics may be bringing to the very nature of inquiry
in the humanities and social sciences, as these are pursued in universities.

But before I do, it may be worth first briefly expounding how the dispute
has emerged against a historical background of political developments in the
wider social and political context and their curricular and ideological effects
on American universities, and second, giving some of the obvious sociological
factors that feed into the disputation.

The wider background history may be utterly familiar, but it bears retell-
ing, if only to put into context the particular cast and character of the contemporary debates that I want to focus on.

The creative turmoil of the universities in the 1960s to a considerable extent
emerged out of a broadly conceived Left politics among students, initially reacting to the draft and, therefore, highly critical of the government's misadven-
tures in Southeast Asia, but then often going on to derive that criticism from a
wider and more fundamental Left critique of capitalism and its effects both on
American (more generally, Western) society and on distant nations. Racial politics ran parallel to this mobilization on campuses and, as we know, produced
one of the more remarkable pieces of legislation in the history of the United

States. I say that it ran "parallel" to the Left politics on campuses initially triggered by the war in Vietnam, but I do not want to give the impression by that term that they were merely contingently or miscellaneously related. An ethos in which racial issues were raised in tandem with conspicuously Left-based mobilizations gave the politics of race a very specific complexion in that decade. Its focus was primarily on a struggle to acquire *rights* hitherto unpossessed by a group defined upon a racial identity, and that *political* focus did not get dispersed to a more broadly *cultural* racial politics, as it did in the decades that followed, especially in the 1980s and 1990s, and which came to be described as "identity politics."" This is a point of some significance and something like this initial restricted political focus dispersing to a broader cultural canvas is also perhaps true of the trajectory of feminist politics from those earlier decades of the 1960s and 1970s to the later decades of the last century.

This is not the occasion to make clear or rigorous what is meant by the term "identity" in the expression "identity politics," but what I do want to stress is that the interest in that expression, however hazy its meaning, derives from a political critique of the perceived limitations of the earlier political radicalism of the Left. Let me trample with great big boots on a lot of subtle distinctions and details—in the time I have, there is no avoiding this—and summarily say that this critique pushed further a criticism that the earlier Left politics had itself made against the complacencies of a liberal universalism, which it felt prevailed in the academic establishment. Such a universalism was said to hide the deep class distinctions that a capitalist society had generated—and the later emergence of identity politics sought to locate a similar complacence in the prevalent conviction among the Left that the only identity that was fundamental was class identity, dismissing all other identities as in one way or other parochializing what should be the more fundamental struggle against the destructive tendencies of capital. The identitarians shared with the Left a rejection of the Enlightenment's liberal legacy in its prevalent orthodox forms, but it insisted that there were forms of disrespect and hatred that had their source in distinctions other than class and material difference, had their source in race, gender, ethnicity, caste, and other such forms of difference. Difference itself, it was argued, must now become a subject of cultural study, over and above a mere struggle for political rights and material improvement, and diversity of identities must be acknowledged as intrinsically worthy, so as to restore dignity and autonomy to groups who had been the target of centuries of cultural contempt over and above material deprivation and exploitation.

This critique caught fire on American campuses, introducing curricular trends and innovations in the social sciences and especially the humanities, and the faculty in these disciplines led the charge, often dismissing more traditional scholars as out of date not only in their thinking but also in their *frameworks* of thinking, something that could only be corrected if the syllabi and the pedagogical methods in these subjects were radically transformed. The old guard often turned defensive in the face of these changes and dug their heels in. "Culture wars" was the term by which such disputation came to be described.

Who was right? It would be impossible (and unsuitable) to even try to adjudicate this question in detail in a short essay of this kind, although looking back on it now from some distance, it does seem as if there was right on both sides. On the one hand, the insistence by the traditional Left on the fundamental nature of class was often wrongly wielded to deny the significance of identity politics and the ameliorations it sought (and to a considerable extent achieved over these later decades) against a longstanding culture of, at worst, contempt for certain minorities (women, being counted as minorities in status if not in numbers) and, at best, insouciance regarding their marginalization. But, on the other hand, the Left seemed to have the right on its side in the following sense at least, a sense which is perfectly compatible with the acknowledgment of the right that may also be found in identity politics and these ameliorations it sought and achieved. The Left could surely rightly claim that such ameliorations as were sought and achieved by identity politics, however right they were, would never have been allowed if they had in any deep way undermined the domination of capital (or to put it less abstractly, the deep and widespread influence of corporations in shaping our societies). If this speculation is right—which, on the face of it, it does seem to be—then there is surely some justification to the claim that class identity is, after all, more fundamental than the other identities that identity politics put on center stage.

I don't want this to come off as some sort of dogmatic recovery of a familiar Left outlook. I think the sort of counterfactual question I am posing could fruitfully be posed inversely too. Thus a feminist identitarian stance may equally pose the question: If such gains as have been made on the class front that undermined the centrality of corporate interests had had the effect of undermining patriarchy, would those gains on the class front be allowed? It is just that I am less certain of how to respond to this conditionally (counterfactually) formulated question, since the first part of the antecedent of the conditional seems to be so remote and unavailable in fact and even when it does become fact, these occasional and partial gains on the class front seem to be so easily and constantly susceptible to being undermined (just think of the chronic instability of social democratic constraints on capital—even in the Scandinavian countries, though there, because they are a peripheral belt of capitalism, there is a little bit more stability). It is really not obvious to me that there is quite the same counterpart instability of the gains made on the gender front.

At any rate, these counterfactual forms of question, I think, are the right ways to raise matters about the relationship between class and other forms of identity, and my rough and general sense remains that when we raise them, there does seem to me to be some point to the idea that the Left was right to stress *this* form of centrality to the concept of class so long as it did not carry it over—as it often did—to an illicit outreach into the realm of moral psychology by ignoring the pervasive disrespect in our societies owing to other differences generated by other identities of gender, race, ethnicity, and caste.

This ecumenical understanding of the rightness and wrongness of the two sides of this dispute was not, however, how things actually played out. There is little doubt that the identitarians won the dispute on the campuses of the nation. As a result, a good deal of the curriculum in a range of disciplines was reshaped over these years, as well as what got counted as important and what irrelevant and arcane or harmful in intellectual inquiry. Some of this was very worthwhile, though there was some justifiable resentment sometimes at the *extent* of the reshaping in some subjects and at the disdain for the old guard, a sort of mirror image of the frustration felt by those excluded and dismissed when fundamental identity issues were for so long simply not on the horizon of discussion. Their victory also had significant effects on the cultural ethos in universities, often for the better, for instance–to mention just one example—by reducing the unreflective sexism on the part of faculty not only in their relations with one another but also in their relations with students, both in and outside of classrooms. In fact, so wide was their victory, that the very term "Left" came now to be owned by identity politics, and the traditional Left began to be described as just that—with the ineliminably dismissive qualifier "traditional."

Though I have been sketching on the American canvas quite narrowly, the issues that I am concerned with in this essay and the political background that prompts them have a wider reach in the academies of what is omnibusly called the "Western" world. My own sense is that the dispute I have been sketching has its parallel in Western Europe and Canada and Australia, though it did not exactly take the form of these culture wars I have been describing but took instead a considerably more theoretically and soberly grounded form in the gradual replacement of secular liberal doctrines with the political doctrine we have come to call "multiculturalism." This doctrine, like secular liberalism itself, emerged in Europe though some centuries later, in the postmigratory scenario of European nations after the Second World War, seeking to build their war-torn economies landed with labor shortages owing to loss of manpower by inviting a labor force from their erstwhile colonies. It is in the crucible of the racial hostilities and discrimination that these immigrant labor minorities and their families suffered that the notion of multiculturalism emerged. The argument for it emerged out of a realization that secular liberalism was insufficient for addressing the very specific humiliations experienced by such minorities. Secular liberalism had been formulated centuries earlier to repair the damage of the civil strife caused by religious and ethnic conflicts in European nations, but it did so by ushering *all* parochial considerations of religion and culture (whether majority or minority) from the orbit of direct influence on the polity. And it was felt this was too blunt an instrument to address directly the particular experience of minorities who turned to their religion and culture as a source of dignity and autonomy in the face of racial and cultural hostility by host majority populations. The demand, therefore, was for far greater latitude than secularism permitted for religious and other cultural minorities to live by their own customs without interference or efforts at reform by the state. When this doctrine traveled from Europe to Canada and the Antipodes, it was applied with a particularly lively intensity both to the minorities that formed the first nation communities of the land but also—as in the old world—to its migrant communities.

I say all this by way of saying that on the theme of diversity as it puts pressure on traditional liberal values in the society at large and in universities in particular, this disputation between multiculturalism and secular liberalism echoed to a considerable extent the culture wars in the United States. But having said that, I would like to pause for a moment to put on record that I find one recent proposal for theoretically resolving such disputation to be quite unconvincing; and it does not at all diminish the great respect in which I hold Charles Taylor's work to point out that the proposal comes from him. In a paper entitled "Why We Need a Radical Re-definition of Secularism," Taylor, noticing that in many parts of the world it is not just right-wing nationalism that has begun to attack multiculturalism but secularism itself that has become a stick with which to beat it, proposes to take that stick away by redefining secularism as *itself a version of multiculturalism*, whereby it is not any longer the state's opposition to religion's direct influence in the polity but rather it is to be seen merely as the state's *neutrality between different religions and cultures*. Though this may be politically well intentioned, I think it is theoretically very badly motivated.

As J. L. Austin once pointed out, there are some terms that have become "hurrah" terms. No side in a dispute wants to give them up. "Democracy" is one such term. "Secularism" is another. And, in fact, I find this proposal to redefine secularism no more intellectually reputable than the Soviet Union's attempt during the long Cold War to redefine democracy as *"people's* democracy" so as to claim it as a description of its own form of government to be contrasted with the merely *"free* democracy" of the Western world. It would be far more intellectually accurate to say that sometimes secularism does bad things, when it becomes a tribal weapon with which to beat up on minorities seeking redress of racial, religious, and ethnic hostility in doctrines such as multiculturalism. In any case, the fact remains that just as much as the so-called culture wars in the United States which remain largely unresolved, the dispute between secular liberalism and multiculturalism is a genuine and ongoing dispute that needs resolution by substantial political negotiation and engagement, not by stipulative redefinition.

I have been keen to stress this entire background and pedigree of the current disputes on campuses partly because I want to stress that this identitarian critique of liberal universalism as well as the traditional Left was primarily mobilized by the faculty of the humanities and the social sciences in their work on urgent social and political issues, and it is the faculty who then quite naturally and gradually shifted the battleground to curricular and pedagogical matters as well, which eventually had the effect of reshaping the cultural ethos of the classroom and of campus life.

But then, looking more closely at the most recent years, once this fallout of the recent past came to be settled in place over these decades, the entire identitarian point of view came to be increasingly owned by *students*, not faculty, and to some extent what we are witnessing today in the contemporary dispute I want to focus on (now that I have retold its historical background in potted form) is an interesting retreat many faculty have made from some of the new developments around the identity politics of diversity and difference that the students on campuses have adopted, in particular from recent efforts on the part of students to put constraints of accountability on freedom in the academy, constraints arising out of (the surely salutary) commitment which universities have adopted in the last few decades to the value of diversity and difference.

What, then, is the current dispute? The problem, as we face it, seems to be this. The commitment to diversity and difference that came to pass as a result of the developments over the last few decade that I have tried to crudely sketch has generated a wide variety of demands, *mostly from students now*—such as the curbing, with sanctions, of the incivility of aggressive hate-mongering speech and even the many "microaggressions," as they are called, that lie just below the surface of seemingly *civil* speech and cause offense to particular groups; such as the creation of safe spaces for minority and even women students facing an insensitive and complacent majoritarian and male ethos; such as the requirement of trigger warnings in the classroom when teaching texts containing material that might offend particular groups (descriptions of rape or of brutal treatment of African Americans in the South, for instance); and so on. Those are the demands on one side. On the other side, there is the claim that all these demands are either direct threats to the freedom of speech or they create an ethos of inhibition of free and open inquiry, discouraging the full expression of the voices and personalities of free inquirers to pursue controversial paths of inquiry which have in the past frequently been the paths that yielded new and fruitful forms of knowledge. And since the pursuit and transmission of knowledge is the chief mission of institutions of higher learning, such inhibitions are particularly unwelcome in such institutions.

Let me begin by putting aside one sort of person on each side of this dispute who I think does not deserve to be taken seriously.

On the side of free speech, I am not going to consider the sort of person who I actually find contemptible, the person who is brazenly inconsistent in his or her championing of free speech. I myself know a few such people, who for instance express high indignation about the threats to free speech that come from what they describe as the "political correctness" that pervades campuses deriving from ideas of diversity and the acknowledgment of historically oppressed minorities, but then are quite prepared to ignore the value of free speech when it comes to the expression of criticism of Israeli government policies toward the Palestinians and the American government's support for such policies. It is obvious that these are people who do not care to protect free speech; they only care to protect the speech that they politically favor. As I said: contemptible.

On the side of diversity, I am not going to consider the sort of person who simply subscribes to the politics of identity and difference as a reflex, just following a trend that is widely in the air, pursuing diversity more out of a sense of not wanting to go against the current political fashion than out of a genuinely compassionate conviction for the sensitivities of disadvantaged groups in our midst. The pejorative term "political correctness" is a good description of such people, and as a term it should be restricted to describing them in particular, not the general politics that recognizes the importance of diversity, which when it is genuine rather than merely a reflex is a humane and worthy form of politics. I should admit that I particularly mention such a person and dismiss him because I fear I might, as a callow youth, have in some small portion been such a person with just such a tendency to unreflectively follow trends—not regarding issues of diversity, but on issues that motivated the more "traditional" Left in the late 1960s.

Putting aside, then, these contemptible or shallow ways of subscribing to the positions on one or other side of the conflict between freedom and diversity, what shall we say of the conflict itself?

Here, first, are some elementary sociological observations. As I have already hinted, the first and obvious thing to notice is that it is the *younger* generations on campus, the students, who are on the side of diversity and are prepared to forgo free speech whenever speech expresses hate and causes offense. Though there are no doubt many faculty (after all, if my remarks setting the background are right, it is the faculty who had generated the underlying politics for these demands) and administrators who are on that side of the dispute and many students on the side of free speech, the older and younger generations by and large do distribute differently, with the former more clearly and insistently and in larger numbers on the side of free speech trumping the demands coming from the politics of identity and diversity.

The historical reasons for this are not hard to find. For all the commitment of some faculty to identitarian ideals in the 1980s and 1990s, the older generations on campus today grew up in the shadow and legacy of McCarthyism, and even after McCarthyism subsided, they experienced the inhibitions on certain kinds of left-wing speech and expression during the long Cold War. It is a reaction to this experience that shapes much of their (I should say "our," since I am part of that generation) deep commitment to free speech. But for the younger generation, the students on our campuses today, all this is lost in the mists of what seems like ancient history. It is certainly not what centrally shapes their experience as it did for us, and so for them there is no such historical ground on which free speech seems to stand with the same compelling centrality. What *they* grew up on is a quite a different kind of politics, a politics of identity battling the complacence of standard liberal universalist ideas which, as I put it earlier, dismissed identities as parochializing sites of mobilization; and even battling traditional Left politics, which, to also repeat, recognized no forms of disrespect that did not owe to class differences, often explicitly downplaying the disrespect that owed to difference of race and gender, and in my own country, the difference of caste in particular. It is this these battles which have reared in them the sensitivities that they want respected even if it means putting aside the protections of freedom of speech.

There is a further element of their experience that fortifies this. They were born into a social setting where social encounters are by no means restricted to face-to-face (or voice-to-voice telephonic) conversations. The internet, in which they participate with far greater relish and ease than the older generations, has undoubtedly increased the freedom with which speech can be aired. But at the same time, the internet—precisely because it is the site of conversations and eavesdropping on conversations that are not only not face to face but are frequently with anonymous interlocutors—can generate a form of abusive discourse on sensitive matters without any identification of the abusive agent behind it. As a result, not only is the younger generation too remote from the history of McCarthyism and the Cold War to see what is so ultimately compelling about free speech for the older generation, but they actually associate free speech with the boundless possibilities of abuse and offense that its exercise can make possible on the new electronic social sites that dominate their social orbit. It is hardly surprising, therefore, that they can quite easily place free speech second when it clashes with what they feel much more strongly about: their genuine sense of the importance of the dignities long under threat by social biases of race, gender, ethnicity, and so on.

So much for the sociology of such disputation. How shall we, then, think of its effect on the nature of knowledge and inquiry, especially in the humanities and social studies, where these demands and sensitivities are most present?

I would like to recklessly make a bold proposal. I suggest that what many of the students are seeking—in their desire to put constraints on liberty or autonomy from this perspective of greater accountability—is a model of inquiry in the humanities (and to some degree even in the social sciences) that is closer to the ideal of what happens in inquiry *in the law*, especially criminal law. This is not how they or anyone else has put it, as far as I know, but it does seem to be implied by the sorts of demands they have made. Let me explain what I mean by "inquiry in the law, especially criminal law."

Take the instruction given to jurors that a defendant must be presumed to be innocent until proven guilty. On the face of it, this seems the wrong instruction to give someone who is in charge of making an inquiry. The usual instruction in inquiry is: keep an open mind. If in inquiry one makes a presumption on one side, then the presumption might cause one to be skeptical of the evidence that is presented by the other side. Why, then, does the juror not get the instruction to keep an open mind instead of presumption of innocence? *The answer, ultimately, lies with some sense that there are prevailing and submerged prejudices that need to be countered.* These prejudices owe to the *practical* as well as the *cognitive* side of the practice of criminal law. On the practical side, there is the obvious prejudice that ordinary people tend to be swayed by those in power and authority (just think of the Milgram experiments), and it is more usual to find prosecutors relying on those in power and authority than the defendants (though criminal cases brought against police brutality are one large exception to this). On the cognitive side there is the prejudice of thinking that if a charge has been brought against someone, there must be something to it, a prejudice often expressed by the cliché, "where there's smoke there's fire." So, to combat these prejudices owing to both practical and cognitive considerations, an instruction of presumption of innocence puts certain normative constraints on inquiry. And this entire constraining model for inquiry carries over in detail to how evidence may be gathered, indeed what constitutes admissible evidence and what does not, what may be said by the witness and what struck from what is said, and so on.

What does this model of inquiry in the law contrast with? Most obviously it contrasts with a longstanding ideal of scientific inquiry (if Kuhn is right, more honored in the breach than in the observance) where there are—at least when scientific inquiry is exemplary—supposed to be no such constraints. You gather whatever evidence you can gather in coming to form and in testing scientific hypotheses in whatever way you feasibly can. In saying this, I am of course not denying what is known to everyone: that, for instance, in the last few decades constraints have come from animal rights concerns about inquiry in laboratories, nor am I denying that there are many experiments that simply cannot be performed on human beings for obvious reasons, and, to repeat, there are also the subtler constraints that Thomas Kuhn described as the unspoken prejudices of orthodoxy or of what he called "normal science." But despite all this, what is traditionally considered exemplary in the natural sciences is inquiry that is to be as unfettered *as is possible*—that is, to proceed without any *ex ante* and *built-in* constraints. But criminal law practice as it has evolved would not be criminal law practice if the constraints that I mentioned earlier were not ex ante built into what we conceive inquiry and investigation in the law to be, and on how it is presented in trials in the courts. And students today are increasingly claiming, I think, that inquiry in the humanities is like inquiry modeled in this way on criminal law rather than as in science.

In methodological debates among scholars in the humanities and some of the social sciences, the ideal of scientific inquiry had been questioned at least since Weber and then Dilthey and then through the entire "verstehen" tradition. But the familiar issues there had to do with the fact that there is a more *interpretative* perspective at work in the humanities rather than explanatory hypothesis-construction as in the sciences. That is not exactly what the students' demands are seeking today. Nor are they pointing to the other familiar element of humanistic study that contrasts with science—that its objects of study, unlike the objects of natural scientific study, are much more pervasively laden with value. The idea is not, or not merely, to say that the subject matter of the humanities is value-laden but rather that the responses that we have to that value laden subject matter may turn on sensitivities that have been sharpened by a greater awareness of the importance of diversity than hitherto existed in our societies with their widespread prejudices against what is anomalous and unconventional, not to mention majoritarian prejudice or, at the very least, majoritarian complacence in society at large. Thus, just as with criminal law, it is the correction of preexisting prejudice owing to one or other social or historical factors that a sort of analog to due process is demanded in inquiry and pedagogy, that is in how the deliverances of inquiry are presented in the classroom and in public. So, to sum up the point, the model of inquiry that I am suggesting is being sought by the young in the last few years is not just a replacement of the scientific model with a more interpretative and value-laden model of inquiry of the verstehen and hermeneutical traditions, but *the quite different model of criminal law with its form of constraints of accountability on the processes and the articulations of the outcomes of investigation.*

Now, the grounds for this suggestion of mine that a new descriptive model for inquiry is emerging from current demands to respect the politics of diversity on campuses, a model based on criminal law, turns crucially on the idea that the latter's instruction to the juror that innocence be *presumed*, is motivated by a desire to correct for natural preexisting prejudices that surface in the context of how crime is legally adjudicated. The politics of diversity makes its normative demands for constraints on the articulations of inquiry in universities to correct a longstanding background of prejudices as well. But someone might argue that the model does not apply because I have misstated, in the first place, the motivations and the justification for instructing the jurors to presume innocence. I must confess to having just made up that justification all on my own. I did not find it in the scholarship and literature on criminal law, which to my surprise, in my searches in it, has very little to say about it explicitly. I just presumed that this was so because the reasons for it are obvious and commonsensical and when I constructed these reasons and motivations I indeed thought I was stating the obvious commonsense on the subject, something anyone would think of if they thought a little hard about why such a presumption was put in place. But there is one article in the literature that is specifically on the subject, and it gives a quite different ground for the presumption than I have done. Alexander Volokh, in an article called "n Guilty Men,"[1] argues that the presumption of innocence is based on the normative premise that it is better that n guilty go free than that one innocent be punished, where n can have a very wide range of values indeed. Jon Elster, who alerted me to this article and who agrees with Volokh's understanding of the motivation behind this "presumption of innocence" instruction to jurors, also argues that the presumption of innocence instruction is really just *synonymous* with the idea of needing a high threshold of evidence for establishing guilt. That is to say, "presume innocence" is just another way of formulating the idea to jurors that the prosecution must be found to have established guilt *beyond a reasonable doubt.* This combination of points (Volokh's and Elster's) amounts to a quite different understanding of the criminal law model from the one I have presented, and if it were correct it would be quite unsuited to describing the model of inquiry that I think is being proposed by the politics of diversity on university campuses.

But I think Volokh and Elster and others who might follow him on this are simply wrong. First of all, it is not quite right to say that "presumed innocence" is synonymous with "guilt must be established beyond reasonable doubt." This is because it seems to me jurors can decide that someone is not guilty if the relatively high threshold (defining reasonable) of evidence is not met and still think the person is not innocent. That is to say, they may well think that "technically" he or she is not guilty (a technicality forced on them by the instruction about guilt requiring a certain threshold of evidence), but they may nevertheless not think he or she is innocent (something, of course, they cannot do anything about in the court, given that instruction). So, we might say, that the logic of criminality assessment is not bivalent. There is no *tertium non datur.* It is not just guilty/innocent. it is guilty/not guilty/innocent. (If I am not mistaken, criminal law in Scotland has even adopted this trio of possible verdicts.)

Now if I am right about this, and the two instructions of presumptive innocence and beyond reasonable doubt are not notational variants of the same substantial idea as Volokh and Elster have claimed, but are substantially different instructions, then I would argue that that exactly explains why Volokh insists that the only motivation for the instruction of presumed innocence is the one he offers. The motivation he offers—that it is far better to let many who are guilty go free than to have one innocent person punished—is a good motivation for instructing the juror to seek a high threshold of evidence for establishing guilt. But it is irrelevant to the other instruction of presumption of innocence, which (since it is not synonymous with the "threshold of evidence" instruction) must have another motivation such as the one I had offered—of countering prejudices that accompany the standard context of criminal trials. And—this is the crucial point of comparison—the students on campuses today are similarly making demands that inquiry and pedagogy must also work now with constraints *with precisely the same motivations of correcting ongoing prejudices*, historically longstanding prejudices on questions of race, gender, sexuality . . . which are present in society at large, so unsurprisingly are present among inquirers and teachers in universities as well. In other words, just as inquiry in criminal law and its presentation in the courts is subject to constraints of how evidence is gathered, what is admissible evidence, what witnesses can and cannot say and what must be struck from what they say, and so on, so also there must be constraints imposed on what can and cannot be pursued in inquiry and what can and cannot be said in the presentation of the outcomes of inquiry in classrooms. All this, as I said, with the same motivation in both cases: to correct for ongoing prejudices, whether in courtrooms or in classrooms.

This is all a relatively *new* development on the methodological horizon of scholarly knowledge and inquiry. Is it a healthy development? Is it the right model for inquiry in the Humanities? Though I have views on the matter, I will not say much by way of response to this question, even as I think it is the question which will become increasingly important to explore and address.

But I will say this. Assuming for the sake of argument that what I have said—about an emerging transformation in the nature of the conduct of inquiry and pedagogy in the direction of a criminal law model rather than a scientific and hermeneutical model—is more or less right, let me close by adding one nuance to this diagnosis that might help to deflate some of the anxieties it prima facie gives rise to.

Suppose it were even the case that we decided to take seriously this new "criminal law" model for how to think about inquiry in the humanities and social sciences that seems to have emerged from the demands of the younger generation on our campuses. I would think that the first thing to notice is that even in criminal law there has in recent years come to be more than one way to understand the sorts of constraints that it places on inquiry and its outcomes and their expression.

In the last several decades, ever since the outreach of criminal law into the realm of *transitional* justice, the possibilities of a quite new model of inquiry emerged even within criminal law. Taking the South African case as conceived by Archbishop Desmond Tutu, Nelson Mandela, and others to be paradigmatic of such a new understanding of criminal law, this new model sometimes even puts aside the very ideal of *forensic* justice because the aspiration—where transitional justice is concerned—is that one has to *live in the future side by side with* the people one was judging and, in any case, much of their crime though active and explicit on the part of a few was, on the part of many, a matter of being complicit. Forensic investigation was therefore beside the point since it actually undermined this idea of engaging with the people one had to live with, even as one judged them. How did it undermine that? Forensic investigation is a *detached* or disengaged form of inquiry, whereas the need was to *engage* with the accused and the adversary, not simply see them in objective terms of evidence. Tutu and his colleagues, therefore, proposed something like this: "We have to live side by side with our past oppressors now, so let us not judge them forensically in a traditional court of law, seeking and presenting evidence in a disengaged mode, while they sit silently in the dock. Let us not assess them in that detached mode, applying our norms and laws; let us *engage* with them, seeking truths about the past through that engagement, trusting them to present the truth of their perpetration of crimes, and look to what correction these confessions make possible for our future together."

All of this has deep relevance to the academy because even if we were to take criminal law as model for how to understand humanistic inquiry, the thought cries out that it is the *transitional justice model* of criminal law which emphasizes engagement rather than the detachment of forensics that better fits inquiry in the humanities and social sciences.

But if that is so, then it is not clear that the constraints of accountability coming from considerations of diversity that the young seek today can be seen—*even by them*—as confronting the demands of liberty that have traditionally been cherished in inquiry. The reason for this is quite straightforward. One can only engage, even with one's adversary, if one is prepared to *hear* their claims, and for that one has to give them the freedom and autonomy to inquire and to speak the deliverances of their inquiry so that we might hear it and engage with it. This point is no doubt very well known and often said by those who resist what is called the "cancel culture" ethos in American universities. But it gains a new point and relevance in the context of discussion of models of inquiry mimicking criminal law inquiry since the notion of engagement is what inquiry in the *transitional* cases of justice introduced into criminal law: the refusal to treat the subjects of judgment as objects by seeing them in purely disengaged or detached terms, *silenced* targets of investigation sitting in the dock. If the model of criminal law that is emerging for humanistic inquiry understands itself along *these* lines, modeled on the transitional rather than the forensic exemplar, a whole sea of controversy that is expressed in the anxious dichotomy of prevalent disputes on campuses—"freedom versus diversity"—can subside. There is sense on each side. That is to say, even if there is right in the demands that push us toward modeling humanistic inquiry on criminal law rather than as in science or hermeneutics, a proper understanding of that model of criminal law, as it is relevant to the humanities or social sciences, would allow for autonomy and liberty—though now liberty would be legitimated not by liberalism's clichés regarding the "marketplace of ideas" but on grounds that link the law itself to a less detached and more engaged understanding of itself and its processes of inquiry.[2]

CHAPTER 17

A CONFEDERACY OF SNITCHES

LAURA KIPNIS

When I read about the downfall of University of Michigan president Mark Schlissel, fired after an anonymous complaint about his consensual though "inappropriate" relationship with a subordinate, my first thought was, "What kind of idiot uses his work email for an affair?" Then I recalled that I myself am the kind of idiot who persists in using my university email account for everything, despite pledging at least once a year to tear myself away from this self-destructive habit. Schlissel, *c'est moi*. The next time I get in trouble, will my employers emulate the classy behavior of the Michigan Board of Regents and release troves of my own embarrassing emails for my enemies to savor and mock?

My next thought: Who was the snitch? I knew none of the players, but my inner Hercule Poiret went right to work, assembling likely suspects in the drawing room of my imagination (betrayed spouse, disappointed paramour, assorted foes and rivals, maligned underlings), cleverly disarming them with my continental charm until the culprit was exposed—most likely by the irrepressible look of creepy satisfaction playing across his or her face. To bring down an apparently much loathed and vastly overpaid university president, even for the stupidest of reasons: what ecstasy!

Among the questions prompted by Schlissel's termination is whether higher education, on the whole, has become a hotbed of craven snitches. From everything I've heard and experienced, the answer is yes.

First let us pause to consider our terms: Was Schlissel's narc a "snitch" or a "whistleblower"? Whistleblowers are generally attempting to topple or thwart the powerful, and Schlissel was certainly powerful. But the reported offense was, in the words of an attorney I spoke with, "a nothingburger." Let us provisionally define snitching as turning someone in anonymously, either for minor or nonexistent offenses, or pretextually. Also: using institutional mechanisms to kneecap rivals, harass enemies, settle scores and grudges, or advantage oneself. Not to mention squealing on someone for social media posts and joining online mobs to protest exercises of academic and intellectual freedom.

This last is a variant of the "social justice snitch," a burgeoning category comprising those who want to defund the police and reform the criminal justice system but are nevertheless happy to feed the maws of a frequently unprocedural and (many say) racist campus justice system. There are, to be sure, right-wing students and organizations dedicated to harassing professors whose politics they object to, but that's to be expected. What's not is the so-called campus left's failing to notice the degree to which the "carceral turn" in American higher ed—the prosecutorial ethos, the resources reallocated to regulation and punishment—shares a certain cultural logic with the rise of mass incarceration and overpolicing in off-campus America. Or that the zeal for policing intellectual borders has certain resonances with the signature tactics of Trumpian America, for which unpoliced borders are equally intolerable. Neoliberal reason is remaking us all, even its putative opponents. But what care social justice types about fostering the carceral university if those with suspect politics can be flattened, even—fingers crossed!—expelled, or left unemployed and penurious?

Americans once famously disliked snitches. Witness the parade of Hollywood liberals who refused to stand or applaud when director Elia Kazan, who'd named names to the House Committee on Un-American Activities in 1952, received an honorary Academy Award in 1999. According to Kazan's autobiography, he named only those who'd already been named or were about to be, and he'd long since come to despise the cultural despotism of the American Communist Party. But he'll still go down in history with "snitch" attached to his name. If only he'd labored in today's academe! He'd be lionized for it.

The carceral campus provides a haven for that formerly reviled personality type, the jailhouse snitch, around whom so many classic prison dramas revolved. The Big House (1930) established the category and delivered a message for the ages: Snitches get stitches. When the privileged twenty-four-year-old Kent (Robert Montgomery), in for carelessly killing someone while driving drunk, starts ratting out his fellow inmates, things don't turn out well for him. In the film's moral universe, only snivelers snitch. Or as the seen-it-all warden opines: "Prison doesn't make you yellow, but if you are already yellow, prison brings it out."

Is this true? Is snitching a function of character, the result of a trait you either possess or don't? Or is it rather that certain institutional contexts, like prisons, incentivize snitching? In higher ed's overfunded, secretive, and ever-expanding punishment infrastructure (hiring for which now vastly outstrips new faculty lines), glutted with vague regulations about everything from romance to comportment to humor, snitching has become a blood sport.

∗ ∗ ∗

I'll begin with my own encounters with the accusation machinery on my campus. I've previously written about being the subject of Title IX complaints by two graduate students over an essay I wrote for (of all places!) the *Chronicle of Higher Education*. But it wasn't just me. Also accused in conjunction with my case were the president of my university, for possibly alluding to me in an op-ed on academic freedom, and my intrepid faculty support person, for speaking at a faculty senate meeting on the subject. I later learned that even more charges had been filed against me because of the charges against him. A few years later, when I wrote a book about these experiences, I was brought up on Title IX complaints *again*; this time the accusers included four of my fellow faculty members. (On all of this I was eventually cleared; the complaints against the other two were dropped.)

Was Title IX designed to combat the scourge of people publishing things you don't like? Presumably not, which hasn't impeded more Title IX investigations from being launched on similar grounds, despite how much criticism my university came under for Title IX overreach. I learned about a creative writing student at a liberal arts college (a place I myself have been invited to speak *on free speech*) found guilty of Title IX violations when another student didn't care for something she'd written. I'd love to provide more details, but despite having transferred to another college, the student was so terrorized by the experience she doesn't want them made public. Which is exactly what makes this subject both impossible to write about and necessary to publicize. Want to muzzle your enemies? Accuse them of something. Title IX officers are standing by.

They're also more than happy to act on third-party complaints. Along with codes making practically everyone on campus a "mandatory reporter" for suspected Title IX violations, a volunteer army of zealots is hot on the trail. One was the roommate of an undergrad I'll call Ann, who witnessed Ann and her boyfriend of three years having a fight. Ann slapped the boyfriend, and the boyfriend slapped her back. Not stellar behavior on anyone's part, but the roommate told Ann she had twenty-four hours to report the boyfriend for relationship violence, or she would. Was she jealous? Ann thought that might have had something to do with it.

Against Ann's wishes, the school charged the boyfriend. Why only him? I wrote extensively in *Unwanted Advances: Sexual Paranoia Comes to Campus* about the proclivity of Title IX officers for reinforcing the gender biases they're supposed to be combatting. The boyfriend is currently awaiting a finding, according to his attorney. (It's also the case that only those with well-off parents can afford attorneys to contest such charges, meaning the outcomes will be entirely unequal. The creative writing student's parents lacked the financial resources to hire an attorney.)

Students snitching on fellow students for anything even sex adjacent is also rampant. Jane Doe, a former Sonoma State University student in its "Depth Psychology" master's degree program, is suing over Sonoma's mishandling of Title IX complaints brought against her by three other students. The three accused Doe, then thirty-one, of sexually harassing them with a sensual dance she'd done during a movement exercise *in class*. The program, which focuses on Jungian psychology, touts itself as emphasizing the integration of scholarship with "embodied practices." The assignment that day—an eleven-person cohort took all their classes together—focused on "authentic movement": Students were supposed to gyrate their hips in a circular fashion and "move like snakes." They were also supposed to ignore cultural norms and challenge themselves to move in ways that might be taboo, to not take anything personally, and to "own your own triggers." They were instructed to watch only their own partners, no one else.

One of Doe's classmates—not her partner, and whose eyes should have been elsewhere—emailed the instructor after class to complain that Doe had been masturbating during the dance. Doe's partner chimed in three days later, seconding the complaints. The third complainant hadn't witnessed Doe's alleged masturbation, but just "hearing about her actions alone was triggering and anxiety producing." All three threatened to withdraw from the program if Doe wasn't punished. Doe contends the three deeply disliked her, wanted her gone, and had also colluded in their statements.

Sonoma State took fifteen months to investigate the case, hence Doe's lawsuit. (According to co-counsel Lara Bazelon, there's currently a small chance the case will go to the Supreme Court.) During those fifteen months, Doe was effectively expelled: banned from classes, thus unable to finish her degree. After she was finally found innocent of lewdness, her relentless accusers hired their own lawyer to appeal the ruling (unsuccessfully). The chancellor's office affirmed that no reasonable person would have found that the alleged conduct constituted sexual harassment, but what snitch worth the time of day is a reasonable person?

Not only do Title IX bureaucracies lack mechanisms for weeding out off-the-wall complaints, but they apparently have no interest in doing so. Anyone who's disliked by anyone is a sitting duck. And even if your target is eventually cleared, so what? The process itself is the punishment.

✳ ✳ ✳

Back to me. Twice exonerated on Title IX allegations, I recently found myself once again ensnared by investigative clutches, this time over my latest book, *Love in the Time of Contagion*. My crime? When I started writing, I'd posted an anonymous Google survey online asking people how their relationships were faring, whether their ideas about love had changed during the pandemic, and other questions in this vein. I got around two hundred responses, often thoughtful and eloquent—people seemed glad for the opportunity to reflect on what they'd been through. Then came an email from my university's Institutional Review Board office. Guess what? Some Stasi acolyte had submitted an anonymous complaint about my little survey: I'd engaged in "human subject research" without approval. (By the way, it turns out there's a webpage *soliciting* complaints about faculty and staff, just to make things more convenient for anonymous snitches.)

Now the IRB people wanted me to get their retrospective permission for a survey I'd already completed and then planned to supervise how I used the results—if they approved the survey in the first place. Given my extreme amateurishness at this kind of thing, their approval seemed doubtful.

As an essayist with fine arts degrees who teaches in a film department, I had only the vaguest idea what an IRB is. If you too are in the dark: It's a review process for scientific and social-scientific research involving human beings. Journalists are exempt, as are people doing oral history or making documentaries. I explained that my type of writing—subjective, frequently ironic—wasn't under their jurisdiction, and I had no idea how I'd use the survey results. I suggested that someone was using the IRB office to harass me because of other things I'd written. Or so I inferred, since at my second Title IX investigation, over my book *Unwanted Advances*, one of the charges was my not getting IRB permission. The team of out-of-town lawyers hired by the university to torment me (at substantial hourly rates, presumably) waved that one away, saying my sort of writing didn't require it. That was how I first learned what an IRB is.

I imagined the current snitch's glee, savoring the idea that I was, once again, wriggling helplessly under the bureaucracy's thumb. The IRB functionary wasn't interested in what the complainant's motives might have been and insisted that I proceed as their supplicant. I responded with some snippy remarks about the territoriality of the sciences—had they somehow declared ownership over the survey method? Over question-asking itself? Why should they get to force me to speak their language? And wasn't this a rather colonial attitude toward the humanities, precisely the sort of marauding, as I understood it, that IRB offices had been invented to curtail?

I had no idea what would happen if I refused to comply. I did glance at the forms they wanted me to fill out, which were mostly scientistic gibberish, but I couldn't bring myself to open the fifty-seven-page manual they'd instructed me to read first. The only question I could confidently answer was whether I was collecting biospecimens. No, not intentionally.

We went back and forth in this vein for two weeks until she finally backed off. The office had concluded my work didn't come under their purview. How many hours I spent on all this I can't say. The whole thing was trivial but also galling. I comforted myself with the old (possibly apocryphal) Algerian proverb: "The man without enemies is a donkey."

＊＊＊

Has anyone stopped to ask whether this is actually what we want the world to look like? Take, for instance, the complaints about gendered speech missteps that are lately swelling the allegation coffers and occupying the swarms of bureaucrats and deanlets on call to aid every manner of snitch. Title IX offices have become the go-to for reporting pronoun errors or faculty members accidentally misgendering students (even when it involves reading a name off a roster, in one case I know of). Or for using a trans author's pretransition name on a syllabus, even when the book in question was published under that name: an older queer art history professor at Pennsylvania State was turned in by younger queer students for doing just that a few years ago (and then temporarily "blew up the internet" by publicly defending himself). The phrase "It's generational" is often heard regarding this upsurge of accusation, a cliché meant to reconcile the apparent contradiction of gender-nonconforming progressives deploying the campus carceral apparatus to enforce their ideas of progressivism and queerness.

The lawyer Samantha Harris, who often defends speech infraction cases, told me that N-word violations are also now a snitch's paradise on earth. There are still, it seems, occasional old school types (often leftists) who persist in thinking that there's a distinction between quoting James Baldwin or Martin Luther King Jr. in full and hurling an epithet. College admissions consultant Hanna Stotland, who specializes in "crisis management," told me that the snitching impulse is taking hold earlier and earlier—she used to have two such cases a year; she's had twenty in the last two years. N-word offenses are a cottage industry here too. High schoolers squirrel away incriminating texts or videos of friends at age fifteen singing along with rap lyrics, then forward them to admissions committees when the friend (or frenemy, rather) gets an athletic scholarship or is admitted to an Ivy. Colleges are so quick to act on the intel, says Stotland, that they'll sometimes retract an offer without even giving the accused student a chance to respond.

＊＊＊

Of course, race is treacherous territory for anyone at the moment, as demonstrated by the lawsuit brought by Timothy Jackson, a professor of music theory, against his employer, the University of North Texas. Jackson formerly headed the Center for Schenkerian Studies, which piqued my interest because it sounds like something from a lost academic novel by Nabokov. I admit to not having heard of Henrich Schenker, a Galician-born Austrian Jew who developed an influential system of music theory and died in 1935. Following the Nazi annexation of Austria, his wife was murdered in Theresienstadt; a number of his Jewish students also perished in the camps. Schenker too would likely have been killed if he'd lived longer.

The trouble started in 2019 when Philip Ewell, a Hunter College professor, delivered a plenary address at the Society for Music Theory called "Music Theory's White Racial Frame." In that talk, Ewell, who is Black, condemned Schenker as an "ardent" and "zealous" racist and indicted music theory as a whole for ignoring Schenker's racism "in order to keep in place racialized systems that benefit whites and whiteness." (A version of the paper is available online.) Not only had Schenker's biological racism "infected and become integral to the white racial frame of music theory," but the scholars who established Schenker studies in the United States also went to great lengths to "whitewash" Schenker, conspiring to conceal his "racial supremacist views."

Among the questions Ewell's paper raises—while nowhere mentioning that Schenker was Jewish—is whether Schenker's musical theories themselves are logically dependent on what Ewell alleges is Schenker's white supremacism. Ewell thinks yes: "As with the inequality of races, Schenker believed in the inequality of tones."

After discussions among the editorial staff, the *Journal of Schenkerian Studies* issued a call for responses to Ewell's address, to be published in volume 12, whose release was delayed for four months due to COVID and came out around the time of the George Floyd protests. Though a third of the responses were pro-Ewell, Jackson's was decidedly critical. He argued that "Schenker's Jewishness complicates any simplistic reduction of 'whiteness' to a monolithic concept." He also argued that Ewell cherry-picked and misread quotations, which he cites in the original German, pointing out nuances he felt Ewell had overlooked. Schenker, Jackson argued, had experienced racism firsthand, and the reception of Schenkerism—tacitly regarded as "Jewish" music theory—was itself complicated by the anti-Semitism of the postwar American academy, which, after all, still had quotas on Jewish admissions. Jackson asks whether "anti-Semitism may implicitly, if not explicitly, underlie attacks on Schenker's legacy now, just as it has in the past." He also points out that Ewell's "scapegoating" of Schenker and the Schenkerians is taking place in the "much broader context of Black anti-Semitism" in the United States, where Jews are "blamed for every conceivable ill." (On the question of Black anti-Semitism he cites Henry Louis Gates, among other sources.)

You could argue that Jackson was just being as polemical as Ewell, who'd denounced the Jewish Schenker as a proto-Nazi (his prose has "Nazi implications") who admired Hitler, but you'd better not argue it these days. All hell broke loose on social media. Ewell's defenders in music theory departments around the country signed petitions denouncing the journal and calling for Jackson to be fired. (Some younger scholars and grad students reported to Jackson feeling pressured to join the condemnations.) According to Jackson's lawsuit, he was also accused of saying "fascist shit" for writing that resources needed to be devoted to increasing the small number of Black music theory students, since few grew up in homes where classical music was appreciated. Ewell called the published responses to his paper "dehumanization," saying he wouldn't read them, although was also angry about not being asked to respond. "They were incensed by my Blackness challenging their whiteness," he told the UNT student paper.

The graduate student editor of the journal, who'd himself initially been skeptical about some of Ewell's arguments—he'd called them "naïve" and "implicitly antisemitic"—quickly posted a lengthy and self-lacerating mea culpa on Facebook in which he revealed that he'd set up a secret meeting with his department chair six months earlier. He had, he said, gone to the chair "as a whistleblower" to report that Jackson was "woefully ignorant about politically correct discourse and race relations." It's a sad document, reeking of professional fear and (according to the correspondence chain in Jackson's affidavit) dissembling. Meanwhile, UNT grad students were on Twitter denouncing Jackson and circulating more petitions demanding that everyone associated with the journal be investigated for past bigotry; seventeen of Jackson's UNT colleagues signed it.

The university swiftly announced that an ad hoc committee was being convened to investigate. They found Jackson guilty of bullying the grad student editor into publishing views he disagreed with and the journal guilty of editorial mismanagement (although the editorial practices followed were the same as they'd always been, said Jackson). Jackson was removed from the journal, and its funding was cut. More troubling to him were that allegedly false and defamatory statements, including by the grad student, were the basis for the decision, which he feels was basically pretextual—the real issue was his critique of Ewell, or, more precisely, the controversy it caused.

The lesson here is not only that universities won't stand up for faculty members who get mobbed for unpopular viewpoints. It's that they'll pile on the reputational wreckage, constitutionally protected speech be damned. Jackson's attorney, Michael Thad Allen, thinks universities now care less about being sued than they fear standing up to social media temper tantrums. UNT's motion to dismiss Jackson's lawsuit was just denied, and the case is proceeding to discovery. We'll see what the courts think.

＊＊＊

Veering from the accepted narratives about race can be career-imperiling, but what's the accepted narrative? The year before Ewell delivered his paper, my partner, a sometimes-intemperate history professor with an apartment in Harlem, became exasperated (when is he not!) about a bunch of noisy white children, possibly the offspring of tourists, overrunning a neighborhood restaurant and creating a ruckus among the mostly Black customers. He posted a satirical mini-rant on Facebook about these future Masters of the Universe, culminating with the pronouncement "I now officially hate white people, and for god's sake I are a white people [sic]." He thought the humor was self-evident.

Nope. Soon came the dreaded email from the Office of Employment Equity on his campus telling him he'd been anonymously reported. He was being charged with discrimination, harassment, and "reverse racism." Which, he argued at his hearing, doesn't exist: Racism is about power, not hatred, in his view. The history experts at OEE overrode him, pronouncing him guilty as charged, notwithstanding that it was apparently white supremacists who'd gotten wind of his post and filed the complaints (all of which, OEE admitted, came from off campus). They also spent the next year harassing him—he got at least three hundred emails accusing him of being a race traitor and worse; Tucker Carlson also kept calling. After his appeal was turned down by the associate VP for human resources, lawyers got involved. FIRE publicized the case. The president of the university intervened and told the OEE to reconsider. Reluctantly, they did, but universities also have plenty of creative ways to punish employees who create bad publicity.

The irony is that my partner was just a bit early to the party—following the summer of 2020 practically everyone was announcing publicly that they hated white people. It turns out you can be on the "right side of history" at the wrong time. Or maybe the whole "right side of history" thing is a narcissistic delusion. Rest assured, today's moral grandstanders will be tomorrow's thought criminals.

＊＊＊

Observe, in all of these scenarios, the bureaucratic mission creep, the territory grabs, the encroachment on the intellectual life of the university. My IRB pals wanted to supervise the humanities; the writing student's Title IX investigator wanted to adjudicate creative writing; my partner's OEE functionaries believed they could override a historian—who's studied, taught, and published on race for decades—about what defines racism. What they ought to do instead is to figure out how to prevent their offices from being hijacked for political grudge matches and personal vendettas. For example: Social media posts don't *have* to be treated as causes for action. *Stop acting on them, and maybe people will stop reporting them.*

After I went public about my own Title IX case, my inbox was flooded with stories about people snitched on for the most bizarre and trivial crap. A grad student had been anonymously reported for sexual harassment because he'd played the words "juicy" and "Girl Scout" during a word game at a party, then snickered. They were on the cards he'd drawn! After being let off with a warning, he speculated the tattler was someone after his spot when summer teaching assignments were handed out. And indeed, resource competition did often figure as possible subtexts in a lot of stories I heard.

One professor who contacted me—I'll call him Dave—was someone prominent in his field who'd been teaching for close to thirty years. A few years earlier Dave had gotten into an argument with the graduate program director in his department during a committee meeting over grad funding. He thought she was trying to prevent one of his students from being nominated for a national grant in order to promote one of her own students instead. Yelling commenced, and the department chair (a woman) told them both to leave the room. In their absence the committee voted to nominate Dave's student for the grant, which she eventually received.

A self-described complainer, Dave complained about the grad director the next day at a faculty meeting. The chair became indignant, adjourned the meeting, then went to the Title IX office to report that Dave was inappropriately hostile to female colleagues and that his complaints amounted to sexual harassment. The Title IX director (a man) told her that nothing she'd described was sexual harassment, and unless she had other evidence of misconduct, his office couldn't investigate.

A few months later Dave got word from the academic senate that a formal grievance had been filed against him by *five* female professors. The associate vice chancellor, a woman, presented the university's case against Dave on behalf of the complainants. In addition to the faculty meeting outburst, now there were reports that he'd engaged in "unwanted physical contact" with female faculty and graduate students by kissing them on the cheek or giving them hello hugs at department parties. The grad students weren't pressing charges but had been enlisted to testify against him.

In addition, there was testimony about Dave's custom of offering pieces of chocolate muffins to staff members. The campus bakery made really good, really large chocolate muffins, which Dave loved, but he couldn't eat a whole one. On those midafternoons when he was in his office and feeling hungry, he'd go to the bakery, buy one, and divide it into quarters, taking one quarter for himself and offering the remaining three quarters to the office or library staff (which included both men and women). Sometimes people turned him down, but usually not.

A couple of his professor-accusers now claimed that offering muffins to the female staff constituted a form of "inappropriate" and "sexually suggestive" behavior. When asked how offering a muffin could be construed as inappropriate, one claimed that a chocolate muffin is a surrogate form of "fecal matter" and that Dave was essentially telling the staff to "eat my shit."

Additionally, one accuser, a feminist theorist (I'm sorry to say), insisted that he'd offered the staff pieces of muffin with his saliva on them, looming over them as they sat at their desks, that he "forced" them to eat the muffin pieces in front of him, and that the entire process was a form of sadistic bullying intended to assert his position as a powerful male. When pressed, this accuser admitted that she'd never herself personally seen Dave offer muffins to any members of the staff.

The hearing went on for two weeks. The transcript ran to twelve hundred pages.

The senate committee cleared Dave of sexual harassment while finding him guilty of disruptive behavior. My question is why the unhinged and obviously pretextual sexual harassment accusations didn't discredit the accusers on all grounds. Instead, the panel recommended that Dave be censured and undergo anger management training, and that his salary be docked 10 percent for a year. The chancellor (a man) followed these recommendations, except he docked Dave's salary for two years. Then Dave's dean imposed additional sanctions, though this was entirely unprocedural: His office would be moved out of his department to another building, he was not to attend faculty meetings or meet with grad students, and he suffered other humiliations. The dean and university lawyers claimed the added strictures weren't technically "disciplinary actions" because they weren't listed among the kinds of disciplinary action described in the faculty handbook. Dave's lawyer pointed out that public flogging wasn't listed among the disciplinary actions either, but if Dave were to be flogged, it would obviously still be a form of punishment. Dave filed another grievance. At the point we were in touch, this had been going on for more than three years, and Dave had spent over $40,000 in legal fees.

Dave struck me as funny and self-aware. Was he also especially disruptive, or just someone who spoke his mind more than was politic? Or was the real problem—as Dave suspected—that certain colleagues simply resented him for being excessively productive and one of the more popular teachers in the department, based on enrollments and evaluations? Were the rather extreme punishments meted out deserved, or due to his having unwisely locked horns with his preceding dean (who'd become a vice chancellor) and also, unfortunately, his current dean?

When I began writing this piece, I wanted to reconnect with Dave to see what had happened with his appeal. Googling his name, I learned he'd died the year after we spoke, at age sixty-three, after battling a serious illness. Had he spent the last year of his life still being hounded by his colleagues, I wondered? According to his obituary, the campus flag was lowered to half-staff in his memory.

* * *

As standards for behavior become narrower and more restrictive, some of those caught in the crosshairs and subject to punishment, lawyers tell me, are the socially maladroit. Some may have Asperger's or be otherwise "on the spectrum," as we now say, treated as blameworthy because of "off" vibes or impediments in reading social cues. I've heard about such instances myself. A young male grad student recently wrote for advice after being accused of making "unwanted advances" to multiple women, though he'd never dated or hooked up in college and was still a virgin at twenty-seven, he revealed. He'd been diagnosed with autism spectrum disorder and hadn't ever figured out sex or dating; his academic future was now in jeopardy given the impossible-to-disprove accusations.

Combing through a batch of heavily redacted OCR complaints against my university—these were appeals of Title IX decisions that had been filed with the Department of Education's Office for Civil Rights over the last decade and obtained by a colleague via FOIA request—I came across more than a few examples of harassment complaints over such matters as a "creepy stare." One case involved a graduate student who, as a dismayed friend wrote in a character testimonial, had an "intense personal style" that was being unfairly transformed into evidence of something sexually untoward. A faculty member wrote to say that other grad students were biased against the alleged starer; other letters testified that the intense gaze wasn't sexual, it was just his personality. But since everyone in the department knew about the allegations, now when the starer merely asked a question at a colloquium, negative inferences circulated about his mental health and character, compounding the bias. (These were, by the way, clinical psychology students.) The student dean stood by his guilty finding, and the OCR appears to have placed the appeal in the circular file.

Not long ago I received a wrenching email from the mother of a former graduate student I'd interviewed and written about in *Unwanted Advances*. He'd been swept up in the same accusation-fest on my campus that I had. In fact, he'd been reported on, he told me, by some of the same people who'd gone after me (friends, he'd once thought) and had been, perhaps, collateral damage in the events I was relating. The charges involved his having made drunken passes (six months apart) at two women in his circle and being, they felt, in various ways invasive. As a result, he was put on disciplinary probation and his funding was cut; he'd needed $100,000 in loans to get through his final year in the program. He felt thrown under the bus by his advisor, who'd recruited then abandoned him, and ostracized by others in the program. (He'd been too depressed to contest the accusations, which he later regretted; some of the details were false or exaggerated, he said, but he hadn't known his department would be informed about them.) He'd obviously been having difficulties at the time and acting in desperate ways, as the student dean's sanctions letter (which I've read many times) makes clear: his "dynamic emotional states," which moved very quickly from sadness to anger, were "perceived as coercive or intimidating" by those he interacted with. Might there have a way to deal with this person more compassionately? No, the university was far more interested in punishing than helping him.

His mother was now writing me to say her son was dead. She thought I'd want to know. The cause of death proved to be "the toxic effects of bromazolam," a designer drug you can get on the internet. She wrote that she thought her son had actually died "because of the toxic effects of a higher education program that caused him nothing but pain and heartbreak." He'd been totally crushed during the worst of it, especially by having been turned on by people he'd thought of as friends and mentors. The "quasi legal administrative processes" their son had been through, his father wrote, had ruined their lives.

His parents had both long thought their son was probably "on the spectrum," but he'd never been formally diagnosed. He was awkward at times and often fuzzy on people's expectations, his father said, adding, "His lack of insight into other people's feelings and motives very likely contributed to his Title IX problems." When we'd met, a few years after the sanctions, he seemed bitter and a little broken. Lives can be destroyed in such casually vicious ways.

* * *

These are a mere smattering of the hundreds of stories I've been told about. There are obviously thousands more that people are too shamed or cowed to disclose. I'm no psychic, but I can predict what will happen when this essay is published. My inbox will be flooded with cases of specious and horrific overblown accusations, sent by people who've been warned that if they talk about what they've been through, even when accused of verifiably false stuff, they'll be punished—charged with "retaliation," then face expulsion or job loss. These effective gag orders mean that administrators will get to keep operating with no public scrutiny, turning ostensibly liberal institutions into cellblocks.

My plan is to feature this new crop of stories in a regular column, or maybe a website, dedicated to the Academic Snitch of the Week. Hey, I know—if we run low on cases, we'll solicit anonymous reports. Warning: We will be naming names. Of the snitches.

Put down the phone, please don't report me. I'm joking. I swear.

CHAPTER 18

FREEDOM GAINED AND FREEDOM LOST IN AMERICAN SCIENCE

JONATHAN R. COLE AND DARIA FRANKLIN

. . . her wings are cut and she is blamed for not knowing how to fly

—Simone de Beauvoir, *The Second Sex*

The American research university has dominated the world of higher learning for the past century. The twentieth century can be called the age of American universities. Our universities have been perhaps the greatest engine of social and economic change that we have witnessed since at least the seventeenth century English scientific revolution. Among the literally thousands of important discoveries: the discovery of the insulin gene, the nicotine patch, antibiotics, the Richter Scale, the origins of computers, the algorithm for Google, the basic RNA science that led to some of the COVID-19 vaccines, the fetal monitor, the pap smear, the cure for childhood leukemia, the methods of scientific agriculture, the electric toothbrush, even the Heimlich maneuver and Gatorade—all came from our research universities.[1] We as a nation have produced scholars and scientists whose work, discoveries, and ideas have transformed the world. Science in the academy is often identified as the institution in our nation that most closely approximates the ideal of universalism.[2] The central question in this essay is: Have we idealized the scientific community? And if so, what are some of the ways that it has harbored and reinforced significant unfreedom within its borders? Freedom matters. Unfreedom matters as well.

The ambiguous word "unfreedom" refers to those mechanisms by which some members of society—the members of the larger society or members of, say the scientific community, impoverish, limit, or eliminate the options of other individuals or groups: *noncoercive threats to freedom*. It is also produced by deep-seated values embedded in cultures—leading individuals and groups to define freedom in ways that, as a matter of course, certain behavior is accepted and becomes normative. Sometimes the opposite of freedom is not coercion but a subtler form of impoverishing of options. This happens often in political economy (as with when freedom is threatened by an authoritarian government) and in the concerns of the environment, where for instance our option of breathing fresh air or drinking clean water, is increasingly under threat, rendering us less free therefore, but where no one is coercing anyone.

Decision making takes place thousands of times each day within the world of science. Not only are critical choices made about the pursuit of scientific inquiry itself and decisions about what to study and what to or not to publish in scientific papers, what lines should be drawn between fact and fiction, or when to end an experiment. But decisions about the fate of scientists themselves—who should be hired, who should be promoted, who should receive honorific recognition, who should receive major increases in salaries, who should receive grants for their research, and who should receive telescope time at national laboratories—are as continual in science as in any other walks of life. Observers of science often idealize it, taking the institution as a model of academic freedom, personal freedom, and a place with few fetters on lines of scientific inquiry. Science is the place to find "truth" without all of the human biases and presuppositions that might affect its pursuit. It is the American institution, which in theory rewards people on the basis of their talents and achievements.

In this essay, we focus on a fuller history of twentieth century American science prior to World War II.[3] Like so much in our history, we tend to hide the ways our nation has fallen short of its ideals of freedom. This is true for science as well. The human side of science is often omitted from its examination. We shall discuss these shortcomings through a lens that looks at the place of women in the scientific community in this formative period. It has become popular sport to enumerate all the ways that research universities fall short of its ideals. But as we discuss the shortcomings in this one area, we do so while recognizing that the American research university has undergone many changes for the better over the past seventy-five years and remains the benchmark for excellence in higher education throughout the world.

The chapter is divided into four parts. First, we limit our discussion here to the Age of Little Science.[4] It is a period of time spanning the first half of the twentieth century. Our focus here is on women and science. Second, while acknowledging the truly extraordinary discoveries made by American science and technology during those years—an age when American science became preeminent in the world—we try to capture ways that "unfreedom" impoverished the options of a huge number of qualified people from entering the scientific enterprise. Third, we inject into the discussion of our history, the broader cultural and political landscape into the analysis of why science continues to fall short of its universalistic ideal. Fourth, and finally, we will discuss how prevailing values and norms created an institutional environment that has made it difficult for some groups, particularly women and people of color, to succeed in doing science. They were "outsiders" rather than "insiders"—they could be *in* science, but they could never be *of* science. The mechanisms that kept them on the margins, as we shall see, were largely in the hands of academic institutions, and less so in the hands of academic scientists.

More specifically, freedom and universalism in science applied only to men until well into the twentieth century. It was an age of white, male, privileged freedom. Women were not part of the measurement of universalism or meritocracy because they were located outside the definition of scientist.[5] Much the same, only more striking, has been true for the apparent contrast between the treatment of African Americans with "white freedom" that simply defined people of color as outside the definition of political liberty in a democratic society—a dilemma for philosophers like Locke and Rousseau and politicians for whom issues of political and social rights and issues of property were salient, while racial unfreedom became a striking anomaly in their work on liberty and freedom.[6] The practices that effectively banned women from regular careers in science after having completed their professional training on an equitable basis did not present a need for institutions and members of the scientific community to reconcile their discriminatory practices with claims of universalism and impartiality because of the presumption that the norms of science, of which universalism is salient, govern the relationship only between scientists themselves, and women were *not* scientists.[7] But during this period, as we shall see, the number of anomalies—women with great talent who were knocking at the door—presented an increasing paradox of how the powers within the institution could claim it was meritocratic when it clearly relegated most women aspiring to be scientists to inferior positions within the community.

As historian Eric Foner has said: "No idea is more fundamental to Americans' sense of themselves as individuals and as a nation than freedom."[8] Since freedom, itself, is a complex set of values, norms, and beliefs, it defies easy definition. But Americans cling to it as a defining quality that sets us apart from other nations, despite the plethora of historical examples of the way freedom in our country has been abridged from well before the American Revolution. But science has been viewed, stereotypically, as one of our institutions that comes closest in practice to our mythical ideal. Let's see how this stereotype, like all, is based partially on fact and also on fiction.

1. The age and the problem

In the age of little science, great, defining discoveries could be made with pencil and paper or, as in biology, in a small laboratory "closet," such as the famous Columbia "fly room."[9] There Thomas Hunt Morgan and his students carried out their now renowned genetics experiments on *Drosophila* fly from 1911 to 1928. In 1931 botanist Barbara McClintock used brown paper bags attached to her belt to capture and scribble down ideas that would subsequently show that chromosomes exchange parts; in the late 1930s physicist turned biologist Max Delbrück started the phage group as a small informal seminar; in 1944 Oswald Avery, Colin MacLeod, and Maclyn McCarty set the stage for the discovery of the structure of the DNA molecule; and in the 1940s George Beadle and Edward Tatum, working with bread mold, discovered the way genes regulate biochemical events in the cells—they formulated the theory of one gene, one enzyme.

During the decades leading up to these discoveries, women were fairly well-represented in secondary and postsecondary education. From 1900 to 1950 the proportion of female high school graduates always outpaced that of men.[10] At the level of the baccalaureate, the proportion of women steadily rose: from 19 percent in 1900 to 41 percent in 1940. Even among PhD recipients, women fared better in 1920 than they did in 1960.[11]

The greater number of women receiving education was one of the new forms of social arrangements and social structures that came with urbanization, industrialization, and bureaucratization of the late nineteenth and early twentieth-century period that led America into modernity. A modern American woman could live and work in the city, attend high school and college, pursue a career in teaching, join a voluntary association or a social movement, or become a foreign missionary.[12] The new woman felt liberated in her choices of lifestyles and fashion, in her manners and morals. She could wear shorter hair and expose her knees, become a flapper or a vamp, listen to jazz, choose professional life over a family, and attend public spaces, such as entertainment centers and department stores. Historian Marilyn Ogilvie explains, "Educational reforms fell in lockstep with political ones. By the early twentieth century, women were active in most fields of science, although certain areas such as the biological and the human sciences were better represented than the physical sciences and mathematics."[13]

The changing social landscape for the definitions of American womanhood did not change the way the state viewed women. The government remained conservative in the assumptions about women's nature and maintained that men and women were different and therefore should be treated differently. In 1905, the Supreme Court in *Lochner v. New York* (198 U.S. 45) addressed the number of hours bakers could work. The result, based on the Court's interpretation of the Fourteenth Amendment, reinforced the right of employers to hire workers for up to ten hours a day and sixty hours a week. Three years later, as part of the Progressive Movement, in the landmark Supreme Court case *Muller v. Oregon* (208 U.S. 412, 1908), the lawyers and social scientists for the plaintiff argued for protective legislation for women. They produced statistical evidence—ultimately included in what we now refer to as the Brandeis brief—illustrating that long hours and strenuous work conditions can harm the procreative function of women. Therefore, protecting women was a matter of state interest:

> That woman's physical structure and the performance of maternal functions place her at a disadvantage in the struggle for subsistence is obvious. This is especially true when the burdens of motherhood are upon her. . . . The physical wellbeing of woman becomes an object of public interest and care in order to preserve the strength and vigor of the race. . . . Still again, history discloses the fact that woman has always been dependent upon man. . . . It is still true that, in the struggle for subsistence, she is not an equal competitor with her brother.

The Court found an exception to Lochner, but it did not overturn it.

Even winning the right to vote in 1920 was no fait accompli. Gaining new political rights and stepping outside the traditional women's roles led to conservative reactions and inspired a new cult of domesticity.[14] Through the 1920s the White House and the courts were not hospitable to reforms and did not provide further legislative support for women. Women's choices were still bound by rules and customs that limited women in most areas of public life. Husbands still controlled family earnings and could determine wives' legal residence; women were barred from entering the majority of professions; they were solely responsible for illegitimate children, yet they had no options for childcare.[15] Even expanded entry into the workforce for women stalled by 1930, and women were largely finding jobs rather than building professional careers. The Depression deteriorated the scant female employment opportunities as women became increasingly seen as competition to men on the tightening labor market. Married women were particularly under attack, since they were assumed to have a partner with income. The results of a poll for *Fortune Magazine* in 1936 revealed that only 15 percent of the nation approved for married women having full-time jobs outside the home.[16]

The women whose stories we examine in this essay began their lives in science in the late 1920s and 1930s. They were the products of the greatest social changes that allowed them to imagine lives outside the home, but they also witnessed how short that life span of opportunities was.

In 1937, commenting on the women's experiences in early twentieth century, literary scholar Marjorie Nicolson wrote: "I find myself wondering whether our generation was not the only generation of women which ever found itself. We came late enough to escape the self-consciousness and belligerence of the pioneers, to take education and training for granted. We came early enough to take equally for granted professional positions in which we could make full use of our training. This was our double glory."[17]

Nicolson's views underlined the gains rather than the resistance to women in the academy during this time of expanded educational opportunities. Universities certainly were hardly receptive to women in almost any capacity, much less as full citizens in the scientific community. As the women we will encounter came of age, there was nothing that approximated shared governance at our top research universities. Most places of higher learning—including women's colleges—were ruled by white men: the benefactors who started the university, the boards of regents, the president, and the leading administrators. There was no protective legislation for members of the faculty. During and after the World War I and the first Red Scare, many faculty members whose political or academic views offended presidents, chancellors, and trustees of universities were unilaterally fired. The AAUP's first Statement of Principles, in 1915, did not weigh heavily in these dismissals.[18] Few universities were deeply committed to the principles of academic freedom and free inquiry.[19]

One would not expect many women to have received tenured positions or honorific recognition within this male bastion of authority and power, even when they clearly merited it. It's hard to win if those with authority refuse to let you play. And that is, of course, what the data tell us. Consider the following facts. Roughly the same number of women won Nobel science prizes between 1994 and 2019 as had won the prize in the previous ninety years. Between 2000 and 2019 more than twice as many women were elected members of the American Philosophical Society as in the previous seventy years. The National Academy honored a majority of its female members after the beginning of the twenty-first century. As of 2025, there are sixty-four recipients of the Fields Medal, the most prestigious award in the field of mathematics given every four years to the most outstanding mathematicians under the age of forty. Only two are women: Maryam Mirzakhani (2014) and Maryna Viazovska (2022). Of the forty-seven recipients of the John Bates Clark Medal for the most outstanding work by an economist under the age of forty, so far only six have been women, and all of them received the award after 2005.[20] Of the leading research universities in the first half of the twentieth century, Columbia's first tenured professor, Ruth Benedict, was elevated to this position in 1937; Harvard awarded tenure to a woman for the first time in 1948, when historian

Helen Maud Cam joined the club of 180 arts and sciences male professors; Yale's first female tenured faculty member, Bessie Lee Gambrill, a specialist in elementary education, received tenure in 1952 after three decades of teaching and doing research at the institution; finally, it took Princeton until 1968 to grant its first tenured position to the sociologist Suzanne Keller. Women, in short, remained part of the scientific "outer circle" throughout most of the twentieth century. One can point to a few exceptions, but on closer inspection, even those extraordinary women of science faced many more life-course obstacles than men.

Let's turn now to two stories and some common "patterns" that we garner from the women of this period.[21] The vignettes below are meant to be suggestive about the world that female scientists faced and their adaptive behavior in the period before World War II. Despite the limitations on their options, the unfreedom that they faced, these women carved out exceptional, if unusual, careers.[22]

2. Short stories of unfreedom

Our stories focus both on the formative years and later career opportunities and choices of two geneticists: Barbara McClintock and Salome Gluecksohn-Waelsch.[23] Both women came of age and contemplated professional careers in the mid-nineteen twenties and thirties. They were finishing their formal education as the country and western world was entering the Great Depression.

Barbara McClintock (June 16, 1902–September 2, 1992)

Barbara McClintock might well be the best known and most celebrated woman scientist in twentieth century America. From the outset of her career as a graduate student at Cornell University, everyone knew they were interacting with a rare intellect, a bit of an odd person, but who had enormous capabilities. She had the right stuff. Her colleagues at Cornell, who also worked as cytologists examining the genetics of maize plants, knew it. "Hell, it was so damn obvious," Marcus Rhoades said of McClintock, "she was something special . . . quick, imaginative, and perceptive. Almost instantly she grasped the significance of a new observation or recently discovered fact."[24] Most others who worked in the field of genetics also knew that they were interacting with someone special—even if many of them could not quite understand what she was doing.

Like most great minds in science, McClintock questioned the received wisdom of the times. There was a general belief among geneticists that the genes on chromosomes were static—they did not move around.[25] McClintock pioneered in the cellular analysis of genetic phenomena in corn. Working alone, she conducted the painstaking work on multiple generations of maize plants. She knew her corn plants. She "had a feeling for the organism," as Evelyn Fox Keller put it. In the 1930s, as a young woman, McClintock, who was not more than five feet two or three, wore wire-rimmed glasses, could be found in her army-like attire meticulously examining her corn at Cold Spring Harbor Laboratory. With exceptional discipline and imagination, and free from the pressures of the dogma of her field, she discovered that certain pieces of chromosome 9 could break off and exchange parts among chromosome pairs. In the 1940s, as a mature scientist, she demonstrated that chromosomes have "switches" that can turn genes on and off and allow them to move to different places on the chromosome.[26] This process is known as "transposition" or "jumping genes." In other terms, she was interested in how genes on a chromosome could move during plant reproduction and how that was affected by mutations.

For this work, McClintock was the third woman elected to the National Academy of Sciences in 1944. So her peers knew how exceptional her scientific originality was. According to McClintock, her election to the NAS at an early age was not a blessing: "I didn't want the academy. . . . I was not elated. I felt caught. I said to myself, 'Caught! Caught! For the first time, I'm caught.' I got into doing interesting things, but I didn't have that same sense of freedom that I'd had. I just knew I couldn't let the women down. You can't walk out. I couldn't walk out the way I'd been walking out."

She saw no hope for women in science at the time. In answering the question of whether there was anything that could be done to change the status of women in science, she insisted: "No, no. I felt that you couldn't change this. The time has to be ripe, and it wasn't ripe. [The walls and barriers were too high.] They were just too high. Why get disturbed? You worked within the particular area you could work within but have your own standards within it to do what you wanted to do. This is where the freedom came in. The barriers meant that I had lots of freedom to walk around them and do something else."

But where did this woman, who turned unfreedoms to freedoms, come from? How did she "make" it? Barbara McClintock was born in Hartford, Connecticut, in 1902, but her family moved to Brooklyn when Barbara was six. She attended public schools and graduated in 1919 from one of New York's best public high schools, Erasmus Hall. Unsurprisingly, McClintock was an excellent student. She especially enjoyed the physics class that she had at Erasmus, which gave her a taste for science. She was quite uncertain in what direction she wanted to turn, but she did intend to go to college. Her mother, a piano teacher, was set against it; her father, an army doctor, who had served in Europe during World War I, got home in time to insist that McClintock go to college. Her family life, where the four children were very much part of the decision-making, proved extremely important in producing the trajectory of her education. It was important that the young women had a means for independence, but the form of work tended to be traditionally gendered work.

As she put it: "I had the support of my father, the complete support. My mother—if she could have done it without raising trouble—she'd have stopped me [from going to Cornell]. It was a real fear on her part that I'd be a professor. My mother hid a lot of ambivalent ideas and one of them was a fear of professional women."[27]

We begin to see the full force of the culture on individual histories when McClintock was at Cornell University, one of the most progressive American universities at the time. After completing her bachelor's degree, she began working on her PhD in the Department of Agriculture. Here she began to encounter "unfreedom." McClintock was able to obtain some highly prestigious postdoctoral fellowships to pursue her work in genetics, but, unlike some of her male colleagues, she was not allowed, for example, to enter the faculty dining room or to hold any significant position at Cornell. She majored in botany, although she had already made friends with a set of exceptionally able Cornell geneticists who were approximately her age. When asked about the vision of her own career, McClintock opined:

> I didn't have any projections. I just figured that a person could do a lot of different things. In those days there was no difficulty in getting jobs. I could do something. You could even wash dishes. But you wouldn't starve. There was absolutely no idea of a career. That was out. I was turned down for fellowships, not all, but some. They didn't think you were going to stay, and therefore it wasn't worthwhile giving it to you. And that was alright with me. I mean, I didn't get mad at that. That was part of the time.

During her early postdoctoral years, McClintock had two exceptionally talented colleagues roughly of her age: Marcus Rhoades, somewhat older, and George Beadle, who was born within a year of McClintock. Since Beadle was so similar to McClintock in age, specialty, and work, consider this one example of the trajectory of a male scientist with a female—Beadle compared with McClintock. He was at Cornell studying maize plants at the same time as McClintock. He too would win a Nobel Prize for his science.

The careers of Beadle and McClintock are illustrative of certain aspect of unfreedom faced by women scientists in those early years. Born in 1903 into a family of farmers in Wahoo, Nebraska, Beadle did his undergraduate work at the University of Nebraska, and then he went to Cornell for graduate study in genetics. He received his PhD in 1931, four years after McClintock received hers. They became part of the maize group at Cornell. McClintock's friendships and work with Beadle and Rhoades lasted while they were at Cornell and for a long time after the group was separated. They were the core of the young faculty. They would construct their own seminars to which they invited young students while denying access to older professors. As McClintock said, "the three of us worked together very, very well." Both Beadle and McClintock received prestigious postdoctoral fellowships. Beadle would spend the four years following his PhD at the California Institute of Technology (Caltech) and would become, in 1936, an assistant professor of genetics at Harvard. No such position was available for McClintock. The University of Missouri, which also had a superb maize group at the time, hired McClintock as an assistant professor in that same year. There she was excluded from faculty meetings, and although her research was progressing very well, she, unlike her male colleagues, was not treated like other male faculty when it came to further opportunities. Uncertain if she would ever gain tenure, McClintock decided to leave. She had written to a colleague: "I have decided that I must look for another job. As far as I can make out, there is nothing more for me here. I am an assistant professor at $3,000 and I feel sure that that is the limit for me." Whether or not the university was prepared to offer her a tenured professorship remains an open question. She moved on to Columbia University for one year in a nonfaculty position and then was offered a research post at Cold Spring Harbor by the prominent Milislav Demerec, the newly appointed director of its Department of Genetics. Demerec had taken his PhD at Cornell, worked on maize genetics before turning to *Drosophila*. He was appointed at the Carnegie Institution by Vannevar Bush, its president, in 1938.[28]

Meanwhile, following his year at Caltech, Beadle moved to Stanford in 1937 as a professor of biology, specializing in genetics. By 1945 he was back at Caltech as chair of its Division of Biology. He remained at Caltech until 1961, well after working with Tatum on the major discovery of "one gene—one enzyme." In 1961, he became the president of the University of Chicago. Finally, while McClintock was only the third woman elected to the National Academy of Sciences in 1944, the same year as Beadle's election, he waited thirteen years (1958) before receiving the Nobel; McClintock waited thirty-nine (1983).

The unfreedom that McClintock experienced took many forms, partly because of the structure of academic life as well as the cultural beliefs about women in science. McClintock experienced significant resistance to her novel ideas. Whether this was a question of appropriate skepticism about what she had produced, ignorance on the part of other scientists, or a common case of a "premature discovery" is difficult to discern. Here is how McClintock expressed the obstacle course that she had to run and her response to it. She was emphatic: "Oh yes, yes. The resistance was because you couldn't communicate. No words would do it. . . . After I got my doctor's degree, I stayed at Cornell to do a job there and it was extraordinary that it wasn't understood. From the genetic point of view, it was so obvious to me and to the people who worked in the Morgan group. . . . It was obvious to them."

Even at Caltech, McClintock felt the difference between her treatment and that toward close colleagues like George Beadle.

> I had been ostracized at that time by everybody in the department. They called me crazy and just irrational. They didn't understand the very basic thing that was being done. And this fellow, who had been with the Morgan group, knew right away that it was basic. And then he explained it to other people and then I was associated with the group again. But it made no difference to me whether or not I was with the group. I was just astounded. That was my first—rather strong—rather difficult experience. And I've had several others. One lasted nearly twenty years, or more.

Asked whether it made any difference to her that the Morgan group thought that this was important and made sense, she responded: "No, no, no. It's just that, older people sometimes you just have to get rid of them. And younger people come in with—I was young—come in with a freed mind, And they were reading that literature that was coming out and the older people weren't. It was too new."

McClintock cited another example of scientific resistance to her ideas, which lasted twenty years: "That's the one that was the controller gene action. That's the one that I had so much trouble with. And only very much later was it understood. Many years later."

In talking with McClintock, she clearly had turned, in her own mind, a set of actual restrictions on her options into its opposite—a sense of freedom. She turned the limits on her options from a negative, career-obstructing events, into a positive. She worked alone, rarely even with the help of an assistant. She often used the word freedom in this context. Here are her responses to several questions about her sense of freedom:

> Well, if you have to think—this is in those days, and now too—you have to think of a career, you select it because you're following what other men have followed. Very few women would have a guide in this respect. You would have to make it if you wanted it. Or you just did what you wanted to do, as I did. So that gave you freedom. Now, another thing. If a man started a profession and went along part-way and then quit, that would be a black mark according to other people. But if a woman did that, no black mark at all, because they were doing it all the time. That is, they were starting something and then getting married and leaving. And nobody blamed them. Nobody called them defective in one way or another in their personality or strength.
>
> The absence of requirements to follow a certain line and continue with it. Also, the ability to move into any direction regardless was free for me. And it

wouldn't have been free for some of the men. I don't think they would have enjoyed ridicule. I didn't care if I had it.

At the conclusion of the interview with McClintock, she was asked almost as an afterthought, how she saw herself doing science. She replied succinctly: "On Mondays through Saturdays I talk to the maize plants; on Sundays, the maize plants talk to me." We believed her.

Here, then, are some of the forms of unfreedom experienced by McClintock relative to her peer George Beadle. During her youth she had to fight against the idea that science could be a home for women; that women could make distinguished discoveries; that her parents, as supportive in many ways as they were, were still divided about a true career for her. When she applied to college, it was Cornell's agriculture school that provided the opening, not the arts and sciences. The paths began to widen even more, since for most women, each of these limitations on their options represented a setback, a defeat, that in their totality, had a cumulative negative effect on their careers. Despite her ability, the prevailing view was that it was a waste of resources to support women because they would almost invariably turn to their domestic lives and leave science. The structure of academic life was solidly against the support of women, regardless of their demonstrated capabilities. There was open gender discrimination. Men who were mostly not colleagues but representatives of the administrative power structure could acknowledge the brilliance of a woman scientist like McClintock, but that did not mean that they would "waste" time and scarce resources on appointments to regular academic lines, and academic tenure was virtually out of the question even for the brightest and most achieving women. Where the scientific community represented faculty members in, for example, professional associations, they would honor women with awards and recognition, but this too was a rarity even for those of greater ability than their male peers. Besides, even when recognized, they often would have to wait longer to receive that recognition. But the academic administrations and boards of trustees were far less likely to recognize exceptional performance by female scientists. They were not afforded the opportunity to do "informal science" with men—the discussions over lunch or at the bar where a great deal of creative thinking took place. Men set the terms of scientific discourse and debate. They produced the scientific paradigms and expected women to work and ask questions within that theoretical structure, even if on second-order problems. They had little tolerance for the iconoclastic "outsider" who happened to be a woman. They had the power and authority to produce conformity within the community.

George Beadle's career parallels McClintock in time, but not in the paths that each would travel. McClintock's options were limited; Beadle's were not.

Beadle had a remarkable but standard career, except for his unusual move to academic administration as president of the University of Chicago. He did not face the prevailing norms about gender and ability as well as the assumptions about women's life priorities; he did not find it difficult, given his talent, to find exceptional positions and rise in the ranks; it was not unusual for him to find recognition within the community that most ambitious scientists covet. The culture of which we speak permeated the society, limiting the options of some while favoring those of others—beginning in childhood and carrying on throughout their lives.

After World War II, even when federal funding for research became available in substantial amounts, women had more difficulty in obtaining research grants, in being successful in the peer review process, achieving positions of leadership within departments and at a national level. Many more subtle forms of the limitation of options confronted them after the evolution to Big Science. But that is not our focus here.

Salome Gluecksohn-Waelsch (October 6, 1907–November 7, 2007)

Salome Gluecksohn, who would become known as Salome Gluecksohn-Waelsch, began her scientific career in Germany, which before Adolf Hitler came to power in the 1930s was the clear international leader in developing outstanding research universities. Born five years after McClintock, she would be a part of the great intellectual migration from Germany to England and the United States after the National Socialists first had laws passed that fired Jewish scientists and scholars and denied them access to any positions at universities.[29]

We include the sketch of Gluecksohn-Waelsch in part because she was an immigrant woman and was also Jewish. The intellectual migration of scientists and scholars, many of whom were Jewish, helped American science grow rapidly. Yet, for some it represented a "double negative," or what is now referred to as the effects of intersectionality.[30]

Gluecksohn-Waelsch was one who managed to emigrate to the United States. She would become one of the world's great geneticists and a leader for some fifty years in the emerging field of developmental genetics. As geneticist Virginia E. Papaioannou put it in her biographical essay on Gluecksohn-Waelsch:

> Her career was remarkable not only for its longevity—she continued experiments well into her 90s—but also for ushering in new ways of approaching developmental biology in mammals. In her studies of the T-complex in mice she made us aware of naturally occurring mutations as nature's own experiments that allowed the investigation of the normal role of genes in the events

of morphogenesis. . . . Throughout the decades that saw a blossoming of the entire field of genetics, Salome Gluecksohn-Waelsch's work tackling some of the most perplexing problems in mammalian genetics firmly established the mouse as model organism, not only for studying development, but also for the eventual application of molecular biology techniques to development. Her published work is a beautifully coherent and rigorous opus.[31]

But for the fact that Gluecksohn-Waelsch had a set of truly exciting and interesting science teachers at university, she might not have turned to science. She became interested in embryology when taking her first course in Berlin and turned to the most exciting experimental embryologist in Germany, Hans Spemann.

The Weimar years in Germany were considered by many intellectuals and scientists as an unusually creative and open time, with opportunities for Jews and others who were typically outsiders. But life for German women of science was little better during the Weimar Republic than it was in the United States. Great women scientists, like the Austrian-Swedish Lise Meitner, a physicist of the first rank, worked with the enormously talented chemist and Nobelist Otto Hahn. But she found herself working in a basement laboratory. Whatever options existed in Weimar narrowed or closed with the triumph of the Third Reich.

Hans Spemann, who would soon receive the Nobel Prize, was, according to Gluecksohn-Waelsch "a strong male chauvinist." One way this was manifested was in the problems he targeted for his male and female PhD students. "You were told what to work on for your PhD thesis. He gave me a problem that was very boring. In retrospect it was an insult to have been given such project for my dissertation. Whereas a young man who was my colleague was given a very exciting problem."[32] After taking her degree, Gluecksohn-Waelsch moved to Berlin, where she was a research assistant in cell biology for a year. When Hitler took power, she and her husband, the young and talented biochemist Rudolph Schoenheimer, moved to the United States, where he took up a position at Columbia's College of Physicians and Surgeons. Salome had no job in the United States for three years. Then, in 1936, she worked as a research associate in L. C. Dunn's Columbia laboratory, a nonfaculty position she held for seventeen years. Widowed in 1941, she married the Columbia biochemist Heinrich Waelsch, with whom she had two children.

In 1955, when Gluecksohn-Waelsch was forty-eight, the Albert Einstein School of Medicine was founded, and Gluecksohn-Waelsch was appointed associate professor of medicine. Three years later she was promoted to full professor. She founded and chaired Einstein's Department of Genetics in 1963. She received many forms of honorific recognition, including election in 1979, at age seventy-one, to the National Academy of Sciences. In fact, in 1988, at the age of eighty-one, Salome Glucksohn-Waelsch received NIH funding for five more years. At the time of this award she had one of the longest continuous grants from the NIH.[33]

Perhaps the best person with whom to compare Glucksohn-Waelsch's work would be L. C. Dunn, with whom she worked for almost two decades. Dunn was an outstanding developmental geneticist who received virtually every honor conceivable except the Nobel Prize. He was not only an innovative scientist who worked and corresponded with leading members of the genetics community, but he also was known for his work as a teacher, textbook author, and humanitarian activist involved with the American Committee for Displaced German Scholars during the 1930s, as well as a vocal critic of the eugenics movement in the Soviet Union.[34]

He was not an exploiter of female scientists. Quite the opposite. But he was working within a social system that limited female scientists' options. There were hiring and promotion rules, such as antinepotism constraints, which prevented married couples from working in the same department or even the university.

If we compare Dunn and Glucksohn-Waelsch's scientific careers we see him as a gifted scientist who had few obstacles to overcome. His path was clear, he followed it, and made notable discoveries, and earned prestigious positions, and honors. Glucksohn-Waelsch, who as his equal or better as a scientist, experienced various forms of unfreedom. Dunn hired women, if only as research associates. He allowed them to work on important research questions and to publish their work under their own names. But he stuck by university rules. These impoverished women's careers. Few within the power structure thought this was unjust. When Glucksohn-Waelsch first came to the United States, her husband was immediately offered a job. When asked whether she expected to have a job opportunity, she reflected on the academic opportunity structure: "No. I didn't have a job in Germany either, because universities had a rule against nepotism. The most I could do was to continue working with Spemann on a joint project, in which my husband would also have been involved. But it was without pay. So, I didn't have a job." Asked whether it was acceptable to work and be a wife but not get paid for it, Glucksohn-Waelsch had this to say:

Here, at Columbia, I worked. But don't forget what time that was. It was the Depression and there was no money. So, I was glad that there was someone who let me work in his lab. And when I came to Dunn I worked in his lab without salary for a year and then he asked me how I would like to have a salary. But there was no NIH, there was no Cancer Society, there were no outside agencies and money didn't exist. That I could perhaps have a better job wasn't anything that occupied my mind. I was perfectly happy working there in Schermerhorn Hall at Columbia, for $1,500 a year, and I really enjoyed the work

thoroughly. It was only later that Heini Waelsch called my attention to the possibility that I could have a faculty appointment. It is not quite true that this
hadn't occurred to me, because I did go to Dunn and tell him that there had
been young men here during my time who had climbed the academic ladder
and I asked him why I still remained a research associate. He told me there
was no chance for advancement for me.

Gluecksohn-Waelsch reflected on where this position originated: "I would think
that it was the University's. In Dunn's case I don't think he theoretically approved
of that position, but he certainly wasn't willing to fight it."[35]

In sum, Salome Gluecksohn-Waelsch, who did make a mark on her field,
overcame various forms of unfreedom that were not affecting men of equal or
lesser talent.

Common conditions and shared experiences

Barbara McClintock and Salome Gluecksohn-Waelsch told us stories about
themselves. These shared experiences were not unusual for female scientists
during the first decades of the twentieth century.[36] The majority of highly successful female scientists saw other women in their departments, while pursuing their doctorate degrees. Biochemist Sarah Ratner, for example, remarked
in the early 1980s, "Everybody is talking about women and the biological professions as if this great interest was born yesterday. And when I was a graduate
student which was really—I began in the early '30s—so that was fifty years ago,
there was a good representation of women." Similarly, describing her graduate
school experience at the University of California physicist Melba Phillips
recalled: "There were at least seven women taking their PhDs. There were
women, and nobody told you not to do [physics because you were a woman]."

Seeing women around, however, did not translate into aspirations for professional scientific careers. The majority of women claimed indifference towards
professional recognition, and they, at best, often aspired to be teachers. Grace
Hopper, a highly prolific early computer scientist who in 1944 worked on a team
that developed the Mark I computer, said: "I fully expected to spend the rest of
my life [teaching at Vassar]." She moved to private industry and became a part
of another team that developed UNIVAC I and then managed the development of the first COBOL compiler, which proved that programming language
based on English was possible. Those women who dared to imagine themselves professional scientists, saw the true state of the field and took a rational
approach. Commenting on her education, Berta Scharrer, who would go on to
cofound the discipline of neuroendocrinology, explained her thinking: "I also
took the precaution of getting those courses that would have made it possible

for me to teach in the gymnasium later on, if no academic possibilities existed. Because the situation for an academic career for a woman was very, very poor at that time. I knew that."

These scientists almost never framed their experiences as careers hindered by gender discrimination. Instead, they attributed their uneven careers, dismal pay (if at all), and slow promotion to factors outside of the institutions. Melba Phillips, for example, understood her professional experiences in the following way: "I don't think that being a woman hindered [my career] particularly. I think that all sorts of circumstances and my own talents and so forth and so on hindered it." Freshwater ecologist, botanist, and limnologist Ruth Patrick, to whom recognition did not come until 1960, opined: "I don't think it was just being a woman, at all. I think it was both [being a woman and working in a marginal subfield]." Sara Ratner, while pursuing her PhD at Columbia University, stated that she experienced no prejudice on the basis of gender. However, she added: "There probably was more anti-Semitism." Grace Hopper spent no time thinking about matters of gender: "At UNIVAC, I was always so busy to get more budget, more people, more computer time, more this and that, fighting for something, trying to put a new idea across. If prejudice was there I never saw it. And it may have been because I never had time to look." When asked why there was a paucity of women in engineering and computing, Hopper responded: "Not in business data processing. In the academic world, yes. In the business world, no. It's much more a woman's world in the business world," and then quipped, "Oh, the academics have all their usual prejudices."

Even when they acknowledged inequalities of treatment and opportunities, these women took unfreedom for granted. It was not a time for activism in the academic world, and they did not see the limitation of their options as reasons to resist the existing order of things. Sarah Ratner framed her position this way:

> And none of the women talked about women's rights or the "professional woman." [Science] was what we wanted to do and so we did it. You know [of the disparate treatment and discrimination], but somehow or other you don't take the bull by the horns. I mean, you wouldn't march up to someone and protest and say, "Why am I not included?" or, "I need more money," something like that. Sometimes I have felt that I was also being exploited. I was very glad to have those positions. They were very good labs, I was learning new things, but I wasn't paid what a man would have been paid. It used to be said—and it still is—that women, particularly married women, that it isn't so important whether they have a salary equal to that of men because they don't need it. And sometimes women themselves would accept the situation.

Berta Scharrer, who was a Jewish immigrant, expressed a similar view of being in the "outer circle": "... all I wanted to do was work and not make waves. It was not necessarily liked that I worked without pay, you see. I was given a room in Cleveland, I was given some space in Denver, and that was already considered a little bit generous on the part of the university."

The limitations at the career level, as these women saw them, had little to do with their relations with colleagues and peers. On the contrary, the women working in those days said they had positive experiences at the individual level. "It is my friendship with people in the scientific world that have been the greatest help to me. And they have been terrific. I mean, all of my colleagues have been great," Ruth Patrick asserted. When Grace Hopper was asked what the environment was like at Yale, where there were only two women, she said: "Everybody but one professor was [receptive of females]." Melba Phillips had a similar experience: "I didn't suffer any discrimination as far as the relationship with the fellows was concerned. I don't think it existed."

Some of the women agreed with McClintock that the lack of institutional freedoms paradoxically resulted in increased freedom to conduct research on their own terms, free from the pressures to work on 'hot' research questions. Berta Scharrer said: "But the advantage was that my time wasn't taken up by anything. You know, I was on no committees. . . . I taught in Cleveland on my own. And the work was awfully nice—I liked to teach."

These patterns, arising from the cultural values in the years of Little Science require further research. An open question is: Were the violations of the norm of universalism a function primarily of faculty values and beliefs or of the institutional values at the university level—or both?

The paradox of individual universalism and institutional particularism

In the past four decades a good deal has been written about the system of social stratification in science. In the 1970s, social scientists explored whether or not the system approximated a universalistic ideal, and much of the empirical work concluded that it did. It also concluded that some of the disparities in recognition resulted from a process of cumulative advantage and disadvantage.[37] Robert K. Merton and Harriet Zuckerman developed the concept of *The Matthew Effect*, taken from the Gospel: "For to everyone who has will more be given, and he will have abundance; but from him who has not, even what he has will be taken away" (Matthew 25:29, RSV).[38] They applied this concept to scientific rewards. *If those who gained by the process were more meritorious to begin with, then the norm of universalism would not necessarily be abridged.* Some social scientists argued that it was futile to imagine that science can follow its own normative prescriptions because social environments, cultures, ideologies, politics, economic incentives, and sensibilities of scientists shape the way science is organized, managed and conducted.[39] Others regarded normative prescriptions and social behavior of scientists as inextricable domains that defined scientific life. According to this view, scientists are not guided by one imperative or another. Rather, to make sense of their work, they rely on flexible "ideological-rhetorical" repertoires and draw from different combinations to account for particular situations and actions.[40]

In the late 1980s it was suggested that universalism could exist at the aggregate level and particularism at the level of individuals.[41] The earlier positions overlooked the combined influence of institutional sorting and of social networks on particular decisions. Although decisions may be based on criteria that are independent of extraneous factors, particularism could enter the system because of scarcity of resources. After the initial sort, or a series of sorts, is made on a population of applicants, aspirants, job seekers, grant applicants, and so on, there still remains a pool of qualified individuals that exceeds by a significant amount the number of positions, honorific awards, or federal grants available for distribution. Although these individuals need not be alike along a host of important dimensions, they all have legitimate claims to be part of the pool of qualified candidates. Given the imbalance between the number of those qualified and the resources and positions available the open question becomes: On what bases do individuals, as representatives of social institutions, make decisions?[42] Examples of this type of particularism can be found in the peer review system—even if it does not eliminate the possibilities of biases based on personal characteristics. Even with peer review, looking beyond the important possibility of outright discrimination, individual reviewers are to some degree basing their decisions on network associations, friendship patterns, institutional loyalties, quid pro quos or tit for tats, authority relationships, old-boy networks, and other decision rules, including the often understated "luck of the reviewer draw."[43]

This distinction between levels of analysis fails to go far enough. In dealing with forms of constrained options facing women in the first half of the past century, we also should consider the distinction between *individual universalism* and *institutional particularism* (table 18.1). Could individual scientists in the system favor opening up positions for women in the academy, while running into strong headwinds from the real power in these institutions—the trustees and presidents of universities? Did these advocates for females in science remain silent in the face of power? These power relations, like all cultural norms, have been, of course, subject to evolution and change. Certainly, from 1890 to World War II there was far less shared governance of universities. Today, presidents rule by authority (largely by the will of the governed). In the past, presidents, trustees, and donors ruled by sheer power. Consider just two examples of attitudes and policies about women in the student body and on the faculty held by prominent presidents.

Charles William Eliot, one of Harvard's great presidents, led the institution from 1869 to 1909. So distinguished a man as Eliot elicited a two-volume biography by novelist Henry James's nephew, of all people. As great as many of Eliot's policies were for the history of higher education, he let his views about women at Harvard be known immediately in his inaugural address:

> The attitude of the University in the prevailing discussions touching the education and fit employments of women demands brief explanation. America is the natural arena for these debates; for here the female sex has a better past and a better present than elsewhere. Americans, as a rule, hate disabilities of all sorts, whether religious, political, or social. Equality between the sexes, without privilege or oppression on either side, is the happy custom of American homes. While this great discussion is going on, it is the duty of the University to maintain a cautious and expectant policy. The Corporation will not receive women as students into the College proper, nor into any school whose discipline requires residence near the school. The difficulties involved in a common residence of hundreds of young men and women of immature character and marriageable age are very grave. The necessary police regulations are exceedingly burdensome. The Corporation are not influenced to this decision, however, by any crude notions about the innate capacities of women. The world knows next to nothing about the natural mental capacities of the female sex. Only after generations of civil freedom and social equality will it be possible to obtain the data necessary for an adequate discussion of woman's natural tendencies, tastes, and capabilities. Again, the Corporation do not find it necessary to entertain a confident opinion upon the fitness or unfitness of women for professional pursuits. It is not the business of the University to decide this mooted point.

Thirty years later President Eliot's views of women continued to be, in the words of Bryn Mawr College's legendary president, M. Carey Thomas, "the old argument of the rural deans." At the inauguration of Caroline Hazard as president of Wellesley College in 1899, among other things, Eliot had this to say about women:

> It would be a wonder, indeed, if the intellectual capacities of women were not at least as unlike those of men as their bodily capacities are. It remains to discover and apply the best means and methods for making a college for women a perfect school of manners. Everybody knows that the influence of women depends more than that of men on bearing, carriage, address, delicate sympathy, and innocent reserve; that manners, in short, are much more important to the influence of women than they have been to the influence of men in the actual

world—not that they ought to have been, but than they have been. A man relies on his strength; a woman on more delicate qualities.

One more example, among the many that we could produce, will suffice to illustrate the prevailing views of people of significant power and influence in the academy at the turn of the twentieth century—and to suggest what the cultural norms were for the women thinking of careers in science or the academy during the first decades of the twentieth century. Here are just some of the words uttered in 1906 by William De Witt Hyde, president of Bowdoin College:

> What, then, is the womanly as opposed to the manly ideal of scholarship? What is the beneficent ordering of intellectual consumption? ... A very important, a very arduous, if less conspicuous and less popular part remains, and probably will remain almost exclusively in the hands of men—the part of productive scholarship. By productive scholarship is meant the power to grasp as a whole some great department of human knowledge; keep abreast of every advance that is made in it; from time to time add some contribution to it, and above all so vitally to incorporate it, so vigorously to react upon it, and so systematically to organize it, that the scholar puts his individual stamp upon it, and compels whoever would master the subject to reckon with the individual form which he has given to it. Productive scholarship of this high sort is very rare, whether in men or women. Its price is very high—in time and strength, in withdrawal from other interests and concentration upon one's chosen subject, in sacrifice of domestic and social claims.[44]

These were the men who held power at our great universities and colleges. They, of course, had their vocal critics in the likes of Thorstein Veblen and the muckraker Upton Sinclair. These two, among others, saw the powerful presidents as part of the larger American plutocracy of the Carnegies, Rockefellers, Morgans, and their crowd, as having too much power in setting university governance structures. Veblen referred to them as "captains of erudition." Sinclair referred to Nicholas Murray Butler, the president of Columbia University, as "Nicholas Miraculous"—"a man with a first-class brain, a driving executive worker, capable of anything he puts his mind to, but utterly overpowered by the presence of great wealth." Butler would run for vice president in 1912 and, of course, Woodrow Wilson moved quickly from the presidency of Princeton to the governorship of New Jersey to the White House. These were members of what C. Wright Mills called "the power elite." They were part of "interlocking directorates." They set the norms and values of the major universities. They carried the cultural imperatives with them and they stamped them on the universities. The faculty, if they thought otherwise about women in the academy (and there are no surveys to confirm this), had little power to affect change—and they rarely tried.

TABLE 18.1 "Little science" typology of norms and values

		Individual level	
		Universalism	Particularism
Institutional level	**Universalism**	George Beadle's quadrant	"Big Science" quadrant
	Particularism	Barbara McClintock's quadrant	Salome Gluecksohn-Waelsch's quadrant

The typology presented in table 18.1 allows us to locate a large portion of women and men of science during the Age of Little Science. Most men would be located in the Beadle quadrant. For these male scientists the institutional norm of universalism was accepted, as was the individual commitment to it. That, of course, would not have been true for many male scientists who were of color or were Jewish, for example. In short, universalism, at the institutional or university level, had yet to become a fully realized normative standard.

The McClintock quadrant represents individuals who experienced formidable institutional limitations on their options even when many individual female scientists were recognized for their ability and achievements by their peers. While this remains an open question, if further research reinforces this observation, it would suggest that the institutional barriers to freedom in science may have been greater than the limitation on options imposed by individuals. One indicator of this is the number of honors received by talented women scientists within their own professional societies or groups—including the virtually all-male National Academy of Sciences. In these situations, peers made the decisions, not administrative authorities. Female scientists received these forms of honorific recognition despite being deprived of standard positions within the university. The power held at the institutional level dominated opposing views held by individual scientists.

The Gluecksohn-Waelsch quadrant represents the vast majority of aspiring female scientists whose options were constrained by other scientists within the community and by powerful leaders of universities. Gluecksohn-Waelsch fits here for the better part of her long career, which she spent in Germany and then at Columbia, without much recognition or opportunities for advancement. Only when she moved to Albert Einstein College of Medicine did she receive recognition for her exceptional scientific work.

Finally, the "Big Science" quadrant represents few scientists during the Age of Little Science, but a space within the community that would increasingly be open to both female and male scientists during the second half of the twentieth century. The typology, although presented in static form, should be seen as part of a dynamic process of changing culture, values, and norms. As the institutions and society changed in term of their values—and as science moved with the larger society—there was greater movement toward institutional universalism, even if individual particularism continues to persist.

The role of culture

There have been many conceptual and empirical efforts to explain differences in career outcomes of men and women scientists. They fall into "emphasis" groups. Most prominent is work on structural constraints related to gender discrimination. But the range of other causal mechanisms is wide. In earlier times, there were those who believed in "proof" of biological, psychological, and physiological differences; those that held to the "sacred spark" theory of innate differences applied to groups rather than individuals; and those who promoted theories of reinforcement and social learning. Later, we have encountered theories of cumulative advantage and disadvantage used to explain various and growing differences in productivity and career outcomes.[45] Related to the idea of cumulative disadvantages is a theory of limited differences—where in a stochastic process over time, the careers of men and women diverge because women experience more, even if small, negative feedbacks than men.[46] These negative "kicks," if you will, accumulate and what were limited or small differences at t_1 become large disparities in scientific productivity and career rewards at t_2. There is a place for each of these mechanisms or sets of variables in the explanatory scheme that affects our tentative conclusions about the causes of gender differences in science.[47]

Here we go beyond these more commonly used concepts and theories to elaborate on and underscore the influence of culture in comparing and understanding scientific careers—specifically the role that noncoercive forms of unfreedom play in shaping the lives of would-be or actual female scientists. These cultural beliefs contribute strongly to the paths taken and not taken by young women considering their own life choices. The culture of which we speak involves the values, morals, and ideas that permeate society or community. As we have seen in our few truncated case histories, cultural values and norms often have led to various forms of unfreedom. Unfreedom begins when girls are told that "girls don't do science," or when they can't imagine a scientist is a female.[48] Unfreedom exists when women scientists are offered inferior laboratory space and support; when they are denied appointments and promotions, especially to tenure; when they experience harassment in the workplace; when male colleagues don't take women's ideas as seriously as men's; when women have a more difficult time getting their ideas published; when it is harder for them to receive research grants or fellowships; when university resources are not provided to balance family life and careers; and when women are excluded from informal networks.

The influence of culture may include both exogenous and endogenous forces: those influences in the broader society and those within the smaller scientific community.[49] These forces produce an ethos for a nation. The ethos of America as a special or exceptional nation, or a city upon a hill as it is taught in our schools and enters our textbooks, is part of our rhetoric and produces in our citizens many false beliefs. It is, nonetheless, a powerful part of our culture and once embedded it is difficult to dislodge. At its worst, these cultural beliefs are exported as hegemonic imperatives. It is to this difficulty to change that we briefly turn.

Who owns the null?

We are born into a culture that provides us with a set of historical beliefs and values that can be easily translated into hypotheses, since few are proven facts or theories. In quasi-scientific experiments we set up the opposite of the belief and then try to overturn it or falsify it. This is referred to as the "null hypothesis." The null hypothesis states the hypothesis of zero difference or equality. This can be contrasted with the research hypothesis that involves a statement of expected differences. For example, suppose that we believe that the scientific community treats women unfairly in hiring, promotions, salaries, and in terms of various forms of honorific recognition. To test this hypothesis, we proceed to set up the null hypothesis: that women are treated fairly in science. To overturn the null—to demonstrate that freedom and equality exist for women in science—we must collect sufficient evidence to demonstrate that the null hypothesis of equality must be rejected, that it is not true. The tests used for demonstrating that the null has been overturned are of no concern here. What is important is that finding sufficient empirical evidence to reject or overturn the null hypothesis, given the limited power of social science theory and our inability to identify adequate methods and techniques that can be applied to complex social situations, is very difficult to do. So, in a society or community that holds a set of beliefs that produces unfreedom, whoever controls the definition of the null hypothesis is apt to carry the day.

Whether or not the challenges to core beliefs and principles rest in the larger political and social arena or within institutions like science, they involve conflicting views of basic principles and what is required to prove that one or another organizing principle in our culture is right or wrong.[50] Today, as in the past, there is a political drama unfolding over who owns the null—who gets to define the "truth" that must be falsified.[51] The attacks come from both the cultural Right and the Left. The questions may range from how much free expression should be tolerated on campuses to what can and cannot be published in scientific papers. This, of course, has been a recurring historical theme at American universities and more generally. If this conflict exists today, the unfreedom of women in science during the days of little science, was believed to be based on "facts." Those facts became part of the cultural norms and the belief system. Behavior was to a significant degree conformed to these normative expectations. If you believe that it is a fact that women are less able to do science than men and because of those beliefs you establish a structure that reinforces your belief, you have the perfect conditions for a self-fulfilling prophecy—and the perpetuation of the prior belief system. Once the self-fulfilling prophecy is established, we have the sources of great inequalities that are justified as a result of inferior competency rather than prejudice or discrimination.

In the years between 1900 and 1950, women were assumed as not up to doing advanced science; it was a male profession. If they did fight against the null, they would find cultural and structural obstacles in every aspect of scientific life, because they turned out to, in fact, work on "smaller" problems; they were less scientifically productive; some got married and had children that hypothetically would end any meaningful career options; and so on. Cultural beliefs about African Americans, about Jews, about immigrants, about women in other fields, dominated the prevailing modes of thinking in the United States. They still do.

To reiterate: It is far simpler to create a fiction and perpetuate it than to overturn it with the facts. Perhaps this is part of what Daniel Kahneman and Amos Tversky referred to as "the status quo bias," but it is undoubtedly more than that. Consider a few examples of cultural beliefs that are taken as facts by many of our citizens that have been extremely difficult to overturn. Think of the small, problematic study that claimed that vaccinations were correlated with increased probability of autism; of the belief that dietary cholesterol can significantly increase heart deaths. Finally, we of course have big lies perpetuated and reinforced as alternative facts that are also hard to overturn once they have been internalized by large sectors of the population. We could enumerate many more examples. However, the beliefs about women and science run deep and are difficult to overturn. Much has been done in the past fifty years to disprove some of these beliefs, but the residues from the nineteenth and twentieth centuries persist.[52]

If we want to examine how ideas, values, and norms form the basis for action and, in many cases, the basis for unfreedom, we ought to more carefully examine both school textbooks and children's books. Even movies and social media provide us with clues. They are the sources, outside of families, of much of the socialization process that young people rely on to form their attitudes and beliefs. They help form the culture. They create the null hypothesis that must be overturned.[53]

✳ ✳ ✳

Each of the scientists pictured in this essay was able to "win" while holding a "losing" hand. They had talent and tenacity. They turned defeat into victory. Even in their triumphs they had to accept and acknowledge the way that science worked against the interests and desires of women in the larger society and within their own community. They were often left out of the "invisible colleges" where a lot of the important conversations about work went on and where the exchange of ideas took place. They tried to turn evidence of unfreedom into its opposite. But most women could not overcome the cultural divides that they faced from early childhood to the building of careers.

Despite the progress that women in science have made since the Second World War, there remain residual effects of the culture of the period of Little Science. There continues today to be residues in our culture that affect the thinking and choices of young women with a great interest in science. Jennifer Doudna (b. 1964), who shared the chemistry Nobel Prize with Emmanuelle Charpentier in 2020 for their revolutionary work in CRISPR gene editing technology, is one example of the continuing influence of these cultural norms. Consider what she says about the early influence of her father on her pathways and of the attitudes toward women in science that she found in the local high school: "I always felt like I was the son that he wanted to have. . . . I was treated a bit differently from my sisters."[54] In high school, after developing an interest in science, her college guidance counselor told her: "No, no, no . . . girls don't do science." Doudna's reaction was: "It hurt me," she says, but she had the fortitude exhibited by our other scientists. She told herself: "I will do it . . . I will show you. If I want to do science, I am going to do it."[55] Sounds a bit like Barbara McClintock.

In the age of little science, women worked in backwater ponds chasing diatoms, rather than in fly rooms breeding drosophila. If they were very talented, they worked alone among the corn plants, not in seats of authority in growing research universities. If they chose to work and were incredibly able, there might be a spot for them at a women's college or as a research associate working in the basement of some makeshift laboratory. Often they could not get proper jobs because of nepotism rules; or because men of science and the administrative authorities thought that they were bound to leave and take up the life of a wife and mother. Or they were thought simply not good enough. A very few, some of whom we have met here, went against the grain. But even those, the most talented and brilliant, were survivors. They often were treated as equals by many colleagues, but administrators, those who held power, did not see them as valued members of the scientific community. The ones that we've met and whose lives we have examined so briefly were rarities. Most opted out, never getting to the starting line. The world they lived in defined them as "outsiders." The culture denied them the belief that they could make it among the men of science. Most were right. Their options were very limited. They suffered from institutionalized unfreedom.

PART VI

MEDIA

CHAPTER 19

EVALUATING THE FAKE NEWS PROBLEM AT THE SCALE OF THE INFORMATION ECOSYSTEM

JENNIFER ALLEN, BAIRD HOWLAND, MARKUS MOBIUS, DAVID ROTHSCHILD, AND DUNCAN J. WATTS

Since the 2016 US presidential election, the deliberate spread of online misinformation, in particular on social media platforms such as Twitter and Facebook, has generated extraordinary interest across several disciplines.[1] In large part this interest reflects a deeper concern that the prevalence of "fake news" has increased political polarization, decreased trust in public institutions, and undermined democracy.[2] A handful of papers have attempted to measure the prevalence of fake news on social media, finding that exposure is rare compared with other types of news content and generally concentrated among older, politically conservative Americans.[3] Despite these findings, many researchers and other observers continue to advocate that deliberately engineered misinformation disseminated on social media is sufficiently prevalent to constitute an urgent crisis.[4] Disagreements over the prevalence and importance of misinformation are difficult to evaluate empirically for three reasons. First, Americans consume news online via desktop computers and, increasingly, mobile devices as well as on television, yet no single source of data covers all three modes. As a result, researchers select data sources on the basis of their availability, which may not correspond with either representativeness or comprehensiveness. For example, many studies rely exclusively on Twitter, whose users are highly unrepresentative of the general population, while even studies that rely on representative online panels omit TV consumption.[5] Second, analyses of fake news often fail to account for how much of it is consumed relative to other types of content, whether related to news or not. Because the volume of online content is so vast, even a very large numerator may constitute only a tiny fraction of the total.[6] Third, even if its prevalence is low relative to other types of content, fake news could be important either because it is disproportionately impactful or because it is concentrated on small subpopulations. While comprehensive measures of prevalence are intrinsically interesting and can indicate how much relative impact different types of content would have to have to dominate, they cannot on their own resolve questions about influence.

Here we address the first two of three challenges, leaving the third for future research. We assembled a unique dataset that drew on three different sources to capture consumption across the two principal modes of news production, TV and online, where we integrate total consumption across the modes by demographic bucket (see the following two sections for a more detailed description of the datasets, definitions of key terms, and estimation methods). Content is defined by the mode on which it is consumed not produced; thus, for example, video consumed on desktop or a mobile device is categorized as online consumption even when it is produced by mainstream TV stations.

Materials and methods

First we measure national TV programming using Nielsen's nationally representative TV panel ($N \approx 100,000$). In addition, we measure local programming using a subset of the national panel ($N \approx 50,000$) sampled from the twenty-five largest local markets. TV news consumption is defined as time devoted to watching any of the roughly four hundred programs that are classified by Nielsen as "news"—a category that includes "hard news" (e.g., evening cable and network news), magazine news (e.g., *Inside Edition* and *Dateline*), morning shows (e.g., *Good Morning America* and *Today*), and entertainment news (e.g., TMZ, Access Hollywood)—and late-night comedy shows (e.g., *The Daily Show* and *The Late Show with Stephen Colbert*), which are frequently viewed as a source of news-related information, especially for younger viewers.[7]

Second, we measure desktop and mobile media consumption (including media consumed through mobile applications) using Comscore's nationally representative desktop and mobile panel, which breaks out total time spent on different types of media sites including news, search, and social media by demographic bucket. Online (mobile and desktop) news consumption is defined as time spent on any article published on one of more than eight hundred websites that primarily cover "hard" news topics like politics, business, and US and international affairs.[8] Correspondingly, fake news consumption is the time spent on one of ninety-eight websites previously identified by researchers, professional fact checkers, and journalists as sources of fake, deceptive, low-quality, or hyperpartisan news.[9] Thus, in accordance with the previous literature, with the notable exception of YouTube, fake news is defined at the publisher or Uniform Resource Locator (URL) level. We further categorize online non-news consumption for the top two thousand domains, ranked by mobile and desktop traffic, into one of twenty-eight Comscore categories (e.g., entertainment, gaming, health, social media, and sports).

Third, we use Nielsen's nationally representative desktop-only web panel (ninety thousand in 2016, decreasing to sixty thousand in 2018), which records individual visits to URLs and the referral URL, to impute passive news consumption (e.g., news snippets, images, headlines, and summaries that appear on a newsfeed or search results page but that the user does not click on) on the top four social media sites (Facebook, YouTube, Twitter, and Reddit) and on the top three search engines (Google, Bing, and Yahoo). For every site except YouTube, we estimated this fraction as the fraction of URLs that are referred to from the platform in question that we classify as news and fake news, respectively. For YouTube, which hosts all of its own content, we computed the fraction of a random sample of 360,000 videos (ten thousand per month, weighted by viewing time) that are classified as "news and politics" in YouTube's internal classification scheme. We further count as online news consumption all time spent on the three major portals: MSN, Yahoo, and AOL. Last, we use a subset of the Nielsen web panel ($N \approx 15,000$) who also appear in the TV panel to estimate the relation between desktop and TV news consumption.

Results

Figure 19.1 shows the breakdown of Americans' daily desktop, mobile, and TV media consumption, measured in minutes per person, over the course of three years spanning January 2016 through December 2018. Figure 19.1a shows this pattern in aggregate, while figure 19.1b and 19.1c shows the same pattern for the youngest (18–24) and oldest (55+) age brackets, respectively. On average, Americans devote over 7.5 hours (460 minutes)/day to media consumption, including TV, streaming video or music, gaming, engaging with social media, or browsing the web either from a desktop or mobile devices (figure 19.1a). This total is relatively stable over the thirty-six-month period of our data, showing seasonal declines during the summers and peaks coinciding with the 2016 presidential election and the presidential inauguration in January 2017 (because the shares devoted to different types of content remain generally stable over time, in subsequent figures we aggregate over time). As expected, younger Americans spend more time on mobile devices and less time watching TV than average (figure 19.1b), whereas the pattern is reversed for older Americans (figure 19.1c); however, the former watch so much less TV than the latter that their total media consumption is about 30 percent less despite their higher mobile usage. Figure 19.1 also reveals three results that directly undercut the conventional wisdom about the prevalence of fake news online and more broadly

Legend:
- TV: Not news
- TV: news
- N/A TV: Fake news
- Mobile: Not news
- Mobile: news
- Mobile: Fake news
- Desktop: Not news
- Desktop: news
- Desktop: Fake news

Media consumption, all (ages 18+)

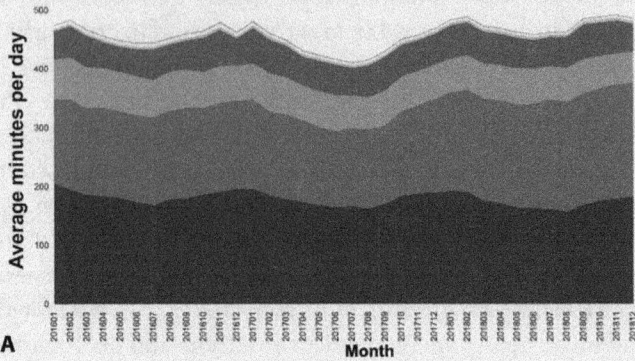

Media consumption, ages 18 to 24

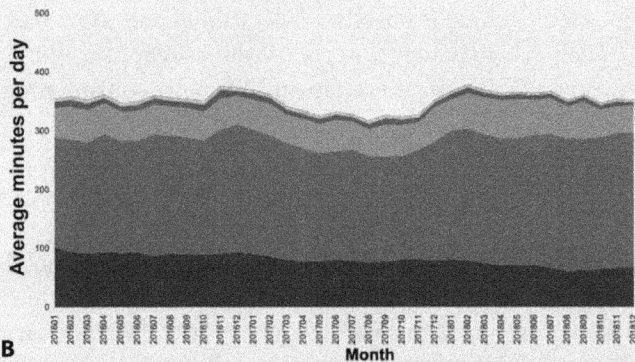

Media consumption, ages 55+

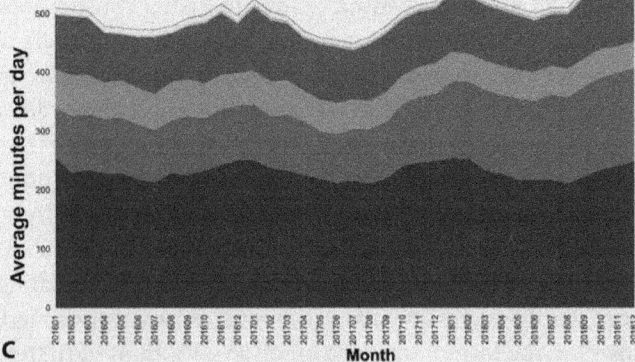

19.1 Overall information consumption by category and platform over time from January 2016 to December 2018. Breakdown of consumption for (A) the entire adult sample, 18 years and older, (B) 18 to 24 years old, and (C) 55 years and older.

question the importance of online news relative to TV news and other types of media consumption.

First, the bulk of daily media consumption is not news related. As expected, young adults spend less time consuming news (colored green) than average and far less time than the oldest group, but in all age groups news consumption is heavily outweighed by non-news consumption (colored blue). Of the 460 minutes per person per day of total media consumption, approximately 400 minutes (86 percent) is not related to news of any kind. Figure 19.2 shows a more detailed breakdown of news and non-news categories of media consumption online and on TV. For online consumption, which includes mobile and desktop, news is dominated by several other categories such as entertainment, social media, and search. Even including passive exposure to news content on social media sites (Facebook, Twitter, Reddit, and YouTube), search engines (Google, Bing, and Yahoo!), and portals (Yahoo!, MSN, and AOL), news accounts for only 4.2 percent of total online consumption. TV news is more prominent, comprising the largest single category of TV consumption and 23 percent of the total. In aggregate, however, TV news is still heavily outweighed by non-news programming such as dramas, documentaries, movies, and sports (Fig. 19.2B). To the extent that Americans are uninformed about politics, economics, and other issues relevant to democracy, the reason may be simply that they are choosing not to inform themselves.[10]

Second, to the extent that Americans do consume news, they do so overwhelmingly by watching TV. Overall, the ratio of TV to online news—including both desktop and mobile devices—is more than five to one (54 minutes versus 9.7 minutes), varying from a minimum of almost two to one for eighteen- to twenty-four-year-olds (9 minutes versus 5 minutes) to a maximum of more than seven to one for those fifty-five years and older (94 minutes versus 13 minutes). Online news (including both mobile and desktop activity) was more prominent in the vicinity of the 2016 election; however, the ratio of TV to online remained similar (the minimum ratio in our thirty-six-month time period is 4.5:1 during December 2016). Drawing on our sample of roughly fifteen thousand individuals who are members of both the Nielsen web and TV panels, Figure 19.3 shows that while essentially everyone is exposed to a substantial amount of daily TV news, 44 percent of the sample is exposed to no online news at all, and almost three quarters spend less than 30 seconds a day reading news online. Because the Nielsen panel records only desktop activity, these figures understate the true consumption of online news (i.e., including mobile). In light of our earlier result that average mobile news consumption is slightly less than desktop news consumption, however, and assuming that the distribution of news consumption is not markedly different on mobile versus desktop devices, then it follows that a majority of Americans spend less than a minute per day reading news online.

Third, fake news consumption (figure 19.1, colored red) is a negligible fraction of Americans' daily information diet. We emphasize here that both our

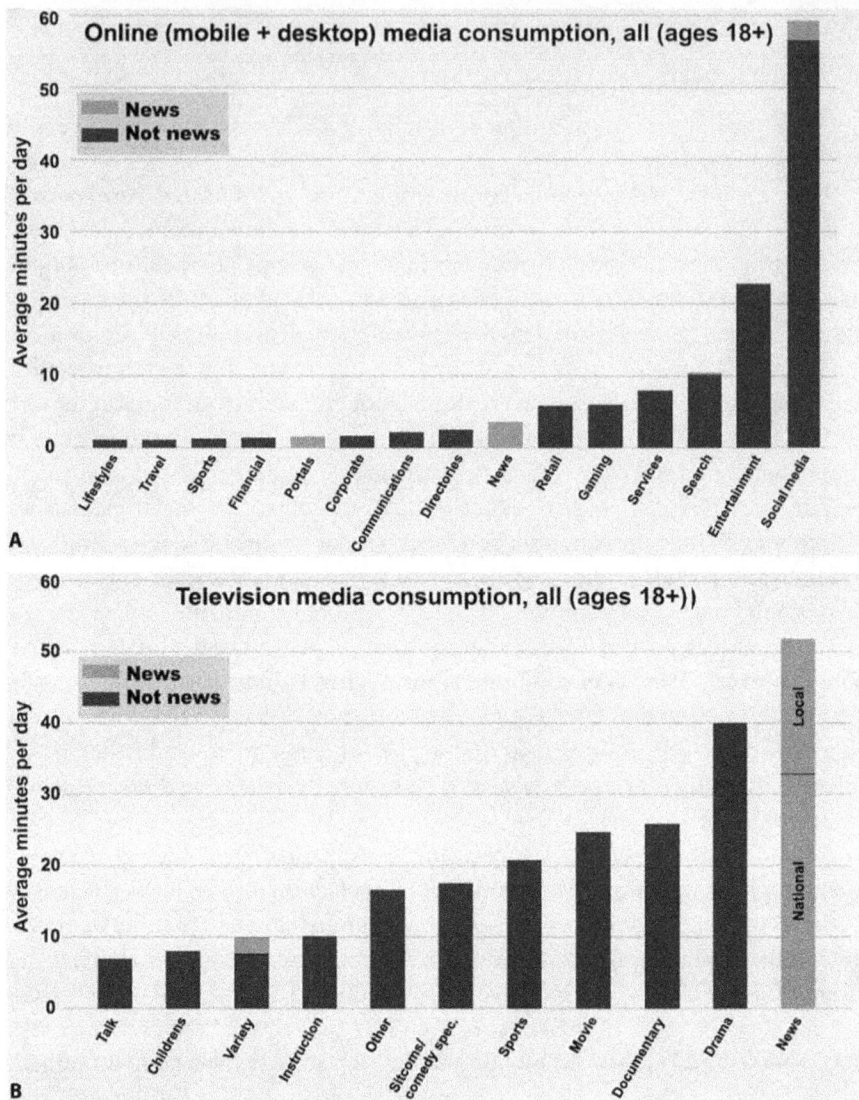

Figure 19.2 Detailed breakdown of overall online and TV media consumption. (*Top*) Online consumption (including mobile and desktop) for the top two thousand sites per applications on Comscore. (*Bottom*) TV consumption by program category.

Total online consumption is 227 minutes per person per day, of which 58 percent is accounted for by the top two thousand sites, while total television consumption is 232 minutes per person per day. To compute news consumption in search and social media, excluding YouTube, we use the share of referrals from the site in question that redirect to news articles as a proxy for the share of time a user is exposed to news-related content on the platform. For YouTube, which does not redirect users to external sites, we randomly sampled ten thousand videos per month (weighted by viewing time) and computed the percentages that were classified as "news and politics." Because portals such as MSN, Yahoo, and AOL almost always display some news-related stories on their landing pages, we count 100 percent of time spent on portals as news consumption. Last, news consumption in the "variety" category of television viewing is computed as 100 percent of time attributed to late-night comedy programs, such as *The Daily Show With Trevor Noah*, which are known to contain commentary on politics and current events. For clarity, the top graph shows only the top fifteen of twenty-eight categories.

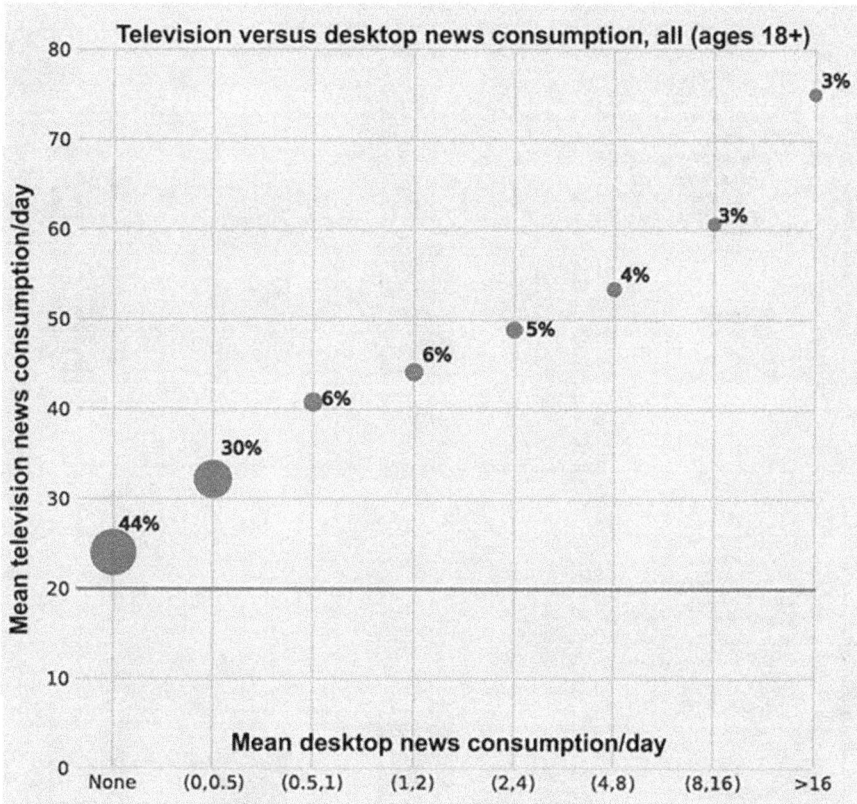

Figure 19.3 Television versus desktop news consumption aggregated over all age categories 18 to 55+. For each month, the overlap panelists are separated into groups corresponding to different ranges of web news consumption. For each group, the mean television
news consumption and group size as a percentage of all panelists are computed. Over-
time averages for the mean television news consumption and size of each group are
calculated by computing the mean television news mean and mean group size over all
thirty-six months. Error bars are SEs obtained via bootstrapping for group size and
group television news consumption, respectively, and are smaller than the symbols.

definition of news and fake news are extremely broad. In the case of news, we
include, for example, morning shows and portals, while our definition of fake
news includes highly biased and hyperpartisan news sites such as Breitbart.com
(corresponding to the "red" and "orange" categories of Grinberg and colleagues)
and outright fraudulent sites (the "black" category).[11] Our estimates of the prevalence of news and fake news therefore likely overstate the true prevalence,
although we also find that adopting stricter definitions makes no discernable
difference to our main conclusions. Figure 19.4 shows a more detailed breakdown of news consumption online and on TV, also broken out by age group.

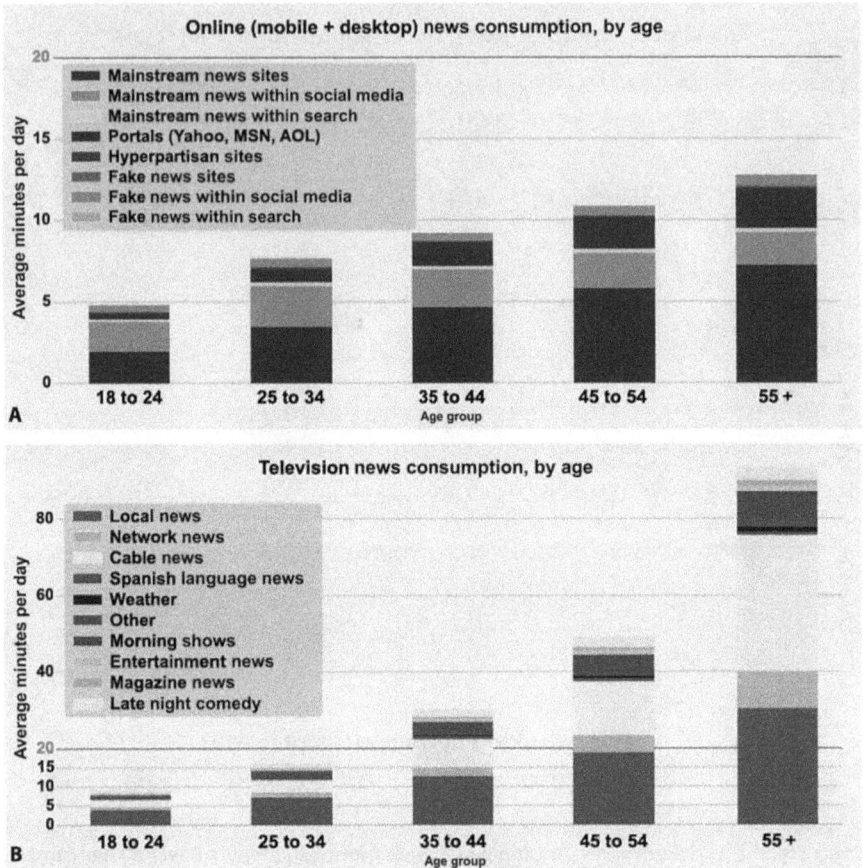

Figure 19.4 News-only consumption by age. Detailed breakdown of news-only consumption by age group for (A) online (including mobile and desktop) and (B) television.

Referring first to online consumption, figure 19.4a shows that fake news stories were more likely to be encountered on social media (dark versus light red) and that older viewers were heavier consumers than younger ones, consistent with previous findings.[12] No age group, however, spent more than an average of a minute per day engaging with fake news, nor did it occupy more than 1 percent of their overall news consumption (i.e., including TV) or more than 0.2 percent of their overall media consumption. Of potential concern, a very small fraction of desktop panelists (1.97%) did consume more fake news than mainstream news; however, this number drops to 0.7 percent when restricting to people who consumed at least one minute of fake news per day. When restricting to just black and red fake news sites (i.e., excluding hyperpartisan sites), these numbers drop to 0.97 and 0.32 percent, respectively. That is, while majority-fake news consumers do exist, they are extremely rare, and most of them consume very little online news of any kind.

Turning to TV, there are no objectively fake news stations of the sort that exist online, that is, that are exclusively or near exclusively devoted to disseminating deliberate falsehoods while masquerading as legitimate news organizations. Including TV news consumption in the previous calculation would therefore reduce the population of majority-fake news consumers even further. Nonetheless, misinformation construed more broadly can also manifest itself in regular news programming in the form of selective attention, framing, "spin," false equivalence, and other forms of bias. Although a detailed analysis of false or misleading content contained in conventional news programming is beyond the scope of this paper, it is nonetheless interesting to examine how much collective attention is paid to different categories of news. Figure 19.4b provides this breakdown, showing first that TV news consumption greatly exceeds online news (red line) and is sharply increasing with age, ranging from less than ten minutes/day (18–24) to more than ninety minutes a day (55+). Local news is the dominant form of news consumption for all age groups except the oldest, for whom national cable news (ranked second overall) is slightly more popular. In turn, the relative dominance of cable news in the 55+ category is driven by a small minority of voracious news consumers, roughly the top 10 percent by consumption. Hard network news (e.g., evening news shows) is ranked third for all age groups, while morning shows are ranked fourth for all age groups but the youngest, which slightly prefers late-night comedy shows. Given the large differences in total news consumption across age groups, the consistency of ranking of different types of news is notable. Also notable given its perceived importance for younger viewers is the limited presence of late-night comedy (less than 5% overall, and less than 7% for the 18–24 cohort).

Discussion

Summarizing, we note that according to at the time of final submission, 2,210 English language publications with "fake news" in the title had appeared since January 2017, compared with just 73 in all the years leading up to and including 2016. Not only has interest in fake news clearly exploded in the past two years, but it has also far outstripped attention to TV news: A comparable count yielded just 329 articles published since 2017 containing either "television news" or "TV news" in their titles, while 708 articles contained "online news," 394 contained "Twitter" or "Facebook" and "news," and 556 contained "social media" and "news." Restricting further to studies that explicitly connect misinformation to a particular platform, yielded 99 results containing both "misinformation" and one of "online" or "social media" or "web" in the title since 2017, but just one result for "misinformation" and "television" or "TV"—an article about the unrealistic survival rates of cardiopulmonary resuscitation on TV shows. This evident focus of the recent research literature on online sources of fake news and misinformation is directionally and proportionately inconsistent with our results in three ways. First, whereas the research treats news consumption as the issue of primary importance, we find that most media consumption, whether online or on TV, is not news related. Second, whereas research on online news—and even more specifically news on social media platforms—markedly outweighs research on TV news, we find that TV news consumption dominates online by a ratio of 5:1 (where the ratio is even more extreme for social media sites). Third, whereas the topic of fake news outstrips all other news-related research, we find that fake news itself is only 1 percent of overall news consumption, substantially lower for Twitter alone.[13] Instead, news consumption is heavily dominated by mainstream news sources both online and on TV.

We emphasize that our results do not imply that fake news is not a problem worthy of attention. Arguably the deliberate circulation of false information with the objective of creating confusion and discord is intolerable in principle and should be combatted at any prevalence greater than zero. Moreover, it is possible that news consumed online could have more impact per minute of exposure than news consumed on TV, or that fake news could have an outsized impact compared with regular news, or that it could have large impacts on certain subpopulations. Last, we note that our definitions of news and fake news are—with the exception of YouTube—dependent on site or program-level classifications. News-relevant content on social media that is not tied to a particular URL, or false or misleading information that is promulgated by generally reliable news sources, would therefore be misclassified by our scheme. We hope that future work will address all of these areas of uncertainty. We note, however, that our methodology was designed to be consistent with previous work, which also has used list-based classification and relied on prevalence (i.e., not impact) to assess importance. On those terms, our finding that fake news is extremely rare, comprising only about one-tenth of 1 percent of Americans' overall daily media diet, suggests that concerns regarding possible threats to democracy should be much broader in scope than deliberately engineered falsehoods circulating on social media. In particular, public ignorance or misunderstanding of important political matters could also arise out of a combination of ordinary bias and agenda setting in the mainstream media and the overall low exposure of many Americans to news content in general, especially in written form.[14] We conclude that future work on misinformation and its potentially corrosive effects on democracy should consider all potential sources of problematic content, as well as the absence of relevant content, not simply the type that is most easily identified and least associated with conventional media interests.[15]

CHAPTER 20

MEASURING THE NEWS AND ITS IMPACT ON DEMOCRACY

DUNCAN J. WATTS, DAVID M. ROTHSCHILD,
AND MARKUS MOBIUS

It is hard to overstate the breadth and intensity of interest directed since 2016 at the issue of false or misleading information (also known as "fake news") circulating on the web in general and on social media platforms such as Facebook and Twitter/X in particular.[1] According to Google Scholar, since January 2017, more than fifteen thousand English language publications with "fake news" in the title have appeared in academic journals spanning economics, political science, computer and information science, communications, law, and journalism. To put this number in perspective, fewer than one hundred such publications appeared in all the years leading up to the end of 2016, while fewer than twelve hundred publications have appeared since 2017 containing "television news" or "TV news."

The origin of this extraordinary surge in interest in a previously sleepy topic was of course the 2016 US presidential election, which, along with other events that year such as Brexit, raised widespread concerns about a possible rise of populist/nationalist political movements, increasing political polarization, and decreasing public trust in the media. Early reporting by journalists quickly focused attention on fake news circulating on social media sites during the election campaign.[2] The philanthropic and scientific communities then responded with dozens of conferences and thousands of papers studying various elements of fake news. Reinforced by continued mainstream media attention and increasing congressional scrutiny of technology companies, the conjecture that the deliberate spread of online misinformation poses an urgent threat to democracy subsequently hardened into conventional wisdom.[3]

In the face of this dominant narrative, a handful of authors have suggested that fake news is less prevalent than breathless references to "tsunamis" or "epidemics" would imply.[4] In an early contribution, Hunt Allcott and Matthew Gentzkow estimated that "the average US adult read and remembered on the order of one or perhaps several fake news articles during the election period, with higher exposure to pro-Trump articles than pro-Clinton articles." In turn, they estimated that "if one fake news article were about as persuasive as one TV campaign ad, the fake news in our database would have changed vote shares by an amount on the order of hundredths of a percentage point," roughly two orders of magnitude less than needed to influence the election outcome. Subsequent studies have found similarly low prevalence levels for fake news relative to mainstream news on Twitter and Facebook. Finally, our own survey of the media consumption landscape, based on a nationally representative sample of TV, desktop, and mobile media consumption, found three main results that undercut the conventional wisdom regarding fake news and also the dominance of online sources of news in general:

1.   News consumption is a relatively small fraction of overall media consumption. Of the more than 7.5 hours per day that Americans spend, on average, watching television of consuming content on their desktop computers or mobile devices, only about 14 percent is dedicated to news ("news" was defined as appearing on one of more than four hundred news-relevant programs, such as the *CBS Evening News*, and more than eight hundred websites, such as that of the *New York Times*, while "consumption" was measured in terms of minutes per person per day watching television or browsing online).

2.   Online news consumption is a small fraction of overall news consumption, which is dominated by TV by a factor of five to one. Even the 18–24 cohort consumes almost twice as much TV news than online news. In striking contrast with the research literature's overwhelming emphasis on online sources of news, we estimate that three in four Americans spend less than thirty seconds a day reading news online, while almost half consume no online news whatsoever.

3.   Fake news is a tiny portion of Americans' information diets. Using our most inclusive definition, less than 1 percent of regular news consumption and less than .10 percent of overall media consumption could be considered fake. Even the heaviest consumers of fake news (the 55+ age group) consume less than one minute of fake news per day on average, compared with 106 minutes of regular news (94 of them on TV) and over 500 minutes of total media consumption.

As has been argued elsewhere,[5] these results on their own do not conclusively demonstrate that fake news does not have meaningful effects on public opinion, political polarization, and trust in institutions. It is possible, for example, that even extremely low rates of exposure to fake or misleading news could have outsized effects, at least on some people, or that equivalent amounts of online and television news consumption have different impacts. Nonetheless, these results do strongly suggest that research on the origins, nature, prevalence, and consequences of misinformation should take a much broader view of the topic than outright false information disseminated on social media or even online.[6] In particular, there are at least three reasons for taking such a broader view.

First, while it is possible that exposure to fake news has more impact than an equivalent amount of exposure to real news, or that online news has more impact than television news, it is equally possible that the opposite is true. For example, recent work has found that subjects rate mainstream publications as more trustworthy than fake or highly partisan sites irrespective of their own partisanship, and that deliberation reduces belief in false headlines but not in true ones, again irrespective of partisan alignment.[7] Likewise, while television consumption can be dismissed as more "passive" than reading, direct comparisons between television and online news and advertising consistently find better recall of televised content, especially for low-involvement consumers.[8] Ultimately, questions of impact are empirical questions and answering those questions will require making comparisons between different types of content and different modes of production.

Second, fake news sites are not the only sources of false information: The mainstream media can also promulgate falsehoods simply by reporting on them.[9] In the lead-up to the 2003 Iraq War, for example, a large majority of media organizations uncritically repeated the administration's false claim that they possessed unequivocal evidence that Saddam Hussein possessed weapons of mass destruction.[10] In August 2009, when Sarah Palin wrote in a blog post that the Affordable Care Act would create "death panels," the claim was repeated in more than seven hundred mainstream news articles even after it was debunked by a variety of fact-checking organizations.[11] More recently, an analysis of Russian disinformation efforts during the 2016 presidential election concluded that these efforts likewise succeeded in reaching the public largely via the credulous reporting of mainstream media outlets.[12] Although the motivations and mechanisms driving misinformation in mainstream media differ from sites that intentionally promote falsehoods, the effects may be many times greater; thus, a proper accounting of the prevalence of false information requires a broad consideration of potential sources.

Third, misinformation is a much broader phenomenon than outright falsehoods. There are many ways to lead a reader (or viewer) to reach a false or unsupported conclusion that do not require saying anything that is unambiguously false. Presenting partial or biased data, quoting sources selectively, omitting alternative explanations, improperly equating unequal arguments, conflating correlation with causation, using loaded language, insinuating a claim without actually making it (e.g., by quoting someone else making it), strategically ordering the presentation of facts, and even simply changing the headline can all manipulate the reader's (or viewer's) impression without their awareness. These practices are pervasive in mainstream professional journalism and are not restricted to political topics, although that is often the focus of research on media bias.[13] Inaccurate and misleading coverage is also pervasive in other areas of journalism, including important domains for public opinion and democracy such as health, science, and business.[14]

For all three reasons, studies of the prevalence of misinformation and its impact on democratic decision making must embrace a much broader conception of the problem that includes biased and potentially misleading information that is embedded in mainstream news content across all major modes of production.[15] Unfortunately, research of this scope and scale is hindered by three interrelated but distinct obstacles. First, research on misinformation and its effects is currently dependent on datasets that are idiosyncratic, one-off, and often small in scale, rendering comparisons across different modes of media consumption, different sample populations, and different time periods difficult to make. Second, much of the relevant data are hard to collect, either because they are scattered across thousands of locations in different formats, or are controlled by private companies (Google, Facebook, Twitter, Microsoft, media companies, etc.) who face large disincentives and limited upsides to sharing data with academic researchers.[16] Third, the relevant academic research is scattered across several disciplines (e.g., economics, marketing, political science, communications, psychology, sociology, computer science, and network science), each with its own set of theoretical frameworks, accepted methodologies, and publishing venues. Collating and reconciling results across these disciplinary boundaries is difficult and often leads to contradictory or incoherent conclusions.[17]

Addressing these shortcomings in existing data and research practices will require a major effort to coordinate scientific communities, data resources, and academic-industry collaborations. Although we are not the first to call for such an effort, our proposal differs from previous instantiations in that it is explicitly focused on the need for shared research infrastructure as well as the opportunities for collaboration and partnership that such an infrastructure may create.

Toward a comprehensive misinformation research agenda

The objective of a comprehensive research agenda to study the origins, nature, and consequences of misinformation on democracy in turn entails assembling four subsidiary components:

1. A large-scale data infrastructure for studying the production, distribution, consumption, and absorption of news over time and across the entire information ecosystem (including the web, television, radio, and other modes of production).
2. A "mass collaboration" model that leverages the shared infrastructure to advance replicable, cumulative, and ultimately useful science.
3. A program for communicating the insights generated by the research to stakeholders outside of the research community (e.g., journalists, policymakers, industry leaders, the public).
4. A network of academic-industry partnerships around data and solutions.

Objective 1: Building a large-scale data infrastructure for studying news

A primary requirement for comprehensive research agenda around misinformation is a shared, open infrastructure for collecting data and running experiments at scale for diverse populations over long timescales. Such an infrastructure would facilitate results that generalize better than prior work and can be more easily implemented in practice. Moreover, the infrastructure would be open, meaning that it would be made available to the research community while also addressing issues of data security, individual privacy, and intellectual property. The information ecosystem can be schematized in four "layers": production, consumption and distribution, absorption and understanding, and action and engagement. Each layer corresponds to a different stage of the process by which information about events and issues affecting a democracy ultimately impacts public opinion, understanding, and civic engagement. Each layer also corresponds to different types of data that derive from distinct sources, typically in different formats and sampled in different ways.

Production (web, TV, radio)
What information is produced, either by online publishers or by TV or radio broadcasters, that could potentially inform and/or influence public opinion? The web alone comprises many thousands of news sources, ranging from large and comprehensive (e.g., the *New York Times*, the *Wall Street Journal*) to small and niche, from neutral to partisan, and including original news publishers as well as aggregators and distributors. As noted earlier, publishers can bias the news they produce in several ways, including selection (what they choose to cover vs. ignore), emphasis (how prominently a given story is featured and for how long), slant (how headlines are written, the tone of the article, the relative emphasis of different facts), and finally outright deception (fake news, propaganda, etc.). To obtain a comprehensive, longitudinal view of

information production, the research community requires a continuously updated catalog of information sources relevant to contemporary issues and political discourse.

Several media databases already exist (e.g., Media Cloud, Event Registry, GDELT, Internet Archive's TV news archive, Newsbank). However, they are not designed to directly support the range of queries that are the focus of many research questions; thus, results typically require substantial investment in postprocessing. In addition, they do not exhibit the kind of methodological transparency that is required for academic research, and/or they do not have the comprehensiveness across the necessary range of site and modes.[18] To illustrate the problem, simple keyword searches (e.g., "Hillary Clinton emails") on unpreprocessed corpora of articles will return many irrelevant articles (i.e., those that contain the keywords but are not about the topic) and will also miss many relevant articles (i.e., those that are on the topic but do not use the exact keywords). Moreover, the results contain no information about features such as partisanship or sentiment that must then be appended by the researcher. Keyword-based search results, in other words, are largely uninformative without a large amount of supplemental data cleaning and analysis. Because this work is typically done in a one-off, nonreplicable manner, simply collecting and storing vast amounts of news data does not on its own do much to accelerate the research process. A central objective for any collective research effort, therefore, is to build data processing pipelines and systems on top of the raw data that make them easily able to be queried by researchers and journalists alike. Included in this objective is also the capability for independent researchers to develop and contribute new modes of querying (e.g., abstracting away from specific stories to broader themes or narratives) as well as new methods for generating relevant metadata (e.g., stance, sentiment, partisan bias, etc.).

Consumption and distribution (desktop and mobile panels)

Much of the information that is produced receives little attention, while some stories resonate with millions. Even comprehensive and well-annotated data on news production, therefore, do not on their own tell us how that information is or is not reaching consumers, let alone how different types of information reaches different types of consumers. Are there groups of people who watch MSNBC in the morning, surf mainstream news during the day, and watch Fox News at night? Do Breitbart and Daily Kos readers also get mainstream news on TV or the web? One potential direction for research on media consumption is to leverage commercial panel providers such as Nielsen, ComScore, Pew Research, and YouGov. Although valuable, these "off-the-shelf" solutions also exhibit some important limitations. In particular, desktop-only panels increasingly suffer from coverage gaps in part because they do not capture mobile activity, and in part because an increasing amount of web traffic is contained in "walled gardens" such as Facebook, within which user activity is visible only to the platform. Ultimately, therefore, it will be necessary to develop new data sources. For example, a dedicated mobile panel would greatly facilitate the measurement of information consumption across social and conventional media, as well as enable linkage to other behaviors of potential interest. In addition, certain modes of consumption—in particular social media (e.g., Facebook, Twitter, Reddit), but also email and messaging services (e.g., WhatsApp)—are also mechanisms for distribution. A proper understanding of consumption, therefore, will also require data on information distribution.

Absorption and understanding (polls, virtual labs)

Just as the publication of a particular piece of information does not guarantee that anyone will see it, so is exposure to information no guarantee of awareness, understanding, or agreement about its meaning.[19] Exposure to disconfirming information may reduce polarization, increase it, or have no effect depending on other factors.[20] Understanding how consumption translates into knowledge and/or beliefs is therefore critical to designing and evaluating possible interventions. Building on advances in nonprobability polling techniques,[21] one could conduct regular panel surveys to probe public knowledge and explore the baselines and shifts in knowledge and attitudes. Polling of this sort could yield indices of facts and sentiment from the general population that could be correlated with media consumption on various issues and, ultimately, civic participation. Understanding of opinion change, influence, and deliberation would also be accelerated via experiments conducted in online "virtual labs."[22]

Action and engagement (admin data, ethnography)

In addition to being an end in itself, knowledge is also important to democracy inasmuch as it translates into political action: voting, community organizing, engagement with legislators, political speech, and protest. An important goal for any comprehensive research agenda is therefore to understand the link between the production, consumption, and absorption of information on the one hand, and action on the other hand. Because "political action" is a multidimensional concept, however, quantifying action is challenging, at a minimum requiring diverse administrative datasets (e.g., voter records, campaign contributions, volunteering, protesting, search, activity on social media, etc.), but also survey and ethnographic data to elucidate levels of engagement in the political process, broadly construed. Alternatively, or in order to get repeated actions or more coverage, researchers could leverage proxies for engagement such as search queries as a proxy for intent or lightweight user actions (following, retweeting, liking, commenting, etc.) as a proxy for interest.[23]

Objective 2: Build a "mass collaboration" model to advance knowledge

Maximizing the value of the data infrastructure just described will also require a "mass collaboration" model in which many researchers leverage the same data assets.[24] Mass collaboration models based on shared infrastructure have an established track record in the physical sciences (e.g., the Sloan Digital Sky Survey, the Large Hadron Collider, the Laser Interferometer Gravitational-Wave Observatory) and also in biology (e.g., the Human Genome Project), but are unfamiliar to many social scientists (the closest model would be surveys such as the General Social Survey, the American National Election Studies, and the Panel Study of Income Dynamics). The ultimate success of any such model is therefore subject to its acceptance by the relevant research community, which cannot be guaranteed *ex ante*. Nonetheless, the model has some advantages over the traditional single investigator model that we believe increase its chances of successful adoption.

1.   It will enable the research community to better leverage the data assets to produce many times the research output that would be possible with a traditional laboratory model in which both data collection/curation and research are conducted in-house.

2.   It lends itself to more comparable research, as researchers can more easily replicate the questions, data, and analytics of previous work, when conducting new inquiries. Often replication efforts are complicated by potentially subtle differences in framing, data, and methods between exploratory and confirmatory studies.

3.   It allows researchers to contribute in a variety of ways, including additional data sources (e.g., text of radio transcripts, social media data); improved methods for processing and/or analyzing existing data (e.g., better named entity extraction or topic identification); appending useful metadata derived from their own research (e.g., content categories, partisanship labels); and direct financial support from research grants to support overhead. By accommodating different types of contributions, a shared infrastructure approach should appeal to a wider range of potential collaborators, thereby also increasing its value to subsequent researchers.

Objective 3: Communicate insights to nonacademic stakeholders

An important facilitator of success in the proposed research enterprise is that it be perceived as both legitimate (i.e., rigorous, transparent, and nonpartisan) and also useful. In addition to gathering and organizing data and coordinating research across many research groups, an important goal is therefore to translate the output of the work for nonacademic audiences. More broadly, it is important to advocate for the importance of the social sciences in addressing critical needs, like information ecosystem design in democracies. Although there are many ways to engage stakeholders outside of academia (e.g., blog posts, white papers), one interesting approach that naturally leverages the existence of a centralized data infrastructure is to expose the data itself via web-based interactive visualizations (a.k.a. "dashboards") that allow journalists, activists, policymakers, researchers, and members of the public to explore the evidence directly. Another benefit of data dashboards is that, in contrast with published research findings, they are dynamic entities that maintain their relevance even in a fast-moving environment. Rather than read a statistic about the prevalence of fake news or the diversity of news consumption as it was when the researchers did their work months or even years ago, for example, a dashboard populated with (nearly) live data could show its prevalence as of yesterday, as well as how it has changed in the past week, month, or year. Visualizing data in a way that is psychologically effective and also scientifically valid is a nontrivial undertaking that requires expertise in statistics, user experience design, and software development as well as the substantive domain in question.[25] Without downplaying the challenges inherent in designing and implementing useful interactive dashboards, we hope that they will help to ground the public debate around misinformation and democracy on rigorous, nonpartisan evidence.

Objective 4: Develop academic-industry partnerships around data and solutions

Modifying the information ecosystem to better support democracy is an example of what has been called solution-oriented social science, meaning that it advances fundamental understanding of the social sciences in the course of solving concrete problems of practical interest.[26] Rather than pursuing a research agenda based purely on theoretical interest, that is, research should address the concrete challenges confronting the participants (e.g., technology and media companies, fact-checking organizations, scientific societies, etc.) in the information ecosystem. To this end, it is critical to foster academic–industry partnerships with the goal of not only understanding but also improving the information ecosystem.

Partnerships could advance solution-oriented research in a variety of ways, including helping to define the research agenda and specific questions, contributing data, providing analytical tools, translating research findings into design principles, and implementing and testing potential solutions. Journalists and media organizations are perfectly situated to ask questions and provide a platform for disseminating results, while technology firms have data that researchers could use, as well as access to analytical tools. For example, voter files offer ground truth voting behavior, search queries correlate with certain offline behaviors, and lightweight user actions (e.g., replying, liking, sharing, and commenting) are a useful proxy for engagement.[27] Finally, beyond harvesting existing telemetry data, the capability to design, implement, and test interventions (e.g., reducing uncivil discourse, increasing relative consumption of high-quality information, etc.) requires direct access to proprietary platforms.

The topic of academic-industry partnerships around data has been of increasing interest to academic researchers, but only limited progress has been made in securing the cooperation of industry partners. Perhaps the most prominent recent example is Social Science One, a commission of senior academics who work with companies (thus far restricted to Facebook) to make preapproved datasets available to researchers while also waiving their right to suppress publication of unfavorable results.[28] Although Social Science One is promising, our proposed approach differs from it by starting first with an independent, researcher-designed, and managed data infrastructure. Because both these models, along with other models that are being developed in the domain of government administrative data and health informatics, have their respective strengths and weaknesses, we see them as complements rather than substitutes.[29]

Research questions

Let us summarize a selection of completed, in-progress, or planned research projects that utilize data of the sort described before. These examples are intended only to illustrate some possibilities and not to limit the scope of the overall research agenda, which we hope will be determined by the collective creativity of a whole research community.

Putting fake news in context

We have quantified fake news consumption across multiple platforms including television, desktop, and mobile web, finding that it constitutes less than .10 percent of total daily media consumption, and less than 1 percent of overall news consumption. Surprisingly, we also find that news consumption in general constitutes a small fraction of overall media consumption (roughly 14 percent) and is heavily biased toward television across all age categories.

Selection vs. framing

Which is more important to the underlying and perceived partisanship of publications: selection (which topics they choose to cover) or framing (what slant they give those topics they select to cover)? In future work, we plan to track and map both activities historically and in real time for daily news events spanning television and online content.

Content overlap in online news

In response to declining revenue, news publishers have reduced costs by replacing original content with copied or slightly edited versions of generic stories provided via wire services (i.e., AP, Reuters). In ongoing work we are attempting to quantify the proportion of news reporting that is either copied or unique, as well as the patterns of content overlap that exist within and between news articles. In future work we will construct networks of publishers characterized by their co-copying patterns, identifying clusters of redundant coverage.

Snippet-based content classification

Prior work on news consumption has relied on classifications of content at the domain or program (e.g., *Today*, *CBS Evening News*) level. This approach, while easy to implement, misclassifies content that is not representative of the domain/program of which it is a part (e.g., news content on late-night comedy shows) or is simply not a part of any domain/program (e.g., user-generated content). In ongoing work, we are developing methods using human labelers to classify content at the "snippet" level, where a snippet is defined as a short piece of text or video, thereby allowing us to compare the proportion of news and misinformation across platforms.

Ideologically segregated consumption

Partisan echo chambers, and selective exposure to partisan news more generally, are of key concern to communication scholars and the public. In ongoing work, we seek to replicate previous findings regarding the ideological segregation of online news exposure over the 2016–2018 interval as well as to compare it with television news consumption.[30]

Comparing survey with behavioral data

Surveys are a vital tool in understanding public opinion and knowledge, but have been shown to overestimate news consumption.[31] We show elsewhere that the bias extends to online and social media-based news consumption and also fails to accurately capture trends.[32] We highlight how behavioral data are more easily adaptable to the wide range of possible results that a researcher may need to answer with different, but related, sets of questions about news consumption.

Measuring awareness and understanding of news events
In ongoing work, we are pulling the top facts from online articles each day and running regular polls that ask whether respondents are aware of a given event, and if so, whether or not they know the facts in question. In addition to measuring the relationship between news coverage and public awareness, this dataset will initiate a larger program of tracking which types of information are absorbed by the news consuming public, and via which channels.

Conclusion

The debate around misinformation and its potentially damaging effects on public opinion, understanding, and democratic decision making is complex and multifaceted. There is not, to our knowledge, any general consensus on what "the problem" is, and even less agreement on what the solution or solutions ought to be. We do not pretend that our approach will resolve these disagreements over what matters and what to do about it. To the extent that such disagreements arise and persist because of the absence of systematic empirical evidence, however, we hope that it will help, in two ways. First, the creation of a shared, open data infrastructure to support research on misinformation and its effect on democracy will reduce existing barriers to producing rigorous, replicable, and ultimately useful science. Second, exposing the data and research insights to external stakeholders via continuously updating interactive visualizations will force interlocutors to confront the world as it is (or at least as it has been measured) rather than how they imagine it to be. Of course, we acknowledge that measurement itself is also imperfect in important ways; however, we do not see these shortcomings as a reason not to rely on data, but rather as a motivation to design better instruments and to collect better data. That data will also be imperfect, and the process of discovering that will in turn motivate better instruments, and so on. Just as no one experiment can settle any complex social scientific question, no one dataset can ever satisfactorily capture everything that we might care about. The process of informing our understanding of the world with evidence will therefore be an ongoing one. Our proposal is simply that we cannot afford not to begin this process.

CHAPTER 21

CLYDE MILLER AND THE INSTITUTE FOR PROPAGANDA ANALYSIS

Fighting Disinformation in the 1930s

ANYA SCHIFFRIN

One of the biggest threats to freedom today is the intense social and political polarization that exists across the world. While anxieties about globalization and growing economic inequality may be the underlying causes, such polarization has been fueled by the spread of false, misleading, or distorted information as well as violent speech on talk radio, right-wing news channels such as Fox, and crony-owned and captured newspapers, as well as the incitement and inflammatory speech commonly found on Facebook, YouTube, WhatsApp, and X.

The right to information is guaranteed in a number of international agreements, and UNESCO has also argued for the right to quality information as an essential part of media freedom.[1] The right to truthful information is even enshrined in the Spanish constitution. It has long been understood that without accurate information societies cannot function, and around the world we have seen the dangers of the polarization of information and the hardening of attitudes. Public policies cannot be made in an environment where there is no agreement on basic facts. In the United States, for example, views on climate change, mask wearing, and the dangers of COVID-19 all relate to politics rather than to science. The poor quality of information and politicization of information have weakened decision making and democracy around the world.

What to do about the breakdown of social trust and how to cope with vast amounts of mis/disinformation (formerly known as "propaganda") is a question that has bedeviled communications scholars for decades. In *Grand Hotel Abyss*, Stuart Jeffries describes how the philosophers of the Frankfurt School tried to understand the rise of Nazism and how German workers could be seduced by it. Theodor Adorno developed the theory of the F-scale and the authoritarian personality. Hannah Arendt wrote extensively about mistrust, the importance of information and the breakdown of societies. In the United States, Columbia University was the center of center of attempts to address "propaganda" by educating audiences to think critically about what they read.

This essay is about the Institute of Propaganda Analysis (IPA), which was based at Columbia University Teachers College and worked on promoting anti-racism education and improving critical thinking skills. Many of the efforts today to address susceptibility to online mis/disinformation have their roots in the work of the IPA and its head, Clyde Miller.

On March 29, 1937, Clyde Miller, a former journalist who had recently been hired by Teachers College as an associate professor of education at an annual salary of $6,700 (about $124,000 in 2025 dollars) and was soon made its head of communications, met with department store owner and philanthropist Edward Filene at the University Club in Boston. Also at the meeting was the public relations pioneer Edward Bernays and Harvard faculty member Kirtley F. Mather.[2] The topic discussed was "education for democracy," and Filene spoke about his worries that Americans were becoming susceptible to propaganda, unable to evaluate information thoughtfully and to make sound assessments. Filene asked for ideas about how to combat the problem. Miller took the request seriously. Collaborating with James Mendenhall from the experimental Lincoln School, Miller drafted a proposal for an institute to study propaganda.[3] The group met again later that year in New York, where Filene offered Miller a $10,000 grant. By the fall, the two had agreed that Filene would provide Miller's educational project at the Teachers College of Columbia University with funding for three years, and together they named it the Institute for Propaganda Analysis.[4] IPA also received funding from the American Jewish Committee, the Whitney Foundation, subscription revenue, and several significant contributions from anonymous individuals.

Miller's vantage point was that public education was the solution to the problem of propaganda. He is often quoted as saying the "American way" to combat propaganda was to understand and explain it, not emulate or suppress it, and this was the stance taken by the IPA. "There are three ways to deal with propaganda—first, to suppress it; second to try to answer it by counter-propaganda; third, to analyze it. Suppression of propaganda is contrary to democratic principles, specifically contrary to the provisions of the United States Constitution. Counter-propaganda is legitimate but often intensifies cleavages. Analysis of propaganda, on the other hand, cannot hurt propaganda for a cause that we consider 'good,'" Miller said in a speech at Town Hall in New York in 1939.[5]

The initial IPA board included sociologist Robert Lynd, later joined by historian Charles Beard and Princeton University psychologist Hadley Cantril, who had researched the audience response to the radio broadcast of H. G. Wells's *War of the Worlds*.[6] Also involved in the IPA were Violet Edwards, sociologists Alfred McClung Lee, and journalist and media critic I. F. Stone, who worked as a researcher after failing to get a job with Harold Ickes.[7] Also in the group was Clyde Beals, who was later stigmatized during the McCarthy era because of his involvement in the Newspaper Guild.[8]

For the next five years, Miller and his colleagues at the Institute for Propaganda Analysis published at least five books, teaching materials, and a weekly bulletin that had more than four thousand subscribers by 1938 and was sent to schools all over the United States.[9] The IPA formed a relationship with *Scholastic* magazine, in 1939 and 1940, producing a series called "What Makes You Think So? Expert Guidance to Help You Think Clearly and Detect Propaganda in Any Form," which was distributed in schools. By the late 1930s, one million school children were using its methods to analyze propaganda, and the IPA corresponded with some 2,500 teachers.[10] By 1939, nearly a thousand copies of the IPA book *Group Leader's Guide to Propaganda Analysis*, by Edwards, had sold, and by 1942 the Institute's most popular book, Alfred McClung Lee and Elizabeth Briant Lee's *The Fine Art of Propaganda: A Study of Father Coughlin's Speeches*, had sold 13,500 copies. Additionally, by that year, the Institute had sold more than eighteen thousand copies of the annual bound volumes of the *Bulletin*. The group was known as one of the leading thinkers of propaganda analysis at a time when the topic was a "virtual obsession," and its efforts were received favorably at first and covered by newspapers such as the *New York Times*, while IPA members made appearances on TV networks like CBS.[11]

The IPA emphasized creating engaged citizens who could think for themselves. and the organization had what historian of communication J. Michael Sproule describes as a "progressive reformist mission of propaganda analysis to help an essentially competent public against the new co-option of communication channels by powerful institutions."[12] Miller and IPA members believed that rational citizens should look closely at sources of information and how they were presented and thus avoid being hoodwinked. This optimistic view of human nature fit squarely with John Dewey's influential ideas of rational and participatory citizens. In taking this stance, the IPA epitomized a branch of communications scholarship that fell out of fashion by the 1940s as the field became dominated by the study of public opinion and methodology influenced by the work of Paul Lazarsfeld and others.[13]

Miller and the IPA studied and tried to counteract all kinds of propaganda—whether from Goebbels, the Communist Party (CPUSA), or PR agencies. They called for an articulation of the techniques used by propagandists and developed an analytical framework for understanding and combatting that era's propaganda.

The use of the word "propaganda" was extraordinarily broad in that era, and so was the IPA's definition "that propaganda is expression of opinions or action by individuals or groups designed to influence opinions or actions of other individuals or groups with predetermined ends."[14] There were of course some critics who questioned their mission and even before World War I, there was discussion about how persuasive propaganda really was.[15] A contemporary piece in *Harpers* accused the IPA of "excess interpretation."[16] But while the IPA had its critics, it proved remarkably influential and many of its ideas are now back in fashion in the study of mis and disinformation online.

For the group that worried about propaganda, the trauma of World War loomed large.[17] Propaganda was viewed as instrumental in gathering public support for the war and governments and the military developed their communications skills and public relations strategies in that period. George Creel served as the head of the Committee on Public Information set up by President Wilson and many journalists, academics joined and produced vast amounts of posters, films, thousands of press releases, songs, slogans, political cartoons and traveling exhibits in order to persuade the public.[18] Walter Lippmann's involvement was well known as was his 1922 book *Public Opinion*, about how opinions which formed, drew on his wartime experiences. Famously, Lippmann coined the term "the manufacture of consent" to describe the process.[19] Edward Bernays, one of the founders of modern public relations, got his start writing for the Committee on Public Information and decided after the war to use propaganda for commercial purposes, including a campaign to get women to start smoking. Thousands of books and articles were devoted to the study of propaganda including Harold Lasswell's *Propaganda Techniques in the World War*. There was a widespread belief that the propaganda of World War I was more powerful than any that had preceded it and scholars sought to understand how the propaganda had worked so effectively on both sides.[20]

The political catastrophes of the 1930s gave these studies new urgency. Faced with fascist regimes taking over much of the world and beaming propaganda globally, US demagogues spouting rhetoric against the government and world Jewry, the rise of Stalinism, and the beginning of the red-baiting that foreshadowed McCarthyism, scholars and journalists struggled to understand how people could fall for lies and overblown rhetoric.[21] The German government used propaganda domestically, but it also emanated from the country as part of its attempts to support appeasement and forestall war. In the United States, German propagandists even wrote speeches for Senator Ernest Lundeen of Minnesota, foreshadowing the way Russian disinformation is circulated today by far-right politicians in the United States and Europe.[22]

While it was clear that Germany's defeat in World War I and dire economic conditions, including widespread unemployment, paved the way for the rise of Adolf Hitler, academics and journalists tried to parse how Nazi propaganda had been so effective in galvanizing public support for the regime. IPA's position was that the interplay of economic conditions and individual tendencies created susceptibility to propaganda. But it saw only one possible solution that was compatible with the freedom of the First Amendment: to educate the public to be aware of it.

IPA's activities

The Leader's Guide to Propaganda Analysis

The IPA wanted people to understand that propaganda didn't appear out of nowhere; it arose from overarching historical, economic, and political patterns and trends that were important to identify. It summarized much of the thinking about media literacy and explained the importance of critical and scientific method.

The "7 Common Propaganda Devices," which are listed in the appendix to this essay, became one of the IPA's most famous interventions, described the techniques used by people spreading propaganda, creating a taxonomy of the different kinds in use, because IPA staffers thought that understanding the techniques of persuasion would fortify people's ability to resist. As well as the taxonomy, the IPA published a foundational document advancing its view that both personal proclivity and social forces induced susceptibility to propaganda. In the lengthy *Leader's Guide to Propaganda Analysis*, IPA's educational director, Violet Edwards, argued that the "common man" was "tragically confused" by overwhelming amounts of information and having to make decisions without first-hand information.

As Edwards wrote, instead of the "town hall" or the "cracker barrel" of yore, where citizens could meet to discuss the topics that affected them personally, citizens had to rely on information from others about how society should be organized and which policies should be pursued far from home, It was a point that had been made by others including Walter Lippmann and later Jacques Ellul, who argued that the common man should rely on journalism to help sift through and distill the excessive information available.[23]

The IPA's 250-page report is a detailed and thoughtful book on propaganda and media literacy. It pulled together much of the then-current thinking on the topic and anticipated much of our contemporary discussion. The IPA discussed confirmation bias and the role of advertising in paving the way for propaganda, and it called for journalists to go into communities and build relationships with their communities to explain the importance of journalism.

Edwards argued that in order to understand the secondhand information on which citizens depend, readers must adopt critical thinking and scientific methods. The IPA hoped that people using its analytical techniques would be able to think rationally about the information they encountered.

IPA's other books and publications

The IPA published analyses of political speeches using little icons—the emojis of the day—after each phrase to explain which technique the speaker was using. One such book analyzed the anti-Semitic radio broadcasts of the infamous Father Coughlin, a Catholic priest in Detroit who was estimated to have thirty million listeners for his broadcasts, which included conspiracy theories about so-called "international Jewry" and President Roosevelt.[24]

Bringing what the IPA described as "the newspaper man's passion for simplifying complicated subjects," Miller published monthly bulletins describing an important topic in the news, analyzing the propaganda techniques used by all sides, and recommending further reading and discussion questions for classrooms. Debunking was inevitably a result of this analysis. Some topics that were analyzed were hysteria about a subversive conspiracy at a Baltimore restaurant; dishonest advertisements paid for by doctors warning against socialized medicine; far-right groups whipped up by weekly broadcasts and taking to the streets, where they were protected by sympathetic police officers; accusations of treason in the US government; a sociology professor who had authored a definitive textbook accused by the business community of being too liberal; and accusations that refugees were getting jobs ahead of Americans. Upton Sinclair, running for governor of California, was the subject of false propaganda newsreels.[25] All of these events took place in the 1930s and 1940s and were the subjects of analysis in the IPA's monthly *Bulletin* for teachers.

The IPA's monthly bulletins also contained teaching guides that included questions and topics for further discussion. These usually related back to the seven propaganda techniques described by the IPA. Like many groups today, the IPA believed that media literacy efforts in schools were essential to spreading their message and techniques. They sought to put students on guard against propaganda and to make them into sophisticated news consumers of information and ideas. The IPA stressed critical thinking and understanding the broader political economy. It outlined techniques for audiences to look for when reading. But it went further than that. In the IPA's monthly bulletins, Miller and colleagues provided detailed analyses of world politics and displayed a broad understanding of the context in which the media operated and how propaganda worked. Rather than simply detail propaganda techniques, Miller exposed the strategies revealed by news coverage of a variety of topics and ana- lyzed the interests of the different players involved. He tackled the growing public relations industry, debates over the rise of chain stores, anti-union press coverage, the quality of evidence presented to the Dies Committee (later known as the House Un-American Activities Committee), as well as tactics used by white supremacists, domestic fascists, and Nazi sympathizers. The IPA analyzed their methods in detail but also provided accurate information in order to do what are now referred to as "debunkings." Looking at the IPA's teaching materials from today's vantage point, it is clear that they belong to a pre-internet era when attention spans were longer and there was an appetite for detailed critiques and analysis.

In the first issue of his monthly bulletin, dated October 1937, Miller drew a historical parallel by comparing the use of propaganda in the Pullman strike of 1894 with that used by Henry Ford and the Johnstown Citizens. In an affi- davit to the Dies Committee, PR firm Hill & Knowlton later disputed the claims made by the IPA about its role in the famously violent Youngstown Steel Strike.

In another bulletin of May 26, 1941, the IPA dissected disinformation about refugees stealing jobs from Americans:

> Persistently since the influx of refugees from the war areas began, a story has bobbed up in numerous American cities about the alleged heartless—and actu- ally unreal—discharging of regular employees by stores to make places for "foreigners." The story usually is anti-Semitic; the store with which it is con- nected has Jewish owners, and Jews are said to get the jobs.
>
> One large store in New York City which has been a victim of the story has spent considerable sums trying to trace the source and find some way of stop- ping it. The efforts have been fruitless. The story keeps reappearing, and mim- eographed leaflets have even been circulated picturing the Jewish manager welcoming a long line of Jewish refugees while turning away another line of fine Nordic types.

One of the things that distinguished the IPA was the breadth of their analysis. Understanding Media ownership and the power of advertisers was part of dis- secting propaganda.[26] In May 1938, *The Bulletin* delved into the techniques of Nazi propaganda and discussed how authoritarian regimes lack the "compet- ing organizations" that create a marketplace of ideas. The IPA argued in part that it's not just propaganda that is a problem, but the state's domination of information flows. "Political, economic, educational and religious spokesmen are able to and, actually do, disseminate rival propagandas. This gives those at whom the rival propagandas are directed some freedom of choice among the alternatives offered them."[27]

Miller used his ideas about propaganda techniques such as "testimonials" and "glittering generalities" and explained how they applied to Nazi propaganda. He discussed the neglect of the German middle class after World War I, arguing that this made them more susceptible to Nazi propaganda, and he singled out such German industrialists as Fritz Thyssen, who funded the NSDAP, for wanting to crush labor and Communism. He also parsed the use of Nazi symbols like swastikas and the othering of Jewish people and dissected how these tropes surfaced in the publications of domestic US Nazi groups like the American Nationalist Confederation, detailing their resemblance to a nineteenth-century white supremacist organization, the White Camelia. Many of the leaders were later put on trial but not imprisoned.[28]

Miller also understood the use of soft power such as ownership and advertising to capture the media.[29] The *Bulletin* devoted two issues to "Newspaper Analysis," returning to the point that in democracies there are "many voices, many opinions and many propagandas." Quoting University of Missouri journalism professor Roscoe Ellard, the *Bulletin* made the point that editors of small-town newspapers cannot afford to lose advertising revenue and so can gradually succumb to pressure from the business community as well as from readers. The result can be a softening of the newspaper's stance, adopting a captured mindset, and self-censorship. Large newspapers that have the pressure to resist are the most "reliable," and the *Bulletin* provided a list of credible newspapers, which included the *New York Times* and the *Baltimore Sun*. Based on a survey of working journalists in Washington, DC, the list of newspapers found to be unreliable included (in first place) the *Chicago Tribune*, which at that time was owned by William Randolph Hearst. The Communist Party's *Daily Worker* also made the unreliable list.

The Springfield Plan and Methodist Federation for Social Action

Meanwhile, the IPA further ruffled feathers by helping design a curriculum aimed at promoting civic engagement and racial and religious tolerance that was piloted in the Springfield, Massachusetts, school district, which had a sympathetic superintendent.[30] Educational sociologist E. George Payne described it and similar programs as an answer to the propaganda that was worsening the "growing menace of racial, religious, political and other prejudices in our country. We have become fully aware that our democracy is falling far short in the realization of our ideals because of these prejudices."[31] Education was viewed as a way to offset the propaganda that had spread prejudice.[32] The Springfield Plan generated "sensational interest" in the United States. It was featured in a March of Time newsreel, *Americans All*, in which Miller had a part, and the plan was the subject of the 1945 Warner Bros film *It Happened in Springfield*. Similar intercultural educational programs were adopted in other cities, including Detroit, New York City, Pittsburgh, Los Angeles, and San Diego.[33]

In Springfield, the program petered out after a few years partly due to criticism by the Catholic Church—which opposed progressive education and ideas emanating from Teachers College and lack of local support as religious tensions rose in Springfield after World War II.[34] By the early '50s, as McCarthyism was under way, there were murmurings that the plan contained "subversive" elements. Miller himself was attacked for being anti-Catholic and criticized in the *Brooklyn Tablet* for lectures he had given to Brooklyn teachers about intercultural education.[35] The incident was featured in a 1948 pamphlet on threats to academic freedom that was published by the New York Teachers Union.[36]

However, although it was phased out in Springfield, the plan's ideas lived on. According to education professor Lauri Johnson, "the Springfield Plan became the most well-publicized intercultural educational curriculum in the 1940s, talked about and emulated by school districts across the country and into Canada."[37]

When the Institute for Propaganda Analysis folded in 1942, Clyde Miller devoted an increasing amount of his time to promoting and disseminate the ideas of the Springfield Plan, but by the early 1950s incessant "red-baiting investigations" brought an end to intercultural education programs.[38]

Criticism outside and inside Columbia University

This broader context is essential to understanding the response to the IPA and to Miller's work, including the attacks by Hearst-owned papers and the investigation of the IPA by the Dies Committee. The committee had been set up to analyze both Communist and fascist activities in the United States; it later became notorious as the House Committee on Un-American Activities, used by Joseph McCarthy after World War II and in the 1950s before finally being disbanded. In January 1940 the IPA devoted an issue of the bulletin to analyzing the Dies Committee.[39]

The committee was often criticized for not going after the domestic far right and for focusing too much on Communism,[40] but this was not the focus of Miller's analysis in the *Bulletin*. Rather, he discussed the testimony given to the committee by many of the witnesses and argued that there was far too little evidence presented and far too much gossip and scandal-mongering. Miller noted that committee chairman Martin Dies and his supporters took the view that "some of his witnesses might be unreliable but insisted, nevertheless, that valuable evidence of Communist activities was being uncovered where none had been suspected."

After the *Bulletin* was published, IPA's president, Kirtley F. Mather of Harvard, signed a letter to Congress calling for the cessation of the committee's activities.[41] This was not the first such letter.[42] A few weeks after the bulletin was published, Dies's deputy, J. B Matthews, announced that an investigation into the IPA had been underway for two years, saying that committee members wanted to understand who was influencing American students.[43]

The IPA ceased publishing the weekly *Bulletin* in 1942, and it disbanded after the United States entered World War II and needed to start producing its own propaganda to galvanize support for the fight against Hitler. In its farewell issue of January 9, 1942, headlined "We Say Au Revoir," the IPA explained that the board of directors had voted to suspend operations. "The publication of its dispassionate analysis of all kinds of propaganda 'good' and 'bad,' is easily misunderstood during a war emergency, and more important, the analyses could be misused for undesirable purposes by persons opposing the government's efforts. On the other hand, for the Institute, as an Institute, to propagandize would cast doubt on its integrity as a scientific body."[44]

This final *Bulletin* expressed satisfaction with the work achieved by the IPA, warned that wartime is usually accompanied by a rise in intolerance, and expressed the hope that the IPA's techniques for analyzing propaganda would be used in the future, which indeed they were. But the ending was not so simple. The United States entered World War II, then transitioned into the Cold War and hurried down the road of McCarthyism—all of which required vast amounts of political messaging (which Miller might have called "propaganda") and sometimes disinformation.

As predicted by Miller, there was apparently no room at Columbia University for the IPA. He was placed on leave in 1944, when the college was facing a financial crisis, and was never brought back to work.[45] In 1948 Miller was officially fired and told it was because of departmental restructuring, but Miller argued that it was because his work had offended William Randolph Hearst.[46] Hearst was known for attacking "Reds" in the universities and schools and even sending in reporters disguised as students to try to uncover left-wing professors in the classroom.[47] His newspaper, *The World Telegram*, had criticized the church group that Miller was involved in. The red-baiting Hearst columnist Frederik Woltman had written nasty articles about the Methodist Federation for Social Action, "accusing the federation of being sympathetic toward the policies of the Soviet Union."[48] Miller protested as soon as they appeared and called on Columbia Journalism School to rescind the Pulitzer Prize it had bestowed on Woltman in 1947.[49]

Many professors during the McCarthy years were let go quietly, and Miller was one of them.[50] He lost his Columbia housing and salary and wrote repeatedly to Columbia's president decrying the "violation of tenure and academic freedom." We may never be certain whether Miller was a victim of the political climate of the 1930s and an early victim of the repressive climate that took hold in the 1950s. Letters in the Central Archives at Columbia University suggest that the dean of Teachers College had long disliked Miller's work and had begun suggesting to Miller as early as 1939 that Miller seek employment elsewhere. After Miller was dismissed, he spoke to the *New York Times*, saying it was a violation of academic freedom, got a lawyer to write Columbia and ask for $100,000 in damages, and asked the American Association of University Professors to write to the provost. The dean of Columbia Teachers College, William Fletcher Russell, responding to the questions about the circumstances of Miller's firing, sent a thirteen-page letter to Provost Albert G. Jacobs on June 29, 1948, outlining the case for firing Miller. Russell's lengthy defense of his decision was that his staff didn't get along with him, Miller was "in no sense a scholar" and had never done much teaching, and the IPA and Springfield Plan had no relation to Teachers College. Russell concluded by saying, "There is no justification for any charge that might be made by Miller that academic freedom or liberty of teaching has been in anyway infringed." The letter seemed to satisfy the administration, which thanked Russell for his "thorough account."[51]

Miller's dismissal from Columbia and the disbanding of the IPA was part of a larger conservative backlash against the idea of "propaganda." Max Lerner, the left-wing journalist who worked at *The Nation* and *PM* but later became far more conservative (like James Wechsler and David Horowitz), described Clyde Miller and the Institute of Propaganda Analysis by saying, "In such a mental climate we have become a nation of amateur detectives looking for concealed propaganda in every effort to awaken America to the real nature of Nazi world strategy. It may be because we have felt cheated and disenchanted by our role in the last war, and are determined never again to be tricked."[52]

As the United States moved into World War II the scholarship shifted, particularly with the invention of modern communications studies, Miller and the IPA fell out of fashion.[53] They began to seem like a Popular Front relic, sort of folksy, old-fashioned lefties with the same breathless, wide-eyed approach of the daily newspaper *PM*.[54] These were people who believed in the "common man" and thought that education would be enough to help them see where their interests lay. They were overshadowed by changes in the Communications field which emphasized polling, public opinion, messaging and stopped using the words "propaganda" or "propaganda studies," instead using terms like "communication" and "communications research."[55] "Scholars like Paul Lazarsfeld championed focus groups and longitudinal panel surveys. Some of these same arguments about the power of propaganda continue today in the discussion about online mis/disinformation.[56]

The Institute for Propaganda Analysis and media literacy programs today

Although Miller's efforts lasted no more than a decade, his legacy lived on. Interest in media trust and media credibility continued and schools in the United Kingdom, Germany, Canada, and Australia, among other countries, launched their own media literacy programs. A number of these were influenced by the work of the IPA, not just in the methods they used but also the language used to describe the problem of propaganda and how to educate people to understand it. As well as teaching media literacy, myriad groups commission research, design curricula, and work with parents, teachers, and legislators to try to pass laws mandating media literacy classes. Librarians are also very involved in teaching media literacy skills. Overall, their efforts tend to be fragmented—and there are not really universal standards or uniform definitions. As a result, such courses may include subjects as varied as online diversity, representation, identifying disinformation, reasoning, and understanding the role of journalism.[57] Even so, there are many points these new groups have in common with the IPA.

The idea that new media are overwhelming audiences, who are no longer able to distinguish truth from falsehoods, came back with a vengeance after the Trump and Brexit votes of 2016 and during the COVID-19 pandemic of 2020. There are of course many ways that today's media literacy efforts are different from those of the IPA. The scale, speed, virality, and financial incentives of today's online dis/misinformation is different from what the IPA contended with, focused as it was on print and radio. Microtargeting and the role of the tech giants is also new.

Even so, the similarities between today's media literacy teaching, now offered all over the world, are worth noting. Today former journalists are at the forefront of much of the news literacy movement and, like Clyde Miller and the IPA, they believe in educating citizens and in school programs that will give students the tools to tell truth from false.[58] The IPA's approach of working with teachers and students to train the next generation to think critically about information is also being tried again.[59]

The concept of "immunizing" or "inoculating" people against false information is a framing still used in the field of media literacy training.[60] Miller and the IPA were believers in John Dewey and strived to create educated citizens, but they also believed in the pre-bunking and inoculation arguments found today. So, too, the IPA's attempts to promote scientific method and rational discourse as a way of countering disinformation are being replicated today.[61]

Miller and IPA made taxonomies of techniques used to dissimulate and confuse people, and so have current scholars of disinformation. To name two:

Claire Wardle, executive director of First Draft, released "Fake News, It's Complicated,"[62] which is now a standard for discussions about the problem. In this paper, Wardle lists the types of mis/disinformation as satire and parody, misleading content, imposter content and fabricated content, false connection, false context, and manipulated content. Her paper with Hossain Derakhshan also included a rubric of who the different actors and targets are such as states targeting states, states targeting private actors, corporates targeting consumers.[63] Also widely cited is the typology from Edson Tandoc, Zhang Lim, and Richard Ling, who reviewed thirty-four scholarly articles published between 2003 and 2017 and came up with a typology that included satire, parody, false images, advertising, and public relations, which sometimes overlap with propaganda.[64]

Part of what is powerful about media literacy efforts is not just the skills but the critical thinking they try to impart. This critical thinking is still core to media literacy efforts today.

Uncertainty about the impact of media literacy training continues and today's discussion often resembles that found in the pages of IPA's *Bulletin*. Social psychologists and others have noted that countering false information with true information is difficult when the people spreading false information refuse to change their ideas when told something is not true, but simply double down on their prejudices.[65] Just as Trump supporters say that factual errors are unimportant because Trump is speaking a larger truth, the *Bulletin* reported on January 1, 1939, that Henry Ford and Father Coughlin as saying that if some information in the *Protocols of the Elders of Zion* was not authentic, it could still be "factual."

Anticipating today's critique by Data & Society founder danah boyd and others of the "backfire" effect of media literacy training, the IPA faced criticism that its techniques would make students cynical.[66] The IPA responded by saying that its teachings were needed to equip students for their future as engaged citizens: "The teacher who acts as a guide to maturity helps her pupils to think critically and to act intelligently on the everyday problems they are meeting. . . . By its very nature [the] process will not build attitudes of cynicism and defeatism."

The 2016 elections and the rise of Facebook and Twitter brought about a renewed interest in propaganda, misinformation, and disinformation and a flurry of commissions, reports, and initiatives.[67] For the tech giants, supporting media literacy efforts became a natural part of efforts to avoid regulation. Given the libertarian bent of many in Silicon Valley (a sharp contrast to Filene's support of good government) it is not surprising that Facebook CEO Mark Zuckerberg, Twitter's Jack Dorsey, and others took the view that they were simply the pipes for other people's content, and it was up to the audience to figure out what was true and what was not.[68] They are especially supportive of initiatives that prompt people to verify their sources before they forward mis/disinformation to others online.[69] The companies funded some media literacy groups, including the LAMP project in New York City, which received funding from Google, Twitter, and Facebook. Facebook and a group of funders also gave $14 million to City University of New York and a consortium of other international institutions, including Sciences-Po in Paris, for a News Integrity Initiative.[70] Despite these grants, the groups doing media literacy training in the United States say that while interest has soared since 2016, funding has not.[71] The tech giants' attempts to avoid regulation in the United States and in Europe have been largely successful. In this they have had intellectual support from free expression groups, such as Committee to Protect Journalists and Access Now, that, like the IPA, are opposed to anything that might impinge on the First Amendment.[72]

Conclusion

Just as Miller and the IPA were criticized for overstating the importance of propaganda, so today many argue that mis/disinformation have little effect and criticize news and media literacy efforts for being unable to demonstrate impact. Access to quality information and a public that is able to discern is important in its own right is agreed, by most reasonable people, to be essential antidotes to the condition of unfreedom.

However, debates about whether or not propaganda or online disinformation have an effect on voting continue, just as they were debated when Paul Lazarsfeld, Bernard Berelson, and Hazel Gaudet published *The People's Choice* saying that their research showed that radio, newspaper and campaign advertising did not affect voting decisions as much as personal interactions and word of mouth.[73]

In his 1962 book on propaganda, Jacques Ellul weighed in on the influence question, summarizing many of the methodological problems that researchers faced when trying to understand media effects and argued that effects must be studied in the context of societies that have been exposed to it over many years.[74] Ellul argued that rather than focus on individual studies or small groups, more can be learned from looking at entire societies that have been subjected to propaganda.[75] In some ways the IPA anticipated Ellul's point of view believing that, in certain contexts, some individuals may be swayed by multiple exposures to mis/disinformation.

Today the rise of the antivaccination movement and the spate of killings by white supremacists who cite phrases used by "conservative media stars" suggest that consumption of incendiary information spread by the media and/or online has an effect on people's emotions.[76] There is also far more research on media effects now than there was twenty years ago, including the natural experiments written about by scholars such as Don Green, Macarten Humphries, Horacio Larreguy, John Marshall, and Dylan Groves. A characteristic of this body of work is that political scientists (like economists) often look for "natural events" such as a period when something starts or finishes or is not available (the arrival of Fox News into a market, the opening or closure of news outlets in a small town, the random placement on the television remote, the boycott of a newspaper, the launch of a pedagogical soap opera aimed at changing behavior). Some of the effects that have been documented are the impact of new information on citizen decision making, the effects of exposure to campaign advertising, voter turnout, the effects of government-controlled media, and a host of other topics.[77]

When understanding media effects and media literacy education, the IPA believed that it was necessary to do more than just verify information and images presented by the media. The sources of the information, the agenda of those sources, and the broader context of the information also matter. Those ideas have had a resurgence today. Teaching people to question what they're told and to think rationally about the information they consume is as essential now as it was in the 1930s. It is also clear from the ongoing pressure on researchers today that the study of propaganda in the academy is as controversial now as it was in Clyde Miller's time. New York University researcher Laura Edelson and Harvard Kennedy School researcher Joan Donovan are just two of the disinformation scholars who have experienced the power and influence of big tech. Lawsuits, subpoenas and House investigations continue and attempts to require media literacy education in public schools have been strongly opposed by the MAGA right. In the Trump era, it is clear that the backlash of the last few years against disinformation researchers turned out to be a just a small part of the larger attack on universities and academic freedom. Sadly, the lessons of the demise of the Institute of Propaganda Analysis are more salient now than when I first began this chapter.

Appendix

Seven propaganda devices described by the Institute for Propaganda Analysis

1. Name-Calling. Based on "hate and fear," the propagandist gives "bad names" "to those individuals, groups, nations, races, policies, practices, beliefs and ideals which he would have us condemn and reject."
2. Glittering generalities. Words are used to "stir up our emotions and befog our thinking. . . . The propagandist identifies his program with virtue by use

of 'virtue words.' Glittering Generalities is a device to make us accept and approve, without examining the evidence."

3. Transfer: "The propagandist carries over the authority, sanction, and prestige of something we respect and revere to something he would have us accept."

4. Testimonial: For instance, "When I feel tired, I smoke a Camel and get the grandest lift."

5. Plain Folks: They "win our confidence by appearing to be people like ourselves." For example, a commercial says, "It's our family's whiskey, neighbor; and neighbor, it's your price."

6. Card Stacking: "The propagandist deploys all the arts of deception to win our support for himself . . . by means of this device propagandists would convince us that a ruthless war of aggression is a crusade for righteousness." "He stacks the cards against the truth. He uses under-emphasis and over-emphasis to dodge issues and evade facts. He resorts to lies, censorship and distortion. He omits facts. He offers false testimony."

7. Bandwagon: "A device to make us follow the crowd to accept the propagandists' program en masse." . . ."Propagandists will appeal to us as Catholics, Protestants, or Jews" and use biases common to a group. "The theme of this type of propaganda may be summed up in the statement, 'Everybody's doing it: come along and follow the great majority, for it can't be wrong.'"

"Some ABC's of Propaganda Analysis" (December 1937)

- **ASCERTAIN** the conflict element in the propaganda you are analyzing. All propaganda contains a conflict element in some form or other—either as cause, or as effect, or as both cause and effect.

- **BEHOLD** your own reaction to this conflict element. It is always necessary to know and to take into consideration our own opinions with regard to a conflict situation about which we feel strongly, on which we are prone to take sides. This information permits us to become more objective in our analysis.

- **CONCERN** yourself with today's propagandas associated with today's conflicts. These are the ones that affect directly our income, business, working conditions, health, education, and religious, political, and social responsibilities. It is all too easy to analyze some old example of propaganda, now having little relation to vital issues.

- **DOUBT** that your opinions are "your very own." They usually aren't. Our opinions, even with respect to today's propagandas, have been largely determined for us by inheritance and environment. . . . We resemble others with similar inheritance and environment and are bound to them by ties of common experience. . . . We tend to distrust the opinions of those who differ from us in inheritance and environment. Only drastic changes in our life conditions, with new and different experiences, associations, and influences, can offset or cancel out the effect of inheritance and long years of environment.

- **EVALUATE**, therefore, with the greatest care, your own propagandas [beliefs]. We must learn clearly why we act and believe as we do with respect to various conflicts and issues—political, economic, social, and religious. . . . This is very important.

- **FIND THE FACTS** before you come to any conclusion. There is usually plenty of time to form a conclusion and believe in it later on. Once we learn how to recognize propaganda, we can most effectively deal with it by suspending our judgment until we have time to learn the facts and the logic or trickery involved in the propaganda in question. We must ask:
  "Who is this propagandist?"
  "How is he trying to influence our thoughts and actions?"
  "For what purpose does he use the common propaganda devices?"
  "Do we like his purposes?"
  "How does he use words and symbols?"
  "What are the exact meanings of his words and symbols?"
  "What does the propagandist try to make these words and symbols appear to mean?"
  "What are the basic interests of this propagandist?"
  "Do his interests coincide with the interests of most citizens, of our society as we see it?"

- **GUARD** always, finally, against omnibus words. They are the words that make us the easy dupes of propagandists. Omnibus or carryall words are words that are extraordinarily difficult to define. They carry all sorts of meanings to the various sorts of men. Therefore, the best test for the truth or falsity of propaganda lies in specific and concrete definitions of the words and symbols used by the propagandist. Moreover, sharp definition is the best antidote against words and symbols that carry a high charge of emotion.

NOTES

Editors' Introduction

1. Akeel Bilgrami and Jonathan Cole, *Who's Afraid of Academic Freedom?* (New York: Columbia University Press, 2015).
2. Antonio Gramsci, *Prison Notebooks* (New York: Columbia University Press, 2011).
3. Although the idea is extensively covered in many of Foucault's writings, the fullest discussion of "normalization" is in part III of *Discipline and Punish* (New York: Vintage Books, [1975] 1995). See also Michel Foucault, *Society Must Be Defended* (New York: Picador, 2003), and *The History of Sexuality*, vol. 1 (New York: Vintage Books, [1976] 1990).
4. Alexis de Tocqueville, *Democracy in America* (Chicago: University of Chicago Press, [1835] 2002).
5. Michael Rosen, *Voluntary Servitude: False Consciousness and the Theory of Ideology* (Cambridge: Polity Press, 1995). For Marx on ideology—and note that he never used the term "false consciousness"—the *locus classicus* is Karl Marx and Friedrich Engels, *The German Ideology*, London: Lawrence and Wishart, [1932] 1974), written in 1845–1846.
6. See Isaiah Berlin, *Four Essays on Liberty* (Oxford: Oxford University Press, 1969).
7. Recognizing this distinctiveness need in no way feed into a certain invidious historical outlook of anthropocentrism that has been much studied ever since Keith Thomas's fine study *Man and the Natural World: Changing Attitudes in England 1500–1800* (London: Allen Lane, 1983).
8. The possession of reason in nonhuman animals is a very large topic with a very large literature in many disciplines. In saying what we have just said, we intend by the term "reason" a rather more full-fledged and self-consciousness-involving use of the term "reason" than the reason that is uncontroversially attributable to animals. This

kind of autonomy-reflecting question that wolves don't ask but we, from a certain age, often do, is a good example of that full-fledgedness and self-consciousness.

9. We say "under certain unusual circumstances" because Al-Jazeera, the television network in question, was producing these subversive broadcasts only while Qatar, where it was based, was keen to assert its rivalry against Saudi Arabia. When that changed, for instance during the period of the invasion of Libya, Al-Jazeera played an entirely different and far from subversive role.

1. Why Freedom to Say Enlarges Freedom to Think

1. John Stuart Mill, *On Liberty*, ed. David Bromwich and George Kateb (New Haven, CT: Yale University Press, 2003), 80.
2. Alexis de Tocqueville, *Democracy in America*, ed. J. P. Mayer, trans. George Lawrence (New York: Harper Perennial, 1988), 254–55.
3. Mill, *On Liberty*, 87.
4. Mill, *On Liberty*, 89.
5. *Selections from Ralph Waldo Emerson*, ed. Stephen E. Whicher (Boston: Houghton Mifflin, 1957), 147.
6. Oliver Wendell Holmes, *The Mind and Faith of Justice Holmes: His Speeches, Essays, Letters and Judicial Opinions*, ed. Max Lerner (New York: Modern Library, 1954), 312.
7. See George Kateb, *Human Dignity* (Cambridge, MA: Harvard University Press, 2011), 6–10.
8. Mill, *On Liberty*, 100–01.
9. Mill, *On Liberty*, 104.
10. Mill, *On Liberty*, 118.
11. James Fitzjames Stephen, *Liberty, Equality, Fraternity*, ed. Stuart Warner (Indianapolis: Liberty Classics, 1993), 30.
12. Søren Kierkegaard, *The Sickness Unto Death*, trans. Walter Lowrie (New York: Anchor Books, 1954), 167.

2. Kant and "Can't": Practical Necessity and the Diminution of Options

1. Luke 10:30–34.
2. Peter Winch, "Who Is My Neighbour?," in *Trying to Make Sense* (London: Basil Blackwell, 1987), quotes at 157, 158, 159.
3. I am quoting loosely in this paragraph from the e-mail in which Akeel Bilgrami and Jonathan Cole invited me to contribute to this volume.
4. Analogous points might also be made about the alleged freedom of women in a patriarchal society.
5. I am indebted in a general way to Bernard Williams, "Practical Necessity," in *Moral Luck: Philosophical Papers 1973–1980* (Cambridge: Cambridge University Press, 1981), 124.
6. See Prabhat Patnaik's and Joseph Stiglitz's contributions to this volume.
7. See Immanuel Kant, *Groundwork of the Metaphysics of Morals*, in Immanuel Kant, *Practical Necessity*, ed. Mary Gregor (Cambridge: Cambridge University Press, 1996), 71–72.

8. But see Williams, "Practical Necessity," 127, for a fierce vindication of the relevant modality. "In face of 'I must,' the other alternatives are no longer alternatives: they become things one cannot do. . . . But how can an alternative be, or become, something I cannot do? Here someone will reach for the weapon of distinguishing senses, and will speak of there being two or more senses of 'cannot,' that which signifies whatever rejection is embodied in the agent's deliberation, and that which expresses what one 'literally' cannot do. But why should we resort to such a distinction of senses? Why should this kind of *cannot* be anything other than *cannot*?"

9. For a helpful discussion of Luther in this context, see Robert Gay, "Bernard Williams on Practical Necessity," *Mind* 98 (1989): 553.

10. See Williams on "incapacities of character," in "Practical Necessity," 129.

11. Christopher Cordner, "Ethical Necessity and Internal Reasons," *Philosophy* 76 (2001): 545. Cordner interprets Williams's view this way: "Ethical requirement must be (somehow) internal to what I find myself deeply to be—must 'speak to' what goes personally deep in me—if ethical requirements are to have real authoritative weight for me. (What I "ought" to do does not seem close enough to me, as it were, for that.) Yet if that authority is not to dissolve into a disposition to act which is merely personal, it must also be intelligible as lying in some sense 'outside' or 'beyond' me. Kant made this double-aspectness of moral requirement perfectly explicit when he spoke of the 'moral law' as both authoritative over us and also lying within us."

12. See Jeremy Waldron, "Who Is My Neighbor?—Proximity and Humanity," *The Monist* 86 (2003): 333.

13. In his essay "Theory and Practice," Kant invites us to consider a simple case of moral choice, involving the benevolent appropriation of funds held on trust that the true owners will never miss. See Immanuel Kant, "On the Common Saying: That may be Correct in Theory, but it is of no Use in Practice," in Kant, *Practical Philosophy*, 287–88.

14. See Kant, *Groundwork of the Metaphysics of Morals*, 71–72.

15. See Williams, "Practical Necessity," 125, for discussion of the way different kinds of imperative might be involved.

16. Winch, "Who Is My Neighbour?," 161.

17. Gay, "Bernard Williams on Practical Necessity," 565–66.

18. See Alfred Archer, "Saints, Heroes and Moral Necessity," *Royal Institute of Philosophy Supplement* 77 (2015): 111. Archer writes, "Moral exemplars often claim to have experienced a sense of internal compulsion. They claim that they felt that they could not have acted otherwise. That they had to act as they did."

19. Robert Cover, *Justice Accused: Anti-Slavery and the Judicial Process* (New Haven, CT: Yale University Press, 1975).

20. *Somerset v. Stewart* 98 ER 499 (1772), as applied in *Lemmon v. People*, 20 N.Y. 562 (1860).

21. *Miller v. McQuerry* 17 F.Cas. 339 (1853), my emphasis.

22. It is said that in 1823 William Webb Ellis, in the middle of a game of soccer, caught the ball in his arms and ran to the goal line, thus inventing rugby as a new code of football.

23. Cover, *Justice Accused*, 122.

24. Compare Williams, "Practical Necessity," 127: "Any notion of necessity must carry with it a corresponding notion of impossibility, and statements in terms of the one can no doubt be recast in terms of the other, but it can make a difference which of them presents itself first and more naturally. In . . . deliberation, there is a significant distinction between two ways in which necessity may enter the structure of my thought. It

may be the case that I conclude that I have to do X . . . because it is the one item to which I attach overwhelming importance. . . . Then, as a consequence of this, Y and Z, alternatives to X, are no longer alternatives—they are things I cannot do. Alternatively, it may be the impossibility that bears the priority. Y and Z, the only alternatives to X, are things that I cannot conceivably do, and are excluded; then consequently, X is what I must, or have to, do."

25. See Jeremy Waldron, "What Can Christian Teaching Add to the Debate About Torture?," *Theology Today* 63 (2006): 330–43; reprinted in Jeremy Waldron, *Torture, Terror and Trade-Offs: Philosophy for the White House* (New York: Oxford University Press, 2010).

26. Joseph Raz, *The Morality of Freedom* (New York: Oxford University Press, 1988), 411.

3. Freedom and Unfreedom in Human Categories: The Case of Multiplicity

1. I will be focusing on two of his works in particular, "Making up People," in *Reconstructing Individualism*, ed. Thomas Heller, Morton Sosna, and David E. Wellbery (Stanford, CA: Stanford University Press, 1986), 222–36, and *Rewriting the Soul: Multiple Personality and the Sciences of Memory* (Princeton, NJ: Princeton University Press, 1998).

2. I say these are *obvious* candidates. But I still classify them as *candidates* rather than as *cases*. In order to vindicate the claim that they truly are mind-independent in the requisite sense implied by scientific realism, we would have to dismiss alternative medical viewpoints according to which human health is to a large extent a function of human emotion. This viewpoint informs traditional Chinese medicine and is shared by contemporary Western-trained medical researcher Gabor Maté in *The Myth of the Normal: Trauma, Illness and Healing in a Toxic Culture* (New York: Penguin Random House, 2022).

3. See, for example, Michel Foucault, *Madness and Civilization: A History of Insanity in the Age of Reason* (New York: Random House, 1965); *The Order of Things: An Archaeology of the Human Sciences* (New York: Random House, 1970); *The Archaeology of Knowledge* (New York: Harper and Row, 1972); *The Birth of the Clinic: An Archaeology of Medical Perception* (London: Tavistock Publications, 1973); *Discipline and Punish: The Birth of the Prison* (London: Penguin Books, 1978).

4. See Carol Rovane, *The Metaphysics and Ethics of Relativism* (Cambridge, MA: Harvard University Press, 2013), ch. 4.

5. See Carol Rovane, *Bounds of Agency: An Essay in Revisionary Metaphysics* (Princeton, NJ: Princeton University Press, 1998).

6. See Bernard Williams, *Ethics and the Limits of Philosophy* (Cambridge, MA: Harvard University Press, 1985).

7. See, for example, Elizabeth Anderson, "Symposium on Amartya Sen's Philosophy: 2. Unstrapping the Straitjacket of Preference—A Comment on Amartya's Sen's Contribution to Philosophy and Economics," *Economics and Philosophy* 17 (2001): 21–38.

8. See https://www.psychiatry.org/psychiatrists/practice/dsm/history-of-the-dsm for the American Psychiatric Association's account of the history of the DSM, from which the quoted passage is drawn.

9. See https://dsm.psychiatryonline.org/doi/book/10.1176/appi.books.9780890425787.

10. For an exhaustive elaboration and defense of this characterization of personal identity, in terms of psychological connectedness and continuity, see Derek Parfit, *Reasons and Persons* (Oxford: Oxford University Press, 1984).

11. I had a firsthand encounter with this attitude in the 1990s when a practicing psychiatrist attended a graduate seminar I was teaching. He reported to me that he had a patient who would surely have been diagnosed with multiple personality disorder by some of his colleagues, whereas *he* was quite sure that such a diagnosis would have been misplaced.

12. See Olivier Dodier, Laurence Patihis, and Mélany Payoux, "Reports of Recovered Memories of Childhood Abuse in Therapy in France," reprinted in *Memory*, August 2019, https://www.tandfonline.com/doi/full/10.1080/09658211.2019.1652654.

13. See, for example, Peter Levine, *Waking the Tiger: Healing Trauma* (Berkeley, CA: North Atlantic Books, 1997). For an excellent study of how thinking about trauma evolved over the course of the twentieth century, see Ruth Leys, *Trauma: A Genealogy* (Chicago: University of Chicago Press, 2000).

14. Two pioneers in developing *nonpsychotherapeutic* approaches to treating trauma—approaches that give due weight to its biological and somatic dimensions—are Peter Levine and Besel van Kolk. See Levine, *Waking the Tiger*, and van der Kolk, *The Body Keeps the Score: Brain, Mind and Body in the Healing of Trauma* (New York: Penguin Books, 2015).

15. Another phenomenon that is often reported in the wake of trauma goes by the name "flashback," which is a vivid experience of traumatic events from the past as if they were happening in the present. Like the term "amnesia," the term "flashback" presupposes a single unified self whose relation to past events in its own life is disturbed, by contrast with the normal relation of *memory*. In the case of amnesia the past events are simply forgotten, whereas in the case of flashback there is a failure to represent the events as having occurred in *in the past* as opposed to occurring in the present. It is commonly recommended that those who suffer from flashbacks should try to *correct for* their phenomenology, by explicitly reminding oneself that they are *just memories*. But I think we should take the phenomenology of flashbacks more seriously than that, by looking for an explanation of *why* the experiences that come in flashbacks *do not present as memories*. One possible explanation follows from the point I made in the text, that trauma gets in the way of processing experiences into full-blown representations of events that are located in both space and time—and this is why if they do not *present* later as memories of such events, but rather as intrusive thoughts. If this explanation is at all on the right track, then the better way to conceive a "flashback" is not as a representation of past events that fails to locate them correctly in time, but rather as a flow of experience that is picking up again, right where it left off when it was interrupted by traumatic overwhelm. So conceived, flashbacks may be occasions for some belated processing (not only cognitive processing, but also emotional processing)—but only provided that they are too traumatic, for if they are, then traumatic overwhelm may simply recur. There are further points to be made here, about *who* is in a position to do this belated processing. As I said at the start of this note, the language of "flashback" tends to take for granted the presence of a single unified self, who both underwent the earlier experience, and who is now undergoing a replay of it, and who is the only self available to do whatever belated processing remains to be done. While this may be the right way to view human beings who have been traumatized by war, natural disaster, etc., it may not be the right way to view human beings who were victims of ongoing childhood sexual abuse from an

early age, insofar as they came to be sites of the severe forms of dissociation that lead to *multiplicity*.

16. See Rovane, *Bounds of Agency*.

17. In the philosophical literature, this is known as a reductionist view of personal identity—a view that Derek Parfit did much to elaborate and defend. But Parfit did not embrace the normative conception of the self, or person, on which the self *constitutes itself* through the thinkings and doings that constitute *it*. See Rovane, *Bounds of Agency*, and Carol Rovane, "Reductionism and the Moral Significance of Personal Identity," in *Derek Parfit's Reasons and Persons*, ed. A. Sautchelli (New York: Routledge, 2020), 227–48, for extended discussions the normative conception, and its implications about self-constitution.

18. In addition to Hacking's history of these developments, see William James's chapter on "Consciousness of Self" in his *Principles of Psychology* for a good summary of how those cases were reported and conceived at the time.

19. See Rovane, *Metaphysics and Ethics of Relativism*, for further discussion of how and why the moral relativist's position is consistent with the *appearance* that there are universal moral truths on which everyone agrees. I clarify there that there are *moral platitudes* that circumscribe the *domain* of the moral, which are universally accepted by all agents who are capable of moral reflection—such as that harm is bad, killing is bad, hindering agency is bad, and arbitrary distinctions among objects of moral concern is bad. But these platitudes cannot be action guiding without the contribution of *thick* moral concepts in Williams's sense. On the matter of child sexual abuse in particular, Hacking surmises that it is a phenomenon that arose in the nineteenth century, with the forms of life that follows upon industrialization. I would surmise, further, that it can arise only in cultures where *privacy* is an important moral value—which then affords the needed cover for what the culture would otherwise be bound, by its other moral commitments, to censure.

20. For a brief summary of some salient points in this history, see David Remnick, "The Assault on Freud," *Washington Post*, February 19, 1984.

21. See Warwick Middleton, "Tipping Points and the Accommodation of the Abuser: Ongoing Incestuous Abuse During Adulthood," *International Journal for Crime, Justice and Social Democracy* 4, no. 2 (2015): 4–17.

4. Freedom and Coercion, Opportunity and the Economy: Neoliberalism, the Individual, and Society

I wish to acknowledge the very helpful comments of Akeel Bilgrami and the editing done by Andrea Gurwitt. I would also like to thank Parijat Lal and Ricardo Pommer Muñoz for their research assistance and multiple insights. Earlier versions of this chapter were presented at a philosophy and social science seminar organized by Jonathan Cole and Akeel Bilgrami at Columbia University on the subject of freedom and coercion; as a lecture delivered on the occasion of the eight hundredth anniversary of the founding of Padua University, as part of a series on freedom; and as a lecture delivered at the Central European University. I am indebted to thoughtful comments and questions raised in those presentations.

1. The subjects of coercion and freedom have been dealt with extensively in the philosophical literature, but not, to my knowledge, as much through the lens of economics. On coercion, see Robert Nozick, "Coercion," in *Philosophy, Science, and Method:*

Essays in Honor of Ernest Nagel, ed. Sidney Morgenbesser, Patrick Suppes, and Morton G. White (New York: St. Martin's Press, 1969), 65–86. On freedom see, e.g., Isaiah Berlin, "Two Concepts of Liberty," in *Four Essays on Liberty* (Oxford: Oxford University Press, 1969), 118–72.

2. Many economists would also argue that all that matters are *outcomes*, not the processes by which they are arrived at.

3. See, for instance, the discussion in Bruce C. Greenwald and Joseph E. Stiglitz, *Creating a Learning Society: A New Approach to Growth, Development, and Social* Progress (New York: Columbia University Press, 2014).

4. The curious aspect of prevailing economic arrangements, say in the United States, is that while the government finances basic (and a considerable amount of applied) research, it then turns over the intellectual property to private companies, which charge prices, well above costs, that generate enormous profits for them. This expands the "freedom" of the owners of the drug companies but constrains the freedom of ordinary citizens who rely on those drugs, often for their very survival. An especially outrageous example occurred during the COVID-19 pandemic, when the basic research behind mRNA vaccines and most of the development work was publicly financed (by the United States and Germany), yet Pfizer and Moderna made tens of billions of dollars in profits. In that particular case, because these drug companies used their control of the intellectual property to restrict production and sale of both vaccines and therapeutics, the virus had a chance to mutate to become more contagious, deadly, or vaccine resistant, even harming those in the advanced countries. It was not in the advanced countries' interests to restrict access to intellectual property, even if it enhanced the profits of a few companies. For a discussion of the restrictions on therapeutics, see Lori Wallach and Joseph E. Stiglitz, "The International Community Must Prioritize COVID Treatment and Test Access," *Scientific American*, November 14, 2022; on vaccines, see Lori Wallach and Joseph E. Stiglitz, "WTO Cannot Continue as Barrier to COVID-19 Medicines," *Newsweek*, June 10, 2022, and Joseph E. Stiglitz, "Vaccinating the World Against COVID-19 Is a No-Brainer," *PLOS Global Public Health*, May 2, 2022. For a discussion in the context of freedom, see Joseph E. Stiglitz, "COVID 19 and Human Freedom," *Project Syndicate*, September 7, 2021.

5. John S. Mill, *On Liberty* (London: Longmans, Green, Reader and Dyer, 1869); Milton Friedman, *Capitalism and Freedom* (Chicago: University of Chicago Press, 1962); Friedrich Hayek, *The Road to Serfdom* (Chicago: University of Chicago Press, 1944).

6. For instance, Bruce C. Greenwald and Joseph E. Stiglitz, "Externalities in Economics with Imperfect Information and Incomplete Markets," *Quarterly Journal of Economics* 101, no. 2 (1986): 229–64, showed that whenever there is imperfect and asymmetric information and/or an imperfect set of risk markets—that is, *always*—there are pecuniary externalities that matter, and the economy is not (Pareto) efficient.

7. This claim was known as the second fundamental welfare theorem. For a general discussion of the reasons it does not hold generally, see Joseph E. Stiglitz, *Wither Socialism?* (Cambridge, MA: MIT Press, 1994).

8. Refer to Stiglitz, *Wither Socialism?*; see also Joseph E. Stiglitz, "Notes on Evolutionary Economics: Imperfect Capital Markets, Organizational Design, Long-Run Efficiency," in *Selected Scientific Papers: Rethinking the Economics of the Public Sector* (2026).

9. The literature establishing this is enormous. Kenneth J. Arrow, "An Extension of the Basic Theorems of Classical Welfare Economics," in *Proceedings of the Second*

Berkeley Symposium on Mathematical Statistics and Probability, ed. J. Neyman (1951), 507–32, and Gerard Debreu, "The Coefficient of Resource Utilization," *Econometrica* 19, no. 3 (July 1951): 273–92, showed that the conditions under which a market economy is efficient were very restrictive—though interestingly, Friedman and his followers paid little attention to the restrictive conditions needed for showing the efficiency of the market; they simply reasserted Adam Smith's claim (one that he qualified) that the pursuit of self-interest would lead, as if by an invisible hand, to the well-being of society. For them, ideology and prior beliefs trumped analytics.

Arrow and Debreu had provided *sufficient* conditions for the efficiency of markets. There followed a long and unsuccessful attempt to find weaker conditions. Arrow and Debreu had found the singular conditions under which markets were in general efficient. Moreover, markets with imperfect information were naturally not competitive, and even small sunk costs could lead to large market power. For an overview, see Joseph E. Stiglitz, "Technological Change, Sunk Costs, and Competition," *Brookings Paper on Economic Activity* 3 (1987): 883–947; Joseph E. Stiglitz, *The Economic Role of the State* (Oxford: Basil Blackwell, 1989); and Joseph E. Stiglitz, *The Selected Works of Joseph E. Stiglitz*, vol. 2, *Information and Economic Analysis: Applications to Capital, Labor, and Product Markets* (Oxford: Oxford University Press, 2013).

10. A claim that has, in general, been disproved, e.g., by Sanford J. Grossman and Joseph E. Stiglitz, "Information and Competitive Price Systems," *American Economic Review* 66, no. 2 (May 1976): 246–53; Sanford J. Grossman and Joseph E. Stiglitz, "On the Impossibility of Informationally Efficient Markets," *American Economic Review* 70, no. 3 (June 1980): 393–408. The preference-shaping role is deeper: just as cooperatives may make individuals more cooperative, current market arrangements may make individuals more selfish.

11. The notion that preferences can be and are shaped is a central pillar of a new strand of behavioral economics that has developed in the past fifteen years. See, for instance, Karla Hoff and Joseph E. Stiglitz, "Striving for Balance in Economics: Towards a Theory of the Social Determination of Behavior," *Journal of Economic Behavior & Organization* 126 (2016): 25–57. For an overview, see Allison Demeritt, Karla Hoff, and Joseph E. Stiglitz, *The Other Invisible Hand: The Power of Culture to Promote or Stymie Progress* (New York: Columbia University Press, 2022). There are some important and subtle distinctions often made between beliefs and preferences, though changes in either affect individual's behavior and the choices they make. Preferences are usually considered as an ordering over deterministic outcomes. Beliefs, on the other hand, relate to judgments about the consequences of certain actions and states of the world; and consequently (and importantly) beliefs affect the distribution over outcomes. Much of the support for the use of the price mechanism is based on beliefs about individual behavior and the functioning of the market economy, beliefs that may be far from correct.

12. Andrea Prat, "Media Power," *Journal of Political Economy* 126, no. 4 (2018): 1747–83. For a broader discussion, see Andrew Kosenko and Joseph E. Stiglitz, "Robust Theory and Fragile Practice: Endogenous Information in a World of Disinformation Part 2: Direct Communication," in *Elgar Companion to Information Economics*, ed. Daphne R. Raban and Julia Wlodarczuk (Cheltenham, UK: Edward Elgar, 2024).

13. The later analysis will suggest limits even on such claims.

14. This is particularly true of those on the Right. Mill, like later neoclassical economists, while recognizing that the presence of externalities might require government intervention, placed insufficient attention on the externalities and public goods that are

central to a twenty-first-century economy. Some of the Chicago economists (like Coase) went so far as to suggest that the markets could deal with externalities and public goods on their own. A huge literature has, by now, discredited this argument.

15. See Ronald Coase, "The Problem of Social Cost," *Journal of Law and Economics* 3 (October 1960): 1–44. He also argued that it didn't make any difference how one assigned property rights. Of course, in the absence of offsetting lump-sum redistributions (which do not exist), the assignment makes a large difference for the distribution of wealth and therefore for social welfare. In the presence of income effects, the assignment also makes a difference for the nature of the equilibrium that emerges.

16. There then becomes no simple way of eliciting how much each individual values the public good, that is, how much he would be willing to pay say the owner of the atmosphere to keep the level of pollutants low. On the other hand, the government can undertake a statistical analysis, calculating the benefits of reduced health care costs and increased life expectancy.

17. On efficiency under costs of enforcing property rights, see Ian A. MacKenzie and Markus Ohndorf, "Restricted Coasean bargaining," *Journal of Public Economics* 97 (January 2013): 296–307. See also Tore Ellingsen and Elena Paltseva, "Confining the Coase Theorem: Contracting, Ownership, and Free-Riding," *Review of Economic Studies* 83, no. 2 (April 2016): 547–86. On private information, see Joseph Farrell, "Information and the Coase Theorem," *Journal of Economic Perspectives* 1, no. 2 (Fall 1981): 113–29. On how seemingly voluntary transactions may be coercive, see Jonathan Harris and Brian Roach, *Environmental and Natural Resource Economics: A Contemporary Approach*, 4th ed. (Abingdon: Routledge, 2018).

18. They made the additional assumption that the (relevant measure of the) utility of any individual could be described by the same function of income. The new welfare economics emerging in the middle of the twentieth century argued that such interpersonal comparisons were not possible, and hence economists shifted their attention to the concept of Pareto efficiency—simply describing situations where no one could be made better off without making someone worse off. Such a framework puts no weight on inequality. Later in this chapter I will discuss the limitations of the Paretian perspective.

19. Joseph E. Stiglitz, *The Price of Inequality: How Today's Divided Society Endangers Our Future* (New York: W. W. Norton, 2012), a development of a brief earlier article in which I suggested ideas along those earlier in this paragraph: Joseph E. Stiglitz, "Of the 1%, by the 1%, for the 1%," *Vanity Fair*, May 2011.

   In some simple models where workers save little and capitalists do much of the savings, a tax on the income of capitalists (intended to reduce inequality) reduces capital accumulation, thereby lowering wages and increasing inequality. But there are policies of reinvesting the tax revenues in human and physical capital (public and private) which, in general, enhance the wellbeing of workers. See J. E. Stiglitz, "Pareto Efficient Taxation and Expenditures: Pre- and Re-distribution," *Journal of Public Economics* 162 (June 2018): 101–19.

20. For a discussion of the nature of the trade-offs in a simple model with a linear income tax, see J. E. Stiglitz, "Simple Formulae for Optimal Income Taxation and the Measurement of Inequality," *Arguments for a Better World: Essays in Honor of Amartya Sen, Volume I, Ethics, Welfare, and Measurement*, ed. K. Basu and R. Kanbur (Oxford: Oxford University Press, 2009), 535–66. For optimal marginal tax rates at the top, see Emmanuel Saez, "Using Elasticities to Derive Optimal Income Tax Rates," *Review of Economic Studies* 68 (2001): 205–29, and Peter Diamond and Emmanuel Saez, "The

Case for a Progressive Tax: From Basic Research to Policy Recommendations," *Journal of Economic Perspectives* 25, no. 4 (Fall 2011): 165–90.

21. Another market failure plays an important role in this obvious result: the inability of the poor to get the resources necessary to expand (efficiently) their opportunity sets because of imperfections in capital markets.

22. See Federico Cingano, "Trends in Income Inequality and Its Impact on Economic Growth," *OECD Social, Employment, and Migration Working Paper 163* (Paris: Organization for Economic Co-operation and Development, 2014); Andrew Berg, Jonathan D. Ostry, and Charalambos G. Tsangarides, "Redistribution, Inequality, and Growth," *IMF Staff Discussion Note 14/02* (Washington, DC: International Monetary Fund, 2014); and Andrew Berg, Prakash Loungani, and Jonathan D. Ostry, *Confronting Inequality: How Societies Can Choose Inclusive Growth* (New York: Columbia University Press, 2019).

23. See, e.g., Stiglitz, "Technological Change, Sunk Costs, and Competition," and Bruce C. Greenwald and Joseph E. Stiglitz, *Creating a Learning Society* (New York: Columbia University Press, 2014).

24. Personal correspondence.

25. As Akeel Bilgrami has pointed out: In fact, it is not obvious that talent can even be specified or conceptualized as such without also specifying what effort is needed to make it flower; and it is only the romantic tradition, which in its outsized commitment to glorifying "genius" presented talent as a self-standing property independent of effort.

26. It is worth noting that Europe does provide restraints, but the United States does not, as long as the monopoly power of the drug company is lawfully acquired.

27. Not all public goods are "pure" in the sense that their benefits are fully accessible to all (without cost); but the argument above holds even if much of the benefits are broadly available. The concept of pure public goods was first formalized by Paul A. Samuelson, "The Pure Theory of Public Expenditure," *Review of Economics and Statistics* 36, no. 4 (1954): 387–89. While most publicly provided goods are not *pure* in the sense defined by Samuelson, the central result that without government intervention there will be underprovision holds more generally. For a discussion of these cases, see Anthony B. Atkinson and Joseph E. Stiglitz, *Lectures on Public Economics* (New York: McGraw-Hill Book Company, 1980).

28. See, e.g., Greenwald and Stiglitz, *Creating a Learning Society* and Bruce C. Greenwald and Joseph E. Stiglitz, "Externalities in Economics with Imperfect Information and Incomplete Markets".

29. See, for instance, Elinor Ostrom, *Governing the Commons: The Evolution of Institutions for Collective Action* (Cambridge: Cambridge University Press, 1990).

30. See J. E. Stiglitz, "Toward a General Theory of Consumerism: Reflections on Keynes' *Economic Possibilities for Our Grandchildren*," in *Revisiting Keynes: Economic Possibilities for Our Grandchildren*, ed. G. Piga and L. Pecchi (Cambridge, MA: MIT Press, 2008), 40–85.

31. An example is the rotation among pharmacies that are open each Sunday in some European countries.

32. Akeel Bilgrami, "The Philosophical Significance of the Commons," *Social Research: An International Quarterly* 88 no. 1 (2021): 203–39.

33. See, e.g., Dilip Abreu, David Pearce, and Ennio Stacchetti, "Toward a Theory of Discounted Repeated Games with Imperfect Monitoring," *Econometrica* 58, no. 5 (September 1990): 1041–63. Note that a structuring of the rules and regulations of a

society (with, e.g., property rights) affects the enforceability of cooperative equilibrium. The (threat of) sanctions imposed in the communities studied by Ostrom suffices to sustain the required coordination.

34. Joseph Stiglitz, "Tapping the Brakes: Are Less Active Markets Safer and Better for the Economy?," paper presented at the Federal Reserve Bank of Atlanta Financial Markets Conference: Tuning Financial Regulation for Stability and Efficiency, April 15, 2014; Michael Lewis, *Flash Boys: A Wall Street Revolt* (New York: W. W. Norton, 2015).

35. This is a central criticism that Hoff and Stiglitz, in "Striving for Balance," provide of, say, the work of those who model individuals as choosing a set of preferences or beliefs or an identity that maximizes a meta-utility function, such as Roland Benabou and Jean Tirole, "Incentives and Prosocial Behavior," *American Economic Review* 96, no. 5 (2006): 1652–78; Roland Benabou and Jean Tirole, "Identity, Morals, and Taboos: Beliefs as Assets," *Quarterly Journal of Economics* 126, no. 2 (2011): 805–55.

36. Akeel Bilgrami has argued that while we are indeed born into and reared and acculturated into families, communities, and other such social contexts, the crucial point is that individuals have freedom to act, so our relationship to these contexts is not as of wolves to packs. This is because, unlike wolves, we possess reason and have the *capacity* to ask, "Do I have reason to do or think what my family or community or social tradition does or thinks? And just having that capacity to ask that *suffices* as grounds to say that we have, in some abstract sense, authorized the social norms we have been reared in. It is not required for authorization that we in each single case exercise that capacity explicitly." Bilgrami thus argues that "even in the case where we have been determined by our social environment, our relationship to that environment and the determination is not that of the wolf to his pack, and that is enough to see us as having a position of freedom that the wolf, by his nature, lacks. In fact, consider an even more strong case of being determined and seemingly unfree: in forming many everyday beliefs we are not exercising any freedom. I hear the patter of raindrops and I form the belief that it is raining. I am not free to *not* form that belief. It is determined that I will form it by the evidence of what I hear. Does it mean that there is no freedom involved at all? I don't think so. The fact is that I have the capacity to find it *thinkable* that it is not raining (because I have the capacity to contemplate that I might be being deceived, that the patter is coming from some other source than rain, etc. I would say that is even true of *seeing* raindrops, an even stronger case of being determined by the evidence to believe that it is raining. I still have the capacity to find it thinkable that I might be wrong—even though the circumstances might be strained for that to happen.) . . . Even when the evidence *compels* me to believe that it is raining, I have a certain capacity for reason as a result of which it is *thinkable* to me that it might not be raining, and that suffices for us to say that we have freedom of belief." He argues that there is not any difference between this situation and "the case of social acculturation into norms." But I remain unconvinced. While *some* individuals within a group are able to come to understand that the lens through which they see the world has been given to them, and decide to accept it or not, for many it is unthinkable to think outside those lenses; the lens is a part of their identity and it is unthinkable that they have another identity.

This skepticism of our ability to transcend biases is reinforced by recent research showing that the introspection required to understand lens formation is difficult to maintain even among those who have the most capacity for it. Mohsen Javdani and Ha-Joon Chang found through an RCT that changing source attributions from mainstream to less mainstream sources reduces economists' reported agreement with statements (with meaningful variation by gender, research area, and undergraduate major—consistent with ideological bias), despite 82 percent professing one should only pay attention to content. Interpretations of these results could vary depending on assumptions about the extent to which respondents' choices are calculated, but given the setting and plausible anonymity, the finding seem more reflective of subconscious biases that the participants do not recognize (as opposed to strategic conformity). See "Who Said or What Said? Estimating Ideological Bias in Views Among Economists" (September 1, 2019), https://papers.ssrn.com/sol3/papers.cfm?abstract_id=3356309.

Even if one has consciously "allowed" oneself to be trained or acculturated into prevailing social norms, different people may feel differently constrained when it comes to bearing the potential costs of rejecting norms. One's background, social standing, and power deeply determine the "budget" one has for deviating from norms, especially when the stakes are substantial. Even if we all have equal ability to question the prevailing norms, our freedom to act on this or update accordingly is far from equally distributed.

37. An experiment provides confirming evidence. Toxic content was randomly hidden on social media; it led to decreased ad and content consumption.

38. Human capital was at the center of economists' traditional discussion of the role of education. And schools do more than screen and signal abilities, as emphasized in more recent literature. This role in shaping individuals was ignored in the standard treatments because the economists' standard model simply *assumed* that individuals' preferences were fixed and given at birth.

39. Bilgrami, "The Philosophical Significance of the Commons."

40. In much of my work I have referred to "constrained Pareto efficiency," Constrained Pareto efficiency simply serves to remind us that we need to take into account imperfections of information and the costs of creating and running markets and of acquiring, processing, and disseminating information.

41. Robert E. Lucas, "The Industrial Revolution: Past and Future," *The Region*, 2003 Annual Report of the Federal Reserve Bank of Minneapolis (2004): 5–20. Lucas went on to say: "The potential for improving the lives of poor people by finding different ways of distributing current production is nothing compared to the apparently limitless potential of increasing production." But he failed to show that achieving a better distribution of income was antithetical to growth, and a key argument in my book *The Price of Inequality* and an immense body of subsequent research is that the opposite is true. America's excessive inequality is adverse to growth. In addition, Lucas failed to show that much, if any, of the fruits of the growth that he cited "trickled down" to those below in a relevant time span. Growth in the United States over the past four decades has left those at the bottom even worse off.

42. Interestingly, Juan-Carlos Córdoba and Geneviève Verdier, using an extended version of Robert E. Lucas's own model in *Models of Business Cycles* (New York: Basil Blackwell, 1987), show that his claim is not true, that societal welfare would have been higher with a more equalitarian distribution. Córdoba and Verdier, "Lucas vs. Lucas: On Inequality and Growth," IMF Working Paper IMF Institute WP/07/17, January 2007.

43. Technically, we might say the world is described by nonstationary stochastic processes.

44. George Stigler and Gary Becker, "De Gustibus Non Est Disputandum," *American Economic Review* 67, no. 2 (March 1977): 76–90.

45. Karla Hoff and Joseph E. Stiglitz, "Equilibrium Fictions: A Cognitive Approach to Societal Rigidity," *American Economic Review* 100, no. 2 (May 2010): 141–46.

46. In modern economics, preferences are inferred from revealed choices. Those choices in turn are based on beliefs about consequences, which in turn depend on cognition. Thus, while there are thought experiments where we could separate out preferences from cognition, in practice, they are intermingled. Indeed, only under restrictive conditions can we describe choices as if individuals were maximizing their expected utility, where we can define a *subjective* probability distribution over the relevant uncertain variables (states of nature). See Leonard J. Savage, *The Foundation of Statistics* (New York: John Wiley, 1954).

47. See, e.g., Abi Adams, Laurens Cherchye, Bram De Rock, and Ewout Verriest, "Consume Now or Later? Time Inconsistency, Collective Choice, and Revealed Preference," *American Economic Review* 104, no. 12 (December 2014): 4147–83.

48. A slightly different vocabulary and perspective may be useful. In standard economics, rationality only means consistency—that if we choose A over B, we consistently do, and that if we prefer A over B and B over C, we prefer A over C (transitive ordering). Standard economics also assumes that we have a complete ordering, that is, we know our rankings of all possible choices, even of things we have not experienced. Within these transitive complete orderings, preferences (choices) cannot exhibit the kinds of irrationalities we often see expressed and sometimes see practiced: Individuals express "preferences" for conflicting things, like eating candy and losing weight. They express preferences only over realizable outcomes.

   But these assumptions are questionable. First, there is no way we can know today how we will feel twenty years from now. (See the discussion in my *Information and Economic Analysis*.) Moreover, we are, as many philosophers have emphasized, fundamentally a different person now than we were then. In addition, outside of economics, within other branches of the social sciences, there are well accepted perspectives saying that individuals have multiple identities, with the identity that is expressed at any moment depending on the context. (See Hoff and Stiglitz, "Striving for Balance," and Demeritt, Hoff, and Stiglitz, *The Other Invisible Hand*.) In that case, individuals' choices may not even exhibit transitivity.

49. These were central ideas in my book *The Price of Inequality*.

50. And that's why it's such a mistake to assess market power in the media by looking just at market power in the market for advertising.

51. Two recent papers have attempted to defend the Washington Consensus policies in Africa, arguing that the poor performance of those adopting the policies in the years before 2000 has been at least partly offset by strong performance since 2000. As Easterly, the author of one of these papers, himself points out, there is no causality in these analyses; for example, the stronger performance may be due to other factors, not appropriately accounted for, like high commodity prices. (Similar objections can be raised to some of the earlier critiques of the Washington consensus policies.) But equally, if there is some mean reversion from recessionary policies induced, say, by extreme austerity, one should expect higher growth rates. Interestingly, Archibong, the author of the other study, fails to note, for instance, that the countries that they labeled were "non-reformers" while doing more poorly in growth rates in the post 2000 era, since by 2019 had grown their incomes more than twice as much as the reformers by the end of the forty-year period beginning in 1980. Belinda Archibong, Brahima Coulibaly, and Ngozi Okonjo-Iweala, "Washington Consensus Reforms and Lessons for Economic Performance in Sub-Saharan Africa," *Journal of Economic Perspectives* 35, no. 3 (Summer 2021): 133–56; Bill Easterly, "In Search of Reforms for Growth: New Stylized Facts on Policy and Growth Outcomes," NBER Working Paper 26318, http://www.nber.org/papers/w26318.

52. For an overview, see Suresh Naidu, Dani Rodrik, and Gabriel Zucman, "Economics After Neoliberalism," *Boston Review*, Summer 2019.

53. Milton Friedman, "A Friedman Doctrine: The Social Responsibility of Business Is to Increase Its Profits," *New York Times Magazine*, September 13, 1970.

54. See Joseph E. Stiglitz, "On the Optimality of the Stock Market Allocation of Investment," *Quarterly Journal of Economics* 86, no. 1 (February 1972): 25–60; Sandy Grossman and Joseph E. Stiglitz, "On Value Maximization and Alternative Objectives of the Firm," *Journal of Finance* 32, no. 2 (May 1977): 389–402; and Sandy Grossman and Joseph E. Stiglitz, "Stockholder Unanimity in the Making of Production and Financial Decisions," *Quarterly Journal of Economics* 94, no. 3 (May 1980): 543–66.

55. This is the central theme of two books I wrote in 2015 and 2020, the first focusing on the US economy, written with colleagues at the Roosevelt Institute, and the second on the European economy, written with the Foundation of European Progressive Studies and Carter Dougherty. See Nell Abernathy, Adam Hersh, Susan Holmberg, Mike Konczal, and Joseph E. Stiglitz, *Rewriting the Rules of the American Economy: An Agenda for Growth and Shared Prosperity* (New York: W. W. Norton, 2015); and Carter Daugherty and Joseph E. Stiglitz, *Rewriting the Rules of the European Economy: An Agenda for Growth and Shared Prosperity* (New York: W. W. Norton, 2020).

56. See, for instance, Joseph E. Stiglitz, *Globalization and Its Discontents* (New York: W. W. Norton, 2002); Joseph E. Stiglitz, *Globalization and Its Discontents Revisited: Anti-Globalization in the Era of Trump* (New York: W. W. Norton, 2017); Andrew Charlton and Joseph E. Stiglitz, *Fair Trade for All: How Trade Can Promote Development* (New York: Oxford University Press, 2005); Joseph E. Stiglitz, *Making Globalization Work* (New York: W. W. Norton, 2006); Dean Baker, Arjun Jayadev, and Joseph E. Stiglitz, "Innovation, Intellectual Property, and Development: A Better Set of Approaches for the 21st Century" (July 2017), https://www.cepr.net/images/stories/reports/baker-jayadev-stiglitz-innovation-ip-development-2017-07.pdf.

57. See Joseph E. Stiglitz, "Regulating Multinational Corporations: Towards Principles of Cross-Border Legal Frameworks in a Globalized World Balancing Rights with Responsibilities," *American University International Law Review* 23, no. 3 (2007): 451–558; and Joseph E. Stiglitz, "Towards a Twenty-First Century Investment Agreement," in *Yearbook on International Investment Law and Policy 2015–2016*, ed. Lise Johnson and Lisa Sachs (Oxford: Oxford University Press, 2017), xiii–xxviii.

58. Even when there were large fixed costs, so that there was a natural monopoly, advocates of unfettered markets claimed that competition *for* the market would replace competition *in* the market, and the resulting equilibrium would be efficient. This doctrine was called "contestability." See William J. Baumol, John C. Panzar, and Robert D. Willig, "Contestable Markets: An Uprising in the Theory of Industry Structure: Reply," *American Economic Review* 73, no. 3 (1983): 491–96. But even with arbitrarily small fixed costs, potential competition could not replace actual competition. See Stiglitz, "Technological Change, Sunk Costs, and Competition," and Greenwald and Stiglitz, *Creating a Learning Society*.

59. Consider, for instance, the following two quotes from *The Wealth of Nations*: "People of the same trade seldom meet together, even for merriment and diversion, but the conversation ends in a conspiracy against the public, or in some contrivance to raise prices," and "Our merchants and masters complain much of the bad effects of high wages in raising the price and lessening the sale of goods. They say nothing concerning the bad effects of high profits. They are silent with regard to the pernicious effects of their own gains. They complain only of those of other people."

60. This is a key idea in my book *Whither Socialism?* (Cambridge, MA: MIT Press, 1994).

5. Capitalism and the Question of Freedom

1. Irfan Habib, "Caste in Indian History," in *Essays on Indian History: Towards a Marxist Perception* (Delhi: Tulika Books, 2017).
2. J. A. Schumpeter, "Karl Marx," in *Ten Great Economists* (New York: Oxford University Press, 1952).
3. A formal presentation of this idea, though it suffers from accepting Say's law and hence the impossibility of any deficiency of aggregate demand, is to be found in R. M. Goodwin, "A Growth Cycle," in *Capitalism, Socialism and Economic Growth: Essays Presented to Maurice Dobb*, ed. C. H. Feinstein (Cambridge: Cambridge University Press, 1967), 54–58.
4. In the Keynesian tradition, it was Joan Robinson who had first raised this question through her concept of the "inflationary barrier." See her *Accumulation of Capital* (London: Macmillan, 1956).
5. This idea of Keynes was expressed as a proposal by Lloyd George, the leader of the Liberal Party, to which Keynes belonged. The British treasury "refuted" the theory behind this proposal through what was called the "Treasury View." The erroneousness of the "Treasury View" was pointed out by Keynes's pupil Richard Kahn in his famous article on the "multiplier," "The Relation of Home Investment to Unemployment," *Economic Journal* 41, no.162 (2005): 172–98.
6. This is what Keynes had to say in his article "National Self-Sufficiency," *Yale Review* 22, no. 4 (June 1933): 755–69: "The decadent international but individualistic capitalism, in the hands of which we found ourselves after the War, is not a success. It is not intelligent, it is not beautiful, it is not just, it is not virtuous—and it doesn't deliver the goods. In short, we dislike it and we are beginning to despise it."
7. "Inequality Is Holding Back the Recovery," *New York Times*, January 13, 2013.
8. For a critique of Thomas Piketty's *Capital in the Twenty-First Century*, see Prabhat Patnaik, "Capitalism, Inequality and Globalization," *International Journal of Political Economy* 43, no. 3 (2014): 55–69.
9. Michal Kalecki had seen the earlier (1930s) fascism as "a partnership of big business with fascist upstarts." See "Political Aspects of Full Employment," in *Selected Essays in the Dynamics of the Capitalist Economy 1933–1970* (Cambridge: Cambridge University Press, 1971).

6. Whither Economic Rights?

1. Prabhat Patnaik, "A Left Approach to Development," *Economic and Political Weekly* 45, no. 30 (July 24, 2010): 33–37. It is worth noting that a similar recent proposal for economic rights being inserted as fundamental rights into a national constitution was rejected in Chile.
2. By "properly so-called," what I am stressing is that the proposal is about fundamental rights, nothing less. The point is not merely that these are not vaguely declared directive principles; they are not rights in any low-profile sense of the term. They are fundamental rights, the deepest commitments of a constitution.
3. This phrase gets a prominent discussion in John Rawls's *A Theory of Justice* (Cambridge, MA: Harvard University Press, 1971). It is also the main theme of his essay "The Priority of Right and Ideas of the Good," *Philosophy and Public Affairs*, 17, no. 4 (Autumn 1988): 251–76. In my essay "Liberalism and Identity," in *Religion in Liberal*

Political Philosophy, ed. Cecile Laborde and Aurelia Bardon (New York: Oxford University Press, 2017), 275–94, I argue that although rights are prior to the good in the sense of providing constraints on the good as expounded before, one nevertheless inevitably has to appeal to the good and often to variable conceptions of the good when one is trying to persuade people with diverse value commitments to embrace one or other right. Even if, as I argue here, a right must have its foundations in deep and fundamental grounds that appeal to the most basic and universal aspects of human nature, the reasons by which one persuades people to adopt a right may have to appeal to *their* specific conceptions of the good, conceptions that may vary among them. There is no inconsistency in this. Foundational grounding and persuasion of people are distinct enterprises.

4. This issue is utterly familiar and has been the topic of a great deal of discussion ever since the earliest formulations of socialist ideals. I will not be taking it up here. If it is not already obvious, the point here is not that socialism does not allow for the existence of any private property, only that it does not allow it as a right and it does not allow it in the form that is defining of relations in a capitalist economic formation.

5. See chapter 10 in my *Secularism, Identity, and Enchantment* (Cambridge, MA: Harvard University Press, 2014) for the relevance of the distinction between thick and thin notions of rationality in the political sphere. Quite apart from the political sphere, speaking quite generally, for human subjects, thin rationality is *not optional*. To be capable of thought and action at all is to exemplify (not perfectly, but considerably) rationality in the thin sense. A massive or considerable failure of thin rationality in our thinking puts into doubt that it is thinking at all. Thin rationality can be codified, but we do not have to be self-consciously applying the codes or to be able to articulate the codes. We simply exemplify them in our thought from whatever early age the capacity for reason grows in us. (In this sense, it is just like our counting, say, marbles—after a certain early age—exemplifying the Peano axioms, without us either articulating them or in any way self-consciously applying them.) What sorts of notions of reason and rationality get counted as thin is an interesting question. Though perhaps no list can (or should) determinately be made, one can safely assume that something like deductive rationality, inductive rationality (that is, rationality roughly codified by inductive logic or "confirmation theory"), and some spare understanding of the codifications of decision theory, fall within thin rationality. But not all "thin" ideas of reason are codified. What I am appealing to here, in stating what underlies autonomy, is something that there is no question of codifying. The autonomy-reflecting question is raised not from the point of view of any codified account of reason; it is rather simply the idea of rationality that is expressed by the most common or garden notion of "reasons." The autonomy-reflecting question is basically asking: "Do I have *reason or reasons* to do or think what the group is thinking and doing?" It is the most general and common exercise of one's reason. Thus, "thin." The sense in which it contrasts with a thick conception of reason is immediately apparent when one puts the question (more thickly) as follows: Do I have a *self-interested reason* to do or think that the group does or thinks?

6. See Carol Rovane, *The Bounds of Agency* (Princeton, NJ: Princeton University Press, 1998), for a detailed account of collective deliberation and rationality and the idea of group agency and personhood.

7. I say "standardly understood" with good reason. There is a tendency, in those who subscribe to liberalism as a doctrine, to seek to accommodate all sorts of dissenting ideas (such as those I mention later in the paragraph) within the doctrine. These efforts

at nonstandard liberalism are bootless and succeed in doing little other than bloating the doctrine to a point that it becomes all things to all and, thus, far less interesting than it is in its standard form, even if the standard doctrine is not in the end plausible.

8. Quentin Skinner, *Hobbes and Republican Liberty* (New York: Cambridge University Press, 2008). The classic paper characterizing liberalism in terms of "negative liberty" and expressing deep anxieties about positive ideals of liberty is Isaiah Berlin's "Two Concepts of Liberty," *Oxford Inaugural Lecture* 2008 (Oxford: Clarendon Press 2008). Rousseau and Marx, and those whom they have influenced, are the explicit targets of Berlin's criticisms of positive liberty.

9. Karl Marx, "On the Jewish Question," is the most cited location for this vehement dismissal of rights, though it also surfaces in *The Communist Manifesto*.

10. Eric Hobsbawm, *The Age of Revolution 1789–1848* (London: Weidenfeld and Nicholson, 1962).

11. In my own case, I have also been grappling with the challenges to the idea of rights that come from Gandhi's somewhat different criticisms of liberalism. Since I am not a liberal, this challenge is partly congenial to me, though its relevance to rights is a subtle and delicate matter. Gandhi, as is well known, accepted the proposals for economic rights in the Karachi Resolution that are invoked by Patnaik. In a curious way, Gandhi reverses the tendency of most liberals, who tend to emphasize the rights of liberty over the rights that would lift people from destitution. But I cannot elaborate on this here.

12. There is a small body of philosophical writing on basic needs and rights. See Len Doyal and Ian Gough, *A Theory of Human Need* (New York: Springer, 1991); H. J. McCloskey, "Human Needs, Rights, and Political Values," *American Philosophical Quarterly* 13, no. 1 (January 1976): 1–11; David Wiggins and Sira Derman, "Needs, Need, Needing," *Journal of Medical Ethics* 13 (1987): 62–68; and David Braybrooke, *Meeting Needs* (Princeton, NJ: Princeton University Press, 1987). I have benefited from these writings as also by conversations with Brian Barry in the graduate seminars he and I taught together at Columbia University.

13. Of course, some relativization may well be necessary despite this assumption of determinacy—those who labor in fields or factories may need to ingest more calories than those who sit at a desk all day long.

14. See Amartya Sen, "Goods and People," in *Resources, Values, and Development* (Malden, MA: Basil Blackwell, 1984), for these criticisms.

15. Of the many writings by Sen elaborating his notion of capabilities, see especially "Well-Being, Agency, and Freedom," *Journal of Philosophy* 82, no. 4 (1985): XXX (these were the Dewey Lectures given at Columbia University in 1984), and *Development as Freedom* (New York: Knopf, 1999).

16. The familiar, relevant classic texts are, of course, G. W. Hegel, *Phenomenology of Spirit* (New York: Cambridge University Press, 2018), and Karl Marx, *Critique of Hegel's Philosophy of Right* (New York: Cambridge University Press, 1977).

17. This qualitative differential in the notion of experience of needs may quite properly be said to extend to related notions of "sentience," "suffering," and so on.

18. Aristotelian *ethics* makes much of a notion of "living well" or "flourishing" that sought precisely to speak to the fact that human animals are set apart from other animals in their experience of even the basic needs by the fact of their possession of reason and freedom. But I will be arguing that those "ethical" conceptions should not carry over into the "political" case for economic rights, since once they enter the political and constitutional arena where the case for rights has to be pressed, to see the fulfillment

of basic needs as part of a richer notion of living well is to weaken that *political* case for their fulfillment.

19. Most explicitly in his "Equality of What?," in *Tanner Lectures on Human Values*, ed. S. M. McMurrin (New York: Cambridge University Press, 1979), and *Inequality Re-Examined* (Oxford: Clarendon Press, 1992).

20. These are two quite separate external sources. Should the external markets in the South even cease to matter, the first source—of supply of primary commodities—remains indispensable.

21. The expression and the idea of "Ulysses and the Sirens" is the theme of a book by Jon Elster, *Ulysses and the Sirens* (New York: Cambridge University Press, 1984), though it was anticipated by Derek Parfit in his example of the Russian Prince in his book *Reasons and Persons* (New York: Oxford University Press, 1984) and some papers by him that preceded that book. But Parfit and Elster are both focused on the moral psychology of individuals, not on politics and rights. I have exploited the idea of Ulysses and the Sirens to characterize a notion of subjective identity that is relevant to politics in various papers of mine, some of which are collected in the section on "Identity" in *Secularism, Identity, and Enchantment*. Elster, in a subsequent book, *Ulysses Unbound* (New York: Cambridge University Press, 2000), is critical of my use of the idea in exploring the notion of identity. But I think the criticism is based on a misunderstanding, as Kryster Bykvist points out in her review of Elster's book in *Ethics* 112 (2002): 375–78. Sometimes rights are described as precommitments. That is intended to capture something like the Ulysses and the Sirens idea, but the word "precommitment" is incoherent since the idea of postcommitments makes no sense.

22. When I say "that is how seriously we have to take rights," I am harking back to the title of Ronald Dworkin's book *Taking Rights Seriously* (Cambridge, MA: Harvard University Press, 2017). Dworkin, however, does not take up the Ulysses and the Sirens feature of rights and is focused much more on their priority over the good, which he is well known to have developed as the idea that rights can *trump* the good.

7. *Roe v. Wade*: Freedom of the Woman Versus Freedom of the Fetus

1. See John M. Riddle, *Contraception and Abortion from the Ancient World to the Renaissance* (Cambridge, MA: Harvard University Press, 1992), 18.

2. Quoted in Angus McLaren, *Reproductive Rituals* (New York: Methuen, 1984), 95.

3. See Geoffrey R. Stone, *Sex and the Constitution: Sex, Religion and Law from America's Origins to the Twenty-First Century* (New York: Liveright, 2017), ch. 9.

4. Clifford Browder, *The Wickedest Woman in New York: Madama Restell, The Abortionist* (New York: Archon Books, 1988), 9.

5. Stone, *Sex and the Constitution*, 187–89.

6. Stone, *Sex and the Constitution*, 189.

7. Stone, *Sex and the Constitution*, 370–74.

8. Linda Greenhouse and Reva Siegel, *Before Roe v. Wade* (London: Kaplan, 2010), 70–71.

9. Stone, *Sex and the Constitution*, 375–76.

10. Stone, *Sex and the Constitution*, 376–78.

11. Stone, *Sex and the Constitution*, 378–83.

12. *Abele v. Markle*, 342 F. Supp. 800, 801–804 (D. Conn. 1972).

13. *Roe v. Wade*, 410 U.S. 113 (1973), 116–17.
14. *Roe v. Wade*, 136–41.
15. *Roe v. Wade*, 147–48.
16. *Roe v. Wade*, 148–50.
17. *Roe v. Wade*, 150–51 (emphasis added).
18. *Roe v. Wade*, 152–53.
19. *Eisenstadt v. Baird*, 405 U.S. 438 (1972), 453. See also *Roe v. Wade*, 152–53.
20. *Roe v. Wade*, 153.
21. *Roe v. Wade*, 153–54.
22. *Roe v. Wade*, 159–60, 162.
23. *Roe v. Wade*, 163–64.
24. *Roe v. Wade*, 221–22.
25. See Stone, *Sex and the Constitution*, 393–95.
26. See Stone, *Sex and the Constitution*, 401–6.
27. Brief for the United States as amicus curiae in *Planned Parenthood of Southeastern Pennsylvania v. Casey*, quoted in David G. Savage, *Turning Right: The Making of the Rehnquist Supreme Court* (New York: John Wiley & Sons, 1992), 456.
28. *Planned Parenthood of Southeastern Pennsylvania v. Casey*, 505 U.S. (1992), 845–46.
29. *Planned Parenthood of Southeastern Pennsylvania v. Casey*, 836.
30. *Planned Parenthood of Southeastern Pennsylvania v. Casey*, 872, 870 (opinion of O'Connor, Kennedy, and Souter).
31. *Planned Parenthood of Southeastern Pennsylvania v. Casey*, 870–72, 874, 877–78 (opinion of O'Connor, Kennedy, and Souter).
32. *Planned Parenthood of Southeastern Pennsylvania v. Casey*, 923 (opinion of Blackmun).
33. *Planned Parenthood of Southeastern Pennsylvania v. Casey*, 923, 943 (opinion of Blackmun).

8. Freedom and Coercion in Public Health

1. M. L. Nixon, L. Mahmoud, and S. A. Glantz, "Tobacco Industry Litigation to Deter Local Public Health Ordinances: The Industry Usually Loses in Court," *Tobacco Control* 13, no. 1 (2004): 65–73.
2. American Lung Association, "Smokefree Air Laws," September 10, 2024, https://www.lung.org/policy-advocacy/tobacco/smokefree-environments/smokefree-air laws.
3. FindLaw, "State Traffic Laws," 2025, https://www.findlaw.com/traffic/traffic-tickets/state-traffic-laws.html.
4. US Department of Labor, Occupational Safety and Health Administration, "Access to Employee Exposure and Medical Records," OSHA 3110, 2020 (revised), https://www.osha.gov/sites/default/files/publications/osha3110.pdf.
5. US Supreme Court, *Jacobson v. Massachusetts*, 197 , 11 (1905).
6. President Dwight D. Eisenhower," Statement by the President on the Polio Vaccine Situation," May 31, 1955, American Presidency Project, https://www.presidency.ucsb.edu/documents/statement-the-president-the-polio-vaccinesituation.
7. A. J. Wakefield, S. H. Murch, A. Anthony, J. Linnell, D. M. Casson, M. Malik, et al., "Ileal-Lymphoid Nodular Hyperplasia, Non-specific Colitis, and Pervasive Developmental Disorder in Children," *The Lancet* 3519, no. 9103 (1998): 637–41; Editors of *The

Lancet, "Retraction—Ileal-Lymphoid Nodular Hyperplasia, Non-specific Colitis, and Pervasive Developmental Disorder in Children," *The Lancet* 375, no. 9713 (2010): 445.

8. M. K. Doll and J. W. Correira, "Revisiting the 2014–15 Disneyland Measles Outbreak and Its Influence on Pediatric Vaccinations," *Human Vaccines & Immunotherapeutics* 17, no. 11 (November 2, 2021):4210–15.

9. National Conference of State Legislature, "States with Religious and Philosophical Exemptions from School Immunization Requirements," updated March 10, 2025, https://www.ncsl.org/research/health/school-immunization-exemption-state-laws .aspx.

10. A. Mandavilli, "How Often Can You Be Infected with the Coronavirus?," *New York Times,* May 16, 2022.

11. R. Klitzman, "Pandemic Politics: What Leaders Should—and Shouldn't—Learn from Napoleon," *STAT* , June 25, 2020, https://www.statnews.com/2020/06/25/napoleon -bonaparte-pandemic-politics-current-leaders/.

12. B. Tolchin, C. Oladele, D. Galusha, N. Kashyap, M. Showstark, J. Bonito, et al., "Racial Disparities in the SOFA Score Among Patients Hospitalized with COVID-19," *PLoS One* 17, no. 16 (2021): e0257608.

13. Centers for Disease Control and Prevention, "Mask Guidance," March 21, 2022, https:// www.cdc.gov/coronavirus/2019-ncov/easy-to-read/mask-guidance.html.

14. E. Nolan, "Patti LuPone Yells at Audience Member Without Mask: 'Get the F** Out,' " *Newsweek,* May 11, 2022, https://www.newsweek.com/patti-lupone-audience-mask company-twitter-viral-company-1705498.

15. S. Banerjee, "Much Relief, Some Concern as Quebec Becomes Last Province to Lift COVID-19 Mask Rules," CBC, May 14, 2022, https://www.cbc.ca/news/canada /montreal/quebec-lastprovince-to-lift-masks-1.6453507.

16. K. O. Ha, "Hong Kong Reports Record Covid Cases as Morgues Near Capacity," *Bloomberg,* February 27, 2022, https://www.bloomberg.com/news/articles/2022-02-27 /hong-kongrecords-26-026-reported-covid-cases-83-deaths.

17. Kaiser Family Foundation, "KFF COVID-19 Vaccine Monitor," April 2022, https://www .kff.org/coronavirus-covid-19/dashboard/kff-covid-19-vaccine-monitordashboard/.

18. H. Razzaghi, A. Srivastav, M. A. de Perio, A. S. Laney, and C. L. Black, "Influenza and COVID-19 Vaccination Coverage Among Health Care Personnel—United States, 2021–22," *Morbidity and Mortality Weekly Report* 17, no. 42 (October 21, 2022): 1319–26.

19. Centers for Disease Control and Prevention, "Influenza and COVID-19 Vaccination Coverage Among Health Care Personnel – United States, 2023-24 Influenza Season," https://www.cdc.gov/fluvaxview/coverage-by-season/health-care-personnel -coverage-2023-24.html#:~:text=Overall%2C%2075.4%25%20of%20HCP%20 reported,%E2%80%9324%20COVID%2D19%20vaccine.

20. US Equal Employment Opportunity Commission, "Section 12: Religious Discrimination," January 15, 2021, https://www.eeoc.gov/laws/guidance/section-12 -religiousdiscrimination.

21. Reuters Fact Check, "Fact Check: Johnson & Johnson's COVID-19 Vaccine Does Not Contain Aborted Fetal Cells," April 1, 2021, https://www.reuters.com/article/factcheck -johnson-aborted/fact-check-johnson-johnsonscovid-19-vaccine-does-not-contain -aborted-fetal-cells-idUSL1N2LU1T9.

22. Cincinnati Children's, "Coronavirus (COVID-19) Vaccines: Myths and Truths," January 2021, https://www.cincinnatichildrens.org/patients/coronavirusinformation /vaccines/bustingmyths.

23. American Medical Association, "Code of Medical Ethics Opinion 7.3.5." https://www .amaassn.org/delivering-care/ethics/research-using-human-fetal-tissue.

24. US Equal Employment Opportunity Commission, "Laws & Guidance," https://www
    .eeoc.gov/laws-guidance-0; "What You Should Know About COVID 19 and the ADA,
    the Rehabilitation Act, and Other EEO Laws," updated March 14, 2022, https://www
    .eeoc.gov/wysk/what-you-should-know-about-covid-19-and-adarehabilitation-act
    -and-other-eeo-laws.

25. D. Watkins, "Pope Francis Urges People to Get Vaccinated Against Covid-19," Vatican
    News, August 21, 2021, https://www.vaticannews.va/en/pope/news/2021-08/pope
    -francisappeal-covid-19-vaccines-act-of-love.html; Redeeming Babel in Partnership with
    the National Association of Evangelicals, COVID Collaborative, the Ad Council, Values
    Partnerships and Public Square Strategies, "Biblical Thinking on the COVID Vaccine,"
    2022, https://www.christiansandthevaccine.com/; First Presidency of the Church of Jesus
    Christ of Latter-day Saints, "The First Presidency Urges Latter-day Saints to Wear Face
    Masks When Needed and Get Vaccinated Against COVID-19," August 12, 2021, https://
    newsroom.churchofjesuschrist.org/article/firstpresidency-message-covid-19-august-2021.

26. Christian Science, "A Christian Science Perspective on Vaccination and Public Health,"
    2022, https://www.christianscience.com/press-room/a-christian-science-perspective
    -onvaccination-and-public-health.

27. Legal Information Institute, *Schenck v. United States. Baer v. Same*, https://www.law
    .cornell.edu/supremecourt/text/249/47.

28. R. Maruf, "Walmart Drops Mask Mandate for Vaccinated Employees," CNN.com. Feb-
    ruary 12, 2022, https://www.cnn.com/2022/02/12/business/walmart-mask-covid-policy
    /index.html; Museum of Modern Art, "Visit Us Safely," 2022, https://www.moma
    .org/visit/tips.

29. The White House, "Briefing Room: Fact Sheet: Biden Administration Announces
    Details of Two Major Vaccination Policies," November 4, 2021, https://www.whitehouse
    .gov/briefing-room/statements-releases/2021/11/04/fact-sheetbiden-administration
    -announces-details-of-two-major-vaccination-policies/.

30. Supreme Court of the United States, *21A240 Biden v. Missouri*, January 13, 2022, https://
    www.supremecourt.gov/opinions/21pdf/21a240_d18e.pdf.

31. G. Vogel, "Sweden's Gamble," *Science* 370, no. 6513 (October 9, 2020): 159–63.

32. T. Carlson, "COVID Lunacy Will End in 2022," transcript, *Tucker Carlson Tonight*,
    January 3, 2021, https://www.foxnews.com/transcript/tucker-covid-lunacy-will-end-in
    -2022.

33. L. Egan, "Trump Calls Coronavirus Democrats' 'New Hoax,'" NBC News, February 28,
    2020, https://www.nbcnews.com/politics/donald-trump/trump-calls-coronavirus
    -democrats-new-hoax-n1145721.

34. B. Jones, "The Changing Political Geography of COVID-19 Over the Last Two Years,"
    Pew Research Center, March 3, 2022, https://www.pewresearch.org/politics/2022/03
    /03/thechanging-political-geography-of-covid-19-over-the-last-two-years/.

35. L. Hill and S. Artiga, "COVID-19 Cases and Deaths by Race/Ethnicity: Current Data
    and Changes Over Time," KFF, February 22, 2022, https://www.kff.org/coronavirus
    -covid-19/issuebrief/covid-19-cases-and-deaths-by-race-ethnicity-current-data-and
    -changes-over-time/.

36. Johns Hopkins University of Medicine, "Coronavirus Resource Center," final data col-
    lection March 10, 2023, https://coronavirus.jhu.edu/.

37. Pew Research Center, "Beyond Distrust: How Americans View Their Government,"
    Pew Research Center, November 15, 2015, https://www.pewresearch.org/politics/2015
    /11/23/beyond-distrust-how-americans-viewtheir-government/.

38. P. Boyle, "Why Do So Many Americans Distrust Science?," AAMC, May 4, 2022,
    https://www.aamc.org/news-insights/why-do-so-many-americans-distrust-science;

World Health Organization, "Infodemic," 2022, https://www.who.int/healthtopics/infodemic#tab=tab_1.

39. United States Holocaust Memorial Museum, "Bibliographies: Medical Experiments," 2022, https://www.ushmm.org/collections/bibliography/medical-experiments.

40. J. Kifner, "Scholar Sets Off Gastronomic False Alarm," *New York Times*, September 8, 2001; R. Klitzman, "Did Facebook's Experiment Violate Ethics?," CNN.com, July 2, 2014.

41. Article One Advisors, "Assessing the Human Rights Impact of Meta's Platforms in the Philippines: Executive Summary for Meta," December 2020, https://about.fb.com/wpcontent/uploads/2021/12/Meta-Philippines_HRIA_Executive-Summary_Dec-2021.pdf.

42. National Kidney Foundation, "Long-Term Risks," 2019, https://www.kidney.org/transplantation/livingdonors/long-term-risks.

43. R. Klitzman, *The Ethics Police? The Struggle to Make Human Research Safe* (New York: Oxford University Press, 2015).

44. D. Kahneman, *Thinking, Fast and Slow* (New York: Farrar, Straus and Giroux, 2013); D. Kahneman and D. Tversky, *Choices, Values, and Frames* (New York: Cambridge University Press, 2000).

9. The Prosecution of Gender Equal Abrahamic Circumcision: Implications for Jews and Muslims

I wish to express my great appreciation to Jonathan Cole, Jerome Davidson, Birgitta Essen, Allan Jacobs, Sara Johnsdotter, Frank Kessel, and Lawrence Sager for their comments and/or editorial suggestions on the original draft of this essay.

1. Richard A. Shweder, "Permitting Gender Equality in Abrahamic Circumcision: The Central Argument—in Retrospect and Reply" and "The Prosecution of Dawoodi Bohra Women: Some Reasonable Doubts," *Global Discourse: An Interdisciplinary Journal of Current Affairs* 12 (2022): 211–44 and 9–27.

2. Philip Lefkowitz, "Khitan and Milah," *Times of Israel*, May 6, 2017. For those who are familiar with his writings, I found the spirit of the Rabbi's admonition reminiscent of Martin Niemoller's famous, rousing, and ominous verse "First they came for . . ."

3. Rosie Duivenbode, "Reflecting on the Language We Use," *Islamic Horizons*, January–February 2018, 54–55.

4. Dorian Lambelet Coleman, "The Seattle Compromise: Multicultural Sensitivity and Americanization," *Duke Law Review* 47 (1998): 717–83.

5. Kavita Shah Arora and Allan J. Jacobs, "Female Genital Alteration: A Compromise Solution," *Journal of Medical Ethics* 42, no. 3 (2016): 158–54.

6. Aasim I. Padela and Rosie Duivenbode, "Morals, Medicine and Female Genital Cutting," Hastings Bioethics Forum, Health and Health Care, November 15, 2017, www.thehastingscenter.org/medicine-morals-female-genital-cutting/.

7. Ingvild Bergom Lunde and Matthew Thomas Johnson, eds., *Gender Equality in Abrahamic Circumcision: Why or Why Not?* Special issue of *Global Discourse: An Interdisciplinary Journal of Current Affairs* 12, no. 1 (2022).

8. David Hackett Fischer, *Albion's Seed: Four British Folkways in America* (New York: Oxford University Press); Colin Woodard, *American Nations: A History of the Eleven Rival Regional Cultures of North America* (New York: Penguin Books, 2012).

9. See, for example, Arthur N. Eisenberg, "Accommodation and Coherence: In Search of a Unified Theory for Adjudicating Claims of Faith, Culture and Conscience," in *Engaging Cultural Differences: The Multicultural Challenge in Liberal Democracies*, ed. Richard A. Shweder, Martha Minow, and Hazel Rose Markus (New York: Russell Sage Foundation Press, 2002), 147–64; Christopher L. Eisgruber and Lawrence G. Sager, "Why the Religious Freedom Restoration Act Is Unconstitutional," *New York University Law Review* 69 (1994):437–76, and "Unthinking Religious Freedom," *Texas Law Review* 74 (1996): 577–614; Cécile Laborde, *Liberalism's Religion* (Cambridge, MA: Harvard University Press, 2017); Michael W. McConnell, "The Origins and Historical Understanding of Free Exercise of Religion," *Harvard Law Review* 1409 (1990): 1437–541; David Souter, concurring opinion in *Church of the Lukumi Babalu Aye, Inc. and Ernesto Pichardo, Petitioners v. City of Hialeah* (508 U.S. 520, 1993).

10. Both quotations are from Eugene Volokh, "Religious Exemptions and the Detroit Female Genital Mutilation Prosecution," *Washington Post*, May 23, 2017.

11. Michael E. Rosman, "Federalism and Female Circumcision in the US," *Global Discourse: An Interdisciplinary Journal of Current Affairs* 12 (2022): 159–66.

12. Rosie Duivenbode, "Criminalizing Medically Unnecessary Child Genital Cutting in Western Countries: The Terms of the Debate and Some Reasons for Caution," *IJIR: Your Sexual Medicine Journal*, November 19, 2021, 21–26; Richard A. Shweder, "The Goose and the Gander: The Genital Wars," *Global Discourse* 3, no. 2 (2013): 348–66; Brussels Collaboration on Bodily Integrity, "Medically Unnecessary Genital Cutting and the Rights of the Child: Moving Toward Consensus," *American Journal of Bioethics* 19, no. 10 (2019): 17–28.

13. For articles calling for the interdiction of all "nonmedical" genital procedures on children, whether male or female, see Yasmin Bootwala, "Exploring Opposition to Ritual Female Genital Cutting Since the First U.S. Federal Prosecution: The 2017 Detroit Case," *International Journal of Impotence Research* 35 (2023): 179–86; Brian D. Earp, "Against Legalising Female 'Circumcision' of Minors: A Reply to 'The Prosecution of Dawoodi Bohra Women' by Richard Shweder," *Global Discourse: An Interdisciplinary Journal of Current Affairs* 12 (2022): 47–76.

14. Seth B. Rozin, "A Dramatic Interpretation of the Fragilities of the FGM Narrative: A Reply to 'The Prosecution of Dawoodi Bohra Women by Richard Shweder,' " *Global Discourse: An Interdisciplinary Journal of Current Affairs* 12 (2022):105–13.

10. Freedom in the American Century and After

1. Eric Foner, *The Story of American Freedom* (New York: W. W. Norton, 1998), 249–52.

2. Gunnar Myrdal, *An American Dilemma: The Negro Problem and Modern Democracy* (New York: Harper & Bros., 1944), 4.

3. Carl Becker, *New Liberties for Old* (New Haven, CT: Yale University Press, 1941), 3; W. B. Gallie, "Essentially Contested Concepts," *Proceedings of the Aristotelian Society* 56 (1955–56): 167–98.

4. Tyler Stovall, *White Freedom: The Racial History of an Idea* (Princeton, NJ: Princeton University Press, 2021).

5. John Dickinson, *Letters from a Farmer in Pennsylvania to the Inhabitants of the British Colonies* (Philadelphia, 1768), 3.

6. Eric Foner, *Reconstruction: America's Unfinished Revolution 1863–1877* (New York: Harper & Row, 1988), 24.

7. James Bryce, *The American Commonwealth*, 2 vols. (London: Macmillan, 1888), 2:635.

8. John Mitchell, "The Workingman's Conception of Industrial Liberty," *American Federationist* 17 (May 1910): 406–7.

9. John A. Ryan, *A Living Wage* (New York: Macmillan, 1906).

10. David A. Corbin, *Life, Work, and Rebellion in the Coal Fields: The Southern West Virginia Miners 1880–1922* (Urbana: University of Illinois Press, 1981), 176–90.

11. Samuel I. Rosenman, ed., *The Public Papers and Addresses of Franklin Delano Roosevelt*, 13 vols. (New York: Macmillan, 1938–1950), 3:422; 6:122–23; 7:232–34, 246–47.

12. David Green, *Shaping Political Consciousness: The Language of Politics in America from McKinley to Reagan* (Ithaca, NY: Cornell University Press, 1987), 121.

13. Rosenman, *Public Papers*, 10:192, 335; 11:287–88.

14. See "The Fifth Freedom," a 1944 advertisement by the Liberty Motors and Engineering Corporation, Library of Congress.

15. *New York Times*, July 25, 1959; Richard M. Nixon, "What Freedom Means to Us," *Vital Speeches of the Day*, September 1, 1959; 677–78; Elaine Tyler, *Homeward Bound: American Families in the Cold War Era* (New York: Basic Books, 2008), 16–18, 162.

16. Louis Menand, *The Free World: Art and Thought in the Cold War* (New York: Farrar Straus and Giroux, 2021), xiv; Gene Slater, *Freedom to Discriminate: How Realtors Conspired to Segregate Housing and Divide America* (Berkeley: University of California Press, 2021), 2.

17. Nikolas Rose, *Powers of Freedom: Reframing Political Thought* (New York: Cambridge University Press, 1999), 65.

18. Ronald Reagan, "Remarks at the Opening Ceremonies of the Statue of Liberty Centennial Celebration in New York," American Presidency Project, University of California, Santa Barbara.

19. Jonathan Franzen, *Freedom* (New York: Farrar Straus and Giroux, 2010).

11. Freedom Through Unfreedom: W. E. B. Du Bois's Theory of Democratic Despotism

1. For all the material quoted in the paragraph, see W. E. B. Du Bois, *Darkwater: Voices from Within the Veil* (New York: Washington Square Press, [1920] 2004), 105–6.

2. Eric Hobsbawm, *The Age of Revolution, 1789–1848* (New York: Vintage Books, 1996), 53.

3. Du Bois, *Darkwater*, 107.

4. Du Bois never mentions the French Revolution in the opening pages of "Of the Ruling of Men" (chapter 6 of *Darkwater*), and I do not claim that he associated eighteenth-century democracy exclusively with the French Revolution. That said, Du Bois's allusions to democratic struggles to restrict menial service; to secure the right of property in handiwork; to regulate public taxes; to redistribute land ownership; and to free trade and barter all point to key moments in the history of the Revolution: for example, to the abolition of serfdom and personal obligations; to the elimination of the guild system; to the incorporation of a "no taxation without representation" principle into "The Declaration of the Rights of Man and Citizen"; to the redistribution of lands owned by the Church; and to the implementation of free market principles. For overviews of the French Revolution that touch on all of these themes see Peter Gay and R. K. Webb, *Modern Europe* (New York: Harper & Row, 1973), ch. 11, and Jeremy

Popkin, *A New World Begins: The History of the French Revolution* (New York: Basic Books, 2019). For a summary of most of the same themes, see Hobsbawm, *The Age of Revolution*, 64–65. For a more recent work that, like Du Bois's World War I–era essay, interprets progressive European political movements of the late eighteenth century as *democratic* movements, see R. R. Palmer, *The Age of Democratic Revolutions: A Political History of Europe and America, 1760–1800* (Princeton, NJ: Princeton University Press, 2014). In their conceptualizations of the ideological orientation animating these movements, Du Bois and Palmer overlap, I believe, although it is clear that Du Bois places greater emphasis on the theme of universal suffrage.

5. Du Bois, *Darkwater*, 106–8.

6. Du Bois, *Darkwater*, 108.

7. It is striking that Du Bois's sense of the nature and importance of this historical juncture persists in *Black Reconstruction* (1935). See, for example, the penultimate paragraph of ch. 14, "The Counter-Revolution of Property," where he writes that "God wept; but that mattered little to an unbelieving age; what mattered most was that the world wept and still is weeping and blind with tears and blood. For there began to rise in America in 1876 a new capitalism and a new enslavement of labor. Home labor in cultured lands, appeased and misled by a ballot whose power the dictatorship of vast capital strictly curtailed, was bribed by high wage and political office to unite in an exploitation of white, yellow, brown and black labor, in lesser lands and "breeds without the law." W. E. B. Du Bois, *Black Reconstruction* (New York: Free Press, [1935] 1998), 634. Du Bois's reference here to "breeds without the law" alludes to Rudyard Kipling's poem "Recessional" (1897). I note, finally, that Du Bois quotes the same line from Kipling's poem in the context of his discussion of the theory of benevolent guardianship in *Darkwater* (see 109).

8. I adapt and develop in greater detail elsewhere Tamar Schapiro's idea of a guiding ideal conception. See Tamar Schapiro, "Kant's Approach to the Theory of Human Agency," in *The Routledge Handbook of Practical Reason*, ed. Ruth Change and Kurt Sylvan (New York: Routledge, 2020), 160–71, and Tamar Schapiro, *Feeling Like It: A Theory of Inclination and Will* (Oxford: Oxford University Press, 2021), ch. 1. For another helpful discussion of the first-person/third-person distinction, see Akeel Bilgrami, "The Political Possibilities of the Long Romantic Period," in *Secularism, Identity, and Enchantment* (Cambridge, MA: Harvard University Press, 2014), 181–201, and Akeel Bilgrami, *Self-Knowledge and Resentment* (Cambridge: Cambridge University Press, 2006), 250–60.

9. For a more detailed discussion of Du Bois's account of the genesis and content of the white supremacist's vicious moral character, see my "Beauty as Propaganda: On the Political Aesthetics of W. E. B. Du Bois," *Philosophical Topics* 49, no. 1 (Spring 2021): 13–34, and my 2021 "Dewey Lecture in Law and Philosophy" at the University of Chicago, https://www.youtube.com/watch?v=Diind3KxndA.

10. For all the material quoted in this paragraph, see Du Bois, "The African Roots of War," 707–8.

11. For all the material quoted in this paragraph, see J. A. Hobson, *Imperialism: A Study* (New York: James Pott & Co., 1902), 6–7, 11, 26, 42.

12. For the material quoted in the paragraph, see Du Bois, "The African Roots of War," 708. For evidence regarding Pliny's career in Africa, see Ronald Syme, "Pliny the Procurator," *Harvard Studies in Classical Philology* 73 (1969): 201–36. For recent discussion of Pliny as a political theorist, see Thomas R. Laehn, *Pliny's Defense of Empire* (New York: Routledge, 2013). As far as I know, there is no evidence that Du Bois read Pliny

in a similar light, but one wonders. In the introduction to his magisterial *Scramble for Africa: White Man's Conquest of the Dark Continent form 1876–1912* (New York: Avon Books, 1991), the historian Thomas Pakenham wrote that there is still no "*general explanation*" of the scramble for Africa "acceptable to historians" (xxii).

13. For the translation and analysis of Weber's famous remark I am wholly indebted to Fritz Ringer, *Max Weber's Methodology: The Unification of the Cultural and Social Sciences* (Cambridge, MA: Harvard University Press, 1997), 153–54, but also his discussion of singular causal analysis in ch. 3). In 1913 Weber read to friends the essay in which these remarks appear ("Die Wirtschaftethik der Welt Religion: Vergleichende religionssoziologische Versuche—Einleitung"); it was first published in 1915, the same year that "The African Roots of War" appeared (see *Max Weber's Methodology*, 179). I am not arguing that Du Bois's essay was written under the influence of Weber, only that Du Bois seems to have relied on an analytical schema similar to one that Weber explicitly articulates.

14 In interpreting Weber's "switches" metaphor in terms of the central role that counterfactual reasoning plays in his approach to "singular causal analysis," I follow Fritz Ringer's reconstruction of Weber's arguments, which he nicely relates to some of the Anglo-American philosophical literature on causal explanation, including the writings of Donald Davidson. (It is striking, however, that Ringer gives no attention to David Lewis's counterfactual analysis of causation.) In emphasizing that for Weber worldviews must acquire efficacy (through, presumably, institutions and practices) in order to be causally significant, I am indebted to Wolfgang Schluchter's reading of Weber, as well to conversation with my colleague Axel Honneth. See Ringer, *Max Weber's Methodology*, ch. 3 and 153–54. See also Wolfgang Schluchter, *The Rise of Western Rationalism: Max Weber's Developmental History*, trans. Guenter Roth (Berkeley: University of California Press, 1981), 25–27.

15. At this stage of his intellectual career, Du Bois leaves open the possibility of a moral, nonexploitative expansion of European capital into Africa. Thus, in the context of envisioning a future, independent African state, he writes, "Capital could not only be accumulated in Africa, but attracted from the white world, with one great difference from present usage: no return so fabulous would be offered that civilized lands would be tempted to divert to colonial trade and invest materials and labor needed by the masses at home, but rather would receive the same modest profits as legitimate home industry offers" (see Du Bois, *Darkwater*, 54). Thanks to Yarran Hominh for drawing my attention to this passage and for pointing out to me that Du Bois later grows skeptical of the vision of a humane capitalism that he embraces in the 1920s and 1930s.

16. For the material quoted in this paragraph, see Hobson, *Imperialism*, 86, 224, 91, 96.

17. Du Bois, "The African Roots of War," 709.

18. For all the material quoted in this paragraph, see Du Bois, "The African Roots of War," 709.

19. Du Bois, *Darkwater*, 105.

20. Du Bois, "African Roots of War," 709, 711; *Darkwater*, 31, emphasis mine.

21. For my appreciation of the differences between Du Bois and Hobson and of the importance of Du Bois's "The African Roots of War" in regard to our understanding of those differences, I am deeply indebted to Jennifer Pitts's groundbreaking scholarship, which she has been kind enough to share with me. See Jennifer Pitts, "The Society of Nations, Imperialism, and the Color Line: Three Conceptions of the International," *Rise of the International*, ed. Richard Devetak and Tim Dunne (New York: Oxford University Press, 2024), 234–54. See, too, Adom Getachew and Jennifer Pitts,

"Democracy and Empire: An Introduction to the International Thought of W. E. B. Du Bois," in *W. E. B. Du Bois: International Thought*, ed. Adom Getachew and Jennifer Pitts (New York: Cambridge University Press, 2021), xv–lvi. I likewise owe a debt to Anthony Brewer's helpful, critical discussion of Hobson in Anthony Brewer, *Marxist Theories of Imperialism: A Critical Survey*, 2nd ed. (London: Routledge, 1990), ch. 4.

22. Du Bois, "The African Roots of War," 709–10.

23. In *Darkwater* Du Bois repeats the point that, in the perspective of the white Christian, white supremacist culture shaping the new democratic nations, the raison d'être of nonwhites is to be dominated and exploited by whites, writing that "slowly but surely white culture is evolving the theory that 'darkies' are born beasts of burden *for* white folk" (Du Bois, *Darkwater*, 29–30, emphasis mine); see, too, W. E. B. Du Bois, "Of the Culture of White Folk," *Journal of Race Development* 7, no. 4 (1917): 439.

24. Considered with respect to late twentieth and early twenty-first century scholarship, Du Bois's explanation of imperialism in terms of white supremacist belief and white culture more generally has obvious affinities to William Appleman Williams's account of the importance of culture to the explanation of imperialism—and, specifically, to the explanation of American imperialism. See William Appleman Williams, *Empire as a Way of Life* (Brooklyn: Ig Publishing, 2007). In Williams's view, "The empire as a territory and as activities dominated economically, politically and psychologically by a superior power is the *result* of empire as a way of life. . . . A way of life is the combination of patterns of thought and action that, as it becomes habitual and institutionalized, defines the thrust and character of a culture and society" (12–13). In a similar vein, but more with an eye to the history of European imperialism, Du Bois's views also find an echo in Edward Said's contention that "neither imperialism nor colonialism is a simple act of accumulation and acquisition. Both are supported and perhaps even impelled by impressive ideological formations that include notions that certain territories and people require and beseech domination, as well as forms of knowledge affiliated with domination: the vocabulary of classic nineteenth-century imperial culture is plentiful with words and concepts like 'inferior' or 'subject races,' 'subordinate peoples,' 'dependency,' 'expansion,' and 'authority.'" See Edward Said, *Culture and Imperialism* (New York: Knopf, 1993), 9. With respect to the particulars of Du Bois's counterfactualist, explanatory strategy, the greatest affinity is to David Eltis's explanation of slavery, which, reminiscent of Du Bois's explanation of imperialism, emphasizes that "the same system that countenanced more rights for workers in Europe (and we might add rising living standards in the long run) also ensured slavery in the Americas. The central practical distinction between the freedom to exploit others and the freedom from exploitation by others is how society defines others. . . . European conceptions of the other ensured that only non-Europeans could be enslaved." See David Eltis, *The Rise of African Slavery in the Americas* (Cambridge: Cambridge University Press, 2000), 223, 280.

25. W. E. B. Du Bois, *The Negro* (Oxford: Oxford University Press, [1915] 2007), 106.

26. Du Bois, "Of the Culture of White Folk," 440–41; Du Bois, *Darkwater*, 31.

27. Du Bois, *The Negro*, 106.

28. In a similar vein, Du Bois takes international socialists in German and America to task, arguing that they "had all but read yellow and black men out of the kingdom of industrial justice. Subtly had they been bribed, but effectively: Were they not lordly whites and should they not share in the spoils of rape? High wages in the United States and England might be the skilfully manipulated result of slavery in Africa and of

peonage in Asia." See Du Bois, *Darkwater*, 34, and "Of the Culture of White Folk,"
443. Later, Du Bois will argue that the unfreedom to which laborers of color are subject ultimately boomerangs on and undermines the freedom that white laborers
enjoy at their expense. In his manifesto for the Second Pan-African Conference, for
example, Du Bois writes, "If we are coming to realize that the great modern problem
is to correct maladjustment in the distribution of wealth, it must be remembered that
the basic maladjustment is the outrageously unjust distribution of world income
between the dominant and suppressed peoples; in the rape of land and raw material,
and in monopoly of technique and culture. And in this crime white labor is *particeps
criminis* with white capital. Unconsciously and consciously, carelessly and deliberately, the vast power of the white labor vote in modern democracies has been cajoled
and flattered into imperialistic schemes to enslave and debauch black, brown and yellow labor, until with fatal retribution, they are themselves today bound and gagged
and rendered impotent by the resulting monopoly of the world's raw material in the
hands of a dominant, cruel and irresponsible few." See W. E. B. Du Bois, *The Crisis* 23,
no. 1 (November 1921): 133. Thanks to Adom Getachew for drawing my attention to
these remarks.

29. Du Bois, *Darkwater*, 34; see, too Du Bois, "Of the Culture of White Folk," 443–45.
30. On January 2, 1916, the *New York Times* published a talk that Bernard Dernburg had
delivered "before a huge audience at Vienna" on December 10, 1915. The speech, to
which Du Bois alludes, was printed under the title " 'England Traitor to the Race'—
Dernburg." For a valuable discussion of Dernburg's career as a colonial administra-
tor, which argues "that colonialism offered the possibility of cooperation between
the representatives of the colonial movement and those they persecuted" (like Dernburg, who was himself of Jewish descent), see Christian S. Davis, *Colonialism, Anti-
semitism, and Germans of Jewish Descent* (Ann Arbor: University of Michigan Press,
2012), ch. 4.
31. Karl Marx, *Capital: A Critique of Political Economy, Volume 1*, trans. Samuel Moore
and Edward Aveling, ed. Frederick Engels (New York: International Publishers, 1967),
714.
32. Du Bois, "The African Roots of War," 713.
33. Hilferding and Luxemburg published their books on imperialism in 1910 and 1913
respectively. See Rudolph Hilferding, *Finance Capital: A Study of the Latest Phase of
Capitalist Development*, trans. Morris Watnick and Sam Gordon (London: Routledge,
[1910] 1981), 319, and Rosa Luxemburg, *The Accumulation of Capital*, trans. Agnes
Schwarzschild (New Haven, CT: Yale University Press, [1913] 1951), 370. V. I. Lenin
wrote *Imperialism, The Highest State of Capitalism* in 1916, and the pamphlet was published in 1917. Nikolai Bukharin, another prominent Marxist theorist, wrote *Imperialism and the World Economy* in 1915, but it was not published until 1917 (regarding
these dates, I follow Brewer, *Marxist Theories of Imperialism*, 109).
34. Du Bois, "African Roots of War," 713.

12. The Denial of Freedom and Punitive Excess

1. David Garland, ed., *Mass Imprisonment* (London: Sage Publications, 2001), 1–3.
2. Erving Goffman, *Asylums: Essays on the Social Situation of Mental Patients and Other
Inmates* (Garden City, NY: Anchor Books, 1961).

3. James B. Jacobs, *The Eternal Criminal Record* (Cambridge, MA: Harvard University Press, 2015).

4. Jeremy Travis, Bruce Western, and Stephens Redburn, eds., *The Growth of Incarceration in the United States: Exploring Causes and Consequences* (Washington, DC: National Academy Press, 2014).

5. Thomas P. Bonczar, *Prevalence of Imprisonment in the U.S. Population, 1974–2001* (Washington, DC: US Department of Justice, 2003); Becky Pettit and Bruce Western, "Mass Imprisonment and the Life Course: Race and Class Inequality in US Incarceration," *American Sociological Review* 69 (2004):151–69; Bruce Western and Becky Pettit, "Incarceration and Social Inequality," *Daedalus* 139 (2010): 8–19.

6. Jeff Manza and Christopher Uggen, *Locked Out: Felon Disenfranchisement and American Democracy* (New York: Oxford University Press, 2006); Robert Brame, Michael G. Turner, Raymond Paternoster, and Shawn D. Bushway, "Cumulative Prevalence of Arrest from Ages 8 to 23 in a National Sample," *Pediatrics* 129 (2012): 21–27; Michelle S. Phelps, "Mass Probation: Toward a More Robust Theory of State Variation in Punishment," *Punishment and Society* 19 (2017): 53–73; Sarah K. S. Shannon, Christopher Uggen, Jason Schnittker, Melissa Thompson, Sara Wakefield, and Michael Massoglia, "The Growth, Scope, and Spatial Distribution of People with Felony Records in the United States, 1948–2010," *Demography* 54 (2017): 1795–818; Peter Hepburn, Issa Kohler-Hausmann, and Angel Zorro Medina, "Cumulative Risks of Multiple Criminal Justice Outcomes in New York City," *Demography* 56 (2019): 1–11.

7. Becky Pettit, *Invisible Men: Mass Incarceration and the Myth of Black Progress* (New York: Russell Sage Foundation, 2012); Christopher Wildeman, "Parental Imprisonment, the Prison Boom, and the Concentration of Childhood Disadvantage," *Demography* 46 (2009): 265–80.

8. This section adapts research reported in Bruce Western, Jessica T. Simes, and Kendra Bradner, "Solitary Confinement and Institutional Harm," *Incarceration* 3 (2021): 26326663211065644.

9. Zhen Zeng, *Jail Inmates in 2017* (Washington, DC: Bureau of Justice Statistics, 2019); Jennifer Bronson and E. Ann Carson, *Prisoners in 2017* (Washington, DC: Bureau of Justice Statistics, 2019).

10 Ronald Goldfarb, *Jails: The Ultimate Ghetto of the Criminal Justice System* (New York: Doubleday, 1975); John Irwin, *The Jail: Managing the Underclass in American Society* (Berkeley: University of California Press, 1985); Issa Kohler-Hausmann, *Misdemeanorland: Criminal Courts and Social Control in an Age of Broken Windows Policing* (Princeton, NJ: Princeton University Press, 2018); Alexandra Natapoff, *Punishment Without Crime: How Our Massive Misdemeanor System Traps the Innocent and Makes America More Unequal* (New York: Basic Books, 2018).

11. Arpit Gupta, Christopher Hansman, and Ethan Frenchman, "The Heavy Costs of High Bail: Evidence from Judge Randomization," *Journal of Legal Studies* 45 (2016): 471–505; Emily Leslie and Nolan G. Pope, "The Unintended Impact of Pretrial Detention on Case Outcomes: Evidence from New York City Arraignments," *Journal of Law and Economics* 60 (2017): 529–57; Paul Heaton, Sandra Mayson, and Megan Stevenson, "The Downstream Consequences of Misdemeanor Pretrial Detention," *Stanford Law Review* 69 (2017): 711–94; Megan T. Stevenson, "Distortion of Justice: How the Inability to Pay Bail Affects Case Outcomes," *Journal of Law, Economics, and Organization* 34 (2018): 511–42.

12. Jeffrey Grogger, "The Effect of Arrests on the Employment and Earnings of Young Men," *Quarterly Journal of Economics* 110 (1995): 51–71; Will Dobbie, Jacob Goldin,

and Crystal Yang, "The Effects of Pre-Trial Detention on Conviction, Future Crime, and Employment: Evidence from Randomly Assigned Judges," *American Economic Review* 108 (2018): 201–40; Christopher Wildeman, Margaret E. Noonan, Daniela Golinelli, E. Ann Carson, and Natalia Emanuel, "State-Level Variation in the Imprisonment-Mortality Relationship, 2001–2010," *Demographic Research* 34 (2016): 359–72; Ariel White, "Misdemeanor Disenfranchisement? The Demobilizing Effects of Brief Jail Spells on Potential Voters," *American Political Science Review* 113 (2019): 311–24.

13. Kristin Turney and Emma Conner, "Jail Incarceration: A Common and Consequential Form of Criminal Justice Contact," *Annual Review of Criminology* 2 (2019): 265–90, at 266.

14. Irwin, *The Jail*, ch. 2; Charles E. Frazier, E. Wilbur Bock, and John C. Henretta, "Pretrial Release and Bail Decisions: The Effects of Legal, Community, and Personal Variables," *Criminology* 18 (1980): 162–81.

15. Bernard E. Harcourt, *Illusion of Order: The False Promise of Broken Windows Policing* (Cambridge, MA: Harvard University Press, 2001); Jeffrey Fagan and Garth Davies, "Street Stops and Broken Windows: Terry, Race, and Disorder in New York City," *Fordham Urban Law Journal* 28 (2000): 457–504; Kohler-Hausmann, *Misdemeanorland*; Natapoff, *Punishment Without Crime*.

16. Preet Bharara, Jocelyn Samuels, Jeffrey Powell, and Emily Daughtry, "CRIPA Investigation of the New York City Department of Correction Jails on Rikers Island," Report of the United States Attorney's Office for the Southern District of New York, 2014; Steve J. Martin, "Seventh Report of the Nunez Independent Monitor," Report of the Court-Appointed Monitor mandated by the Consent Judgment in *Nunez v. City of New York et al.*, 2018.

17. Jennifer Gonnerman, "Before the Law," *New Yorker*, October 6, 2014; "Kalief Browder, 1993–2015," *New Yorker*, June 7, 2015.

18. Homer Venters, *Life and Death in Rikers Island* (Baltimore: Johns Hopkins University Press, 2019), ch. 2.

19. Craig Haney, Joanna Weil, Shirin Bakhshay, and Tiffany Lockett, "Examining Jail Isolation: What We Don't Know Can Be Profoundly Harmful," *Prison Journal* 96 (2016): 126–52.

20. Western, Simes, and Bradner, "Solitary Confinement."

21. Tedd Robert Gurr, "Historical Trends in Violent Crime: A Critical Review of the Evidence," *Crime and Justice* 3 (1981): 295–353.

22. Loïc Wacquant, *Punishing the Poor: The Neoliberal Government of Social Insecurity* (Durham, NC: Duke University Press, 2009); Michelle Alexander, *The New Jim Crow: Mass Incarceration in the Age of Colorblindness* (New York: New Press, 2010); cf. David Garland, "Penal Controls and Social Controls: Toward a Theory of American Penal Exceptionalism," *Punishment & Society* 22 (2020): 321–52.

23. This section adapts research reported in Hannah Pullen-Blasnik, Jessica T. Simes, and Bruce Western, "The Population Prevalence of Solitary Confinement," *Science Advances* 7 (2021): eabj1928, and Western, Simes, and Bradner, "Solitary Confinement."

24. Allen J. Beck, *Use of Restrictive Housing in U.S. Prisons and Jails, 2011–12* (Washington, DC: US Department of Justice, 2015).

25. Nan D. Miller, "International Protection of the Rights of Prisoners: is Solitary Confinement in the United States a Violation of International Standards," *California Western International Law Journal* 26 (1995): 139–72; Elizabeth Vasiliades, "Solitary

Confinement and International Human Rights: Why the U.S. Prison System Fails Global Standards," *American University International Law Review* 21 (2005–2006): 71–100; Sharon Shalev, "Solitary Confinement: The View from Europe," *Canadian Journal of Human Rights* 4 (2015): 143–65; Craig Haney, "Restricting the Use of Solitary Confinement," *Annual Review of Criminology* 1 (2018): 285–310.

26. Ram Subramanian and Alison Shames, "Sentencing and Prison Practices in Germany and the Netherlands: Implications for the United States," *Federal Sentencing Reporter* 27 (2014): 33–45; Beck, *Restrictive Housing.*

27. Liman Program & ASCA, *Time-in-Cell: The ASCA-Liman 2014 National Survey of Administrative Segregation in Prison* (New Haven, CT: Yale Law School, 2015); Holly Foster, "The Conditions of Confinement in Restrictive Housing," in Frost, Natasha A., Carlos E. Monteiro, and M. Garcia, eds., *Restrictive Housing in the U.S.: Issues, Challenges, and Future Directions* (Washington, DC: National Institute of Justice, 2016), 85–116).

28. See, e.g., Lorna A. Rhodes, *Total Confinement: Madness and Reason in the Maximum Security Prison* (Berkeley: University of California Press, 2004).

29. Rhodes, *Total Confinement*; Keramet Reiter, *23/7: Pelican Bay Prison and the Rise of Long-Term Solitary Confinement* (New Haven, CT: Yale University Press, 2016).

30. Alison Liebling, *Prisons and Their Moral Performance: A Study of Values, Quality, and Prison Life* (Oxford: Oxford University Press, 2004); Rhodes, *Total Confinement.*

31. Liman Program & ASCA, *Administrative Segregation, Degrees of Isolation, and Incarceration: A National Overview of State and Federal Correctional Policies* (New Haven, CT: Yale Law School, 2013).

32. Stuart Grassian, "Psychopathological Effects of Solitary Confinement," *American Journal of Psychiatry* 140 (1983):1450–54, and "Psychiatric Effects of Solitary Confinement." *Washington University Journal of Law & Policy* 22 (2006): 325–84.

33. See Haney, "Restricting the Use," and Peter Scharff Smith, "The Effects of Solitary Confinement on Prison Inmates: A Brief History and Review of the Literature," *Crime and Justice* 35 (2006): 441–528.

34. Gresham M. Sykes, *The Society of Captives: A Study of a Maximum Security Prison* (Princeton, NJ: Princeton University Press, 2007), 79.

35. Devah Pager, "The Mark of a Criminal Record," *American Journal of Sociology* 108 (2003): 937–75.

36. Samuel H. Pillsbury, "Creatures, Persons, and Prisoners: Evaluating Prison Conditions Under the Eighth Amendment," *Southern California Law Review* 55 (1981): 1099–1131; Jonathan Simon, "The Second Coming of Dignity," in *Mapping the New Criminal Justice Thinking*, ed. Sharon Dolovich and Alexandra Natapoff (New York: New York University Press, 2017), 275–307; William W. Berry and Meghan J. Ryan, "Eighth Amendment Values," in *The Eighth Amendment and Its Future in a New Age of Punishment*, ed. Meghan J. Ryan and William W. Berry (New York: Cambridge University Press, 2020), 64–75.

37. Jessica T. Simes, *Punishing Places: The Geography of Mass Imprisonment* (Oakland: University of California Press, 2021).

38. Phillip Atiba Goff, Jennifer L. Eberhardt, Melissa J. Williams, and Matthew Christian Jackson, "Not Yet Human: Implicit Knowledge, Historical Dehumanization, and Contemporary Consequences," *Journal of Personality and Social Psychology* 94 (2008): 292–306; Phillip Atiba Goff, Matthew Christian Jackson, Brooke Allison Lewis DiLeone, Carmen Marie Culotta, and Natalie Ann DiTomaso, "The Essence of

Innocence: Consequences of Dehumanizing Black Children," *Journal of Personality and Social Psychology* 106 (2014): 526–45.

39. William J. Bennett, John DiIulio, and John P. Walters, *Body Count: Moral Poverty . . . and How to Win America's War Against Crime and Drugs* (New York: Simon & Schuster, 1996), 27.

14. Persuasion, Manipulation, and Unfreedom

1. I am thinking here of Raphael Samuel, Gareth Stedman Jones, Anna Davin, Sally Alexander, and the editorial team at *History Workshop Journal: A Journal of Socialist Historians.*

2. On opinion and belief, see Leon Wieseltier, "Reason and the Republic of Opinion," *New Republic*, November 12, 2014.

3. Daniel Kahneman, *Thinking, Fast and Slow* (New York: Farrar, Straus and Giroux, 2011).

4. Alexis de Tocqueville, *Democracy in America*,(New York: Everyman's Library, 1994), chs. 7–9, esp. 414, 418.

5. Isaiah Berlin, "Two Concepts of Liberty" (1958), in *Four Essays on Liberty* (New York: Oxford University Press, 1969); see also Isaiah Berlin, *Personal Impressions* (Princeton, NJ: Princeton University Press, 2014).

6. Czeslaw Milosz, *The Captive Mind* (New York: Vintage Books, [1953] 1990).

7. Milovan Djilas, *The New Class: An Analysis of the Communist System* (New York: Harcourt Brace Jovanovich, 1957), and *Conversations with Stalin* (London: Rupert Hart Davis, 1962).

8. Karl Popper, *The Open Society and Its Enemies* (London: Routledge & Kegan Paul, 1945).

9. John Stuart Mill, *On Liberty* (London: John W. Parker and Son, 1859); *Abrams v. United States*, 250 U.S. 616 (1919): "when men have realized that time has upset many fighting faiths, they may come to believe even more than they believe the very foundations of their own conduct that the ultimate good desired is better reached by free trade in ideas—that the best test of truth is the power of the thought to get itself accepted in the competition of the market, and that truth is the only ground upon which their wishes safely can be carried out."

10. Pano Kanelos, "We Can't Wait for Universities to Fix Themselves. So We're Starting a New One," November 8, 2021, The Free Press, https://bariweiss.substack.com/p/we-cant-wait-for-universities-to.

11. Robert Noggle, "The Ethics of Manipulation" (2020), https://plato.stanford.edu/entries/ethics-manipulation/.

12. Plutarch, "Pericles," in *Greek Lives*, trans. Robin Waterfield (Oxford: Oxford University Press, 1998).

13. Plato, *Phaedrus*, 271c.

14. Thomas Hobbes, *De Cive*, 10.11.

15. Condorcet, *Sketch of the Historical Progress of the Human Mind*, ed. Steven Lukes and Nadia Urbinati (New York: Cambridge University Press, 2012).

16. Karl Marx, *Early Writings*, ed. Lucio Colletti (London: Penguin Books, 1975).

17. See Michael Brock, "We Must Educate Our Masters," *Oxford Review of Education* 4, no. 3 (1978): 221–32.

18. George Orwell, "Such, Such Were the Joys" (1952), http://www.george-orwell.org/Such,_Such_Were_The_Joys/0.html.
19. Eli Pariser, *The Filter Bubble* (New York: Penguin Books, 2015); Nigel Shadbolt and Roger Hampson, *The Digital Ape: How to Live in Peace with Smart Machines* (London: Scribe, 2018).

15. Ridicule and Argument

1. Jon Elster, "Obscurantism and Academic Freedom," in *Who's Afraid of Academic Freedom*, ed. Akeel Bilgrami and Jonathan R. Cole (New York: Columbia University Press, 2015), 81–96.
2. Andrew May, *Fake Physics: Spoofs, Hoaxes, and Fictitious Science* (Berlin: Springer, 2019), 123.
3. As an aside, entrapment is usually viewed as *legally* acceptable if the target person is provided only with the *opportunity* to engage in criminal behavior, but not if an additional *inducement* is offered.
4. For a full overview, see https://areomagazine.com/2018/10/02/academic-grievance-studies-and-the-corruption-of-scholarship/.
5. The article is now retracted, but the following statement can still be found on the internet: "The reining in or 'leashing' of men in society [can] be understood pragmatically on a metaphorical level with clear parallels to dog training 'pedagogical' methodologies. By properly educating human men (and re-educating them, when necessary) to respect women (both human and canine), denounce rape culture, refuse to rape or stand by while sexual assault occurs, de-masculinize spaces, and espouse feminist ideals—say through mandatory diversity and harassment training, bystander training, rape culture awareness training, and so on, in any institutions that can adopt them (e.g. workplaces, university campuses, and government agencies)—human men could be 'leashed' by a culture that refuses to victimize women, perpetuate rape culture, or permit rape-condoning spaces."
6. See https://areomagazine.com/2019/01/05/academic-freedom-or-social-justice-what-kind-of-university-is-portland-state/.
7. These rules cannot be accessed by outsiders on the Portland State University website. They can be accessed as part of a video presentation by Brendan Maddux on the theme "Portland State University Institutional Review Board (IRB)." It is very detailed and has the appearance of authenticity. I shall treat it as credible. However, there are indications that it may be somewhat dated.
8. Brian Barry, "Review of Robert Nozick, *Anarchy, State and Utopia*," *Political Theory* 3 (1975): 332.
9. Many, including the original article, are collected on https://physics.nyu.edu/faculty/sokal/.
10. Jacques Derrida, "Sokal et Bricmont ne sont pas sérieux," *Le Monde*, November 20, 1997.
11. There are ninety-three references to Searle as SARL in Jacques Derrida, *Limited Inc* (Evanston, IL: Northwestern University Press, 1977).
12. Anthony Kenny, *Brief Encounters* (London: SPCK, 2018), 112.
13. Jon Elster, *Ulysses Unbound* (New York: Cambridge University Press, 1997), ch. 3.
14. Marcel Proust, *À la recherche du temps perdu* (Paris: Gallimard, 1987), 1:314–15.

16. Is Wokeism Changing the Nature of Inquiry?

1. Alexander Volokh, "n guilty men," *University of Pennsylvania Law Review* 146 (1997): 173–218.
2. For a scrutiny and critique of the marketplace metaphor attributed to Oliver Wendell Holmes and the metainductive argument in John Stuart Mill, from which it derives, see my "Liberalism and the Academy," in *Secularism, Identity, and Enchantment* (Cambridge, MA: Harvard University Press, 2014). See also David Bromwich's essay in this volume.

18. Freedom Gained and Freedom Lost in American Science

This collaboration resulted from equal contributions by each author. We want to thank particularly Harriet A. Zuckerman for her work on women in science and who (with Jonathan R. Cole) conducted many of the extensive interviews quoted in this essay.

1. For a detailed discussion of these university-based discoveries, see part II of Jonathan R. Cole, *The Great American University: Its Rise to Preeminence, Its Indispensable National Role, Why It Must Be Protected* (New York: Public Affairs, 2012).
2. Universalism, one of the four basic norms of science, defined originally by Robert K. Merton, refers to the belief that the scientific community judges truth claims and the substance of discoveries on the content of the claims and the demonstration of their validity, *not* on any of one or more particular ascribed characteristic of the scientist: race, gender, nationality, and so on.
3. When Jonathan Cole began to study women in science during the mid-1970s, few other social scientists focused on their treatment within the scientific community. His interest in women in science, in particular, derived from a more theoretical interest in how the reward system of science fell short of its normative ideal of universalism. Today much has changed, including the publication of biographical and autobiographical accounts of female scientists, of great success stories that led women to produce scientific breakthroughs, and accounts of the way women continue to draw the short end of the stick within the community. It is no longer a lonely enterprise. We are indebted to the historians of science Margaret W. Rossiter and Londa Schiebinger, physicist Evelyn Fox Keller, philosopher Sandra G. Harding, and many other female scholars for their groundbreaking work on women in science.
4. In his book *Little Science, Big Science* (New York: Columbia University Press, 1963), historian of science Derek de Solla Price showed that 80 to 90 percent of all scientists who ever lived were alive in the 1960s. He defined this historic evolution of science as a movement from "little science" to "big science."
5. We have shied away from using the term "meritocracy." In recent years its meaning has taken on a level of confusion that we prefer not to interfere with the understanding what we mean here by "universalism." The term "scientist" was first introduced in print by the English historian of science William Whewell, in 1834, when upon reviewing Mary Somerville's treatise *On the Connexion of the Physical Sciences* he proposed to replace the then common "men of science" to "scientist." At that time the term caused scholarly disagreements. The term did not become commonly accepted until 1882. For a more detailed discussion, see David Wootton, *The Invention of*

Science: A New History of the Scientific Revolution (New York: HarperCollins, 2015), 27–28.

6. For a full discussion of racism and political and social freedoms, see Tyler Stovall, *White Freedom: The Racial History of an Idea* (Princeton, NJ: Princeton University Press, 2021).

7. Within academia, most fields were not favorable to women.

8. Eric Foner, *The Story of American Freedom* (New York: W. W. Norton, 1998), 1.

9. The fly room, described as a dingy, closet-like space, still exists at Columbia. Several Nobel Prize winners did their work in these cramped quarters, which was filled with excitement and some resentments during its operation. But limited space did not limit original thought.

10. In 1920, 60.5 percent of all high school graduates were women ($n = 311,000$). In 1950, the proportion of women was smaller, at 52.4 percent, but women were still better represented then men ($n = 2,889,000$). See Thomas D. Snyder, *120 Years of American Education: A Statistical Portrait* (Washington, DC: National Center for Education Statistics, US Department of Education, 1993).

11. In 1920, 15 percent of all doctorate degrees were conferred to women. In 1960, the proportion of women with PhDs was 10 percent. *Earned Degrees Conferred, 1869-70 Through 1964-65* (Washington, DC: Digest of Education Statistics, National Center for Education Statistics, US Department of Education, March 2014).

12. Marilyn Ogilvie, *Women, Science, and Myth: Gender Beliefs from Antiquity to the Present* (Palo Alto, CA: ABC-CLIO, 2008).

13. These new freedoms were accessible to mostly white and affluent women. Women of color and working-class women remained bound to low-paying menial jobs and housework.

14. For a detailed discussion, see Megan McDonald Way, *Family Economics and Public Policy, 1800s–Present: How Laws, Incentives, and Social Programs Drive Family Decision-Making and the US Economy* (New York: Springer, 2018). 134.

15. See Sara Evans, *Born for Liberty* (New York: Simon & Schuster, 1997).

16. H. Erskine, "The Polls: Women's Role," *Public Opinion Quarterly* 35, no. 2 (1971): 275–90. It has to be noted that despite the stagnant economy and limited opportunities, married women still managed to make some progress in gaining employment through the depression decade. See Winifred D. Wandersee Bolin, "The Economics of Middle-Income Family Life: Working Women During the Great Depression," *Journal of American History* 65, no. 1 (1978): 60–74.

17. Marjorie Nicolson, *A University Between Two Centuries* (Ann Arbor: University of Michigan Press, 1937), 414.

18. *AAUP Bulletin* 1, no. 1 (December 1915): 17–39.

19. Cole, *The Great American University.*

20. Susan C. Athey (2007); Esther Duflo (2010); Amy Finkelstein (2021); Emi Nakamura (2019); Melissa Dell (2020); Stephanie Stantcheva (2025).

21. All women who appear in this essay were interviewed by Harriet Zuckerman and the senior author (long-term colleagues in developing the sociology of science) of this essay during the years between 1978 and 1982. For a variety of reasons, these interviews, which remain in the form of recordings and their transcripts—as well as a good deal of biographical information—have been used in only a few essays. We will refer to those interviews and other sources in this section of the essay. Support for that interview project came from the National Science Foundation. The sample was by no means a random or stratified random sample. Eminent women are oversampled. The male

scientists interviewed were roughly matched to the women in terms of discipline and professional age, but they too were not randomly selected within groups. All of the scientists quoted in this essay are no longer alive. We have chosen to use their names, which we would not have done if they were alive today.

22. Because of the cultural norms and the values within the United States at the time, most women self-selected themselves out of science as an occupation. But that self-selection was based on perceptions of the proper role for women in society and the absence of values of inclusion in academic science.

23. In this essay we rarely compare the careers of the women and men, except to highlight the sharp differences in the opportunity structures and power within the scientific community.

24. Marcus Rhoades, "The Early Years of Maize Genetics," in *The Dynamic Genome: Barbara McClintock's Ideas in the Century of Genetics*, ed. Nina Fedoroff and David Botstein (New York: Cold Spring Harbor Laboratory Press, 1992), 1–29.

25. The system that a scientist chooses to work on can be of essential importance to the results achieved. Those cytologists who chose the maize plant took on a very difficult system, primarily because you only had one or two "crops" each year to examine in experiments and analysis. Those early geneticists who chose Drosophila as a system, as the Morgan lab did, could breed the fruit flies many more times in a short period of time to examine hypotheses or theories of the gene. That gave them a definite advantage in making rapid scientific advance—if they had people of rare curiosity and intellect working on the system.

26. She published her findings over several years but gave her presentation in Cold Spring Harbor Symposium in 1951. Barbara McClintock, "The Origin and Behavior of Mutable Loci in Maize," *1947–1948 Carnegie Yearbook* (Washington DC: Carnegie Institution of Washington, 1948), 155–69; Barbara McClintock, "The Origin and Behavior of Mutable Loci in Maize," *Proceedings of the National Academy of Sciences of the United States of America* 36, no. 6 (1950): 344–55.

27. Cole and Zuckerman interview with Barbara McClintock, July 10, 1981, Cold Spring Harbor. (Subsequent quotations from McClintock are from the same source.) A supporting father and a somewhat reluctant mother was not an uncommon motif in the interviews that Cole and Zuckerman produced. It seems that in a disproportionate number of cases, fathers without sons, treated their female children (or at least one of them) as if they were a son.

28. Cole and Zuckerman interview with Barbara McClintock. Perhaps ironically, the position she obtained was offered to her by the prescient Vannevar Bush, then the president of the Carnegie Institution in Washington, DC. Bush was an exceptional "truffle-dog" for smelling out talent. He and others saw McClintock's brilliance, understood the resistance to her discoveries in parts of the scientific community when she discovered transposons, and offered her a full-time staff position at Cold Spring Harbor. He was willing to support this unique scientist who began her quest to find a "controlling mechanism" that produced the mutable loci of genes in maize plants. Of course, this was the same Vannevar Bush who would lead much of the nation's scientific World War II science effort, become a confident of Franklin D. Roosevelt, and write the transformative science policy document *Science: The Endless Frontier—A Report to the President by Vannevar Bush, Director of the Office of Scientific Research and Development, July 1945* (Washington, DC: United States Government Printing Office, 1945).

29. There is a good deal of literature on the intellectual migration in the 1930s and 1940s from Germany and parts of Europe controlled by National Socialism. Perhaps the single best source for autobiographical essays about the migration by those who went through it can be found in Donald Fleming and Bernard Bailyn's *Intellectual Migration* (Cambridge, MA: Belknap Press of Harvard University, 1969). The migration of over half of Germany's top physicists and other renowned scientists was only part of the story. Among the scientists who left were Leo Szilard, Max Delbrück, Enrico Fermi, and, of course, Albert Einstein. Among the other creative minds that left Germany, Austria, Poland, Russia, Italy, and France were writers and playwrights Thomas Mann and Bertold Brecht; artists Wassily Kandinsky and Max Ernst; architects Ludwig Mies van der Rohe and Water Gropius; art historians Erwin Panofsky and Walter Friedlaender; and composers Paul Hindemith, Bela Bartók, Arnold Schoenberg, and Igor Stravinsky, among many others. Social scientists such as Paul F. Lazarsfeld and Theodor Adorno also saw the writing on the wall. Some did not, and they suffered under Hitler's rule. There were also the children of the émigrés, who went on to distinguished careers. Gerhard Sonnert and Gerald Holton, *What Happened to the Children Who Fled Nazi Persecution* (New York: Palgrave Macmillan, 2006), and Laura Fermi, *Illustrious Immigrants: The Intellectual Migration from Europe 1930–41* (Chicago: University of Chicago Press, 1968), have written about the general phenomena, while Hannah Gray has recounted her experiences in an exceptionally fine autobiography, *An Academic Life* (Princeton, NJ: Princeton University Press, 2018).

30. This term was coined by Columbia legal scholar Kimberlé Crenshaw in 1989 in "Demarginalizing the Intersection of Race and Sex: A Black Feminist Critique of Antidiscrimination Doctrine, Feminist Theory, and Antiracist Politics," *University of Chicago Legal Forum* 1 (1989): 139–67.

31. Virginia E. Papaioannou, "Salome Gluecksohn-Waelsch. 6 October 1907–7 November 2007," *Biographical Memoirs of Fellows of the Royal Society* (London: Royal Society Publishing, 2019), 67. This memoir is an excellent detailed description of Waelsch's scientific contributions.

32. Quoted from Harriet Zuckerman, Jonathan R. Cole, and John T. Bruer, eds., *The Outer Circle: Women in the Scientific Community* (New York: W. W. Norton, 1991), 72.

33. Zuckerman, Cole, and Bruer, eds., *The Outer Circle*, 71.

34. The papers of L. C. Dunn can be found in the archives of the American Philosophical Society. We have used some of the online material from those archives here, but for more detailed and very interesting correspondences of Dunn, see this archival material.

35. These quotes are taken from parts of the interview with Waelsch conducted by Harriet Zuckerman and Jonathan R. Cole and published in Zuckerman, Cole, and Bruer, eds., *The Outer Circle*, 81–83.

36. Harriet Zuckerman and Jonathan Cole interviewed seven women and two men who were born before 1910. It is difficult to conclude that the patterns that we have identified would hold for a larger and more varied population of female scientists of this period. As noted, we are here discussing patterns based on a small number of high-achieving female scientists. The scientists interviewed included Barbara McClintock (1902), genetics; Sara Ratner (1903), biochemistry; Berta Scharrer (1906), endocrinology (immigrant, Jewish); Grace Hopper (1906), computer science; Salome Gluecksohn-Waelsch (1907), genetics (immigrant); and Melba Phillips (1907), physics. The two men were Chandra Subrahmanyan (1910), astrophysics (immigrant); and Tjalling Koopmans (1910), mathematics and economics (immigrant).

37. See Stephen Cole's and Jonathan R. Cole's work in the 1970s. Jonathan Cole and Stephen Cole, "Measuring the Quality of Sociological Research: Problems in the Use of the 'Science Citation Index,'" *American Sociologist* 6, no. 1 (February 1971): 23–29; Jonathan Cole and Stephen Cole, "The Ortega Hypothesis," *Science* 178, no. 4059 (Oct. 27, 1972): 368–75.

38. Robert K. Merton, "The Matthew Effect in Science." *Science* 159, (1968): 56–63.

39. See, for example, Marlen Blissett, *Politics in Science* (Boston: Little, Brown and Company, 1972); Ian I. Mitroff, "Norms and Counter-Norms in a Select Group of the Apollo Moon Scientists: A Case Study of the Ambivalence of Scientists," *American Sociological Review* 39 (1974): 579–95.

40. Michael Mulkay, *Science and the Sociology of Knowledge* (New York: Routledge, 1979).

41. Jonathan R. Cole, "The Paradox of Individual Particularism and Institutional Universalism," *Social Science Information* 28, no. 1 (1989): 51–76.

42. The process described here applies to college admissions at highly selective colleges. See Jonathan R. Cole, *Toward a More Perfect University* (New York: PublicAffairs, 2016).

43. Cole, "Paradox."

44. William De Witt Hyde, *The College Man and the College Woman* (Boston: Houghton, Mifflin, 1906), 206.

45. The concept of cumulative advantage and disadvantage was first developed by Robert K. Merton. Since Merton introduced the concept, many others have used it. See especially Thomas DiPrete and Gregory Eirich, "Cumulative Advantage as a Mechanism for Inequality: A Review of Theoretical and Empirical Developments," *American Review of Sociology* 32 (2006): 271–97.

46. Jonathan R. Cole and Burton Singer, "A Theory of Limited Differences: Explaining the Productivity Puzzle in Science," in Zuckerman, Cole, and Bruer, eds., *The Outer Circle*, 277–310.

47. For an overview of more resent theories and empirical evidence, see Jo Handelsman et al., "More Women in Science," *Science* 309.5738 (2005): 1190–91.

48. In the late 1960s and 1970s, when asked to draw a picture of a scientist, elementary school children depicted almost exclusively males. See D. W. Chambers "Stereotypic Images of the Scientist: The Draw-A-Scientist Test," *Science Education* 67 (1983): 255–65). The meta-analysis of similar experiments across the five decades showed that more children depicted scientists as being female, but the share of children who depicted a scientist as a woman decreased among older children. D. I. Miller, K. M. Nolla, A. H. Eagly, and D. H. Uttal, "The Development of Children's Gender-Science Stereotypes: A Meta-Analysis of 5 Decades of U.S. Draw-a-Scientist Studies," *Child Development* 89 (2018): 1943–55.

49. Exogenous factors include broad social belief systems, societal values, norms of behavior, and expectations within society that become embedded through socialization and other means into the minds of most of a society's people. Endogenous factors are here more localized to the values, and norms, and culture within the scientific community. Sometimes these are consistent with exogenous factors; sometimes they are at variance with them.

50. For an extended discussion of this idea, see Jonathan R. Cole, "Dilemmas of Choice Facing Research Universities," in *Research Universities in a Time of Discontent*, ed. Jonathan R. Cole, Elinor G. Barber, and Stephen R. Graubard (Baltimore: Johns Hopkins University Press, 1993), 11–23. This follows closely those earlier ideas.

51. This theme of who owns the null has been implicit in many works of contemporary literature. The best depiction of this conflict can be found in David Mamet's play

Oleana. Philip Roth made it a theme in *The Human Stain*, and it is a central theme in J. M. Coetzee's novel *Disgrace*.

52. Many studies examine how cultural and structural factors impede the progress of women in science and academia, among them Sue Rosser, ed., *Women, Science, and Myth: Gender Beliefs from Antiquity to Present* (Palo Alto, CA: ABC-CLIO, 2008); Ruth Watts, *Women in Science: Social and Cultural History* (New York: Routledge, 2007); Donna Haraway, *Primate Visions: Gender, Race, and Nature in the World of Modern Science* (New York: Routledge, 1990); Sally Gregory Kohlstedt, "Sustaining Gains: Reflections on Women in Science and Technology in the 20th Century United States," *NWSA Journal* 16, no. 1 (2004): 1–26; and C. Cronin and A. Roger, "Theorizing Progress: Women in Science, Engineering, and Technology in Higher Education," *Journal of Research in Science Teaching* 36, no. 6 (1999): 639–61.

53. See, for example, Jonathan R. Cole, "The Two Cultures Revisited," *The Bridge on Engineering Partnerships* 26, nos. 3–4 (1996): 194–215. See also work done by the historian Donald Yacovone, who has been studying the way race has been portrayed historically in textbooks. When you examine the treatment of science in the most widely adopted secondary school textbooks, the first thing one notices, is the almost total absence of a discussion of science. If you want to understand "antiscience," you might begin here. When you compare the content devoted to the pop culture (e.g., Madonna) to that of women scientists, there is simply no comparison. As might be expected, there is virtually no mention of a woman scientist at all other than an occasional passing reference to Maria Curie. Not only does Madonna win hands down over all references to women, but also over any discussion of Watson and Crick's discovery—or the myriad other revolutionary scientific discoveries in the twentieth century, except perhaps for the creation of the atomic bomb. When authors of these texts were asked why this was so, the authors almost invariably replied that the publisher "told me that science doesn't sell." Moreover, the authors of these texts knew very little about science in general and about women in science in particular. The reference to the sales factor also suggests what goes into history texts is often driven by their commodification and by another factor—the power of state boards that control the purchasing of texts for schools and public libraries in their state. Thus, Texas has a significant impact on the content of texts by suggesting that the state will not adopt a text with unless certain content is modified or dropped. That includes the way women are portrayed.

54. Walter Isaacson, *The Code Breaker: Jennifer Doudna, Gene Editing, and the Future of the Human Race* (New York: Simon & Schuster, 2021), 6. Doudna had already published an autobiography about her life and discoveries. See Jennifer Doudna and Samuel Sternberg, *A Crack in Creation: Gene Editing and the Unthinkable Power to Control Evolution* (New York: Houghton Mifflin Harcourt, 2018). Both books are worth reading for the lucidity of their explanations of the science and for insight into the personal challenges and encounters that Doudna faced during the drive to discover CRISPR gene editing.

55. Doudna and Sternberg, *A Crack in Creation*, 31.

19. Evaluating the Fake News Problem at the Scale of the Information Ecosystem

This chapter was originally published as Jennifer Allen et al., "Evaluating the Fake News Problem at the Scale of the Information Ecosystem," *Science Advances* 6 (2020): eaay3539. Reprinted with permission from AAAS.

1. H. Allcott and M. Gentzkow, "Social Media and Fake News in the 2016 Election," *Journal of Economic Perspectives* 31 (2017): 211–36; K. Shu, A. Sliva, S. Wang, J. Tang, and H. Liu, "Fake News Detection on Social Media: A Data Mining Perspective," *ACM SIGKDD Exploration Newsletter* 19 (2017): 22–36; D. M. J. Lazer, M. A. Baum, Y. Benkler, A. J. Berinsky, K. M. Greenhill, F. Menczer, M. J. Metzger, et al., "The Science of Fake News," *Science* 359 (2018): 1094–96; S. Vosoughi, D. Roy, and S. Aral, "The Spread of True and False News Online," *Science* 359 (2018): 1146–51; C. Shao, P.-M. Hui, L. Wang, X. Jiang, A. Flammini, F. Menczer, and G. L. Ciampaglia, "Anatomy of an Online Misinformation Network," *PLOS One* 13 (2018): e0196087; A. Guess, B. Nyhan, and J. Reifler, "Selective Exposure to Misinformation: Evidence from the Consumption of Fake News During the 2016 US Presidential Campaign," European Research Council (2018); M. Stella, E. Ferrara, and M. De Domenico, "Bots Increase Exposure to Negative and Inflammatory Content in Online Social Systems," *Proceedings of the National Academy of Sciences U.S.A.* 115 (2018): 12435–40; N. Grinberg, K. Joseph, L. Friedland, B. Swire-Thompson, and D. Lazer, "Fake News on Twitter During the 2016 U.S. Presidential Election," *Science* 363 (2019): 374–78; A. Guess, J. Nagler, and J. Tucker, "Less Than You Think: Prevalence and Predictors of Fake News Dissemination on Facebook," *Science Advances* 5 (2019): eaau4586; G. Pennycook and D. G. Rand, "Fighting Misinformation on Social Media Using Crowdsourced Judgments of News Source Quality," *Proceedings of the National Academy of Sciences U.S.A.* 116 (2019): 2521–26.
2. N. Persily, "Can Democracy Survive the Internet?," *Journal of Democracy* 28 (2017): 63–76; J. Tucker, A. Guess, P. Barberá, C. Vaccari, and A. Siegel, "Social Media, Political Polarization, and Political Disinformation: A Review of the Scientific Literature," 2018, https://papers-ssrn-com.ezproxy.cul.columbia.edu/sol3/papers.cfm?abstract_id =3144139; G. L. Ciampaglia, "Fighting Fake News: A Role for Computational Social Science in the Fight Against Digital Misinformation," *Journal of Computational Social Science* 1 (2018): 147–53; K. Clayton, S. Blair, J. A. Busam, S. Forstner, J. Glance, G. Green, A. Kawata, et al., "Real Solutions for Fake News? Measuring the Effectiveness of General Warnings and Fact-Check Tags in Reducing Belief in False Stories on Social Media," *Political Behavior* 42 (2019): 1073–95.
3. Allcott and Gentzkow, "Social Media and Fake News"; Grinberg et al., "Fake News on Twitter"; Guess, Nagler, and Tucker, "Less Than You Think."
4. S. Aral and D. Eckles, "Protecting Elections from Social Media Manipulation," *Science* 365 (2019): 858–61; J. Roozenbeek and S. van der Linden, "The Fake News Game: Actively Inoculating Against the Risk of Misinformation," *Journal of Risk Research* 22 (2019): 570–80.
5. S. Wojcik and A. Hughes, "Sizing up Twitter Users," Pew Research Center, 2018, https://www.pewinternet.org/2019/04/24/sizing-up-twitter-users/; A. Mitchell, "Americans Still Prefer Watching to Reading the News–and Mostly Still Through Television," Pew Research Center, 2018, https://www.journalism.org/2018/12/03/americans-still-prefer -watching-to-reading-the-news-and-mostly-still-through-television/.
6. D. J. Watts and D. Rothschild, "Don't Blame the Election on Fake News. Blame It on the Media," *Columbia Journalism Review*, 2017, https://www.cjr.org/analysis/fake-news -media-election-trump.php.
7. L. Feldman, "The News About Comedy: Young Audiences, *The Daily Show*, and Evolving Notions of Journalism," *Journalism* 8 (2007): 406–27.
8. S. Athey, M. M. Mobius, and J. Pál, "The Impact of Aggregators on Internet News Consumption," 2017, https://papers-ssrn-com.ezproxy.cul.columbia.edu/abstract =2897960.

9. Grinberg et al., "Fake News on Twitter."

10. S. Edgerly, E. K. Vraga, L. Bode, K. Thorson, and E. Thorson, "New Media, New Relationship to Participation? A Closer Look at Youth News Repertoires and Political Participation," *Journalism & Mass Communication Quarterly* 95 (2018): 192–212.

11. Grinberg et al., "Fake News on Twitter."

12. Guess, Nyhan, and Reifler, "Selective Exposure to Misinformation"; Grinberg et al., "Fake News on Twitter"; Guess, Nagler, and Tucker, "Less Than You Think."

13. Grinberg et al., "Fake News on Twitter."

14. M. E. McCombs and D. L. Shaw, "The Agenda-Setting Function of Mass Media," *Public Opinion Quarterly* 36 (1972): 176–87; R. Puglisi and J. M. Snyder, "Empirical Studies of Media Bias," in *Handbook of Media Economics*, ed. S. P. Anderson, J. Waldfogel, and D. Stromberg (Amsterdam: North-Holland, 2015), 1:647–67; G. King, B. Schneer, and A. White, "How the News Media Activate Public Expression and Influence National Agendas," *Science* 358 (2017): 776–80.

15. Watts and Rothschild, "Don't Blame the Election on Fake News."

20. Measuring the News and Its Impact on Democracy

This chapter was originally published as Duncan J. Watts, David M. Rothschild, and Markus Mobius, "Measuring the news and its impact on democracy," *Proceedings of the National Academy of Sciences* 118, no. 15 (2021): e1912443118.

1. H. Allcott and M. Gentzkow, "Social Media and Fake News in the 2016 Election," *Journal of Economic Perspectives* 31 (2017): 211–36; K. Shu, A. Sliva, S. Wang, J. Tang, and H. Liu, "Fake News Detection on Social Media: A Data Mining Perspective," *ACM SIG-KDD Exploration Newsletter* 19 (2017): 22–36; J. Tucker, A. Guess, P. Barberá, C. Vaccari, and A. Siegel, "Social Media, Political Polarization, and Political Disinformation: A Review of the Scientific Literature," 2018, https://papers-ssrn-com.ezproxy.cul.columbia .edu/sol3/papers.cfm?abstract_id=3144139; D. M. J. Lazer, M. A. Baum, Y. Benkler, A. J. Berinsky, K. M. Greenhill, F. Menczer, M. J. Metzger, et al., "The Science of Fake News," *Science* 359 (2018): 1094–96; S. Vosoughi, D. Roy, and S. Aral, "The Spread of True and False News Online," *Science* 359 (2018): 1146–51; C. Shao, P.-M. Hui, L. Wang, X. Jiang, A. Flammini, F. Menczer, and G. L. Ciampaglia, "Anatomy of an Online Misinformation Network," *PLOS ONE* 13 (2018): e0196087; A. Guess, B. Nyhan, and J. Reifler, "Selective Exposure to Misinformation: Evidence from the Consumption of Fake News During the 2016 US Presidential Campaign," European Research Council (2018); M. Stella, E. Ferrara, and M. De Domenico, "Bots Increase Exposure to Negative and Inflammatory Content in Online Social Systems," *Proceedings of the National Academy of Sciences U.S.A.* 115 (2018): 12435–40; N. Grinberg, K. Joseph, L. Friedland, B. Swire-Thompson, and D. Lazer, "Fake News on Twitter During the 2016 U.S. Presidential Election," *Science* 363 (2019): 374–78; A. Guess, J. Nagler, and J. Tucker, "Less Than You Think: Prevalence and Predictors of Fake News Dissemination on Facebook," *Science Advances* 5 (2019): eaau4586; G. Pennycook and D. G. Rand, "Fighting Misinformation on Social Media Using Crowdsourced Judgments of News Source Quality," *Proceedings of the National Academy of Sciences U.S.A.* 116 (2019): 2521–26; S. Aral and D. Eckles, "Protecting Elections from Social Media Manipulation," *Science* 365 (2019): 858–61.

2. C. Silverman, "This Analysis Shows How Viral Fake Election News Stories Outperformed Real News on Facebook," BuzzFeed News, November 16, 2016, https://www .buzzfeednews.com/article/craigsilverman/viral-fake-election-news-outperformed -real-news-on-facebook.

3. Aral and Eckles, "Protecting Elections"; J. Roozenbeek and S. van der Linden, "The Fake News Game: Actively Inoculating Against the Risk of Misinformation," *Journal of Risk Research* 22 (2019): 570–80.

4. Allcott and Gentzkow, "Social Media and Fake News"; Grinberg et al., "Fake News and Twitter"; Guess et al., "Less Than You Think"; D. J. Watts and D. Rothschild, "Don't Blame the Election on Fake News. Blame It on the Media," *Columbia Journalism Review*, 2017, https://www.cjr.org/analysis/fake-news-media-election-trump.php; B. Nyhan, :Why Fears of Fake News Are Overhyped," *Medium*, February 4, 2019, https://link.medium.com/MgiT8vLJUW; J. Allen, B. Howland, M. Mobius, D. Rothschild, and D. J. Watts, "Evaluating the Fake News Problem at the Scale of the Information Ecosystem," *Science Advances* 6 (2020): eaay3539.

5. Aral and Eckles, "Protecting Elections."

6. Watts and Rothschild, "Don't Blame the Election on Fake News."

7. Pennycook and Rand, "Fighting Misinformation on Social Media"; B. Bago, D. G. Rand, and G. Pennycook, "Fake News, Fast and Slow: Deliberation Reduces Belief in False (but Not True) News Headlines, *Journal of Experimental Psychology: General* 149 (2020): 1608–13.

8. W. P. Eveland, M. Seo, and K. Marton, "Learning from the News in Campaign 2000: An Experimental Comparison of TV News, Newspapers, and Online News," *Media Psychology* 4 (2002): 353–78; J. H. Walma van der Molen and T. H. A. van der Voort, "Children's Recall of Television and Print News: A Media Comparison Study," *Journal of Educational Psychology* 89 (1997): 82–91; M. Dijkstra, H. E. J. J. M. Buijtels, and W. F. van Raaij, "Separate and Joint Effects of Medium Type on Consumer Responses: A Comparison of Television, Print, and the Internet," *Journal of Business Research* 58 (2005): 377–86.

9. T. E. Patterson, *How America Lost Its Mind: The Assault on Reason That's Crippling Our Democracy* (Norman: University of Oklahoma Press, 2019).

10. D. Miller, ed., *Tell Me Lies: Propaganda and Media Distortion in the Attack on Iraq* (London: Pluto Press, 2003); W. Lance Bennett, R. G. Lawrence, and S. Livingston, *When the Press Fails: Political Power and the News Media from Iraq to Katrina* (Chicago: University of Chicago Press, 2008).

11. B. Nyhan, "Why the 'Death Panel' Myth Wouldn't Die: Misinformation in the Health Care Reform Debate," *The Forum* 8, no. 1 (2011), https://www.degruyterbrill.com/document/doi/10.2202/1540-8884.1354/html; R. G. Lawrence and M. L. Schafer, "Debunking Sarah Palin: Mainstream News Coverage of 'Death Panels,' " *Journalism* 13 (2012): 766–82.

12. Y. Benkler, R. Faris, and H. Roberts, *Network Propaganda: Manipulation, Disinformation, and Radicalization in American Politics* (New York: Oxford University Press, 2018).

13. AllSides, "How to Spot 11 Types of Media Bias," https://www.allsides.com/media-bias/how-to-spot-types-of-media-bias; S. Mullainathan and A. Shleifer, "The Market for News," *American Economic Review* 95 (2005): 1031–53; M. Gentzkow and J. M. Shapiro, "What Drives Media Slant? Evidence from US Daily Newspapers," *Econometrica* 78 (2010): 35–71.

14. B. G. Southwell, E. A. Thorson, and L. Sheble, *Misinformation and Mass Audiences* (Austin: University of Texas Press, 2018); S. Dentzer, "Communicating Medical News—Pitfalls of Health Care Journalism," *New England Journal of Medicine* 360 (2009): 1–3; W. Glazer, "Scientific Journalism: The Dangers of Misinformation," *Current Psychiatry* 12 (2013): 33–35; D. A. Scheufele and N. M. Krause, Science Audiences,

Misinformation, and Fake News," *Proceedings of the National Academy of Sciences U.S.A.* 116 (2019): 7662–69; P. Rosenzweig, *The Halo Effect* (New York: Free Press, 2007).

15. Patterson, *How America Lost Its Mind*; Benkler, Faris, and Roberts, *Network Propaganda*.

16. G. King and N. Persily, "A New Model for Industry-Academic Partnerships," *PS: Political Science and Politics* 53 (2018): 703–9.

17. D. J. Watts, "Should Social Science Be More Solution-Oriented?," *Nature Human Behavior* 1 (2017): 0015.

18. W. Wang, R. Kennedy, D. Lazer, and N. Ramakrishnan, "Growing Pains for Global Monitoring of Societal Events," *Science* 353 (2016): 1502–3.

19. Tucker et al., "Social Media, Political Polarization, and Political Disinformation"; D. C. Mutz, *Hearing the Other Side: Deliberative Versus Participatory Democracy* (New York: Cambridge University Press, 2006).

20. D. M. Kahan et al., "The Polarizing Impact of Science Literacy and Numeracy on Perceived Climate Change Risks," *Nature Climate Change* 2 (2012): 732–35; C. A. Bail et al., "Exposure to Opposing Views on Social Media Can Increase Political Polarization," *Proceedings of the National Academy of Sciences U.S.A.* 115 (2018): 9216–21.

21. W. Wang, D. Rothschild, S. Goel, and A. Gelman, "Forecasting Elections with Nonrepresentative Polls," *International Journal of Forecasting* 31 (2015): 980–91; A. Gelman, S. Goel, D. Rivers, and D. Rothschild, "The Mythical Swing Voter," *Quarterly Journal of Political Science* 11 (2016): 103–30.

22. D. J. Watts, "Computational Social Science: Exciting Progress and Future Directions," *Bridge Frontiers of Engineering* 43 (2013): 5–10.

23. C. Wells and K. Thorson, "Combining Big Data and Survey Techniques to Model Effects of Political Content Flows in Facebook," *Social Science Computing Review* 35 (2017): 33–52; T. Konitzer, D. Rothschild, S. Hill, and K. C. Wilbur, "Using Big Data and Algorithms to Determine the Effect of Geographically Targeted Advertising on Vote Intention: Evidence from the 2012 US Presidential Election," *Political Communication* 36 (2019): 1–16; C. Budak and D. J. Watts, "Dissecting the Spirit of Gezi: Influence vs. Selection in the Occupy Gezi Movement," *Sociological Science* 2 (2015): 370–97.

24. M. J. Salganik, I. Lundberg, A. T. Kindel, and S. McLanahan, "Introduction to the Special Collection on the Fragile Families Challenge," *Socius* (2019), https://journals.sagepub.com/doi/10.1177/2378023119871580.

25. J. Mackinlay, "Automating the Design of Graphical Presentations of Relational Information," *ACM Transactions on Graphics* 5 (1986): 110–41; M. Hegarty, "The Cognitive Science of Visual-Spatial Displays: Implications for Design," *Topics in Cognitive Science* 3 (2011): 446–74.

26. Watts, "Should Social Science Be More Solution-Oriented?"; M. Prasad, "Problem-Solving Sociology," *Trajectories* 28 (2016): 17–21; M. Western, "We Need More Solution-Oriented Social Science: On Changing Our Frames of Reference and Tackling Big Social Problems," *Impact of Social Sciences Blog*, June 26, 2016, http://eprints.lse.ac.uk/67288/; D. E. Stokes, *Pasteur's Quadrant: Basic Science and Technological Innovation* (Washington, DC: Brookings Institution Press, 1997).

27. B. C. Burden, "Voter Turnout and the National Election Studies," *Political Analysis* 8 (2000): 389–98; S. Goel, J. M. Hofman, S. Lahaie, D. M. Pennock, and D. J. Watts, "Predicting Consumer Behavior with Web Search," *Proceedings of the National Academy of Sciences U.S.A.* 107 (2010): 17486–90; H. Choi and H. Varian, "Predicting the

Present with Google Trends," *Economic Record* 88 (2012): 2–9; SSRC, "To Secure Knowledge: Social Science Partnerships for the Common Good," https://www.ssrc.org/to-secure-knowledge.

28. King and Persily, "A New Model for Industry-Academic Partnerships."
29. See, e.g., https://www.aisp.upenn.edu and https://saildatabank.com.
30. E. Pariser, *The Filter Bubble: What the Internet Is Hiding from You* (New York: Penguin Books, 2011); C. R. Sunstein, *Republic: Divided Democracy in the Age of Social Media* (Princeton, NJ: Princeton University Press, 2018); M. Gentzkow and J. M. Shapiro, "Ideology and Online News," in *Economic Analysis of the Digital Economy*, ed. A. Goldfarb, S. M. Greenstein, and C. E. Tucker (Chicago: University of Chicago Press, 2015), 169–90; E. Bakshy, S. Messing, and L. A. Adamic, "Exposure to Ideologically Diverse News and Opinion on Facebook," *Science* 348 (2015): 1130–32; S. Flaxman, S. Goel, and J. M. Rao, "Filter Bubbles, Echo Chambers, and Online News Consumption," *Public Opinion Quarterly* 80 (2016): 298–320.
31. M. Prior, "The Immensely Inflated News Audience: Assessing Bias in Self-Reported News Exposure," *Public Opinion Quarterly* 73 (2009): 130–43; M. Prior, "The Challenge of Measuring Media Exposure: Reply to Dilliplane, Goldman, and Mutz," *Political Communication* 30 (2013): 620–34.
32. T. Konitzer et al., "Comparing Estimates of News Consumption from Survey and Passively Collected Behavioral Data," March 4, 2020, https://ssrn.com/abstract=3548690.

21. Clyde Miller and the Institute for Propaganda Analysis: Fighting Disinformation in the 1930s

1. http://www.unesco.org/new/en/unesco/events/prizes-and-celebrations/celebrations/international-days/world-press-freedom-day/previous-celebrations/2012/2012-themes/difficulty-in-the-access-to-quality-information-undermines-media-freedom/.
2. David Greenberg, *Republic of Spin: An Inside History of the American Presidency* (New York: W. W. Norton, 2016), 109.
3. J. Michael Sproule, *Propaganda and Democracy: The American Experience of Media and Mass Persuasion* (New York: Cambridge University Press, 1996), 130. The Lincoln School was part of a well-known group of progressive private schools in New York City that later merged with Horace Mann and was replaced by New Lincoln School, which then later merged with Walden School on West Eighty-Eighth Street. Lincoln School was founded in 1917 and affiliated with Columbia Teachers College. For more information see John Heffron, "The Lincoln School of Teachers College: Elitism and Educational Democracy," in *Schools of Tomorrow, Schools of Today: What Happened to Progressive Education?*, ed. Susan F. Semel and Alan R. Sadovnik (New York: Peter Lang, 1999).
4. Danielle Allen and Justin Pottle, "Democratic Knowledge and the Problem of Faction," Knight Foundation White Paper, 2018.
5. Clyde R. Miller, *How to Detect and Analyze Propaganda: An Address Delivered at Town Hall*, pamphlet, February 20, 1939.
6. Sproule, *Propaganda and Democracy*; Greenberg, *Republic of Spin*, 208.
7. Violet Edwards wrote some of the IPA materials but is not usually mentioned in accounts of the IPA's work. We hope to rectify this lacuna in the future once we have done more research. J. Michael Sproule had dinner with Violet Edwards and her husband in December 1982 and emailed me that: "Violet idolized Miller and cherished

her work with the Institute. [Her husband] Hal [on] the other hand seemed to have been chiefly happy for escaping the red baiting which surrounded the IPA. He was coauthor of the Institute's second book, *War Propaganda and the United States*, with James Wechsler, his friend who was somewhat less successful in remaining under the radar."

    According to I. F. Stone's biographer Don Guttenplan, Stone began work in May 1939 and, after having traveled to California to do interviews, wrote the IPA *Bulletin* issue on the Associated Farmers which had been founded to stop farm workers from joining unions. Guttenplan describes how Stone attacked the Associated Farmers for false populism, saying it was essentially a "front for West Coast banks, utility companies, railroads and big growers intended to stop cannery workers and migrant pickers from joining unions." D. D. Guttenplan, *American Radical: The Life and Times of I. F. Stone* (New York: Farrar, Straus and Giroux, 2009), 143.

8. Philip M. Glende, "'We Used Every Effort to Be Impartial': The Complicated Response of Newspaper Publishers to Unions, American Journalism," *American Journalism* 29, no. 2 (2012): 37–65.

9. Elizabeth Briant Lee and Alfred McClung Lee, "The Fine Art of Propaganda Analysis—Then and Now," *ETC: A Review of General Semantics* 36, no. 2 (Summer 1979): 117–27.

10. Sproule, *Propaganda and Democracy.*

11. Sproule, *Propaganda and Democracy*, 133; "Propaganda Study Is Aim of Institute," *New York Times*, October 10, 1937; "T. F. Woodlock Will Appear on CBS Television Program," *Wall Street Journal*, December 12, 1941.

12. J. Michael Sproule, "Progressive Propaganda Critics and the Magic Bullet Myth," *Critical Studies in Mass Communication* 6, no. 3 (1989): 225.

13. Kenneth Cmiel, "On Cynicism, Evil, and the Discovery of Communication in the 1940s," *Journal of Communication* 46, no. 3 (1996): 88–107.

14. Hadley Cantril, "Propaganda Analysis," *English Journal* 27, no. 3 (March 1938): 217–21.

15. Richard J. John and Heidi Tworek, "Publicity, Propaganda, and Public Opinion; From the Titanic Disaster to the Hungarian Uprising," in *Information: A Historical Companion*, ed. Ann Blair, Paul Duguid, Anja-Silvia Goeing, and Anthony Grafton (Princeton, NJ: Princeton University Press, 2021), 211–37.

16. Bernard DeVoto, "The Fallacy of Excess Interpretation," *Harper's*, June 1, 1938, 109–12.

17. Todd Gitlin, "Media Sociology: The Dominant Paradigm," *Theory and Society* 6, no. 2 (September 1978): 210.

18. Greenberg, *Republic of Spin*, 110.

19. Greenberg, *Republic of Spin*, 109; Walter Lippmann, *Public Opinion* (New York: Harcourt, 1922).

20. Brett Gary, *The Nervous Liberals: Propaganda Anxieties from World War I to the Cold War* (New York: Columbia University Press, 1999).

21. John and Tworek, "Publicity, Propaganda, and Public Opinion."

22. Heidi Tworek, *News from Germany: The Competition to Control World Communications, 1900–1945* (Cambridge, MA: Harvard University Press, 2019); Bradley Hart, *Hitler's American Friends: The Third Reich's Supporters in the United States* (New York: Thomas Dunne Books, 2018), 104; Yochai Benkler, Robert Faris, and Hal Roberts, *Network Propaganda* (Oxford: Oxford University Press, 2018).

23. As Richard R. John notes, "yet by the time Lippman published the *Phantom Public* he had more or less given up on the common man (and woman) altogether."

24. Alfred McClung Lee, *The Fine Art of Propaganda: A Study of Father Coughlin's Speeches* (New York: Harcourt Brace & Co., 1939); Alan Brinkley, *The End of Reform: New Deal Liberalism in Recession and War* (New York: Vintage Books, 1996); Abba Hillel Silver, "Father Coughlin," *Jewish Telegraphic Agency*, May 6, 1934; Donald Warren, *Radio Priest: Charles Coughlin, the Father of Hate Radio* (New York: Free Press, 1996).

25. Greg Mitchell, "A Look Inside Hollywood and the Movies: Democracy in Action, How the Studios Torpedoed Upton Sinclair's Run for Office," *Los Angeles Times*, October 31, 1993.

26. Adam Maksl, Stephanie Craft, Seth Ashley, and Dean Miller, "The Usefulness of a News Media Literacy Measure in Evaluating a News Literacy Curriculum," *Journalism & Mass Communications Educator* 72, no. 2 (2017): 228–41.

27. Institute for Propaganda Analysis, *Bulletin* 1, no. 8 (May 1938).

28. Hart, *Hitler's American Friends*.

29. Institute for Propaganda Analysis, *Bulletin* 1, no. 5 (February 1938).

30. Lauri Johnson, " 'One Community's Total War Against Prejudice': The Springfield Plan Revisited," *Theory and Research in Social Education* 34, no. 3 (2006): 301–23.

31. E. George Payne, "Significant Developments in Education," *Journal of Educational Sociology* 3 (February 1946): 395–97.

32. A flavor of the time can be found in Clarence I. Chatto, "Education for Democratic Living," *Journal of Education* 127, no. 6 (September 1944): 189–91. Chatto describes ninth graders interviewing foreign-born resident of the city and writing their biographies and other groups of students making books about folk music. "Children learn to be good citizens of tomorrow by learning to be good citizens of the school today. They learn to accept other Americans as comrades and equals by doing just that on the school playground and in the classroom."

33. Johnson, "One Community's Total War Against Prejudice"; Payne, "Significant Developments in Education."

34. Daniel Bresnahan, "The Springfield Plan in Retrospect," PhD diss. (Teachers College, Columbia University, 1971), 43. He describes the hostility of some Catholics in Springfield to public schools as dating back to the 1870s. Nor did they join attempts by Protestants and Jews in the 1930s to form a council of churches.

35. Correspondence between Philip Horowitz and Clyde Miller, Center for the Study of Popular Culture records, Box 113, Folder 1, Hoover Institution Archives, 1930s.

36. Celia Lewis, Vera Shlakman, and Louis Jaffe, *Academic Freedom in a Time of Crisis* (New York: New York Teachers Union Local 555, 1948).

37. Johnson, "One Community's Total War Against Prejudice," 302.

38. Johnson, "One Community's Total War Against Prejudice," 317.

39. Interestingly, the scholar A. J. Bauer writes that Miller "privately sent Dies information supporting other investigations in hopes of being spared from investigation himself." Personal correspondence, January 28, 2021.

40. Michael Heale, "Red Scare Politics: California's Campaign Against Un-American Activities, 1940–1970," *Journal of American Studies* 20, no. 1 (1986): 5–32.

41. Special to the *New York Times*, February 23, 1941.

42. Kenneth Heineman, "Media Bias in Coverage of the Dies Committee on Un-American Activities, 1938–1940," *The Historian* 55, no. 1 (1992): 37–52.

43. Special to the *New York Times*, February 23, 1941.

44. Institute for Propaganda Analysis, *Bulletin* 4 (January 9, 1942).

45. Columbia University Academic Appointment records for Clyde R. Miller, 1929–1948.

46. *New York Herald Tribune*, "Teachers College Drops Dr. Miller," May 8, 1948; *New York Times*, "Dr. Miller Gives Version of Ouster at Columbia," May 8, 1948.

47. Edward Alwood, *Dark Days in the Newsroom: McCarthyism Aimed at the Press* (Philadelphia: Temple University Press, 2007).

48. *New York Times*, May 8, 1948.

49. IPA files at Butler Library, Columbia University.

50. Ellen Schrecker, *No Ivory Tower: McCarthyism and the Universities* (Oxford: Oxford University Press, 1986).

51. Columbia University Central Files Series 1: 1895–1971 of the archives at Butler, Boxes 352, 217, 412.

52. Roger L. Geiger and Max Lerner, *Ideas for the Ice Age: Studies in a Revolutionary Era* (New York: Taylor & Francis, [1941] 2020). Interestingly, correspondence between David Horowitz's Communist schoolteacher father and Clyde Miller can be found in the Hoover Institute archives, as well as a pamphlet on free speech from the New York teacher's union. See Scott Sherman, "David Horowitz's Long March," *The Nation*, July 3, 2000.

53. See Cmiel, "On Cynicism, Evil, and the Discovery of Communication in the 1940s"; Sproule, *Propaganda and Democracy*; and Gitlin, "Media Sociology."

54. Anya Schiffrin, "We Are Against People Who Push Other People Around: A Study of the Newspaper *PM*," BA thesis (Reed College, 1984).

55. Cmiel, "On Cynicism, Evil, and the Discovery of Communication in the 1940s," 90.

56. John and Tworek, "Publicity, Propaganda, and Public Opinion," 46.

57. Alison Head, Barbara Fister, and Margy MacMillan, "Information Literacy in the Age of Algorithms," *Project Information Literacy*, Knight Foundation, 2020.

58. Many of the groups currently active were founded by journalists with a passion for educating the public about the importance of journalism and the role of journalists. These include Howard Schneider, the former *Newsday* editor who went on to direct Stony Brook's Center for News Literacy, and Alan Miller, a former *Los Angeles Times* reporter who founded the News Literacy Project.

    The News Literacy Program has revived its Newsroom-to-Classroom initiative so that teachers around the United States can bring journalists into their classrooms to talk about how journalists gather information and what makes journalism different from other kinds of information.

59. In the United States, media literacy efforts are often fragmented and inconsistent, which contributes to the difficulty of measuring their impact. Nor have they been well funded. Indeed, one study of media literacy funding put the amount at a mere $12 million between 2006 and 2016.

60. Johnson, "One Community's Total War Against Prejudice."

61. Gordon Pennycook and David G. Rand, "Who Falls for Fake News? The Roles of Bullshit Receptivity, Overclaiming, Familiarity, and Analytic Thinking," *Journal of Personality* 88, no. 2 (2019): 185–200.

62. Claire Wardle, "Fake News, It's Complicated," *First Draft*, February 16, 2017.

63. Claire Wardle and Hossein Derakhshan, *Information Disorder: Toward an Interdisciplinary Framework for Research and Policy Making* (Strasbourg: Council of Europe, 2017).

64. Edson Tandoc, Zhang Lim, and Richard Ling, "Defining 'Fake News,' " *Digital Journalism* 6, no. 2 (2017): 1–17.

65. Brendan Nyhan and Jason Reifler, "The Effect of Fact-Checking on Elites: A Field Experiment on U.S. State Legislators," *American Journal of Political Science* 59, no. 3 (2015): 628–40.

66. danah boyd, "You Think You Want Media Literacy . . . Do You?" *Medium*, March 9, 2018.

67. Chris Barr, "20 Projects Will Address the Spread of Misinformation Through Knight Prototype Fund," *Knight Foundation*, June 22, 2017.

68. Nicholas Thompson and Fred Vogelstein, "Inside the Two Years That Shook Facebook—and the World," *Wired*, February 12, 2019; Emily Bell, "Facebook Is Eating the World," *Columbia Journalism Review*, March 7, 2016.

69. See Sarah Perez, "Google's New Media Literacy Program Teaches Kids How to Spot Disinformation and Fake News," *TechCrunch*, June 24, 2019; Facebook Journalism Initiative, "Investing in U.S. Media Literacy Initiatives," June 24, 2020, https://www.facebook.com/journalismproject/media-literacy-initiatives.

70. Madhumita Murgia, "Facebook Launches $14m Collaborative News Literacy Project," *Financial Times*, April 3, 2017.

71. Author interviews with media literacy proponents in 2019.

72. For a strong defense of this position, see Nadine Strossen, *Hate: Why We Should Resist It With Free Speech, Not Censorship* (New York: Oxford University Press, 2018), and Suzanne Nossel, *Dare to Speak: Defending Free Speech for All* (New York: Dey Street Books, 2020).

73. Paul F. Lazarsfeld, Bernard Berelson, and Hazel Gaudet, *The People's Choice: How the Voter Makes Up His Mind in a Presidential Campaign* (New York: Columbia University Press, 2020).

74. Jacques Ellul, *Propaganda: The Formation of Men's Attitudes* (New York: Vintage Books, 1962), 259.

75. Ellul, *Propaganda*.

76. Jeremy Peters, Michael M. Grynbaum, Keith Collins, Rich Harris, and Rumsey Taylor, "How the El Paso Killer Echoed the Incendiary Words of Conservative Media Stars," *New York Times*, August 11, 2019.

77. Horacio Larreguy and John Marshall, "The Incentives and Effects of Independent and Government-Controlled Media in the Developing World," in *Oxford Handbook of Electoral Persuasion*, ed. Elizabeth Suhay (Oxford: Oxford University Press, 2019), 590–617.

CONTRIBUTORS

Akeel Bilgrami is the Sidney Morgenbesser Professor of Philosophy at Columbia University. He has published books on the nature of linguistic meaning and reference, on self-knowledge, on secularism and identity, and on the commons.

David Bromwich is Sterling Professor of English at Yale University. He is a literary scholar interested in Romantic criticism and poetry, eighteenth-century moral philosophy, and political writing. He has published widely on these topics.

Noam Chomsky, Institute Professor and Professor of Linguistics Emeritus at MIT, pioneered the field of modern linguistics and has written and lectured on linguistics, philosophy, intellectual history, contemporary issues, international affairs and US foreign policy. His work also has influenced the fields of cognitive science, philosophy, psychology, computer science, mathematics, childhood education, and anthropology.

Jonathan R. Cole is John Mitchell Mason Professor of the University and Provost and Dean of Faculties Emeritus at Columbia University. He is one of the pioneering scholars in the field of sociology of science. His scholarly attention has also focused on issues in higher education, and he has written several books and articles on the topic.

Jon Elster is Robert K. Merton Professor Emeritus of the Social Sciences at Columbia University. He is a political philosopher interested in reason and rationality and their roles in politics and public life. Elster's research interests include the theory of individual and collective choice, the philosophy of the social sciences, the theory of distributive justice, and the history of social thought.

Eric Foner is DeWitt Clinton Professor Emeritus of History and Columbia University. He has focused on the intersections of intellectual, political, and social history and the history of American race relations. He is one of only two persons to serve as president of the Organization of American Historians, American Historical Association, and Society of American Historians.

Daria Franklin is a PhD candidate in sociology at Columbia University. She studies mechanisms of change in constraining political and organizational environments, and in the ways culture and ideology structure professional identities.

Robert Gooding-Williams is Brooks and Suzanne Ragen Professor of Philosophy at Yale University. His areas of research interests include social and political philosophy, the history of African American political thought, nineteenth-century European philosophy, existentialism, and aesthetics.

Michael Ignatieff is Professor of History and former Professor and Rector at Central European University. He is an author, literary critic, and politician who represented the Etobicoke-Lakeshore riding in the Canadian House of Commons (2006–2011) and who served as leader of the Liberal Party (2008–2011). Ignatieff is most known for his international commentary on contemporary issues of democracy, human rights, and governance.

Laura Kipnis, Professor Emerita in the Department of Radio/TV/Film at Northwestern University, is a cultural critic/essayist and former video artist whose work focuses on sexual politics, aesthetics, shame, emotion, acting out, moral messiness, and various other crevices of the American psyche. She is the author of *Love in the Time of Contagion: A Diagnosis* and *Unwanted Advances: Sexual Paranoia Comes to Campus*.

Robert Klitzman, MD, is Professor of Psychiatry at Columbia University Irving Medical Center. He focuses on ethical, psychological, and social aspects of decision making among patients, providers, and others concerning genetics, HIV, end of life care, and other areas. He has published extensively, drawing on multidisciplinary methods to examine ethical, psychological, and social issues in a variety of contexts in medicine and psychiatry.

Prabhat Patnaik is Professor Emeritus in the Centre for Economic Studies and Planning at Jawaharlal Nehru University. He is a political economist specializing in macroeconomics. His books include *Accumulation and Stability Under Capitalism*, *The Value of Money*, *Re-envisioning Socialism*, *A Theory of Imperialism*, and *Capitalism and Imperialism: Theory, History, and the Present*, coauthored with Utsa Patnaik.

Carol Rovane is Violin Family Professor of Philosophy at Columbia University. Her research focuses on several interrelated topics: the first person, personal identity, relativism, the foundations of value, group vs. individual responsibility, and some new problems for liberal theory. She has published widely on these subjects.

Anya Schiffrin is a senior lecturer and the director of the Technology, Media, and Communications specialization at Columbia University. She writes on journalism and development, has conducted investigative reporting in the Global South, and has published extensively over the last decade on the media in Africa. She has also become focused on solutions to the problem of online disinformation.

Richard Shweder is Harold H. Swift Distinguished Service Professor of Human Development at the University of Chicago. A cultural anthropologist, he has published extensively on cultural psychology, psychological anthropology, comparative human development, and diversity in child and adolescent development. Most recently he has been examining the scopes and limits of pluralism and the multicultural challenge in Western liberal democracies.

Jessica T. Simes is Associate Professor of Sociology at Boston University. Her scholarship broadly examines the consequences of mass incarceration for communities and neighborhoods in the United States. Her research has focused on racial inequality and health disparities in criminalizing and punitive experiences.

Joseph E. Stiglitz is University Professor and Co-President of the Initiative for Policy Dialogue at Columbia University. Chief economist of the Roosevelt Institute, he has made major contributions to macroeconomics and monetary theory, development economics and trade theory, public and corporate finance, theories of industrial organization and rural organization, and theories of welfare economics and income and wealth distribution. In 2000 he was awarded the Sveriges Riksbank Prize in Economic Sciences in Memory of Alfred Nobel for his analyses of markets with asymmetric information.

Geoffrey R. Stone, Edward H. Levi Distinguished Service Professor at the University of Chicago, is a legal scholar and noted First Amendment scholar. He published numerous works on constitutional law, free speech, and liberty. He has also written amicus briefs for constitutional scholars in a number of Supreme Court cases. Stone served as Dean of the Law School (1987–1994) and Provost of the University of Chicago (1994–2002).

Jeremy Waldron is Professor of Law and University Professor at New York University. A legal philosopher, he has written extensively on jurisprudence and political theory, publishing numerous books and articles on theories of rights, constitutionalism, the rule of law, democracy, property, torture, security, homelessness, and the philosophy of international law.

Duncan Watts is the Stevens University Professor and Penn Integrates Knowledge University Professor at the University of Pennsylvania. He is a computational social scientist interested in social and organizational networks, collective dynamics of human systems, web-based experiments, and analysis of large-scale digital data, including the production, consumption, and absorption of news. His coauthors, Jennifer Allen (New York University), Baird Howland (University of Pennsylvania), Markus Mobius (Microsoft), and David Rothschild (Microsoft), study news consumption, misinformation, and social networks from economic, computational, and political perspectives.

Bruce Western is the Bryce Professor of Sociology at Social Justice and Director of the Justice Lab at Columbia University. He studies the relationship between political institutions and social and economic inequality. He has long-standing interests in criminal justice policy, incarceration, and the effects of incarceration on poor communities. His research has analyzed labor unions and their effects on income inequality and trends in income inequality and mobility in the United States.

GPSR Authorized Representative: Easy Access System Europe, Mustamäe tee 50, 10621 Tallinn, Estonia, gpsr.requests@easproject.com